SOCIOLOGY

SOCIOLOGY

A Brief Introduction

THIRD EDITION

ALEX THIO
OHIO UNIVERSITY

 LONGMAN

An imprint of Addison Wesley Longman, Inc.

New York • Reading, Massachusetts • Menlo Park, California • Harlow, England
Don Mills, Ontario • Sydney • Mexico City • Madrid • Amsterdam

Sociology: A Brief Introduction, Third Edition

Acquisitions Editor: Alan McClare
Developmental Editor: Ann Torbert
Supplements Editor: Tom Kulesa
Project Coordination and Text Design: Thompson Steele Production Services
Cover Design: Kay Petronio
Photo Researcher: Julie Tesser
Electronic Production Manager: Eric Jorgensen
Manufacturing Manager: Hilda Koparanian
Electronic Page Makeup: Thompson Steele Production Services
Printer and Binder: RR Donnelley & Sons Company
Cover Printer: Phoenix Color Corp.

For permission to use copyrighted material, grateful acknowledgment is made to the copyright holders on pages 381–382, which are hereby made part of this copyright page.

Library of Congress Cataloging-in-Publication Data

Thio, Alex.
   Sociology : a brief introduction / Alex Thio. — 3rd ed.
      p.   cm.
   Includes bibliographical references (p.) and index.
   ISBN 0-673-98111-8
   1. Sociology.   I. Title.
   HM24.T495   1997
   301—dc20   96-16015
                                          CIP

ISBN 0-673-98111-8

12345678910—DOW—99989796

Brief Contents

Detailed Contents

Preface

Like its previous editions, this book is designed to help students have fun learning sociology. We live in a period of rapid social change, and it is an exciting time to be studying sociology. We will explore many of the ongoing social changes in this new edition of *Sociology: A Brief Introduction*. It is a major revision packed with current information and new ideas from sociological research. I have, however, continued to present the essentials of sociology without a loss of substance or concreteness. In pruning away those topics that are not central to learning about sociological issues, I have concentrated on major areas in depth, with enough lively details to maintain student interest. Although this text is relatively short, it provides instructors and students with the full range of sociological analyses and issues. To ensure that students learn a great deal from this brief text, I have retained the more successful features of my full-length book. I have also tried to convey the excitement I feel about sociology.

FEATURES

A unique blend of style and substance makes this text stand out from the rest. This distinguishing feature and others make the book easier for students to learn sociology.

Solid Scholarship

There is a great deal of substance to the text. All analyses are based on empirical studies or data-informed theories, or both. In addition, no attempt has been made to gloss over or water down complex sociological issues, such as the phenomenological theory of deviance or the causes of upward and downward mobility in global society. Such issues are confronted head-on but explained in a clear and interesting fashion.

Current Research

Special care has been taken to present the most recent findings from the sociological literature. Sociology is a fast-growing field, reflecting the significant changes that have recently taken place all over the world. Thus, many studies cited in this text are as recent as the mid-1990s. Many current events reported in the nation's first-rate newspapers and newsmagazines are also discussed to demonstrate the relevancy of sociology to today's world.

Social Diversity

The diversity of U.S. society, including various racial and ethnic groups as well as women and men of various social classes, is presented in a balanced way. In regard to minorities and women, the text does not focus only on their problems; their strengths and achievements are also revealed, as in Chapter 10 (Families), where Native American, African American, Hispanic American, and Asian American families are discussed.

Global Analyses

All chapters contain analyses of how peoples around the world live or how their lives affect ours in the United States. Such global analyses enhance and deepen our understanding of other cultures. The analyses also help us gain special insight into our own society by looking at it more objectively—from the outsider's point of view.

Critical Thinking

In every chapter a list of myths and realities about social behavior is offered to promote truly critical thinking. Many students tend to assume that sociology is merely common sense—that there is nothing new in sociology or that whatever is there they have known all along. In this text students will find some of their firmest assumptions challenged and will start to look at the familiar world around them with a critical, fresh eye.

Theoretically Illuminating

The three major sociological perspectives are introduced in the first chapter and then consistently applied in *all* the other chapters, which is unique to this text. The application of these theoretical approaches to a specific subject in each chapter is balanced, substantive, and interesting. One can learn more about society from the three perspectives than from one or two only. Together, the three illuminate different facets of society, providing a broader and more realistic view of each subject. Other theoretical views, especially feminist theory, are also presented where appropriate.

Lively Writing

The writing style is second to none. It is simple, direct, and vibrant, making sociology come alive. Many professors have described the writing as clear and engaging. Numerous students have commented that they enjoyed reading the book.

NEW TO THIS EDITION

A great number of substantive changes have been made, as follows:

- The book has been extensively revised and updated.
- There is a new chapter on social interaction in everyday life.
- A global analysis is provided in *all* chapters.
- The three major sociological perspectives—functionalism, conflict perspective, and symbolic interactionism—are presented in *every* chapter.
- The number of tables and figures has been increased, with some U.S. and global maps added, to reinforce the points made in the text.
- Many new topics have been introduced throughout the text. The most significant are listed below.

Chapter 1   The Essence of Sociology
New sections on:
- The importance of studying social diversity in the United States.
- The significance of analyzing the global diversity of today.
- The nature of sports as seen through the functionalist, conflict, and symbolic interactionist perspectives.
- How sociology can enrich our lives.

Chapter 2   Society and Culture
New sections on:
- The nature of institutions.
- Postindustrial societies.
- The global influence of the U.S. pop culture.
- Multiculturalism in the United States.
- Culture clash around the globe.
- A global analysis of culture.
- The three sociological perspectives on culture.

Chapter 3   Socialization
New sections on:
- Freud's theory of psychosexual development.
- Kohlberg's theory of moral development.
- The feminist theory of gender development.
- The three sociological perspectives on socialization.
- A global analysis of socialization.
- Are we puppets of society?

Chapter 4   Social Interaction in Everyday Life
This is a new chapter. Some of the subjects covered are unique to this text, such as:
- The functionalist perspective on interaction.
- The conflict perspective on interaction.
- A global analysis of communication.
- U.S. diversity in communication.
- How women and men tend to speak different "genderlects."
- How men and women play the gendered game of proxemics.
- The art of managing impressions.
- Humorology: subverting reality with humor.

Chapter 5   Groups and Organizations
New sections on:
- How to classify organizational theories.
- The nature of organizations as seen through the three sociological perspectives.
- The feminist model of organizations.
- A global analysis of organizations.

Chapter 6   Deviance and Control
New sections on:
- Drug abuse.
- Power theory.
- Phenomenological theory.
- Classifying deviance theories into functionalist, conflict, and symbolic interactionist perspectives.
- An analysis of deviance around the world.

Chapter 7   U.S. and Global Stratification
New sections on:
- Feminist perspective on poverty.
- Popular beliefs about welfare.
- Reforming welfare programs.
- Social classes in global society.
- Social mobility in global society.
- The symbolic interactionist perspective on stratification and class.

Chapter 8   Race and Ethnicity
New sections on:
- Northern and Western European Americans.
- Using the three sociological perspectives to analyze race and ethnicity.
- A global analysis of racial and ethnic relations.

Chapter 9   Gender and Age
New sections on:
- Sexual harassment.
- The three sociological perspectives on gender inequality.

♦ A global analysis of gender inequality.
♦ The three sociological perspectives on age and aging.
♦ A global analysis of aging.

Chapter 10   Families
New sections on:
♦ A global analysis of families.
♦ The symbolic interactionist perspective on the family.
♦ Gay and lesbian marriages.
♦ Native American families.
♦ African American families.
♦ Hispanic American families.
♦ Asian American families.

Chapter 11   Education and Religion
New sections on:
♦ The conflict theory about education as inequality reinforcer and cultural imperialism.
♦ The symbolic interactionist perspective on education.
♦ Schools in Belgium, Finland, France, and Japan.
♦ The three sociological perspectives on the nature of religion.
♦ New trends in U.S. religion.

Chapter 12   Economy and Politics
New sections on:
♦ The nature of capitalism as seen through the three sociological perspectives.
♦ The economies of Canada, Latin America, Western Europe, Eastern Europe, Russia, China, and Southeast Asia.
♦ A global analysis of political violence.
♦ Government responses to international and domestic terrorism.
♦ The three sociological perspectives on war.

Chapter 13   Health and Population
New sections on:
♦ A global analysis of health.
♦ Sexism in medical research.

Chapter 14   Environment and Urbanization
New sections on:
♦ A primary cause of environmental problems.
♦ The megacities of the world.
♦ The three sociological perspectives on urbanization.
♦ Causes of urban problems.
♦ The future of U.S. cities.

Chapter 15   Collective Behavior and Social Change
New sections on:
♦ A global analysis of social change.

♦ How the theories of social change are related to the three sociological perspectives.

LEARNING AIDS

An effective system of learning aids is incorporated into the text to motivate students and facilitate learning. Students are encouraged to think about the materials by themselves or by discussing important issues in class. It is frequently through such active involvement, as opposed to passive acceptance of what one reads, that students begin to sharpen their thinking skills. Then the understanding and absorption of ideas presented in the text will come easily.

Chapter-Opening Vignettes

Along with a chapter outline and a myths and realities box, each chapter opens with a thought-provoking story. This will stimulate students' interest as well as fix their attention on the main themes of the chapter.

Stimulating Graphics

Colorful figures, tables, maps, and beautiful photos are interspersed throughout the book. They are designed not only to spark student interest but, more importantly, to reinforce comprehension and retention of the points made in the text.

Discussion-and-Review Questions

In every chapter there are questions at the end of each main section. Instructors can use them as a springboard for lively discussion in class. Students can use them to review the main ideas that have just been discussed, before moving on to the next topic. However the questions are used, students will learn more as active thinkers than as passive recipients of ideas and facts.

Chapter Summaries

Each chapter ends with a full summary in a question-and-answer format. The standard form of summary in an introductory text tends to turn students into passive consumers of knowledge. In contrast, the question-and-answer format encourages students to become actively involved, by inviting them to join the author in thinking about important issues. Students who have actively thought about what they have read will more easily understand and remember it later.

Key Terms

The most important words are boldfaced and defined when introduced. They are listed and defined again at the end of each chapter, with a page cross-reference to facilitate study. All key terms with their definitions are also presented in the Glossary at the end of the book.

Suggested Readings

In line with the currency of the material in the text, up-to-date books and articles for further reading are listed at the end of each chapter. These sources enable students to seek additional knowledge about the subject matter of each chapter. Most readings are readily available in school libraries.

SUPPLEMENTS

Accompanying this text is a highly useful support package for instructors and students.

Societies: A Multi-Cultural Reader

A collection of relatively brief articles, all related to cross-cultural issues, has been assembled by Peter Morrill of Bronx Community College. There are two to three readings for each chapter in the text. The great variety of topics covered will help students appreciate cultural diversity within the United States and will also illustrate how ways of life in other societies can differ from the familiar world they know. Each reading begins with a short introduction that relates the material to key concepts in the text and each chapter ends with a set of study questions.

Instructor's Manual

Prepared by Peter Morrill of Bronx Community College, this manual provides chapter outlines, learning objectives, a complete summary of chapter topics, and an extensive set of classroom discussion questions keyed to main topics. Each chapter also includes demonstrations, projects, and applications that are designed to develop the thinking skills of students. The *Instructor's Manual* ends with an extensive list of audiovisual aids and their sources. The goal of the manual is to enable instructors to show students how to think effectively about sociological topics. In addition, students are helped not only to master the material of the course but also to take an active role in learning it.

Test Bank

The *Test Bank,* also prepared by Peter Morrill, contains over 1100 multiple-choice, true/false, short-answer, and essay questions. The *Test Bank* is available as a printed manual and on Testmaster. Testmaster is Longman's computerized test-generating system. It produces customized tests and allows instructors to scramble questions and add new ones. Testmaster is available for use with IBM PC and compatibles, and the Macintosh.

Study Guide

A *Study Guide,* also prepared by Professor Morrill, is a substantial book in its own right. Each chapter opens with an outline of the chapter in the text, a list of learning objectives, a detailed review of the material designed to get the student deep into the particulars of the chapter, and numerous questions and answers to check the student's knowledge.

Hyper-Soc™

We offer a customized version of Hyper-Soc™, a combination classroom demonstration software and hypertext student tutorial program. Available for IBM and compatible computers. (For more information, please contact your Longman sales representative.)

Transparency Acetates

Our **Sociology Transparency Acetate Package** offers full color figures, tables and graphics from a wide variety of sources, including this text. Free upon qualified adoption.

Sociology Laser Disk

The Addison Wesley Longman Sociology laser disk includes short video programs and over 70 graphs and charts for classroom use. The eight video programs stimulate interest and can be used to launch class discussion or lectures. Free to qualified adopters.

ACKNOWLEDGMENTS

I am extremely grateful to the numerous instructors all over the country who have adopted the past editions of this text. I am equally thankful for the invaluable help from many colleagues at various universities and colleges in reviewing the manuscript for the current edition. Unsolicited responses from adopters and insightful criticisms and suggestions from reviewers have helped me produce the best brief text on introductory sociology today. The reviewers for this edition include:

Martha Shwayder,
Metropolitan State College of Denver

Jennifer Solomon, Winthrop University

Patricia Dorman, Boise State University

Michael Kimmel, State University of New York at Stony Brook

Diane Levy, University of North Carolina at Wilmington

Rose Jensen, Lynchburg College

Michael Goslin, Tallahassee Community College

Robert Tournier, College of Charleston

I am also thankful to Professor Peter Morrill. His tireless pursuit of appropriate articles for the book of readings, *Societies,* and his work on the *Study Guide, Test Bank,* and the *Instructor's Manual* have contributed immensely to the text's support package.

I owe a special debt to Alan McClare, Longman's sociology editor, for making it easy and fun to work on this project. A lot of thanks also goes to Ann Torbert, the developmental editor, for greatly enhancing the quality of this revision. I am grateful, too, to Andrea Fincke, the project editor, for efficiently guiding the production of the book.

Finally, I am grateful to my wife and children for their understanding and patience. They have made it possible for me to take a great deal of pleasure, without much guilt, in writing this book.

Alex Thio

About the Author

Alex Thio (pronounced TEE-oh) is Professor of Sociology at Ohio University. Of Chinese heritage, born in Penang, Malaysia, he grew up in a multicultural environment. He acquired fluency in Mandarin (modern standard Chinese), two Chinese dialects (Fukienese and Hakka), Malay, and Indonesian. He also picked up a smattering of English and Dutch.

Professor Thio attended primary school in Malaysia and high school in Indonesia. He then came to the United States and worked his way through Central Methodist College in Missouri, where he majored in social sciences and took many literature and writing courses. Later, he studied sociology as a graduate student at the State University of New York at Buffalo, and completed his doctorate while working as a research and teaching assistant.

Dr. Thio regularly teaches courses in introductory sociology, deviance, social problems, and criminology. Aside from teaching, he enjoys writing. He has written many articles, as well as the popular texts *Sociology,* Fourth Edition (1996) and *Deviant Behavior,* Fourth Edition (1995), both of which were published by HarperCollins. The author is deeply grateful for the feedback he often receives from faculty and students, which he believes improves significantly the quality of his books. If you have any comments, suggestions, or questions, please write him at the Department of Sociology, Ohio University, Athens, OH 45701 (Internet: athio@ohiou.edu).

He lives with his wife, Jane, and their daughters, Diane and Julie, in Athens, Ohio. His hobbies include reading, moviegoing, and traveling.

SOCIOLOGY

THE ESSENCE OF SOCIOLOGY

Myths and Realities

MYTH: *Life must be more stressful in densely populated states such as New York and New Jersey than in wide-open areas such as Montana and Wyoming. Not surprisingly, people in the densely populated states are more likely to commit suicide.*
REALITY: People in the densely populated states have *lower* suicide rates. (p. 7)

MYTH: *Problems, especially crises, are bad. They are sources of failure and misery.*
REALITY: Problems, even crises, are not necessarily bad. They can be good, providing opportunities for enhancing our lives. (p. 24)

MYTH: *College men who have a hard time getting dates and have little or no sexual experience are more likely than others to rape their dates.*
REALITY: Sexually active men who can easily get dates are more likely to rape their dates. (p. 126)

MYTH: *Because mental ability declines with age, older people are less productive than younger ones.*
REALITY: On most measures of productivity, older workers are as productive as younger ones, despite some decline in the older workers' perception and reactive speed. (p. 205)

MYTH: *Since we have the highest divorce rate in the world, the marriage rate must be very low in the United States.*
REALITY: The United States has one of the highest rates of marriage in the world. (p. 223)

At 10 A.M. Pacific time on the first Tuesday of October 1995, television sets across the United States were tuned in to hear the jury's verdict on O. J. Simpson, who was accused of murdering his ex-wife Nicole Brown and her friend Ronald Goldman. As they heard that Simpson was found not guilty, most African Americans erupted with joy, while most whites gasped with dismay. To many whites, considerable evidence suggested that Simpson committed the murders. To many African Americans, though, the evidence could not be trusted because of the bungling of the police department, including detective Mark Fuhrman's apparent willingness to manufacture evidence. However, long before any evidence was presented at trial, both groups had already formed conflicting opinions. According to a Gallup poll taken more than a year earlier, 68 percent of whites believed Simpson was guilty but 60 percent of blacks believed him innocent (Cose, 1995).

Why do white and African Americans see the same case differently? Is it because blacks are so much more likely than whites to be targets of police harassment that they have developed a negative view of the U.S. criminal justice system? Such questions deal with the diverse and complex world in which we live. There are many other questions about that world: Why do wars break out between nations? How does the economy of one nation depend on that of another? Why are some marriages successful while others end in divorce? How will a college education affect your income? Are men naturally more aggressive than women? Do cities make people callous and rude? Answers to such questions can be found in **sociology,** the systematic, scientific study of human society, as you will see in the following chapters.

THE STUDY OF SOCIAL LIFE

Virtually everybody has something to say about social behavior. Because we observe it around us every day, many people assume that they know all about it. But, as Otto Larsen (1981) has noted, "Living in a family or working in an organization does not automatically make one a sociologist any more than swimming in the sea makes one an oceanographer or being an animal breeder makes one a geneticist." Sociologists have a special way of looking at human behavior and special tools for studying it.

More Than Common Sense

To many people, sociology appears to be a laborious study of the obvious, an expensive way to discover what everybody already knows. To these people, sociology is merely common sense. But sociology is more than common sense because it is largely based on scientific evidence. Often ideas or beliefs derived from common sense turn out to be false, contradicted by facts from sociological research. See, for example, "Myths and Realities" at the opening of this chapter, which demonstrates some differences between common sense and sociological facts.

Sociological findings such as those that contradict commonly held myths may surprise you. Of course, not every finding in sociology is surprising. In fact, some confirm what you have known all along. You should not be surprised, therefore, to learn from sociology that there is more joblessness among blacks than whites or that there are more poor people than rich people in prison. But many other commonsense ideas have turned out to be false, like the ones in the chapter-opening box. By systematically checking commonsense ideas against reliable facts, sociology can tell us which popular beliefs are myths and which are realities.

Sociology can also help clarify the confusion that sometimes arises from common sense. You may have read that "birds of a feather flock together" but also that "opposites attract." You may have heard the encouraging message that "absence makes the heart grow fonder," but you may still remember the discouraging warning, "out of sight, out of mind." When confronted with such conflicting commonsense ideas, how can we tell which are correct and which are false? We can get the answer from sociological research. It has shown, for example, that the effect of someone's absence on another depends on the strength of the initial relationship. If two people have loved each other deeply like Romeo and Juliet, absence would make their hearts grow fonder, but a high school romance tends to disintegrate, because such relationships are usually not deep and serious enough to begin with (Kohn, 1988).

In sum, it is not true that sociology is only common sense. If it were, we wouldn't bother to study sociology. Why would we spend our time learning something we already know? Common sense requires only a willingness to believe what it tells us. It cannot tell us whether those beliefs have any basis in fact. But sociology can. This is one of the reasons that sociology is exciting. It enables us to see that what has long been familiar—or just "common sense"—may turn out to be unfamiliar or uncommon. While common sense gives us familiar and untested ideas, sociology offers factually supported ideas as well as the excitement of discovering something new about ourselves.

Analyzing Social Diversity

For centuries many people have followed the ancient Greek philosopher Plato's advice, "Know thyself," by looking into themselves rather than at others. Sociology suggests that we can know *ourselves* better by studying *others*. By doing so, we can see how others are similar to us in some ways and different in other ways. By a small leap of imagination, we may see that we are likely to behave similarly if we find ourselves under the same social condition.

Our society offers great diversity in race, ethnicity, class, gender, age, sexual orientation, and other social characteristics. Studying these differences provides us with an excellent opportunity to know one another and gain insight into how society operates. We can learn much, for example, from people who experience **social marginality**—being excluded from mainstream society—such as racial or ethnic minorities, women, the poor, the homeless, older persons, gays, people with disabilities, and so on. Generally, these people are acutely aware of how powerfully their lives are affected by various social conditions such as prejudice and discrimination. Their social marginality constantly reminds them of how difficult it is for them to make it in a society that treats them like outsiders. On the other hand, we can also see how the social advantages enjoyed by members of mainstream society make it easier for them to succeed. In short, the study of social diversity can reveal the various ways in which society influences the lives of different individuals, including our own.

Exploring the Global Village

We can gain further insight into ourselves and our society by going beyond our national boundaries to study other societies. Today, the whole world has become a **global village**, a closely knit community of all the world's societies. Whatever happens in a faraway land can affect our lives here.

Consider the various ways in which **economic globalization**—the interrelationship of the world's economies—can influence economic life in the United States: The abundance of low-paid workers in relatively poor countries tends to decrease the wages of American workers because their employers want to reduce production costs, including wages, in order to compete. The abundance of low-paid foreign workers also encourages U.S. corporations to produce inexpensive products by building factories and hiring workers abroad. This may increase plant closings, unemployment, low-wage employment, poverty, and community breakdown in the United States. On the other hand, economic globalization may have some positive consequences for the U.S. economy. Competing with foreign firms here and abroad forces U.S. corporations to become more efficient and productive. Shifting low-skilled jobs from the United States to poor nations is likely to raise those countries' incomes, making them bigger markets for U.S. goods. Globalization induces each country to specialize in what it does best, a poor country, for example, making shoes and a rich country producing computer software. Competition in the global market may increase the availability of well-made but inexpensive products in all nations.

Given the importance of globalization in our lives, we can never emphasize enough the significance of studying other societies. As Peter Berger (1992) says, "One can be an excellent physicist without ever having stepped outside one's own society; this is not so for a sociologist. . . . Thus sociologists must look at Japan in order to understand the West, at socialism in order to understand capitalism, at India so as to understand Brazil, and so on." In brief, by guiding us through the global village, sociology enables us to understand our lives better by opening our eyes to social forces that we may not see from looking at our society alone.

Sociology as a Science

The goal of science is to find order in apparent chaos. Scientists search for a pattern in what, on the surface, may look like random variations. They look for regularity, something that appears over and over, across time and space. Observation is usually a key element in this search. It is true that scientists, like everyone else, have preconceived ideas, beliefs, and values, and

Studying the differences in society in such characteristics as race, ethnicity, class, gender, and age enables us to understand others better, to gain insight into how society operates, and ultimately to know ourselves better.

they use intuition to understand the world. But scientific methods require scientists to put aside existing views of what the world should be like and to rely, above all, on observation.

When scientists discover a pattern in the world, they describe it in the form of a **hypothesis,** a tentative statement of how various events are related to one another. Then they test the hypothesis against systematic observations, producing evidence for or against it. Hypotheses must be related to one another in order to explain a broader range of phenomena. A set of logically related hypotheses that explains the relationship among various phenomena is called a **theory.** A good theory will apply to a wide range of existing observations and suggest testable predictions about what can be observed in the future.

Suppose we are investigating the causes of revolutions. We find that most of the Asian and African nations gained their independence by revolting against their various European colonial rulers in the late 1940s and 1950s. Despite their differences, we come across some similarities among all those revolutions, which historians have called the "revolutions of rising expectations." In those countries, the living conditions had improved but the people did not find the improvement adequate. They were enraged by the discrepancy between what was and what they felt ought to be. From these similarities, we could devise the hypothesis that revolutions are caused by a discrepancy between expectations and reality. If we test this hypothesis against systematic observations of other revolutions and find that the evidence consistently supports our hypothesis, then we have a theory of revolution.

We would, however, have proven our theory to be only tentatively, rather than absolutely, true. A scientific theory is always open to revision in the light of new evidence. Scientific findings are always subject to verification or refutation by other scientists. If the findings cannot be duplicated by other scientists, they are suspect. Scientists usually check whether their findings confirm or contradict those of their colleagues. This procedure increases the chances that mistakes, oversights, or biases will be detected. It ensures the objectivity of science.

The Sociological Imagination

To understand human behavior, sociologists stand back and look "from the outside" at individuals as members of society, rather than "inside them" to examine their thoughts, personalities, or motivations. Sociologists have long found that no matter how personal our experiences are, they are influenced by **social forces**—forces that arise from the society of which we are a part. Social forces exist outside the individual in the form of social relationships such as those we share with friends, relatives, and people in educational, economic, religious, and other institutions. C. Wright Mills (1959b) referred to the ability to see the impact of social forces on individuals, especially on their private lives, as the **sociological imagination.** Through social forces, society exercises so much power on individuals that we can effectively see it through their behavior.

Consider the case of suicide. It is reasonable to assume that those who kill themselves are frustrated and unhappy, since happy people rarely want to die. But suicide cannot be explained that simply. This explanation does not tell us why, for example, people who live in wide-open areas have much higher suicide rates than those who live in crowded areas (see Figure 1.1). There is no evidence that those who live in wide-open areas are more unhappy. How, then, do we account for the difference in suicide rates?

The sociological imagination leads us to look not at the individual personalities of those who commit suicide, but at social forces. When French sociologist Emile Durkheim (1897) examined suicide in the late nineteenth century, he detailed variations in the rates of suicide among various countries and groups. These rates constitute social, not individual, facts; to explain them, Durkheim turned to social forces. The force that he found to have a great impact on suicide was **social integration,** the degree to which people are tied to a social group. When there is either excessive or inadequate social integration, suicide rates are likely to be high.

In the past, when elderly Inuit* committed suicide, the cause was usually extreme social integration. Obedient to the values and customs of their society, they did what they were expected by others to do: killing themselves when they could no longer contribute to the economy of their community. Similarly, Hindu widows used to follow the tradition of their society by ceremoniously throwing themselves onto the funeral pyres of their husbands. These ritual suicides were called *suttee* (literally, "good women"). The Hindu widows and elderly Inuit apparently felt pressured to commit suicide. If the Hindu widows did not kill themselves, they might be scorned as "bad women." If the elderly Inuit refused to kill themselves, they might be stigmatized as "selfish."

On the other hand, a lack of social integration can also be found in high suicide rates. Divorced and widowed people, for example, are more likely than married people to be isolated from others and to receive little affection or moral support when they have problems. In other words, they are more likely to experience *inadequate* social integration. As a result, they are also more likely than married people to commit suicide. Similarly, people who live in sparsely populated states such as Montana and Wyoming are more isolated from others than those who live in densely populated states such as New York and New Jersey. Greater isolation tends to make people more individualistic, more dependent on themselves than on others. This individualism may underlie the higher rate of suicide in the wide-open areas. By relying on themselves to solve their personal problems, people tend to be too subjective and emotional to find a viable solution (Thio, 1995).

Suicide is an extreme, exceptional act, but all around us we can see ordinary actions that are also molded by social forces. The distribution of income in

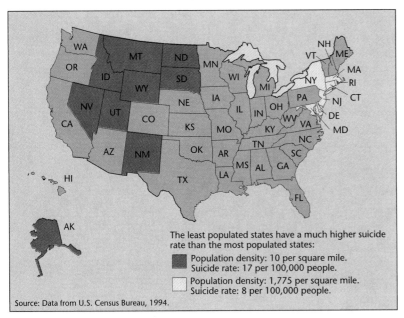

FIGURE 1.1
Suicide More Common in Wide-Open Areas

A social cause of suicide is relative isolation from others. Having to rely on themselves to solve personal problems, people tend to be too subjective and emotional to find a viable solution. This may explain why suicide rates are generally higher in sparsely populated areas.

The least populated states have a much higher suicide rate than the most populated states:

- Population density: 10 per square mile. Suicide rate: 17 per 100,000 people.
- Population density: 1,775 per square mile. Suicide rate: 8 per 100,000 people.

Source: Data from U.S. Census Bureau, 1994.

---

*Inuit are popularly called "Eskimo," a derogatory term meaning "eater of raw meat."

the United States is a social fact. Your family's position in that distribution is one of your social characteristics. This characteristic influences your way of living and your chances in life—such as the likelihood that you will pursue a successful career. Our private worlds can never be totally sealed off from the larger world of society and global community. The technology, economy, customs, ideals, beliefs, government, and politics in the United States, as well as those in other countries—all are social characteristics and represent social forces that help shape our lives.

Questions for Discussion and Review

1. How does sociology differ from common sense?
2. Why is it important to study the diversity in the United States and the world?
3. What is the nature of sociology as a science?
4. How does the sociological imagination clarify the influence of social forces on the experiences of individuals?

THE DEVELOPMENT OF SOCIOLOGY

Sociology as a formal field of study has a very short history. Of course, centuries before Christ was born, thinkers such as Plato and Socrates had thought and argued about social behavior. But most of them did not make systematic observations to test their speculations against reality. They were social philosophers, not sociologists. The field of sociology emerged in the nineteenth century, when European social philosophers began to use scientific methods.

Two factors combined to convert some philosophers into sociologists: the social upheavals of nineteenth-century Europe and the advancement of the natural sciences. The Western world was radically altered during the nineteenth century as the Industrial Revolution brought new industries and technologies and new ways of living. Almost overnight, societies that had long been rural and stable became industrialized, urbanized, and chaotic. They confronted problems such as the exploitation of factory workers, the migration of people from farms to cities, congestion and poverty in the cities, crowded and squalid housing, broken families, and rising crime. Meanwhile, the European political order had been shaken. In the aftermath of the French Revolution, many people began to question the legitimacy of their monarchies and the authority of their churches, demanding greater

freedom for the individual. Many social philosophers felt challenged to find solutions to their societies' new problems and to understand how and why such radical change could occur. At the same time, the natural sciences were highly respected, because they were providing ways to both explain and control aspects of the physical world. Some social philosophers looked on natural science as a model for how they might go about understanding and controlling the social world.

As sociology developed, these two urges—to improve the world and to apply scientific methods to the study of society—continued to motivate sociologists.

The Pioneers of Sociology

The nineteenth-century French philosopher Auguste Comte (1798–1857) is sometimes called the father of sociology. He coined the word "sociology" in 1838 to refer to the scientific study of society. Comte believed that every society goes through three stages of development: religious, metaphysical, and scientific. According to Comte, reliance on superstition and speculation characterizes the religious and metaphysical stages, and neither is adequate for understanding society. What is needed, he argued, is scientific knowledge about society based on social facts, just as scien-

Auguste Comte (1798–1857) was the first to argue for the need for scientific knowledge about society. He is regarded as the father of sociology.

tific knowledge about the physical world is based on physical facts. He envisioned a science of society with two branches: *statics,* the study of the organization that allows societies to endure, and *dynamics,* the study of the processes by which societies change. During the scientific stage, Comte believed, sociologists would develop a scientific knowledge of society and would guide society in a peaceful, orderly evolution. Such a task was soon initiated by Harriet Martineau (1802–1876), the world's first woman sociologist in England. She translated Comte's writings, studied British and U.S. societies, and suggested that societal progress could be achieved by eradicating slavery, the oppression of women, and worker exploitation (Hoecker-Drysdale, 1992).

Herbert Spencer (1820–1903), an Englishman, had a different view of how society works. He believed that a society can be compared to a living organism. Each part of an animal—its heart, lungs, brains, and so on—has its own function to perform, yet all the parts are interdependent; a change in one part affects all the others. Moreover, each part contributes to the survival and health of the animal as a whole. If one organ becomes diseased, others adapt by working harder to ensure the animal's survival. Similarly, in Spencer's view, each part of a society performs its own function and contributes to the survival and stability of the whole. The family, religion, the government, and industry are all seen as parts of one "organism," society.

Spencer concluded that society, if left alone, corrects its own problems; it tends naturally toward health and stability. Social problems work themselves out through the process of natural selection called "survival of the fittest." The phrase suggests that rich, powerful, or otherwise successful people—the "fittest"—have been "selected" by nature to be what they are. On the other hand, poor, weak, or otherwise unsuccessful individuals—the "unfit"—have been doomed, by nature, to failure. If government interferes with this natural process by helping the unfit, society will suffer because the efforts of its successful people will be wasted. According to Spencer, the best thing government can do about social problems is to leave them alone. The fate of society, in his view, is governed by laws of nature. If nature is left to do its job without government interference, society will not only survive but evolve to become better.

Where Spencer saw harmony and stability, Karl Marx (1818–1883) observed underlying conflict, exploitation, and the seeds of revolution. According to Marx, a German who spent much of his life writing in England, Spencer's stable, interdependent society was a myth. The primary feature of society, Marx claimed, is not stability and interdependence but conflict and

competition. He saw every society, past and present, as marked by social conflict.

In particular, Marx claimed that the primary feature of society is **class conflict,** the struggle between capitalists, who own the means of production, and the proletariat, who do not. These two classes, he said, are inevitably locked in conflict. The laborers, far from being naturally unfit, are destined to overthrow the capitalists and establish a classless society in which everyone will work according to ability and receive according to need.

Marx did not believe, as did Spencer, that the differences between laborers and capitalists are determined by natural selection. On the contrary, Marx believed that they are determined by the economic system. In fact, he argued, the economic system determines a society's religious beliefs, its values, and the nature of its educational system, government, and other institutions. He urged people not to let society evolve on its own but to change it.

Despite their differences, both Marx and Spencer, like Comte, recognized the value of science in the study of society, but they did not actually use scientific methods. They merely argued about how society

Emile Durkheim (1858–1917) pioneered the systematic application of scientific principles to sociology. He was the first to use statistical methods to test hypotheses.

worked and how its troubles might be eased. It was Emile Durkheim (1858–1917) who pioneered the systematic application of scientific methods to sociology. His ideas about suicide, discussed earlier, were not based on speculation. In his study of suicide, he made a research plan and collected a large mass of statistical data on suicide in various European countries. Then he analyzed the data in order to discover the causes of suicide. He not only used systematic observation but also argued that sociologists should consider only what they could observe and should look at "social facts as things." They should not look, he said, to "the notions" of people in order to explain society. People's subjective experiences should not be a concern of sociologists.

In contrast, the German sociologist Max Weber (1864–1920) believed that sociologists must go beyond what people do, beyond what can be observed directly. He argued that individuals always interpret the meaning of their own behavior and act according to these interpretations. Sociologists must therefore find out how people feel or what they think about their own behavior. To do this, according to Weber, sociologists should adopt a method he called **Verstehen** (pronounced fair-SHTAY-in)—empathetic understanding of their subjects. By mentally putting themselves into the position of their subjects, sociologists could obtain an "interpretive understanding" of the meanings of particular behavior. Then, he said, they should test this understanding through careful observation.

Sociology in the United States

By the turn of the twentieth century, sociology had made its way from Europe to the United States. Like their European predecessors, the first U.S. sociologists tried to understand and solve the problems of their time, problems such as crime and delinquency, broken homes, poor neighborhoods, and racial problems. But they dealt with social problems differently. The Europeans were more interested in developing large-scale social theories. So they examined the fundamental issues of social order and social change, trying to discover the causes of social problems as a whole. In contrast, the U.S. sociologists were more pragmatic. They were more inclined to focus on specific problems, such as prostitution or juvenile delinquency, and to treat each problem separately. To study and solve these problems, they developed scientific, quantitative methods (Ross, 1991).

A good example was Jane Addams (1860–1935), one of the founders of U.S. sociology and social work. In Chicago, she set up and directed a center for social reform and research, which she named Hull House. Most of the social activists working at Hull House were

Jane Addams (1860–1935) conducted scientific research on social problems with the aim of eliminating or alleviating them. She was the only sociologist ever to have received a Nobel Prize.

women. They often exchanged ideas and interests with the predominantly male sociologists at the University of Chicago. The chief goal of Hull House was to solve social problems using sound sociological theory. The "Chicago School" sociologists also were interested in applying sociological theory to social problems, but they emphasized theory and research. Thus, their achievements in social reform were not as successful as those of the truly applied sociologists of Hull House.

In their projects, Addams and her colleagues would first identify a certain problem, then gather data documenting the nature of the problem and formulate a social-action policy based on the data. Their final step was to organize citizens and lobby political and community leaders to eliminate or alleviate the problem. They dealt with a wide array of social ills, including poverty, worker exploitation, child labor, juvenile delinquency, unjust laws, and difficulties faced by working women and the elderly. A new research technique called "mapping" was used. It involved seeking information on an urban population's demographic characteristics (such as age, sex, occupations, wages, and housing conditions) and then presenting the geographic distribution of those characteristics on a map. By applying research in this way, Addams was able to play a significant role in establishing many government programs—most notably Social Security, the Children's Bureau, the Immigrant Bureau, Workers'

Compensation—and various government regulations affecting health and safety standards. In 1931, Addams was awarded the Nobel Peace Prize (Deegan, 1988; Ross, 1991).

For about 40 years after the turn of this century, most U.S. sociologists focused on studying and solving social problems. However, the prosperity that followed the Second World War masked many social problems, causing the reformist fervor to begin to cool. Some sociologists turned their attention to general theories of society. The idea grew that sociology should be a *basic science,* seeking knowledge only, not an *applied science,* which puts knowledge to use. Moreover, many people believed that sociology must be objective and free of values. This left no room for a commitment to reform society according to certain values. From about 1945 to 1965, sociology was dominated by the attempt to develop scientific methods that could be applied to the study of societies and social behavior. During these two decades, sociologists developed increasingly sophisticated research techniques.

In the 1960s, however, the ideal of objective, value-free knowledge came under fire in just about all fields, including sociology. Renewed awareness of poverty and years of social unrest—marked by race riots, student revolts, and controversy about the Vietnam War—put pressure on sociologists to attack society's ills once again. Meanwhile, attitudes toward the major theoretical perspectives in sociology were also shifting. The conflict perspective, which emphasizes social conflict as a constant fact of social life, was becoming popular at the expense of the functionalist perspective, which stresses the persistence of social order.

Sociology in the United States has thus developed into a diverse discipline. Today, it is both a basic and an applied science, and sociologists use both objective and subjective methods. The soaring number of sociologists—from only about 3,000 in the 1960s to about 20,000 today—has further splintered sociology into numerous specialties, such as mathematical sociology, organizational research, and race and ethnic relations. Each of these specialties has been differentiated into many subspecialties. The specialty of race relations, for example, has broken down into studies of blacks, Hispanics, Asians, and other specific minorities in the United States (Blalock, 1984; Collins, 1986; Gans, 1989). Underlying this diversity are certain theoretical perspectives that sociologists employ to study and understand social behavior. We will examine three major ones in the next section.

Questions for Discussion and Review

1. How did Karl Marx's understanding of nineteenth-century European society differ from that of Herbert Spencer?

2. How did the development of U.S. sociology differ from the work of European sociologists?

MAJOR PERSPECTIVES IN SOCIOLOGY

Sociologists approach the study of human society in different ways. They can look at the "big picture" of society to see how it operates. This is a **macro view,** focusing on the large social phenomena of society such as social institution and inequality. Sociologists can also take a **micro view,** zeroing in on the immediate social situations where people interact with one another. From these two views sociologists have developed various **theoretical perspectives,** each a set of general assumptions about the nature of society. There are three well-known theoretical perspectives in sociology: the functionalist and conflict perspectives, which both provide a macro view of society, and the symbolic interactionist perspective, which offers a micro view.

Functionalist Perspective

Both Spencer and Durkheim provided ideas that inspired the **functionalist perspective,** which focuses on social order. According to this perspective, each part of society—the family, the school, the economy, the state—performs certain functions for the society as a whole. Moreover, all the parts are interdependent. The family, for example, depends on the school to educate its children, and the school, in turn, depends on the family or the state to provide financial support. The state, in turn, depends on the family and school to help children grow up to become law-abiding, taxpaying citizens. Out of these interdependent parts of society comes a stable social order. If something happens to disrupt this social order, its parts will adjust in a way that produces a new stability. Suppose the economy were in bad shape, with high rates of inflation and unemployment. The family would adjust, perhaps by spending less and saving more. Schools would probably offer fewer programs and might emphasize vocational training to help students find work. The state might try to cut its budget. As a result, a new social order would emerge.

However, what holds the society together, enabling all of its parts to produce social order? The answer, according to functionalists, is **social consensus,** a condition in which most members of the society agree on what would be good for everybody and cooperate to achieve it. Durkheim assumed that social consensus can come about in the form of either mechanical or organic solidarity.

Mechanical solidarity is a type of social cohesion that develops when people do similar work and have similar beliefs and values. It exists in relatively small-scale, traditional societies. An example is a society in which almost everyone works at farming and believes in the same gods.

In contrast, **organic solidarity** is a type of social cohesion that arises when the people in a society perform a wide variety of specialized jobs and therefore have to depend on one another. Organic solidarity is characteristic of complex, industrialized societies. The people in a U.S. city, for example, are likely to hold many very different types of jobs, to have grown up with different family customs, to hold varying beliefs and values. There are bankers, teachers, engineers, plumbers, and many other businesses, professions, and occupations. Among these people there will probably be atheists and Christians, Jews and Muslims, reactionaries and radicals, and everything in between. Thus, mechanical solidarity among the city's people is not likely to be strong. They cannot be bound together by conformity to the same ideas and ideals. But they can be more easily bound together by their need for each other. The banker needs the worker who deposits and borrows money, and both need the storekeeper, who needs the trucker who delivers food, who needs the mechanic and gas station attendant, and so on. The complex ties of dependence seem virtually endless. These people are bound together by organic solidarity.

During the 1940s and 1950s, the functionalist perspective became widely accepted by U.S. sociologists. In its European origins, functionalism was used to help explain the society as a whole—to clarify how order and stability were maintained. U.S. sociologists, on the other hand, have been more interested in discovering the functions of specific types of human behavior.

The most prominent among these U.S. sociologists is Robert Merton (1957). He classified functions into two types: manifest and latent. **Manifest functions** are those that are intended and seem obvious; **latent functions** are unintended and often unrecognized. The manifest function of going to college, for example, is to get an education, but going to college also has the latent function of enabling many students to find their future spouses. Another latent function is to force students to learn the valuable lesson of negotiating their way through bureaucratic mazes in order to get things done. After four years of learning to master preregistration, financial aid forms, major and general education requirements, course schedules, add-and-drop policies, and dormitory preference forms, you will find it easier to work in even the most formidable business bureaucracy (Galles, 1989).

Throughout this book we will see many examples of the usefulness of the functionalist perspective, but by itself it cannot lead to a complete picture of social events. It has also been criticized for focusing on the positive functions of a social event, such as sports, and ignoring the negative. Similarly, the application of functionalism to analyze society has been criticized for being inherently conservative; in effect, it justifies the status quo. By emphasizing what every current aspect of society does for its citizens, functionalism encourages people to dismiss social change as "dysfunctional" (harmful), even though change may, in fact, produce a better society.

Conflict Perspective

The conflict perspective produces a portrait of society strikingly different from that offered by functionalism. Whereas functionalism emphasizes society's stability, the **conflict perspective** portrays society as always changing and always marked by conflict. Functionalists tend to focus on social order, to view social change as harmful, and to assume that the social order is based largely on people's willing cooperation. In contrast, proponents of the conflict perspective are inclined to concentrate on social conflict, to see social change as beneficial, and to assume that the social order is forcibly imposed by the powerful on the weak. They criticize the status quo.

The conflict perspective originated largely from Karl Marx's writings on class conflict between capitalists and the proletariat. For decades U.S. sociologists tended to ignore Marx and the conflict perspective because the functionalist perspective dominated their view of society. Since the turbulent 1960s, however, the conflict perspective has gained popularity. Generally, conflict is now defined more broadly. Whereas Marx believed that conflict between *economic* classes was the key force in society, conflict theorists today define social conflict to mean conflict between any unequal groups or societies. Thus, they examine conflict between whites and blacks, men and women, one religious group and another, one society and another, and so on. They emphasize that groups or societies will have conflicting interests and values and will compete with each other. Because of this perpetual competition, society or the world is always changing.

Feminist Theory The conflict perspective leads sociologists to ask such questions as: Which groups are more powerful and which are weaker? How do powerful groups benefit from the existing social order, and how are weaker groups hurt? How do the powerful preserve their privileges, and how do the weaker challenge them? Some sociologists have in recent decades applied these kinds of questions to

Conflict theorists look at conflicting interests and values between unequals and see such competition as the source of social change. Thus, even conflict between parents and adolescents can be seen as beneficial in changing the status quo.

the experiences of women. As a result, they have fashioned a **feminist theory,** a form of conflict theory that explains human life from the experiences of women. Details of the theory vary from one sociologist to another. But they suggest in one way or another how women's lives differ from men's (Lengermann and Niebrugge-Brantley, 1992), with the assumption that these gender differences shape the lives of all of us.

First, women's experiences are said to *differ* from those of men. There is a diversity of feminist views on what the gender differences are. However, most agree that being interested in bearing and caring for infants, being gentle rather than tough, and being peaceful rather than violent toward others are among the socially learned characteristics that distinguish some women from men. To feminists, these feminine values are at least equal, if not superior, to traditional masculine values. They deserve to be respected and recognized as valuable alternatives to, rather than as undesirable departures from, male values. But men have long regarded these traits as less valuable, which reinforces the devaluation of women's social position.

Second, feminist theory holds that women's position in most social situations is *unequal* to that of men. Compared with men, women have less power, freedom, respect, or money. Such gender inequality comes from the widely held sexist belief that women are inferior to men. It may also originate from the traditional role that women play as unpaid caregivers for husbands and children.

Third, feminist theory views women as *oppressed*—restrained, subordinated, controlled, molded, or abused—by men. This is the essence of **patriarchy**—

"a system of domination in which men exercise power over women" (Kimmel, 1992). The oppression may involve overt physical violence against women, such as rape, wife abuse, or incest. It may assume more subtle forms such as unpaid household work, underpaid wage work, sexual harassment in the workplace, and the standards of fashion and beauty that reduce women to men's sexual playthings (Lengermann and Niebrugge-Brantley, 1992).

According to feminist theory, then, women are not only different from men but also unequal to men and oppressed by men. But what is the cause of all this? According to *liberal feminists,* the problem of gender differences, inequalities, and oppressions can be traced to *socialization*—the process by which society transmits its cultural values to its members through the family, school, and media (see Chapter 9: Gender and Age). To *socialist feminists,* gender inequalities originate from the need of *capitalism* to enhance profits by turning women into wives, housewives, and mothers. In these roles, women are forced to serve as unpaid caregivers (for husbands and children) to ensure a productive male workforce, and also serve as consumers of goods and services (for the household) to keep the economy going. To *radical feminists,* because only women can bear children and men are naturally aggressive, men use their *aggression* to force women to raise children and depend on men for security (Abbott and Wallace, 1990; Bart, 1991).

Feminist theory assumes that, given those negative experiences, women are bound to challenge the status quo by seeking gender equality in education, career, marriage, and other areas of life. The theory is therefore useful for understanding the changes that have been taking place in the lives of both women and men throughout society. The theory has also been criticized for overemphasizing the oppressiveness of patriarchy. According to critics, not all men are oppressors and not all women are victims. In fact, in critics' views, most women are far from being victims of their fathers, husbands, and sons but instead receive love, assistance, and other benefits from them. In the same way, the conflict perspective itself has been criticized for overly stressing social conflict and other negative aspects of society while ignoring the order, stability, and other positive aspects of society.

Symbolic Interactionist Perspective

Both functionalist and conflict perspectives focus on larger social forces of order, conflict, and patriarchy, forces that simultaneously affect huge numbers of people across the country. In contrast, the **symbolic interactionist perspective** directs our attention to the details of a specific situation and of the interaction between individuals in that situation. The combination of these countless interactions in various situations is seen to constitute society. We can trace the origins of symbolic interactionism to Max Weber's argument that people act according to their interpretation of the meaning of their social world. But it was George Herbert Mead (1863–1931), a U.S. philosopher, who introduced symbolic interactionism to sociology in the 1920s.

According to symbolic interactionism, people assign meanings to each other's words and actions. Our response to a person's action is therefore determined not by that person's action in and of itself but by our *subjective interpretation* of that person's action. When we speak to a friend, an observer can easily give an objective report of the words we have said. But our friend's response will depend not on the list of words we spoke but on our friend's interpretation of the entire interaction, and our friend's response is at the same time influencing what we are saying. If our friend perceives by the way we speak that we are intelligent, this interpretation may make our friend respect and admire us and, perhaps, respond more positively to what we are saying. If we, in turn, catch this interpretation, we may feel proud and speak more confidently. In other words, the exchange is a *symbolic interaction*. It is an interaction between individuals that is governed by their interpretation of the meaning of symbols. In this case, the symbols are primarily spoken words. But a symbol can be anything—an object, a sound, a gesture—that points to something beyond itself. The marks on this paper are symbols because they point to something—they mean something—beyond black squiggles.

The symbolic interactionist perspective suggests two things. First, people do not respond directly to physical "things." Rather, they respond to their *own* interpretations of them. Second, because people constantly impose interpretations—on the world in general, on other people, themselves, and even their own interpretations—and then act accordingly, human behavior is fluid, always changing. How we act is constantly being altered by how we interpret other people's actions and their reactions to our own behavior. In other words, human behavior is not real in and of itself but becomes real only after it has been subjected to "reality construction," the process by which we interpret what a given action means and respond to it in accordance with the interpretation.

The symbolic interactionist perspective is very useful for understanding why and how we interact with others, something that we do during most of our waking hours. But the perspective has been criticized for ignoring the larger issues of national and international order and change. It has also been faulted for ignoring the influence of larger social forces such as social institutions, groups, cultures, and societies on individual interactions.

A Multiple View

After thinking about those three perspectives, you may ask, "Which one is right?" The answer can be found in the following story from sociologist Elliot Liebow (1993):

> Mr. Shapiro and Mr. Goldberg had an argument they were unable to resolve.
>
> It was agreed that Mr. Shapiro would present the case to a rabbi.
>
> The rabbi said to Mr. Shapiro, "You are right."
>
> When Mr. Goldberg learned of this, he ran to the rabbi with his version of the argument. The rabbi said to him, "You are right."
>
> Then the rabbi's wife said to the rabbi, "You told Mr. Shapiro he was right and you told Mr. Goldberg he was right. They can't both be right!"
>
> The rabbi said to his wife, "You are right too."

As the rabbi would say, each of the three perspectives in sociology is right in its own way. Each shows what our world looks like, but only when viewed from a certain angle. (See Table 1.1 for a review of the key features of each perspective.)

Though different, the three perspectives are not really incompatible. To some extent, they are like different perspectives on a house. Looked at from the front, the house has a door, windows, and a chimney on top. From the back, it has a door and a chimney on top, but probably fewer windows and maybe a porch. From the top, it has no doors or windows, but it has a chimney in the

TABLE 1.1
How the Three Perspectives Differ

TYPES OF PERSPECTIVES	Subject Under Focus	Nature of Society	Maintenance of Social Order
Functionalist Perspective	Social order or stability	Consists of interdependent groups pursuing common goals	Through social consensus, whereby people agree to cooperate in order to contribute to social order
Conflict Perspective	Social conflict or change	Made up of conflicting groups, each pursuing its own interest	Through coercion, social order is imposed by the powerful on the weak
Symbolic Interactionist Perspective	Interaction between individuals	Composed of individuals whose actions depend on interpreting each other's behavior	Through constant negotiations between individuals trying to understand each other's actions and reactions

middle. It is the same house, but it looks very different, depending on one's perspective. Similarly, whether we see functions, conflict, or interaction depends on the position from which we are looking. Each perspective is useful because we cannot take everything about the complex social world into account at once. We need some vantage point. Each perspective tells us what to look for, and each brings some aspect of society and human behavior into sharper focus. Brought together, these diverse perspectives can enrich our sociological knowledge of the world.

Suppose we want to study the interaction between whites and blacks or between upper- and lower-class people. Each perspective can be useful. Functionalist and conflict perspectives can clarify how the interaction is affected by larger social forces, such as the popular belief in democracy and equality, the long history of racial prejudice, or the differences in lifestyle or power between rich and poor. On the other hand, symbolic interactionism can give us a richer, more detailed view of specific interactions and an understanding of why people who are exposed to the same social forces behave in different ways. Moreover, the three perspectives can be used to check each other to see if we have overemphasized any one perspective and missed the complex reality of the world in which we live. In the next section, we will see how the three perspectives can be used to shed light on sports.

Questions for Discussion and Review

1. What is a theoretical perspective, and what are the main features of the three perspectives sociologists use today?

2. How do the basic assumptions of the conflict perspective differ from those of functionalism?

3. Why isn't any one of the three perspectives better than the others?

SPORTS: ILLUSTRATING THE THREE PERSPECTIVES

The influence of sports reaches far and wide. Sports are particularly popular in our leisure-oriented society. Most of us have had some experience with athletics, as participants or spectators. Schools, from kindergarten to college, provide many sports opportunities. Newspapers carry more news about sports than about politics, the economy, crime, or practically any other event. Radio and television newscasts rarely go on the air without a sports report. Football, basketball, baseball, and other games are often broadcast in their entirety, preempting regular programming. Sports exert so much influence on our lives that our everyday speech is full of sports imagery: "struck out," "touch base," "ballpark figure," "game plan," "teamwork," "cheap shot," "go all the way," and so on.

What, then, is the nature of this powerful aspect of our lives? From the three sociological perspectives, we can see that sports are beneficial to society in some ways, harmful in other ways, and like any other social interaction, governed by individuals' definitions of each other's actions.

To functionalists, sports help athletes develop such qualities as skill and ability, diligence and self-discipline, mental alertness, and physical fitness, which help athletes ensure success in the larger society.

Sports as Beneficial to Society

According to the functionalist perspective, sports contribute to the welfare of society by performing at least three major functions.

First, sports are conducive to success in other areas of life. Being competitive, sports inspire athletes to do their utmost to win, thereby helping them to develop such qualities as skill and ability, diligence and self-discipline, mental alertness, and physical fitness. These qualities can ensure success in the larger society. In the words of General Douglas MacArthur: "Upon the fields of friendly strife are sown the seeds that, upon other fields, on other days, will bear the fruits of victory." By watching athletes perform, spectators also learn the importance of hard work, playing by the rules, and working as a team player, characteristics that help ensure success in a career and other aspects of life.

Second, sports enhance health and happiness. Participants can enjoy a healthy and long life. The health benefit is more than physical. It is also psychological. Runners and joggers, for example, often find that their activity releases tension and anger as well as relieving anxiety and depression. Moreover, many people derive much pleasure from looking upon their participation as a form of beauty, an artistic expression, or a way of having a good time with friends. Similarly, sports improve the quality of life for the spectators. Fans can escape their humdrum daily routines, or find pleasure in filling their leisure time. They can savor the aesthetic pleasure of watching the excellence, beauty, and creativity in an athlete's performance. The fans can therefore attain greater happiness, life satisfaction, or psychological well-being (Smith, 1993).

Third, sports contribute to social order and stability. This is because sports serve as an integrating force for society as a whole. Sports are in effect a social mechanism for uniting potentially disunited members of society. Through their common interest in a famous athlete or team, people of diverse racial, social, and cultural backgrounds can feel a sense of homogeneity, community, or intimacy that they can acquire in no other way. Athletes, too, can identify with their fans, their community, and their country.

Sports as Harmful to Society

According to the conflict perspective, sports are harmful to society in a number of ways, reflecting the conflict between the interests of the relatively powerful and those of the powerless (the ruling class vs. the masses, team owners vs. sports audience, whites vs. blacks, or men vs. women).

First, by serving as an integrating force, sports effectively act as an opiate, numbing the masses' sense of dissatisfaction with capitalist society. Involvement in sports as spectators tends to distract low-paid or unemployed workers from their tedious and dehumanizing jobs or frustrating joblessness. At the same time, sports tend to promote what Marx called "false consciousness," attitudes that support the established society rather than question it. The mostly working-class "soccer hooligans" in England are a good example. After their team loses in international soccer games, they often show "an exaggerated, embarrassing patriotism, a violent nationalism" by attacking foreigners (Buford, 1992). To divert their citizens' attention from their miserable lives, governments of many poor countries also seize any opportunity that arises to whip up the masses into a frenzy of patriotic support for their teams. Such a nationalist frenzy can be carried to extremes as it was in 1969 when Honduras and El Salvador went to war against each other after a World Cup soccer match.

Second, sports encourage deviant behavior. This has much to do with the overemphasis on winning. In sports, as the legendary football coach Vince Lombardi said, "winning isn't everything, it's the only thing!" Not surprisingly, athletes have been known to use illicit drugs to enhance performance. In contact sports such as hockey, football, and basketball, players often gratuitously assault their opponents. Even beautiful and graceful sports like figure skating can produce violence, as the whole world saw when Tonya Harding's associate whacked rival Nancy Kerrigan's leg. All this, however, serves the interests of the powerful, such as wealthy team owners and college sports administrators. They can more easily control and exploit the masses and consumers, who generally find the violence and other ruthlessly competitive actions in sports very exciting, so that they will spend a lot of time and money watching.

Third, sports reinforce social, gender, and racial inequalities in society. With regard to social inequality, the overemphasis on competition and winning has caused the loss of something that all participants can enjoy equally—namely, the original elements of play and fun in sport activities. This has turned many people into "couch potatoes," who spend more time watching than playing sports. Sports, then, have become big business, with powerful owners of professional teams exploiting the public and government. Aside from making enormous sums of money from the fans, team owners receive many tax breaks as well as enjoying the enviable position of being the only self-regulated (in effect, unregulated) monopoly in the nation. Team owners have further professionalized and bureaucratized sports. This in turn has generated an elitist system, in which a very tiny number of owners and players become tycoons and superstars and the huge number of potential players are turned into mere spectators.

It is true that over the last two decades sports participation among women has risen sharply, thanks to the women's liberation movement and the 1972 law that prohibits sex discrimination in school sports. Nevertheless, in most colleges and universities, more funds continue to be spent on men's sports, especially football and basketball, than on women's athletic programs. Because of gender bias, men are even more likely than women to get top management and coaching jobs even in *women's* programs (Diesenhouse, 1990). Sports are still considered a "man's world," in which women's leadership skills are devalued. Even the skills of superb

Training and facilities for women's teams have improved since passage of the 1972 law, Title IX of the Educational Amendment Act, which prohibits sex discrimination in school sports. Ironically, however, Title IX has brought about a drop in the number of female coaches and administrators.

women athletes are discounted as the media often describe female athletes as "pretty," "slim," "attractive," "gracious," and "lovely," as opposed to male athletes being "brilliant," "cool," "courageous," "great," or "tough." In glorifying masculinity, sports further encourage male athletes to commit rape, sexual harassment, or wife beating (Nelson, 1994).

On the surface, the huge numbers of remarkably successful black athletes today may cast doubt on the existence of racial inequality in sports. But African Americans do suffer from racism in various ways. We can detect it in the racial patterns of playing positions in professional sports—blacks tend to be in the less important positions, while whites are more likely to be in the central, more important positions. In football, for example, blacks tend to play such peripheral positions as offensive tackle, running back, and defensive back, while whites are more likely to be in the central positions of quarterback, center, offensive guard, and linebacker. Racism is most visible in the virtual absence of African Americans in top positions as owners, managers, and coaches of professional teams.

Most significantly, sports help perpetuate the high rate of poverty among African Americans. Traditionally, widespread and severe job discrimination has caused many poor African American youths to work extremely hard developing athletic skills in order to make it in college and professional sports, which explains why most of the best athletes in the country are black. Today the enormous attention given by the white-dominated media to black superstars further encourages many poor black youths to give their all to athletics. The media apparently have also influenced parents. As Arthur Ashe (1992) found from a survey, black families are six times more likely than white families to encourage their sons to pursue a career in sports. But such an intense concentration on sports has diverted attention from academics. This is tragic because, given the same hard work, it is far easier to become a professional in business, government, education, or any other ordinary field. The odds of turning professional in sports are extremely small. Only one or two percent of high school players with college athletic scholarships will end up as pros, while nearly 100 percent of their non-athlete peers with scholarships for academic achievement will become professionals in other, non-athletic pursuits. This is why Ashe once urged black youths to spend two hours in the library for every hour spent on the athletic field (Ashe, 1977).

Sports as Symbolic Interaction

While functionalist and conflict perspectives focus on the larger, societal issues of sports, which affect most people, symbolic interactionism homes in on the smaller, immediate issue of how athletes—or other individuals involved in a sport, such as coaches and fans—behave. According to this third perspective, if we define a situation as real it is real in its consequences. This means, for example, that if athletes define a game as one that they will win, they will likely win it. Let us take a closer look at how definition influences performance.

Great coaches know that they can get their athletes to perform well by drumming certain ideas into their heads. Foremost is the idea that the players are winners so that they will think only of winning and never about the possibility of losing. Chances are great that they indeed will win, because the image of themselves as winners will force them to concentrate only on the moves that ensure winning. This is basically the technique Jack Nicklaus, perhaps the greatest golfer of all time, uses to enhance his performance. Before every shot, he forms a mental picture in which he sees three things: (1) the target area the ball lands in, (2) the flight path of the ball to the target area, and (3) himself using the appropriate swing for that particular shot (Vealey and Walter, 1993). In short, if athletes define themselves as winners, they are more likely to win. By the same token, if athletes define themselves as losers, they will very likely lose.

Whatever the content of self-definition, it does not necessarily come from within the person. It is more likely to originate from social interaction. Children under 10, for example, often evaluate how "good" or "bad" they are at a sport from what their significant others (parents, teachers, or coaches) say to them. Thus children would describe themselves in ways such as "I know I am a good runner because my mom says I am" or "I don't think that I'm a very good soccer player because my coach is always yelling at me" (Horn and Lox, 1993).

Indeed, how others see us when they interact with us can shape how we define ourselves. But just as we often get our self-definition from our social environment, others also get their image of us from *their* environment. In interacting with an African American athlete, for example, a coach tends to stereotype the athlete as naturally gifted in sports. This stereotype, part of the popular belief about blacks in U.S. society, has a significant impact on the coach's interaction with the black athlete. Most commonly, the coach will impose a higher standard of performance on the black athlete than on a white athlete. And the black athlete will be forced to work harder in order to achieve that higher standard, which may partly explain why black athletes usually outshine their white peers on the same team. Similarly, gender bias in the larger society has often led parents and teachers to discourage young women from playing basketball, soccer, and other so-called male sports, defining women who want to compete in these games as unfeminine. As a result, many women have responded by avoiding these sports and choosing the so-called female sports such as aerobic dancing, swimming, gymnastics, or tennis. The popular definition of some sports as "masculine" and others as "feminine" can also influence the spectators. "Masculine" sports such as football and soccer, for example, are more likely to cause fan violence than are "feminine" sports such as gymnastics and swimming.

We have observed how the three sociological perspectives can shed light on different aspects of sports. Combined, the perspectives can offer not only a *fuller* but also a *balanced* view of the subject. The combination of functionalist and conflict perspectives, for example, provides the balanced view that sports are *both* beneficial and harmful—rather than either totally beneficial or totally harmful. Symbolic interactionism can also balance either of the other two perspectives. Consider, for example, the conflict perspective's assumption that the British soccer hooligans' violence is an expression of patriotism. This cannot be taken to mean that the violence *completely* or *only* reflects the hooligans' patriotism, because we know from symbolic interactionism that fans' violence may *also* reflect a unique interaction between players and spectators. In basketball, football, and other popular U.S. sports, players of both teams frequently score some points, thrilling the fans. By contrast, points are rarely scored in soccer. In a typical game, fans of the losing team are repeatedly put through the wringer of waiting with heightened expectation for a goal that never comes. The accumulation of these repeated disappointments at the end of the game is likely to trigger violence among fans, such as the British soccer hooligans, who are already frustrated by their working-class lives.

In conclusion, it is important to consider each of the three different perspectives. Together, they can offer not only a fuller but also a balanced view of sports.

Questions for Discussion and Review

1. What are the differences between the functionalist and conflict perspectives on sports?
2. What is the nature of sports as seen through the symbolic interactionist perspectives?

MAJOR RESEARCH METHODS

From the three major sociological perspectives, we can draw many ideas about how social forces shape our lives. Yet these ideas are merely idle guesswork unless they are backed up by scientific facts. The need for facts is one important reason why sociologists conduct research. The purpose of social research, however, is not only to check the presumed validity of existing theories about people and society. It also is to produce information that describes our lives and to develop new theories that explain how our lives are influenced by various social forces. Thus, the production of sociological knowledge depends heavily on social research. It involves the use of four basic methods: survey, observation, experiment, and analysis of existing data.

Survey

Of the four research methods, the **survey**—a research method that involves asking questions about opinions, beliefs, or behavior—is most frequently used by sociologists. Suppose we want to know what led people to have sex for the first time. We could take a survey, and we would find, as Table 1.2 shows, that women had different reasons than men for having their first sexual experience. Or suppose a theory suggests that students' social class and geographical background (urban, rural, or suburban) are related to their sexual behavior. Survey data could be collected to determine whether this might be true.

Sampling   To take a survey, we first select a **population,** the entire group of people to be studied. We can choose a population of any size, but all of its members must have something in common. Thus, a population may consist of all Americans above the age of 100, or all U.S. congresswomen, or all of the students at a large university, or all U.S. citizens, or all of the people in the world.

TABLE 1.2
Reasons for Having Sex the First Time

Reasons given by ...	Women		Men	
	%	**n**	**%**	**n**
Affection for partner	48	913	25	283
Peer pressure	3	57	4	61
Curiosity/readiness for sex	24	456	51	781
Wanted to have a baby	1	19	0	0
Physical pleasure	3	57	12	184
Under influence of alcohol/drugs	0	0	1	15
Wedding night	21	399	7	107
Total	100%	1901	100%	1531

SOURCE: Adapted from Robert T. Michael, John H. Gagnon, Edward O. Laumann, and Gina Kolata, *Sex in America: A Definitive Survey* (Boston: Little, Brown, 1994), p. 93.

If a population is relatively small, all of its members can be approached and interviewed. If a population is very large, it would cost too much time and money to contact all of its members. In such a case, we need a **sample,** a relatively small number of people selected from a larger population. The sample, however, must accurately represent the entire population from which it is drawn. Otherwise, the information obtained from the sample cannot be generalized to the population.

If a sample is to be representative, all members of the population must have the same chance of getting selected for the sample. Selection in effect must be random, which is why a representative sample is often called a **random sample.** A crude way to select a random sample is to throw the names of an entire population into a hat, mix them up, and then pull out as many names as needed for a sample. This method may be too cumbersome to use if the size of the population is very large. There are more sophisticated and convenient techniques for drawing random samples from large populations. The most commonly used are systematic and stratified sampling.

Systematic sampling is the process of drawing a random sample systematically, rather than haphazardly. This involves using a system, such as selecting every tenth or hundredth person in the population. But *stratified sampling* is used when the population can be divided into various strata or categories, such as males and females or rural, urban, and suburban residents. To draw a stratified sample, we have to know what percentage of the population falls into each of the categories used and then select a random sample in which each category is represented in exactly the same proportion as in the population. Suppose we know that the population of a city is 52 percent female and 48 percent male; then our stratified sample should also be 52 percent female and 48 percent male. Thus **stratified sampling** can be defined as the process of drawing a random sample in which various categories of people are represented in proportions equal to their presence in the population.

Questionnaires and Interviews   Given a representative sample, we can ask its members about their opinions, attitudes, or behavior. This is usually done by using self-administered questionnaires, personal interviews, or telephone interviews.

In using *self-administered questionnaires*, the researcher simply gives or sends the people in the sample a list of questions and asks them to fill in the answers themselves. Usually the list consists of true-false or multiple-choice questions. The respondents are asked to answer "yes," "no," or "don't know" or to check one

of the answers such as "single," "married," "divorced," or "widowed."

Personal interviews may be either structured or unstructured. In structured interviews, the researcher asks standardized questions that require respondents to choose from among several standardized answers, comparable to those in self-administered questionnaires. But in unstructured interviews, open-ended questions are asked and respondents are allowed to answer freely, in their own words.

The telephone can be used to conduct interviews, hence called *telephone interviews*. Telephone interviewing has recently become popular in survey research and is routinely used in many public opinion polls. An even more convenient method, computer-assisted telephone interviewing, has become increasingly popular. The U.S. Census Bureau and commercial survey firms are already using this method.

Observation

It is obvious from the preceding section that in surveys we depend on others to tell us what has happened. By contrast, in observation we rely on ourselves to go where the action is—and to watch what is happening. There are two ways to observe an ongoing activity. In **detached observation,** we observe as outsiders, from a distance, without getting involved. As detached observers, we may watch children playing in a schoolyard or bring them into a room and watch from behind a one-way mirror. Detached observation has

How important is a college education today—very important, fairly important, or not too important?

"We spent a lot of money educating him, so if you want Junior's opinion, you'll have to pay for it."

the advantage of making it less likely that the subjects will be affected by the observer. But it has at least one disadvantage: the detached observer has difficulty perceiving and understanding subtle communication among the subjects. The detached observer behind a one-way mirror might not see some important facial expressions or understand the emotions attached to some unconventional symbols.

The second type of observation avoids this problem. In **participant observation,** researchers take part in the activities of the group they are studying. Sometimes they conceal their identity as researchers when they join the group. This enhances

Detached observation is one method of gathering data. From behind a one-way mirror, researchers unobtrusively note interactions among preschool children. Since the subjects can be themselves, they behave as they would under normal circumstances, not changing their behavior to please the observer, which enhances the validity of the study's results.

the chances that the unknowing subjects will act naturally. If the subjects knew they were being observed, they might change their behavior. As members of the group, the researchers have the opportunity to observe practically everything, including whatever secret activities are hidden from outsiders. As a result, the researchers may discover some surprising facts about their subjects. Consider, for example, the following classic case of participant observation involving a concealed-researcher identity.

Most people assume that if men engage in homosexual acts, they must be homosexuals. If you make this assumption, the results of Laud Humphreys's (1970) classic research may surprise you. Humphreys concealed his identity as a researcher by offering to serve as a lookout for men engaging in homosexual activity in public restrooms, so that the police would not arrest them. Because he was not suspected of being an outsider, Humphreys also succeeded in secretly jotting down his subjects' automobile license plate numbers, which he used to trace their addresses. A year later, he disguised himself, visited those men at their homes, and found that they were mostly conservative lower-class married men who were seeking the homosexual experience as a means of releasing tension. They considered themselves straight and masculine. Humphreys has been severely criticized for being unethical in his deception. He has argued, though, that had he not concealed his identity, it would have been impossible to get scientifically accurate information, because his subjects would have behaved differently or would have refused to be studied.

Many sociologists do identify themselves as researchers to the people they study. They do not worry that their true identity will change their subjects' behavior. They are not overly concerned that subjects will hide secrets from them. Usually they strive to minimize these problems by not getting too deeply involved with their subjects while simultaneously establishing a good rapport with them. This is not easy to accomplish. Nevertheless, such efforts have paid off, as can be indicated by some sociological insights that have emerged from their work. Herbert Gans (1982), for example, became a participant observer in a poor Italian neighborhood in Boston in the late 1950s. On the surface, the neighborhood looked like a badly organized place, an urban jungle of its period. Yet Gans discovered that it was a well-organized community—an urban village rather than a jungle—where the residents enjoyed close social relationships with one another.

Whether carried out with detachment, with participation as a disguised member, or with participation as a known researcher, observation has the advantage of providing firsthand experience with natural, real-life situations. The wealth of findings derived from this experience are useful for developing new theories. Gans's data, for example, can be used to suggest the theory that many poor neighborhoods in the city are actually well-organized communities. This very advantage, however, is also a disadvantage. Because rich findings from observation techniques are largely relevant to one particular case study but not generalizable to other cases, they may not be used for testing theories. To test theories, sociologists usually use surveys, which we have discussed, or experiments.

Experiment

Actually, a theory can be tested only indirectly, not directly. It must be translated into a hypothesis or a series of related hypotheses that are directly testable—more specific statements that can be demonstrated to be either true or false. To test a hypothesis, researchers first specify what they assume to be the independent variable ("cause") and the dependent variable ("effect"). Then they create a situation in which they can determine whether the independent variable indeed causes the dependent variable. They are, in effect, conducting an **experiment,** a research operation in which the researcher manipulates variables so that their influence can be determined.

Consider an experiment conducted by Frank Prerost and Robert Brewer (1980). These researchers wanted to test the hypothesis that human crowding reduces the appreciation of humor. They assumed that people in a crowded situation tend to feel uncomfortable, which in turn makes it hard to laugh. To create a crowded condition, the experimenters put six college students in a relatively small room. They also put six other students in a larger room—a less crowded situation. Both groups were asked to rate 36 written jokes for funniness, using a seven-point scale from 0 for "not funny at all" to 6 for "extremely funny." The researchers found what they had hypothesized: students in the cramped situation gave the jokes a lower rating than did those with more "elbow room."

Quite often sociologists design controls to ensure that a hidden third variable is not producing the apparent effect of the independent variable. To do this, they generally select two groups of people who are similar in all respects except for the way they are treated in the experiment. One group, called the **experimental group,** is exposed to the independent

variable; the second, called the **control group,** is not. If the researchers find that the experimental group differs from the control group with respect to the dependent variable, they may reasonably conclude that the independent variable is the cause of this effect.

Robert Rosenthal (1973) and his colleague Lenore Jacobson, for example, wanted to test the theory of the self-fulfilling prophecy. In applying this theory to the classroom, they hypothesized that teachers' expectations influence student performance. That is, if a teacher considers certain students unintelligent and expects them to do poorly in class, the students will do poorly. If the teacher regards other students as intelligent and expects them to perform well, they will perform well. To test this hypothesis, Rosenthal and Jacobson gave all the children in an elementary school an IQ test. Then, *without looking at the test results,* they randomly chose a small number of children and told their teachers—falsely—that these children had scored very high on the test. The intention was to make the teachers expect these supposedly "bright" children to show remarkable success later in the year. Thus, the experimental group consisted of these "bright" children, who were exposed to high teacher expectations; the control group included the rest of the pupils. Eight months later, the researchers went back to the school and gave all the children another test. They found that the experimental group did perform better than the control group. They concluded that teacher expectations (the *independent variable*) were indeed the cause of student performance (the *dependent variable*).

Analysis of Existing Data

So far we have discussed methods for collecting data from scratch. Sometimes it is unnecessary to gather new information because of the availability of "old" data, collected by someone else. Sometimes it is simply impossible to conduct an interview, observation, or experiment because the people we want to study are long dead. Thus, sociologists often turn to analysis of existing data, which may be in the form of secondary analysis or content analysis.

In **secondary analysis,** the sociologist searches for new knowledge in the data collected earlier by another researcher. Usually, the original investigator had gathered the data for a specific purpose and the secondary analyst uses them for something else. Suppose we want to study religious behavior by means of secondary analysis. We might get our data from an existing study of voting behavior conducted by a political scientist. This kind of research typically provides information on the voters' religion along with education, income, gender, and other social characteristics. The political scientist may try to find out from this research whether, among other things, men are more likely than women to vote in a presidential election and whether the more religious are more politically active than the less religious. As secondary analysts, we can find out from the same data whether women attend church more often than men.

The data for secondary analysis are usually quantitative, presented in the form of numbers, percentages, and other statistics, such as the percentage of women as compared to the percentage of men attending church once a week. But some of the existing information is qualitative, in the form of words or ideas. This can be found in virtually all kinds of human communication—books, magazines, newspapers, movies, TV programs, speeches, letters, songs, laws, and so on. To study human behavior from these materials, sociologists often resort to **content analysis**, searching for

specific words or ideas and then turning them into numbers.

How can we carry out "this marvelous social alchemy" (Bailey, 1994) that transforms verbal documents into quantitative data? Suppose we want to know whether public attitudes toward sex have indeed changed significantly in the last 20 years. We may find the answer from comparing popular novels of today with those of the past to see if one is more erotic than the other. We should first decide what words will reflect the nature of eroticism. After we settle on a list of words such as "love," "kiss," and "embrace" to serve as indicators of eroticism, we will look for them in a novel. Finally, we will count the number of times those words appear on an average page, and the number will be used as the measure of how erotic the novel is. In repeating the same process with other novels, we will see which ones are more erotic.

Table 1.3 summarizes the key characteristics of the major research methods used in sociology, with their advantages and disadvantages.

TABLE 1.3
Major Research Methods in Sociology

Method	Characteristics	Advantages	Disadvantages
Survey	Selecting a representative sample of people and asking them to fill out questionnaires, interviewing them in person or on the phone	Self-administered questionnaires inexpensive and useful; greater response from subjects in personal interviews; phone interviews convenient	Questionnaires not returned; personal interviews costly in time and money; phone interviews discourage subjects' cooperation
Observation	Observing subjects' activities as a detached outsider, or as a participating member identifying or concealing oneself as researcher to subjects	Providing firsthand experience with natural, real-life situations, useful for developing new theories	Findings largely relevant to one particular case, not generalizable to other cases nor useful for testing theories
Experiment	Manipulating variables to determine their influence on the subjects in the field or in a laboratory	Relatively easy to test theories by determining the relationship between independent and dependent variables	Observer's presence in the field may influence subjects; subjects may not behave the same outside the laboratory as inside
Analysis of existing data	Secondary analysis involves studying someone else's quantitative data; content analysis entails examining and converting qualitative into quantitative data	Both secondary and content analysis save much time and money; content analysis also unobtrusive to subjects and uniquely suitable for historical research	Both secondary and content analysis not sufficiently valid and reliable because the interpretation of data tends to be subjective

1. How do sociologists use surveys to study human behavior?
2. How does detached observation differ from participant observation?
3. How do you conduct an experiment to determine whether one variable causes another?
4. How does secondary analysis differ from content analysis?

HOW SOCIOLOGY CAN ENRICH OUR LIVES

Sociology can be used for at least three major purposes. First, it can be used as an *intellectual exercise*, pursued for its own sake, for the pleasure of tickling our curiosity, or for producing scientific knowledge. Second, sociology can be used as a *general guide* for understanding our lives. It encourages us to be more conscious of the society in which we live, actively participating in it while critically evaluating its popular assumptions, understanding how it operates, and appreciating its diversity in race and ethnicity, gender, sexual orientation, and other social characteristics. Third, sociology can be used for *pursuing a specific career* in government (to help fight crime, improve education, reduce poverty, or solve some other social problem) or in the private sector (as a sociology teacher, social researcher, social critic, political analyst, political lobbyist, sociological consultant, or some other position that requires sociological knowledge). However it is used, sociology can *enrich our lives* with its perspectives and insights.

One of the most useful insights to be gained from sociology is that problems, whether intellectual, personal, societal, or global, can be seen as opportunities. Common sense causes us to see problems as problems, but we can get out of this negative view of problems by letting the global perspective in sociology transport us to another culture. In the Chinese culture, the word for crisis consists of two characters, *wei ji*, meaning "danger" and "opportunity." Through this cross-cultural perspective, we may want to stop seeing problems as problems and start looking for opportu-nities instead. On the surface, these opportunities may not appear real but merely a perception. However, through the symbolic interactionist perspective, sociologists have long known the self-fulfilling prophecy that if people define something as real it is real in its consequences. (We will see more of this idea in Chapter 4: Social Interaction in Everyday Life.) Similarly, if we believe that problems are full of opportunities, we will likely find—and use—these opportunities to solve the problems.

The same sociological perspective also offers the useful insight that *our own interpretation* of the world around us affects our lives more than what the world does to us. Suppose someone insults us. We may interpret the insult in a "commonsensical way," as a justification for us to be angry at the individual; or we may define the insult in a sociological way, as a product of social circumstances—such as poverty, unemployment, family problems, or having difficulties with work, family, or some other aspect of social life. Both interpretations affect our lives, but differently. The commonsensical interpretation makes us feel vengeful or even violent toward the individual, but the sociological one makes us feel fortunate (for not having the problems ourselves), tolerant, or compassionate. In a larger sense, the commonsense interpretation tends to worsen social life, whereas the sociological interpretation tends to improve it. Witness how Dr. Martin Luther King, Jr. improved race relations in a nonviolent way, without advocating retaliatory action against racist individuals. This is an example of sociological imagination at work. It enables us to see the individual's problem from the social-structural standpoint (as represented by the functionalist and conflict perspectives), attributing the problem to social forces rather than blaming the victim.

There are many other specific ways sociological perspectives and insights can be used to enrich our lives, as we will see in the following chapters.

1. For what purposes can sociology be used?
2. How do you apply a sociological perspective or insight to some aspects of your life?

CHAPTER REVIEW

1. *How does sociology differ from common sense?* While common sense produces familiar and untested ideas, sociology provides factually supported ideas and the excitement of discovering something new about ourselves. *Why is it important to study groups and societies* *different from ours?* By studying others, we can understand our lives better, because others may open our eyes to social forces that we have not seen before. *What is the nature of sociology as a science?* As a science, sociology seeks to discover relationships between one

event and another, describe these relationships in the form of hypotheses and theories, and dig out evidence to see if it supports or refutes these hypotheses and theories. *How does the sociological imagination help us understand our lives better?* It shows the influences of social forces on our private lives.

2. *Plato and Socrates discussed social issues. Were they sociologists?* No, they were social philosophers, who thought and argued about the nature of the world but did not test their ideas against systematic observation. *What led to the transformation of social philosophy into sociology?* Seized with the desire to solve social problems and impressed with the contributions from the natural sciences, some nineteenth-century social philosophers tried to apply the scientific method to the study of society in the hope of curing social ills. This attempt to replace philosophical speculation with the scientific method of systematic observation transformed social philosophy into sociology.

3. *What did Spencer mean when he said society is like a living organism?* In Spencer's view, each part of society, like each organ of an animal, performs its own function. If one part of society has problems, the other parts will adapt to the situation, ensuring the survival of the entire society. *What did Marx mean by class conflict?* Marx was referring to the struggle between the class of capitalists, who own the means of production, and the proletariat, who perform the labor. *What is the difference between* Verstehen *and Durkheim's objective approach?* Verstehen requires sociologists to adopt an attitude of understanding or empathy toward their subjects in order to understand how people interpret their own behavior; Durkheim, who pioneered the application of scientific methods to sociology, argued that sociologists should deal solely with observable aspects of human behavior.

4. *How did the early U.S. sociologists differ from their European predecessors?* The European sociologists were primarily interested in explaining the nature of society as a whole—the causes of social stability and change. In the United States, interest shifted to the study of specific social problems. Later, U.S. sociologists emphasized the search for sociological knowledge rather than its application to social problems, but their interest in social reform grew again during the 1960s. *What is the nature of modern sociology?* Modern sociology is a diverse discipline, one that is both a basic and an applied science and that uses both objective and subjective methods of investigation.

5. *What are the basic ideas of the functionalist perspective?* It focuses on social order and assumes that the various parts of a society are interdependent, forming a social structure in which each part serves a function that helps ensure the survival of the whole. *How does the conflict perspective differ from functionalism?* Whereas functionalism focuses on social order and stability, the conflict perspective emphasizes social conflict and change, showing how one group dominates another. *What are the basic ideas of feminist theory?* Women are different from, unequal to, and oppressed by men, which compels women to challenge the status quo of gender prejudice and discrimination. *What is a symbolic interaction?* It is an interaction between individuals that is governed by their interpretations of each other's actions. *What is the nature of sports as seen through the three perspectives?* Sports appear to be beneficial to society in some ways, harmful in other ways, and similar to any other social interaction.

6. *What research methods do sociologists use?* There are four major methods: survey, which gathers information on a population through interviews or questionnaires; observation, which provides firsthand experience of the subject being studied; experiment, which allows the researcher to manipulate variables; and secondary and content analyses, which use existing data.

7. *How can sociology enrich our lives?* It can do so by using insights from such perspectives as the global, symbolic interactionist, and social-structural perspectives.

KEY TERMS

Class conflict   Marx's term for the struggle between capitalists, who own the means of production, and the proletariat, who do not. (p. 9)

Conflict perspective   A theoretical perspective that portrays society as always changing and always marked by conflict. (p. 12)

Content analysis   Searching for specific words or ideas and then turning them into numbers. (p. 23)

Control group   The subjects in an experiment who are not exposed to the independent variable. (p. 22)

Detached observation   A method of observation in which the researcher observes as an outsider, from a distance, without getting involved. (p. 20)

Economic globalization   The interrelationship of the world's economies. (p. 5)

Experiment A research operation in which the researcher manipulates variables so that their influence can be determined. (p. 22)

Experimental group The subjects in an experiment who are exposed to the independent variable. (p. 22)

Feminist theory A form of conflict theory that explains human life from the experiences of women. (p. 13)

Functionalist perspective A theoretical perspective that focuses on social order. (p. 11)

Global village A closely knit community of all the societies in the world. (p. 11)

Hypothesis A tentative statement about how various events are related to one another. (p. 6)

Latent function A function that is unintended and often unrecognized. (p. 12)

Macro view A view that focuses on the large social phenomena of society, such as social institutions and inequality. (p. 11)

Manifest function A function that is intended and seems obvious. (p. 12)

Mechanical solidarity A form of social cohesion that develops when people do similar work and have similar beliefs and values. (p. 12)

Micro view A view that focuses on the immediate social situations where people interact with one another. (p. 11)

Organic solidarity A type of social cohesion that arises when people in a society perform a wide variety of specialized jobs and therefore have to depend on one another. (p. 12)

Participant observation A method of observation in which the researcher takes part in the activities of the group being studied. (p. 21)

Patriarchy A system of domination in which men exercise power over women. (p. 13)

Population The entire group of people to be studied. (p. 19)

Random sample A sample drawn in such a way that all members of the population have an equal chance of being selected. (p. 20)

Sample A relatively small number of people selected from a larger population. (p. 20)

Secondary analysis Searching for new knowledge in the data collected earlier by another researcher. (p. 22)

Social consensus A condition in which most members of society agree on what is good for everybody to have and cooperate to achieve it. (p. 11)

Social forces Forces that arise from the society of which we are a part. (p. 6)

Social integration The degree to which people are tied to a social group. (p. 7)

Social marginality Being excluded from mainstream society. (p. 5)

Sociological imagination C. Wright Mills's term for the ability to see the impact of social forces on individuals, especially on their private lives. (p. 6)

Sociology The systematic, scientific study of human society. (p. 4)

Stratified sampling The process of drawing a random sample in which various categories of people are represented in proportions equal to their presence in the population. (p. 20)

Survey A research method that involves asking questions about opinions, beliefs, or behavior. (p. 19)

Symbolic interactionist perspective A theoretical perspective that directs our attention to the details of a specific situation and of the interaction between individuals in that situation. (p. 14)

Systematic sampling The process of drawing a random sample systematically, rather than haphazardly. (p. 20)

Theoretical perspective A set of general assumptions about the nature of society. (p. 11)

Theory A set of logically related hypotheses that explains the relationship among various phenomena. (p. 6)

Verstehen Weber's term for empathetic understanding of the subjects studied by sociologists. (p. 10)

SUGGESTED READINGS

Andersen, Margaret L. 1993. *Thinking About Women: Sociological Perspectives on Sex and Gender*, 3rd ed. New York: Macmillan. A sociological perspective on the lives of women; a useful counterbalance to most sociological studies, which claim to deal with people in general but in fact focus on men only.

Hoover, Kenneth R. 1995. *The Elements of Social Scientific Thinking*, 6th ed. New York: St. Martin's. A short, readable introduction to the research process; excellent for beginning students.

Ross, Dorothy. 1991. *The Origins of American Social Science*. New York: Cambridge University Press. Shows how the early U.S. sociologists, along with economists and political scientists, sought to model their new discipline on the natural sciences.

Wolfe, Alan. 1995. "Realism and Romanticism in Sociology," *Society,* January/February, pp. 56–63. An interesting discussion of the two conflicting tendencies in sociological analysis.

Wrong, Dennis. 1994. *The Problem of Order: What Unites and Divides Society.* New York: Free Press. Analyzes the basic sociological issues of order and conflict in society.

SOCIETY AND CULTURE

Myths and Realities

MYTH: *In the Middle East, the religions of Jews and Arabs are so different that they have hardly anything in common.*
REALITY: Since the Jews, who founded Judaism and Christianity, and the Arabs, who founded Islam, used to be pastoral people, we can find in each religion the image of a god who looks after his people, in the same way that a shepherd looks after his flock. (p. 35)

MYTH: *Aside from being useful for communication, language is only a tool with which people express their thoughts.*
REALITY: Language is more than that. It can determine, or at least influence, how we think. (p. 43)

MYTH: *People in the United States have given up the work ethic. They are more interested in having fun than in working hard.*
REALITY: Americans now work harder than before, having increased their work week from 40.6 hours 15 years ago to 46.8 hours today. While working harder, though, they also enjoy themselves more—on the job and off. (p. 44)

MYTH: *In India, the Hindus refrain from killing cows for food, simply because they consider the animals sacred.*
REALITY: The reason has to do with more than the Hindu belief in the sacredness of cows. India's peasant economy depends heavily on the cows performing various services, without which massive numbers of people would starve to death. (p. 51)

n Sheeb, Eritrea, across the Red Sea from Saudi Arabia, 18-year-old Hamida Mohammed displayed to a foreign journalist all the regalia of her recent marriage. They included elaborate gold bracelets on each wrist, a heavy steel watch, and an ornate mask—finely embroidered with metallic thread—that revealed only her eyes during the three days of her wedding feast. She is a member of the nomadic Rashaida tribe, who live in tents, move frequently, and raise goats and sheep as their main livelihood. Following a tribal custom, Mrs. Mohammed's husband had to "buy" her for marriage, paying a high bride price, of which those items were only a part. Her husband probably paid about 40,000 birr (about $7,000) in cash and several camels to her parents, in addition to jewelry and a wedding dress for her and a three-day ceremonial feast. Because of this high cost, far fewer Rashaida men today take more than one wife. The bride, however, has to be a virgin. Only on the last night of the multiday feast was Mrs. Mohammed, who had never met her husband until then, allowed to sleep with him. The tribal chief explained how the men go about ensuring chastity among female teenagers: "We try to make them marry at 15, so they are not tempted to get pregnant. If a daughter gets pregnant in the bush, we kill her. If we meet a Tigrayan man (of a neighboring tribe) playing with one of our women, we take a knife and kill him" (Perlez, 1992).

Mrs. Mohammed's life differs strikingly from ours in the United States. This is largely because she lives in a radically different kind of society and culture. In this chapter we examine what society and culture are and how they shape human life.

COMPONENTS OF SOCIETY

Society is a collection of interacting individuals sharing the same way of life and living in the same territory. Societies, especially large ones such as the United States, are highly complex. They have so many diverse characteristics—their customs, religions, politics, economies, families, schools, and so on—that we may despair of making sense of what they are like. Nevertheless, sociologists have long been aware of certain patterns in the way societies operate. Most important, all societies can carry on in the face of differences and conflicts among their members because they have developed certain building blocks—the foundation of society—called statuses, roles, groups, and institutions.

Statuses

To the general public, "status" often means prestige. But to sociologists, **status** is a position in society. People usually behave in accordance with their statuses. Interacting with a friend, you are likely to be relaxed, informal, uninhibited. But talking with a professor, you are more likely to be a bit stiff and to act in a formal, inhibited way. The status of being a student differs from the status of being a friend.

In our complex society, we have so many statuses that it is impossible to name them all. Some we are born with: we are born male or female or into some racial group. These statuses of gender and race as well as age are called **ascribed statuses.** They are given to us independent of what we do. All other statuses result from what we do. We earn them in some way. You must *do* something to gain the status of a student or college graduate or married person or countless other things. These are called **achieved statuses,** which are attained through our own actions. In modern societies such as the United States, achieved statuses have grown in influence at the expense of ascribed statuses. In place of a king or queen who inherits the position, for example, we have a president who must win the office.

Statuses are sometimes ranked, with one being considered higher than the other. In U.S. society, for example, the position of doctor is ranked higher than

Ascribed statuses are given to us independently of what we do. Achieved statuses result from our own actions. For example, Elizabeth Dole's position as president of the American Red Cross is an achieved status and her status as a white, female, or fiftyish person is ascribed.

that of plumber. In a family, the father's status is higher than the son's. But other statuses are merely different, not higher or lower. A sociology major's status is different from but essentially equal to another student's status as a history major.

Despite our many statuses, we are usually influenced by only one status when we interact with another person. If a woman interacts with her husband at home, she will behave primarily as a wife, not as a banker, employer, PTA leader, or athlete. Because the status of wife dominates her relationship with her husband, it is called the **master status** in this interaction. All of her other statuses—as a banker, employer, and so on—are less relevant to the interaction; hence, they are called **subordinate statuses.**

The nature of a society may determine which status becomes the master status. In an extremely racist society, race is the master status and all others are subordinate to it. A white person interacting with a black physician would therefore use race as the master status and profession as the subordinate status. As a result, the white person would not be likely to treat the black physician with the respect usually given doctors. In such a case, the black doctor would encounter **status inconsistency,** the condition in which the same individual is given different status rankings, one high because of the victim's profession and the other low because of race.

In our society the master statuses of race and gender also influence the way others treat us. Research has shown that blacks in interracial groups and women in mixed company, compared with their white and male colleagues, are often given fewer opportunities to interact, are less likely to have their contributions accepted, and usually have less influence over group decisions. This "interaction disability," as imposed by the master statuses of race and gender, is difficult to overcome unless the minorities appear highly cooperative and agreeable to the majority. The influence of race and gender also appears in many other areas of social life, as we will see in Chapter 8 (Race and Ethnicity) and Chapter 9 (Gender and Age).

Even physical appearance can function as a master status. More specifically, physical attractiveness has a profound impact on how individuals are perceived and treated by others. Research has shown, for example, that attractive individuals are expected by college students to be more capable at most tasks than unattractive ones. Similar studies have found that teachers tend to expect attractive schoolchildren to be smarter than unattractive ones and that many people perceive attractive adults to be more likable, friendly, sensitive, and confident. Not surprisingly, according to the latest study, people considered "good looking" earn, on average, about 10 percent more than those viewed as "homely," even though both groups have similar education, employment experience, and other characteristics. This phenomenon is not limited to occupations where looks play a big part, such as modeling or acting. It also exists in jobs where appearance cannot conceivably enhance employer profits, such as bricklaying, factory work, and telemarketing (Harper, 1993; Jackson, Hunter, and Hodge, 1995).

Roles

Every status has rights and obligations. Children enjoy the right of receiving food, shelter, and love from their parents, but they are expected to show respect, obedience, gratitude, and affection in return. In other words, every status carries with it a **role,** a set of expectations of what individuals should do in accordance with their particular status. Because of your status as a student, you act in certain ways that are part of the student role. Thus, status and role seem like two sides of the same coin. But they are distinguishable. A status is basically static, like a label on a bottle. A role is dynamic, shaped by specific situations and persons.

Consider the role of nurse. In an emergency, nurses must be cool and professional, but they are also expected to convey warmth and concern to their patients. With doctors, nurses are expected to be obedient; with patients' relatives, they may be authoritative. The behaviors demanded by the role change with the situation.

In addition, various people play the same role differently, just as various actors perform the same role on the stage in diverse ways, even though they are working from the same script. The script—the set of expectations about how a person with a particular status should behave—is the **prescribed role.** How a person actually carries out the role is the **role performance.** The prescribed role of college student calls for attending classes, reading, thinking, and learning, but students differ in how and to what extent they fulfill these expectations. They may understand the prescribed role differently and be more or less successful in fulfilling those expectations. They may simply differ in their manner of carrying out the role. Thus, some students may expect to get straight A's while others would settle for B's and C's. The ambitious ones would study harder. No matter how each individual defines and performs the student role, however, commitment to it is far from total. In fact, most students do not strongly identify with their role as students. The reason is that many other roles—such as friend, date, worker, and athlete—compete for the student's time.

Indeed, all of us play many roles every day. Some of these are bound to impose conflicting demands. The role of judge prescribes an emotionless, objective attitude; the role of father requires emotional involvement. Usually, the conflicting demands of these roles present no particular problem because a person plays one role at a time. But if a judge found his or her daughter in court as the defendant, there would be a conflict. Similarly, if you are a student athlete, you will find yourself in conflict when your professor gives an exam on the day your coach wants you to play a game away from your school. When we are expected to play two conflicting roles at the same time, we experience **role conflict.** Even a single role may involve conflicting expectations and thus produce what is called a **role strain.** Supervisors are expected to be friendly with their workers, to be one of them. But they are also expected to be part of management and to enforce its rules. Professors, too, are torn between the expectation to teach classes and the expectation to do research. Role conflict or strain is usually stressful, causing anxiety and other psychological aches and pains (Coverman, 1989; Voydanoff and Donnelly, 1989).

Groups

When people interact in accordance with their statuses and roles, they form a **social group,** a collection of people who interact with one another and have a certain feeling of unity. A group can be a family, a class, or two businesspersons trying to strike a deal. A group differs, though, from a **social aggregate,** a number of people who happen to be in one place but do not interact with one another, such as the audience in a theater or the pedestrians on a street. Groups are so important to our daily lives that no society can survive without them.

There are two major types of groups: primary and secondary. A **primary group** is a group whose members interact informally, relate to each other as whole persons, and enjoy their relationship for its own sake. Families, friends, neighbors, and the like are primary groups. They are durable, often lasting for years.

By contrast, a **secondary group** is a group whose members interact formally, relate to each other as players of particular roles, and expect to profit from each other. A secondary group may consist of a sales clerk and a customer. In such a group, there are hardly any emotional ties, the communication is bound by formalities, and each person is interested only in getting what they themselves want, such as something to sell or buy. Once this self-centered goal is accomplished, the group dissolves.

Primary groups are more common in traditional, preindustrial societies. But secondary groups are more prevalent in modern, industrial societies. (We will discuss these two types of groups in greater detail in Chapter 5: Groups and Organizations.)

Institutions

Society cannot survive without social institutions. A **social institution** is a set of widely shared beliefs, norms, or procedures necessary for meeting the basic needs of society. The most important institutions are the family, education, religion, economy, and politics. They have stood the test of time, serving society well. The family institution leads countless people to produce and raise children to ensure they can eventually take over from the older generation the task of keeping society going. The educational institution teaches the young to become effective contributors to the welfare—such as the order, stability, or prosperity—of society. The religious institution fulfills spiritual needs, making earthly lives seem more meaningful and therefore more bearable or satisfying. The economic institution provides food, clothing, shelter, employment, banking, and other goods and services that we need to live. The political institution makes and enforces laws to prevent criminal and other similar forces from destabilizing society.

In ensuring the survival of society, institutions further make life much easier for individuals. They are like the map of a country. With the map, we can easily find our way driving from one place to another. Without the map, we may have to spend much time

Social institutions are sets of widely shared beliefs, norms, and procedures needed to meet the basic needs of society. The educational institution teaches young people the skills they need to become effective contributors to the order and prosperity of society.

exploring through trial and error different ways of reaching our destination. Similarly, with institutions, we know what to do in our lives. The institutions in our society help us do many things. If we want to have a family we probably will have a few children rather than 10 or 20. If we want to pursue a career in science, law, medicine, or some other field, we can go to school instead of studying by ourselves. If we seek spiritual fulfillment we can find guidance from various religions rather than endlessly searching for God on our own. If we need employment we are free to find the best job possible instead of being forced by government to accept a low-paid, unpleasant one. If we want to have a good government, we are allowed to vote or run for office rather than risk our lives by starting a revolution. These are only a few of the countless benefits we can enjoy by simply following the guidance of institutions.

Because institutions are so useful, it is not surprising that they tend to be *conservative*, resisting change or supporting the status quo. People generally support institutions with the attitude "if it ain't broke, why fix it?" Supporting the status quo, however, also involves helping to perpetuate the domination and exploitation of the powerless by the powerful and other social injustices in society. Institutions also tend to be *integrated* in that they depend on one another as parts of a unified whole. The family and educational institutions in the United States, for example, teach young people the values of hard work, competition, free enterprise, and democracy. These values sustain the capitalistic and democratic activities of economic and political institutions, which in turn provide the family and educational institutions with employment, income, public funding, and social order. But the

degree of institutional conservatism and integration varies from one society to another.

Generally, institutions are more conservative and integrated in traditional, preindustrial societies than in modern, industrial societies. Being more conservative and integrated, the institutions in traditional societies are less likely to generate social problems such as the high rates of family violence, drug abuse, or crime. At the same time, however, the institutions in traditional societies are more likely to suppress individual freedom and creativity, forcing people to conform to age-old traditions, with threats of harsh punishment for nonconformity.

Questions for Discussion and Review

1. What are statuses, and how do they influence our behavior?
2. How do prescribed roles differ from role performance?
3. How do social groups and primary groups differ from social aggregates and secondary groups?
4. What important things do institutions do for society?

SOCIETIES IN SOCIOCULTURAL EVOLUTION

Since they first appeared on earth, most human societies have gone through different stages of **sociocultural evolution,** the process of changing from a

Hunter-gathers move about in search of food. Limited food sources limit the size of the population in these societies, and division of labor is largely based on gender. Here, a San woman of Africa, with children, dips for water from the roots of a tree.

technologically simple society to a more complex one, with significant consequences for social and cultural life. In the most technologically simple societies, the methods of producing food are so primitive and inefficient that practically the whole population is forced to do the same kind of work—food production—to survive. Social and cultural opportunities—such as meeting people with various ways of life and enjoying a wide range of entertainments—are therefore extremely limited. In the most technologically advanced societies, where highly efficient methods are used in food production, only a tiny number of farmers are needed to produce enough food to support the whole population. This frees the overwhelming majority of people to pursue numerous other kinds of work, creating a huge and complex array of social and cultural opportunities. Food-producing technology, then, is the driving force behind sociocultural evolution. Societies can be classified into different types according to the technologies they use to produce food—and the stages of sociocultural evolution they are in (Lenski, Lenski, and Nolan, 1995).

Hunting-Gathering Societies

Hunting-gathering societies hunt animals and gather plants as their primary means for survival. Throughout 99 percent of humankind's presence on earth, or until about 10,000 years ago, all societies survived by using simple tools such as spears to hunt wild animals, fishing, and using human hands to gather wild roots, fruits, birds' eggs, wild bees' honey, and the like. Today, less than 0.1 percent of the world's people live this way. Among the few remaining hunting-gathering societies are the !Kung* of South Africa, the Batek Negritos of Malaysia, and the Alyawara of central Australia.

Hunter-gatherers move about a great deal in search of food, but they cover only a small area. Because their food sources are thus so limited, hunting-gathering societies are very small, each having only 20 to 50 people. Their division of labor is based on gender: men usually do the hunting; women, the gathering. Contrary to popular belief, though, hunter-gatherers do not live in total isolation and eat only wild foods. For thousands of years, they have also practiced some herding and farming or have traded with herders and farmers (Headland and Reid, 1989). But hunting and gathering remain their *primary* subsistence technology.

The lives of hunter-gatherers are not necessarily hard. In fact, because their needs are simple, they may work only two or three hours a day. It has been estimated that a family can easily collect enough wild cereal grain in three weeks to feed itself for a year. Sometimes the food must be processed. Some nuts, for example, require roasting and cracking. Hence, hunter-gatherers may spend more time preparing food than finding it (Hawkes and O'Connell, 1981). Nevertheless, they still have so much leisure time that Marshall Sahlins (1972) has called them the "original affluent societies."

Hunting-gathering societies fall into two categories: one with an "immediate-return system," and the other with a "delayed-return system." In the first,

---

*The ! represents a click, a speech sound not used in English.

people go hunting or gathering and eat the food on the same day; they do not store it for later use. In the delayed-return system, food is elaborately processed and stored. In the immediate-return societies, the people do not even store food for emergencies, and they tend to share their food with one another. Sharing, in fact, is a central norm and value in these societies. The more successful hunters are denied the opportunity to build prestige and wealth with their skills. They are expected to be self-deprecating about their hunting success, and boasting is met with scorn. Because no one hoards, no one acquires great wealth. And because there are few possessions to fight about, hunter-gatherers are unlikely to engage in warfare. If a strong and skilled hunter tries to dominate others, he can be secretly killed, because there is no effective means of protection (like the police in other societies) and because everyone has easy access to poisoned arrows, spears, or other hunting weapons. As a result, the !Kung and other hunting-gathering societies with immediate-return systems are generally the most egalitarian in the world. On the other hand, those societies with delayed-return systems, such as the aborigines of Australia, are marked by inequality because stored food can be turned into durable and exchangeable goods—hence leading to the accumulation of wealth and power (Woodburn, 1982).

Both systems, however, are patriarchal. Men exclude women from hunting activities. They even impose strict and extensive taboos on menstruating women, prohibiting them from touching any man and from handling such "male" things as bows, arrows, and fishing gear. They believe that menstruating women are dangerous to men, that the women may cause sickness, injury, or loss of magical power in the man they touch (Woodburn, 1982; Kitahara, 1982).

Pastoral Societies

Pastoral societies domesticate and herd animals as their primary source of food. In deserts, mountains, and grasslands, plants are difficult to cultivate, but animals can easily be domesticated for use as a food source. About 10,000 years ago, some hunter-gatherers began to specialize in the domestication of animals. Today there are a number of pastoral societies, mostly in the deserts and highlands of North and East Africa, the Middle East, and Mongolia. The Africans specialize in keeping cattle; the Arabs, camels and horses; and the Mongols, various combinations of horses, cattle, camels, goats, and sheep. These peoples are different racially and far apart geographically, yet they show a considerable degree of cultural uniformity.

Unlike hunter-gatherers, pastoralists accumulate a surplus of food. One result is that pastoral societies can be far larger than hunting-gathering bands. Another result is the emergence of marked social inequality, based on the size of an individual's herd and the number of a man's wives. Some anthropologists argue that animal holdings represent an unstable form of wealth because, as a herder puts it, "Owning animals is like the wind. Sometimes it comes and sometimes it doesn't." When a disaster such as an epidemic or a severe drought strikes, the wealthy herders are assumed to suffer such great losses that social inequality cannot be maintained. But in his study of the Komachi pastoralists in south-central Iran, sociologist Daniel Bradburd (1982) found that disasters cannot wipe out inequalities in animal wealth. "While disasters befall rich and poor alike, they do not befall each with quite the same effect," Bradburd explains. "A poor man who loses half his herd frequently finds it reduced to a size from which recovery is impossible; on the other hand, a wealthy man who loses half his herd will frequently be left with enough animals to rebuild the herd without great difficulty."

Usually, pastoral peoples are constantly on the move, looking for fresh grazing grounds for their herds. Consequently, they become fiercely independent and inclined to scorn land boundaries. They also become rather warlike, and some use horses to enhance their war-making capabilities. They are just as likely to raid settled villages as they are to attack each other. The aim of such aggression is to increase their livestock as well as to warn others against encroachment. Sometimes they take captives and use them as slaves. Their religious beliefs reflect the pastoral way of life. The Hebrews who founded Judaism and Christianity and the Arabs who founded Islam used to be pastoral people, and in each religion we can find the image of a god who looks after his people in the same way that a shepherd looks after his flock. The Mongols have a religious taboo against farming, believing that plowing and planting offend the earth spirit. The African cattle herders, very proud of their pastoralism, regard horticulture as degrading toil. The non-Islamic tribes of the Hindu Kush mountains, on the borders of Afghanistan and Pakistan, treat their goats as sacred animals capable of appeasing the gods and mountain spirits (Parkes, 1987).

Horticultural Societies

Horticultural societies produce food primarily by growing plants in small gardens. About 10,000 years ago, while some hunter-gatherers became pastoralists, others became horticulturalists. Horticulturalists do their gardening by hand, with hoes and digging sticks. Because their soil cannot support continuous intensive

In pastoral societies animals are domesticated for use as a major source of food. Since pastoralists can accumulate a surplus of food, social inequality develops in their societies. Because they are on the move in search of fresh grazing grounds for their herds, pastoralists have also become fiercely independent and tend to disregard land boundaries.

farming, many horticulturalists rely on slash-and-burn cultivation. They clear an area in the forest by slashing undergrowth and cutting trees, allowing them to dry, and then burning them off, leaving ashes that help fertilize the soil. This procedure also ensures that the plot will be free of weeds. After two or three years of growing crops, the soil becomes exhausted, so new fields are slashed and burned.

Unlike pastoralists, horticulturalists live in permanent settlements. Like pastoralists, their society is marked by a sexual division of labor: men clear the forest, and women do the cultivation. Because horticulturalists can produce a food surplus, their societies are usually larger than those of hunter-gatherers. The existence of a surplus also gives rise to inequality in many horticultural societies, where the men can enjoy great prestige by possessing many gardens, houses, and wives.

Warfare, too, becomes common. Many tribes in a forest often raid each other, torturing, killing, or occasionally eating their captives. Victorious warriors receive great honors. They preserve and display their defeated enemies' skulls and shrunken heads, much as athletes in other societies show off their trophies. In advanced horticultural societies, warriors hold power as well as prestige. These societies are usually divided into a small, powerful warrior nobility and a large mass of powerless common people. This social inequality is reflected in religion. Horticultural societies generally believe in capricious gods who must be worshiped. And they perform religious rituals to appease not only the gods but also the spirits of their dead ancestors, perhaps because in permanent settlements the living remain physically close to their dead. Today, there are still some horticulturalists in the trop-

ical forests of Africa, Asia, Australia, and South America.

Agricultural Societies

Agricultural societies produce food primarily by using plows and draft animals on the farm. About 5000 years ago, the invention of the plow touched off an agricultural revolution that radically transformed life in the Middle East and eventually throughout the world. When a field is plowed, weeds are killed and buried efficiently, fertilizing the soil. At the same time, nutrients that have sunk too deep for the plants' roots to reach are brought closer to the surface. Thus, the coming of the plow allowed peasants to obtain crop yields many times larger than the horticulturalists obtain with their hoes. If farmers use animals to pull their plows, then their productivity is increased further. As a result, unlike horticulturalists, farmers can cultivate a piece of land continuously and intensively.

The giant leap forward in food production enables large populations to emerge in agricultural societies. Because each farmer can produce more than enough food for one person, some people are able to give up farming and become tailors, shoemakers, tanners, and weavers. These people help cities emerge for the first time.

The towns, cities, and farms in an agricultural society come under the control of a central government, usually headed by a dictator with the power to enslave or even exterminate large numbers of people. This centralization of political control, coupled with the possession of valuable property, provides a strong stimulus for warfare. The common people who fight for their leader tend to believe that the leader has divine power. They also believe in a family of gods in which one is the high god and the others are lesser gods. This hierarchy seems to mirror the peasants' experience with various levels of government officials, from the tax collector at the bottom to the leader at the top. In fact, agricultural societies past and present have the greatest inequality of all types of society. Agricultural societies still predominate today as relatively poor countries in Africa, Asia, and Central and South America.

Industrial Societies

Industrial societies produce food for their subsistence primarily by using machinery. Since the Industrial Revolution started in England about 250 years ago, many agricultural societies have become industrialized and use machinery to till their lands. Today's industrial societies are relatively rich and can be found in Western Europe, North America, and parts of Asia (Japan, South Korea, Taiwan, and Singapore). Industrialism has been fueled by the use of increasingly powerful energy sources—flowing water, steam, internal combustion, electricity, and atomic fission—to power more and more efficient machines to do the work that had been done mostly by humans or animals in the past. Consequently, only a tiny number of farmers are needed to produce enough food for the rest of the population. This phenomenon triggers an exodus into towns and cities, creating huge urban centers across the country. There, huge masses of people work in numerous industries, producing an abundance of remarkable new things and experiences. In this century alone we have seen the invention and proliferation of automobiles, telephones, radios, movies, television, jet airliners, nuclear reactors, computers, fax machines, and other high-tech devices. All these and other modern technologies have affected our lives significantly.

For one thing, the functions of institutions have changed. The family alone no longer provides gainful employment for adults, education for children, and religious worship for both. These functions have been taken over by business companies, schools, and churches, synagogues, mosques, or temples. The economy is vast and powerful because virtually everybody depends on this institution for survival. The educational institution is equally powerful in another way: it serves all school-age youngsters, not just a few from wealthy families, which makes for a prosperous and democratic society. Religion, however, has lost its earlier influence as the dominant, unquestioned source of moral authority; this institution now faces challenges from the varying beliefs of a more diverse population.

Second, human life has greatly improved. People are much healthier and live considerably longer. The standard of living has risen sharply for most people. Social inequality has declined significantly, though the income gap between rich and poor was very great in the early stages of industrialism. Gender inequality has similarly declined. And political, religious, and other freedoms have become more easily attainable.

Third, war has become less likely to break out between industrial societies than between preindustrial societies. This change has much to do with the fear that modern weapons, such as nuclear bombs, can wreak massive, unthinkable destruction on warring nations. Not surprisingly, the former Soviet Union and the United States have avoided a nuclear war, choosing instead the "cold" war. But in the less industrialized world, where weapons are unlikely to destroy an entire nation, wars continue to be common. Fighting is particularly likely to erupt between tribes or ethnic groups within a nation-state, such as the recent war between the Tutsi and Hutu tribes in Rwanda or among the Serbs, Muslims, and Croats in Bosnia. In these conflicts, one party can become victorious without totally destroying itself in the process.

Fourth, human relations have become weaker and more impersonal. Instead of working with family members on the farm as in agricultural societies, most people in industrial societies are employed away from home and thrown into contact with others they hardly know. Their social life also revolves increasingly around secondary groups rather than primary groups. Interaction with strangers becomes more and more common. All this has led to a rise in individual concerns and a decline in social solidarity. But life has also become more interesting and challenging: greater social diversity offers experiences of meeting new people with different ways of life and enjoying their distinctive entertainment, food, and the other aspects of their subcultures.

Postindustrial Societies

Since the early 1970s, the most advanced and richest industrial countries—the United States, Canada, Japan, and the Western European nations—seem to have begun emerging as **postindustrial societies,** the type that produces food for subsistence primarily by using high technology. It is impossible to predict with accuracy when those societies will become mostly postindustrial. But we can be certain that it will not take thousands or even hundreds of years as it did for each of the earlier societal types to appear, because the speed of sociocultural evolution is remarkably greater today. It will be only a matter of a number of decades, some time during the next century, that the United States will transform into a

One of the characteristics of industrial society is increasing impersonalization in society, as people are employed away from home and are thrown in daily contact with others they hardly know. This impersonalization has led to a rise in individual concern and a decline in social solidarity.

primarily postindustrial society. The United States has already shown some unmistakable signs that it is in transition from industrialism to postindustrialism.

In recent years, biotechnology has made food production far more efficient than ever. When a mass-produced hormone called BST (bovine somatotropin) is injected into cows, milk production increases by 30 or even 40 percent. By the year 2000, the use of BST will so sharply reduce the number of cows needed to meet the U.S. milk requirements that the number of commercial dairy farms could be cut in half. In the late 1980s, seven genetically identical bull calves were produced from human-made embryos in Texas. This means that large numbers of cattle, pigs, and sheep can be cloned from a single embryo to produce uniformly healthier animals and higher-quality, lower-fat, and tastier meat. Fish have also been genetically altered to mature faster. Applying genetic engineering to plants has produced supertomatoes that have a built-in resistance to parasites, viruses, and herbicides. Various vegetables and fruits can be genetically made pest-resistant, disease-resistant, and frost-resistant. Some biotechnologists are even trying to engineer the lowly potato so that it will have better protein than beef. When these high-tech strategies become commonplace, far fewer people will be needed to farm, and the United States will truly become the leading postindustrial society (Naisbitt and Aburdene, 1990).

By relieving people of physical labor, high technology has also begun to transform the nonfarm economy from one that produces things to one that provides services or information. Over the last few decades increasing numbers of *manufacturing* jobs have been eliminated and growing numbers of *service* jobs have been created. We have increasingly allowed

less industrialized societies to produce our goods, largely because they can do so more cheaply while we focus instead on designing and marketing the products. At about the same time, the proportion of Americans with a college education has shot up to more than 50 percent, the highest in the world. Consequently, the demand for service jobs has increased sharply, and the demand has been met through an explosion of knowledge, particularly with the proliferation of computers. The numerous managerial, administrative, and technical jobs created by computer usage, along with product design and marketing, are high-wage service jobs. However, less educated workers, who used to earn high wages in the steel, auto, and other manufacturing industries, have largely been left out in the cold. When they move out of manufacturing, they are forced to settle for low-paying service jobs. Obviously, higher education is the key to success in the increasingly postindustrial, knowledge society.

The transition to postindustrialism has begun to influence our lives in at least four ways:

First, more and more people have been moving from large cities to small towns and rural areas. In industrial societies, workers must live close to their work, swarming into places that become larger cities. In our emerging postindustrial society, however, the cities are declining because urbanites are attracted to the quality of life in less populated places: low crime rates, inexpensive housing, recreational opportunities, and a return to community values. The migration is facilitated by computers, fax machines, E-mail, and Federal Express, which enable people to work anywhere. In the United States there are now over 20 million full-time home-based businesses and as many as five million people work at home in computer-related jobs. Their numbers continue to grow (Naisbitt and Aburdene, 1990).

Second, the blind faith industrial societies place in science and technology is increasingly questioned in our emerging postindustrial society. Constant exposure to a high-tech environment has increased the realization that science is limited, and that it may not offer us the meaning of life. This has prompted hosts of people to seek spirituality. Since spiritual experience tends to be intensely personal and less dependent on an organized religion, mainstream churches that have long dominated the religious scene are declining in membership. More and more people are turning inward to seek spiritual guidance without submitting themselves to the outside authority of traditional religious organizations. An important reason for this shift to the individuality of faith is the fact that people who have computer and other high-tech jobs tend to spend considerable time alone.

Third, individuals enjoy more power or freedom than before. Citizens receive so much information through television and other telecommunications on government activity that they can prevent misconduct among their leaders. Computers enable individuals to keep tabs on their government more efficiently than the government can keep tabs on all of them. With global television, fax machines, and computer networks, it seems difficult for a repressive and dictatorial government to emerge in a postindustrial society. The government can seize radio or television stations and suppress the press, but individual citizens can still get information from one another or from abroad through fax, the Internet, and other telecommunications that the government cannot control (Watson, 1995).

Fourth, there tends to be more gender equality. Postindustrialism depends on brain power more than does industrialism. Since women are just as likely as men to attend college today, they can be expected to be as likely to command high positions in the service or information economy. Well-educated women can advance fastest in the forefront of the emerging postindustrial, information industry. At Apple Computer, for example, the proportion of women managers had risen to 30 percent in 1989 and is expected to reach 50 percent—parity with men—before the end of this decade (Naisbitt and Aburdene, 1990).

In conclusion, the main characteristics of various societal types just discussed are presented in Table 2.1.

Questions for Discussion and Review

1. What are the differences among hunting-gathering, pastoral, and horticultural societies?
2. How do industrial societies differ from agricultural societies?
3. What consequences does our emerging postindustrial society have for our lives?

COMPONENTS OF CULTURE

Culture is a design for living or, more precisely, a complex whole consisting of objects, values, and other characteristics that people acquire as members of society. When sociologists talk about cultures, they usually are not talking about sophistication or knowledge

Culture consists of both tangible objects (material culture) and intangible activities such as knowledge, norms and values, and language (nonmaterial culture), which can differ markedly from one culture to the next. Here, a Geisha girl in Japan shows both material culture in the form of clothing and hair accessories and nonmaterial culture in terms of the norm of beauty expressed in her white body makeup and traditional costume.

TABLE 2.1
Societies in Various Stages of Sociocultural Evolution

Societal Type	When First Appeared, Where Today	Food-Producing Technology	Sociocultural Life
Hunting-Gathering Societies	When human life began on earth; extremely few remain, in South Africa, Malaysia, Australia	Spears or other simple tools for hunting, hands for gathering wild plants	Gender-based division of labor, men hunting and women gathering; generally, most egalitarian in the world
Pastoral Societies	About 10,000 years ago; few today, in deserts and highlands of North and East Africa, Middle East, Mongolia	Domesticating and herding animals	Fiercely independent; warlike; religions reflecting value of pastoralists' animals; great social inequality
Horticultural Societies	About 10,000 years ago; few today, in tropical forests of Africa, Asia, Australia, South America	Simple hand tools (hoes, digging sticks)	Warlike and highly inegalitarian, warrior nobility dominating common people; inequality reflected in worship of capricious gods
Agricultural Societies	About 5,000 years ago; still numerous, relatively poor countries in Africa, Asia, Central and South America	Plows and draft animals	Create diverse occupations; cause cities to emerge; rulers believed to have divine power over common folk; many gods; most inegalitarian in the world
Industrial Societies	About 250 years ago; many still exist, rich countries in Western Europe, North America, parts of Asia (Japan, South Korea, Taiwan, Singapore)	Machinery	Create huge urban cities; educational and economic institutions more influential than in earlier types; religion no longer dominant; living condition greatly improved; wars less likely; human relations weaker, more impersonal
Postindustrial Societies	Began to emerge about 1970; still in process of becoming fully postindustrial; led by the United States, Canada, Japan, and other richest nations	High technology (biotechnology, genetic engineering)	Increasing replacement of manufacturing by service, knowledge, information jobs; large cities in decline; blind faith in science questioned; more power and freedom for the individual; increased gender equality

of the opera, literature, or other fine arts—so-called "high culture." While only a small portion of a population may be sophisticated, all members of a society possess a culture. Nor is culture the same as society, although the two terms are often used interchangeably. Society consists of people interacting with one another as citizens of the same country. But culture consists of (1) abstract entities—such as ideas—that influence people and (2) tangible, human-made objects

that reflect those ideas. The tangible objects make up what is called the **material culture,** which includes every conceivable kind of physical object produced by humans, from spears and plows to cooking pots and compact discs. Objects reflect the nature of the society in which they were made. If archaeologists find that an ancient society made many elaborate, finely worked weapons, then they have reason to believe that warfare was important to that society. In their study of contemporary societies, however, sociologists are more interested in **nonmaterial culture,** the intangible aspect of culture. It includes *knowledge and beliefs* (its cognitive component), *norms and values* (normative component), and *signs and language* (symbolic component).

Knowledge and Beliefs

Culture helps us develop certain knowledge and beliefs about what goes on around us. **Knowledge** is a collection of relatively objective ideas and facts about our physical and social worlds. Knowledge can be turned into technology, and as such it can be used for controlling the natural environment and for dealing with social problems. The high standard of living in modern societies may be attributed to their advanced knowledge and sophisticated technology. Knowledge is best exemplified by science. On the other hand, **beliefs** are ideas that are more subjective, unreliable, or unverifiable. They may include, for example, the idea that God controls our lives. The best example of beliefs is religion, which we discuss in Chapter 11 (Education and Religion).

Norms and Values

Each culture has its own idea not only about what is important in the world but also about how people should act. This is the normative component of a culture, made up of its norms and values. **Values** are socially shared ideas about what is good, desirable, or important. These shared ideas are usually the basis of a society's **norms,** social rules that specify how people should behave. Whereas norms are specific rules dictating how people should act in a particular situation, values are the general ideas that support the norms. Thus the specific U.S. norm against imprisoning people without a trial is based on the general American value of freedom. Parents are required by a norm to send their children to school because society places a high value on mass education. We are allowed to criticize our government because we value freedom of speech. Even a norm as mundane as that against pushing to the head of a line is derived from a general value, one that emphasizes fairness and equal treatment for all.

Values and norms also vary from culture to culture. Because they are subjective, a value and its norms considered good in one society may appear bad in another. If someone says to us, "You have done an excellent job!" a U.S. norm requires that we say "Thank you." This may be traced to the value our

society places on fair exchange: you scratch my back and I'll scratch yours, so if you praise me, I'll thank you for it. In China, however, the same praise will elicit a self-effacing response like "Oh, no, not at all" or "No, I've done poorly." The reason is that humility ranks high in the Chinese value system. Thus, we might consider the Chinese odd for being unappreciative, and the Chinese might regard us as conceited for being immodest.

Values and norms also change together over time. Forty years ago, most Americans supported the norm of school segregation because they considered racial inequality desirable. Today the norm has given way to school integration because the value has leaned toward racial equality. In China before the late 1970s, ideological purity ("We would rather have a poor country under socialism than a rich one under capitalism") was the country's reigning value. One of its resulting norms was to send professors, students, scientists, and other intellectuals to farms to learn equality from the peasants. After the late 1970s, the new value of pragmatism ("It doesn't matter if the cat is white or black as long as it catches mice") took over, and one of its accompanying norms has been to send many intellectuals abroad to learn modernization from the West.

Norms   Day in and day out, we conform to norms. They affect all aspects of our lives. As a result, we are usually not aware of them. If someone asked why we say "Hi" when greeting a friend, we might be inclined to answer, "How else?" or "What a silly question!" We hardly recognize that we are following a U.S. norm. This fact will dawn on us if we discover that people in other societies follow quite different customs. Tibetans and Bhutanese, for example, greet their friends by sticking out their tongues. They are simply following their own norms.

These norms are **folkways,** "weak" norms that specify expectations about proper behavior. It's no big deal if we violate folkways; nobody would punish us severely. The worst might be that people would consider us uncouth, peculiar, or eccentric—not immoral, wicked, or criminal. Often society turns a blind eye to violations of folkways. When we go to a wedding reception, we are expected to bring a gift, dress formally, remain silent and attentive during the ceremony, and so on. If we violate any of these folkways, people may raise their eyebrows, but they will not ship us off to jail.

Much stronger norms than folkways are mores (pronounced MORE-ayz). **Mores** are "strong" norms that specify normal behavior and constitute demands, not just expectations. Violations of mores will be severely punished. Fighting with the bridegroom, beating some of the guests, and kidnapping the bride would be violations of mores, and the offender would be dealt with harshly. Less shocking but still serious misbehaviors, such as car theft, shoplifting, vandalism, and prostitution, also represent violations of mores.

In modern societies, most mores are formalized into **laws,** norms that are specified formally in writing and backed by the power of the state. Violations of these mores are considered illegal or criminal acts, punishable under the law. Some folkways—such as driving safely, mowing the lawn, or no liquor sale on Sundays—may also be turned into laws. Laws can effectively control our behavior if they are strongly supported by popular beliefs. If there is not enough *normative support*—support for the norms—the laws are hard to enforce, as in the case of legal prohibitions against prostitution, gambling, and teenage drinking.

In fact, all kinds of norms play an important role in controlling behavior, and society has various methods of enforcing them. These enforcement measures are called **sanctions,** rewards for conforming to norms or punishments for violation of norms. Positive sanctions, or rewards, range from a word of approval for helping a child across a street to public adulation for rescuing someone trapped in a burning building. Negative sanctions, or punishments, can be as mild as a dirty look for heckling a speaker or as severe as execution for murder. Some sanctions are applied by formal agents of social control such as the police and judges, but most often sanctions are applied informally by parents, neighbors, strangers, and so on.

Values By regularly rewarding good actions and punishing bad ones, the agents of social control seek to condition us to obey society's norms. If they are successful, obedience becomes habitual and automatic. We obey the norms even when no one is around to reward or punish us, even when we are not thinking of possible rewards and punishments. But human beings are very complicated and not easily conditioned, as animals are, by rewards and punishments alone. Thus, sanctions are not sufficient to produce the widespread, day-to-day conformity to norms that occurs in societies all over the world. To obtain this level of conformity, something more is needed: the values of the culture.

Because norms are derived from values, we are likely to abide by a society's norms if we believe in its underlying values. If we believe in the value our society places on freedom of religion, we are likely to follow the norm against religious intolerance. If employers cling to the traditional belief that a woman's place is in the home, they will violate the norm against job discrimination by not hiring married

women. In developing countries, parents often carry on the norm of producing many babies because they continue to hold to the traditional value of big, extended families. Why do values have such power over behavior? There are at least three reasons: (1) our parents, teachers, and other socializing agents teach us our society's values so that we feel it is right and natural to obey its norms, as we will see in Chapter 3 (Socialization); (2) values contain an element of moral persuasion—the achievement value, for example, in effect says, "It's good to be a winner; it's bad to be a loser"; (3) values carry implied sanctions against people who reject them (Spates, 1983).

People are not always conscious of the values instilled in them, nor do they always know why they obey norms. Sometimes norms persist even after the values from which they are derived have changed. Why, for example, do we shower a bride and groom with rice (or birdseed) after a wedding? It seems the proper thing to do, or a pleasant thing to do, or a vague sign of wishing the newlyweds well. In fact, the norm is derived from the high value our ancestors placed on fertility, which was symbolized by rice. Over time, a norm can become separated from the value that inspired it and come to be valued in itself. We may follow the norm simply because it seems the "thing to do."

Values are not directly observable, but we can infer them from the way people carry out norms. When we see that the Japanese treat their old people with respect, we can safely infer that they put great value on old age. When we learn that the Comanche Indians were expected to save their mothers-in-law during a raid by an enemy before trying to save their own lives, then we conclude that the Comanche placed a high value on mothers-in-law. When we see that many U.S. women are dieting, some to the point of becoming anorexic, we know that our culture places an enormous value on slenderness as the model for feminine beauty (Mazur, 1986).

Language

The components of culture that we have discussed so far—norms and values as well as knowledge and beliefs—cannot exist without symbols. A **symbol** is a word, gesture, music, or anything that stands for some other thing. A key example is language.

The Importance of Language Symbols enable us to create, communicate and share, and transmit to the next generation the other components of culture. It is through symbols that we are immersed in culture and, in the process, become fully human. We can better appreciate the importance of symbols, and particularly language, from Helen Keller's (1954) account of her first step into the humanizing world of culture. Blind and deaf, she had been cut off from that world until, at the age of seven, she entered it through a word:

> Someone was drawing water and my teacher placed my hand under the spout. As the cool stream gushed over one hand she spelled into the other the word water, first slowly, then rapidly. I stood still, my whole attention fixed upon the motion of her fingers. Suddenly I felt a misty consciousness as of something forgotten—a thrill of returning thought; and somehow the mystery of language was revealed to me. I knew that "w-a-t-e-r" meant the wonderful cool something that was flowing over my hand. The living word awakened my soul, gave it light, hope, joy, set it free! There were barriers still, it is true, but barriers that could in time be swept away.

Once Helen Keller understood that her teacher's hand sign meant water, once she understood what a word was, she could share her world with others and enter into their world, because she could communicate through symbols. All words are symbols; they have meaning only when people agree on what they mean. Communication succeeds or fails depending on whether people agree or disagree on what their words mean. Helen Keller's experience is a vivid example of the general truth that almost all human communication occurs through the use of language.

The Sapir-Whorf hypothesis has encouraged people to study the relationship between culture and language. Studies of the language of societies that are surrounded by ice much of the year have found numerous terms for the word ice, which enable these people to communicate with each other important information about the texture, strength, and depth of the ice around them.

The Influence of Language According to many social scientists, language does more than enable us to communicate. It also influences the way we perceive the world around us. Edward Sapir (1929) was the first to hold this view. Human beings, he said, live "at the mercy of the particular language which has become the medium of expression for their society." Sapir also wrote that language has "a tyrannical hold upon our orientation to the world." When societies speak a different language, "the worlds in which societies live are distinct worlds, not merely the same world with different labels attached to it."

This view was developed by Sapir's student Benjamin Whorf (1956) and became known as the *Sapir-Whorf hypothesis*. It holds that language predisposes us to see the world in a certain way. Sometimes, the hypothesis is put even more strongly: language molds our minds, determining how we think about the world. Whorf found, for example, that the language of the Hopi Indians of the southwestern United States has neither verb tenses to distinguish the past and the present nor nouns for times, days, seasons, or years. Consequently, according to Whorf, Hopi- and

English-speaking people perceive time differently. Although we see the difference between a person working *now* and the same person working *yesterday*, the Hopi do not because their language makes no distinction between past and present. In his novel *1984*, George Orwell (1949) provided a dramatic presentation of the possibilities of the Sapir-Whorf hypothesis. In the dictatorship portrayed in the novel, a language called *Newspeak* has been created. Among other things, Newspeak has no word for freedom, so that people cannot even think about freedom, much less want it.

The Sapir-Whorf hypothesis has nevertheless stirred controversy. A common criticism is that the hypothesis overemphasizes the power of language. According to the critics, language only influences—rather than determines—how we think. If language determined thought, people who spoke different languages would always think differently, and it would be impossible for us to comprehend English translations of foreign languages. But the critics do admit that language does have some influence on cognition. This is why people who speak different languages sometimes think differently, so that they cannot see eye-to-eye on some issues. Virtually all social scientists, then, agree that language influences perception and thinking, though they disagree on how much the influence is.

The Sapir-Whorf hypothesis has further stimulated studies of language with the aim of understanding culture. An important finding is that the Garo of northeast India, who live in an environment full of ants, have more than a dozen words for different kinds of ants but no general term for "ant." The Garo apparently find it useful to distinguish one kind of ant from another. Ants play so small a role in our lives that our language makes no distinction between them. We lump them all together in one word, and to most of us one ant looks just like another. On the other hand, in the United States, which is full of cars, there are many different words for the automobile, such as *sedan, convertible, coupe, fastback, wagon, bus, van,* and *truck.* To people in another society with few automobiles, a car is a car, period (Whiteford and Friedl, 1992).

Questions for Discussion and Review

1. How do sociologists define "culture" differently than the general public does?
2. What are cultural values and norms, and how do they combine with sanctions to control people's behavior?
3. How does the language you use influence the way you see the world?

U.S. Culture

We can understand culture better by analyzing three aspects of the U.S. culture: basic values, multiculturalism, and pop culture.

Basic Values

According to sociologist Robin Williams (1970), 15 basic values dominate U.S. culture: success, hard work, efficiency, material comfort, morality, humanitarianism, progress, science, external conformity, individualism, in-group superiority, equality, freedom, patriotism, and democracy. Most of these values, such as success, hard work, and efficiency, are clearly related to one another, showing **cultural integration,** the joining of various values into a coherent whole. But at the same time the integration is never perfect in any society. If you take another look at Williams' list of U.S. values, you will see that the value given to *efficiency*

and *success* often clashes with considerations of *morality* in the business world: Should companies pursuing efficiency and success sell unsafe products, engage in deceptive advertising, or violate price-fixing laws? Or should they resist these immoralities and risk losing out to competitors? The conflict between efficiency/success and morality shows a lack of cultural integration. But this should not be surprising, because the cultures of large, modern industrial societies are generally less integrated than those of small, traditional ones (Archer, 1985; Bohannan, 1995).

Moreover, some of the values Williams identified have been changing. For example, Americans work harder than ever before. In the past 15 years, the typical adult's leisure time has shrunk by 40 percent—down from 26.6 hours to 16.6 hours a week—and the work week has swelled by 15 percent—up from 40.6 hours to 46.8 hours (Lipset, 1990b). A more recent study also shows Americans working much harder as a result of the greater demands of employers and the rise of addictive consumerism (Schor, 1991). More time is also spent in pursuit of leisure, as indicated by the significant increase in personal expenditures on recreation over the last decade (U.S. Census Bureau, 1994).

Related to working harder is a greater interest in individual success. Concern with this personal value, however, has apparently caused a decline in community life and social responsibility. In relentlessly pursuing their personal ambitions, Americans have little or no time left for their families, friends, and communities, finding themselves "suspended in glorious, but terrifying, isolation" (Bellah et al., 1986). Moreover, increased concern with one's own welfare has fostered a strong sense of individual rights but a weak sense of obligation to the community. Most U.S. citizens, for example, demand their right to be tried by a jury of their peers, but if asked to serve on such juries many strive to evade the call. Consequently, a group of social thinkers called "communitarians" has emerged to encourage social responsibility. They urge that we move beyond the isolated self by spending more time with our families, seeking meaningful rather than casual relationships, and working to improve community life (Etzioni, 1993).

Multiculturalism

The U.S. culture consists of many subcultures such as European and African American subcultures. The coexistence of numerous subcultures can develop into **multiculturalism,** a state in which all subcultures are equal to one another in the same society. Mindful of the U.S. democratic ideal of equality for all, African

Americans, women, gays, and other minorities have since the early 1990s struggled to move multiculturalism closer to reality. They remind others that the United States is far from a "melting pot," where various subcultural groups are supposed to join together to form one single people as suggested by the U.S. national motto, *e pluribus unum,* or "out of many, one." Instead, the advocates of multiculturalism argue, minorities are forced to adopt the white European male subculture as if this subculture were superior to the others.

Consider, for example, U.S. history. Written mostly by white European males, it has for the last two centuries largely ignored minority contributions to the development of this nation and concentrated instead on the exploits of white European males. For example, many white European males such as Christopher Columbus are presented as heroes even though they brought death, disease, and suffering to Native Americans, African Americans, and other minorities. To counter **Eurocentrism,** the view of the world from the standpoint of European culture, some multiculturalists have proposed the adoption of **Afrocentrism,** the view of the world from the standpoint of African culture. But most simply want better recognition of minority achievements and a more realistic assessment of white-European-male actions than have so far been presented. This presumably would help create an egalitarian society where all subcultures will be treated as respectfully as the white-European-male subculture.

Some traditionalists have criticized multiculturalism for encouraging divisiveness in an already increasingly divisive society. Their reasoning is that members of each subculture would identify with only their own group rather than the whole nation. Intergroup conflict or even violence is expected to get worse. Other traditionalists have also criticized Afrocentrism for being as limiting as Eurocentrism because it is said to deprive black children of a wide range of views necessary for success in a highly diverse U.S. society (Lind, 1995).

But such criticisms seem unwarranted. First, the divisiveness has largely stemmed from minority frustration born out of feeling treated as second-class citizens. Thus, genuine recognition of minorities as equal to white European males may help reduce frustration and hence divisiveness. Second, critics are right for finding fault with Afrocentrism if it is offered as *the only* view for black school children to learn. But Afrocentrism—or any other minority-centered view—can be useful if offered as one of the many views available for learning. It not only can foster self-esteem but also can challenge Eurocentrists to stop ignoring minority contributions and exaggerating white European males' exploits.

In fact, appreciation of multiculturism has increased significantly in U.S. society. Commissioned by Congress to help bolster students' competency in core subjects, the university professors and schoolteachers of the National Standards for United States History published in late 1994 a multiculturalist teachers' guide for fifth through twelfth graders. In the guide, the views and stories of blacks, Native Americans, women, and ordinary people are added to conventional history. "History comes alive with these stories," says the co-director of the project. "America's beginnings were not just a simple tale of civilization

U.S. history books are increasingly being broadened and enlivened by the inclusion of stories of blacks, Native Americans, women, and ordinary people. One such story is that of Frederick Douglass (1817–1895). Born a slave, he went North as a young man, where he worked, wrote his autobiography, and eventually bought his freedom with the proceeds of abolitionist lectures he gave. After obtaining his freedom, Douglass published a newspaper, recruited black regiments to fight for the North during the Civil War, and was consulted by President Lincoln several times on the problems of slavery. In 1872, Douglass was the first black vice-presidential candidate, on the ticket of the Equal Rights Party.

meeting savages. It was really far more messy and far more interesting" (Hancock, 1994).

Pop Culture

Popular culture consists of relatively unsophisticated artistic creations that appeal to a mass audience. Examples include movies, TV shows, musical performances, and other entertainments that attract large audiences. The U.S. pop culture reflects as well as influences our society.

A Mirror of the Status Quo   In 1992, then-Vice President Dan Quayle publicly criticized prime-time television for promoting single motherhood when TV character Murphy Brown bore a child out of wedlock. In 1995, Senator Bob Dole and others also blasted the entertainment industry for undermining U.S. values with movies and music that glorify violence and loveless sex. The critics saw moral decay in U.S. pop culture. But analysis reveals the pop culture to be more traditional than its critics give it credit for.

Unwed mothers, for example, rarely appear on prime-time TV—Murphy Brown is an exception. Even so, she does not represent most real-life unwed mothers, who, unlike her, are very young or poor. The virtual absence of poor unwed mothers as TV characters reflects the popular belief that they are immoral and thus a threat to traditional family values. A similar belief about homosexual couples also keeps them almost entirely off prime-time television. Instead, what is routinely presented is the traditional family: a heterosexual, monogamous couple and their children with a lot of familial love, as portrayed in "Home Improvement" and "The Fresh Prince of Bel-Air."

Popular movies and music may also seem morally offensive, with their violence, sex, and vulgar language. But generally they reaffirm old values. Consider these top films in the early 1990s: *Pretty Woman, Ghost, Goodfellas, Home Alone, Forrest Gump,* and *Jurassic Park.* They show, respectively, a Beverly Hills version of the old movie *My Fair Lady* starring a spirited prostitute with the proverbial heart of gold, a fantasy romanticizing widowhood, a classic gangster story, a funny kid caper, a triumph of traditional virtues, and a resurrection of the old Frankenstein movie with dinosaurs. Providing escapist entertainment, all these movies support the status quo, just as the old ones did before the rebellious 1960s. What about the extremely violent, obscene, or subversive music from the "gangsta" rapper Ice-T or Geto Boys? Such music is far from being really *popular* culture. It attracts considerable media attention, but its appeal to music consumers is extremely limited, which

explains why, of the 1250 albums produced by Warner Music U.S. in 1994, only 15 are violent rap. Far more popular are Whitney Houston's love songs, Arrested Development's hip-hop, R.E.M.'s "Everybody Hurts," and other basically pleasant music (Pareles, 1994; Weinraub, 1995). In a nutshell, today's popular movies, series TV, and music mostly mirror the conservative times in which we live.

A Feminist View   From the feminist perspective we can also see how the popular culture reflects the patriarchy of our society. At the 1993 movie award ceremony, Hollywood ostentatiously paid a special tribute to women in movies, proclaiming "Oscar Celebrates Women and the Movies" as the theme of the widely watched ceremony. But the facts seemed to show otherwise, prompting a female film critic to say, "That Oscar theme is a joke, because men are now playing *all* the best roles. They get the macho roles *and* the sweet-sensitive roles, and they play the sexual pinups too" (Corliss, 1993).

The reason is that the mass audience, under the influence of patriarchy, prefers movies that put women in their place. That's why Hollywood tends to produce blockbuster movies in which women play major roles as predators or sex kittens. Explaining the predator role, Jon Avnet, director of *Fried Green Tomatoes,* observed, "The general feeling is that if a woman is bright, aggressive and successful, she's got to be a bitch." Explaining the sex kitten role, Callie Khouri, screenwriter of the feminist buddy movie *Thelma & Louise,* said, "Hollywood is trying to resexualize its women back into submission.... The women who do best in this society are the ones who are the most complacent in the role of women as sexual commodity, be it Madonna, Julia Roberts or Sharon Stone" (Corliss, 1993; Walters, 1995).

Global Reach   As a reflection of U.S. society, the pop culture exerts a powerful influence on the world. U.S. movies, television, music, novels, and fashion have never been more dominant globally than in the 1990s. U.S. movies in particular are the most popular around the world. Of the world's 100 most-attended films in 1993, for example, 88 were American. These cultural products are now the United States' second-biggest export after aircraft (Rockwell, 1994).

This U.S. dominance has stirred some fear that U.S. pop culture may destroy the traditional values of foreign countries (Patterson, 1994). Some critics even argue that the bone-crunching, eyeball-popping violence on the screen may provoke violence on the streets. But the very popularity of U.S. movies tends to reflect the nature of foreign cultures. Apparently, foreign audiences find the American movie violence highly exciting, but regard it as pure entertainment rather than as a model for actual violence. This may partly explain why street violence is relatively rare in Hong Kong, though the movies made there are even more violent than those made in the United States. Many foreign governments also do not seem as concerned as we are about movie violence. Fundamentalist Islamic governments, for example, often deface posters of semiclothed women but not lurid pictures of mayhem. The U.S. films would not have become hits around the world if they did not touch some global need for highly exciting and entertaining violence.

Another indication of how U.S. movies respond to the cultures of foreign audiences is the globalization of Hollywood in the 1990s. The U.S. movie industry is no longer as parochial as it used to be. Nowadays the French and the Japanese own some U.S. studios or invest heavily in U.S. films. Hollywood gets half of its profits from abroad, and it "boasts an Austrian named Schwarzenegger as its biggest star, a Belgian named Van Damme close behind in action films, and a Chinese, Bruce Lee, as an honorable ancestor" (Rockwell, 1994).

Questions for Discussion and Review

1. To what extent do your personal values agree with the list of cultural views identified by Williams?
2. According to advocates of multiculturalism, what is wrong with the "melting pot" concept of U.S. culture?
3. What social conditions does the U.S. pop culture reflect?

A GLOBAL ANALYSIS OF CULTURE

The world is full of cultures. But are cultures universally the same in some ways? Do cultural differences cause international conflict and violence? These are some of the questions of global significance that we will address here.

Cultural Universals

Everywhere on the planet, human beings are the product of the same evolutionary process, and all of us have the same set of needs that must be met if we are to survive. Some, such as the need for food and shelter, are rooted in biology. Others—such as the need for clothing, complex communication, social order, and esthetic and spiritual experiences—are basic necessities of human social life. Human cultures are the means by which people everywhere meet these needs. Because these needs are universal, there are **cultural universals**—practices found in all cultures as the means for meeting the same human needs.

These universals appear in both material and nonmaterial cultures. To meet their need for food, all peoples have some kind of food-getting technology, such as food gathering, hunting, or farming. To meet their need for shelter, people in all societies build some kind of housing, such as a grass hut, igloo, wooden house, or brick building. To meet their need for complex communication, all societies develop symbols and language. To meet their need for esthetic and religious experiences, peoples all over the world create art forms—such as music, painting, and literature—and believe in some kind of religion. In fact, George Murdock (1945) found more than 60 cultural universals, including incest taboos, myths, folklore, medicine, cooking, bodily adornment, feasting, dancing, and so on.

Since the early 1980s a new Darwinian theory called **sociobiology** has emerged to argue that human behavior is genetically determined. One of the sociobiologist's tasks is to explain how humans have acquired the cultural universals. With regard to incest taboos, for example, the leading sociobiologist Edward Wilson (1980) argues that "human beings are guided by an instinct based on genes" to avoid having sex with their mothers, fathers, or other close relatives. In order to perpetuate and multiply themselves, our genes, in effect, tell us to stay away from incest. If we do not, our offspring will become less fit than ourselves and less able to produce children. Through the logic of natural selection, then, individuals who avoid incest pass on their genes to more descendants than do those who practice incest. In other words, the prohibition on incest exists practically all over the world because it serves to maximize the fitness and reproductive success of humans.

Most sociologists, however, find the sociobiological argument difficult to accept. In their view, if humans were already compelled by their genes to avoid incest, why would virtually every society in the world bother to prohibit it? Sociologists have, instead, suggested two reasons for the incest taboo. First, the taboo brings about marital alliances among many groups that are useful for security against famine and foreign attack. Second, the taboo ensures family stability—without the taboo, sexual rivalry could tear the family apart.

Cultural universals are practices found in all cultures as the means for meeting human needs. Though the form it takes differs from culture to culture, dance is one of the more than 60 cultural universals.

Culture Clash

While cultural universals reflect the *general* means by which all societies meet their common needs, the *specific* content of these means varies from culture to culture. For example, religion is a cultural universal, but its specific content varies from one culture to another, as can be seen in the differences among Christianity, Islam, Judaism, Confucianism, and so on. These religions, along with other values, norms, and languages, constitute the specific cultures of various societies. These cultures can be classified into larger groupings called "cultural domains," popularly known as civilizations. There are, according to Samuel Huntington (1993), about eight cultural domains in the world today (see Figure 2.1).

The differences among these cultural domains can be expected to generate most of the conflict around the globe. As Huntington (1993) observes, in the new world emerging from the ashes of the Cold War, the dominating source of international conflict will no longer be political or economic but instead cultural. Huntington offers a number of reasons, such as the following:

First, differences among cultures are real and basic. Cultural differences do not necessarily mean conflict or violence, but differences have for centuries produced the most violent conflicts.

Second, the world is shrinking, increasing interactions between peoples of different cultures. This reinforces awareness of differences between cultures (such as American and Japanese cultures) and commonalities within a culture (such as the Western culture). This partly explains why the U.S. reacts far more negatively to Japanese investment here than to larger investments from Canada and Western Europe.

Third, economic modernization and social changes are destroying local traditions, the longstanding source of identity for much of the world. Religion has moved in to fill the gap, often in the form of fundamentalist religious movements.

Fourth, Western notions of individualism, human rights, democracy, and the separation of church and state often run counter to Islamic, Confucian, Buddhist, Latin-American, and other cultures. As Harry Triandis (1989) found in a review of 100 comparative studies of cultural values in different societies, "the values that are most important in the West are least important worldwide." This culture clash may explain why Western efforts to promote those values often provoke charges of "human rights imperialism" from the rest of the world (Huntington, 1993).

Because of these forces, culture clash may create more conflict and violence in the world. This may not happen if peoples learn to understand each other's cultures, especially the ways people in a different culture see their own interests. But there is a strong resistance to such an understanding. It exists in the form of ethnocentrism. Let us analyze ethnocentrism and how we can deal with it.

Ethnocentrism

Almost from the time we are born, we are taught that our way of life is good, moral, civilized, or natural. At the same time we learn to feel that other peoples' ways of life are not. The result is **ethnocentrism,** the attitude that one's own culture is superior to those of others.

Ethnocentrism exists to one degree or another in every society. People in North America consider it psychologically unhealthy that children in non-Western traditional countries sleep with their parents until they reach puberty. On the other hand, people in traditional countries tend to find it cruel for North Americans to let their elderly parents live by themselves. Ethnocentrism can also become so deeply ingrained in our bodies that we can become physically ill if we eat something our culture defines as sickening. Try eating toasted grasshoppers, which the Japanese relish, or ants, which some tribes in Brazil eat with gusto. But many Asians and Africans recoil from cheese, a favorite American food, because they find it too smelly (Harris, 1985).

Ethnocentrism can serve as a glue to hold a society together. By declaring among themselves, "We're the greatest," people tend to feel a strong sense of unity as a nation. Usually, nations keep their ethnocentrism to themselves. But ethnocentrism can go overboard, leading to global violence, as suggested in the preceding section.

Cultural Relativism

Although ethnocentrism is universal, it can be suppressed with **cultural relativism,** the belief that a culture must be understood on its own terms. By looking at others' cultures from their own perspective, we can understand why they do things the way they do.

Such an understanding can bring a bonanza of profits to U.S. business operations around the globe. In our legalistic, rule-oriented culture, a written contract is usually required for conducting business. Once a contract is signed, negotiation should more or less cease. But to succeed in Greece, U.S. businesspeople have to look at the contract from the Greek point of view: The contract is only a charter for serious negotiations, which will stop only after the work is completed. In the Arab world, success in business requires acceptance of the Muslim view that a person's word when given in a special kind of way is just as binding as, if not more so than, most written contracts (Morgan, 1989).

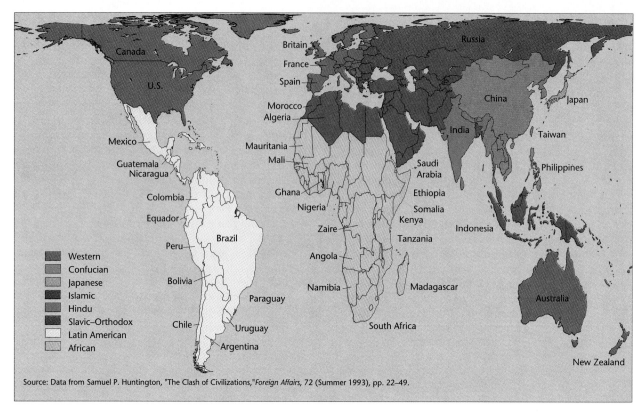

FIGURE 2.1
Cultural Domains of the World

Cultural relativism can also contribute to international peace. Soon after Bill Clinton took office as president in 1993, he repeatedly pressured the Chinese government to correct its human rights abuses (which involve mistreating political dissidents). The pressure seriously strained U.S.–China relations. Clinton obviously refused to see the problem from China's perspective. To the Chinese, President Clinton should not interfere in other countries' internal affairs and should focus on the United States' own human rights problems such as poverty, racism, and police brutality against African Americans. Finally, Clinton seemed to adopt cultural relativism, and came around to the Chinese view. He stopped pressuring China on its human rights problem and started focusing on the task of increasing U.S. exports to China. The U.S.–China relations began to improve.

But Clinton was criticized for kowtowing to China by ignoring its human rights abuses. This raises the question of how far cultural relativism should be carried out. Should ethical judgment be suspended when others engage in such horrors as infanticide, cannibalism, torture, or genocide? Only extremists would answer yes, arguing that no matter how repugnant they themselves find these horrors, their duty is only

to understand them from others' perspective, without passing judgment on them. They would pursue the "live and let live" policy. But most cultural relativists would condemn the horrors, because, to them, cultural relativism requires only understanding a culture on its own terms, *not* also abandoning their moral conscience. (Berreby, 1995).

Questions for Discussion and Review

1. What are cultural universals?
2. Why is culture clash likely to increase global conflict in the new world order?
3. What is the nature of ethnocentrism and cultural relativism?

PERSPECTIVES ON CULTURE

We have so far taken a close-up look at various aspects of culture. We may now step back, view culture as a whole, and ask, "What is the essence of culture?" The answer is important because a few years from now you may easily forget all the details about culture but not the essence of culture. Many answers can be found in sociology as well as anthropology. But it should suffice to know three major themes of culture from the three sociological perspectives.

Functionalist Perspective

According to the functionalist perspective, culture serves the important function of meeting human needs, ranging from the basic needs for food and shelter to the higher needs for psychological security, social harmony, and spiritual fulfillment. The most central function of culture is to ensure social order and stability. As functionalists see it, without culture, human society cannot survive. All this may seem obvious, because the evidence is all around us. But the functionalist approach can help explain seemingly puzzling cultural practices. Consider how a key component of India's Hindu culture—the belief in cows as sacred—serves the function of saving human lives and therefore ensuring social order.

In India, which has the largest number of cattle in the world, there are many poor and starving people; yet the slaughter of cows is forbidden. Moreover, their 180 million cows are treated like gods and goddesses. They are given right of way in the street. They are even affectionately retired to "old-age homes" when they begin to become infirm. Why doesn't India feed starving humans by killing these animals for food? The popular explanation is simply that the Hindus consider their cows sacred. But why do they consider their cows sacred?

The reason suggested by the functionalist perspective is that the sacred cows serve several important, practical functions. First, they produce oxen, which Indian farmers desperately need to plow their fields and pull their carts. Second, when the cows die naturally, their beef is eaten by the poor lower castes and their hides are used by non-Hindu Indians to maintain one of the world's largest leather industries. Third, the cows produce an enormous amount of manure, which is used as fertilizer and cooking fuel. Fourth, the cows are tireless scavengers, eating garbage, stubble, and grass between railroad tracks, in ditches, and on roadsides. Thus, it costs nothing to raise the cows, while they provide many things of value. In fact, India's peasant economy depends heavily on the cows. If the Indians ate their cows, many more people would starve to death. In short, by enabling the cows to do all those things, the Hindu belief in their sacredness ultimately serves the function of saving the lives of people, thereby helping to ensure social order and stability in India (Harris, 1985).

Conflict Perspective

While functionalism shows the positive side of culture, the conflict perspective reveals the negative side. At least two related ideas can be found in the conflict perspective.

First, culture reflects the interests of the rich and powerful in society. As Marx said, "The ruling ideas of society are the ideas of the ruling class." The value of competitiveness in our society, for example, benefits the powerful in two ways. One, it stimulates higher worker productivity, which enables employers to reap larger profits. Two, it discourages the poor and powerless from being resentful against the rich and powerful. If they believe in competition, the powerless will feel that the powerful deserve their riches and privileges because of great intelligence and hard work. Therefore, the poor are likely to envy rather than resent the rich, while blaming themselves for being poor. The powerless, in effect, join the powerful in supporting the status quo of social inequality.

Second, culture protects the status quo from the alienating effects of social and economic oppression. Suffering discrimination, exploitation, and poverty, some of the powerless may reject the competitive value as a hoax. But other values may still come to the rescue of the powerful. The most pertinent values are beliefs in morality and conformity, which may partly explain why most of the poor do not threaten social order by committing crime. Other, more tangible aspects of the culture further deflect the alienating impact of oppression from the powers that be. As Marvin Harris (1995) notes, such cultural artifacts as the movies, television, radio, and organized sports can effectively distract and amuse the exploited citizenry. This is similar to how the ruling elite in the ancient Roman empire controlled the masses by letting them watch gladiatorial contests and other circus spectaculars.

Symbolic Interactionist Perspective

Both functionalist and conflict perspectives provide a structural view of culture as largely capable of *constraining* us. For functionalists, culture effectively forces us to depend on it because of the important functions it performs for us. Without these functions, we can hardly survive. To conflict theorists, culture oppresses the poor and the powerless by manipulating them into supporting the status quo of social inequality. Both functionalist and conflict theorists seem to offer a theme familiar to watchers of the *Frankenstein* or *Jurassic Park* movies: Humans have through evolution created culture to free themselves from biological constraints, only to lose that freedom to the constraints of their own creation, namely, culture.

By contrast, symbolic interactionists are more likely to portray humans as being *free* to create and change culture. To them, culture is a set of shared understandings that people use to coordinate their activities. More specifically, culture is both a *guide* to social interaction and a *product* of interaction. As a guide to humans, culture is fixed, but as a product of humans, it is ever-changing. As Howard Becker (1982) explains, "On the one hand, culture persists and antedates the participation of particular people in it; indeed, culture can be said to shape the outlooks of people who participate in it." On the other hand, culture has "to be reviewed and remade continually, and in the remaking it changes."

As a guide, culture enables us to think and behave without first having to question the meaning of every thought and behavior. We do not, as Becker (1982) suggests, have to rack our brains for a new economic system every time we go to the grocery store. But culture has not always been a perfect or useful guide because the social environment changes continuously. A generation ago, most people bought their food at corner grocery stores, butcher shops, or poultry and fish stores. In those days, the shopping culture required the store owners or employees to serve the customers. But that culture is no longer a useful guide today. Due to the rise of giant corporations capable of opening hundreds of stores across the country, most of us now buy our food in supermarkets, which requires a different way of shopping—we have to serve ourselves. In fact, many cultural practices in U.S. society change every 20 or 30 years. So, when new social conditions arise, people get together to create culture.

In sum, while functionalist and conflict theorists are more likely to emphasize the importance of culture as a *constraint* on human behavior, symbolic interactionists tend to stress the importance of culture as a *product* of human creation. Together, both concepts of culture contribute much more than each alone does to our understanding of culture.

Questions for Discussion and Review

1. How can the functionalist perspective be used to explain the cultural value of the "sacred cow" in India?
2. According to the conflict perspective, how is culture related to social inequality?
3. How does the symbolic interactionist view of culture differ from the two other perspectives?

CHAPTER REVIEW

1. *What are the basic components of society?* They are statuses, roles, groups, and institutions. Statuses are the social positions occupied by individuals in a society. Roles are the expectations of what people should do in accordance with their statuses. Groups are collections of people who interact and have a feeling of unity. And institutions are sets of widely shared beliefs, norms, or procedures for meeting the basic needs of society.

2. *What kinds of society can be found in various stages of sociocultural evolution?* They include hunting-gathering, pastoral, horticultural, agricultural, industrial, and postindustrial societies. Hunter-gatherers hunt animals and gather plants as their primary means for survival. Pastoralists domesticate and herd animals as their primary source of food. Horticulturalists produce food primarily by growing plants in small plots of land. Agricultural societies produce food primarily by using plows and draft animals on the farm. Industrial societies produce food for their subsistence primarily by using machinery. And postindustrial societies produce food for subsistence primarily by using high technology.

3. *What is culture?* It is a design for living. It consists of material culture, which includes all the things produced by members of a society, and nonmaterial culture, which comprises knowledge, beliefs, norms, values, and symbols. *What are norms and values?* Norms are social rules dictating how to behave. There are two types: folkways, which simply expect us to behave properly, and mores, which practically force us to behave morally. Both are derived from values, socially shared ideas about what is good, desirable, or important. *How does language affect our lives?* Language influences our perception and thinking as well as reflecting our social life.

4. *What are the basic U.S. values?* They include success, hard work, efficiency, material comfort, morality, humanitarianism, progress, science, external conformity, individualism, in-group superiority, equality, freedom, patriotism, and democracy. *What do advocates of multiculturalism want?* They want an egalitarian society where all subcultures are treated equally. *What is the nature of U.S. pop culture?* The pop culture reflects the status quo and patriarchal influence in the United States, as well as the increasing global acceptance of U.S. culture.

5. *What are cultural universals?* They are practices that are found in all cultures as a means for meeting the same human needs. *Why can culture clash be expected to generate more global conflict and violence?* A number of reasons: (1) Cultural differences are real and basic. (2) The world is shrinking. (3) Modernization is destroying local traditions. (4) The West's efforts to promote its own culture have provoked resistance from non-Western societies. *What should we do to understand other cultures?* We should get rid of ethnocentrism, the attitude that our own culture is superior to that of others, and adopt cultural relativism, which means judging other cultures on their own terms. Cultural relativism, however, should be tempered with moral conscience.

6. *What can we learn from the functionalist perspective on culture?* Culture serves important functions for meeting human needs so as to ensure social order and stability. *What does the conflict perspective suggest about culture?* Culture reflects the interests of the rich and powerful, helping to perpetuate social inequality. Culture also protects the status quo from the alienating effects of social and economic oppression. *What is the symbolic interactionist view on culture?* While recognizing culture as a useful guide to social interaction, symbolic interactionists emphasize the importance of humans creating and changing cultures to respond to new social conditions.

KEY TERMS

Achieved status   A status that is attained through an individual's own actions. (p. 30)

Afrocentrism   The view of the world from the standpoint of African culture. (p. 45)

Agricultural society   A society that produces food primarily by using plows and draft animals on the farm. (p. 36)

Ascribed status   A status that one has no control over, such as status based on race, gender, or age. (p. 30)

Belief   An idea that is relatively subjective, unreliable, or unverifiable. (p. 41)

Cultural integration   The joining of various values into a coherent whole. (p. 44)

Cultural relativism   The belief that a culture must be understood on its own terms. (p. 49)

Cultural universals   Practices found in all cultures as the means for meeting the same human needs. (p. 47)

Culture   A design for living or a complex whole consisting of objects, values, and other characteristics that people acquire as members of society. (p. 39)

Ethnocentrism   The attitude that one's own culture is superior to those of others. (p. 49)

Eurocentrism   The view of the world from the standpoint of European culture. (p. 45)

Folkways   Weak norms that specify expectations about proper behavior. (p. 41)

Horticultural society   A society that produces food primarily by growing plants in small gardens. (p. 35)

Hunting-gathering society   A society that hunts animals and gathers plants as its primary means for survival. (p. 34)

Industrial society   A society that produces food for its subsistence primarily by using machinery. (p. 37)

Knowledge   A collection of relatively objective ideas and facts about the physical and social worlds. (p. 41)

Laws   Norms that are specified formally in writing and backed by the power of the state. (p. 42)

Master status   A status that dominates a relationship. (p. 31)

Material culture   Every conceivable kind of physical object produced by humans. (p. 40)

Mores   Strong norms that specify normal behavior and constitute demands, not just expectations. (p. 41)

Multiculturalism   A state in which all subcultures are equal to one another in the same society. (p. 44)

Nonmaterial culture   The intangible aspect of culture. (p. 41)

Norms   Social rules that specify how people should behave. (p. 41)

Pastoral society   A society that domesticates and herds animals as its primary source of food. (p. 35)

Popular culture   A collection of relatively unsophisticated artistic creations that appeal to a mass audience. (p. 46)

Postindustrial society   A society that produces food for subsistence primarily by using high technology. (p. 37)

Prescribed role   A set of expectations held by society regarding how an individual with a particular status should behave. (p. 32)

Primary group   A group whose members interact informally, relate to each other as whole persons, and enjoy their relationship for its own sake. (p. 32)

Role   A set of expectations of what individuals should do in accordance with a particular status of theirs. (p. 31)

Role conflict   Conflict between two roles being played simultaneously. (p. 32)

Role performance   Actual performance of a role. (p. 32)

Role strain   Stress caused by incompatible demands built into a role. (p. 32)

Sanction   A reward for conformity to norms, or punishment for violation of norms. (p. 42)

Secondary group   A group whose members interact formally, relate to each other as players of particular roles, and expect to profit from each other. (p. 32)

Social aggregate   A number of people who happen to be in one place but do not interact with one another. (p. 32)

Social group   A collection of people who interact with one another and have a certain feeling of unity. (p. 32)

Social institution   A set of widely shared beliefs, norms, or procedures necessary for meeting the basic needs of a society. (p. 32)

Society   A collection of interacting individuals sharing the same way of life and living in the same territory. (p. 30)

Sociobiology   A new Darwinian theory that human behavior is genetically determined. (p. 47)

Sociocultural evolution   The process of changing from a technologically simple society to a more complex one with significant consequences for social and cultural life. (p. 33)

Status   A position in a group or society. (p. 30)

Status inconsistency   The condition in which the same individual is given different status rankings. (p. 31)

Subordinate status   A status that does not dominate a relationship; the opposite of master status. (p. 31)

Symbol   A word, gesture, music, or anything that stands for some other thing. (p. 42)

Value   A socially shared idea about what is good, desirable, or important. (p. 41)

SUGGESTED READINGS

Drucker, Peter F. 1993. *Post-Capitalist Society.* New York: HarperCollins. An analysis of how an industrial, capitalist society has been changing into a postindustrial, knowledge society.

Etzioni, Amitai. 1993. *The Spirit of Community: Rights, Responsibilities, and the Communitarian Agenda.* New York: Crown. Shows how individualism has adversely affected American life and proposes how the society can benefit from a renewed spirit of mutuality.

Lenski, Gerhard, Jean Lenski, and Patrick Nolan. 1995. *Human Societies,* 7th ed. New York: McGraw-Hill. Uses the perspective of sociocultural evolution to analyze various types of societies, including those that have been briefly discussed in this chapter.

Schor, Juliet B. 1991. *The Overworked American.* New York: Basic Books. Shows the American work ethic as more powerful than ever, as evidenced by longer working hours and less leisure time.

Weinstein, Deena. 1991. *Heavy Metal: A Cultural Sociology.* New York: Lexington. An insightful sociological study of a controversial specimen of American pop culture.

SOCIALIZATION

Myths and Realities

MYTH: *Infants will not die as long as they are well fed.*
REALITY: Despite being well fed, infants can become developmentally impaired and even die if deprived of human contact. (p. 60)

MYTH: *To be a genius, you must be born one.*
REALITY: Geniuses such as Einstein and Picasso are not only born but made. Since childhood they worked intensely to develop their potential abilities under the guidance of parents who valued learning and achievement. (p. 60)

MYTH: *Born with the ability to have feelings, children do not have to learn how to be happy, fearful, or anxious.*
REALITY: Emotions are not innate; they must be learned. Through parents and other caretakers, children learn to feel happy when receiving a compliment, fearful when being threatened, or anxious when facing uncertainties. (p. 64)

MYTH: *If working parents are more committed to career than to parenting, they will fail to socialize their children adequately.*
REALITY: Although working parents cannot spend much time at home with their children, they are more likely than traditional parents to promote their children's understanding and mature behavior rather than unthinking obedience. (p. 68)

MYTH: *Schools only help students develop their potential as creative, independent individuals by teaching them knowledge and skills.*
REALITY: Schools also mold students into social conformity. This includes the "hidden curriculum" of training students to be patriotic, to believe in their country's cultural values, and to obey its laws. (p. 69)

Soon after three-year-old Rebecca and her family moved to another town, her mother wanted to find a good pediatrician for her. She talked to many new neighbors and friends, and they all recommended the same doctor. After seeing Rebecca undergo a physical checkup for about five minutes, the mother was extremely pleased at how well her little girl was responding to the doctor. He was very friendly, talking gently to her and explaining everything he was doing. When it was time for him to test her reflexes, he said, "Rebecca, I'm going to hit your knee very lightly with a hammer." Immediately Rebecca let out a blood-curdling scream. Shaken and puzzled, the doctor turned to her mother and asked, "What did I do wrong?"

"Her father," said the mother, "is a carpenter" (Espinosa, 1992).

Actually, Rebecca is just like all of us. To a significant degree, she is a product of **socialization,** the process by which a society transmits its cultural values to its members. Socialization is carried out through society's agents, such as parents and teachers. Without socialization, Rebecca could not have become a truly human being, a person who could take part in society and its culture like most children her age. Simultaneously, though, Rebecca has developed through socialization a **personality**—a fairly stable configuration of feelings, attitudes, ideas, and behaviors that characterizes an individual—different from that of most of her peers. As we have seen, unlike other children Rebecca reacts fearfully to the word "hammer." She obviously associates the physician's harmless little hammer with the carpenter's powerful hammer, a result of being socialized by a carpenter father.

Does this mean that children are like clay waiting to be shaped in one way or another? The roles of *nature* (what we inherit) and of *nurture* (what we learn) in making us what we are have long been argued. To the seventeenth-century philosopher John Locke, the mind of a child was like a *tabula rasa* (blank slate). People became what they were taught to be. By the second half of the nineteenth century, a quite different view was popular. Instead of looking to nurture—what people are taught—to explain human behavior, many social scientists looked to nature—what people inherit. The pendulum of opinion has swung back and forth ever since. In retrospect, the debate may sometimes seem fruitless, but we have learned from it.

THE SIGNIFICANCE OF HEREDITY

Obviously, we do inherit something of what makes us who we are. But what? Physical traits such as skin color and sex are inherited, but how they affect human behavior and personality depends to a great extent on what society makes of them.

People also appear to inherit temperament—an inclination to react in a certain way. Some people are inclined to be active, nervous, or irritable, but others, although brought up in a similar environment, tend to be passive, calm, or placid. Psychologists have found that even infants show consistent temperaments. Some are active most of the time, whereas others move rather little. Some cry and fuss a lot, and others rarely. These differences may influence personality development. Very active infants, for example, are more likely than passive ones to become aggressive and competitive adults.

The role of heredity in determining intelligence and aptitude is more controversial. **Intelligence** is the capacity for mental or intellectual achievement, such as the ability to think logically and solve problems. **Aptitude** is the capacity for developing physical or

We inherit much of our physical makeup, including eyes, hair, and skin color. But much debate swirls around the question of whether we inherit nonphysical characteristics such as intelligence, aptitude, and personality. Sociologists maintain that although nature sets limits on what we can achieve, socialization plays a large role in determining what we do achieve.

social skills, such as athletic prowess. The *extent* to which intelligence in particular is inherited has been the subject of some of the most bitter, emotional debates in all of social science. Richard Herrnstein and Charles Murray (1994) assume that more than half of our intelligence comes from the genes. But most social scientists consider intelligence to be largely learned from social environment. The debate is far from settled. For our purposes, what is significant is that, although nature sets limits on what we can achieve, socialization plays a very large role in determining what we do achieve. Whatever potential is inherited may be enhanced or stunted through socialization.

Question for Discussion and Review

1. Can heredity influence personality? Why or why not?

THE SIGNIFICANCE OF SOCIALIZATION

What makes socialization both necessary and possible for human beings is the lack of **instincts,** biologically inherited capacities for performing relatively complex tasks. Whatever temperament and potential abilities human infants may be born with, they are also born helpless, depending on others for survival. What may

be more surprising is the extent to which traits that seem very basic and essential to "human nature" also appear to depend on socialization. Evidence of the far-reaching significance of socialization comes both from case studies of children deprived of socialization and from instances in which children are socialized into geniuses.

Impairing Development

Since the fourteenth century there have been more than 50 recorded cases of "feral children"—children supposedly raised by animals. One of the most famous is "the wild boy of Aveyron." In 1797 he was captured in the woods by hunters in southern France. He was about 11 years old and completely naked. The "wild boy" ran on all fours, had no speech, preferred uncooked food, and could not do most of the simple things done by younger children (Malson, 1972; Lane, 1976). The French boy was obviously deprived of socialization. In the U.S., there have also been three well-known similar instances.

Anna was born in Pennsylvania in 1932 to a young unwed mother, a fact that outraged the mother's father. After trying unsuccessfully to give Anna away, the mother hid her in the attic and fed her just enough to keep her alive. Anna was neither touched nor talked to, neither washed nor bathed. She simply lay still in her own filth. When she was found in 1938 at the age of 6, Anna could not talk or walk. She could do nothing but lie quietly on the floor, her eyes vacant and her face expressionless. Like Anna, Isabella was a child born to an unwed mother in Ohio. Her grandfather kept her and her deaf-mute mother secluded in a dark room. When Isabella was discovered in 1938, she was 6 years old. She showed great fear and hostility toward people. Unable to talk, she could only make a strange croaking sound (Davis, 1947).

Genie, who was found in California in 1970, had been deprived of normal socialization for nearly 13 years—twice as long as Anna and Isabella. Since birth, Genie had been isolated in a small, quiet room. During the day she was tied to her potty seat, able only to flutter her hands and feet. At night, her father would straitjacket and cage her in a crib with an overhead cover. He would beat her if she made any noise. He never spoke to her except to occasionally bark or growl like a dog at her. Her terrified mother, forbidden to speak to Genie, fed her in silence and haste. Discovered at age 13, Genie could not stand straight, was unable to speak except whimper, and had the intelligence and social maturity of a 1-year-old (Pines, 1981; Rymer, 1993).

These four cases are, to say the least, unusual. But even less severe forms of deprivation can be harmful. In 1945, researcher René Spitz (1945) reported that children who received little attention in institutions suffered very noticeable effects. In one orphanage, Spitz found that infants who were about 18 months old were left lying on their backs in small cubicles most of the day without any human contact. Within a year, all had become physically, mentally, emotionally, and socially impaired. Two years later, more than a third of the children had died. Those who survived could not speak, walk, dress themselves, or use a spoon.

Creating Geniuses

While the lack of normal socialization can destroy minds, specialized socialization can create geniuses. A young woman named Edith finished grammar school in four years, skipped high school, and went straight to college. She graduated from college at age 15 and obtained her doctorate before she was 18. Was she born a genius? Not at all. Ever since she had stopped playing with dolls, her father had seen to it that her days were filled with reading, mathematics, classical music, intellectual discussions and debates, and whatever learning her father could derive from the world's literature. When she felt like playing, her father told her to play chess with someone like himself, who would be a challenge to her (Hoult, 1979).

Like Edith, many geniuses have been deliberately subjected to a very stimulating environment. A well-known example is Norbert Wiener, a prime mover in the development of computers and cybernetics. He entered college at age 11 and received his Ph.D. from Harvard at 18. According to his father, Norbert was "essentially an average boy who had had the advantage of superlative training." Another example is Adragon Eastwood DeMello, who graduated with a degree in mathematics from the University of California at age 11. When he was a few months old, his father gave up his career as a science writer to educate him (Radford, 1990). In his study of Einstein, Picasso, Gandhi, and other world-renowned geniuses in various fields, Howard Gardner (1993) found that they were all born into families that valued learning and achievement, with at least one loving and supportive adult.

Those people may have been born with a *potential* for becoming geniuses, but that potential was transformed into reality only through extraordinary socialization. Without socialization, no infant can naturally grow into a genius. Consider ace test pilot Chuck Yeager. He may have been born fearless. But, if his parents had been overprotective and kept him from jumping off barns, he might never have grown up to be the first flier to break the sound barrier.

Questions for Discussion and Review

1. What will happen to children if deprived of socialization?
2. How can children become geniuses?

THEORIES OF PERSONALITY DEVELOPMENT

Children go through various processes of socialization that help them develop their personalities. We can learn much about these processes from a number of theorists and researchers.

Freud: Psychosexual Development

One of the most influential theories of how children develop their personalities is that of Sigmund Freud (1856–1939). In his view, personality consists of three parts: the id, ego, and superego. The **id** is the part of personality that is irrational, concerned only with seeking pleasure. The id is our inborn desire to live, enjoy ourselves, make love, or celebrate life in one way or another. But such desires cannot be successfully fulfilled unless we have learned *how* to fulfill them. Thus we have learned innumerable ways to live as best we can. The knowledge that results from this learning

Many individuals known as geniuses have been deliberately subjected to a stimulating environment, so that their potential for genius can grow and blossom. The movie Searching for Bobby Fischer *explored the issue of whether an individual with extraordinary talent should focus solely on developing that talent or be allowed to live a more "normal" life.*

becomes the **ego,** the part of personality that is rational, dealing with the world logically and realistically. In trying to help us enjoy ourselves, our ego tells us that there is a limit to our id satisfaction. If we want to satisfy our sexual desire, we cannot simply make love anywhere, such as on a street corner. This limit to our self-enjoyment is imposed by society in the form of rules and injunctions—"You should not do this.... You should not do that." Our acceptance of these rules and injunctions becomes the cornerstone of the **superego,** the part of personality that is moral; it is popularly known as conscience. The ego, in effect, advises the id to obey the superego so that we will enjoy life in a socially acceptable way.

Freud proposed that those three parts of personality develop through a series of five stages in childhood. Influenced by interaction with parents, these early experiences will have a significant impact on adult personalities. If childhood experiences are positive, adults may turn out to be normal. But a difficult childhood may later create personality problems, as noted in Table 3.1.

It is impossible to scientifically observe and measure the id, ego, and superego. These concepts are nonetheless useful for understanding human personality. They are also sociologically significant in at least two ways. One is the emphasis on the family as a crucial determinant of personality development. Another is the way the superego develops from acquiring society's norms and values.

Piaget: Cognitive Development

From close observation of children, Swiss psychologist Jean Piaget (1896–1980) concluded that they pass through certain stages of *cognitive* (mental or intellectual) development:

1. *Sensorimotor stage (birth to age 2):* Infants lack language and cannot think to make sense of their environment. In their view, something exists only if they can see or touch it. Thus, to the young child, a parent no longer exists when leaving the child's field of vision. Unlike older children, who interact with the world by using their brains, infants use their senses and bodily movements to interact with the environment. Infants, for example, use their hands to touch, move, or pick up objects, and they put things in their mouths or suck on some objects.

2. *Preoperational stage (ages 2 to 7):* Children are not yet capable of performing simple intellectual operations. "Precausal," they cannot understand cause and effect. When Piaget asked 4-year-olds what makes a bicycle move, they replied that the street makes it go. When he asked 6-year-olds why the sun and moon move, the youngsters said that the heavenly bodies follow us in order to see us. These children are also *animistic:* they attribute humanlike thoughts and wishes to the sun and moon. Moreover, they are egocentric, seeing things from their own perspective only. If we ask a young boy how many brothers he has, he may correctly say "One."

TABLE 3.1
Freud's Stages Of Psychosexual Development

	Characteristics	**Personality Problems**
Oral stage (birth to age 1)	Infant is at the mercy of the id because the ego and superego have not emerged; seeks pleasure through oral activity such as sucking.	If the drive for oral pleasure has been overindulged or frustrated, the adult may be excessively interested in oral pleasures, such as eating, smoking.
Anal stage (ages 1 to 3)	Infant seeks pleasure from holding in and pushing out feces. The ego emerges, aided by toilet training, through which the child learns self-control and self-dependence.	If toilet training and other self-control lessons are overly strict, the child may be either extremely messy and wasteful or too concerned with order, cleanliness, or possessions.
Phallic stage (ages 3 to 6)	Child feels sexual love for opposite-sex parent, and learns that this desire must be suppressed. Through learning restrictions, the child internalizes the parent's ideals and morals, and thus superego develops.	If the superego fails to develop adequately, the adult is inclined to engage in unconventional or antisocial activities.
Latency stage (ages 6 to 11)	The id quiets down, and the child focuses on developing intellectual and social skills. The ego and superego become stronger.	If many problems happen in this stage, the adult may become withdrawn or extremely individualistic.
Genital stage (adolescence)	Interest in sex develops, and the habits of modesty and sympathy give way to pleasure in exhibitionism and aggressiveness; but gradually the adolescent learns to cope with these problems.	If frustrations repeatedly occur without resolution, the adult may have difficulties getting along sexually with others, and, if married, may have marital or parenting problems.

But if we ask him, "How many brothers does your brother have?" he would say, "None." He has difficulty seeing himself from his brother's perspective.

3. *Concrete operational stage (ages 7 to 12):* By now children can perform simple intellectual tasks, but their mental abilities are restricted to dealing with concrete objects only. If children between the ages of 8 and 10 are asked to line up a series of dolls from the tallest to the shortest, they can easily do so. But they cannot solve a similar problem put verbally—in abstract terms—such as "John is taller than Bill; Bill is taller than Harry; who is the tallest of the three?" The children can correctly answer this question only if they actually see John, Bill, and Harry in person.

4. *Formal operational stage (ages 12 to 15):* Adolescents can think and reason formally (abstractly). They can follow the form of an argument while ignoring its concrete content. They know, for example, that if A is greater than B and B is greater than C, then A is greater than C—without having to know in advance whether the concrete contents of A, B, and C are vegetables, fruits, animals, or whatever can be seen or touched.

Today's sociologists find Piaget's studies useful for understanding how children learn new cognitive skills—such as perception, reasoning, or calculation—as they grow up. Social forces such as family and education, though, are also assumed to influence cognitive development. Piaget's different stages of cognitive development, summarized in Figure 3.1, do *not* correspond to different levels of intelligence. Young children are not necessarily less innately intelligent than older ones. They just think about things in a different way. Contrary to Piaget's assumption, however, young children can be *taught* through intensive socialization to think like older ones. Nevertheless, research has proved Piaget right for suggesting that virtually all children go through the sequence of mental development he laid

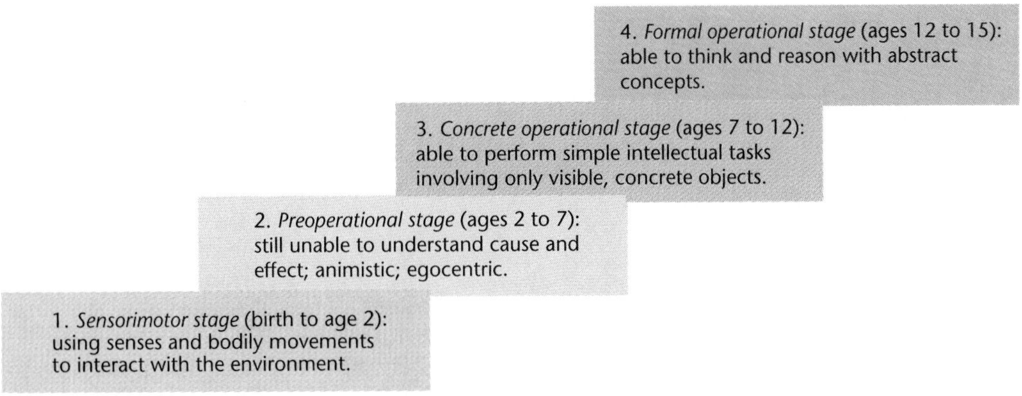

4. *Formal operational stage* (ages 12 to 15): able to think and reason with abstract concepts.

3. *Concrete operational stage* (ages 7 to 12): able to perform simple intellectual tasks involving only visible, concrete objects.

2. *Preoperational stage* (ages 2 to 7): still unable to understand cause and effect; animistic; egocentric.

1. *Sensorimotor stage* (birth to age 2): using senses and bodily movements to interact with the environment.

FIGURE 3.1
Piaget's Stages of Cognitive Development

out. For example, all children think concretely before thinking abstractly, rather than the other way around.

Kohlberg: Moral Development

According to U.S. psychologist Lawrence Kohlberg (1981), children go through three levels of moral development. This idea came from his research on how youngsters of different ages deal with moral dilemmas. The children were presented with a hypothetical situation: A man did not have the money to buy a drug that might save his dying wife. He became desperate and broke into a store to steal the drug. Should he have done that?

Some children answered yes; others no. But Kohlberg was more interested in asking further the crucial question *why* they thought so. He found three distinct patterns of response, each reflecting a certain level of moral development.

At the first level, most of the children under age 10 have a **preconventional morality,** the practice of defining right and wrong according to the *consequence* of the action being judged. The consequence involves reward or punishment. Thus, some of these children said that it was all right to steal the drug because it could save the wife (reward), while others regarded the stealing as wrong because the offender could be arrested (punishment).

At the second level, between ages 10 and 16, children have a **conventional morality,** the practice of defining right and wrong according to the *motive* of the action being judged. Thus, most of these children said that they could not blame the man for stealing the drug because of his love for his wife.

At the third level, most young adults have a **post-conventional morality,** the practice of judging actions by taking into account the importance of *conflicting norms*. Some of these adults supported the stealing but still believed in the general principle about the wrongfulness of stealing. They felt that the man was justified in stealing the drug for his wife but also believed that the stealing was not right. Other adults opposed the drug theft but were nevertheless sympathetic to the thief. To such adults, the ends do not justify the means but the compassionate husband cannot be completely blamed for stealing the drug. In a word, adults are more likely than youngsters to appreciate the conflict between norms in a moral dilemma.

This view of moral development, outlined in Figure 3.2, has been criticized for being applicable to males more than females, because it was based on research that used males only. According to Carol Gilligan (1982), Kohlberg focuses on men's interest in *justice*, which is impersonal in nature, and neglects women's lifelong concern with *relationships*, which are personal. In Gilligan's view, there is a different course for most females' moral development. It involves progressing from an interest in one's own survival to a concern for others. Thus women are said to have achieved a great deal of moral maturity if they have developed a compassionate concern for others.

Sociology of Emotions: Affective Development

From the sociological study of emotions, we can see how children are socialized to develop their **emotional intelligence,** the ability to identify and manage their

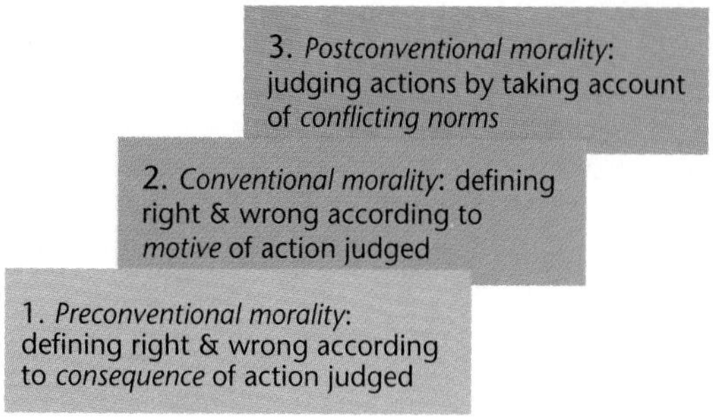

3. *Postconventional morality:* judging actions by taking account of *conflicting norms*

2. *Conventional morality:* defining right & wrong according to *motive* of action judged

1. *Preconventional morality:* defining right & wrong according to *consequence* of action judged

FIGURE 3.2
Kohlberg's Levels of Moral Development

affect (feelings), which is crucial for functioning well as members of society (Goleman, 1995).

Human emotions abound, ranging from such basic feelings as fear, anger, and happiness to more refined emotions, such as frustration, love, and jealousy. Children are taught how to *identify* these feelings because they cannot by themselves know what they are. Suppose a little boy at a day-care center engages in such expressive behaviors as fidgeting, sulking, biting, or kicking while waiting for his mother to pick him up. He may learn from an adult that what he feels is anger. Here is how such a scenario may occur (Pollak and Thoits, 1989):

BOY [RESTLESS]: My mom is late.
STAFF MEMBER: Does that make you *mad?*
BOY: Yes.
STAFF MEMBER: Sometimes kids get *mad* when their moms are late to pick them up.

The adult, in effect, teaches the child to identify an emotion by making a causal connection between a stimulus event (mother being late) and an emotional outcome (boy being angry). Through socialization—not only by parents and other caretakers but also by television, movies, and other mass media—children learn that a compliment is expected to give pleasure, a threat is expected to arouse fear, and uncertainty is expected to give rise to anxiety. While they learn that it is logical to feel resentful toward someone who has mistreated them, they also learn that it is not logical to feel affectionate toward that person. It is crucial for children to acquire this emotional logic. Failure to do so is popularly considered a symptom of mental disorder. If 10-year-olds tell you with a big smile that their mother has just died, you may suspect them of being mentally ill (Rosenberg, 1990).

Children also learn how to *manage* their emotions in at least three ways. First, they learn how they *should* feel. For example, they should love their parents, or they should feel guilty for displeasing their parents.

Second, children learn how to *display* or *conceal* emotions. They should look happy at a wedding, look sad at a funeral, or appear reverent at a religious service. Sometimes, children learn to display an emotion that they do not have in them or conceal a feeling that they do have. If a grandparent gives them a present they do not like, they are taught to show how much they like it. If they dislike their teachers, they learn to conceal the negative feeling.

Finally, while they learn to display or conceal certain emotions, children also learn how to *change* some feelings in themselves. When children are feeling sad, they may learn to manipulate that feeling by, for example, telephoning or visiting a friend (Rosenberg, 1990).

Feminist Theory: Gender Development

From feminist theory we can see how boys and girls develop different **gender identities,** people's images of what they are socially expected to be and do on the basis of their sex. Under the influence of a patriarchal society, gender development involves socializing males to be dominant over females.

A major source of gender development is the family. In a patriarchal society, child care is assigned primarily to the mother, and children consequently spend much time with her. During the first two years or so after birth, children of both sexes lack self-awareness, and see themselves as a part of their mothers. But beginning at about age three, when children begin to see themselves as separate individuals, girls and boys start to develop different gender identities. Girls continue to identify with their mother because they are of the same sex. Girls consequently develop the traditionally feminine appreciation for relationships and nurturance. On the other hand, boys begin to differentiate themselves from their mothers because of sexual difference. Further influenced by their father's dominant role in the family, boys try to suppress the feminine traits they have acquired from their mother, learn to devalue anything they consider feminine, and identify with their fathers by being independent and aggressive.

Another important source of gender development is the school. Also influenced by patriarchal society, teachers tend to socialize girls to see themselves as less important than boys, and boys to see themselves as more important than girls. Thus teachers praise boys' contributions more lavishly and call on boys more frequently. Teachers also tend to socialize girls to be quiet and polite and boys to be assertive and aggressive. This involves, among other things, accepting answers that boys shout out but reprimanding girls for "speaking out of turn" (Wood, 1994).

The mass media also help socialize girls to be submissive and boys to be dominant. Analyzing 80

TV series and 555 characters in 1990, the National Commission on Working Women found a preponderance of women working as secretaries and homemakers and a world of young, beautiful, and scantily dressed women. Even in advertisements that portray women as being in charge of their own lives, the women are shown "literally being carried by men, leaning on men, being helped down from a height of two feet, or figuratively being carried away by emotion" (Sidel, 1990).

Questions for Discussion and Review

1. In Freud's view, what does personality consist of and how does it develop?
2. According to Piaget, what mental abilities develop from birth through adolescence?
3. How does moral development differ between males and females?
4. How do children learn to identify and manage their emotions?
5. How does feminist theory explain the development of gender identity?

PERSPECTIVES ON SOCIALIZATION

The preceding section has focused on how children develop their various personalities. Here we turn our attention to the nature of socialization.

Functionalist Perspective

To functionalists, socialization serves a number of functions for society. By far the most important is the function of ensuring social order. With socialization, the norms and values of society can be instilled within the child. Society in effect can become a part of the individual's innermost being. It is therefore natural for socialized individuals to support their society, such as working to contribute to its prosperity and obeying the law to help ensure its stability. In addition, socialized individuals keep society going, after the older generation dies. Without socialization, anarchy would likely reign, threatening the survival of society.

Socialization also provides important psychological benefits. Most parents enjoy holding and cuddling infants as well as watching and helping them play and learn. As children grow older, their love and respect for parents are also highly valued. Socialization of children further teaches parents to be patient, understanding, and self-sacrificing, qualities useful for enhancing human relations in society.

Socialization further serves an economic function for the family. Although this function has sharply declined in significance in modern Western societies, it is still very important for many traditional communities around the globe. First, children are socialized to grow up to support parents in old age. Second, in many peasant villages, children are crucial contributors to the family's economic well-being. In Javanese villages in Indonesia, for example, girls aged 9 through 11 contribute about 38 hours of valuable work per week, while boys aged 12 to 14 put in 33 hours a week. Much of the work involves making handicrafts, processing foods for sale, and working in petty trade. Further, the children, especially girls, do most of the rearing of their younger siblings, so that their mothers can go out to work (Harris, 1995). This child labor, however, can alternatively be seen from the conflict perspective, as a case of exploitation of the powerless by the powerful.

Conflict Perspective

Viewed from the conflict perspective, socialization can be harmful to children. Because children have to depend heavily on adults to survive, an enormous power accrues to parents. Parents are therefore tempted to exploit and abuse children. Examples of child exploitation include child labor and child slavery, which are more prevalent in poor countries, and the use of children for pornographic profit, more common in rich countries. Child abuses range from beating to raping to killing them. Every year over two million children in the U.S. are abused, including roughly 1300 killed by their parents (Thio, 1995).

Occupying the top of the age hierarchy, parents usually regard children as their personal possessions, denying them many rights that adults enjoy as members of society. Consider the right to "physical integrity." In virtually all societies, children do not have that right, as physical punishment is widely considered appropriate for disciplining children. This contrasts with the world of adults, where, for example, U.S. Army sergeants may *not* discipline recruits by hitting them (Leach, 1994).

It is understandable from the conflict view that powerful people usually justify their maltreatment of subordinate individuals under their control. Thus, adults often defend physical punishment by saying "it is for their own good." In an extremely poor region in northeast Brazil, parents tend to commit infanticide by withholding medical assistance from infants who at birth have been considered not healthy or strong enough. Some of the reasons given by the parents for this infant killing are: "It is best for them to die" and "It is a blessing that the child will soon be an angel" (Harris, 1995). In Western societies, when extremely

Children learn to understand their own emotions and, by extension, others' emotions. Through socialization, a boy, for example, learns that a threat from his mother is expected to arouse fear.

stressed or depressed parents commit suicide they tend to kill their young children first, rationalizing that the family will be happily reunited in the hereafter (McCormick, 1994).

In sum, the conflict perspective reveals the dark side of socialization as exploitative and abusive, reinforcing age inequality at the expense of children. It complements the functionalist view of socialization as a positive force in society.

Symbolic Interactionist Perspective

Not concerned with the larger issue of whether socialization is a positive or negative force in society, symbolic interactionists focus on how children develop a "self"—a sense of who they are—from interaction with their parents and other people in their lives.

Cooley: The Looking-Glass Process

U.S. sociologist Charles Horton Cooley (1864–1929), a founder of symbolic interactionism, viewed society as a group of individuals helping each other to develop their personalities. According to Cooley, the core of personality is the concept of oneself, the self-image. And self-image, Cooley said, is developed through the "looking-glass process":

> *Each to each a looking glass*
> *Reflects the other that doth pass.*

We, in effect, acquire a **looking-glass self,** the self-image that we develop from the way others treat us. Their treatment is like a mirror reflecting our personal qualities. According to Cooley, if we have a positive image, seeing ourselves as intelligent or respectable, it is because others have treated us as such. Just as we cannot see our own face unless we have a mirror in front of us, so we cannot have a certain self-image unless others react to our behavior.

The self-image that emerges from the looking-glass process can affect our personality and behavior. If children have a favorable self-image, they tend to be self-confident, outgoing, or happy, and behave relatively well, get good grades, and even show great creativity. If youngsters have a poor self-image, they are inclined to be timid, withdrawn, or unhappy. The consequences are likely to be, among other things, delinquent behavior and lower academic achievement (Gecas, 1981).

Mead: The Role-taking Process

Like Cooley, George Herbert Mead (1863–1931), the other founder of symbolic interactionism, assumed that the development of a self-concept is made possible by interaction. But while Cooley stressed the importance of using others as mirrors by observing their reactions to our behavior, Mead emphasized the significance of getting "under the skin" of others by taking their roles.

According to Mead, children develop their self-concept in three stages. First, during their initial two years, they go through the *preparatory stage* by simply imitating other people in their immediate environment. When they see their mother reading a newspaper, they will pretend to read it too. When they see their father talk on the phone, they may later pick up the phone and talk on it. In this imitation stage, how-ever, they are not yet playing the role of father or mother, because they do not have any idea of what they are doing. They simply learn to act like others without knowing the meanings of those actions.

Then, at about age three, children begin to go through the *play stage* by taking the roles of **significant others**—people who have close ties to a child and exert a strong influence on the child. Children pretend to be their mother and father, examples of their significant others, while they play. In this world of make-believe, they learn to see themselves from their parents' perspective. In the process, they internalize their parents' values and attitudes, incorporating them into their own personalities. When they tell their baby dolls not to be naughty, they, in effect, tell themselves not to be naughty.

As they grow older, children also come into contact with doctors, nurses, bus drivers, sales clerks, and so on. These people outside the family circle are not as significant as the parents, but they are representative of society as a whole. Mead called them **generalized others,** people who do not have close ties to a child but do influence the child's internalization of the values of society. By this time, children pass through the *game stage* by playing the roles of the generalized others. In this third stage, they learn to internalize the values of society as a whole. Participation in organized games such as baseball and basketball also promotes this internalization. These games involve a complex interaction among the players that is governed by a set of rules. When they play such games, children are, in effect, playing the game of life. They are learning that life has rules too.

Internalized social values become only one part of our personality, which Mead called *the me*. Whenever we feel like obeying the law, following the crowd, and the like, we are sensing the presence of the me. It represents society within our personality. On the other hand, a portion of our personality cannot be easily "invaded" by society, no matter how often we have played childhood games. Mead referred to this part of our personality as *the I*. It is basically spontaneous, creative, or impulsive. Unlike the me, which makes all of us look alike in our behavior, the I makes each of us unique. These two aspects of personality are complementary: without the I, there would be no individual creativity or social progress; without the me, there would be no social order or individual security. Both are inevitable and necessary.

With his concept of the me, Mead greatly advanced the sociological understanding of how human personality emerges from social interaction. But he has been criticized for failing to explain where the I comes from. According to Norbert Wiley (1979), the I develops from both the me and *the we*. Infants first develop the me in

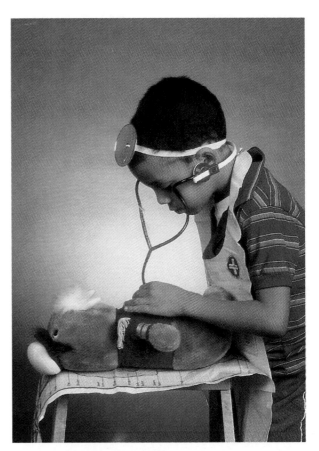

George Herbert Mead emphasized role-taking, by which children internalize the values and attitudes of significant others. Children imitate their parents, without actually knowing the meanings of their actions; then, in play, they pretend to be their parents, thus internalizing parental values. The boy in this photo is taking the role of a doctor, a generalized other, and thus is beginning to be a part of the larger society outside his own family.

about the same way as Mead indicated, except at a younger age. Through this me infants identify with their parents so totally that they feel themselves an inseparable part of their parents. Then, through a tactile, giggly love experience between parents and infants, which Wiley calls a *we experience*, the adults are, in effect, saying to the youngsters, "You exist; you are a different person; and I love the person you are." The infant then learns to see itself as independent from its parents, at which point it develops the I. Figure 3.3 summarizes the stages of self development according to the symbolic interactionist theories of Mead and Wiley.

FIGURE 3.3
Stages of Self Development

Questions for Discussion and Review

1. In what ways can socialization be functional?
2. In what ways can socialization be exploitative or abusive?
3. How do children develop the I and the me?

AGENTS OF SOCIALIZATION

Every society tries to socialize its members. It slips the task into the hands of several groups and institutions, which sociologists call the *socializing agents* of society. Some of them, including the family and school, are in a sense appointed by society to transmit its cultural heritage to the young. Other agents, including the peer group and mass media, are not appointed by society. Their socialization of children is mostly unintentional.

The Family

The family is the most important socializing agent, especially during the first few years of life. A review of various studies has concluded that warm, supportive, moderately restrictive family environments usually produce happy and well-behaving children; cold, rigid, and overly restrictive families tend to cause youngsters to become rebellious, resentful, and insecure (Gecas, 1981).

Various social forces, however, influence the way parents socialize their children. The most significant of these forces is social class. Research has long shown that lower-class families tend to be more authoritarian and strict than middle-class families. In authoritarian fami-

lies, parents tend to train children to respect and obey parental authority. On the other hand, middle-class parents are more permissive and lenient, emphasizing the value of independence. Compared with lower-class mothers, middle-class mothers are also more child-centered and sensitive to the child's feelings. For example, they spend considerably more time in mutual play with their 3-year-olds. And if a child while playing pretends to make a toy puppy bite off a larger toy's head, they refrain from jumping in with the accusatory remark, "Oh, that's terrible!" They instead respect the child's feeling by saying something like "Wow! It looks as if the baby doggy is really angry at the daddy doggy" (Farran and Haskins, 1980; Crossen, 1991).

As an agent of socialization, the family has changed a great deal over the last 30 years. In the past, young children were regarded as innocent and teenagers as immature, so they were protected from what were considered the evils and temptations of the world outside the family. Today, young children are considered competent rather than innocent. Thus, even 4- or 5-year-olds are taught about AIDS and child abuse and provided with "toys" that simulate pregnancy. Similarly, teenagers are no longer considered immature, but sophisticated in the ways of the world, knowledgeable about sex, drugs, crime, and much more. Teenagers are consequently left to fend for themselves, with little guidance or supervision from adults (Elkind, 1992). This is particularly true for children whose parents seem more committed to career than parenting. But these children are more likely than traditional children to learn understanding and mature behavior instead of unthinking obedience (Greenberger and Goldberg, 1989).

The School

At home children are treated as unique, special persons. At school, they are treated more impersonally, the same as all their schoolmates. One of their first tasks at school is to learn to fit in by getting along with others. In fact, the schools often provide children with their first training in how to behave in secondary groups.

Whereas socialization by families often contributes to the diversity of society, the schools are more likely to contribute to uniformity. Society, in effect, officially designates schools as its socializing agents. They are expected both to help children develop their potential as creative, independent individuals and to mold them into social conformity—two goals that seem contradictory. To meet the first goal, the school teaches its formal curriculum of academic knowledge and skills. The pursuit of this goal becomes increasingly important as students rise to progressively higher educational levels. By cultivating their intellectual capabilities,

The cultural heritage is passed on directly from parents to children, which is why the family is the prime socializing agent of society. The family teaches the child to behave as the society expects. Since their parents follow Navajo traditions, these children are socialized to behave differently than if they were raised in a city where Navajo traditions had been set aside.

students are expected to become intelligent citizens capable of making a living and contributing to the prosperity of their society.

The pursuit of the second goal—social conformity—is more earnest at the lower grade levels. It involves teaching history and civics. But also important is the "hidden curriculum," training students to be patriotic, to believe in their country's cultural values, and to obey its laws. It is also implicit in classroom rituals (such as the Pledge of Allegiance), in demands that classroom rules be obeyed, in the choice of books assigned in English classes, and in a host of other activities (such as glorification of the competition and discipline of sports).

The Peer Group

As children grow older, they become increasingly involved with their **peer group,** a group whose members are about the same age and have similar interests. As a socializing agent, the peer group differs from the family and school. Whereas parents and teachers have more power than children and students, the peer group is made up of equals.

The peer group teaches its members several important things. First, it teaches them to be independent from adult authorities. Second, it teaches social skills and group loyalties. Third, the peer group teaches its members the values of friendship and companionship among equals—values that are relatively absent in the socialization received from authority figures like parents and teachers. On the other hand, a peer group can

socialize its members to thumb their noses at authorities and adults. If there is a rule against bringing toys from home to nursery school, some children will ignore it, and some may even end up getting into trouble with the law one day. But many others may only innocently poke fun at adults behind their backs (Elkin and Handel, 1988; Corsaro and Eder, 1990).

Freeing themselves from the grip of parental and school authorities, peer groups often develop distinctive subcultures with their own values, symbols, jargon, music, dress, and heroes. Whereas parents and teachers tend to place great importance on scholastic achievement, adolescent peer groups are likely to put a higher premium on popularity, social leadership, and athletic attainment (Corsaro and Rizzo, 1988). The divergence between parental and peer values does not necessarily lead to a hostile confrontation between parents and teenagers.

In fact, most youngsters are just as friendly with parents as with peers. They simply engage in different types of activities—work and task activities with parents but play and recreation with peers. Concerning financial, educational, career, and other serious matters, such as what to spend money on and what occupation to choose, they are inclined to seek advice from parents. When it comes to social activities, such as whom to date and what clubs to join, they are more likely to discuss them with peers (Sebald, 1986). This reflects the importance placed by the peer group on "other-directed behavior," looking to others for approval and support as opposed to reliance on personal beliefs and traditional values. Peer groups, in effect, demand conformity at the expense of independence and individuality. Early

The influence of the peer group varies at different ages. Early adolescents are most willing to accept conformity and thus are most deeply involved with peer groups.

understand stories without visual illustration. This is because watching television usually makes people feel passive. Third, through its frequent portrayal of violence, television tends to stimulate violence-prone children to actual violence, to make normal children less sensitive to violence in real life, and to instill the philosophy that might makes right. Finally, television destroys the age-old notion of childhood as a discrete period of innocence. It reveals the "secrets" of adulthood that have been hidden from children for centuries. The spectacle of adults hitting each other, killing each other, and breaking down and crying teaches them that adults do not know any better than children (Cullingford, 1993; Clark, 1993; Kolbert, 1994).

On the other hand, television has the redeeming quality of enlarging young children's vocabulary and knowledge of the world (Josephson, 1987). Moreover, whatever negative effects TV may have on young children, they are likely to dissipate with older children. Thus, beginning age 12, youngsters will increasingly find commercials unreal and misleading. With more sophistication, older teenagers also take TV violence for what it is—fake and intended for entertainment only (Freedman, 1986; Rice et al., 1990).

adolescents are most willing to accept conformity; hence, they are most deeply involved with peer groups. As young people grow into middle and late adolescence, their involvement with peers gradually declines because of their growing independence. When they reach the final year of high school, they tend more to adopt adult values, such as wanting to get good grades and good jobs (Steinberg, 1994; Larson, 1994).

The Mass Media

The *mass media* include popular books, magazines, newspapers, movies, television, and radio. Today, television has become the prime source of information about the world, more than parents or teachers. It has been found to affect children in certain ways.

First, children may come to expect their lives, their parents, and their teachers to be as exciting as those portrayed on television. Even the widely praised "Sesame Street" makes children expect their schools to be fast-paced and entertaining. Thus, children are likely to be disappointed, finding their parents inadequate and their teachers boring. Second, television tends to impoverish its young viewers' creative imagination. If they watch TV frequently, they may find it difficult to create pictures in their own minds or to

Questions for Discussion and Review

1. Why is the family the most important agent of socialization?
2. What is the hidden curriculum of the school, and how does it help ensure social order?
3. Why are many adolescents more influenced by their peer group than by their family?
4. How does television influence children?

ADULT SOCIALIZATION

The socialization process does not stop at the end of childhood. It continues with the emergence of adulthood and stops only when the person dies.

Learning New Roles

Being socialized includes learning new roles. Like children, adults learn many new roles as they go through various stages of life. At the same time, adults' specific socialization experiences do differ from those of children. We can see this in the three types of socialization that all of us undergo.

One is **anticipatory socialization,** the process by which people learn to assume a role in the future. Many young children learn to be parents in the future by playing house. Young adults prepare themselves for their future professions by attending college. Generally, as people get older, they tend to be less idealistic or more practical. Many first-year medical students, for example, expect to acquire every bit of medical knowledge and then to serve humanity selflessly. Toward the end of their medical schooling, they usually become more realistic: they will strive to learn just enough to pass exams and look forward to a lucrative practice as a reward for their years of hard work. In brief, as people get closer to the end of their anticipatory socialization, their earlier idealism gradually dies out, to be replaced by realism.

Like children, adults also go through **developmental socialization,** the process by which people learn to be more competent in playing their currently assumed role. This is much like receiving on-the-job training. Children learn their currently acquired roles as sons or daughters, students, and members of their peer groups. Adults learn their newly assumed roles as full-time workers, husbands, wives, parents, and so on. The learning of these roles can mold adult personality. For example, the more complex the worker's job, the more likely the worker will experience self-direction in the workplace and end up valuing autonomy in other aspects of life. On the other hand, the more simple and routine the work, the more likely the individual will be supervised by some higher-up and eventually will value conformity (Kohn, 1980).

A third form of socialization is less common: **resocialization,** the process by which people are forced to abandon their old self and to develop a new self in its place. It happens to adults more often than to children. Resocialization can take place in prisons, mental institutions, POW camps, military training centers, and religious cults. Such settings are **total institutions,** places where people are not only cut off from the larger society but also rigidly controlled by the administrators. Resocialization in total institutions is usually dehumanizing.

In a state mental institution, for example, the staff tends to treat patients as if they were objects rather than humans. The staff may verbally or physically abuse them, or prevent them from talking to the staff unless spoken to first. The staff may also enter the patients' rooms and examine their possessions at any time. The staff may even monitor the patients' personal hygiene and waste evacuation in the bathroom. Such dehumanization is intended to strip the patients of whatever self-concept they have brought into the institution from their prior social life. Then rewards and punishments are used to mold them into docile conformists. Such patients usually develop "institutionalism"—a deep sense of hopelessness, pervasive loss of initiative, deterioration of social skills, and an inability to function in larger society (Thio, 1995).

Continuing Development

As we saw earlier, Freud suggested that once the adult personality has been molded by childhood experiences it stops growing or changing. But his student, Erik Erikson (1902–1994), theorized that personality continues to develop throughout the life span. According to Erikson, personality development goes through eight stages, as shown in Figure 3.4. In each stage, people are faced with a crisis that must be resolved, with either a positive or a negative result.

The first five preadult stages parallel Freud's. According to Erikson, the child normally develops a sense of *trust* during what Freud called the oral stage, *autonomy* during the anal stage, *initiative* during what Freud called the phallic stage, *industry* during the latency stage, and *identity* during adolescence. Negative childhood experiences, however, lead to mistrust, doubt, guilt, feelings of inferiority, and confusion. Consider, for example, how trust and mistrust develop. During the oral stage, from birth to age 1, the totally helpless infant must depend on an adult to survive. If the infant's need for life-sustaining care is well met, the infant will develop a sense of trust in others; otherwise, mistrust will develop.

After people enter adulthood, they will, in Erikson's view, go through three more stages of development. In early adulthood, which lasts from ages 20 to 40, people face the crisis of having to resolve the conflicting demands for love and work. They usually meet the demand for love by falling in love, getting married, and raising a family. If they are too attached to their families, they may not be able to achieve great success in their careers. But if they are too eager to work extremely hard, they risk losing intimacy with and incurring isolation from their families. In this stage, the young adult is confronted with the conflict between enjoying *intimacy* and suffering *isolation*.

In middle adulthood, which lasts from ages 40 to 60, people become acutely aware that their death will come, that their time is running out, and that they must give up their youthful dreams to start being more concerned with others rather than themselves. Usually, they choose to be what Erikson calls "generative"—nurturing or guiding the younger generation. This gives them an elevating sense of productivity and creativity, of having made a significant contribution to others. On the other hand, they are

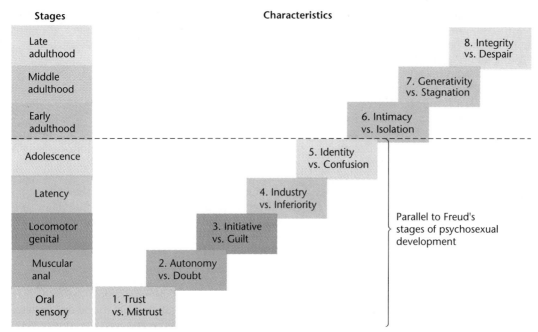

FIGURE 3.4
Erikson's Stages of Psychosocial Development

also inclined to continue hanging on to their youthful dreams, to try to be active and feel young again. Because this is difficult to fulfill at this stage, the individuals risk getting weighed down with a depressing sense of disappointment, stagnation, and boredom. In short, the middle-aged adult is faced with the conflict between *generativity* and *stagnation*.

In late adulthood, from age 60 until death, people find themselves in conflict between achieving *integrity* (holding oneself together) and sinking into *despair* (emotionally falling apart). Those who are able to maintain the integrity of the self are likely to have accepted whatever they have attained so far. But those who sink into despair regret that their lives have been full of missed opportunities and that the time is just too short for them to start another life. Death "loses its sting" for those who have learned to hold themselves together and to accept death as the ultimate outcome of life. But those who fall apart emotionally cannot accept death and are gripped with fear of it.

Feminists have criticized Erikson's theory for applying to men more than to women. The crisis of having to choose between intimacy and isolation, for example, is less likely to confront women in early adulthood because they have long been socialized to appreciate personal relationships. But research has established that most people do experience the two conflicting forces in most of the stages (Varghese, 1981; Ochse and Plug, 1986). Especially significant to sociology is Erikson's emphasis on society's influence on personality development. He observes, for

example, that teenagers in modern societies have a hard time solving their identity crisis because they are bombarded with a staggering array of lifestyle and career choices unimaginable in traditional societies.

Aging and Dying

Also unlike traditional societies, modern societies do not adequately socialize individuals for old age. In traditional societies, old people are more valued and respected. It is quite an accomplishment to survive into old age in a traditional society, where most people die relatively young. Further, the experiences that the elders have accumulated over the years are invaluable to younger generations, because their societies change so little and so slowly that old knowledge and values do not seem to lose their relevance. Since the aged in these societies live with their children and grandchildren, are given an honored role, and are often observed to dispense wisdom and advice, young people are easily socialized to accept old age when they themselves become old.

In modern societies, old people typically live alone. By not living with their old parents and grandparents, younger people have little chance of learning how to grow old gracefully. Although they may visit their old relatives often, they do not relish the prospect of growing old themselves, because they believe that the aged live an unrewarding, lonely, or even degrading life.

Our culture has traditionally not taught us to accept death as natural and unavoidable. The old have consequently felt afraid to die. But in recent years, many have learned to face death calmly.

Modern societies also have come up short in socialization for death. In traditional societies, people see their loved ones die at home, handle their corpses, and personally bury them. But in modern societies, we seldom witness a dying scene at home because most deaths occur in hospitals. As Sherwin Nuland (1994) says, "We have created the method of modern dying. Modern dying takes place in the modern hospital, where it can be hidden, cleansed of its organic blight, and finally packaged for modern burial." The method of modern dying has in effect robbed us of the important realization that death is the natural culmination of life. Not surprisingly, many of us find death frightening, as research by Elisabeth Kübler-Ross (1969) has suggested.

Kübler-Ross found that terminally ill patients usually go through five stages of reaction, from the time when they discover they are dying to the final moment of death. She refers to the first stage as *initial denial* because upon being told that they are dying, patients usually express disbelief: "No, not me; it just can't be me." At the second stage—*anger*—they believe they are dying but get angry with family, doctor, and God, protesting, "Why me?" When they move into the third stage—*bargaining*—they are no longer angry and ask God to let them live just a little longer in return for good behavior. In the fourth stage—*depression*—they can no longer postpone their death, so they sink into deep depression. Finally, in the fifth stage—*acceptance*—they feel calm and ready to die. But most patients do not make it to the final stage.

Because our elderly population is increasing, we will see many more deaths in our lives. Common sense

would suggest that this should make us less afraid of the "horsemen of death." But it is not the number of deaths but *how society treats death* that affects our feelings about the end of life. We will likely continue to fear death as long as our society continues to depersonalize it, rendering it more distant and more forbidding than in traditional societies (Nuland, 1994).

Questions for Discussion and Review

1. How do anticipatory and developmental socialization differ from resocialization?
2. What are Erikson's three development stages of adult life, and what personal crisis does each stage contain?
3. Why is the fear of death relatively common in modern societies?

A GLOBAL ANALYSIS OF SOCIALIZATION

All over the world, socialization appears largely the same in some ways and different in other ways. Researchers rarely study socialization with a global approach, but the existing findings reveal some interesting similarities and differences.

In a study of three significantly different cultures—American, French, and Japanese—researchers found similarities in how mothers respond to their 5-month-olds. When infants cry, mothers respond with nurturance. If the babies simply vocalize, showing no distress, mothers will respond with imitation. Mothers generally respond more to infants' vocalizing than to infants' looking (Bornstein et al., 1991). Such uniformities across different societies suggest the influence of biological factors on socialization.

But most of the studies that have been conducted suggest the powerful influence of culture on socialization. This is most vivid in the differences between the West and the rest of the world. First, young children in the West are supposed to play, whereas their peers in many non-Western countries are expected to work. As has been suggested, Javanese children in Indonesian villages, although only 9 years old, already work to contribute substantially to family income. Even younger children, 4 or 5 years old, also work, though mostly taking care of younger siblings while mothers work on the farm. In many African agricultural societies, the importance of child caregivers is so keenly felt that women with infants often recruit relatives' children from distant villages to help out (Morelli and Tronick, 1991).

Second, in the West, responsibility for the daily care and long-term upbringing of children is often left entirely to parents. Increasingly, therefore, strangers such as childcare workers take care of children for money more than from affection. This kind of socialization tends to foster individualism in the charges. By contrast, in much of the rest of the world, extended family groups, clans, and even communities pitch in to care for each other's children. This kind of socialization is more likely to develop trust in others and thereby attachment to groups (Leach, 1994).

Third, Western parents start socializing their children to be self-reliant at an extremely young age—virtually right after birth. Babies are placed in a crib, often in their own room. But, at least initially, the trauma of being left alone causes the infant to cry at bedtime or upon waking up. By contrast, infants in many non-Western societies are spared that trauma. They are allowed to sleep with their parents, often until age 5 or 6 (Harrison, 1992). With this sleeping arrangement, the children may have a slow start in learning to be on their own. But they are effectively socialized to develop a strong sense of security. This may partly explain why the insurance industry, which is supposed to meet customers' need for security about their future, is not as prosperous in non-Western countries as it is in Western countries.

Fourth, Western parents begin earnestly socializing children to curb their impulses and behave well at a very young age—before age 4. This may have much to do with Westerners' assumption that people are born bad, as suggested by Judeo-Christian beliefs

Whereas the "job" of young children in the West is to play, young children in many non-Western countries, such as this child in Mozambique, are also expected to work, mostly taking care of younger siblings.

about being born sinners or by Freud's widely accepted idea about being born with the id. By contrast, in Japan, China, and other East Asian societies, children are assumed to be innately good and therefore given much freedom to do what they want. This parental indulgence and permissiveness toward children usually gives way to strict disciplining after age 4. From then on, the content of Asian and Western socialization also differs. Asian parents tend to emphasize emotional control, filial piety, politeness to others, and other traits that promote social relationships and conformity. On the other hand, Western parents stress spontaneity, autonomy, assertiveness, and other characteristics that promote individual freedom and creativity (Papousek and Papousek, 1991; Harrison, 1992).

Questions for Discussion and Review

1. In what ways is childhood socialization about the same throughout the world?
2. In what ways does childhood socialization vary from Western to non-Western societies?

ARE WE PUPPETS OF SOCIETY?

Through socialization we internalize the norms and values of society. Does this imply that we become puppets of society, individuals who basically enjoy giving up freedom and following the rules society sets down? The answer is yes and no.

In many respects, we do behave like society's puppets. We are glad to follow society's expectation that we be friendly to our friends and love our parents. We are happy to do many other similarly nice things every day as expected of us by society. It just happens that we enjoy doing all these things because others have made us happy by responding positively when we do them. Living in a highly individualistic society, though, we do not see ourselves as society's puppets when we act in these ways.

But we may also do things differently than dictated by society. We may get drunk, fool around a bit too much, protest what we perceive to be a social injustice, or do other similar things that raise others' eyebrows. By engaging in such activities, we express the unsocialized aspect of our "self," no longer behaving like puppets. Dennis Wrong (1961) has suggested that we can never be puppets all the time because it is impossible to be entirely socialized. There are at least four reasons why socialization can never turn us into total puppets:

First, we have certain "imperious biological drives" that always buck against society's attempt to mold us in its image.

Second, the socializing influences are not always consistent and harmonious with one another. Our ethnic group, social class, and professional and occupational associations may not socialize us in the same way. They may teach conflicting roles, norms, and values.

Third, even if society could consistently and completely socialize us, we would still violate its laws and rules. In the very process of learning to obey the rules, we may also learn how to break them without getting caught, which is a great temptation for most if not all people. Even some of the most "respectable" citizens have committed crimes.

Finally, if we were completely socialized, we would become extremely unhappy and probably neurotic or psychotic. This is why, as Sigmund Freud said, civilization tends to breed discontent in the individual. No normal persons want their drives for self-expression, freedom, creativity, or personal eccentricity to be totally suppressed.

Questions for Discussion and Review

1. In what ways do we behave like society's puppets?
2. What aspects of human life prevent socialization from turning us into total puppets?

CHAPTER REVIEW

1. *What is socialization?* It is the process by which a society transmits its cultural values to its members. *Can either nature or nurture alone explain human behavior?* No. Both heredity and environment make us what we are. The importance of heredity can be demonstrated by how our temperament, intelligence, and aptitude influence the development of our personality. The significance of socialization can be seen in the case studies of children who are feral, isolated, institutionalized, or gifted.

2. *How do various theories explain the development of personality?* To Freud, personality develops from the interaction of the id, ego, and superego during childhood. To Piaget, children develop mentally in stages, from using sensorimotor skills in infancy to thinking abstractly in adolescence. To Kohlberg, children develop morally from a low, preconventional level of judging right and wrong to higher levels. The sociology

of emotions demonstrates how children learn to develop emotionally by identifying and managing their feelings through interaction with others. Feminist theory shows how children develop different gender identities under the influence of patriarchal society.

3. *What do the three major sociological perspectives tell us about socialization?* According to functionalists, socialization helps ensure social order as well as providing psychological and economic benefits. To conflict theorists, socialization reinforces age inequality, leading to child exploitation and abuse. The symbolic interactionist perspective suggests that children learn to see themselves from the way others see them and from the roles of others with whom they interact.

4. *What is distinctive about each of the major socializing agents?* The family is the most important socializing agent for the child. The school is charged both with

helping children develop their potential as independent individuals and with securing their conformity to social norms. The peer group socializes its members as equals, offering a set of values largely different from that presented by adult authorities. The mass media, particularly television, influence the child's values and behavior, but this influence tends to wear off as the child grows up.

5. *Does socialization stop with the end of childhood?* No. Adults continue to experience socialization as children do. They go through anticipatory socialization, developmental socialization, and resocialization. According to Erikson, adults continue to go through three more stages of psychosocial development after having come out of five preadult stages. Each stage involves struggling to resolve a crisis. *How does modern society deal with aging and dying?* Not very well. Generally, the aged are not as highly respected in modern societies as in traditional ones. Death is also not treated as a normal, eventually inevitable part of life to be accepted.

6. *What can a global analysis of socialization reveal?* Socialization is similar and different from society to society, suggesting the influence of both biological and cultural factors.

7. *Are we puppets of society?* Yes, to the extent that we enjoy doing many things in accordance with social norms, but no, to the extent that we occasionally engage in activities frowned on by others.

KEY TERMS

Anticipatory socialization The process by which people learn to assume a role in the future. (p. 71)

Aptitude The capacity for developing physical or social skills. (p. 58)

Conventional morality Kohlberg's term for the practice of defining right and wrong according to the *motive* of the action being judged. (p. 63)

Developmental socialization The process by which people learn to be more competent in playing their currently assumed role. (p. 71)

Ego Freud's term for the part of personality that is rational, dealing with the world logically and realistically. (p. 61)

Emotional intelligence The ability to identify and manage one's own *affect* (feelings). (p. 63)

Gender identity People's image of what they are socially expected to be and do on the basis of their sex. (p. 64)

Generalized others Mead's term for people who do not have close ties to a child but do influence the child's internalization of the values of society. (p. 67)

Id Freud's term for the part of personality that is irrational, concerned only with seeking pleasure. (p. 60)

Instincts Biologically inherited capacities for performing relatively complex tasks. (p. 59)

Intelligence The capacity for mental or intellectual achievement. (p. 58)

Looking-glass self Cooley's term for the self-image that we develop from the way others treat us. (p. 66)

Peer group A group whose members are about the same age and have similar interests. (p. 69)

Personality A fairly stable configuration of feelings, attitudes, ideas, and behaviors that characterizes an individual. (p. 58)

Postconventional morality Kohlberg's term for the practice of judging actions by taking into account the importance of *conflicting norms*. (p. 63)

Preconventional morality Kohlberg's term for the practice of defining right and wrong according to the *consequence* of the action being judged. (p. 63)

Resocialization The process by which people are forced to abandon their old self and to develop a new self in its place. (p. 71)

Significant others Mead's term for people who have close ties to a child and exert a strong influence on the child. (p. 67)

Socialization The process by which a society transmits its cultural values to its members. (p. 58)

Superego Freud's term for the part of personality that is moral; popularly known as conscience. (p. 61)

Total institutions Places where people are not only cut off from the larger society but also rigidly controlled by the administrators. (p. 71)

SUGGESTED READINGS

Gardner, Howard. 1993. *Creating Minds: An Anatomy of Creativity Seen Through the Lives of Freud, Einstein, Picasso, Stravinsky, Eliot, Graham, and Gandhi.* New York: Basic Books. Shows how the family and other social forces affected the development of these seven geniuses.

Gilligan, Carol, et al. (eds.). 1990. *Making Connections.* Cambridge, Mass.: Harvard University Press. A series of research reports on how U.S. society encourages adolescent girls to change from being confident about what they know and see to being uncertain and hesitant.

Goleman, Daniel. 1995. *Emotional Intelligence.* New York: Bantam Books. Shows what emotional intelligence is and how it contributes to success in school, career, or life in general.

Nuland, Sherwin B. 1994. *How We Die: Reflections on Life's Final Chapter.* New York: Knopf. Offers insight into how death has become frightening and lonely to modern society.

Rymer, Russ. 1993. *Genie: An Abused Child's Flight from Silence.* New York: HarperCollins. Details how the atrocious deprivation of socialization affected Genie and how her case led to conflicts among linguists, psychologists, social workers, and others who claimed to help her.

SOCIAL INTERACTION IN EVERYDAY LIFE

Myths and Realities

MYTH: *To avoid misunderstanding, especially in conversation with foreigners, it is always wise to say directly what's on our mind, such as saying "yes" to mean "yes."*
REALITY: Directness in speech may be good for transmitting information, but *indirectness* is common in many other countries. The Japanese, for example, may say "yes" to mean "no" when asked "Would you agree to do business with us?" This is their way of trying to save others from disappointment or embarrassment. (p. 85)

MYTH: *All over the world it is natural for people to nod their heads to mean "yes" and shake them to mean "no."*
REALITY: Body language varies from one culture to another. In the United States, we, of course, nod our heads to mean "yes" and shake them to mean "no." But in Bulgaria, head nodding means "no," and head shaking means "yes." (p. 85)

MYTH: *Because they speak the same language, men and women can easily understand each other.*
REALITY: They are likely to use the same language differently: men for the purpose of *giving information*; women for *expressing feelings*. Thus, men tend to misunderstand women by taking literally what women say, and women tend to misunderstand men by reading emotional meanings into what men say. (pp. 87–88)

MYTH: *The world "out there" is by itself real.*
REALITY: The world out there is not real without being defined as real by us. (p. 93)

John and Mary, a married couple, teach college in different cities. They spend three days a week far away from each other. People frequently express sympathy with remarks such as "That must be rough" or "How do you stand it?" Mary readily accepts their sympathy, saying things like "We fly a lot." Sometimes she reinforces their concern: "The worst part is packing and unpacking all the time." But John reacts differently, often with irritation. He emphasizes the advantages of his marriage: as professors, he and his wife have four-day weekends together, long vacations throughout the year, and four months off in the summer. They even benefit from those days when they are separated because they can do their work without interruption. All this is true, but Mary is surprised that her husband reacts differently than she does. He explains that he senses condescension in others' expression of concern, as if they were implying, "Yours is not a real marriage. I pity you, and look down on you, because my wife and I do not have your kind of misfortune." In a nutshell, John tends to see others as adversaries but Mary does not (Tannen, 1990).

What John and Mary experience is **social interaction,** the process by which individuals act toward and react to others. Interactions can be classified into three types, roughly reflecting the three major perspectives in sociology. John tends to engage in **oppositional interactions,** treating others as competitors or enemies. Mary, on the other hand, tends to have **supportive interactions,** treating others as supporters or friends. This gender difference reflects the different social worlds in which John and Mary live. Reflecting the conflict perspective, John's world is more hierarchical and dominance-oriented, in which a man must be either one-up or one-down. To men, life is more like a contest, with social interactions being an arena where "people try to achieve and maintain the upper hand if they can, and protect themselves from others' attempts to put them down and push them around" (Tannen, 1990). Reflecting the functionalist perspective, however, Mary's world is more egalitarian and sharing-oriented, in which there is a greater tendency to nurture relationships by seeking and giving confirmation and support. To women, life is more like "a community, a struggle to preserve intimacy and avoid isolation" (Tannen, 1990).

Both of those two perspectives are structural, suggesting that people more or less passively follow the dictates of their world. To symbolic interactionists, all interactions, whether oppositional or supportive, are also *symbolic,* in which people actively interpret each other's actions and reactions and behave in accordance with the interpretation. Thus John and Mary react differently to the same comments from others because they *interpret* the comments differently.

In sum, the three perspectives spotlight different patterns of social interaction. Functionalism focuses on the supportive nature of interaction; the conflict perspective, the oppositional nature; and symbolic interactionism, the symbolic or interpretive nature.

FUNCTIONALIST PERSPECTIVE

According to functionalists, there are two types of supportive interaction: exchange and cooperation. An **exchange** is an interaction in which two individuals offer each other something in order to obtain a reward in return. **Cooperation** is an interaction in which two or more individuals work together to achieve a common goal.

Exchange

If you help a friend study for an exam and your friend, in turn, types a paper for you, you have engaged in an exchange. The reward we expect to get for what we do for others may be material, such as salary or a gift, or it may be nonmaterial, such as a word of praise or gratitude. We find exchanges in all types of situations. Representatives of nations trade votes at the United Nations, employees exchange their labor for a salary, friends exchange advice and gratitude, children trade toys, and so on.

Social exchanges are usually governed by the norm of *reciprocity*, which requires that people help those who have helped them. If a favor has been extended to us, we will be motivated to return the favor. Conversely, if others have not been helpful to us, we are not likely to be helpful to them. Therefore, if social exchanges are fair, the social structure involved tends to be solid. The exchange reinforces the relationships and provides each party in the exchange with some needed good. But if exchanges are seen as unfair, the social structure is likely to be shaky. A friendship in which one person constantly helps another, expecting but not getting gratitude in return, is likely to be short-lived.

But friends cannot be too fussy about the fairness of exchange, unless they want the relationship to be something less than friendship. If you give someone five dollars and expect to get exactly the same amount back from that person later, chances are that he or she is not your friend. Thus, in exchanges between classmates, co-workers, or business associates who are not friends, the participants give benefits with the expectation of receiving precisely comparable benefits in return. In friendships, however, members actively avoid the exactly equitable exchange because it seems too impersonal, businesslike, or unsentimental. Instead, they work out complicated exchanges of noncomparable benefits. Such an exchange would occur if you were to offer help and consolation to a friend who is ill and later received $100 from that friend when you were broke.

Cooperation

In an exchange, a task can be adequately performed by only one of the parties. In cooperation, an individual needs another person's help to do a job or to do it more effectively. Within this broad category of interactions, there are some differences (Nisbet, 1977).

When neighbors come together to help a family whose house has just burned down or been destroyed by a tornado, that is *spontaneous cooperation*. This is the oldest type of cooperation, but it is unpredictable.

Over time, some forms of cooperation occur frequently enough for them to become customary in society. It was a custom in parts of the U.S. frontier, for example, for neighbors to work together to build a barn. This type of cooperation, *traditional cooperation*, brings added stability to the social structure.

Because modern societies such as the United States include people with diverse traditions, they are more likely to depend on a third type of cooperation, *directed cooperation*. It is based on the directions of someone in authority. We are directed by government, for example, to abide by the law and pay taxes. But in return the government provides us with such services as education, police protection, and national defense.

A fourth type of cooperation is equally useful in complex modern societies: *contractual cooperation*. It does not originate from tradition or authority but from voluntary action. Nor does it happen spontaneously; it involves, instead, some planning. In contractual cooperation, individuals freely decide, for example, whether to embark on a business project together, and they spell out the terms of the cooperation.

Questions for Discussion and Review

1. What is the difference between exchange and cooperation?
2. What are the different types of cooperation?

CONFLICT PERSPECTIVE

Oppositional interaction can be competition or conflict. **Competition** is an interaction in which two individuals follow mutually accepted rules, each trying to achieve the same goal before the other does. **Conflict** is an interaction in which two individuals disregard any rules, each trying to achieve his or her own goal by defeating the other.

Traditional cooperation adds stability to the social structure. Although traditional cooperation still exists among people such as the Amish, most people in the United States have come to depend on the directed cooperation of someone in authority.

Competition

In a competition, some degree of cooperation exists because the competitors must cooperate with each other by "playing the game" according to the rules. In a boxing match, for example, the fighters must cooperate by not hitting each other on certain parts of the body—by not turning the fight into a free-for-all. In politics, candidates competing for the same office must cooperate by following certain rules, the major one being that all contenders, especially the losers, must accept the outcome.

It is widely believed that competition brings out the best in us. The economic prosperity of Western capitalist nations, as opposed to the lower standard of living in formerly communist countries, is often attributed to the high value placed on competition. Compelled to compete fiercely with Japan and other countries in the global market, U.S. industries seem to have become more efficient and productive. It is apparently true that competition can stimulate economic growth. Certain types of professionals, such as athletes, politicians, and lawyers, are also known to thrive on competition. In our everyday life, however, we usually perform less well—or more poorly—when we are trying to beat others than when we are working with them.

Several scholars who reviewed over 100 studies conducted from 1924 to 1981 that dealt with competition and cooperation in classrooms found that in 65 of the studies, cooperation promoted higher achievement than competition. In only eight studies did competition induce higher achievement; 36 studies showed no statistically significant difference. Research on college students, scientists, and workers has pro-

duced further data challenging the popular belief in the benefits of competition (Kohn, 1986; Azmitia, 1988). Competition seems to hamper achievement primarily because it is stressful. The anxiety that arises from the possibility of losing interferes with performance. Even if this anxiety can be suppressed, it is difficult to do two things at the same time: trying to do well and trying to beat others. Competition can easily distract attention from the task at hand. Consider a teacher asking his pupils a question. A little girl waves her arm wildly to attract his attention, crying, "Please! Please! Pick me!" Finally recognized, she has forgotten the answer. So she scratches her head, asking, "What was the question again?" The problem is that she has focused on beating her classmates, not on the subject matter (Kohn, 1986).

Conflict

In competition, the contestants try to achieve the same goal in accordance with commonly accepted rules. The most important rule is usually that competing parties should concentrate on winning the game, not on hurting each other. When competing parties no longer play by these rules, competition has become conflict. In conflict, defeating the opponent, by hook or by crook, has become the goal. To use an extreme contrast, we can see competition in sports and conflict in wars.

Conflict exists in all kinds of social situations. It occurs between management and labor, whites and blacks, criminals and police, but also between friends, lovers, family members, and fellow workers. It can both harm and help a social structure. Wars between nations and violent confrontations between hostile groups clearly are harmful. Yet war may also unify members of a society. This is most likely to occur if various segments of society, such as leaders and the ordinary people, agree that the enemy is a real menace to the entire country, that it warrants going to war and defending the nation, and that internal conflict, if any, can be resolved (Markides and Cohn, 1982). Thus, the Vietnam War divided the American people because many did not agree with their government that South Vietnam was worth defending. In contrast, the Second World War was a unifying force because virtually all the United States population looked upon the threat of Nazi Germany and Japan in the same light. Conflict can also stimulate needed change. Consider the black-white conflict in the United States. Spearheaded by the civil rights movement in the 1960s, this conflict has led to greater equality between the races.

Questions for Discussion and Review

1. How does competition differ from conflict?
2. How would you prevent competition from becoming conflict?

SYMBOLIC INTERACTIONIST PERSPECTIVE

Both functionalist and conflict perspectives enable us to see the different forms of interaction by watching from a distance how people interact. What we get from these perspectives is the *outside* view of interaction. We do not do know what is going on *inside* people when they interact. To symbolic interactionists, we can learn much about interaction by analyzing people's interpretations of each other's actions.

Interpreting Supportive Interaction

Erving Goffman (1971) referred to supportive interactions as "supportive interchanges," "mutual dealings," or "acts of identificatory sympathy." Examples range from "the congratulations at marriage, the careful commiserations at divorce, and the doleful condolences at deaths" to "the neighborly act of lending various possessions and providing minor services" to inquiries about "another's health, his experience on a recent trip, his feelings about a recent movie." To symbolic interactionists, all these acts should *not* be taken at face value because they are not what they appear to be.

When people ask us "How are you?" they are not really interested in finding out the condition of our health in the same way as our doctor is. Instead, if they are strangers, they may actually mean to say "you can trust me," "I want to know you," or "I want to be your friend." If they are already our friends, they may mean to express their joy at seeing us, their desire to reaffirm our friendship. There are many other possible meanings, depending on the people and circumstances we encounter. All such meanings shape interaction in everyday life.

Interpreting Oppositional Interaction

While supportive interaction usually involves individuals of about the same social status, oppositional interaction tends more to involve people of different statuses. In such a situation, the higher-status person tends to be disrespectful toward the lower-status person. One common way of showing this disrespect involves symbolically invading the personhood of the lower-status person.

Consider, for example, the interaction between men and women in a sexist society. Since they are generally given a higher status than women, men tend more to stare at women than vice versa. Men are also more likely to touch women's bodies, such as letting their hands rest on women's shoulders, while women rarely reciprocate. When members of both sexes participate in a group discussion, men are far more likely to interrupt women than the other way around. In one study, only 4 percent of the interruptions in male-female conversations came from women, and 96 percent came from men (Karp and Yoels, 1993).

Question for Discussion and Review

1. What is the symbolic interactionist view of supportive and oppositional interaction?

INTERACTION AS SYMBOLIC COMMUNICATION

We have just seen how power, respect, and other aspects of social relationships are communicated with symbols, such as words and gestures. Without symbolic communication, humans would have to interact

In a competition between two or more individuals or groups, each tries to achieve the same goal before the other does. But competition involves some cooperation, since competitors such as these football players must cooperate with each other by playing the game according to the rules.

like other animals. Symbolic communication, then, is the essence of human interaction.

The Nature of Human Communication

Animals communicate, too. If you try to catch a seagull, it will call out "hahaha! hahaha!" to signal its friends to watch out for an intruder. A squirrel may cry out to warn other squirrels to flee from danger. But these signal systems are not symbols, and animal communication differs in fundamental ways from human communication.

First, symbols are *arbitrary.* The meaning of a word is not determined by any inherent quality of the thing itself. Instead a word may mean *whatever* a group of humans has agreed it is supposed to mean. If you do not speak Chinese, you would not know that *gou* is the Chinese word for dog. There is no inherent connection between the word and the thing itself. The Spaniards, after all, call the same animal *perro,* and the French call it *chien.* Even "dingdong" is an arbitrary symbol: a bell may sound like "dingdong" to us, but not to the Germans, to whom a bell sounds like "bimbam." The meaning of a word is "socially constructed" because it is determined by people through their social experiences as members of a specific society. It is no wonder that there are a great many different symbols in human communication to represent the same thing. Animals, on the other hand, do not arbitrarily produce different symbols to indicate the same thing because their communication is largely determined by instinct. This is why, for example, all

seagulls throughout the world make the same sound to indicate the presence of danger. Unlike humans, they cannot express a particular thought in more than one way (Cowley, 1988).

Second, animal communication is a closed system, but human communication is an *open system.* Each animal species can communicate only a limited set of messages, and the meaning of these signals is fixed. Animals can use only one signal at a time—they cannot combine two or more to produce a new and more complex message. A bird can signal "worms" to other birds but not "worms" and "cats" together. Animal communication is also closed in the sense of being stimulus-bound; it is tied to what is immediately present in the environment. The bird can signal "worms" only because it sees them. It is impossible for an animal to use a symbol to represent some invisible, abstract, or imaginary thing. As philosopher Bertrand Russell said, "No matter how eloquently a dog can bark, he cannot tell you that his parents are poor but honest." In contrast, we can blend and combine symbols to express whatever ideas come to mind. We can create new messages, and the potential number of messages that we can send is infinite. Thus, we can talk about abstractions such as good and evil, truth and beauty. It is this creative character of language that leads many people to believe that language is unique to humans. Language also makes possible the exchange of ideas through the information superhighway around the world.

Human communication is not only verbal, involving the use of words. It is also nonverbal, consisting of kinesics and proxemics. **Kinesics** (pro-

cathy®   **by Cathy Guisewite**

nounced ki-NEE-sicks) is "body language," the use of body movements as a means of communication, such as smiling to express happiness at seeing someone. **Proxemics** (pronounced procks-EE-micks) is the use of space as a means of communication. It is an example of proxemics when we snuggle up to an intimate to express affection or when we avoid touching a stranger to show respect.

A Global Analysis of Communication

Whether human communication is verbal or nonverbal, it is conducted differently in different societies. Let us see how people in other countries communicate differently than we do.

Global Diversity in Verbal Communication In some cultures where people like to talk a lot, a listener's silence is often assumed to indicate agreement. Once an Egyptian pilot radioed ahead to the Cyprus airport for permission to land. Receiving no response, the pilot took the silence to mean "permission granted." But as the pilot brought the plane in for landing, the Cypriot air force opened fire. Obviously, to the Cypriots, the silence meant "permission denied" (Tannen, 1986).

But between equally talkative cultures there are also differences in conversational style. In our society we tend to believe that even in casual conversation only one person should speak at a time. Yet in many other countries, it is normal for a listener to chime in when someone is talking, in order to show enthusiastic participation or involvement with others. Such logic seems to elude many people in the United States. In the late 1980s, the U.S. president's wife, Nancy Reagan, complained to the press about Raisa Gorbachev, wife of the Soviet president: "From the moment we met, she talked and talked and *talked*—so much that I could barely get a word in, edgewise or

otherwise." Probably unaware of the "one speaker at a time" ethic, Mrs. Gorbachev might have been wondering why her U.S. counterpart never said anything—and made her do all the conversational work (Tannen, 1990; Tannen, 1994a).

When we talk, we tend to express directly what is on our mind. People in many other cultures are more likely to speak indirectly. In Asia, if you visit an acquaintance on a hot day and feel thirsty, you would not ask your host point-blank, "May I have a glass of water?" Instead, you would convey the same request by saying, "Isn't it hot today?" In Japan, if at the end of a lengthy business meeting you ask, "Do you then agree to do business with us?" the Japanese will always say "yes" even if they mean "no." They are reluctant to say "no" directly, in order to save others' face and spare them embarrassment. Used to directness in speech, many of us cannot understand how "yes" can possibly mean "no." But Japanese can say "yes" in a certain way to mean "yes," and say "yes" in another way to mean "no."

Global Diversity in Nonverbal Communication
Like verbal communication, body language varies from one culture to another. People in the United States nod their heads to mean "yes" and shake them to mean "no." But in Bulgaria, head nodding means "no," and head shaking means "yes." The Semang of Malaya thrust their heads forward to signal "yes" and cast their eyes down to signal "no." When North Americans use a thumb and forefinger to form a circle, they mean "A-OK," but the same gesture is considered obscene in Brazil and other countries.

In proxemics, the amount of space we take up around us also varies from one society to another. In North America, when we talk to a person whom we do not know well, we ordinarily stand about three feet away. If one person moves in closer than that, the other would find it too close for comfort. This may

Nonverbal communication may involve proxemics, the use of space as a means of communication. The proxemics found in Arab cultures, for example, differs from that characteristic of North Americans. When conversing with people we do not know, we usually stand about three feet apart, but Arabs tend to maintain a closer conversational distance.

reflect the North American values of individual independence and privacy. But South Americans and Arabs are inclined to stand much closer. In "invading" others' space, they do not mean to be rude. On the contrary, they are expressing their desire for human connection.

U.S. Diversity in Communication

Both verbal and nonverbal communication also vary from one group to another within our own diverse society.

Verbal Communication in the United States Various groups speak English with different accents. The Midwestern accent is different from the New York accent, which is distinct from the Southern accent, which is distinguishable from the New England accent, and so on. Accents also vary within each of these regional categories. Different races and classes have their own accents. Most interestingly, there are variations in English usage and conversational style.

The middle class seldom uses the double negative ("I can't get no satisfaction"), whereas the working class often does. The middle class rarely drops the letter "g" in present participles ("doin'" for "doing," "singin'" for "singing"), perhaps because they are conscious of being "correct." The working class often drops the "g," probably to show that they are not snooty. They also tend to say "lay" instead of "lie," as in "Let's lay on the beach," without suggesting a

desire for sex. On the other hand, the middle class has a weakness for euphemism. To them, drunks are "people with alcohol problems," and a prison is a "correctional facility." They also tend to choose words that they consider sophisticated—"vocalist" instead of "singer," or "as of this time" rather than "now." The upper class distinguishes itself by its tendency to use such words as "tiresome" or "tedious" instead of "boring" (Fussell, 1992).

Inner-city blacks speak a dialect that their white counterparts may find hard to understand. Here is an example of how "Black English" was used to explain why God cannot be black:

> Why? I'll tell you why. 'Cause the average whitey out here got everything, you dig? And the [black man] ain't got shit, y'know? Y'understan'? So—um—for— in order for *that* to happen, you know it ain't no black God that's doin' that bullshit (Nanda, 1994).

The quote can be roughly translated into: "No way God can be black. If he was, he wouldn't have screwed up our lives." To some whites, Black English is deficient, but for its speakers it is a lively, useful tool for communication in the inner city.

Similarly, whites often say things in everyday conversation that would sound peculiar to Apache Indian listeners. Whites would say to mere acquaintances or even strangers, "Hello, my friend! How're you feeling?" Apaches would not call somebody "my friend" unless that somebody is truly a friend. They would not ask mere acquaintances how they feel, because it is considered an invasion of personal privacy, reflecting an unnatural curiosity about others' inner feelings. Also to Apaches, whites' frequent use of the other's name ("Glad to see you, *Mary*," "How you doing, *Joe*?") smacks of disrespect because a personal name is the individual's sacred property (Nanda, 1994).

Nonverbal Communication in the United States

In his classic study of a Chicago slum, Gerald Suttles (1970) found some ethnic diversity in the use of body language and personal space:

> The other ethnic groups think it odd that a group of Mexican men should strike a pose of obliviousness to others, even their nearby wives and children. Puerto Ricans, on the other hand, are disparaged because they stand painfully close during a conversation.... Whites say that [African Americans] will not look them in the eye. The [African Americans] counter by saying that whites are impolite and try to "cow" people by staring at them.

But among whites themselves, when talking with members of the same sex, men are less likely than women to look at others. Researchers have observed a series of casual conversations between two subjects of the same sex. In these studies men often "looked outward, away from each other, and around the room, rather than directly at each other," while women more frequently looked straight at each other. The men did occasionally look at each other, but their eye contact did not last as long as that among women. What does this gender difference mean? It is possible that, to men, looking at others as long as women do seems like staring, hence a hostile action, a threat, which they try to avoid. But it is more likely that, by looking away from each other, men may be avoiding friendly connection or intimacy, which women tend more to seek and express by looking at others (Tannen, 1990; 1994a). This has much to do with the nature of the world in which men live, which differs from that of women. Let us explore these two worlds and see how they affect the communication between the sexes.

Questions for Discussion and Review

1. In what ways does human communication differ from animal communication?
2. How does communication differ from one society to another?
3. How do various groups in the United States differ in communication?

COMMUNICATION BETWEEN WOMEN AND MEN

In the world of women, connection and intimacy are the primary goals of life, and individuals cultivate friendship, minimize differences, seek consensus, and avoid the appearance of superiority. On the other hand, status and independence are the primary goals of life in men's world, so individuals seek status by telling others what to do, attain freedom from others' control, avoid taking orders, and resist asking for help. Thus, when the two sexes communicate with each other, women tend to use the language of connection and intimacy, and men the language of status and independence. Both may use the same English language, but in effect they speak and hear different dialects called **genderlects,** linguistic styles that reflect the different worlds of women and men (Tannen, 1990; 1994a).

Speaking Different Genderlects

Failure to understand each other's genderlects can spell trouble for intergender communication. Consider a married couple, Linda and Josh. One day Josh's old high school buddy from another city called to announce that he would be in town the following month. Josh invited him to stay for the weekend. When he told Linda that they were going to have a houseguest, she was upset. Often away on business, she had planned to spend that weekend with Josh alone. But what upset her the most was that Josh had extended the invitation without first discussing it with her. Linda would never make plans without first checking with Josh. "Why can't you do the same with me?" Linda asked. But Josh responded, "I can't say to my friend, 'I have to ask my wife for permission'!" To Josh, who lives in the men's world of status, checking with his wife means seeking permission, giving up his independence, or having to act like a kid asking his mom if it's OK to play with a friend. In Linda's female world of connection, checking with her husband has nothing to do with permission. In fact, Linda likes to tell others, "I have to check with Josh," because it makes her feel good to reaffirm that she is involved with someone, that her life is bound up with someone else's (Tannen, 1990). In short, Linda and Josh speak and hear different genderlects, one having to do with connection and intimacy, the other with status and independence.

There are other ways the different genderlects can throw a monkey wrench into the communication between women and men. Accustomed to speaking for the purpose of giving *information* only, men tend to misunderstand women by taking literally what women say. On the other hand, women, more habituated to talking for the purpose of expressing *feelings,* tend to misunderstand men by reading emotional meanings into what men say. Thus women and men tend to communicate at cross-purposes. If a woman says to her husband, "We never go out," he may upset her by responding, "That's not true. We went out last week." The husband fails to grasp the feeling the wife tries to convey. In saying "we never go out," she in effect says something like "I feel like going out and doing something together. We always have such a fun time, and I enjoy being with you. It has been a few days since we went out." If on another occasion the woman asks her husband, "What's the matter?" and gets the answer, "I'm OK," she may respond by saying, "I know something's wrong. What is it? Why aren't you willing to share your problem with me? Let me help you." The wife fails to understand that, by saying "I'm OK," her husband means "I am OK; I can deal with my problem. I don't need any help, thank you" (Gray, 1992). In his male world, dealing with one's own problems is a hallmark of independence, which he tries to assert, and getting help from others is a sign of weakness, which he tries to avoid.

Genderlects are not confined to communication between intimates. They also influence communication in public. Sitting alone in a dining room where bank officers had lunch, sociolinguist Alice Deakins listened to what they were talking about at adjacent tables. When no woman was present, the men talked mostly about business and rarely about people. The next most popular topics were food, sports, and recreation. When women talked alone, their most frequent topic was people, especially friends, children, and partners in personal relationships. Business was next, and then health, including weight control. Together, women and men tended to avoid the topic that each group liked best and settle on topics of interest to both, *but they followed the style of the men-only conversations.* They talked about food the way men did, focusing on the food and restaurant rather than diet and health. They talked about recreation the way men did, concentrating on sports figures and athletic events rather than exercising for weight control. And they talked about housing the way men did, dealing mostly with location, property values, and commuting time, rather than whether the house is suitable for the family, how safe is the neighborhood for the children, and what kinds of people live next door. In other words, in public communication between the sexes, the male genderlect tends to dominate, mostly centering on things and activities, thus ignoring the female genderlect, which primarily concerns people and relationships (Tannen, 1990; 1994a).

Playing the Gendered Game of Proxemics

In gender-mixed groups, men's proxemics differs from women's. Men usually sprawl with legs spread apart and hands stretched away from the body, taking up considerable space around them. Women are more likely to draw themselves in, using only little space with "ladylike" postures, such as closing or crossing the legs and placing the hands near the body.

A more direct way for men to dominate women in proxemics involves invading their personal space. As has been suggested, men often let their hands rest on women's shoulders but women rarely do the same to men. A similar proxemic domination prevails in interactions of mutual affection. When an intimate couple walks down the street, the man may place his arm around the woman's shoulders, but the woman is far less likely to put her arm around the man's shoulders. Doesn't this merely reflect the fact that the man is usually taller so that it would be uncomfortable for the sexes to reverse positions? No. The same ritual of man playing the powerful protector and woman the helpless protected is often observed when both are of about the same height or even when the man is slightly shorter. If the man is too short to stretch his arm around the woman's shoulders, they still will not reverse positions but will instead settle for holding hands. If a tall woman does put her arm around a shorter man's shoulders, chances are that she is a mother and he is her child (Tannen, 1990; 1994a). In the world of gender inequality, a man is likely to cringe if his girlfriend or wife treats him like a child by putting her arms around his shoulders.

Even in the most intimate moments between a man and a woman, male domination reigns. When both lie down in bed, he typically lies on his back, flat and straight, but she lies on her side, her body nestled against his. She further places her head on his shoulder, and he his arm around her. It is a picture of unequal relationship, with the man appearing strong and protective and the woman weak and protected (Tannen, 1990; 1994a).

Questions for Discussion and Review

1. What are genderlects, and how do they affect the communication between women and men?
2. How do men and women play the gendered game of proxemics?

The proxemics of body language differs between women and men. In gender-mixed groups, men are likely to sprawl, in open positions, whereas women are likely to draw themselves in, in "lady-like" postures.

DRAMATURGY: INTERACTION AS DRAMA

Underlying the diversity of communication that we have just analyzed is the same tendency for people everywhere to interact with others as if they were performing on the stage of a theater. Shakespeare captured the essence of social interaction as a staged drama with his famous line: "All the world's a stage, and all the men and women merely players." U.S. sociologist Erving Goffman (1922–1982) developed the theatrical analogy into **dramaturgy,** a method of analyzing social interaction as if the participants were performing on a stage.

Behaving Like Actors

When we interact, we behave like actors by following a script that we have learned from our parents, teachers, friends, and others (see Chapter 3: Socialization). The script essentially tells us how to behave in accordance with our statuses and roles (Chapter 2: Society and Culture). But the stage analogy does have limitations. On stage, the actors have a clearly written and detailed script that allows them to rehearse exactly what they will say and do. In real life, our "script" is far more general and ambiguous. It cannot tell us precisely how we are going to act or how the other person is going to react. It is therefore much more difficult, if possible at all, to be well rehearsed. In fact, as we gain new experiences every day, we constantly revise our script. This means that we have to improvise a great deal, saying and doing many things that have not crossed our minds before that very moment.

One example is how women used to react to a pelvic examination in the office of a gynecologist. Women dreaded this event, when they had to subject their most private body areas to "public" scrutiny, very often by a male physician. The occasion was potentially embarrassing to both doctor and patient. How best to minimize this risk? One way was revealed in a classic study by James Henslin and Mae Biggs (1971). They analyzed the data on several thousand pelvic examinations that Biggs had observed as a trained nurse. A typical examination unfolded like the scenes in a play:

In the prologue, the woman enters the waiting room and thus assumes the role of patient. In the first act, she is called into the consulting room, where she describes her complaints. The doctor assumes his role by responding appropriately, listening closely, asking the necessary questions, and discussing the patient's problems. If a pelvic examination is indicated, he so informs the patient and then departs, leaving the patient in the nurse's hands.

The second act begins as the nurse ushers the patient into an examining room and asks her to disrobe. At the same time, the nurse tries to help the patient make the transition from a dignified, fully clothed person to little more than a scientific specimen. The patient appears nervous. The nurse is sympathetic and reassuring. The nurse shows the patient where to leave her clothes and how to put on her hospital gown. The interaction with the nurse creates a strictly clinical situation.

The third act is the examination itself. Lying on the table with her body covered, the patient is transformed into a "nonperson," the object of the doctor's scrutiny. She cannot see the doctor, who sits on a low stool. She also avoids eye contact with the nurse. She simply stares at the ceiling and says little or nothing. Similarly, the doctor tries to refrain from talking. All this serves to desexualize the situation, reassuring everybody that it is only a medical examination.

The fourth and final act begins as the examination ends. The doctor leaves, allowing the patient to dress in solitude. Then, fully clothed, she is ushered back into the consulting room, where both doctor and patient resume the roles they have played in the first act. Now the doctor again treats his patient as a person, and the patient behaves as though nothing

unusual has happened. Finally, she departs, going back to her everyday roles.

This analysis suggests that, despite the lack of a script showing how doctor and patient should interact, they nevertheless manage, with the help of the nurse, to play their roles. We also learn that each participant tries to save the other's "face" with what Goffman calls "*tactful blindness*" to an embarrassing situation, acting as if it did not exist. This mutual cooperation makes it possible for the performance to go on. According to Goffman, the performance is the heart of social interaction and as such involves *presenting the self* to the other.

Presenting the Self

In presenting our "self" to others, we are the actors and they the audience. They also do the same, with themselves as actors and us as audience. The playing of these two opposite roles by each participant in social interaction ensures that when each performs poorly in presenting the self the audience will empathize, ignore the flaw, and form the impression desired by the actor. One will help the other pull off the performance because of the expectation that the favor will be returned. This explains the avoidance of embarrassment through tactful blindness in many situations comparable to the pelvic examination. If our houseguest stumbles on

In dramaturgical analysis, the participants are seen as actors and an audience. In presenting ourselves in job interviews, for example, we are like actors trying to display our positive aspects and conceal the negative ones from our audience, the interviewer.

arrival or belches after dinner, we usually pretend not to see or hear the contretemps.

Although others want to help us succeed with our self-presentation, we still strive to do so on our own. Generally, we try to display the positive aspects of ourselves and conceal the negative ones. When we date someone for the first time, we will shower and dress properly and use a deodorant to mask any unpleasant smell. When we listen to a story, we try to be "all ears," but even if we become bored to the point of yawning we cover our mouths with our hands. In conversation we try to say the right thing and avoid saying the wrong thing. In fact, to ensure a smooth interaction, we often have to say or do things we truly don't want to. That is why store clerks appear friendly even to pesky customers, or a polite person laughs at bad jokes. Doesn't all this destroy our true self, self-identity, or dignity? No, because we maintain what Goffman calls **role distance,** the separation of our role playing as outward performance from our inner self. Thus we may outwardly appear servile to some people but inwardly scorn them.

The outward performance is similar to what the actor does *onstage*, and the inward feeling is comparable to what the actor does *backstage*. Goffman takes this stage analogy seriously in his analysis of self-presentation, which he divides into "front-region" (or "frontstage") performance and "back-region" ("backstage") behavior. In the front region, people present their selves in ways expected by others, the audience. In the back region, they reveal their true selves, with no concern for the audience. Often the backstage behavior contradicts the frontstage performance. Consider, for example, the goings-on in a funeral home. The body-preparation room is the backstage where the funeral director and staff often show no respect to the dead, such as by joking about the corpse or complaining about its size or smell. But in the frontstage interaction with the bereaved family and friends, the mortuary personnel exhibit great respect to the deceased. Even though in the back region they have drained and stuffed the corpse, in the front region the personnel never touch it, always respectfully keeping a distance from the casketed body (Turner and Edgley, 1990).

Onstage performances are not necessarily dishonest, nor intended only to manipulate or fool the audience. Often we do present who we really are. Generally, onstage performance is more honest with families and friends than with strangers. But even with strangers dishonest performance cannot be pulled off without the apparent collusion of the audience. In fact, the appearance of mutual cooperation between performer and audience is an important characteristic of interaction rituals.

Performing Interaction Rituals

In religious rituals, the worshipers perform certain acts to show reverence to the deity. Similarly, in **interaction rituals,** the participants perform certain acts to show reverence to each other. Some people may not genuinely feel reverent but only pretend to show reverence with the intent of manipulating others. But, in dramaturgy, they can be said to be engaged in an interaction ritual because the essence of interaction rituals is the *appearance* or *display* of reverence rather than actual reverence. Just as anybody can participate in religious rituals whether or not they truly believe in God, anybody can participate in interaction rituals. The only requirement is that the participant act as if the other's self is sacred, producing an action that exudes respect for the other.

Interaction rituals are performed every day. In a restaurant, on a sidewalk, or some other public place, any two strangers can be observed quickly glancing at each other and then just as quickly looking away. The split-second eye contact suggests that the two strangers consider each other worthy, important, or respectful enough to have their presence recognized. Their next-moment withdrawal of attention from each other expresses even greater respect for each other. They in effect treat each other like gods. As Goffman (1967) observed, "This secular world is not so irreligious as we might think. The individual is a deity of considerable importance. He walks with some dignity and is the recipient of many little offerings [such as the fleeting eye contact from strangers]."

Without the rituals, interaction in everyday life would be difficult, if not impossible. Imagine how you would feel if strangers kept staring at you. But violations of interaction rituals do occur. A common violation involves *loss of poise,* such as spilling a drink at a friend's apartment. Another form of interaction-ritual violation involves *incorrect identification*, as when we get someone's name wrong or say "How's your wife?" to a man whose wife has died. A third form of violation involves *situational impropriety,* such as dressing improperly at a social event or giving sad news to a happy couple at their wedding. When these and other ritual violations occur, everybody will pitch in by doing what Goffman calls "remedial work of various kinds." The culprit is likely to say "excuse me" or "I'm sorry," or provide excuses ("The drink sure made me a little drunk") or disclaimers ("I *don't mean* to be insensitive, but I have tell you something"). Others will graciously accept the apologies, excuses, or disclaimers. In doing so, they help the ritual violator "save face," rescuing the individual from embarrassment so that the derailed interaction can be put back on track. There are, however, strategies for preventing the problems in the first place, helping the self get the desired impression from others, as we will see in the next section.

Questions for Discussion and Review

1. What does Goffman mean by "tactful blindness"? How does it help ensure the success of a pelvic examination?
2. How do individuals present themselves to others?
3. What are interaction rituals? How can the rituals be violated?

THE ART OF MANAGING IMPRESSIONS

In Goffman's dramaturgy, all performances in social interaction are aimed at creating a desired impression. The performer can achieve the objective by *using defensive measures* with the help of the audience. The audience assists by *offering protective measures.*

Defensive Measures by Performers

Goffman divides these measures into three types. The first has to do with *dramaturgical loyalty,* in which members of a team of performers support each other before an audience or keep their team secrets from outsiders. One basic technique for developing loyalty is to foster "high in-group solidarity within the team." Another is to change audiences periodically to prevent the performers from becoming so attached to a few audience members that other members are ignored. This is why bank managers and church ministers are often shifted from one place of operation to another.

The second defensive measure has to do with *dramaturgical discipline.* This requires self-control, such as refraining from laughing about matters that are supposed to be serious and from taking seriously matters that are supposed to be humorous. Dramaturgical discipline also involves managing one's face and voice to display appropriate feelings and conceal inappropriate ones. In dealing with a pesky customer, for example, disciplined performers suppress their annoyance with a cheerful smile and a friendly voice.

The third defensive measure is *dramaturgical circumspection.* This involves carefully looking for the right things to do to ensure success in performance. One tactic is to limit the size of the audience. As salespersons often find, it is easier to sell to an unaccompanied customer than a customer with one or more companions. Another tactic is to adapt a performance

to the "information condition" at hand, relaxing the performance when we are with those we have known for a long time, while choreographing the performance when among those new to us. One should also adjust one's presentation to the nature of the thing presented to the audience. For example, clothing merchants take extreme care not to make exaggerated claims about their merchandise because customers can test it by sight and touch, but furniture salespersons need not be so careful because few customers can judge what lies behind the varnish and veneer of the product shown.

Protective Measures by Audience

By themselves, these defensive techniques of impression management cannot guarantee success. The performer also needs to have the audience cooperate. According to Goffman, the audience has the "tactful tendency" to act in a protective way to help the performers carry off their show.

First, audience members tend to stay discreetly away from the backstage unless invited. Otherwise, the audience will know what goes on in the backstage, and the frontstage performance will be ruined because the audience will find it unreal—contradicted by the backstage goings-on. If audience members want to enter the back region, they will give the performers some warning, in the form of a knock or a cough, so that the performers will stop activities that are inconsistent with their frontstage performance.

Second, if the performers commit a social blunder, the audience usually will tactfully "not see" it. Audience tact is so common that we may even find it among mental hospital patients, well-known for their unconventional behavior. To illustrate, Goffman (1967) cites this research report:

> [Once] the staff, without consulting the patients, decided to give them a Valentine party. Many of the patients did not wish to go, but did so anyway as they felt that they should not hurt the feelings of the student nurses who had organized the party. The games introduced by the nurses were on a very childish level; many of the patients felt silly playing them and were glad when the party was over.

According to Goffman, audiences are motivated to act tactfully for one of several reasons: (1) immediate identification with performers, (2) desire to avoid a scene, or (3) ingratiating themselves with performers for purposes of exploitation. Goffman regards the third as the best explanation for audience tactfulness, citing for illustration the case of successful prostitutes "who are willing to enact a lively approval of their clients' sexual performance."

Goffman found that social performances involve defensive measures on the part of the performers, with cooperative assistance from the audience. At a dinner party, for example, the guests—the audience—often will stay discreetly away from the backstage area—the kitchen—to help the hosts maintain the frontstage performance of ease, elegance, and control.

Questions for Discussion and Review

1. How can performers obtain the desired impression from the audience?
2. How does the audience help performers pull off the show?

THE SOCIAL CONSTRUCTION OF REALITY

In discussing interaction as symbolic communication or staged performance, we have focused on how people interact with *others*. But while interacting with others, people are also simultaneously interacting with *themselves*, somewhat like talking to themselves. In this internal interaction, people create in themselves an image of the other person and then interact with *this image* rather than the other person. Thus, when people are interacting outwardly with the other person, they are in reality interacting inwardly with their own image. All this refutes the popular belief that the world "out there"—such as the other person—is by itself real. If the world out there is real without being defined as real by us, we will all interact in the same way with the other person. But we do not, because we are not really interacting with the same person but, instead, with our own different images of that person.

In brief, reality does not exist "out there," in the form of the other person, but within ourselves, in the form of our image of that person. Nevertheless,

reality cannot be created in a social vacuum; it is *socially* constructed through social interaction. Our past as well as current encounters with others help us develop all the ideas, feelings, or attitudes that shape our image of the other person at a given moment. Let us take a closer look at this **social construction of reality,** the process by which people create through social interaction a certain idea, feeling, or belief about their environment.

Thomas Theorem: Creating Reality with Definition

After constructing reality, we do not just let the reality lie idle within ourselves. We act it out by doing something in accordance with the constructed reality. This is what sociologist W. I. Thomas (1863–1947) had in mind when he made the famous pronouncement known today as the **Thomas theorem:** "If people define situations as real, they are real in their consequences." In other words, people are able to turn their socially constructed, inner reality (perception, idea, belief, attitude, or feeling) into socially observable, outer reality (behavior, action, or activity).

If people believe that God exists, God is just as real to them as are humans, things, ideas, and other features of their social and physical world. They will *act as if God is real* by worshiping God. Similarly, if people believe that they will become successful in the future, they will *do something to make it real,* such as by working hard, which will likely lead to success. This second illustration suggests two ways in which situations defined as real are real in their consequences: working hard *now* and achieving success *later*. This is why the Thomas theorem is sometimes called the self-fulfilling prophecy (Chapter 1: The Essence of Sociology). But many instances also resemble the first example: definition of the situation produces only one kind of consequence, such as worshiping God now. In sum, if we define something "out there" as real, we will act as if it is real or do something to make it real.

Ethnomethodology: Exposing Hidden Reality

We have just seen how the Thomas theorem focuses on the outer, behavioral consequences of defining situations. But we are not shown the inner, subjective reality. To delve into that reality, we need **ethnomethodology,** the analysis of how people define the world in which they live. Taken from Greek, *ethno* means "folk" and *methodology* a systematic or standard method. So *ethnomethodology* literally means "folk method," implying that the method is popular, traditional, conventional, or widely shared.

But what exactly is the folk method people use to define their world in everyday interaction? To find out, Harold Garfinkel (1967), the founder of ethnomethodology, asked his students to interact with relatives, friends, and others in an "antifolk," antitraditional, anticonventional manner. From such experiments, the students and Garfinkel discovered that the folk method generally involves *defining the world in a vague, ambiguous manner*, leaving out a lot of specific details. Consider the following two interactions: one involving a student and her husband; the other between a student and the student's friend.

> On Friday my husband remarked that he was tired.
> I asked, "How are you tired? Physically, mentally, or just bored?"
> "I don't know, I guess physically, mainly," he responded.
> "You mean that your muscles ache or your bones?" I asked.
> A little irritated, he said, "I guess so. Don't be so technical."

> FRIEND: How are you?
> STUDENT: How am I in regard to what? You mean my health, my finances, my school work, my sex life, my peace of mind, my . . .
> FRIEND: Look! I was just trying to be polite. Frankly, I don't give a damn how you are.

Why do people interacting with one another define things vaguely and leave out the details? The reason is *the popular assumption that people understand one another without the specific details.* But this assumption of shared understanding, or the folk method based on it, is so often employed, widely shared, and taken for granted that most people are not aware that it exists. Only when it is questioned, as in the examples given above, do they suddenly recognize not only that they have long held it, but also that it can be incorrect. As a consequence, they may become irritated, angry, dumbfounded, or embarrassed. Such negative reactions show the discomfort of having their cherished and taken-for-granted assumption taken away. Not surprisingly, Garfinkel found the same negative reactions in many other experiments in which he instructed his students to bargain for small items in supermarkets, violate the rules in playing tic-tac-toe, or move increasingly closer to someone in conversation until nearly nose-to-nose with them. Again, these experiments demonstrate through the subjects' negative reactions that their cherished assumption of shared understanding can be questionable.

But we may not need Garfinkel's experiments to discover the shakiness of the shared-understanding assumption. As was previously discussed, women and men do not always share the same understanding even when they use the same words to communicate. When we interact with people of different racial, ethnic, religious, or other backgrounds, we are also likely to find that they, like Garfinkel's students, do not share our definition of the situation. Generally, the more diverse the society, the more untenable the assumption of shared understanding.

This is particularly true in today's global village, where people of different cultures often interact. Without cross-cultural understanding, we may erroneously assume that people in other countries share the same definitions of situations. We may believe, for example, that it is polite to inquire about a man's wife, but to do so in Saudi Arabia would provoke an angry reaction because the Saudis consider the inquiry rude. Similarly, we may think that giving such gifts as a letter opener or a clock to a college friend is a nice gesture of friendship. But in Latin America the presentation of the letter opener may be construed as our desire to sever the relationship, and in China the clock may be taken as our wish for the person to die soon. In instances such as these, people in other cultures effectively expose as untenable our socially shared assumption that we understand one another. Simultaneously, we also question the same assumption held by the foreigners, in about the same manner as Garfinkel's students did to their subjects. When this happens, both interactants—we and the foreigners—may be dumbfounded, angry, irritated, or embarrassed.

Humorology: Subverting Reality with Humor

Like ethnomethodology, **humorology**—the study or practice of humor—can undermine our widely shared assumptions about our world. But, while ethnomethodologists make people feel bad, humorologists make them feel good. Consider the following joke from a Woody Allen movie:

> A boy goes to a psychiatrist, saying, "Doctor, you must help us, my brother thinks he's a chicken."
>
> The psychiatrist exclaims, "You must have him committed at once."
>
> But the boy retorts, "We can't, we need the eggs."

With this joke, the humorologist *subverts* our conventional assumption that shared understanding exists between us and others just as it does between the psychiatrist and the boy. In addition, humorology can subvert not only the assumption about shared understanding but myriad other conventional realities, involving friendship, sex, marriage, politics, and virtually all other aspects of human life. In doing so, humor makes us laugh.

But what is it about humor that makes us laugh? The clue can be found in the fact that almost all jokes contain an *incongruity* between two realities, usually a conventional and an unconventional one. These two realities represent conflicting definitions of the same situation. To make people laugh, we first make them clearly aware of their taken-for-granted conventional definition of a situation and then surprise them by contradicting that definition with an unconventional one. Take another look at the Woody Allen joke cited above. The first sentence sets up a situation to be defined. In the second, the psychiatrist defines the situation to mean that the boy is normal, thereby reinforcing the audience's conventional belief that people who consider their relatives abnormal are normal themselves. But the last sentence, also aptly called the punch line, crushes the psychiatrist's definition with the unexpected reality that the boy himself is abnormal. More generally, the punch line shatters the popular belief with the unconventional reality that people who appear normal can indeed be abnormal. A similar incongruity exists in the following joke from a study by Murray Davis (1993):

> My wife comes home and says, "Pack your bags. I just won $20 million in the California lottery."
>
> "Where are we going, Hawaii, Europe?" I ask jubilantly.
>
> She says, "I don't know where you're going, Doug, as long as it's out of here."

The first two sentences set up in our mind the conventional assumption that the married couple will share the joy of winning the lottery. The punch line strikes down that assumption with the unexpected, unconventional reality that a presumably loving wife wants to be free from her husband.

The reality in the punch line does not always have to be unconventional. It can be any kind of reality as long as it is incongruous with the one just presented. The punch line in the following joke, for example, is hardly unconventional but does unexpectedly contradict a reality previously defined—though with purposeful ambiguity (Davis, 1993):

> QUESTION: [Former Soviet president] Gorbachev has a long one, [former U.S. president] Bush has a short one, the Pope has one but doesn't use it, and Madonna doesn't have one. What is it?
>
> ANSWER: A last name.

The question leads the audience to expect a risqué answer, only to be contradicted by an innocent one.

Questions for Discussion and Review

1. How do people interact with themselves?
2. How can we create realities with definitions?
3. What is the socially constructed reality that guides interaction and how do ethnomethodologists expose that reality?
4. How does humor make people laugh?

CHAPTER REVIEW

1. *How do the three perspectives differ in dealing with social interaction?* The functionalist perspective focuses on the supportive types of interaction: exchange and cooperation. The conflict perspective deals with the oppositional types: competition and conflict. Both perspectives are structural, offering the outside, objective view of interaction. But the third, symbolic interactionist perspective delves into the subjective world of social interactants. While the structural perspectives concentrate on the objective, external characteristics of supportive and oppositional interactions, symbolic interactionism penetrates into the subjective, internal meanings of these interactions.

2. *How does human communication differ from animal communication?* Animal communication is largely governed by instincts. It is also a closed system, tied to the immediate present, enabling animals to communicate only a limited set of messages. In contrast, human communication is socially constructed, arbitrarily determined by people through their social experiences. It is also an open system, where people are able to create an infinite number of messages.

3. *How does communication differ globally?* Verbal communication varies from one society to another. There is, for example, a greater adherence to the "one speaker at a time" rule in the United States than in other countries. Nonverbal communication also differs; making a circle with a thumb and forefinger has a positive meaning in the United States, but a negative one in Brazil and other countries. *What is the U.S. diversity in communication like?* Various groups use the same language with different accents, words, and sentences as well as conversational styles. Group differences also exist in the use of body language and personal space. *How do women and men differ in communication?* They tend to use different genderlects, one emphasizing connection and intimacy and the other status and independence. The sexes also differ in proxemics, with men more likely to dominate women by invading their personal space.

4. *What is the dramaturgical view of interaction?* Interaction involves people acting toward each other as if they were performers and audiences in a theater. *How do people present themselves to others?* They display the positive sides of themselves and conceal the negative ones. This frontstage behavior, designed to create a desired impression in others, may differ from backstage activities, where the performers can reveal their true selves. *What is the essence of interaction rituals?* This is a show of reverence or respect among people engaged in social interaction. *What is the art of impression management?* To create a desired impression in others, we must use defensive measures but with others offering protective measures.

5. *What is the Thomas theorem?* If people define, see, or believe something "out there" as real, they will act as if it is real or do something to make it real. *What can we learn from ethnomethodology?* When people interact with one another they define their world in an ambiguous manner, leaving out considerable specific details. They assume that everybody understands them without the specific details. *What is the nature of humor that makes people laugh?* Humor consists of the surprising subversion of a conventional or widely accepted reality by an unconventional or unexpected one.

KEY TERMS

Competition An interaction in which two individuals follow mutually accepted rules, each trying to achieve the same goal before the other does. (p. 81)

Conflict An interaction in which two individuals disregard any rules, each trying to achieve his or her own goal by defeating the other. (p. 81)

Cooperation An interaction in which two or more individuals work together to achieve a common goal. (p. 81)

Dramaturgy A method of analyzing social interaction as if the participants were performing on a stage. (p. 89)

Ethnomethodology The analysis of how people define the world in which they live. (p. 94)

Exchange An interaction in which two individuals offer each other something in order to obtain a reward in return. (p. 81)

Genderlects Linguistic styles that reflect the different worlds of women and men. (p. 87)

Humorology The study or practice of humor. (p. 95)

Interaction ritual The form of interaction in which the participants perform certain acts to show reverence to each other. (p. 91)

Kinesics The use of body movements as a means of communication; also called body language. (p. 84)

Oppositional interaction The interaction in which the participants treat each other as competitors or enemies. (p. 80)

Proxemics The use of space as a means of communication. (p. 85)

Role distance Separating the role-playing as outward performance from the inner self. (p. 91)

Social construction of reality The process by which people create through social interaction a certain idea, feeling, or belief about their environment. (p. 93)

Social interaction The process by which individuals act toward and react to others. (p. 80)

Supportive interaction The interaction in which the participants treat each other as supporters or friends. (p. 80)

Thomas theorem Sociologist W. I. Thomas's famous pronouncement that "If people define situations as real, they are real in their consequences." (p. 93)

SUGGESTED READINGS

Davis, Murray S. 1993. *What's So Funny? The Comic Conception of Culture and Society.* Chicago: University of Chicago Press. A sociological study of how humor reveals various aspects of social and cultural life.

Goffman, Erving. 1959. *The Presentation of Self in Everyday Life.* New York: Doubleday. The sociological classic on the dramaturgical analysis of social interaction.

Karp, David. A., and William C. Yoels. 1993. *Sociology in Everyday Life,* 2nd ed. Itasca, Ill.: Peacock. An excellent review of the current knowledge about social interaction in various situations and settings.

Tannen, Deborah. 1994. *Gender and Discourse.* New York: Oxford University Press. An insightful sociolinguistic study of the gender differences in communication.

Wood, Julia T. 1992. *Spinning the Symbolic Web: Human Communication as Symbolic Interaction.* Norwood, N.J.: Ablex. Shows the nature of human communication as seen through the symbolic interactionist perspective.

GROUPS AND ORGANIZATIONS

Myths and Realities

MYTH: *If two groups of people have become hostile to each other, it is virtually impossible for friendship to develop between them.*
REALITY: If they have to work together to solve a common problem, friendship will likely emerge. (pp. 100–101)

MYTH: *When we look for a job we can get more help from our close friends than from mere acquaintances.*
REALITY: Acquaintances are more effective in helping us find a job. We may already be aware of the job openings known to our friends, but we may not know of the many other job opportunities our acquaintances can tell us about. (p. 102)

MYTH: *In a group situation, you will never accept someone else's view when you are certain it is wrong.*
REALITY: The pressure to conform can make you accept that view if it is held by the majority. (p. 103)

MYTH: *If you are a nice, compassionate person, you would help a victim whether other people are around or not.*
REALITY: You would be less likely to help a victim when others are present than when you are alone with the victim. (p. 104)

MYTH: *It's always nice to be your own boss: in small businesses owned and managed by the workers themselves, the workers generally have an easy, pleasant life.*
REALITY: Although workers in such small organizations are highly satisfied with their jobs, they tend to work too hard and often suffer stress and burnout as a result. (p. 111)

Afemale university president was expecting a visit from a male member of the board of trustees. When her secretary told her that the visitor had arrived, she left her office to greet him at the reception area. Before ushering him into her office, the woman handed a letter to her secretary and said, "I've just finished drafting it. *Do you think you could* type it right away? I'd like to get it out before lunch. And *would you please do me a favor* and hold all calls while I'm meeting with Mr. Smith here?" After they were inside her office, with the door closed, Mr. Smith told her that he thought she had spoken inappropriately to her secretary. "Remember," he said, "*You're* the president!" To Mr. Smith, the president seemed self-deprecating and lacking in self-confidence, not giving orders like a man (Tannen, 1994b).

Mr. Smith didn't get it. He did not realize that many women can effectively run an organization without playing a macho game of domination with their subordinates. In fact, the egalitarian style of management, as shown by the university president's expression of respect to her secretary, has made many female managers more successful in running organizations than their male counterparts who throw their weight around. To get a deeper insight into this female approach to management, let us first analyze the basic characteristics of groups and organizations.

SOCIAL GROUPS

In a classic experiment, Muzafer Sherif (1956) took a group of white, middle-class, 12-year-old boys to a summer camp at Robbers' Cave State Park in Oklahoma. Sherif pretended to be a caretaker named Mr. Musee. For the first three days, the boys lived on one site at the camp and became acquainted. Then they were separated. Half of the boys were given one cabin and one set of activities, and the other half, another. Soon each group of boys had chosen a name, one group calling itself the "Eagles" and the other, "Rattlers." Each group had its own insignia on caps and T-shirts, its own jargon, and jokes and secrets.

Each band of boys, in short, had formed a **social group**—a collection of people who interact with one another and have a certain feeling of unity. A social group is more than either a social aggregate or a social category. A **social aggregate** is just a number of people who happen to be in one place but do not interact with one another, such as the boys when they first arrived at the camp. A **social category** is a number of people who have something in common but neither interact with one another nor gather in one place. Men as a whole constitute a social category. So do women as a whole, college students as a whole, and so on. A social category becomes a social group when the people in the category interact with one another and identify themselves as members of the group.

Thus, the boys at Robbers' Cave were members of a social category—12-year-old boys— but they became a social group when they began to interact with one another and consider themselves members of the Eagles or the Rattlers. A closer look at Sherif's experiment can give us a clearer idea of the significance of groups.

In-Groups and Out-Groups

A few days after Sherif had put the boys in separate cabins, he arranged for the groups to compete against each other in baseball, tug of war, and other games. The winners of the games were awarded points toward a prize—camp knives. At first, the Eagles and Rattlers were very friendly with each other, but soon the games turned into fierce competitions. The two groups began to call each other stinkers, sneaks, and cheaters. They raided each other's cabins, and scuffles became common.

The boys' behavior showed that in forming each group, the youngsters set up a boundary between themselves as an in-group and the others as an out-group. An **in-group** is the group to which an individual is strongly tied as a member, and an **out-group** is the group of which an individual is not a member. Every social group defines a boundary between itself and everyone else to some extent, but a cohesive in-group has three characteristics. First, members of the in-group normally use symbols such as names, slogans, dress, or badges to identify themselves so that they will be distinguishable from the out-group. As we have seen, one group of boys in Sherif's experiment called itself the Eagles, and the other, Rattlers. Second, members of a cohesive in-group view themselves in terms of positive stereotypes and the out-group in negative stereotypes. Sherif's boys, for example, liked to say things like, "We are smart, and they are dumb!" We can also witness similar social behavior among college students: rating their own fraternities, sororities, or organizations higher in prestige than someone else's and disparaging others as "objectionable." Third, the in-group is inclined to compete or clash with the out-group.

Sherif's experiment showed how easily loyalty to an in-group can generate hostility toward an out-group and even aggression when there is competition for some resource (in this case, prizes). Competition with another group can also strengthen the unity within each group. But there was another phase in Sherif's experiment. He set up situations in which the groups had to work together to solve a common problem. When the camp's sole water tank broke down, he told the groups to work together to repair it. As they cooperated, friendships began to emerge between Eagles and Rattlers. In short, cooperation between groups eroded the hostility and divisions that competition had spurred.

Reference Groups

In-groups can become **reference groups,** a group that is used as the frame of reference for evaluating one's own behavior. Members of a street gang, for example, may evaluate themselves by the standards of the gang and feel proud about a successful mugging. This positive self-evaluation reflects the *normative effect* of a reference group whose members share the same view of themselves. If other members of your reference group (say, your parents) have high self-esteem, you too are likely to share that norm and have high self-esteem. The normative effect basically involves imitating the reference group. However, reference groups can also have *comparison effects* and *associative effects* on self-appraisals. If most of your classmates shine in academic achievement, you are likely to compare yourself with them. As a result, you may have a negative self-evaluation, feeling that your academic performance is not up to par. Being associated with the brilliant group, though, may make you feel proud of yourself, "basking in reflected glory" (Felson and Reed, 1986).

These reference groups are at the same time in-groups. But we do not have to be members of a group in order to use it as our reference group. As a student,

you might have professional athletes as your reference group. If that is the case, you will probably judge your athletic skills to be inadequate—even if they are excellent compared with those of most amateurs—and perhaps you will work harder in an effort to meet professional standards.

Whether we are members of reference groups or not, they frequently exert a powerful influence on our behavior and attitudes, as has been suggested. In fact, their impact became well known long ago, after Theodore Newcomb (1958) published his study of the students at Bennington College, a very liberal college in Vermont. Newcomb found that most of the students came from conservative families and that most of the freshmen were conservative. A small minority remained conservative throughout their time at the school. But most became more liberal the longer they stayed at the college. These students, Newcomb concluded, used the liberal faculty or older students as their reference group, whereas the minority continued to look to their conservative families as their reference group.

Primary and Secondary Groups

It is not at all surprising that some students used their families as a reference group. After all, families are the

"Of course you're going to be depressed if you keep comparing yourself with successful people."

Source: Drawing by Wm. Hamilton; © 1991 The New Yorker Magazine, Inc.

As members of a primary group, these sorority sisters have strong emotional ties. They interact informally and relate to one another as unique persons.

best examples of the groups Charles Cooley (1909) called *primary* chiefly because they "are fundamental in forming the social nature and ideals of the individual." In **primary groups** the individuals interact informally, relate to each other as whole persons, and enjoy their relationship for its own sake. This is one of the two main types of social groups. In the other type, **secondary groups,** the individuals interact formally, relate to each other as players of particular roles, and expect to profit from each other.

Families, peer groups, fraternities, sororities, neighbors, friends, and small communities are all examples of primary groups. They are marked by what are called *primary relationships.* Communication in these relationships is not limited by formalities. The people in a primary group interact in an informal way, and they relate to each other as unique, whole persons. Moreover, they enjoy the relationship for its own sake.

These characteristics become clearer when we compare them with those of *secondary relationships.* The people in a secondary group do not know each other personally. They may have little face-to-face interaction. If they interact, they do so formally. They relate to each other only in terms of particular roles and for certain practical purposes.

Consider salesclerks and their customers. In these secondary groups, there are likely to be few if any emotional ties, and the people know little about each other. Their communications are bound by formalities. Salesclerks are not likely to kiss their customers or to cry with them over the death of a relative. The clerk will treat the customer as a customer only—not as a person who is also a mother of three, a jazz lover, a victim of an airplane hijacking, or a person who

laughs easily but worries a lot. In contrast, we expect our families to treat us as whole persons, to be interested in our experiences, preferences, and feelings. The clerk is also likely to treat one customer much like another. We expect this attitude in a clerk, but the same attitude in our family or friends would hurt our feelings. Finally, the clerk and the customer have a relationship only because each has a specific task or purpose in mind: to buy or sell something. They use their relationship for this purpose. The relationship among family members, in contrast, is not oriented to a particular task but is engaged in for its own sake. In fact, if we believe that a person in a primary group is interested in us only as a means to some end, we are likely to feel "used." Parents are hurt if they feel their children are interested only in the food, shelter, and money the parents provide.

Primary relationships—with our relatives, friends, or neighbors—are very precious to us. As research has shown, they are particularly helpful when we are going through stressful life events. They help ease recovery from heart attacks, prevent childbirth complications, make child rearing easier, lighten the burden of household finances, and cushion the impact of job loss by providing financial assistance and employment information. However, primary relationships are not always more beneficial than secondary relationships. Our close friends cannot help us get as good a job as our acquaintances can. Our friends move in the same social circle as we do, but our acquaintances, to whom we have only weak ties, move in different circles. Hence, we may already be aware of the job openings known to our friends, but we may not know of the many other job opportunities our

Instrumental leaders are primarily concerned about achieving goals. Expressive leaders are more concerned with their followers' feelings, making sure that harmony and cohesiveness can prevail in the group. A small group such as this softball team needs both types of leadership from its coach to function effectively.

acquaintances can tell us about (Granovetter, 1983; Bridges and Villemez, 1986).

Group Leadership

In most groups, there are two kinds of leaders. **Instrumental leaders** are those who achieve their group's goal by getting others to focus on task performance. They may say something like "Let's get to work!" or "I think we're getting off the track." Such tactics show the leaders as overseers, whose exchange with followers involves a unidirectional downward influence and a weak sense of common fate. Although this kind of leadership can get the group to move toward a goal, it can also rub people the wrong way. Not surprisingly, most people tend not to like their instrumental leaders.

On the other hand, most people tend to like their **expressive leaders,** who achieve group harmony by making others feel good. This second type of leader is more concerned with members' feelings, making sure that everybody is happy, so that cohesiveness can reign in the group. The exchange between such leaders and their followers reflects a partnership, characterized by reciprocal influence, a strong sense of common fate, and mutual trust, respect, and liking. A group needs both types of leaders to function effectively.

Group Conformity

Because they are seen as competently performing certain tasks for the group, leaders are usually given an **idiosyncrasy credit,** the privilege that allows leaders to deviate from their group's norms. The rank and file, however, are expected to conform. In a group, the pressure to conform is so powerful that individual members tend to knuckle under: going along with the majority even though they privately disagree with it. This point has been driven home by Solomon Asch's (1955) classic experiments. Asch brought together groups of eight or nine students each. He asked them to tell him which of the three lines on a card was as long as the line on another card, as shown in Figure 5.1. In each group only one was a real subject—the others were the experimenter's secret accomplices who had been instructed to give the same obviously wrong answer. Asch found that nearly a third of the subjects changed their minds and accepted the majority's answer even though they were sure that their own answer was correct and the others' answer was wrong.

The group to which Asch's subjects felt compelled to conform were strangers. The pressure to conform is even greater among people we know. It usually gives rise to what Irving Janis (1982) calls **groupthink,** the tendency for members of a cohesive group to maintain consensus to the extent of ignoring the truth. Groupthink may lead to disastrous decisions, with tragic consequences. It caused President Kennedy and his top advisers to approve the CIA's unsound plan to invade Cuba. It caused President Johnson and his advisers to escalate the Vietnam War. It caused President Reagan and his advisers to get involved in the Iran-Contra affair. In each case a few members had serious doubts about the majority decision but did not speak out.

It is even more difficult to voice dissent if the leader rules with an iron hand. About 30 years ago, when

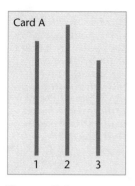

FIGURE 5.1
Would You Conform?
Asch's experiments suggest that if you are asked privately which line on card A is as long as the line on card B, there is a 99 percent chance that you will correctly pick line 2. But if you find yourself in a group in which all the other members choose line 3—an obviously wrong answer—there is about a 33 percent chance that you will yield to the group pressure to conform by choosing 3.

Nikita Khrushchev, ruler of what was then the Soviet Union, came to the United States, he met with reporters at the Washington Press Club. The first anonymous written question he received was: "Today you talked about the hideous rule of your predecessor, Stalin, who killed thousands of his political opponents. You were one of his closest aides and colleagues during those years. What were you doing all that time?" Khrushchev's face turned red. "Who asked that?" he shouted. No one answered. "Who asked that?" he shouted again. Still no answer. Then Khrushchev said, "That's what I was doing: keeping my mouth shut" (Bennis, 1989). Leaders can indeed prevent groupthink by encouraging and rewarding dissent. Interestingly, the greater the disagreement among group members, the better their collective decision. This is because "with more disagreement, people are forced to look at a wider range of possibilities" (Bennis, 1989).

Group Size

Aside from pressuring people to conform, social groups also cause them to behave in other ways. This has a lot to do with the specific size of groups. The smallest group is a *dyad,* which contains two people. A dyad can easily become the most cohesive of all the groups because its members are inclined to be most personal and to interact most intensely with each other. This is why we are more willing to share our secrets in a dyad than in a larger group, secrets such as our parents getting divorced or a relative having been committed to a mental hospital. A dyad, however, is also the most likely to break up. If just one person

leaves, the group will vanish. Such a threat does not exist for a *triad,* a three-person group. If one member drops out, the group can still survive. A triad also makes it possible for two people to gang up on the third or for one member to patch up a quarrel between the other two. But triads lose the quality of intimacy that is the hallmark of dyads; as the saying goes, "Two's company, three's a crowd."

If more people join a triad, the group will become even less personal, with each individual finding it extremely difficult to talk and relate to each of the other members. The upshot is the emergence of many different coalitions (made up of two against one, two against three, three against one, and so on) and many mediating roles for various conflicting subgroups. The reason is that even a small growth in the size of a group increases dramatically the number of relationships among its members. If a dyad, for example, grows into a seven-person group, the number of possible relationships will shoot up from one to 966 (Hare, 1962). Generally, as a group grows larger, it changes for the worse. Its members become less satisfied, participate less often in group activities, are less likely to cooperate with one another, and are more likely to misbehave. Even the Japanese, universally known for their politeness, may become rude on a crowded train. This is because an increase in group size makes it difficult to maintain interpersonal relationships and individual recognition (Mullen et al., 1989; Levine and Moreland, 1990).

There are other, more fascinating effects of group size. In a dyad or triad, the host usually has the edge over the visitor, with the host more likely to get his or her own way. Thus a businesswoman can strike a better deal if she invites the other person to her office. But such territorial dominance—the "homecourt advantage"—may disappear if the group is larger than a triad. In public places, a large group may also inhibit an individual from helping someone in distress. Over 50 studies have shown consistently that people are less likely to help a victim if others are around than if they are alone with the victim. A major reason is that the knowledge that others are present and available to respond allows the individual to shift some of the responsibility to others. The same factor operates in "social loafing": as the size of a group performing a certain task increases, each member tends not to work as hard (Latané and Nida, 1981).

Questions for Discussion and Review

1. What characteristics of social groups make them different from social aggregates and categories?
2. What are some social functions of in-groups and reference groups?

3. Why are primary groups fundamental for human existence?
4. How does the concept of groupthink help explain experiences you have had in social groups?
5. How does group size affect our behavior?

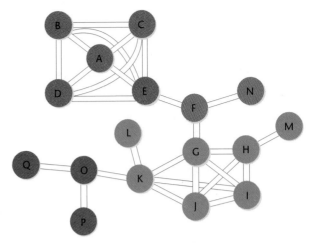

FIGURE 5.2
A Social Network
In this network, the individuals A, B, C, D, and E are directly linked to one another. But through E's friendship with F, the other four members (A, B, C, and D) are indirectly connected to F, and all five of them (A, B, C, D, and E) are also indirectly linked to G, H, I, and so on. Thus a social network can consist of both directly and indirectly connected individuals.

SOCIAL NETWORKS

Regardless of size, groups can develop **social networks,** webs of social relationships that link individuals or groups to one another. We are all involved in numerous networks. Since birth, we have been constantly developing or expanding our networks by forming social ties with various people who come into our lives. As soon as we were born, our parents drew us into their networks, which became our own. When we began to attend school, we started to develop social ties with children in our neighborhoods, with our schoolmates and teachers, and with children in our churches, synagogues, or other places of worship. As adults, we often get into all kinds of networks, such as those at the college we attend, the place where we work, and the social organizations we belong to. These networks, however, are quite different from the ones that we joined before we turned 17 or 18. Our current adult networks are more diffuse, more loosely organized, and made up of weaker social ties.

Individuals are not the only ones joining and developing social networks. Groups, organizations, and even whole nation-states also forge ties with each other. That is why there are numerous intergroup networks (for example, among lawyers, judges, doctors, business executives, and other professional groups), intercommunity networks (such as the U.S. Conference of Mayors), and international networks (such as the United Nations).

Characteristics

To make it easier to see what networks look like, sociologists use such devices as points (technically called *nodes*) and lines (or *links*) to represent them. A point can be a person, group, or nation-state. A line can be any kind of social relationship connecting two points. The relationship can be a friendship; an exchange of visits; a business transaction; a romantic entanglement; the flow of information, resources, influence, or power; or an expression of such feelings as affection, sympathy, or hostility.

Consider what your college network may look like. Let's make A in Figure 5.2 represent you and B, C, D, and E your friends. The lines show that all five of you are *directly* connected to one another. Your college network also comprises 12 other people, namely, F through Q. This is because four of you—A, B, C, and D—are *indirectly* tied, through E, to those individuals. Because of your (A's) friendship with E and E's friendship with F, you belong to the same network as F and all the other individuals, whom you may not know. Thus, a social network can consist of both directly and indirectly connected individuals. Because each of the numerous individuals to whom you are indirectly linked knows, directly and indirectly, numerous other people, you may ultimately belong to a network involving millions of people all over the world. This is especially true today, because easily accessible air travel has made it possible for people from many different countries to establish links with one another.

Given the massive network to which we belong, we should not be surprised to meet a total stranger in some faraway city, state, or foreign country and discover that the stranger happens to know somebody that we know. On such an occasion, that stranger and we are likely to exclaim, "What a small world!" Indeed, a series of classic experiments have demonstrated how small our world really is. In one of those studies, the wife of a divinity-school student who lived in Cambridge, Massachusetts, was selected as a "target person." Her name, address, occupation, and other facts about her were printed in a booklet. Copies of this booklet were randomly distributed to a group of people in Wichita, Kansas. They were asked to send it directly to the target person only if they knew her personally. If she was a stranger to them, they were asked to send the booklet to friends or acquaintances who they thought might know her. Interestingly, many (30 percent) of the booklets sent by strangers did finally reach the target, after passing through the hands of only about five intermediaries (Milgram, 1967; Travers and Milgram, 1969).

Effects

A social network usually acts as a support system for its members. It helps members maintain good physical and mental health or prevent physical and mental breakdown. It also reduces the risk of dying prematurely or of committing suicide. There are several reasons for this. Our friends, relatives, and co-workers, as part of our social network, can make us feel good by boosting our self-esteem despite our faults, weaknesses, and difficulties. Being more objective than we are about our own problems, they can open our eyes to solutions that we are too emotionally distressed to see. The companionship and camaraderie from our network, fortified by frequent participation in joint recreational activities, can bring us joy while chasing away loneliness, worries, and trouble. Finally, our friends and relatives often give us *instrumental support*—money and service—to help us cope with our problems. All these social-psychological factors have a physiological impact on our health: They keep our blood pressure and heart rate at low levels, presumably by lowering our brain's secretion of stress hormones (Lin, 1982; House et al., 1988; Pescosolido and Georgianna, 1989).

On the other hand, our intimates place many demands on our time and personal resources. They can irritate us by criticizing us or invading our privacy. This is why in a study of the social networks of 120 widows, the women reported that more than two-thirds of the people who made their lives more difficult were their friends and relatives. In fact, these negative experiences seem to drag down people's sense of well-being more than the positive experiences of receiving social support can raise it up. Negative encounters usually have a stronger impact than positive ones, because an argument sticks out like a sore thumb against a background of generally pleasant experiences. Thus, a pleasant exchange at a wedding that is already filled with strife between in-laws can restore only a little peacefulness, but a single heated

exchange at an otherwise tranquil wedding can ruin the whole experience (Fischman, 1986).

In sum, social networks can have both positive and negative consequences for people's lives.

Questions for Discussion and Review

1. What does a social network consist of?
2. How can social networks affect our lives?

FORMAL ORGANIZATIONS

Of the various kinds of social groups that we have discussed, secondary groups are the most likely to develop into **formal organizations**, groups whose activities are rationally designed to achieve specific goals. Not all secondary groups become formal organizations, though. Some secondary groups are small and transitory, without explicitly stated goals and rules. A salesclerk and customer interact on a temporary basis to achieve a generally known but unstated objective without following any explicitly described rules for carrying out the business transaction. This is not a formal organization. Other secondary groups are large and more permanent and have explicit goals and working procedures. Government agencies, for instance, often last well beyond their members' lifetimes, and are large and complex. Their goals and rules must be stated explicitly so that the work of their many members can be coordinated. These agencies, along with hospitals, colleges, business firms, political parties, the U.S. Army, the Sierra Club, and the like, are examples of formal organizations.

Goals and Means

The importance of goals cannot be emphasized enough. Without them, organizations would not have come into being. Goals can help an organization determine what to do and offer guidelines for measuring performance—how successful it is in meeting its goals. While most organizations fall by the wayside if they fail to realize their goals, some organizations continue to exist, even to thrive on their failure to achieve their goals. Government agencies that enforce drug laws, for example, continue to exist because they fail to put drug traffickers out of business.

Whether they achieve their goals or not, all organizations develop certain common means for achieving them. Generally, they engage in *rational planning*. They must decide what specific tasks are necessary to realize the goals, who are best qualified to carry out the tasks,

A social network acts as a support system for its members. Although friends can often place demands on our time and resources, at the same time they boost our self-esteem, provide companionship and activity, and often give instrumental support to help us through tough times.

and how to coordinate the various tasks to avoid costly conflict and achieve high efficiency.

More specifically, first, through a *division of labor,* different tasks are assigned to workers with different skills. This makes it easier for an organization to attain its goals than if all workers perform the same task. But the division of labor may get out of hand, with one worker producing an item (say, a car door) that cannot be fitted into another item (a car body) made by someone else. Thus an organization must establish a *hierarchy of control,* which makes a supervisor, a manager, and other administrators responsible for overseeing and directing workers to ensure that various activities are properly coordinated. Administrators must deal with workers in accordance with a set of *formalized rules,* without showing any favoritism. Strict adherence to the rules may explain why formal organizations typically appear impersonal. The rules themselves may also explain why organizations appear to have a life of their own and can outlive original members. Because the rules stipulate how replacements are to be found, organizations do not collapse when certain personnel leave.

Power and Involvement

According to Amitai Etzioni (1975), virtually every organization includes "higher participants" (such as the administrators) and "lower participants" (the rank and file). The function of the higher participants is to exercise power over the lower participants so that the latter will help the organization achieve its goals. Three kinds of power are available to higher participants: (1) *coercive power,* the use of physical force; (2) *remunerative power,* the use of material rewards such as money and similar incentives to ensure cooperation; and (3) *normative power,* the use of moral persuasion, the prestige of a leader, or the promise of social acceptance. There are also three kinds of involvement by lower participants: (1) *alienative,* in which they do not support the organization's goals; (2) *calculative,* which means they are moderately supportive; and (3) *moral involvement,* in which they strongly support the organization.

From these kinds of power and involvement, Etzioni constructed the following typology of organizations:

Kinds of Power	Kinds of Involvement		
	Alienative	**Calculative**	**Moral**
Coercive	1	2	3
Remunerative	4	5	6
Normative	7	8	9

Of the nine types, only three—1, 5, and 9—represent the huge majority of organizations. These, then, are the most common types; the remaining six are rare. Etzioni called the three most common types *coercive organizations* (type 1), *utilitarian organizations* (type 5), and *normative organizations* (type 9).

Coercive Organizations Prisons, concentration camps, and custodial mental hospitals are examples of coercive organizations. In each, force or the threat of force is used to achieve the organization's main goal: keeping the inmates in. The inmates obviously do not enjoy being imprisoned; they will run away if they have the chance. They are alienated from the organization and do not support its goals at all. Understandably, the higher participants—such as prison administrators—have to act tough toward the inmates, seeking compliance by threatening solitary confinement if they try to escape. In brief, in this kind of organization, coercion is the main form of power used, and the involvement by lower participants is alienative.

Utilitarian Organizations   Factories, banks, and other businesses are all utilitarian organizations in Etzioni's classification. The higher participants use incentives such as money to ensure that lower participants work to achieve the organization's goals. The rank and file tend to be moderately supportive of those goals. They are likely to calculate whether it is worth their while to work hard, asking "What's in it for me?" In general, the more attractive their remuneration—in money, fringe benefits, or working conditions—the more committed lower participants are to the organization. Thus, the major form of power used in utilitarian organizations is remunerative, and the typical form of involvement by lower-level participants is calculative.

Normative Organizations   If Mormons do not pay their tithes, they may be denied access to religious services, but they are not subject to arrest and imprison-

ment. If a political party wants you to vote for its candidates, it may send you letters, phone you, or knock on your door, and it will certainly advertise; but it does not offer you money. Churches and political parties are examples of a type of organization very different from coercive and utilitarian organizations. Their power over lower participants is based on persuasion, exhortation, social pressure, public recognition, or a leader's appeal. This normative power is sufficient because most of the participants generally want to do what the organization is asking; they are strongly committed to its goals. For this reason, normative organizations are sometimes called *voluntary associations*. In addition to religious organizations and political organizations, examples include colleges, social clubs, and charitable organizations. In Etzioni's terms, their primary form of power is normative, and involvement by the rank and file is moral.

Mixed Organizations   In fact, no organization relies entirely on just one type of power. All three types can be found in most organizations. Still the majority do use one type of power far more than the other two. Prisons, for example, may use normative power through rehabilitation programs, but still rely mostly on coercion. A business may use speeches to inspire its workers, but it depends mostly on wages to ensure their involvement.

Though rare, some organizations do depend on two types of power to about the same degree. A good example is combat units, which rely heavily on both normative and coercive powers. First, they apply normative powers through basic training, military

In Etzioni's classification of formal organizations, those that use incentives such as money to ensure that participants work to achieve the organization's goals are utilitarian organizations. In general, the more attractive the remuneration offered, in terms of money, fringe benefits, or working conditions, the more committed the rank and file are to the organization's goals.

schools, and patriotic pep talks. Second, although it is not practical for the military to offer huge sums of money to induce soldiers to risk life or limb, it can apply effective coercion by withdrawing furloughs from uncooperative members and by imprisoning or executing deserters.

An Evaluation The Etzioni typology is useful for knowing the characteristics of practically all organizations. It also explains why some organizations flounder while others sail smoothly. As Etzioni suggests, organizational effectiveness depends on running an outfit for what it is. A prison managed like a coercive organization, a business firm like a utilitarian organization, or a political party like a normative organization can be expected to do well. On the other hand, a prison run like a political party or a business firm operated like a prison would likely be in trouble.

However, because Etzioni concentrates on what goes on inside organizations, his typology ignores environmental, contextual, or external influences. Outside factors do affect organizations significantly. For example, societal and cultural differences make Swedish prisons less coercive than U.S. prisons. Also because of social and cultural differences, Japanese firms are run more like normative organizations, whereas U.S. companies are managed more like utilitarian organizations.

Classifying Organizational Theories

All around us, we find organizations using the types of control Etzioni described. Much as we might try to stay in the warmer world of friends and family, we cannot escape these organizations and their power. How the organizations use power affects how they operate as well as our ability to achieve goals we share with them.

There have been many attempts to analyze just how organizations operate and what types of operation are most efficient. Under what circumstances, for example, can an organization do without moral persuasion? What is the most effective way to offer remunerative rewards? How should managers and workers interact if the organization is to be effective? Answers can be found in organizational theories.

A great number of theories have been proposed since the early part of this century. Some describe what organizations are like; most suggest what they *should* be like to achieve their goals. These organizational theories can be classified into three types according to how they may have been influenced by the three major sociological perspectives. (1) Theories that may be considered functionalist portray organizations as conflict-free, harmonious systems in which members

can be encouraged through "scientific management" or "human relations" to work harder to achieve the organizational objective. (2) Organizational theories influenced by the conflict model emphasize the importance of social equality for attaining organizational success. (3) Theories that may be regarded as symbolic interactionist focus on organizational culture as members' shared definitions of their life in the organization or depict bureaucracy as the embodiment of the West's "rational" worldview. We analyze these three types of theories in the following sections.

Questions for Discussion and Review

1. What are the principal features of a formal organization?
2. How do coercive, normative, and utilitarian organizations differ from each other?
3. In general, what do organizational theories tell us?

FUNCTIONALIST PERSPECTIVE

For functionalists, organizations are essentially free of human conflict. Members come together to cooperate in achieving a common goal. Given such a harmonious environment, members can be induced to increase their productivity for the betterment of everybody in the organization. Two well-known theories have been proposed to show how.

Scientific Management

Early in this century, U.S. engineer Frederick Taylor (1911) published the first systematic presentation of what was soon called *scientific management*. Taylor assumed that the primary goal of an organization is to maximize efficiency. For a manufacturing company, this means getting maximum productivity, the highest possible output per worker per hour. The achievement of this goal, Taylor argued, depends on three elements: maximum division of labor, close supervision of workers, and an incentive system of piecework wages.

To obtain maximum division of labor, production must be broken down into numerous simple and easy-to-perform tasks. Each of these is then defined down to the tiniest detail, so that it can be completed in the shortest time possible. One of Taylor's specific recommendations was that zigzag motions of the hands must be avoided; workers should begin and complete their motions with both hands simultaneously. To ensure that the task is properly carried out, the worker must be closely and continuously supervised. Taylor suggested that there be four types of supervisors—setting-up boss, speed boss, quality inspector, and repair boss—and that the supervisors in turn be controlled by a planning department. Finally, to be sure they work as hard as possible, workers should be paid by the piece: the more units each produces, the higher the pay.

Today, many companies still apply Taylor's basic principles. Productivity appears to decline if the basic points of this model are not applied to some degree. Scientific management works particularly well in the world of production, where the work is mostly routine. But the theory ignores many aspects of organizations and human behavior. It looks only at the *official* organization, the formal relationships between workers and supervisors. Most sociologists have criticized the theory for treating human beings as machines, arguing that such treatment contributes to worker dissatisfaction and ultimately to lower productivity.

Human Relations

In the early 1930s, industrial psychologist Elton Mayo (1933) challenged practically all the assumptions of the scientific management theory. His argument consists of several points: (1) Workers' productivity is not determined by their physical capacity but by their "social capacity," their sensitivity to the work environment. No matter how fast they *can* do their jobs, they will not produce a lot if their fellow workers frown on the idea of working too fast. (2) Noneconomic rewards, such as friendship with co-workers and respect from management, play a central role in determining the motivation and happiness of workers. Thus, wages are less important than Taylor claimed. (3) The greatest specialization is not the most efficient division of labor. Extreme specialization creates problems for those coordinating the work. Supervisors are hard put to know all the details of very specialized tasks. (4) Workers do not react to management and its incentives as isolated individuals but as members of a group. They will reject management's offer of high pay for maximum productivity if their fellow workers are against working too hard.

These points make up the *human relations theory.* In contrast to scientific management, it emphasizes that productivity depends on social forces, especially the informal relations among workers. The key to increased productivity is not official organization, as Taylor assumed, but **informal organization,** a group formed by the informal relationships among members of an organization—based on personal interactions, not on any plan by the organization.

Empirical support for this theory came from a classical study at the Hawthorne plant in Chicago in the

The scientific management model of industrial organization suggests that a company can achieve maximum productivity if its workers do a simple repetitive task under close supervision. Scientific management works best in manufacturing companies, where the work is mostly routine, but it has been criticized for treating workers as machines.

1930s (Roethlisberger and Dickson, 1939). The study showed that workers increased their productivity regardless of changes in the physical environment. Productivity went up, for example, when the experimenter brightened the workplace, but it also went up when he dimmed the lights. The researchers concluded that the employees worked harder because the presence of the researcher made them feel important; management seemed to be treating them as people, not mere machines. Another study at the same plant examined whether output was determined by financial incentives. Surprisingly, it was shaped by an informal norm. The norm forbade working too hard as well as working too slowly. Anyone working too hard was ridiculed as a "rate buster," and anyone working too slowly was scorned as a "chiseler." As a result, each worker tried to produce as much as the other workers, rather than trying to meet management's goals. These studies have clearly shown that informal relations can increase worker productivity.

The human relations theory covers parts of the organization ignored by scientific management, but it too has limitations. First, it exaggerates the importance of the informal group life at the workplace. Most workers will not wake up every morning feeling that they cannot wait to go to work in order to be with their co-workers. They are more interested in their families and friends outside the workplace. Second, informal social relations may create more pleasant conditions in the plant, but they cannot significantly reduce the tediousness of the manual job itself. While a person may enjoy working with certain individuals, it cannot transform an inherently boring job into an exciting one. Relations with co-workers, though, may be more significant to white-collar and professional workers, whose jobs often involve a great deal of interaction with co-workers, than to blue-collar workers.

Questions for Discussion and Review

1. What are the basic features of the scientific management theory?
2. What is the essence of the human relations theory?

CONFLICT PERSPECTIVE

According to the conflict perspective, the major problem with the scientific management and human relations theories is that they fail to take into account the reality of conflict in organizations. Given the inequality in income, status, and other rewards between management and workers, the lower participants cannot be expected to give their all to fulfill the higher participants' wish for maximum productivity. The inequality severely limits how far management can successfully use scientific management or human relations to manipulate workers into superproducers. By contrast, the practice of *equality* can help ensure organizational success. This is the main point of the collectivist and feminist models of organization, which have been influenced by the conflict perspective.

Collectivist Model

According to Karl Marx, capitalist organizations—or business corporations—are the capitalists' tool for exploiting the working class. Eventually, Marx claimed, the corporations will be abolished in a class-less, communist society. They will be replaced by collectivist organizations, in which managers and workers work together as equals and for equal pay. The workers would be much more productive than the exploited ones of today. In the meantime, an approximation of this organizational model exists to some extent in the United States.

The typical U.S. corporation is bureaucratic, paternalistic, or undemocratic: those on the top dictate to those below, and those at the bottom may not choose who is above them or who influences their decisions. Power, then, flows from the top down. By contrast, in a collectivist organization, power flows from the bottom up. In the United States, this element of the collectivist model can be seen in some 5000 "alternative institutions" established during the 1970s. These free schools, free medical clinics, legal collectives, food cooperatives, communes, and cooperative businesses are a legacy of movements during the 1960s against authority and "the Establishment." These enterprises are collectively owned and managed, without any hierarchy of authority. They tend to be in craft production and other special niches of the economy that exempt them from directly competing with conventional companies. Most are quite small, averaging six employees, but this size helps preserve full worker participation. The workers are highly satisfied with their jobs and strongly identify with their firms. Because they are also owners, the workers tend to work too hard and often suffer stress and burnout as a result (Rothschild and Russell, 1986).

The collectivist idea of giving workers control over their jobs has also been tried on a limited basis in some 90 percent of the 500 largest U.S. corporations as a way to combat worker alienation and low productivity. In these companies small groups of employees work together as equals, similar to what are known in Japan as "quality circles." They do not await orders from the top but take the initiative. They are encouraged with rewards and recognition—merit raises, cash bonuses, and bulletin-board praise—to contribute ideas on how to increase productivity and sales. They operate with the "open door" policy, whereby employees report directly to top management. This policy further encourages employees to work harder because it makes them feel important and respected. Practically all the companies that have implemented quality circles are in the manufacturing sector of the economy. Good examples are IBM and General Motors. The quality-circle style of worker participation has also invaded the service sector in such areas as the insurance business. Collectivist practices such as these can boost not only worker morale but also productivity, as demonstrated in the successful operation of a Honda auto plant and other Japanese businesses in the United States (Rothschild and Russell, 1986; Scott, 1986; Florida and Kenney, 1991).

Feminist Model

We have seen how the collectivist model of organization achieves success through social equality, also popularly known as *participatory democracy*. The model proposed by feminist theorists does more than simply get everybody to work together as equals. The feminist model also calls for personal, emotional support from each other, as typically exists in a group of close friends. Instead of urging people to leave their personal problems behind when coming to work, as do most conventional organizations, the feminist model tolerates—even encourages—the opposite. The equality espoused in the feminist model is personal, subjective, or spontaneous. This is in contrast to the impersonal, objective, or rule-oriented type of equality found in organizations that have hired women and minorities only because federal law has forced them to do so.

The feminist model originates from studies of predominantly female organizations as well as female executives of conventional, gender-mixed organizations. An example is Judy Rosener's (1990) landmark study. In comparing 456 successful female executives with their male counterparts in similar positions at similar companies, Rosener found significant gender differences in leadership styles. Men tend more to prefer a "command and control" way of dealing with subordinates—relying on orders, appeals to self-interest, rational decision making, and rewards for manipulative purposes. By contrast, women are more likely to prefer an intuitive, anti-hierarchical style. They are more willing to share power, ask for guidance from subordinates, and humanize their workplace, as demonstrated to some degree by the female university president in the vignette at the beginning of this chapter. In another study, Sandra Morgen (1994) found that the women who work at feminist health clinics generally cater to each other's *personal* needs, not just the instrumental, "bottom line" needs of the organization. Considerable "personal sharing" goes on in the organization: Members not only tend to greet each other with hugs and kisses, but also share personal problems rather than leave them at home. Not surprisingly, members identify closely with their organizations, committed with heart and soul to them.

We should be careful, however, not to stereotype all women as having the same organizational style. Personal, subjective, or spontaneous egalitarianism does not exist exclusively among women or equally among all women. Some men have it, and some women do not. It is only as a group that women are more likely than men to have that kind of organizational style. This gender difference is far from innate, but rather, is largely a product of socialization.

Generally, females are more likely than males to have learned from parents, peer groups, schools, and various social experiences the values of supporting and nurturing others, protecting long-term relationships, seeking solutions where everyone wins, and sharing emotions. For example, boys tend more to play in packs such as hierarchical sports teams, where they learn how to compete, take criticism, and win, but girls are more likely to play in leaderless groups, where they learn to get along, be fair, and reach consensus (Heim and Golant, 1993; Rothschild and Davies, 1994).

Questions for Discussion and Review

1. What is the most important characteristic of a collectivist organization?
2. What does a feminist organization look like?

SYMBOLIC INTERACTIONIST PERSPECTIVE

The basic ideas of many organizational theories can be related to the symbolic interactionist perspective. Here we analyze two such theories. One that is relatively new emphasizes the significance of organizational culture, suggesting that the way people define the situation they are in shapes their organizations. The other theory is older and well known as Weber's theory of bureaucracy, which essentially portrays bureaucracy as the embodiment of the Western—or the male—definition of rationality as the proper way to run an organization.

Organizational Culture: Shared Definitions

Over the last decade many new organizational theories have emerged, variously labeled as cultural, interpretive, or hermeneutic. All are related to the symbolic interactionist perspective. *Cultural theories* emphasize how organizational members' values or beliefs, which reflect how they interpret the world around them, influence their behavior in the organization. *Interpretive theories* focus on the individual's "perspective on life in organizations." And *hermeneutic theories* show how interpretations of the meanings of organizational documents influence members' interactions (Morgan, 1989; Aldrich, 1992; Turner, 1992). Roughly translated into the language of symbolic interactionism, all of these theories essentially say that organizational culture, popularly called "corporate culture," consists of members' shared definitions of what the organization is like and therefore significantly affects what goes on in the organization.

Studies of corporate culture often reveal why some organizations succeed while others fail in achieving their goals. Tandem, a successful computer manufacturer, was found to owe its success largely to the widely shared belief among its employees that it is a wonderful company to work for. Slogans extolling the company as an outstanding employer appear on T-shirts and bulletin boards and are spread by word of mouth. A related belief is that everybody is treated equally, suggested by the absence of name tags and reserved parking spaces. When questioned by researchers, Tandem employees also revealed the relative lack of hierarchy with comments such as, "Everyone here, managers, vice-presidents, and even janitors, communicate on the same level. No one feels better than anyone else" (Morgan, 1989). Organizational culture cannot exist, though, without real support such as in the form of recognitions and rewards. If Tandem's employees were not given enough praise and salary raises for their hard work, its gung-ho culture would disappear.

Bureaucracy: Embodiment of "Rational" Worldview

According to Max Weber, modern Western society makes a specific form of organization necessary: **bureaucracy,** a modern Western organization defined as being rational in achieving its goal efficiently. "In the place of the old-type ruler who is moved by sympathy, favor, grace, and gratitude," Weber (1946) said, "modern culture requires ... the emotionally detached, and hence rigorously 'professional' expert." In every area of modern life there is a tendency toward **rationalization,** Weber's term for the process of replacing subjective, spontaneous, informal, or diverse ways of doing things with a planned, objective, unified method based on abstract rules. Applied to organizations, rationalization means the development of bureaucracies.

What specifically is bureaucracy? It is an organization that differs sharply from a collectivist organization, as shown in Table 5.1. It is as rational as a machine, as Weber (1946) wrote:

> The fully developed bureaucratic mechanism compares with other organizations exactly as does the machine with the non-mechanical modes of production. . . . The strictly bureaucratic administration succeeds in eliminating from official business, love, hatred, and purely personal, irrational, and emotional elements which escape calculation.

By squeezing out the human element of emotion, bureaucracy is, in Weber's view, the most efficient form of organization. This can be so if, as symbolic interactionism suggests, organization members define the machine-like rationality as reasonable, legitimate, acceptable, or agreeable.

However, this definition is increasingly rejected in today's socially diverse organizations. As our previous discussion on feminist theory suggests, women are likely to define the emotionless, impersonal, or dehumanizing form of rationality as *irrational*. They tend more to define the subjective, personal, or empathetic form of rationality as *rational*. With increasing female participation in organizations, we can expect bureaucracies to become increasingly humanized like the feminist organizations that we have analyzed. The Japanese also define the Western impersonal form of rationality as *unreasonable* for

TABLE 5.1
Bureaucratic versus Collectivist Organization

Bureaucratic Organization	Collectivist Organization
1. Maximum division of labor.	1. Minimum division of labor
2. Maximum specialization of jobs—monopolization of expertise.	2. Generalization of jobs—diffusion of expertise.
3. Emphasis on hierarchy of positions—justifying reward differentials.	3. Striving for egalitarianism—restricting reward differentials.
4. Authority in individual officeholders; hierarchical control; bureaucratic elitism.	4. Authority in collectivity as a whole; democratic control; subordinate participation.
5. Formalization of fixed and universal rules.	5. Primacy of ad hoc decisions.
6. Worker motivation through direct supervision.	6. Worker motivation through personal appeals.
7. Impersonality as ideal of social relations in organization.	7. Comradeship as ideal of social relations in organizations.

running organizations. And they define their own traditional values of mutual obligations and loyalties as *reasonable,* because they help, among other things, strengthen a company's lifetime commitment to its employees and employee commitment to the company. This may explain why those traditional and emotional values that Weber regarded as obstacles to achieving organizational efficiency have made Japanese companies rank among the most efficient in the world.

Although bureaucracy is not the most efficient form of organization in the world, it is still most efficient in predominantly individualist cultures such as that of the United States. Still, bureaucracy is also deficient in some ways. We will discuss both the efficient and deficient aspects of bureaucracy in the following section.

Questions for Discussion and Review

1. How does organizational culture contribute to corporate success?
2. What are the major characteristics of Weber's bureaucratic model of organization?

———

THE REALITIES OF BUREAUCRACY

All the organizational theories we have discussed are basically **normative theories,** theories that suggest what we *should* do to achieve our goals. Table 5.2 out-

lines what each of the theories prescribes as the key to achieving organizational efficiency. Here we focus on what bureaucratic organizations are really like. Despite widespread dislike of bureaucracy, this form of organization is still pervasive. Most people in the United States continue to work in bureaucracies, and even more must deal with bureaucratic organizations when they enroll in school, have a phone installed, pay a hospital bill, or handle any number of other countless arrangements that are part of living in a modern Western society. The prevalence of bureaucratic organization affects both the small details of everyday life and the overall function of the government and economy. The benefits and problems of bureaucracy are thus worth a closer look.

Bureaucratic Benefits

If so many people do not like bureaucracies, why does this kind of organization continue to exist? In part, it is because they are not all bad. Even red tape has its advantages: one person's "red tape" can be another person's safeguard against problems. The process of getting a government permit to open a hazardous waste dump may seem an endless, expensive obstacle course of paperwork to the company that wants to operate the dump. But to people living near the proposed site, the rules and regulations that make up that red tape may seem the best guarantee of proper precautions to safeguard their health.

Similarly, the impersonality of bureaucracies, especially in government, is sometimes welcome. If you need a government-subsidized student loan, you are

TABLE 5.2
Organizational Theories: How to Achieve Efficiency

Functionalist Perspective
- Scientific Management: Maximize division of labor, supervision of workers, and wage incentive
- Human Relations: Foster informal relations among workers

Conflict Perspective
- Collectivist Model: Encourage workers to participate as equals in management of organization
- Feminist Model: Encourage both equality and emotional closeness among all members

Symbolic Interactionist Perspective
- Organizational Culture: Develop positive culture with recognition and reward
- Bureaucratic Theory: Squeeze out human emotion by defining for members the organization's rules and regulations regarding division of labor, differentiation of authority, and hiring based on competence

The chief source of the efficiency of bureaucracies is reliance on impersonal rules. Rules ensure that employees treat equally all the people they serve. Unfortunately, the consequences of bureaucratic efficiency may be rigidity on the part of personnel, such as being unable to help customers with unusual needs.

probably glad that impersonal rules—not political pull or personal friendships—determine whether or not you can obtain the loan. Bureaucracy encourages equality and discourages discrimination.

Even for employees, bureaucracies may bring some benefits. The widely held assumption that bureaucracies tend to stifle individual creativity and imagination seems groundless. Data collected by sociologist Melvin Kohn (1983) suggest that bureaucracies make their workers intellectually flexible, creative, and open-minded. Kohn defined bureaucrats as people who work in large organizations with complicated hierarchies of authority, and nonbureaucrats as people who work in small organizations with only one level of supervision. Kohn found that, compared with nonbureaucrats, bureaucrats demonstrated a higher level of intellectual performance on tests administered by an interviewer. Bureaucrats also placed greater intellectual demands on themselves during their leisure time. They were more likely than nonbureaucrats to read books and magazines, attend plays and concerts, and go to museums. They also put greater value on self-direction, rather than conformity, and were more likely to take personal responsibility for whatever they did. Finally, they were more open-minded and more receptive to change than the nonbureaucrats.

Skeptics may argue that the bureaucrats' wonderful traits did not *result* from working in a bureaucracy. Perhaps the bureaucrats were better educated, more intellectually flexible, and more receptive to change in the first place. This argument assumes that bureaucracies hold some special attraction for people with these qualities. But because most people believe that

bureaucracies suppress creativity, this assumption is far from convincing.

Kohn contended that bureaucracies themselves encourage the development of the positive traits he found in their employees. The more complex a job is, argued Kohn, the more intellectually flexible the worker becomes, and employees of bureaucracies tend to have more complex jobs than those with comparable education who work for an organization with just one or two levels of supervision.

Bureaucratic Problems

In Weber's view, bureaucracy is inescapable but not very likable. "It is horrible," he once said, "to think that the world would one day be filled with nothing but those little cogs, little men clinging to little jobs and striving toward bigger ones" (Bendix, 1962). Finding a person to say a good word about bureaucracy is about as hard as finding a landlord who likes rent control. Why? Because of certain problems often associated with bureaucracy.

The first problem has to do with rules and regulations. Since they are based on what is already known, rules cannot tell us what to do about the unanticipated. Blind adherence to rules can therefore wreak havoc in people's lives. If we have lost an important document like our I.D. card, bureaucrats cannot do anything for us that requires the presentation of the document. A more common problem is the tendency of bureaucracies to produce a seemingly endless array of rules and regulations. Public bureaucracies, in particular, are notorious for mountains of rules, all of which slow action by officials and fall like an avalanche on private citizens and businesses that must comply with them. The nation's small businesses alone spend an immense amount of money every year just to complete government forms.

Another problem is that bureaucracy tends to grow unnecessarily bigger. This problem has been called **Parkinson's Law:** "Work expands to fill the time available for its completion." The author of this "law," C. Northcote Parkinson, believed that the natural tendency of bureaucracy is to grow and to keep on growing by at least six percent a year. Wanting to appear busy or important or both, officials increase their workload by writing many memos, creating rules, filling out forms, and keeping files. Then, feeling overworked, they hire assistants. At the same time, powerful incentives—such as bigger salaries, more perquisites, higher status, and greater power—encourage officials to increase their agency work forces, budgets, and missions. As a result, many bureaucrats are doing the same thing at great cost to taxpayers. As the director of Vice President Al Gore's project on reducing the federal bureaucracy said, "As a rule, virtually any task being done by government is being done by 20 or more agencies" (Church, 1993).

There is yet another bureaucratic problem: deadwood tends to pile up. This problem is known as the **Peter Principle:** "In every hierarchy every employee tends to rise to their level of incompetence." Competent officials are promoted and, if they prove to be competent in their new jobs, promoted again. The process continues until they are promoted to a position in which they are incompetent. And there they remain as deadwood until they retire. The bureaucracy functions only because there are always employees still proving their competence before they are promoted beyond their abilities. Like Parkinson's Law, however, the Peter Principle is based on impressionistic observation rather than rigorous scientific research. Both problems are widely thought to be common, but precisely how common is not known.

The Future of Bureaucracy

Bureaucracy will probably continue to thrive. Many organizations in the United States seem to be getting larger, as suggested by the growth of big government agencies, multinational corporations, multicampus universities, and agribusinesses. Large organizational size usually leads to greater bureaucratic control, requiring numerous workers to follow standard rules and operating procedures so that chaos can be avoided.

At the same time, less bureaucratic control is imposed on higher-ranked technical experts and specialists within giant organizations. There is also less administrative control throughout the corporations on the frontier of technology. In many successful U.S. corporations today, highly trained specialists already enjoy a large degree of autonomy. They resent taking orders from managers who have less technical knowledge. Because of the increasing shift from manual to knowledge work in the composition of the U.S. work force, pressure will grow to replace the bureaucratic, hierarchical bureaucracies with much flatter, more egalitarian organizations made up of numerous smaller units with six to ten employees each. In fact, there is some evidence in the early 1990s that the information revolution has begun to force many centralized bureaucracies, from education to business, to give way to this collectivist, egalitarian model. Some public schools, for example, are managed by teams of teachers and parents rather than bureaucrats. Increasing female participation in organizations also contributes to the replacement of bureaucratic control with egalitarian cooperation.

In sum, bureaucracy appears to be moving in two seemingly opposite directions. On the one hand, bureaucracy will probably increase in *form*, with more and more organizations becoming giant bureaucracies across the United States and around the globe. On the other hand, the *content* of bureaucracy will become increasingly anti-bureaucratic, with more and more participants working as equals.

Questions for Discussion and Review

1. What are the benefits of bureaucracies?
2. What bureaucratic problems do Parkinson's Law and the Peter Principle illustrate?
3. What changes seem to be happening in today's bureaucracies?

A GLOBAL ANALYSIS OF ORGANIZATIONS

It is important to look at organizations from a global perspective. Without that perspective, we would have believed Weber's *erroneous* assumption that the traditional non-Western organization cannot be as efficient as Western bureaucracy.

Writing about organizations around 1910, Weber, like most Westerners of that time, did not have the same global sensitivity that many of us have today. Thus, he tended to see in non-Western traditionalism only its *negative* aspects, such as hiring the boss's incompetent relative rather than the best-qualified person. But today, a more sensitive global analysis can reveal the *positive* aspects of non-Western traditionalism, such as the cooperation and commitment demonstrated by Japanese organizations.

Basically, the Japanese traditional culture is group-oriented rather than individual-centered as in the West. As group members rather than independent individuals, Japanese tend to have stronger relations with one another. Therefore, at the heart of the Japanese organization is concern with group achievement. Employees begin each workday by singing their company song or reciting slogans of devotion to their company. They work in sections of eight to ten people, headed by the *kacho* (section chief). Each section, now well known as a "quality circle," does not await orders from the top but takes the initiative, and all its members work together as equals. Personnel of different sections often get together to discuss how best to achieve company objectives. Executives, then, rubber stamp most of the decisions made by employees at the section level. Workers, moreover, look upon their company as their family because they enjoy the security of permanent employment. Executives also feel secure and regard their company as their family. Not surprisingly, both workers and executives are strongly committed to their company and work hard to make it highly efficient and productive.

Traditionalism has also contributed to organizational efficiency in other East Asian societies such as South Korea and Taiwan. But why can't it do the same in many developing countries? The answer is hard to find because most research has focused on the negative aspects of their traditionalism. If the focus of research is shifted to the positive, then we may find out what prevents the clan-centeredness and personal ties from building efficient organizations in traditional African, Latin American, and other developing countries. Interestingly, in the meantime, these countries have begun to learn from the Japanese model of organization. In fact, many organizations in the West have already done so by becoming more humanized or less impersonal.

Japanese companies are collectivist organizations. They are often run like families, encompassing every aspect of a worker's life. Employees may begin each day singing their company song, reciting slogans of devotion to the company. Here, workers at a Mitsubishi shipbuilding yard do group gymnastics at the start of the workday.

Question for Discussion and Review

1. How can a global analysis help us understand organizations better?

CHAPTER REVIEW

1. *What is a social group?* It is a collection of people who share some characteristics, interact with one another, and have some feeling of unity. *What are in-groups and out-groups?* An in-group is a group to which a person is strongly tied as a member. An out-group is a group of which an individual is not a member. *What is a reference* *group?* A group that people use as a guide for their behavior. *What are primary and secondary groups?* A primary group is one whose members interact informally, relate to each other as whole persons, and enjoy their relationship for its own sake. In a secondary group, the individuals interact formally, relate to each other as

players of particular roles, and expect to achieve some practical purpose through the relationship.

2. *What is the nature of group leadership?* Leadership can be *instrumental*, trying to achieve goals by focusing on task performance. It can also be *expressive*, being concerned with others' psychological well-being and working to enhance it. *Why are leaders less likely than followers to conform to the group?* Because leaders usually enjoy an idiosyncrasy credit extended to them by followers. *Does the size of a group matter?* Yes. The larger a group, the more impersonal it becomes, the more difficult it is for one member to influence another, or the less likely a member is to help someone in distress.

3. *What draws us into a social network?* Friendship, business transactions, sexual contacts, expressions of admiration, or some other kind of social relationship. *Can networks affect our lives?* Yes. The smaller, denser networks of friends and relatives can help us maintain good health by giving us social support. But they can also make our lives miserable by putting many demands on our time and personal resources, criticizing us, and invading our privacy.

4. *What is a formal organization?* It is a group whose activities are rationally designed to achieve specific goals. *What are the most common types of organizations?* According to Etzioni, they are coercive, utilitarian, and normative organizations.

5. *According to scientific management theory, what must an organization do to achieve its goal?* It must have maximum division of labor, close supervision of workers, and a piecework system of wages. *How does the human relations theory differ?* Whereas scientific management focuses on the official organization and the effect of wages on efficiency, the human relations theory emphasizes the influence of social forces—in particular the informal relations among workers—on job satisfaction and productivity.

6. *What does a collectivist organization look like?* Its members participate as equals in the management of the organization. *What does a feminist organization look like?* In addition to practicing equality, the feminist organization fosters close personal relations among its members.

7. *What are the principal characteristics of a bureaucracy?* A bureaucracy is characterized by a division of labor, a hierarchy of authority, the hiring of employees on the basis of impersonal procedures and technical qualifications, and a reliance on formal, written rules. *What*

are some of the benefits of bureaucracy? When tasks are stable and routine, bureaucracies are very efficient; their reliance on rules and their impersonality can protect people from the exercise of arbitrary power and favoritism. In addition, bureaucracies may foster among their workers intellectual flexibility, creativity, and openness to change. *What are the problems of bureaucracy?* Bureaucracies tend to produce an ever-increasing number of rules, grow unnecessarily larger, and retain incompetent officials. *What changes can be seen in bureaucracy?* Bureaucracies seem to increase in size but are becoming more egalitarian.

8. *How does a global perspective enhance our understanding of organizations?* It enables us to see how non-Western traditionalism can contribute to organizational efficiency.

KEY TERMS

Bureaucracy A modern Western organization defined by Max Weber as being rational in achieving its goal efficiently. (p. 113)

Expressive leaders Leaders who achieve group harmony by making others feel good. (p. 103)

Formal organization A group whose activities are rationally designed to achieve specific goals. (p. 106)

Groupthink The tendency for members of a cohesive group to maintain consensus to the extent of ignoring the truth. (p. 103)

Idiosyncrasy credit The privilege that allows leaders to deviate from their group's norms. (p. 103)

Informal organization A group formed by the informal relationships among members of an organization—based on personal interactions, not on any plan by the organization. (p. 110)

In-group The group to which an individual is strongly tied as a member. (p. 100)

Instrumental leaders Leaders who achieve their group's goal by getting others to focus on task performance. (p. 103)

Normative theories Theories that suggest what we *should* do to achieve our goals. (p. 114)

Out-group The group of which an individual is not a member. (p. 100)

Parkinson's Law The observation that "work expands to fill the time available for its completion." (p. 116)

Peter Principle   The observation that "in every hierarchy every employee tends to rise to their level of incompetence." (p. 116)

Primary group   A group whose members interact informally, relate to each other as whole persons, and enjoy their relationship for its own sake. (p. 102)

Rationalization   Max Weber's term for the process of replacing the subjective, spontaneous, informal, or diverse ways of doing things with a planned, formally unified method based on abstract rules. (p. 113)

Reference group   A group that is used as the frame of reference for evaluating one's own behavior. (p. 101)

Secondary group   A group whose members interact formally, relate to each other as players of particular roles, and expect to profit from each other. (p. 102)

Social aggregate   A number of people who happen to be in one place but who do not interact with one another. (p. 100)

Social category   A number of people who have something in common but neither interact with one another nor gather in one place. (p. 100)

Social group   A collection of people who interact with one another and have a certain feeling of unity. (p. 100)

Social network   A web of social relationships that link individuals or groups to one another. (p. 105)

SUGGESTED READINGS

Biggart, Nicole Woolsey. 1989. *Charismatic Capitalism: Direct Selling Organizations in America.* Chicago: University of Chicago Press. An interesting sociological study of direct-selling organizations such as Tupper, Amway, and Mary Kay.

Czarniawska-Joerges, Barbara. 1992. *Exploring Complex Organizations: A Cultural Perspective.* Newbury Park, Calif.: Sage. An interpretation of what goes on within an organization from the standpoint of the participants.

Hearn, Jeff, et al. (eds.). 1989. *The Sexuality of Organization.* Newbury Park, Calif.: Sage. An analysis of the relationships between gender relations and organizational life, focusing on such subjects as sexual harassment in the workplace and the self-image of women managers.

Waring, Stephen P. 1991. *Taylorism Transformed: Scientific Management Theory Since 1945.* Chapel Hill: University of North Carolina Press. A historical analysis of the organizational model of scientific management.

Zeitlin, Maurice. 1989. *The Large Corporation and Contemporary Classes.* New Brunswick, N.J.: Rutgers University Press. An analysis of how managers have taken over the control of corporations from their owners.

6

DEVIANCE AND CONTROL

Myths and Realities

MYTH: *Strangers don't care about us as much as our relatives, friends, and acquaintances. No wonder that strangers are more likely to kill us.*
REALITY: Strangers are less likely to kill us. Most murder victims were related to or knew their killers. (p. 123)

MYTH: *"Guns don't kill, people do." Therefore, it is futile to outlaw the possession of guns.*
REALITY: Of course, guns by themselves cannot kill, nor can their absence reduce the motivation to kill. But, were guns less available, potential murderers would use less-lethal weapons, which would result in fewer deaths. (p. 124)

MYTH: *Drug abuse is common in the United States, involving all kinds of people such as the rich and the poor as has been the case for many years.*
REALITY: Since the early 1980s drug abuse has worsened among the lower class, particularly the socially and economically oppressed minorities, but it has declined among the middle class. (p. 124)

MYTH: *Deviance is always harmful to society.*
REALITY: Deviance can bring benefits to society if it occurs within limits. (p. 129)

MYTH: *The U.S. criminal justice system is by any measure soft on criminals.*
REALITY: Our country appears soft on criminals because extremely few criminals are apprehended and punished. But compared with other democracies, the United States is tougher for imprisoning proportionately more criminals and imposing longer prison terms. (p. 138)

If you thumb through a newspaper or magazine, you might come across a story such as this: In 1988 Jeffrey Dahmer murdered three people. He first met a 14-year-old boy at a bus stop and asked him to pose nude for photos. Soon after they arrived at Dahmer's apartment, Dahmer had sex with the boy, drugged him, strangled him, dismembered him, and smashed his bones with a sledgehammer. Several months later, Dahmer picked up a 23-year-old man at a gay bar, had oral sex with him, drugged him, and butchered him. Later in the same month, Dahmer strangled another, 24-year-old man and then kept his head after having boiled it to remove the skin and painted the skull. Dahmer later told the police that he saved skulls of only the most handsome victims so that he would not forget them. By 1991, when he was arrested, the police found in Dahmer's apartment at least 15 dismembered bodies, a head in the refrigerator and a heart in the freezer, and a blue barrel of acid for leftovers (Matthews, 1992).

With crimes such as this popping up in the media, we may regard deviants as creatures who are foreign to us. But deviance is widespread, although most is far from as gruesome as Dahmer's. Even in a society of saints, as Durkheim long ago suggested, its rules will be broken. Virtually everybody has committed some deviant acts such as those listed in Table 6.1. What, exactly, is deviance?

TABLE 6.1
Common Offenses Punishable by Fines or Jail Terms

- Gambling illegally, such as betting on a sport event or political election.
- Evading taxes, such as failing to report or exaggerating deductible expenses.
- Committing computer crime, such as copying software illegally.
- Serving alcohol to minors.
- Drinking in public, where prohibited.
- Possessing marijuana in small quantities for personal use.
- Committing adultery in states where illegal.
- Patronizing a prostitute.
- Appearing nude in public, such as nude sunbathing, where prohibited.
- Stealing TV signals, such as with a satellite dish.
- Speeding or other moving-traffic violations.
- Parking illegally.
- Smoking in public, where ordinance prohibits it.
- Failing to recycle where required.

SOURCE: Adapted from Stephen J. Adler and Wade Lamber, "Common Criminals: Just About Everyone Violates Some Laws, Even Model Citizens," *Wall Street Journal*, March 12, 1993, p. A6.

WHAT IS DEVIANCE?

Deviance is generally defined as any act that violates a social norm. But the phenomenon is more complex than that. How do we know whether an act violates a social norm? Is homosexuality deviant—a violation of a social norm? Some people think so, but others do not. There are at least three factors involved in determining what deviance is: time, place, and public consensus or power.

First, what constitutes deviance varies from one historical period to another. In the last century in the United States, opium and cocaine were legal and easily available common drugs; today their use is a criminal offense. Nowadays in most countries cigarette smoking is legal, but in the seventeenth century it was illegal. In fact, in some countries at that time, smokers were punished harshly: in Russia their noses were cut off and in Hindustan their lips sliced off (Goode, 1989).

Second, the definition of deviance varies from one place to another. A polygamist (a person with more than one spouse) is a criminal in the United States but not in Saudi Arabia and other Muslim countries. Prostitution is illegal in the United States (except in some counties in Nevada), but legal in Denmark, Germany, France, and many other countries.

Third, whether a given act is deviant depends on public consensus. Murder is unquestionably deviant because nearly all societies agree that it is. In contrast, long hair on men is not generally considered deviant. Public consensus, however, usually reflects the vested interests of the rich and powerful. As Marx would have said, the ideas of the ruling class tend to become the ruling ideas of society. Like the powerful, the general public tends, for example, to consider bank robbery to be a serious crime but not fraudulent advertising, which serves the interests of the powerful.

In view of those three determinants of deviant behavior, we may more precisely define **deviance** as an act considered by public consensus or by the powerful at a given time and place to be a violation of some social rule.

Question for Discussion and Review

1. What determines whether a person has violated a social norm?

EXAMPLES OF DEVIANCE

There exists a wide gamut of deviance, ranging from the relatively trivial, such as bad manners at the dinner table, to the extremely serious, such as murdering a person. Here we discuss the more serious ones.

Homicide

Homicide is mostly a "personal" crime, far more likely to be committed against acquaintances, friends, or relatives than against strangers, as shown in Figure 6.1. Swayed by common sense, we may find this

Deviance is an act that is considered by public consensus to be a violation of some social rule or norm. What constitutes deviance varies by time and place. For example, cigarette smoking was illegal and harshly punished in some countries in the seventeenth century. Although smoking is legal in most countries these days, it is coming to be less commonly accepted in many public places.

Relationship of homicide victim and offender
(cases of unknown relationship excluded)

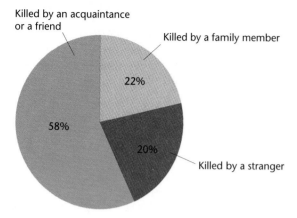

Source: Data from Kathleen Maguire and Ann L. Pastore, (eds.), *Source of Criminal Justice Statistics—1993* (Washington, D.C.: Government Printing Office, 1994), pp. 380–381.

FIGURE 6.1
Most Victims Know Their Killers

incredible. But as sociologists Donald Mulvihill and Melvin Tumin (1969) explained, "Everyone is within easy striking distance from intimates for a large part of the time. Although friends, lovers, spouses, and the like are a main source of pleasure in one's life, they are equally a main source of frustration and hurt. Few others can anger one so much." As a crime of passion, homicide is usually carried out under the overwhelming pressure of a volcanic emotion, namely, uncontrollable rage.

Homicide occurs most frequently during weekend evenings, particularly Saturday night. This holds true largely for lower-class murderers, but not for middle- and upper-class offenders, who tend to kill on any day of the week. One apparent reason is that higher-class murders are more likely than lower-class homicides to be premeditated, hence less likely to result from alcohol-induced quarrels during weekend sprees. Research has also often shown that most U.S. murderers are poor, including semiskilled workers, unskilled laborers, and welfare recipients (Parker, 1989).

Whatever their class, murderers most often use handguns to kill. Perhaps seeing a gun while embroiled in a heated argument incites a person into murderous action. As Shakespeare wrote, "How oft the sight of means to do ill deeds, makes ill deeds done." Of course, firearms by themselves cannot cause homicide, nor can their absence reduce the motivation to kill. It is true that "Guns don't kill, people do." Still, were guns less available, less dangerous weapons such as fists or knives might be used instead. Thus many heated arguments might result in aggravated assaults rather than murders, thereby reducing the number of fatalities. But given the enormous number of guns in private hands, it is not surprising that far more deaths result from gun attacks in this country than in Canada, Britain, and other industrialized countries, where there are considerably fewer guns per person.

The easy availability of guns has contributed to a stunning upsurge in killings by teenagers. Since 1985, the homicide rate has declined among older adults, but has soared among youngsters under age 18, as shown in Figure 6.2. Most of these killings take place in large cities' poor neighborhoods, where many teenagers carry guns, a new phenomenon since 1985 (Fox, 1994; Blumstein, 1995).

Drug Abuse

In the United States drug abuse has steadily declined since the early 1980s among the middle class. But it has increased in the lower class, particularly among socially and economically oppressed minorities. The reasons include lack of education, lack of jobs, and despair from being poor or discriminated against. Less obvious is the experience of being treated as the enemy in their own society's war on drugs. Instead of being provided with drug education and treatment, poor and minority drug users are often arrested or imprisoned. In 1989, for example, African Americans

FIGURE 6.2
Souring Rates of Teen Homicides

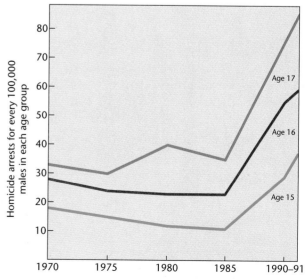

Source: Data from Northeastern University, National Crime Analysis Program, 1992.

constituted only 12 percent of the U.S. population, but they made up 40 percent of all arrests for various drug offenses (Currie, 1993).

But why would the poor abuse drugs in the first place? Reviewing various studies, Elliott Currie (1993) found at least four reasons. First, drugs can fulfill the need for *status*. In the larger, conventional society, the poor are denied legitimate avenues for attaining esteem and respect. Therefore, in the poor neighborhood a drug culture that serves as an alternative source of respect has developed. "Being in the drug culture is just like being a movie star," Currie (1993) explains. "So many people depend on you, want to stop you in the street. . . . You are a very important person."

Second, drugs can help the user *cope* with the harsh, oppressive realities of poverty. As Currie (1993) writes, "drugs become a way of getting away from daily problems, medicating emotional anguish, relieving stress, escaping pain."

Third, drugs can provide a sense of *structure* (purpose) to shattered lives. In the absence of steady work or stable family life, the poor cannot find the sense of structure that the nonpoor have. As a substitute, drug use helps relieve monotony and purposelessness among the poor.

Fourth, the absence of social and economic opportunities has for decades or generations made life so hopeless and purposeless that the poor communities are *saturated* with illicit drugs. Given this environment, it is easy to drift passively into drug use without considering its consequences.

Rape

Rape involves the use of force to get someone to do something sexual against his or her will. It is a common problem in the United States, but exactly how common? And why is it common?

Incidence and Characteristics   Every year only about 110,000 cases of rape in the United States are reported to the police, but the actual number of rapes is considerably higher, running into the millions. According to a recent survey, 22 percent of women aged 18 to 59 reported having been forced to have sex at least once since age 13 (Michael et al., 1994). This 22 percent translates into about 15 million women as victims of forced sex. Most of these incidents are not even legally defined as rapes, let alone reported to the police. A major reason is that, as shown in Figure 6.3 , the overwhelming majority of the cases involve intimates such as lovers and close friends, whereas the concept of rape is popularly associated with strangers or mere acquaintances.

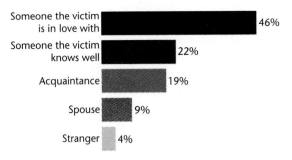

Source: Data from Robert T. Michael, John H. Gagnon, Edward O. Laumann, and Gina Kolata, *Sex in America: A Definitive Survey* (Boston: Little, Brown, 1994).

FIGURE 6.3
The Men Who Force Sex on Women

In the same survey, while 22 percent of the women said they had been forced to have sex, only about 3 percent of the men admitted to having committed forced sex. Why do the overwhelming majority of men fail to acknowledge what some women see as forced sex? The apparent reason, again, has much to do with the fact that most cases of forced sex involve intimates. Consider the following two scenarios given by Michael and his colleagues (1994):

One involves a married man coming home late after drinking a lot of beer with the guys. He wants sex, but his wife cringes when he gets near. She obviously does not want sex. He does, and has his way. He does not think it was forced, but she does. Another illustration involves two young people on a date. She touches his hand, his arm, then even his thigh while they are talking at dinner. She thinks she is only trying to get to know him. But he thinks she wants sex. Later, when he makes his move, she says "no." But he thinks she means "yes." He believes the sex was consensual. To her, it was forced.

But why do such husbands and dates fail to see they have committed forced sex? The reason seems to lie in the traditional, patriarchal belief that men should be aggressive to win a woman's heart. Resulting from such aggression gone out of control, forced sex is an extension of the traditional pattern of male sexual behavior. The belief about the importance of male aggressiveness is embedded in the culture that encourages rape.

The Culture of Rape   The culture of rape reveals itself through at least three prevailing attitudes toward women.

First, women traditionally have been treated like men's property. If a woman is married, she is, in effect, her husband's property. Thus in most countries and some states in the United States, a man cannot be prosecuted for raping his wife. The reasoning seems to be: How can any man steal what already belongs to

The culture of rape is evident in three prevailing attitudes toward women: that women should be treated as property, that women are objects of sexual aggression and masculinity contests, and that women want to be raped. Men who hold these attitudes are likely to misunderstand or ignore women's signals regarding sexual consent.

him? The property logic may also explain the difficulty of getting a man convicted for raping a "cheap, loose woman" or a known prostitute. Such a female is considered as if she were every man's property, because she has had sex with many men. If a "good" woman is raped, we often say that she has been "ravaged," "ravished," "despoiled," or "ruined," as if she were a piece of property that has been damaged.

Globally, when conquering armies destroy the conquered population's property, they also tend to rape the women as if they were part of that property. During World War II, German soldiers raped massive numbers of Jewish and Russian women after occupying many villages and cities in Europe, and the Japanese army systematically raped women and girls as it invaded Korea, China, and various Southeast Asian countries. Most recently, the Serbian soldiers in Bosnia raped thousands of Muslim women as part of their "ethnic cleansing" campaign.

Second, women are treated as if they are objects of masculinity contests among men. To prove his manhood, a man is culturally pressured to have sex with the largest number of women possible. The pressure to play this masculinity game often comes from friends who ask things like: "Did you score?" "Had any lately?" If the answer is "no," they may say, "What's the matter? Are you gay or something?" Such social pressure tends to make young men want to show off their "masculine" qualities, such as aggressiveness, forcefulness, and violence. Even without peer pressure, the popular belief in sexual conquest as a badge of masculinity already encourages men to be aggressive toward women. If women say "no," men are expected to ignore this response or even translate it into really meaning "yes." Such lessons in sexual conquest often

come from the stereotype of the movie or television hero who forcefully, persistently embraces and kisses the heroine despite her strong resistance and is rewarded when she finally melts in his arms.

In real life, such sexual aggression can easily lead to rape. This is why many sociologists regard rape as an extension of the socially approved, conventional pattern of male sexual behavior. It is also not surprising that members of the Spur Posse, a group of high school boys in California who competed with one another by scoring points for sexual conquests, were only jailed for a few days in 1993 on charges of molesting and raping girls as young as 10. It is also no wonder that other winners of the masculinity game, such as college men with considerable sexual experience, are more likely to rape their dates than the so-called losers, who have little or no sexual experience (Kanin, 1983; Schur, 1984).

Third, there is a popular myth that, deep down, women want to be raped. This myth is often expressed in various ways: "she asked for it"; "she actually wanted it"; "she lied about it (or consented to sex but later decided to 'cry rape')"; and "she was not really hurt (or it was only a form of sex, though without her consent)." In essence, the victim is held responsible for the rape. The victim is assumed to have done something that provoked the man to rape her. That "something" involves being in the "wrong" place (walking alone at night); wearing the "wrong" clothes (short shorts, miniskirts, or some other sexy dress); turning the man on (letting him kiss or pet her); or having "an attitude" (behaving assertively or independently) (Brinson, 1992).

Because of this blame-the-victim assumption, defense attorneys for alleged rapists tend to portray the victim as a willing partner. In one case, the victim was accused of having a "kinky and aggressive" sex life. In another case, the victim was said to be "sexually voracious" and to have "preyed on men" (Lacayo, 1987). The willing-victim myth is a major motivating force behind many rapes. In a study of convicted rapists, 59 percent denied their guilt and blamed their victims instead. They insisted that their victims seduced them, meant "yes" while saying "no" to the sexual assault, and eventually relaxed and enjoyed the rape. Not surprisingly, men who believe this dangerous myth about women are more likely to rape them (Scully and Marolla, 1984).

Corporate Crime

Corporate crimes are committed by company officials without the overt use of force, and their effect on the victims is not readily traceable to the offender. If a miner dies from a lung disease, it is difficult to prove beyond reasonable doubt that he dies *because* the employer violated mine safety regulations. Corporate crimes may be perpetrated not only against employees but also against customers and the general public. Examples include disregard for safety in the workplace, consumer fraud, price-fixing, production of unsafe products, and violations of environmental regulations. Compared with traditional "street crime," corporate crime is more rationally executed, more profitable, and less detectable by law enforcers. In addition, crime in the executive suite is distinguished from crime in the street by three characteristics that help explain the prevalence of corporate crime.

The Criminal's Noncriminal Self-Image   Corporate criminals often see themselves as respectable people rather than common criminals. They maintain their noncriminal self-image through *rationalization.* Violators of price-fixing laws, for example, may insist that they are helping the nation's economy by "stabilizing prices" and serving their companies by "recovering costs." In their book, there is no such crime as price-fixing.

The noncriminal self-image is also maintained through *seeing oneself as a victim rather than an offender.* Corporate criminals argue that they were just unlucky enough to get caught for doing something that practically everyone else does. As a convicted tax offender said, "Everybody cheats on their income tax, 95 percent of the people. Even if it's for $10 it's the same principle" (Benson, 1985).

The noncriminal self-image is further maintained through *denial of criminal intent.* Corporate criminals may admit that they committed the act that landed them in prison, but regard their acts only as mistakes, not something motivated by a guilty, criminal mind.

THE WALL STREET JOURNAL

"The upside of what I'm proposing is a huge profit. The downside is 800 hours of community service."

As a convicted tax offender said, "I'm not a criminal. That is, I'm not a criminal from the standpoint of taking a gun and doing this and that. I'm a criminal from the standpoint of making a mistake, a serious mistake" (Benson, 1985).

The Victim's Unwitting Cooperation   Primarily due to lack of caution or knowledge, many victims unwittingly cooperate with the corporate criminal. In a home improvement scheme, victims do not bother to check the work history of the fraudulent company that solicits them, or they sign a contract without examining its content for such matters as the true price and the credit terms. Some victims purchase goods through the mail without checking the reputation of the firm. Doctors prescribe untested drugs relying only on the pharmaceutical company's salespeople and advertising. It may be difficult for victims to know they are victimized, even if they want to find out the true nature of their victimization. Average grocery shoppers, for example, are hard put to detect such unlawful substances as residues of hormones, antibiotics, pesticides, and nitrites in the meat they buy.

Society's Relative Indifference   Generally, little effort is made to catch corporate criminals. On the rare occasions when they are caught, they seldom go to jail. Their pleas for mercy are heard after they promise to repay their victims or to cooperate in prosecutions against others. They insist that a long prison term will do no good because their lives are already in ruins. Thus, in the more than a dozen convictions for Wall Street insider trading in the late 1980s, most defendants were merely put on probation or sentenced to prison for less than six months. From 1987 through 1992, federal agents charged a staggering 95,045 white-collar and corporate executives with various bank and S&L frauds, but more than 75 percent of these charges were dropped from prosecution (Pizzo and Muolo, 1993). Even when convicted of crimes that caused the deaths of many workers or customers, corporate

Mental illness is extremely common, although most of our mental disorders are not serious. Virtually all of us have experienced a brief bout of anxiety or depression, as appears to be the case of the mother in this picture. Sociologists have long pointed to the role of social forces in the development of mental disorder.

offenders have never been sentenced to death, let alone actually executed, though numerous lower-class criminals have been executed for killing only one person.

Mental Disorder

Mental disorder is far more common than popularly believed. According to the latest surveys, about 19 percent of U.S. adults suffer from a mental disorder serious enough to require psychiatric help or hospitalization, and the figure for adolescents is ten percent (Myers et al., 1984; Robins et al., 1984; Lewinsolhn et al., 1993). The most common disorder is phobia (such as fear of heights or enclosed spaces), followed by depression and alcoholism (Regier et al., 1993). In fact, all of us have been or will be mentally ill in one way or another. Of course, most of our mental disorders are not serious at all. We occasionally come down with only a brief bout of anxiety or depression, "the common cold of mental ailments."

The types of mental disorder that sociologists and psychiatrists study are more serious. They include **psychosis,** typified by loss of touch with reality, and **neurosis,** characterized by a persistent fear, anxiety, or worry about trivial matters. A psychotic can be likened to a person who thinks incorrectly that 2 plus 2 is equal to 10 but strongly believes it to be correct. On the other hand, a neurotic can be compared to a person who thinks correctly that 2 plus 2 is equal to 4 but constantly worries that it may not be so (Thio, 1995).

Sociologists have long suspected that certain social forces are involved in the development of mental disorder. The one that has been most consistently demonstrated by many different studies to be a key factor in mental illness is social class: the lower the social class, the higher the rate of mental disorder.

This finding, however, has prompted two conflicting explanations. One, known as *social causation,* suggests that lower-class people are more prone to mental disorder because they are more likely to have the following experiences: being subjected to social stress, such as unemployment, family problems, or threat of criminal victimization; suffering from psychic frailty, infectious diseases, and neurological impairments; and lacking quality medical treatment, coping ability, and social support. The other explanation, called *drift,* suggests that the heavy concentration of mental disorder in lower-class neighborhoods results from the downward drift of mentally ill people into the neighborhood, coupled with the upward movement of mentally healthy people out of it. This explanation means that being a member of the lower class is a consequence rather than a cause of mental illness. Both explanations have been found to have some basis in fact. In general, the evidence for the drift theory comes from studies of major mental illnesses, especially schizophrenia. The early onset of such illnesses can cause job loss and downward mobility (Jones et al., 1993; Rodgers and Mann, 1993; Fox, 1993). But the evidence for social causation comes from studies of less severe disorders such as depression and phobia. These problems are more likely to result from the social stresses of lower-class lives (Kessler, Price, and Wortman, 1985; Link, Lennon, and Dohrenwend, 1993).

Questions for Discussion and Review

1. What does it mean to call homicide a personal crime?
2. Why do the poor abuse drugs?
3. What is the culture of rape and how does it encourage rape?
4. What distinguishes corporate crime from street crime?
5. How common is mental disorder in the United States, and what does social class have to do with the disorder?

FUNCTIONALIST PERSPECTIVE

Most scholars other than sociologists generally attribute deviance to a certain biological or psychological abnormality in the individual. But sociologists have long assumed that there is nothing physically or mentally wrong with most deviants. This assumption is a legacy of the French sociologist Emile Durkheim (1858–1917), one of the founders of functionalism in the discipline. For him, deviance is not only normal but also beneficial to society.

Durkheim: Functionalist Theory

According to Durkheim, deviance can serve a number of functions for society:

First, deviance helps *enhance conformity* in society as a whole. Norms are basically abstract and ambiguous, subject to conflicting interpretations. Even criminal laws, which are far more clear-cut than other norms, can be confusing. The criminal act a deviant commits and is punished for provides other citizens with a concrete example of what constitutes a crime. From deviants we can learn the difference between conformity and deviance, seeing the boundary between right and wrong more clearly. Once aware of this boundary, we are more likely to stay on the side of "right-ness."

Second, deviance *strengthens solidarity* among law-abiding members of society. Differing values and interests may divide them, but collective outrage against deviants as a common enemy can unite them. Because deviance promotes social cohesion that decreases crime, Durkheim (1915) described it as "a factor in public health, an integral part of all healthy societies."

Third, deviance *provides a safety valve* for discontented people. Through relatively minor forms of deviance, they can strike out against the social order without doing serious harm to themselves or others. As Albert Cohen (1966) suggested, prostitution may serve as a safety valve for marriage in a male-dominated society, because the customer is unlikely to form an emotional attachment to the prostitute. In contrast, a sexual relationship with a friend is more likely to develop into a love affair that could destroy the marriage.

Fourth, deviance can *induce social change*. Martin Luther King, Jr., and other civil rights leaders were jeered and imprisoned for their opposition to segregation, but they moved the United States toward greater racial equality.

There is a limit, however, to the validity of Durkheim's functionalist theory. If deviance is widespread, it can threaten social order in at least two ways. First, it can wreck interpersonal relations. Alcoholism tears apart many families. If a friend flies into a rage and tries to kill us, it will be difficult to maintain a harmonious relationship. Second, deviance can undermine trust. If there were many killers, robbers, and rapists living in our neighborhoods, we would find it impossible to welcome neighbors into our home as guests or babysitters. Nevertheless, Durkheim's theory is useful for demolishing the commonsense belief that deviance is always harmful. Deviance can bring benefits if it occurs within limits.

Merton: Strain Theory

In the 1930s U.S. sociologist Robert Merton agreed with Durkheim that deviance is "an integral part of all healthy societies." However, rather than seeing deviance as a *cause* of social solidarity, as Durkheim did, Merton regarded deviance as a normal *consequence* of a culture's contribution to a prosperous social order.

According to Merton, U.S. culture places too much emphasis on success as a valued goal. From kindergarten to college, teachers prod students to achieve "the American Dream." Parents and coaches pressure even Little League players not just to play well but to win. The media often glorify winning not only in sports but in business, politics, and other arenas of life. All this motivates people to work hard, thereby contributing to society's prosperity. But at the same time not all people are provided with equal opportunities (such as good jobs) for success. There is, then, an inconsistency between too much emphasis on the success *goal* and too little emphasis on the availability of legitimate *means* for achieving that goal. Such inconsistency produces a strain among people in the lower classes, pressuring them to achieve success through what Merton calls *innovation*—using illegitimate means of achieving success, such as committing robbery or selling drugs.

But most people do not resort to innovation as a response to the goal-means inconsistency. In addition to innovation, four other responses are possible, depending on whether the cultural goal of success and institutionalized means are accepted or rejected (see Table 6.2):

1. *Conformity,* the most popular form of response, involves accepting both the cultural goal of success and the use of legitimate means for achieving that goal.

2. *Innovation,* the response described earlier, involves accepting the goal of success, but rejecting the use of socially accepted means to achieve it, turning instead to unconventional, illegitimate methods.

3. *Ritualism* occurs when people no longer set high success goals but continue to toil as conscientious, diligent workers.

4. *Retreatism* is withdrawal from society, caring neither about success nor about working. Retreatists include vagabonds, outcasts, and drug addicts.

5. *Rebellion* occurs when people reject and attempt to change both the goals and the means approved by society. The rebel tries to overthrow the existing system and establish a new system with different goals and means. An example would be attempting to replace the current U.S. competitive pursuit of fame and riches with a new system that enhances social relations through cooperation.

Merton's theory is useful for explaining the higher rates of robbery, theft, and other property crimes among lower-class people. But the theory fails to explain embezzlement, tax fraud, and other white-collar crimes. As a functionalist, Merton assumes that the same value—belief in *material* success—is shared throughout our society. But this assumption runs counter to the pluralistic and conflicting nature of U.S. society, where many groups differentiated by class, gender, ethnicity, or religion do not share the same values. Some groups are more interested in pursuing strong relationships than "big bucks."

Hirschi: Control Theory

A functionalist like Merton, U.S. sociologist Travis Hirschi (1969) assumed that the family, school, and other social institutions can greatly contribute to

TABLE 6.2
Merton's Typology of Responses to Goal-Means Inconsistency
In U.S. society, according to Merton, there is too much emphasis on success but too little emphasis on the legitimate means for achieving success. Such inconsistency may cause deviant behavior, yet various people respond to it differently.

Response	Success goal	Legitimate means
1. Conformity	+	+
2. Innovation	+	−
3. Ritualism	−	+
4. Retreatism	−	−
5. Rebellion	− +	− +

NOTE: + signifies accepting; − rejecting; and − + rejecting the old and introducing the new.

SOURCE: By permission of The Free Press, a Division of Macmillan, Inc., from *Social Theory and Structure* by Robert K. Merton. Copyright 1957 by The Free Press; copyright renewed 1985 by Robert K. Merton.

social order by controlling deviant tendencies in all of us. If such control is lacking or weak, in Hirschi's view, people will commit deviant acts.

According to Hirschi, the best control mechanism against deviance is our bond to others or, by extension, society. He proposed four types of social bond:

1. *Attachment to conventional people and institutions.* Teenagers, for example, may show this attachment by loving and respecting their parents, making friends with conventional peers, liking school, or working hard to develop intellectual skills.

2. *Commitment to conformity.* This commitment can be seen in the time and energy devoted to conventional activities—getting an education, holding a job, developing an occupational skill, improving professional status, building a business, or acquiring a reputation for virtue.

3. *Involvement in conventional activities.* Following the maxim that "idleness is the devil's workshop," people keep themselves so busy doing conventional things that they do not have time to take part in deviant activities or even to think about deviance.

4. *Belief in the moral validity of social rules.* This is the conviction that the rules of conventional society

should be obeyed. People show this moral belief by respecting the law.

Many studies have supported Hirschi's theory that the lack of social bond *causes* deviance. But most of these studies have ignored, as does the theory, the fact that the lack of bond can also be the *effect* of delinquency. Just as the loss of bond can cause youths to commit delinquency, so delinquency can cause youths to lose their bond to society.

Braithwaite: Shaming Theory

While Hirschi sees how society controls us through bonding, Australian sociologist John Braithwaite (1989) looks at how society controls us through shaming. Shaming involves an expression of disapproval designed to evoke remorse in the wrongdoer. There are two types of shaming: disintegrative and reintegrative. In **disintegrative shaming**, the wrongdoer is punished in such a way as to be stigmatized, rejected, or ostracized, in effect, banished from conventional society. It is the same as stigmatization. **Reintegrative shaming** is more positive and involves making wrongdoers feel guilty while showing them understanding, forgiveness, or even respect. It is the kind of shaming that affectionate parents administer to their misbehaving child. It involves "hating the sin but loving the sinner." Thus reintegrative shaming serves to reintegrate—welcome back—the wrongdoer into conventional society.

Reintegrative shaming is more common in communitarian societies (marked by strong social relationships or interdependence), such as Japan. Disintegrative shaming is more prevalent in less communitarian societies (characterized by weaker social relationships), such as the United States. Whereas reintegrative shaming usually discourages further deviance, disintegrative shaming tends to encourage more deviance. This is one reason why crime rates are higher in the United States than in Japan. Braithwaite concludes by arguing that the United States can significantly reduce its crime rates if it emphasizes reintegrative shaming in dealing with criminals, as Japanese society does, rather than stigmatization.

Braithwaite may be correct that reintegrative shaming can reduce crime, especially if it is applied to first-time offenders who have committed relatively minor crimes. But it can hardly have the same positive impact on hardened criminals with little sense of shame for their crimes.

Questions for Discussion and Review

1. According to Durkheim, in what ways can deviance benefit society?
2. How did Merton explain the high crime rate in the United States?
3. How does Hirschi's control theory explain deviance?
4. In Braithwaite's view, how is shaming related to society and deviance?

The use of stocks is an example of disintegrative shaming, in which a wrongdoer is punished in such a way as to be stigmatized or rejected by conventional society. Shaming theory suggests that disintegrative shaming is less effective in controlling deviance than reintegrative shaming, in which wrongdoers are made to feel guilty at the same time as they are shown understanding and forgiveness and welcomed back into conventional society.

CONFLICT PERSPECTIVE

Functionalists assume the importance of social consensus for explaining deviance. Thus, for Durkheim, deviance is functional to society as a whole and hence to virtually all groups in it. To Merton, nearly all Americans worship money as their god. To Hirschi, a bond to society is always a desirable goal for everybody if they want to avoid deviance. And to Braithwaite, shaming is a widely shared value in communitarian societies. By contrast, conflict theorists assume the importance of social conflict—as in the form of inequalities or power differentials—for explaining deviance.

Conflict Theory

Many people assume that the law is based on the consent of citizens, that it treats citizens equally, and that it serves the best interest of society. If we simply read the U.S. Constitution and statutes, this assumption may indeed be justified. But focusing on the *law on the books,* as William Chambliss (1969) pointed out, may be misleading. The law on the books does indeed say that the authorities ought to be fair and just. But are they? To understand crime, Chambliss argued, we need to look at the *law in action,* at how legal authorities actually discharge their duty. After studying the law in action, Chambliss concluded that legal authorities are actually unfair and unjust, favoring the rich and powerful over the poor and weak.

Richard Quinney (1974) blamed unjust law directly on the capitalist system. "Criminal law," said Quinney, "is used by the state and the ruling class to secure the survival of the capitalist system." This involves the dominant class doing four things: First, it defines as criminal those behaviors (robbery, murder, and the like) that threaten its interests. Second, it hires law enforcers to apply those definitions and protect its interests. Third, it exploits the subordinate class by paying low wages so that the resulting oppressive life conditions virtually force the powerless to commit what those in power have defined as crimes. Fourth, it uses these criminal actions to spread and reinforce the popular view that the subordinate class is dangerous, in order to justify its concerns with making and enforcing the law. These factors and the relationships among them are shown in Figure 6.4. The upshot of these four related factors is the production and maintenance of a high level of crime in society (Quinney, 1974).

To Marxists, the capitalists' ceaseless drive to increase profit by cutting labor costs has created a large class of unemployed workers. These people become

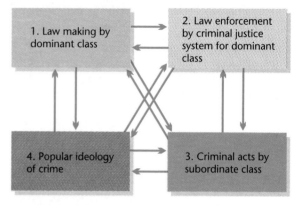

Source: Data from Richard Quinney, *The Social Reality of Crime* (Boston: Little, Brown, 1970).

FIGURE 6.4
Quinney's Conflict Theory
These four factors influence one another, helping to produce and maintain a high level of crime in society.

what Marxists call **marginal surplus population**—superfluous or useless to the economy—and they are compelled to commit property crimes to survive. Marxists argue that the exploitative nature of capitalism also causes violent crimes (such as murder and assault) and noncriminal deviance (such as alcoholism and mental illness). As Sheila Balkan and her colleagues (1980) explained, economic "marginality leads to a lack of self-esteem and a sense of powerlessness and alienation, which create intense pressures on individuals. Many people turn to violence in order to vent their frustrations and strike out against symbols of authority, and others turn this frustration inward and experience severe emotional difficulties."

Marxists further contend that the monopolistic and oligopolistic nature of capitalism encourages corporate crime, because "when only a few firms dominate a sector of the economy they can more easily collude to fix prices, divide up the market, and eliminate competitors" (Greenberg, 1981). Smaller firms, unable to compete with giant corporations and earn enough profits, are also motivated to shore up their sagging profits by illegal means.

Conflict theory is useful for explaining why most laws favor the rich and powerful and why the poor and powerless commit most of the unprofitable crimes in society (such as murder, assault, and robbery). The theory is also useful for explaining why crime rates began to soar after the formerly communist countries in Russia and Eastern Europe embraced capitalism. But the theory has been criticized for implying that all laws are unjust and capitalism is the source of all crimes.

Power Theory

It seems obvious that power inequality affects the quality of people's lives. The rich and powerful live better than the poor and powerless. Similarly, power inequality affects the quality of *deviant* activities likely to be engaged in by people. Thus, the powerful are more likely to perpetrate profitable crimes, such as corporate crime, while the powerless are more likely to commit unprofitable crimes, such as homicide and assault. In other words, power—or the lack of it—largely determines the *type* of crime people are likely to commit.

Power can also be an important *cause* of deviance. More precisely, the likelihood of powerful people perpetrating profitable crimes is greater than the likelihood of powerless persons committing unprofitable crimes. It is, for example, more likely for bank executives to quietly rob customers than for jobless persons to violently rob banks. Analysis of the deviance literature suggests three reasons why deviance is more common among the powerful (Thio, 1995).

First, the powerful have a *stronger deviant motivation.* Much of this motivation stems from **relative deprivation**—feeling unable to achieve relatively high aspirations. Compared with the powerless, whose aspirations are typically low, the powerful are more likely to raise their aspirations so high that they cannot be realized. The more people experience relative deprivation, the more likely they are to commit deviant acts.

Second, the powerful enjoy *greater deviant opportunity*. Obviously a rich banker enjoys more legitimate opportunities than a poor worker to make money. But suppose they both want to acquire *illegitimately* a large sum of money. The banker will have access to more and better opportunities that make it easy to defraud customers. The banker further has a good chance of getting away with it because the kind of skill needed to pull off the crime is similar to the skills required for holding the bank position in the first place. In contrast, the poor worker would find his or her illegitimate opportunity limited to crudely robbing the banker, an illegitimate opportunity being further limited by a high risk of arrest.

Third, the powerful are subjected to *weaker social control*. Generally, the powerful have more influence in the making and enforcement of laws. The laws against higher-status criminals are therefore relatively lenient and seldom enforced, but the laws against lower-status criminals are harsher and more often enforced. Not a single corporate criminal, for example, has ever been sentenced to death for marketing some untested drug that "cleanly" kills many people. Given the lesser control imposed on them, the powerful are likely to feel freer to use some deviant means to amass their fortunes and power.

There is some evidence to support this theory, presented in greater detail elsewhere (Thio, 1995). In the United States, for example, there are about six industrial deaths caused by corporate violations of safety regulations for every one homicide committed by a poor person. In Great Britain, the ratio of industrial deaths to homicides is seven to one (Box, 1983). It is difficult, however, to get direct data on powerful deviants. Compared with their powerless counterparts, powerful deviants are more able to carry out their deviant activities in a sophisticated and consequently undetectable fashion.

Feminist Theory

Many theories about deviance are meant to apply to both sexes. But feminists argue that those theories are actually about men only. Consequently, the theories may be valid for male behavior but not necessarily for female.

Consider Merton's strain theory. First, this theory assumes that people are inclined to strive for material success. This may be true for men but not necessarily for women. In a patriarchal society, women have been socialized differently from men. Consequently, women are traditionally less interested in achieving material success, which often requires "one-upmanship," and more given to attaining emotional fulfillment through close, personal relations with others. Second, the strain theory assumes that women who have a strong desire for economic success but little access to opportunities are as likely as men in similar circumstances to commit a crime. Nowadays, given the greater availability of high positions for women in the economic world, the number of ambitious women in the "men's world" is on the rise. But, faced with the lack of opportunities for greater economic success, these women have not been as likely as men to engage in deviant activities. And finally, the strain theory explicitly states that Americans are likely to commit a crime because their society overemphasizes the importance of holding high success goals while failing to provide the necessary opportunities for all of its citizens to realize those goals. But this may be more relevant to men than to women. Despite their greater lack of success opportunities, women still have lower crime rates than men (Beirne and Messerschmidt, 1995).

The lack of relevancy to women in strain and other conventional theories of deviance stems from a male-biased failure to take women into account. In redressing this problem, feminist theory focuses on women. First, the theory deals with women as *victims*, mostly of rape and sexual harassment. The crimes against women are said to reflect the patriarchal society's attempt to put women in their place so as to perpetuate men's dominance.

Feminist theory also looks at women as *offenders*. It argues that the recent increase in female crime has not been great enough to be significant. This is considered to reflect the fact that gender equality is still far from being a social reality. Like employment opportunities, criminal opportunities are still much less available to women than men; hence, women are still much less likely to engage in criminal activities. When women do commit crimes, they tend to be the types of crimes that reflect women's subordinate position in society: minor property crimes, such as shoplifting, passing bad checks, welfare fraud, and petty credit-card fraud. In fact, recent increases in female crime primarily involve these minor crimes, largely reflecting the increasing feminization of poverty—more women falling below the poverty line. Not surprisingly, most women criminals are unemployed, without a high school diploma, and single mothers with small children. They hardly fit the popular image of the newly empowered, liberated women, who benefit from any increase in gender equality. There is no significant increase in female involvement in more profitable crimes, such as burglary, robbery, embezzlement, and business fraud (Day and Chesney-Lind, 1988; Weisheit, 1992; Miller, 1995).

Feminist theory is useful for understanding female deviance. But its focus on female deviance cannot be generalized to male deviance.

Questions for Discussion and Review

1. How does conflict theory explain the nature of laws and the cause of deviance?
2. How does the power theory explain why deviance is more prevalent among the powerful?
3. How does feminist theory differ from other theories?

SYMBOLIC INTERACTIONIST PERSPECTIVE

Both the functionalist and conflict perspectives portray deviance as a *product* of society. In contrast, symbolic interactionists see deviance as a *process* of interaction between the supposed deviant and the rest of society. And that process of interaction involves subjective interpretations that shape the world of deviance.

Differential Association Theory

According to Edwin Sutherland (1939), deviance is learned through interactions with other people. Individuals learn not only how to perform deviant acts but also how to define these actions. Various social groups have different norms; acts considered deviant by the dominant culture may be viewed positively by some groups. Each person is likely to be exposed to both positive and negative definitions of these actions. An individual is likely to become deviant if the individual engages in **differential association**, the process of acquiring through interaction with others "an *excess* of definitions favorable to violation of law over definitions unfavorable to violation of law" (Sutherland, 1939).

Suppose a father tells his children that "it's all right to steal when you are poor." He is giving them a pro-deviant definition. On the other hand, if the father tells his children that "it's wrong to steal," he is providing an anti-deviant definition. If the youngsters pick up a greater number of pro-deviant definitions, they are likely to become deviant.

While definitions play a crucial role in becoming deviant, Sutherland emphasized more the importance of social interaction because it is the source of definitions. Thus, Sutherland also stressed that deviance will arise if interactions with those who define deviant behavior positively outweigh interactions with those who define it negatively. Which definitions are most influential depends not just on the frequency and duration of the interactions but also on the strength of the relationship between the interactants.

Sutherland developed his theory to explain various forms of deviance, including white-collar crimes such as tax evasion, embezzlement, and price-fixing. All these misdeeds were shown to result from some association with groups that viewed the wrongdoings as acceptable. Still, it is difficult to determine precisely what differential association is. Most people cannot identify the persons from whom they have learned a pro-deviant or anti-deviant definition, much less whether they have been exposed to one definition more frequently, longer, or more intensely than the other.

Labeling Theory

Most theories focus on the *causes* of deviance. In contrast, the labeling theory, which emerged in the 1960s, concentrates on *societal reaction* to rule violation and the impact of this reaction on the rule violator.

According to labeling theorists, society tends to react to a rule-breaking act by labeling it deviant. Deviance, then, is not something that a person does but merely a label imposed on that behavior. As Howard Becker (1963) said, "Deviance is *not* a quality of the act the person commits, but rather a consequence of the application by others of rules and sanctions to an 'offender.' The deviant is one to whom that label has successfully been applied; deviant behavior is behavior that people so label." The label itself has serious and negative consequences for the individual, even beyond any immediate punishment.

Once a person is labeled a thief or a delinquent or a drunk, the individual may be stuck with that label for life and be rejected and isolated as a result. Finding a job and making friends may be extremely difficult. More important, the person may come to accept the label and commit more deviant acts. Labeling people as deviants, in short, can push them toward further and greater deviance.

Much earlier, Frank Tannenbaum (1938) noted this process of becoming deviant. According to him, children may break windows, annoy people, steal apples, and play hooky—and innocently consider these activities just a way of having fun. Edwin Lemert (1951) coined the term **primary deviance** to refer to these violations of norms that a person commits for the first time and without considering them deviant. Now suppose parents, teachers, and police consider a child's pranks to be a sign of delinquency. They may "dramatize the evil" by admonishing or scolding the child. They may even go further, hauling the child into juvenile court and labeling the child as bad, a delinquent—a deviant. The child may develop a bad self-image and try to live up to this self-image by becoming increasingly involved in deviant behavior. Lemert used the term **secondary deviance** to refer to such repeated norm violations, which the violators themselves recognize as deviant. Secondary deviants are, in effect, confirmed or career deviants.

Labeling theory helps us understand how secondary deviance might develop, and it sensitizes us to the power of labels. But the theory has been criticized for at least two reasons. First, it cannot explain why primary deviance occurs in the first place. Second, it cannot deal with deviance that occurs in secret; unknown to others, it cannot be labeled deviance. Without the label, logically the theory cannot define it as deviance.

Phenomenological Theory

Phenomenologists delve into people's subjectivity (called *phenomenon*), including their consciousness, perception, feelings, and opinions about deviance. To really understand deviance, phenomenologists say, we must study people's subjective interpretations of their own deviant experiences.

According to labeling theory, tagging a person as deviant can make the person deviant. A social drinker who gets labeled as "a man who can hold his liquor" can become alcoholic because people begin to pressure him to live up to that image.

Generally, phenomenological studies have revealed that deviants tend to see themselves and their deviance in some positive way and then behave accordingly. This is what Harold Garfinkel (1967) found in his classic study of Agnes, a hermaphrodite (a person with both male and female sex organs). Agnes was raised as a boy until high school. At 17 she developed an attractive female figure. By then she dropped out of school, left home, moved to another city, and tried to begin a new life as a woman. A year later, she went to the UCLA medical center to request a sex-change operation. Garfinkel interviewed her extensively before she underwent surgery.

Garfinkel found that Agnes saw herself as a normal woman and did her best to convince others that she was. She told Garfinkel that she was merely a normal woman who happened to have a physical defect comparable to any other deformity such as a harelip or clubfoot. Like any other normal person with a deformity, she felt that it was only natural for her to want to have hers—the male organ—removed. Her self-concept as a normal woman further led her to claim that, as a sexual organ, her penis was "dead," that she had no sexual pleasure from it and felt no sexual attraction to women. She wanted it to be replaced by a surgically constructed vagina. Her self-concept as a normal woman also caused her to make sure that others would not suspect her of having the male organ, so she always wore a bathing suit with a skirt and she never undressed in her female roommate's presence.

In his more recent analysis of murderers, robbers, and other criminals, Jack Katz (1988) also found a similarly positive self-perception that conflicts with society's negative view of the deviant. Murderers, for example, tend to see themselves as morally superior to their victims. In most cases of homicide, because the victims have humiliated them, the killers have felt outraged and considered the killing a justifiable way of defending their identity, dignity, or respectability.

Phenomenological theory is useful for understanding the subjective world of deviants. But it is doubtful that all, or even most, deviants have a positive view of themselves and their deviance. Some are bound to develop a negative self-image from having been condemned or ridiculed by society, as suggested by labeling theory.

The key points of each of the theories presented under the three sociological perspectives are summarized in Table 6.3.

Questions for Discussion and Review

1. How does differential association lead to deviance?
2. What occurs when some people move from primary to secondary deviance?
3. What does phenomenological theory tell us about deviants?

CONTROLLING DEVIANCE

After discussing various perspectives and theories about deviance, we need to deal with the more practical issues that concern many people today, namely, how to control deviance. As discussed in Chapter 3 (Socialization), society transmits its values to individuals through socialization. If families, schools, and other socializing agents do their jobs well, then individuals internalize the values of their society, accepting society's norms as their own. They tend to become conformists and law-abiding citizens.

Internalization through socialization is the most efficient way of controlling deviance. It produces unconscious, spontaneous self-control. As a result, most people find it natural to conform to most social norms most of the time. Violating the norms makes them feel guilty, ashamed, or at least uncomfortable. They act as their own police officers.

Nevertheless, for reasons suggested by the various theories that we have discussed, a few people commit serious crimes, and everyone deviates occasionally, at least from some trivial norms. Thus, control by others is also needed to limit deviance and maintain social order.

Social Control

Social control is the process by which individuals are pressured by society to conform to social norms. It may be either informal or formal. Teachers, peer groups, and even strangers enforce *informal* controls through frowning, gossip, criticism, or ridicule. When deviant acts are serious, *formal* controls are usually imposed by police, judges, prison guards, and other law-enforcement agents.

In small, nonindustrialized societies, informal control is the primary or only means of handling deviance. It may involve such mild expressions of disapproval as a frown, scowl, or scolding, as in modern industrialized societies. But it may also call for more serious punishment, such as beating, maiming, or killing. Such informal control is administered on a private basis, usually by the aggrieved party. The Mayan Indians of south Mexico believe that you should kill a person who has wronged you. The Ifugao of the Philippines consider it necessary for any "self-respecting man" to do away with an adulterer caught red-handed. Violence in these societies is nonetheless quite rare—as are adultery and other deviances—apparently a testament to the effectiveness of informal control. The deterrent effect of informal control in traditional societies is greater than that of formal control in modern societies. As Donald Black (1983) pointed out, in the 1950s the rape incidence among the Gusii of Kenya shot up after the British colonial government prohibited traditional violence against the rapist and started to use British law to deal with the criminal.

But in large, industrialized societies, there is an extensive system of formal control. Perhaps formal control has become more important in modern nations because they have become more heterogeneous and more impersonal than traditional societies. This societal change may have increased social conflicts and enhanced the need for formal control, popularly called the "criminal justice system."

TABLE 6.3
Perspectives and Theories of Deviance

Functionalist Perspective

- *Durkheim's functionalist theory*   Deviance benefits society by enhancing conformity, strengthening social solidarity, safely releasing discontent, and inducing social change.

- *Merton's strain theory*   U.S. crime rate is high because the society emphasizes the importance of success without providing equal opportunities for achieving it.

- *Hirschi's control theory*   The absence of social bonds causes deviance.

- *Braithwaite's shaming theory*   Disintegrative shaming causes deviance.

Conflict Perspective

- *Conflict theory*   For Chambliss, law enforcement favors the rich and powerful over the poor and weak. For Quinney, the dominant class produces crime by making laws, enforcing laws, oppressing subordinate class, and spreading crime ideology. For Marxists, deviance and crime stem from the exploitative nature of capitalism.

- *Power theory*   Because of stronger deviant motivation, greater deviant opportunity, and weaker social control, the powerful are more likely to engage in profitable deviance than the powerless in unprofitable deviance.

- *Feminist theory*   Critical of conventional theories for being largely inapplicable to women, while suggesting that the status of women as victims and offenders reflects the continuing subordination of women in patriarchal society.

Symbolic Interactionist Perspective

- *Differential association theory*   Deviance arises if pro-deviant definitions outweigh anti-deviant definitions acquired in social interactions.

- *Labeling theory*   Being labeled deviant by society leads people to see themselves as deviant and live up to this self-image by committing more deviance.

- *Phenomenological theory*   Looking into people's subjective interpretation of their own experiences is key to understanding their deviant behavior.

Criminal Justice

The criminal justice system is a network of police, courts, and prisons. These law enforcers are supposed to protect society, but they are also a potential threat to an individual's freedom. If they wanted to ensure that not a single criminal could slip away, the police would have to deprive innocent citizens of their rights and liberties. They would restrict our freedom of movement and invade our privacy—by tapping phones, reading mail, searching homes, stopping pedestrians for questioning, and blockading roads. No matter how law-abiding we might be, we would always be treated like crime suspects—and some of us would almost certainly fall into the dragnet.

To prevent such abuses, the criminal justice system in the United States is restrained by the U.S. Constitution and laws. We have the right to be presumed innocent until proven guilty, the right not to incriminate ourselves, and many other legal protections. The ability of the police to search homes and question suspects is limited. Thus, our freedom, especially from being wrongly convicted and imprisoned, is protected.

In short, the criminal justice system faces a dilemma: If it does not catch enough criminals, the streets will not be safe; if it tries to apprehend too many, people's freedom will be in danger. Striking a balance between effective protection from criminals and respect for individual freedom is far from easy. This may be why the criminal justice system is criticized from both the right and the left, by one group for coddling criminals and by the other for being too harsh.

Both criticisms have some merit. Most criminals in the United States are never punished. Of the 35 million crimes committed every year, less than half—about 15 million more serious crimes—are reported to the police. Out of these serious crimes, only 20 percent (3 million) result in arrest and prosecution. Of these three million prosecuted, two million are convicted, of which 25 percent (500,000) are sent to prison. Ultimately, then, *less than 2 percent* of the original 35 million offenders are put behind bars (Anderson, 1994). Moreover, most of these prisoners do not serve their full terms because they are released on parole. The average prisoner serves only about one-third of the sentence.

Does this mean that the U.S. criminal justice system is soft on criminals? Not necessarily. The United States treats convicted criminals more severely than any other democratic nation. It has the dubious distinction of being the No. 1 jailer in the world (see Figure 6.5). Since the early 1980s the U.S. prison population has more than doubled to over one million inmates. With the 1994 "three strikes and you're out" law (which mandates life sentences for a third violent crime), the prison population is expected to continue growing. Imprisonment is also generally longer than in other democratic countries. The length of imprisonment is generally measured in months and weeks in Sweden, but in years in the United States. The United States is also the only industrialized nation in the West that still executes convicted murderers.

Does the comparatively harsh treatment in the United States help to decrease crime rates? Apparently not. Although the number of people behind bars has more than doubled since the early 1980s, the rate of crime has remained about the same (U.S. Census Bureau, 1994). In addition, the rate of **recidivism**—repeated commission of crimes—is extremely high. As Figure 6.6 shows, about eight out of every ten prisoners have served time before. Although these recidivists constitute a small minority of the criminal population, they have committed most of the crimes in society. The prisons are in effect "crime schools," producing tougher, more motivated criminals. Such schools are expensive, though: it costs more to send a person to prison than to college. A number of states have hired private companies to run some of their prisons at far lower cost. Nonetheless, because of wide-

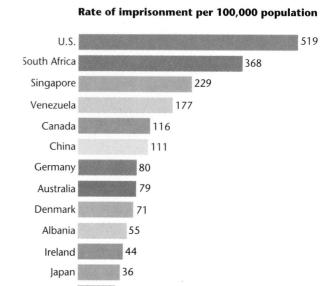

FIGURE 6.5
Imprisonment: A Global View

Rate of imprisonment per 100,000 population

U.S.	519
South Africa	368
Singapore	229
Venezuela	177
Canada	116
China	111
Germany	80
Australia	79
Denmark	71
Albania	55
Ireland	44
Japan	36
India	23

Source: Data from the *Sentencing Project*, 1994.

spread belief that crime is getting out of control, there is increased outcry to "lock 'em up and throw away the key." The general public today is far more interested in using prisons to punish criminals than to deter crime.

The War on Drugs

Over the last 15 years or so, the drug problem in the United States has become considerably worse. In 1981, there were about three million drug addicts; today the figure is around six million. The number of drug-overdose deaths and drug-related homicides has soared in cities across the country, even in the midst of an eight-fold increase in the federal budget for the war on drugs (Massing, 1993). The drug war is obviously a colossal failure. Most drug experts attribute the failure to the government's emphasis on law enforcement over drug education and treatment. But why the emphasis on law enforcement? A likely reason is a lack of concern for the welfare of the poor and minorities. Witness the fact that the drug war is waged largely against poor African Americans and Hispanics, who are much more likely than affluent whites to be arrested and convicted for drug offenses.

Failure of the law-enforcement approach has led to calls for legalization of drugs. Advocates of legalization contend that, like Prohibition (of alcohol) in the

FIGURE 6.6
Recidivists Outnumber First-Timers in Prison

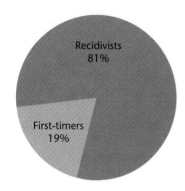

Source: Data from U.S. Bureau of Justice Statistics, 1994.

1920s, the current drug laws do more harm than good. They are said to generate many crimes, including homicides, and to encourage police corruption. By legalizing drugs, the proponents argue, the government can take away obscene profits from drug traffickers, end police corruption, and reduce crime drastically. Finally, legalizers believe that with legalization the huge amount of money currently spent on law enforcement can be used for drug treatment and education, which will dramatically reduce drug abuse.

Those who oppose legalization respond that, if drugs are legalized, drug use and addiction will skyrocket. As William Bennett (1989), a former national drug-control policy director, says, "After the repeal of Prohibition, consumption of alcohol soared by 350%." Sociologist Elliott Currie (1993) also argues that legalization cannot solve the problem of widespread drug abuse and crime, because legalizers, just like the drug warriors, ignore the root cause of the problem, which is poverty, racism, or inequality. Thus, Currie proposes that the government eradicate the cause of the problem by providing employment to all, increasing the minimum wage, expanding the Job Corps, increasing health care for the poor, offering paid family leave, providing affordable housing, and reducing social inequality.

Questions for Discussion and Review

1. What is the difference between formal and informal control?
2. In what ways can the criminal justice system balance the need to catch criminals with the need to respect individual freedom?
3. Can the war on drugs be won?

A GLOBAL ANALYSIS OF DEVIANCE

An analysis of deviance around the world reveals societal differences in a number of deviant activities (Thio, 1995).

First, homicide is generally more likely to occur in poor than in rich countries, suggesting that poverty is a major contributing factor. Among rich countries, the United States has the highest homicide rate, largely because the poverty rate is considerably higher than in Western Europe, Canada, and Japan. But the ratio of property crimes to violent crimes is generally higher in rich than in poor countries. While poverty serves as a strong *motivation* for committing a crime, property crimes cannot occur without the necessary *opportunities*, namely, properties being available as targets for robbery or theft. Since such opportunities abound in more prosperous countries, more property crimes can be expected.

Second, prostitution has recently become a fast-growing global industry. Many unemployed women in formerly communist Russia and Eastern Europe have flocked to more prosperous Western Europe to sell sex. Some of these women, however, have been tricked into prostitution with promises of singing, dancing, modeling, or waitressing jobs from pimps posing as businessmen in their home countries. More women from poor Asian countries have been lured with promises of legitimate jobs into Japan and Western Europe only to be sold to brothels. Large numbers of Thai and Filipino prostitutes that remain in their home countries cater to local men as well as to hordes of Japanese and Western men on organized sex tours. Most of these prostitutes come from poor villages. Thus, poverty, along with exploitation by richer countries, contributes to the sex trade.

Third, suicide is generally more common in modern than in traditional societies. But among modern societies, countries such as Finland, Denmark, and Austria suffer higher rates of suicide than do the United States, Spain, and Italy. The higher suicide rate seems related to greater social equality. In societies with greater equality, people are less subjected to social regulation, a key contributor to suicide. As Durkheim (1915) suggested, less regulated individuals are more encouraged to expect too much from life and thus become more liable to greater frustration when expectations fail to materialize.

Fourth, organized crime differs across societies. Members' loyalty to the crime organization seems stronger in Japan and Hong Kong than in the United States and Italy. The syndicates in Hong Kong, Japan, Italy, and Russia have penetrated legitimate business and politics more deeply, compared with those in the

United States. Not surprisingly, antisyndicate measures fail more frequently in those countries than in the United States. There is one important similarity between U.S. organized crime and its counterparts in other countries. They all serve as a "crooked ladder of upward mobility" for the ambitious poor, who can become rich by joining a syndicate.

Question for Discussion and Review

1. How do some deviances vary from society to society?

CHAPTER REVIEW

1. *What is deviance?* It is an act considered by public consensus or by the powerful at a given time and place to be a violation of some social rule.

2. *In what ways does homicide occur?* Homicide involves nonstrangers more than strangers. It most frequently takes place during weekend evenings, especially for lower-class offenders. Guns are often used to commit homicide, and their easy availability has contributed to a startling upsurge in teen homicide.

3. *Who is more likely to abuse drugs and why?* Drug abusers tend to be the poor, for several reasons: drugs can meet their need for status, help them cope with their harsh lives, and provide them a sense of purpose. An additional reason is easy access to drugs.

4. *How common is rape in the United States?* Rape is very common: About 22 percent of women, or 15 million, have been forced to have sex. Most of these rapes are committed by lovers and other intimates rather than by strangers. *What is the culture of rape?* It encourages men to rape women by treating women as if they are men's property, as if they are the trophies of men's masculinity contests, and as if they want to be raped.

5. *How does corporate crime differ from street crime?* Corporate crime is more rationally executed, more profitable, and less detectable. Corporate offenders do not see themselves as criminals, their victims unwittingly cooperate with them, and society does little to punish them.

6. *What group is more likely than others to be mentally ill?* The poor are more likely to be mentally ill. There are two conflicting explanations: One is the stressful life of the poor. The other is that the mentally ill move into lower-class neighborhoods and the healthy ones, out of them.

7. *What does Durkheim's functionalist theory tell us about deviance?* Deviance helps enhance conformity, strengthen social solidarity, provide a safe release for discontent, and induce social change. *According to Merton's strain theory, what is the cause of deviance?* U.S. society emphasizes the importance of success without providing equal opportunities for achieving it. One possible response to this inconsistency is deviance. *How are Hirschi's and Braithwaite's theories similar and how are they different?* Both assume that social control leads to conformity, and, therefore, the absence of control causes deviance. According to Hirschi, the absence of control arises from a lack of social bonds. To Braithwaite, the absence of control comes from disintegrative shaming.

8. *What does conflict theory say about deviance?* According to Chambliss, law enforcement favors the rich and powerful over the poor and weak. In Quinney's view, the dominant class produces crime by making criminal laws, hiring enforcers to carry out the law, oppressing the subordinate class into deviance, and spreading the ideology that the lower class is crime-prone and dangerous. Marxists argue that the exploitative nature of capitalism produces violent crimes and noncriminal deviances. *How does the power theory explain deviance?* The powerful are more likely to engage in profitable deviance than the powerless in unprofitable deviance because the powerful have a stronger deviant motivation, greater deviant opportunity, and weaker social control. *What is the feminist theory of deviance?* Conventional theories may be relevant to men but not women. Women are likely to be victims of rape and sexual harassment, which reflects men's attempt to put women in their place. Although female crime has recently increased, it is not significant because most of the increase involves minor property crimes with very little profit, reflecting the continuing subordinate position of women in a patriarchy.

9. *How does differential association lead to deviance?* Deviance occurs if interactions with those who define deviance positively outweigh interactions with those who define it negatively. *How is being labeled deviant likely to affect people?* The label may cause them to look upon themselves as deviant and to live up to this self-

image by engaging in more deviant behavior. *What insight about deviance does phenomenological theory offer?* We can understand deviance better by looking into people's subjective interpretation of their own deviant experiences.

10. *How does society control deviance?* Society controls deviance through socialization, supplemented by formal and informal social control. Informal control is more common in traditional societies, and formal control is more common in modern societies. Informal control, however, seems more effective in deterring deviance. *Is the U.S. criminal justice system soft on criminals?* It appears so because extremely few criminals are apprehended and punished, but compared with other democracies, the U.S. imprisons proportionately more people and imposes longer prison terms. *How does the government wage the war on drugs?* It focuses its efforts on law enforcement against drugs rather than treatment and education. Failure of the drug war has led some to advocate legalizing drugs, arguing it would take away obscene profits from drug traffickers, end police corruption, and reduce crime drastically. Opponents respond that legalization will cause rampant drug use and addiction without reducing crime.

11. *How does deviance differ across societies?* Homicide is more likely to occur in poor countries, or in rich countries with high rates of poverty. Property crimes are more prevalent in rich countries because targets for such crimes are more abundant. Prostitution flourishes in poor countries as a result of poverty and exploitation by richer countries. Suicide is more common in more modern and egalitarian societies. Organized crime is stronger and more a part of legitimate business and politics in other countries than in the United States, but serves as an avenue to success for the ambitious poor in all countries.

KEY TERMS

Deviance An act that is considered by public consensus or by the powerful at a given place and time to be a violation of some social rule. (p. 123)

Differential association The process of acquiring through interaction with others "an *excess* of definitions favorable to violation of law over definitions unfavorable to violation of law." (p. 134)

Disintegrative shaming The process by which the wrongdoer is punished in such a way as to be stigmatized, rejected, or ostracized. (p. 131)

Marginal surplus population Marxist term for unemployed workers who are superfluous or useless to the economy. (p. 132)

Neurosis The mental disorder characterized by a persistent fear, anxiety, or worry about trivial matters. (p. 128)

Primary deviance Norm violations that a person commits for the first time and without considering them deviant. (p. 135)

Psychosis The mental disorder typified by loss of touch with reality. (p. 128)

Rape The use of force to get someone to do something sexual against his or her will. (p. 125)

Recidivism Repeated commission of crimes. (p. 138)

Reintegrative shaming Making wrongdoers feel guilty while showing them understanding, forgiveness, or even respect. (p. 131)

Relative deprivation Feeling unable to achieve a relatively high aspiration. (p. 133)

Secondary deviance Repeated norm violations that the violators themselves recognize as deviant. (p. 135)

Social control The process by which individuals are pressured by society to conform to social norms. (p. 136)

SUGGESTED READINGS

Braithwaite, John. 1989. *Crime, Shame, and Reintegration.* Cambridge: Cambridge University Press. Explains how *reintegrative* shaming prevents deviance, while *disintegrative* shaming encourages deviance.

Friedman, Lawrence M. 1993. *Crime and Punishment in American History.* New York: Basic Books. Reveals how the United States has repeatedly lost the "war against crime" from the colonial period to today.

Goode, Erich, and Nachman Ben-Yehuda. 1994. *Moral Panics: The Social Construction of Deviance.* Cambridge, Mass.: Blackwell. Explains why people react with unreasonable fear to a nonexistent or relatively harmless threat.

Sterling, Claire. 1994. *Thieves' World: The Threat of the New Global Network of Organized Crime.* New York: Simon & Schuster. Shows how criminal organizations around the world engage in such activities as credit card scams, weapon deals, drug-running, and contract killings.

Thio, Alex. 1995. *Deviant Behavior,* 4th ed. New York: HarperCollins. A comprehensive and, according to a UCLA professor writing in the journal *Teaching Sociology,* "remarkably well-written text that takes the student two steps beyond most extant texts."

U.S. AND GLOBAL STRATIFICATION

Myths and Realities

MYTH: *As the world's leading democratic society, the United States has the most equal distribution of income.*
REALITY: Although the U.S. income distribution is more equal than that of developing countries, it is less so than most other industrial nations, such as Japan, Sweden, and Germany. (p. 145)

MYTH: *Given the great diversity in the U.S. population, various groups are bound to disagree on whether a particular occupation is desirable or not.*
REALITY: Virtually all groups, rich or poor, rate occupations in the same way. Even people in other countries evaluate occupations in the same way. (p. 146)

MYTH: *Homelessness is a new phenomenon in the United States.*
REALITY: There have always been homeless people in the United States. (p. 154)

MYTH: *Most of the poor people in the United States are on welfare.*
REALITY: Only about one-third of the poor are on welfare. (p. 155)

MYTH: *As many rags-to-riches stories in the media show, it is not uncommon for a poor man's child to become a millionaire in this land of opportunity.*
REALITY: It is uncommon for a poor person in the United States to become a millionaire. The success experienced by many involves moving only a little way up the economic ladder. (p. 156)

Robert Swanson was already relatively rich 10 years ago, but since then he has become even richer. A decade ago, when he founded a semiconductor firm, he paid himself a salary of $125,000. Today, the 53-year-old California entrepreneur earns $360,000 a year, and his net worth has soared to $15 million. He revels in being a very rich man, often driving around in a new Porsche. By contrast, Mary Huntley found the 1980s a time of stagnation rather than success. In 1982, the 41-year-old medical technologist from Fort Wayne, Indiana, took home $24,000 a year. Today, she makes only $34,000, which, because of inflation, is less than what she earned a decade ago. An avid moviegoer, she has to skip evening shows in favor of half-price matinees. "For me," says Huntley, "50 cents is 50 cents" (Hawkins, 1992).

"Those who have, get." This old saying suggests that in every society some people, like Robert Swanson, get more rewards than others, like Mary Huntley. The specific nature of the rewards varies from one society to another. The rewards may be in the form of wealth, power, prestige, or whatever is highly valued by the society. All over the world, these rewards are distributed unequally. This patterned inequality is called **social stratification,** the division of society in such a way that some people get more rewards than others.

THE BASES OF STRATIFICATION

Of the many different rewards people can receive in life, sociologists have long identified three as the most important bases of stratification in the United States: wealth, power, and prestige. These three are, respectively, economic, political, and social rewards. They usually go together. People who are rich are also likely to have political power and social prestige. But possession of one reward does not guarantee enjoyment of others. Compared with teachers, some garbage collectors may make more money but have less prestige and power.

Wealth

In the last century, Karl Marx divided industrial society into two major classes and one minor class: the *bourgeoisie* (capitalists), the *proletariat* (workers), and the *petite bourgeoisie* (small capitalists). Marx differentiated them on the basis of two criteria: whether they own the "means of production"—tools, factories, offices, and stores—and whether they hire others to work for them. Capitalists are those who own the means of production and hire others. Workers neither own the means of production nor employ others; hence they are forced to work for capitalists. Small capitalists own the means of production but do most of the work themselves.

Examples are shopkeepers, doctors, lawyers, and other self-employed persons. Marx considered these people a minor, transitional class because he believed that they would eventually be forced down into the working class when their means of production were taken over by giant corporations.

In Marx's view, exploitation characterizes the relationship between the two major classes: capitalists and workers. Capitalists, bent on maximizing profit, compel workers to work long hours for little pay. Such exploitation was indeed extreme in Marx's time. Consider his description of child laborers:

> Children of nine or ten years are dragged from their squalid beds at two, three, or four o'clock in the morning and compelled to work for a bare subsistence until ten, eleven, or twelve at night, their limbs wearing away, their frames dwindling, their faces whitening, and their humanity absolutely sinking into a stone-like torpor, utterly horrible to contemplate (Marx, 1866).

Marx believed that eventually workers would rise in revolt and establish a classless society of economic equals. But his prophecy of revolution has not materialized in any highly developed capitalist economy. Writing in the 1860s, Marx failed to foresee that the exploitation of workers would ease and that a large, prosperous class of white-collar workers would emerge, as it has in the United States.

Karl Marx believed that capitalists sought to maximize profit by exploiting workers. He saw the appalling working conditions in English factories in the mid-nineteenth century. Women and children were employed for long hours at low pay. Conditions in the United States were not much better, as shown here in a famous photograph of child laborers in the early twentieth century.

Even so, the United States still suffers from glaring economic inequalities. According to the latest data available, the richest 20 percent of the population earns *nearly 45 percent* of the nation's total income. In contrast, the poorest 20 percent has *only about 4 percent* of the national income (see Figure 7.1). In fact, the U.S. income inequality is the greatest in the industrial world (Wright, 1995; Bradsher, 1995).

Power

Power—the ability to control the behavior of others, even against their will—is associated with wealth. Most sociologists agree that people with more wealth tend to have more power. This is evident in the domination of top government positions by the wealthy. Higher-income persons are also more likely to feel a strong sense of power. Thus, they are more likely to be politically active, working to retain or increase their power. Meanwhile, lower-income people are more likely to feel powerless to influence major political decisions. They are therefore more indifferent to politics and less likely to participate in political activity— a reaction likely to exacerbate their lack of power.

FIGURE 7.1
Unequal Income Distribution in the United States

Share of nation's income

Richest fifth	44.6%
2nd-richest fifth	24%
Middle fifth	16.5%
2nd-poorest fifth	10.5%
Poorest fifth	4.4%

Source: Data from U.S. Census Bureau, 1994

It is clear that power is distributed unequally. To what extent? A lot? A little? Power cannot be identified and measured as easily as wealth because people with power do not always express it. As a result, sociologists disagree about how it is distributed.

Both Marxist and elite theorists argue that a very small group of people holds most of the power in the United States. According to *Marxist theorists,* that group consists of capitalists. Even if they do not hold office, say Marxists, capitalists set the limits of political debate and of the government's actions, protecting their own interests. This is why large corporations, through heavy political campaign contributions and congressional lobbying, are able to hold down their taxes and avoid government regulation. According to *elite theorists,* a lot of power resides in the **power elite,** a small group of individuals who hold top positions in the federal government, military, and corporations and who have similar backgrounds, values, and interests.

In contrast to both Marxist and elite theorists, *pluralist theorists* argue that power is not tightly concentrated, but widely dispersed—more or less equally distributed among various competing groups. The power of big business, for example, is balanced by that of big labor, and government actions are ultimately determined by competition and compromise among such diverse groups. Even ordinary citizens have the power to vote anyone into office or out of it.

In sum, while Marxists and elitists see a great deal of inequality in power distribution, pluralists see very little. Both views may be correct. Most of the power in U.S. society is concentrated at the top, but the elite is not all-powerful. It is subject to challenge by voters from below. It is true that the general public is usually powerless—because it is not organized. But occasionally, when people feel strongly enough about an issue to make their wishes known, as they did in opposition to the Vietnam War in the 1960s, the government does change policy to follow public opinion.

Prestige

A third basis of social stratification is the unequal distribution of prestige. Following Max Weber's lead, sociologists call this kind of stratification a **status system,** a system in which people are stratified according to their social prestige.

Prestige differs from wealth and power. Wealth and power are objective entities: an individual can have them regardless of what other people think of the individual. But prestige is subjective, depending on how the individual is perceived by others. If the individual is rich and powerful but is seen by others as unworthy of respect, the individual has low prestige. The boss of an organized crime syndicate may make millions and exercise awesome power, but he might never acquire prestige because most people refuse to hold him in esteem—and they cannot be forced to do so. On the other hand, many college professors may not be rich and powerful, but they do enjoy more prestige than the crime boss. Why the difference? The answer has much to do with occupation.

For many years, sociologists have found that people have very definite ideas about the prestige of various occupations. In 1947 a team of sociologists asked a large random sample of the U.S. population to evaluate 90 occupations on a scale from "excellent" to "poor." Since then, similar surveys have been periodically taken using different representative samples. The result has always been the same: occupations that require more *education* and offer higher *income* than others are generally given higher prestige scores. Figure 7.2 shows a recent occupational ranking. Almost everybody, rich or poor, has rated the occupations in the same way. Even people in many other countries—some industrialized and some not—have been found to rank occupations in the same way (Hodge, Siegel, and Rossi, 1964; Treiman, 1977).

Occupation is only one of a person's many statuses among those based on age, race, and gender. These statuses may create **status inconsistency,** the condition in which the same individual is given different rankings, such as being high in occupation but low in ethnicity. An African American lawyer and a female executive, for example, have high occupational status, but they may have less prestige because of prejudice against their race or gender. People plagued with status inconsistency usually experience considerable stress. They resent the source of their status inconsistency. They think of themselves in terms of their higher status and expect others to do the same. But others may treat them in reference to their lower status. Consequently, people with status inconsistency are likely to support liberal and radical movements designed to change the status quo.

Questions for Discussion and Review

1. What is social stratification?
2. How are economic rewards distributed in the United States?
3. In what ways is the power basis of stratification different from the system of prestige?

THE U.S. CLASS STRUCTURE

The inequality in the United States can be observed in the way the society is divided into different social classes, forming a distinctive class structure.

Identifying Classes

Sociologists have long defined **social class** as a category of people who have about the same amount of income, power, and prestige. But how do we know who is in which class? There are three different methods for identifying a person's class.

Reputational Method One way of finding out which classes people belong in is through using the **reputational method,** identifying social classes by selecting a group of people and asking them to rank others. These selected individuals, or informants, typically have been living in the community for a long time and can rank many other residents on the basis of their reputation. If these "judges" are asked to rank a man whom they know to be a public drunk, they will put him in a lower-class category. If they are asked to rank a woman whom they know as a respectable banker, they will place her in an upper-class category.

The reputational method is useful for investigating the class structure of a small community where everybody knows practically everybody else. But it has several disadvantages. First, the reputational method cannot be applied to large cities because it is impossible to find individuals who know thousands of other people. Second, it is impossible to generalize the findings from one community to another because the informants can judge only their own community. Third, it is impossible to find unanimity among the reputation judges in a community. There are always cases in which an individual is considered upper-class by one judge but lower-class by another.

Subjective Method To find out the class structure of a large population, we can use the **subjective method,** identifying social classes by asking people to rank themselves.

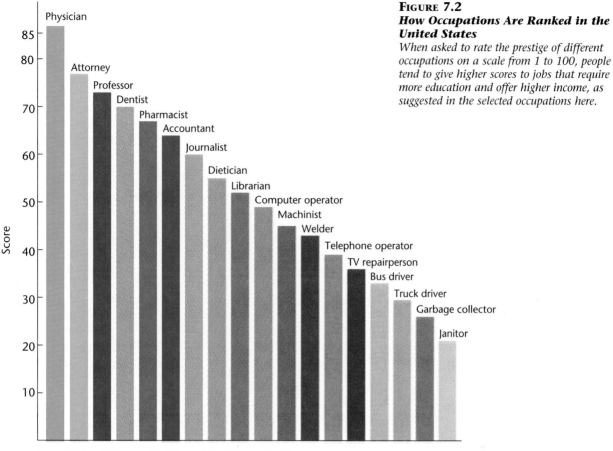

FIGURE 7.2
How Occupations Are Ranked in the United States
When asked to rate the prestige of different occupations on a scale from 1 to 100, people tend to give higher scores to jobs that require more education and offer higher income, as suggested in the selected occupations here.

Source: Data from NORC, *General Social Surveys, 1972–1994*, pp. 881–889.

In using this method, sociologists have long discovered that, if asked whether they are in the upper, middle, or lower class, the overwhelming majority of people will identify themselves as in the middle class. Both "upper class" and "lower class" have connotations offensive to democratic values. To call oneself upper-class is to appear snobbish. To call oneself lower-class is demeaning. As a result, many millionaires would call themselves middle- rather than upper-class; meanwhile, many low-income people such as maids and laborers would also regard themselves as middle-class. But, if given "working class" as a fourth choice, many people will identify themselves as in the working class rather than the middle class.

Thus, the weakness of the subjective method is twofold. The result depends heavily on how the question is asked, and respondents may lie about their social class. Despite these problems, the subjective method has at least two advantages. First, it can be used to investigate large cities or even an entire society. Second, it is useful for understanding and predicting behaviors that are strongly affected by attitudes. If self-employed auto mechanics, electricians, and plumbers identify themselves with the upper class, they can be expected to hold politically conservative views and to vote Republican, just as upper-class people tend to do.

Objective Method   Both subjective and reputational methods rely on people's perceptions of class. The third method depends on objective criteria, such as how much people earn annually. The **objective method** involves identifying social classes by using occupation, income, and education to rank people.

Like the subjective method, the objective method is useful for identifying the classes of a large population. It has another advantage as well: sociologists can easily obtain the needed data on occupation, income, and education from the Bureau of the Census or by mailing questionnaires to the people themselves.

The objective method has at least one disadvantage, though. In using objective criteria such as income and education, we can distinguish clearly between the top and the bottom of the class ladder, but it is difficult to differentiate the huge number of people near the middle. Researchers are therefore forced to establish an *arbitrary* boundary between classes—say, choosing 12 years of education rather than 11 or 13 to distinguish between the middle and working classes. As a consequence, many people who are said to be *middle*-class in one study turn out to be *working*-class in a different study.

Class Profiles

The three methods of identifying classes have been used in many studies with roughly the same result: In the United States, about 3 to 5 percent of the population are in the upper class, 40 to 50 percent in the middle class, 30 to 40 percent in the working class, and 15 to 20 percent in the poor, lower class. Sociologists disagree about the precise boundaries of these classes, but most accept these broad estimates of their sizes.

The Upper Class   Though it is a mere 3 to 5 percent of the population, the upper class possesses at least 25 percent of the nation's wealth. This class has two segments: upper-upper and lower-upper. Basically, the upper-upper class is the "old rich"—families that have been wealthy for several generations—an aristocracy of birth and wealth. Their names are in the *Social Register,* a listing of acceptable members of high society. A few are known across the nation, such as the Rockefellers, Roosevelts, and Vanderbilts. Most are not visible to the general public. They live in grand seclusion, drawing their incomes from the investment of their inherited wealth. In contrast, the lower-upper class is the "new rich." Although they may be wealthier than some of the old rich, the new rich have hustled to make their money like everybody else beneath their class. Thus, their prestige is generally lower than that of the old rich. The old rich, who have not found it necessary to "lift a finger" to make their money, tend to look down on the new rich.

However its wealth is acquired, the upper class is very, very rich. They have enough money and leisure time to cultivate an interest in the arts and to collect rare books, paintings, and sculpture. They generally live in exclusive areas, belong to exclusive social clubs, rub elbows with one another, and marry their own kind—all of which keeps them so aloof from the masses that they have been called the *out-of-sight class* (Fussell, 1992). More than any other class, they tend to be conscious of being members of a class. They also command an enormous amount of power and influence in government and business, affecting the lives of millions.

The Middle Class   The middle class is not as tightly knit as the upper class. Middle-class people are distinguished from those above them primarily by their lesser wealth and power, and from those below them by their white-collar, nonmanual jobs.

This class can be differentiated into two strata by occupational prestige, income, and education. The *upper-middle class* consists mostly of professional and business people with high income and education, such as doctors, lawyers, and corporate executives. The *lower-middle class* is far larger in size and much more diverse in occupation. It is made up of people in relatively low-level but still white-collar occupations, such as small-business owners, store and traveling salespersons, managers, technicians, teachers, and secretaries. Though having less income and education than the upper-middle class, the lower-middle class has achieved the middle-class dream of owning a sub-urban home and living a comfortable life.

The Working Class   The working class consists primarily of those who have little education and whose jobs are manual and carry little prestige. Some working-class people, such as construction workers, carpenters, and plumbers, are skilled workers and may make more money than those in the lower reaches of the middle class, such as secretaries and teachers. But their jobs are more physically demanding and, especially in the case of factory workers, more dangerous. Other working-class people are unskilled, such as migrant workers, janitors, and dishwashers. There are also many women in this class working as domestics, cleaning ladies, and waitresses, and they are the sole breadwinners in their households. Because they are generally underpaid, they are often called the *working poor.*

The Lower Class   This class is characterized by joblessness and poverty. It includes the chronically unemployed, welfare recipients, and the impoverished aged. These people suffer the indignity of living in run-down houses, wearing old clothes, eating cheap food, and lacking proper medical care. Very few have finished high school. They may have started out in their youth with poorly paying jobs that required little or no skill, but their earning power began to drop when they reached their late twenties. A new lower class has emerged in recent decades: skilled workers in mechanized industry who have become unskilled workers in electronically run factories. They have first become helpers, then occasional workers, and finally the hard-core unemployed.

Most members of the lower class are merely poor. But they are often stigmatized as "the underclass," a term conjuring up images of poor people as violent criminals, drug abusers, welfare mothers who cannot stop having babies, or able-bodied men on welfare who are too lazy to work.

The Influence of Class

One of the most consistent findings in sociology is that people in different classes live differently. In fact,

Top: In general, the middle class does not have inherited wealth and must earn the money for its lifestyle. Middle-class people can be wealthy if they own a successful business or rise to the top of their profession. But others in the middle class are not well-off, such as schoolteachers, church ministers, and middle-level managers.
Bottom: The lower class is mostly jobless and poor. It includes the chronically unemployed, welfare recipients, and impoverished older people.

the influence of class is so great and pervasive that it is taken into account in nearly every sociological study. This is why we have discussed the impact of class on childhood socialization, verbal communication, and mental illness in previous chapters. We will also examine class differences in religion, politics, and other human behaviors in later chapters. Here we focus on how social class affects life chances and lifestyles.

Life Chances Obviously, the rich have better houses, food, and clothes than the middle class, who, in turn, live in more comfortable conditions than the poor. The upper classes can also devote more money, and often more time, to nonessentials like giving lavish parties; some rich people even spend more

money on their pets than most people earn from their jobs. Their choices are often wider, and their opportunities greater, than those of the lower classes. In other words, the upper classes have better **life chances**— the likelihood of living a good, long, or successful life in a society.

We can see the impact of class on life chances in the *Titanic* tragedy, which took 1500 lives in 1912. On the night the ship sank into the Atlantic Ocean, social class was a major determinant of who survived and who died. Among the females on board, 3 percent of the first-class passengers drowned, compared with 16 percent of the second-class and 45 percent of the third-class passengers. All passengers in first class were given the opportunity to abandon ship, but those in third class were ordered to stay below deck, some of them at the point of a gun (Lord, 1981; Hall, 1986).

Less dramatic but just as grim is the common finding in many studies that people in the lower classes generally live shorter and less healthy lives than those above them in the social hierarchy. An infant born into a poor family is much more likely to die during its first year than an infant born into a nonpoor family. For adults, too, mortality rates are higher among men and women of the lower classes than among those of the higher classes. People of the lower classes are also more likely to die from syphilis, tuberculosis, stomach ulcers, diabetes, influenza, and many other diseases (Gilbert and Kahl, 1993).

Lifestyles **Lifestyles**—tastes, preferences, and ways of living—may appear trivial in comparison to life chances. But studying lifestyle differences among people also shows the importance of social class in our lives. Let us see how class shapes lifestyles.

Upper- and middle-class people are likely to be active outside their homes—in parent-teacher associations, charitable organizations, and various community activities. They are also likely to make friends with professional colleagues or business contacts, with their spouses helping to cultivate the friendship. In fact, they tend to combine their social and business lives so much that friendships are no longer a personal matter but are used to promote careers. In contrast, working-class people tend to restrict their social life to families and relatives. Rarely do they entertain or visit their friends from work. Although male factory workers may "stop off for a beer with the guys" after work, the guys are seldom invited home. Many working-class men and women are also quite reluctant to form close ties with neighbors. Instead, they often visit their parents, siblings, and other relatives, which has prompted Lillian Rubin (1976) to describe the extended family as "the heart of working-class social life." Some observers believe that this kin-oriented sociability arises because working-class people feel less secure in social interactions, fearing or distrusting the outside world (Gilbert and Kahl, 1993).

People in different classes also tend to prefer different magazines, newspapers, books, television programs, and movies. Whereas the working class and lower-middle class are more likely to read the *National Enquirer* and watch soap operas or professional wrestling, the upper-middle class is more likely to read *Time* or *Newsweek* and watch public-television programs. The upper class does not go for TV viewing at all. When the richest 400 persons were asked what they thought about TV's evening entertainment offerings, their typical responses were condescending: "very mediocre," "99 percent hogwash," "juvenile, boring and insulting" (Hacker, 1983). More generally,

compared with higher classes, working-class people read less; attend fewer concerts, lectures, and theaters; participate less in adult education; and spend less on recreation and are more likely to watch television, work on their cars, take car rides, play cards, and visit taverns.

Questions for Discussion and Review

1. What methods can be used to study social class, and what are their strengths and weaknesses?
2. What are the distinguishing features of various social classes in the United States?
3. How does social class influence life chances and lifestyles?

POVERTY IN THE UNITED STATES

Consider the case of a single mother with three children, who earns $15,000 a year. Is she poor? The government says no, because her income is above the official poverty line of $14,763 for a family of four. But critics would say that the woman is definitely poor. Who is right depends on which definition one chooses to accept.

What Is Poverty?

To determine the number of poor people, the U.S. government first defines poverty as the lack of minimum food and shelter necessary for maintaining life, which sociologists call **absolute poverty.** The government then decides what income is needed to sustain that minimum standard of living and sees how many people fall below it. This method of determining poverty originates from the research that Mollie Orshansky did for the Social Security Administration in the early 1960s. Because she found that the average family then spent a *third* of its income on food, she determined the poverty line by multiplying the cost of the Agriculture Department's cheapest recommended food plan by *three.* Her resulting figures, which varied with family size, were officially adopted in 1969. Since then, those figures have been simply raised every year to take inflation into account. Thus, for 1993, the "poverty line" for a four-person family was $14,763, and 15.1 percent of the population—over 39 million of the U.S. population—were considered poor. Figure 7.3 shows how the U.S. poverty rate has changed over the past 35 years.

Those figures have stirred a controversy. Conservative critics argue that the figures *overestimate* the extent of poverty because they do not count as income the many noncash benefits, such as food stamps, school lunches,

FIGURE 7.3
The U.S. Poverty Rate

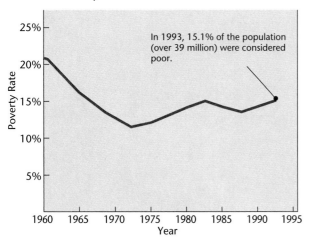

In 1993, 15.1% of the population (over 39 million) were considered poor.

Source: Data from U.S. Census Bureau, 1994.

housing subsidies, and medical assistance, that the poor receive from the government. These noncash benefits account for two-thirds of government programs for the poor. If these benefits were added to cash incomes, many "poor" people would rise above the poverty line—and hence no longer be poor.

Liberal critics, on the other hand, contend that the official rate *underestimates* the extent of poverty because it is based on the outdated assumption that the average U.S. family today spends a third of its income on food, as it did more than 30 years ago. Actually, it now spends only a fifth of its income on food, largely because of increases in nonfood costs such as taxes, medical expenses, and child care. In other words, the family today needs a much higher income than the family of 30 years ago in order to stay out of poverty. Failing to take this into account, the government excludes from its poverty statistics many families that are actually poor.

Recently, however, poverty experts at the National Academy of Sciences recommended to the government that both the liberal and conservative criticisms be taken into account, namely, by *deducting* nonfood costs from family income as well as *adding* noncash benefits to the income. If this recommendation is adopted, it will likely increase the official poverty rate because the nonfood costs are higher than noncash benefits (Pear, 1995a).

Poverty can further be found more prevalent than officially reported if it is defined in terms of how people live relative to—that is, in comparison with—the majority of the population. According to a widely accepted *relative definition* of poverty, those who earn less than half of the nation's median income are poor because they lack what is needed by most people to live a decent life. By this definition, for more than 30

years, the percentage of the nation living in poverty has been much higher than what has been reported by the government. These poor people are said to live in **relative poverty,** a state of deprivation resulting from having less than what the majority of the people have. The psychological impact of relative poverty seems far greater in the United States than in other countries. In many developing countries, the poor may not find themselves too bad off because most people around them are just as poor. But it is tougher to be poor in a sea of affluence, such as the United States, where many people blame the poor for their poverty, stereotyping them as lazy. In a poll taken by New York Times/CBS News (1994), for example, more people attributed poverty to "lack of effort" than to "circumstances beyond one's control."

Feminist Perspective on Poverty

Poverty affects women more than men, creating a social phenomenon that sociologists call the **feminization of poverty,** a huge number of women bearing the burden of poverty, mostly as single mothers or heads of families. Compared with other industrial nations, the United States has the largest gender gap in poverty (see Figure 7.4). The reason is that U.S. women are much more likely than their foreign counterparts to be both unemployed and heads of

FIGURE 7.4
The Gender Gap in Poverty: A Global View

Ratio of women's to men's poverty rate*

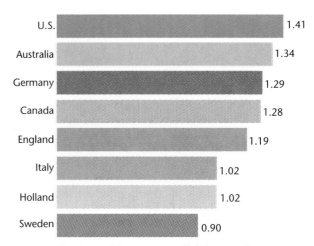

*If a ratio exceeds 1, women are more likely than men to be poor: 1.41, for example, means that women are 41% more likely than men to be poor.

Source: Data from Lynne M. Casper, Sara S. McLanahan, Irwin Garfinkel, "The Gender-Poverty Gap: What We Can Learn from Other Countries," *American Sociological Review*, Vol. 59 (August 1994), p. 597.

Absolute poverty is the lack of minimum food and shelter necessary for maintaining life. But poverty can also be relative: a state of deprivation resulting from having less than what the majority of the people have. Poor Americans find their poverty all the more disheartening when they see the vivid contrast between their lives and the lives of the wealthy. The conditions of the poor worsen when prosperous Americans, who tend to blame the poor for their poverty, are reluctant to support social programs, whether public programs funded by tax dollars or private programs funded by charitable giving.

families with children (Casper, McLanahan, and Garfinkel, 1994). In fact, single mothers constitute the largest proportion of the poor adult population in the United States. In 1993, about 46 percent of single-mother families were poor, compared with only 7 percent of two-parent families (U.S. Census Bureau, 1994). Thus, the feminization of poverty mostly involves poor women maintaining a household.

The problem can be attributed to several changes in U.S. society. Increases in divorce, separation, and out-of-wedlock birth have caused a growing number of women to become heads of poor households. The increase in divorced fathers not paying child support, along with reduction in government support for wel-

fare, has caused many more female-headed households to fall below the poverty line. Living longer than men has further contributed to a growing number of elderly women living alone in poverty.

But most important, according to feminists, women as a group are more vulnerable than men to poverty because of the sexist and patriarchal nature of the society. Unlike men, who often can escape poverty by getting a job, women tend to remain poor even when they are employed. Why? Because in the gender-segregated labor market, women are much more likely to work in low-paid, low-status jobs. By socializing women to become wives and mothers, feminist theory suggests, the patriarchal society further discourages them from developing educational and occupational skills. This is likely to cause poverty among divorced women or widows, even those from relatively affluent families (Gimenez, 1990; Pearce, 1993).

Causes of Poverty

There are two kinds of theories about general poverty. One essentially blames the poor for their poverty. The other is sociological in nature.

"Blame the Poor" Theories   These theories assume that there are plenty of opportunities for making it in the United States. The poor are believed to have failed to grab the opportunities by not working hard. Attempts have long been made to find the source of this self-defeating behavior. Political scientist Edward Banfield (1974) claimed to have found it in the present-oriented outlook among the poor, who, he said, live for the moment, unconcerned for the future. Earlier, anthropologist Oscar Lewis (1961) had found about the same lifestyle among the poor families that he studied. He found the poor to be fatalists, resigning themselves to being poor and seeing no way out of their poverty. They were said to have developed a "culture of poverty," characterized by a series of debilitating values and attitudes, such as a sense of hopelessness and passivity, low aspirations, feelings of powerlessness and inferiority, and present-time orientation. According to Lewis, this culture of poverty is passed on from one generation to another. All this, then, was assumed to discourage the poor from working hard, which, in turn, continues to keep them poor.

But there are holes in the blame-the-poor theories. For one thing, the poor are not necessarily averse to working hard. Most are likely to work hard if given the opportunity. But the problem is that, even if they have the opportunity, they are likely to remain poor because of low wages. In fact, the "working poor" account for 40 percent of those who fall below the poverty line. Also, in fully 60 percent of all poor families, at least one person works (Roberts, 1993). Another flaw in the blame-the-poor explanation is that it confuses cause and effect. The self-defeating values that Banfield and Lewis found among the poor may well be the effect, not the cause, of poverty.

Sociological Theories   According to a functionalist theory, society creates and maintains poverty because benefits can be derived from it. Poverty is assumed to perform some positive functions for society, such as the following:

1. Poverty makes it possible for society's "dirty work" to be done. Most people will stay away from many

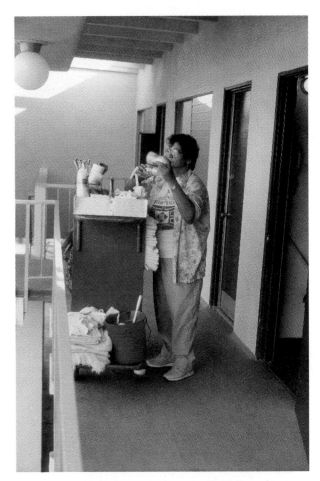

Many poor people remain poor not through lack of hard work but because of low wages. The "working poor," many of whom work at relatively unskilled jobs, account for four of every ten people who fall below the poverty line.

boring, underpaid, or unpleasant jobs such as washing dishes, scrubbing floors, and hauling garbage. Poor people are compelled to take such jobs because they cannot find better ones.

2. By working as maids and servants, poor people make it easier for the affluent to pursue their business and professional careers.

3. Poverty creates jobs for social workers and other professionals who serve the poor. It also produces jobs for police and other law enforcers who protect others from the poor (Gans, 1971).

But this functionalist theory still cannot explain how society has created poverty in the first place. Such an explanation can be found in conflict theory: It suggests that the inegalitarian nature of society makes inevitable the unequal distribution of economic opportunities, with the poor getting "the short end of the stick." Receiving few or no opportunities, the poor are bound to be poor and to remain so.

Why the Poor Become Poorer In recent years the poor have gotten *poorer,* particularly in big cities. Again, there are two contrasting explanations. One is sociological, attributing the increase in poverty to forces beyond the control of the individual. Over the last 30 years the middle class has largely left the cities for the suburbs, taking much of the tax base with them. Many well-paying, low-skilled jobs in manufacturing industries have also left the cities. As a result, the poor who are left behind jobless have become poorer.

According to another explanation, a new version of the old "blame the victim" theory, poor people have gotten poorer because they do not want to work. There are still many jobs that match their skills, such as working in sweatshops, in fast-food restaurants, and as maids or servants. But poor people today consider these jobs demeaning and prefer to be on welfare instead, not seeing the first jobs as stepping-stones from which to advance. Such an attitude is said to scorn the traditional view that almost any honest job, however unpleasant, confers independence and therefore dignity, and is better than taking something for nothing (Mead, 1992).

Questions for Discussion and Review

1. How does the rate of poverty depend on its definition?
2. What are characteristics and causes of the feminization of poverty?
3. How do different theories explain the causes of poverty?

HOMELESSNESS IN THE UNITED STATES

No one is sure about the number of homeless in the United States. There are only estimates and they vary widely—or wildly. Former President Bush's administration estimated the homeless to be about 300,000 in the late 1980s, but for the same period the Clinton administration put the estimate at seven million (Filer, 1990; DeParle, 1994). Generally, conservatives give low estimates, while liberals provide high estimates. A careful, nonpartisan analysis by sociologist Christopher Jencks (1994) shows the number to be between 300,000 and 400,000.

Who Are the Homeless?

The homeless are among the extremely poor. They are by definition people who sleep in streets, parks, shelters, and places not intended as dwellings, such as bus stations, lobbies, or abandoned buildings.

According to Peter Rossi's (1989) study of the Chicago homeless, most of the subjects are African American men in their middle thirties with an educational attainment largely similar to that of the general population. Most have never married; if they have, their marriages have failed. Most held their last steady job more than four years ago. Although a third of the homeless studied had worked at some time in the previous month, the jobs were only temporary, involving low skills and paying low wages (Rossi, 1989). Other studies have further indicated that only about one-sixth of the homeless are female-headed families with children, one-fourth of the homeless are mentally ill, and one-third are alcohol or drug abusers (Jencks, 1994).

Homelessness is not new. There have always been homeless people in the United States. But the homeless today differ in some ways from their counterparts of the 1950s and 1960s. More than 30 years ago, most of the homeless were old men, only a handful were women, and virtually no families were homeless. Today, as has been suggested, the homeless are younger, and include more women and families with young children. Today's homeless are also more visible to the general public because they are much more likely to sleep on the streets or in other public places in great numbers. They also suffer greater deprivation. Although the past homeless men on Skid Row were undoubtedly poor, their average income from casual and intermittent work was three to four times more than what the current homeless receive. In addition, many of the elderly homeless men in the past had small but stable pensions, which today's homeless do not have (Rossi, 1989).

Causes of Homelessness

The causes of homelessness can be categorized into two types: larger social forces and personal characteristics. One social force is the shortage of inexpensive housing for poor families and poor unattached persons. This shortage began in the 1970s and accelerated in the 1980s. Another social force is the decreasing demand for unskilled labor in the 1980s, which resulted in extremely high unemployment among young men in general and blacks in particular. A third social force is the erosion of public welfare benefits over the last two decades. These three social forces do not directly cause homelessness. They merely enlarge the ranks of the extremely poor, thereby increasing the chances of these people becoming homeless.

Certain personal characteristics may explain who among the extremely poor are more likely to become homeless. These characteristics have been found to include chronic mental illness, alcoholism, drug addiction, serious criminal behavior, and physical health problems. Most of the extremely poor do not become homeless because they live with their relatives or friends. But those who suffer from any of the personal disabilities just mentioned are more likely to wear out their welcome as dependents of their parents or as recipients of aid and money from their friends. After all, their relatives and friends are themselves likely to be extremely poor and already living in crowded housing (Rossi, 1989; Baum and Burnes, 1993). We should be careful, though, not to exaggerate the impact of personal disabilities on homelessness. To some degree, personal disabilities may be the consequences rather than the causes of homelessness (Snow and Anderson, 1993).

Questions for Discussion and Review

1. Who are the homeless?
2. What causes homelessness?

It is popularly believed that welfare encourages dependency, that most welfare recipients are so dependent on the system that they will never voluntarily leave it. But the fact is that most recipients stay on welfare less than two years, and welfare benefits do not seem generous enough to encourage dependency.

WELFARE IN THE UNITED STATES

Contrary to popular belief, most of the poor in the United States are not on welfare. Only about one-third are. Moreover, most people on welfare are children. There are about 15 million, of whom 5 million are single mothers and 10 million their children. Thus the large majority—two-thirds—of the welfare recipients are children. Since the economic recession that began in 1989, the welfare roll has increased steadily (U.S. Census Bureau, 1994; Dowd, 1994). This has in turn increased taxpayer and government opposition to the welfare system.

Beliefs About Welfare

In one survey a national sample of people in the United States were asked, "Do you think government spending on *welfare* should be increased, decreased, or kept about the same?" The most popular response was "*decreased.*" But many people do not realize that the proposed welfare cuts will affect mostly children. This is why, when asked about government spending on *poor children*, far more people said they wanted the government to *increase* it (Dowd, 1994).

If the real target of public opposition is not the children, it is their single mothers. In the same survey just mentioned, a large majority (87 percent) of the general public want welfare recipients to be required to work. It is widely assumed that welfare encourages dependency, that most welfare recipients are so dependent on the system that they will never voluntarily leave it (Toner, 1992).

But the fact is that most recipients (about 70 percent) stay on welfare less than two years. Moreover, welfare benefits do not seem generous enough to encourage dependency. An average three-member family on welfare receives only about $380 a month, and the benefit has declined over the last 20 years (Bane and Ellwood, 1994).

Reforming Welfare

Nevertheless, efforts have been made to end welfare dependency. The Clinton administration has proposed that single mothers who have been on welfare for more than two years be required to join a work program. Those who stay in the program may continue to receive aid as long as they are seeking private-sector jobs. By contrast, Republican leaders want the federal government to abolish its welfare programs and replace them with "block grants" to state governments. The states are expected to eliminate welfare within two years even if the recipients cannot find private jobs.

By late 1995 about 32 states had introduced some welfare changes, affecting half of the nation's 15 million people on welfare. Some of those states impose work requirements and time limits, while others deny additional benefits to women who have more children while on welfare (Pear, 1995b). It is likely that many more poor families will be denied benefits or lose what they now have. But will all this spur poor adults to lead more productive lives and provide their children with better role models, as the reformers assume? Critics do not think so. They argue that the government continues to avoid solving the real problem. The solution lies in providing "good job training, adequate child care, and decent wages at the end of the road," which would enable many poor single mothers to leave welfare. But such programs would cost more than $50 billion, which the government is not willing to spend (Abramovitz and Piven, 1994).

Questions for Discussion and Review

1. What does the public think about welfare?
2. What do you think is the best idea for solving the welfare problem?

SOCIAL MOBILITY IN U.S. SOCIETY

In virtually all societies there is some **social mobility**—movement from one social standing to another. The amount of mobility, though, varies from one society to another. Generally, there is more mobility in the more industrialized societies than in less developed societies. Sociologists have long discovered certain patterns and causes of social mobility.

Patterns

Social mobility can take several forms. **Vertical mobility** involves moving up or down the status ladder. The upward movement is called *upward mobility* and downward movement, *downward mobility*. The promotion of a teacher to principal is an example of upward mobility, and demotion from principal to teacher is downward mobility. In contrast to vertical mobility, **horizontal mobility** is movement from one job to another within the same status category. If a teacher leaves one school for a similar position at another, the teacher is experiencing horizontal mobility.

Mobility can also be intragenerational or intergenerational. When an individual moves from a low position to a higher one, it is called **intragenerational mobility** (or *career mobility*)—a change in an individual's social standing. A manager who becomes the vice president of a company illustrates intragenerational mobility. When a person from a lower-class family gets a higher-status job, as in the case of a factory worker's daughter becoming company vice president, it is called **intergenerational mobility**—a change in social standing from one generation to the next.

Of those various forms of mobility, upward intergenerational mobility has attracted the most attention from sociologists. Their research has primarily focused on the question of how much such mobility exists in the United States. This interest is understandable because we revel in stories about the son of a poor person becoming president, as politicians and journalists proclaim, "Only in America." This may be an exaggeration, but it reflects the high place that upward mobility holds in U.S. values. Rags-to-riches tales make people feel good about their country, and they make interesting stories. By publicizing them, the media reinforce the vision of the United States as a land of opportunity, where through sheer hard work the son of a janitor can become a millionaire. This view of the United States is further reinforced by the experience of those who have achieved moderate, but real, upward mobility.

But is this picture accurate? Is upward mobility common? Until the 1970s, the answer was yes and no: yes because numerous people climbed a little way up the social ladder; no because very few people rose from rags to riches. In the last few decades, however, the rich have gotten richer and the poor poorer. As Figure 7.5 shows, the share of national income in the hands of the richest portions of the U.S. population has gone up, but the income share of the poorest groups has gone down. Today the salary of a typical chief executive of a large U.S. company is *120 times* that of a manufacturing worker, compared to only 35 times in 1974 (Frank and Cook, 1995). The middle classes have been hurting, too. While corporate presidents and chairpersons have been riding high, many mid-level management and technical jobs have been lost. Middle managers and highly educated technicians are said to have become insecure and vulnerable in their jobs. They have increasingly shared with high-school-trained assembly-line workers and office clerks the same feelings of uncertainty, insecurity, and anxiety about their jobs and incomes. They have become what Secretary of Labor Robert Reich (1994) calls "the anxious class."

FIGURE 7.5
The Rich Get Richer . . .

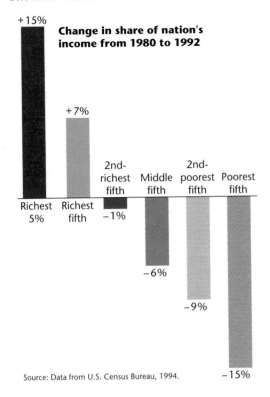

Change in share of nation's income from 1980 to 1992

+15% Richest 5%

+7% Richest fifth

−1% 2nd-richest fifth

−6% Middle fifth

−9% 2nd-poorest fifth

−15% Poorest fifth

Source: Data from U.S. Census Bureau, 1994.

Sources

Why, in the pursuit of the American Dream, are some people upwardly mobile while others stay in the same position or fall behind? There are two major factors determining the chances for upward or downward mobility: structural changes in the society and individual characteristics.

Structural Mobility Sometimes large changes in society enable many people to move up or down the social ladder at the same time. The result is **structural mobility,** social mobility related to changes in society. As we have suggested, much of the downward mobility of blue-collar workers over the last two decades is due to the decline of manufacturing industries and labor unions, which have long shored up wages and benefits for workers without much education and high-level skills. As for the downward mobility of many well-educated managers and technicians in recent years, it can be attributed to the increased globalization of the U.S. economy. Pressured by international competition, many U.S. corporations have tried to be "lean and mean" by greatly reducing their size and expenses.

In the earlier part of this century, however, most of the structural mobility was upward rather than downward. This kind of structural mobility can be traced to at least four sources: First, there was a tremendous expansion of the industrial economy. In 1900, agricultural workers made up nearly 40 percent of the labor force, but massive industrialization has reduced the proportion to only 4 percent today. At the same time, many unskilled jobs were gradually taken over by machines, but replaced by numerous higher-status jobs—clerical, service, business, and professional jobs. This created the opportunity for large numbers of people from farming and blue-collar families to get into those higher-status occupations (Blau and Duncan, 1967; Kerckhoff, Campbell, and Winfield-Laird, 1985).

A second source of structural mobility has been the dramatic increase in the educational attainment of the population. High school enrollment exploded from a mere 7 percent of the appropriate age group in 1900 to over 90 percent today. College enrollment jumped from only a quarter of a million in 1900 to over 12 million today. Thus, more people achieved the knowledge and skills needed to fill higher-status jobs (Featherman and Hauser, 1978; Davis, 1982).

A third source of structural mobility has been the lower birth rates in the higher classes than in the lower classes. In the early part of this century, professional and other white-collar workers had relatively few children, but manual workers, especially farmers, had many. As the economy expanded, there were many more new professional positions. Because there was a shortage of higher-status people to fill all those higher-status jobs, it provided the lower classes with an opportunity to take them.

A fourth source of structural mobility has been the large influx of immigrants into this country. Immigrants usually have taken lowly jobs as laborers on farms, in factories, and in mines, pushing many native-borns into higher-status occupations. When children of immigrants grew up, they too had the opportunity as native-borns to become upwardly mobile. It is no accident that the world's most prosperous societies—Israel, Canada, Australia, and the United States—have had unusually large numbers of immigrants (Tyree et al., 1979; Tyree and Semyonov, 1983).

All in all, as a result of a rapidly industrializing economy, increasing education, lower birth rates in the higher classes, and considerable immigration, many people whose parents were factory or farm workers came to fill higher-status jobs. In today's increasingly postindustrial society, however, higher-status jobs require much more education and skill than before.

Individual Mobility Even when structural mobility opens up higher-status positions, some people move

One source of structural mobility in the United States has been the influx of immigrants into this country willing to take lowly jobs as laborers on farms, in factories, and in mines, which enables many native-borns to move into higher-status occupations.

up and some do not. Let us take a closer look at this **individual mobility,** social mobility related to an individual's personal achievement and characteristics.

Among the characteristics that influence individual mobility are racial or ethnic background, gender, education, occupation, place of residence, and sheer luck. More specifically, being African American, Mexican American, Puerto Rican, Native American, or female decreases the chances for upward mobility. (In later chapters we look at these inequalities in detail.) College graduates are much more likely than the uneducated to be upwardly mobile. White-collar workers are more likely than blue-collar workers to experience upward career mobility. People who live in urban areas have a greater chance of upward mobility than those

who live in rural areas. Finally, sheer luck often acts as the force pushing a person up the status ladder.

Some of the personal characteristics are *achieved,* such as education, talent, motivation, and hard work. Others are *ascribed,* such as family background, race, and gender. As has been suggested, both achieved and ascribed qualities have a hand in determining who gets ahead in U.S. society. But the popular belief in equal opportunity would lead us to expect career success to be attained through achievement more than ascription. Is achievement, then, really the more powerful determining force in upward mobility? According to most sociological studies, achievement may appear on the surface to be the predominant factor, but it is at bottom subject to the influence of ascription. It is well-known that the more education people have, the more successful they are in their careers. But the amount of education people have is related to their family background. Thus, compared with children from blue-collar families, white-collar children can be expected to get more education—and then have a better chance for career mobility.

Questions for Discussion and Review

1. What are the different patterns of mobility?
2. What structural and individual characteristics influence social mobility?

GLOBAL STRATIFICATION

We have so far discussed social stratification that exists within a society, namely, our own, but stratification also exists among various nations. In today's **world system**—a network of commercial and other relationships among all the members of the world's community—nations can be divided into three broad classes that correspond to the upper, middle, and lower classes within a society. Sociologist Immanuel Wallerstein (1987) refers to those three classes of countries in terms having to do with their position of economic power and influence in the world system. Thus countries with the greatest influence are said to be in the *core* of the world system, those with less influence are in the *semiperiphery* of the system, and those with the least influence are in the *periphery.*

Global Classes

The United States, Western European countries, and Japan are **core countries,** the world's upper class, the

America. Their economies are highly specialized, producing and exporting to core countries only a few raw materials or foodstuffs, such as oil, copper, sugar, or coffee. Their governments tend to be unstable.

In between those two types of societies are **semiperipheral countries,** the world's middle class, relatively affluent societies in the middle of global stratification, also known as newly industrialized countries. Examples are South Korea, Taiwan, Mexico, and Brazil. These countries are more industrialized and richer than peripherals but less industrialized and rich than cores. Their economies are also more diversified than those of peripherals but less diversified than those of cores.

What about the former Soviet Union and Eastern Europe, which have splintered into many independent nations? Most of these nations, such as Russia, Ukraine, and Poland, appear more industrialized than the typical peripheral country. These countries may be considered semiperipheral. But a few, such as Tajikistan and Uzbekistan, are more like peripheral countries and may be considered as such. Figure 7.6 illustrates the distribution of these three classes of countries in the world.

Interclass Relations

Traditionally, core countries exploit peripheral countries in the world system, just as the upper class exploits the lower class within a given society. The cores often buy raw materials from the peripherals at a very low price and then use these raw materials to manufacture goods to sell back to the peripherals for a large profit. The profit, however, is mostly sent back to the cores rather than invested in the peripherals. Consequently, the peripherals remain poor and economically underdeveloped. The semiperipherals also exploit the peripherals in about the same way. Brazil, for example, gets cheap oil, gas, and agricultural commodities from Bolivia, a poor peripheral; Bolivia in turn buys more expensive manufactured goods from Brazil.

This kind of exploitative trading has been going for a long time—even centuries in some cases. But, according to the world system theory, in the last 40 years new forms of exploitation have emerged under the guise of generosity or commercial cooperation. They have, however, served the latent function of enabling some peripheral countries to industrialize and improve their economies. By taking advantage of the cheap labor, core countries have transferred technology to the peripherals by building and operating factories there, helping the peripherals to industrialize. Moreover, eager to turn peripherals into markets for products from the cores, the rich countries have instituted foreign aid programs to

One of the most effective determinants of individual upward mobility is education. Thus, individual upward mobility is largely due to achievement, although it is also subject to the influence of ascription because the amount of education people have is related to their family background.

most industrialized and richest societies, popularly known as industrialized or developed countries. They have highly diversified economies, producing practically anything from corn to microchips. They also have a very high standard of living, stable governments, and a great deal of individual freedom.

Countries with the least influence in the world are called **peripheral countries**—the world's lower class, relatively poor societies, popularly known as developing countries. These are the predominantly agricultural countries in Africa, Asia, and Latin

FIGURE 7.6
Global Stratification

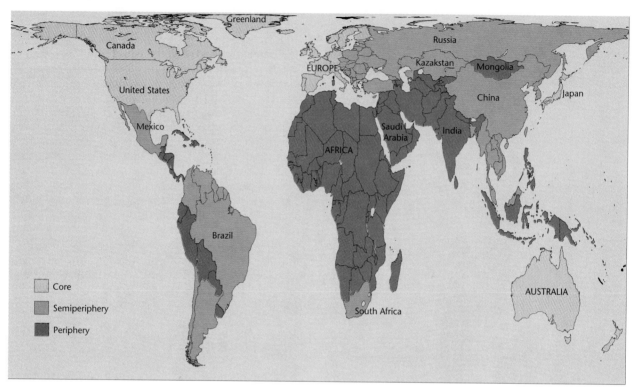

Core

Semiperiphery

Periphery

help the poor countries increase their agricultural and industrial productivity. All this has significantly helped Japan, South Korea, Taiwan, and others to transform into affluent core or semiperipheral countries.

In short, as members of the stratified world system, various classes of nations are interrelated and influence each other's fortunes. The ability of one country to influence another suggests that the class structure of the world system is dynamic rather than static, fluid and changing rather than rigid and fixed.

International Inequality

Global stratification clearly suggests inequality among nations. This inequality appears in many different forms, the most important of which have to do with economic conditions and quality of life.

By definition, economic conditions are better in relatively rich countries than in poor ones, but the disparity between rich and poor appears extreme. Although they constitute only about 20 percent of the world's population, richer countries have well over 80 percent of global income and other economic opportunities. These disparities reflect other disparities such as those in productivity, trade, savings, and investment. The richest 20 percent of the world population have 84.7 percent of the world's GNP (gross national

product—the total value of all the goods and services produced by a nation, including those exported). In sharp contrast, the bottom 20 percent of the world population have only 1.4 percent of the GNP. The global inequality appears even worse in other economic indicators: the poorest fifth have less than one percent of world trade, domestic savings, and domestic investment, way below the over–84 percent enjoyed by the richest fifth (United Nations, 1994).

Such global disparities are indeed extreme. Even so, they are expected to get even worse. Over the last 30 years, the share of world income for the richest fifth has risen from 70 to 85 percent, while the meager share for the poorest fifth has dropped from 2.3 to 1.4 percent. To appreciate how much the gap between the global rich and poor has widened, look at Figure 7.7. It shows that in 1960, the world's top fifth was 30 times richer than the bottom fifth, but by 1991 the top fifth became 61 times richer. In other words, the gap between the world's rich and poor has widened by more than 100 percent.

A similar gap exists in regard to the quality of life. The United Nations (1994) finds that, compared with poor developing countries, affluent industrial countries have considerably higher income per person, far greater longevity, and a much higher rate of literacy. While the world's affluent enjoy a better life, the poor bear the cost of global inequality.

FIGURE 7.7
The Widening Gap Between the World's Rich and Poor

Ratio of income shares
Richest 20% compared to
poorest 20% of the
world population.

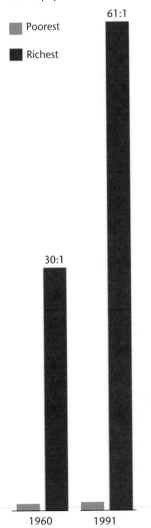

Source: United Nations, *Human Development Report 1994.*

In the world system of social stratification, one of the conditions necessary for peripheral countries to turn into semiperipherals is the ability to attract foreign investment with an abundance of cheap labor. Factories that produce clothing and various manufactured goods in countries like South Korea, Taiwan, and Mexico have broadened the industrial base of those countries and helped move them up in the global stratification system.

Mobility in Global Society

To move up or down in the global class system depends not only on foreign influence but also on the domestic conditions of a country.

Let us first consider how *peripheral countries can turn into semiperipherals*. One condition is that the peripherals must already have a number of factories that manufacture goods rather than only farms and mines that produce food and raw materials. Examples are some Latin American countries. Let's say that the price of their primary exports (raw materials) declines so as to cause high unemployment and other economic problems. The peripherals that have already established adequate industrial bases are then able to expand these bases to produce more goods and sell them to core and semiperipheral countries. This is partly how Brazil and Argentina, already relatively industrialized as early as the 1950s, have changed from peripherals to semiperipherals. Another condition for becoming semiperipheral is the ability to attract foreign investment with an abundance of cheap labor, thus broadening the industrial base with the addition of many more manufacturing plants. This is partly how South Korea and Taiwan, which used to be poor peripherals, have moved up into the semiperipheral class. The third condition for peripherals is a nationwide pursuit of economic development through social or political changes. China, for example, has become semiperipheral largely because its socialist government has turned largely capitalist and given its citizens the freedom to create personal wealth, an opportunity seized with a vengeance.

Semiperipheral countries can transform into cores if they meet at least two requirements: First, they must have developed an advanced technology that can turn out products at a lower cost than their competitors. Second, they must have large affluent markets, such as North America and Western Europe, for their products. This is how Japan, Spain, and Italy have achieved the status of core countries over the last 30 years or so. On the way to joining them are some newly industrializing countries such as East Asia's "four small tigers" (South Korea, Taiwan, Hong Kong, and Singapore), which have penetrated the rich core markets with their electronics, cars, computers, and other high-tech goods.

Finally, *core countries may lose their upper-class status in the world system.* In recent decades the United States seems to have fallen a notch or two from its preeminent core status. One major source of this slip is **deindustrialization**, the loss of numerous factory jobs as a result of relocating a massive number of manufacturing plants to peripheral countries. U.S. deindustrialization peaked in the midst of a deep economic recession in the early 1980s. As it slowed significantly by the mid-1980s, **reindustrialization**—the proliferation of unstable, low-skilled, or low-paying jobs—swept across the economy. Most victims of deindustrialization are forced to seek such jobs, in effect having to compete with poorly paid workers in labor-cheap countries (So, 1990). This has raised the specter of the United States eventually becoming a poor country (Chomsky, 1993; Luttwak, 1994).

Questions for Discussion and Review

1. How are the world's social classes related to each other?
2. How do economic condition and quality of life differ among nations?
3. What are the general forces that push some nations up or down in the global stratification system?

PERSPECTIVES ON STRATIFICATION

Social stratification is in essence social inequality, contrary to the U.S. belief in equality. Functionalists argue that it is necessary. Conflict theorists disagree. Symbolic interactionists, however, are more interested in how differences in status and power influence social interaction.

Functionalist Perspective

Kingsley Davis and Wilbert Moore (1945), in the most influential tenet of the functionalist view, said that stratification is necessary. Davis and Moore were trying to explain why stratification exists in all societies. The reason, they said, is that stratification serves a useful, positive function—in effect, a function necessary for the survival of a society.

What is this function? According to Davis and Moore, stratification motivates people to work hard by promising them such rewards as money, power, and prestige. The amount of rewards depends on two things: how important a person's job is to society and how much training and skill are required to perform that job. A physician, for example, must receive more rewards than a garbage collector, not only because the physician's job is more important than the garbage collector's but also because it requires more training and skill. Without this system of unequal rewards, many jobs important to society would never be performed. If future physicians knew they would be paid and respected just as much as garbage collectors, they would not bother to spend years studying long hours at medical school. In brief, stratification is necessary for society because it ensures that "the most important positions are conscientiously filled by the most qualified persons."

Conflict Perspective

The Davis-Moore theory has encountered much criticisms. Some critics argue that it is difficult to see why such large inequalities are necessary to fulfill the functions Davis and Moore described. Why is it functional, for example, to pay a corporate executive two or three times more than the president of the United States? The functionalist theory suggests that the corporate executive's job is more important. But is it really? Many people may disagree. Even the physician's job is not necessarily more important than the garbage collector's, because uncollected refuse can pose a serious problem to a society. The functionalist theory also fails to take into account the inherent interest of certain jobs. The intrinsic satisfaction of being a doctor far outweighs that of being a garbage collector. Why, then, should the doctor be given more rewards?

In addition, according to Melvin Tumin (1953), stratification is dysfunctional rather than functional. First, by limiting the opportunities of those who are not in the privileged class, stratification restricts the possibility of discovering and exploiting the full range of talent in society. When some intelligent teenagers are too poor to stay in school and never develop their talents fully, society loses. Second, stratification helps maintain the status quo of social injustices, such as denying the poor, minorities, and women the opportunities for good jobs. Third, because the stratification system distributes rewards unjustly, it encourages the less privileged to become hostile, suspicious, and distrustful. The result may be social unrest and chaos.

Symbolic Interactionist Perspective

According to symbolic interactionists, social inequality largely determines how people interact with one another. Generally, when interacting with a lower-status person, higher-status people tend to show off their power, either consciously or unconsciously. A common example involves calling lower-status persons by their first names. At work, our bosses call us by our first names, but we do not call them by their first names unless we get their permission first. When we go to see a doctor, he or she calls us by our first names, but we address him or her as "doctor." By readily using lower-status persons' first names, higher-status people try to be personal, but in doing so they disregard whether the lower-status persons may prefer to be shown respect instead (Karp and Yoels, 1993). In summary, interaction between unequals tends to involve "superiors" using various symbols of power to put "inferiors" in their place.

Questions for Discussion and Review

1. How does the functionalist theory of stratification differ from the conflict approach?
2. How do status differences affect symbolic interaction?

TOWARD SOCIAL EQUALITY

Both functionalist and conflict theorists assume that inequality is here to stay. Functionalists believe that stratification will persist because it is necessary. Conflict theorists also believe that inequality will continue, but because the powerful will not give up their privileged positions. Mickey Kaus (1992) argues that social equality *can* be achieved.

According to Kaus, it is futile to pursue equality of money, income, or wealth in a capitalist society such as the United States unless capitalism is eliminated. But so long as we want to preserve capitalism, we are inevitably saddled with income inequality, selfishness,

or even greed. These nasty aspects of capitalism are the price of enjoying the prosperity that capitalism brings to the country. In fact, capitalism can generate prosperity only because it depends on money inequality as a spur to work—the more you work the more money you make. The success of capitalism also depends on *vast* inequality as a spur to risk-taking—people, especially greedy ones, will gamble their money on an economic venture because they will get rich if it succeeds. Finally, capitalism thrives on income inequality because most people do not resent the rich, because they have their own dreams of getting rich themselves. It is, therefore, impossible to get rid of income inequality in order to achieve equality.

Although income equality cannot be achieved, *social* equality can. To Kaus, social equality is a situation where people respect one another regardless of their wealth or lack of it. They have equal pride in being a citizen and treat one another as equals. There are no feelings of superiority among the rich, and there is no servile behavior among the nonrich. But "money talks," especially in a capitalist society, where wealth exerts a great influence on the other two aspects of inequality—prestige and power. Recognizing this problem, Kaus calls for government action "to *restrict the sphere of life in which money matters,* and enlarge the sphere in which money *doesn't* matter." The aim is to restrain the influence of wealth, to prevent money inequality from translating into social inequality.

The primary way to do this is through social institutions, where the capitalist principle of the marketplace ("rich beat poor") is replaced by the principle of equality of citizenship. Thus Kaus would create, or reinforce, essentially egalitarian institutions, such as the military draft; mandatory national service (caring for the infirm elderly, tutoring the illiterate, maintaining or patrolling public spaces); more public financing of political campaigns; a national health care system; expanded day care (where toddlers of ordinary workers mix with those of company executives); revived schools, parks, museums, post offices, libraries, and mass transit. In these spheres of life the rich and nonrich can interact, so that they can rediscover "the esthetics of democracy"—the joy of mingling with people of all classes while feeling equal as simply citizens.

Questions for Discussion and Review

1. According to Kaus, what is social equality?
2. How can it be achieved?

CHAPTER REVIEW

1. *What are the bases of social stratification?* Wealth, power, and prestige. The unequal distribution of these social rewards constitutes social stratification.

2. *How equal is the distribution of wealth in the United States?* Very unequal. The richest 20 percent of the population earn about 45 percent of the total national income, and the poorest 20 percent earn less than 5 percent. *How is power distributed in the United States?* Very unequally, according to Marxist and elite theorists. They argue that power is concentrated in the hands of a very few people. In contrast, pluralist theorists contend that power is widely dispersed among competing groups. *What is an important source of prestige in the United States?* Occupation.

3. *How do we know who is in which social class?* We may use the reputational method, asking a selected group of people to rank others; the subjective method, asking people how they rank themselves; or the objective method, ranking people according to such criteria as income, educational attainment, and occupation. *How is the U.S. population distributed into social classes?* About 3 to 5 percent are in the upper class, 40 to 50 percent in the middle class, 30 to 40 percent in the working class, and 15 to 20 percent in the lower class. *How does social class affect our lives?* People of different classes have different life chances and lifestyles.

4. *What is poverty?* Poverty can be absolute or relative. Absolute poverty is the lack of minimum food and shelter necessary for maintaining life. Relative poverty is having less than the majority of the people. *What is the feminization of poverty?* It refers to the huge number of women bearing the burden of poverty, mostly as single mothers. *What causes poverty?* To some social scientists, personal weaknesses and the "culture of poverty" cause people to be poor. To sociologists, however, society's need for "dirty work" to be done and its inegalitarian nature cause poverty. *Why have the poor gotten poorer in large cities?* Sociologists find the cause in forces beyond the control of the individual, but others blame the poor for not wanting to work.

5. *Who are the homeless?* Extremely poor, most are African American men in their middle thirties, but a few are single mothers with children, mental patients, or alcohol or drug abusers. *What causes homelessness?* A combination of social forces and personal disabilities.

6. *What does the public think of the welfare system?* A large segment of the public do not like welfare because they believe that it encourages dependency. *What has been proposed to deal with the welfare problem?* The Clinton administration wants welfare recipients to work; Republicans agree but want to minimize federal involvement by turning welfare programs back to the states.

7. *Is upward mobility common in the United States?* Before the 1970s, upward mobility was common, but mostly within the middle segment rather than from "rags to riches." In the last few decades, however, the rich have gotten richer and the poor poorer. *What factors influence the opportunity for social mobility?* Structural factors of social mobility include the decline of manufacturing industries in recent decades and an expanding economy, increasing education, low fertility among higher classes, and massive immigration in earlier periods. Individual characteristics include social and ethnic background, gender, education, occupation, and luck.

8. *What is the world system approach to global stratification?* The world is divided into three classes: The most industrialized and wealthy nations make up the upper class known as the core of the world system, the poor countries constitute the lower class known as the periphery, and nations that are in between are the middle class known as the semiperiphery. *What is global inequality?* The extreme disparity in economic conditions and quality of life between rich and poor nations. *What is the dynamic nature of global stratification?* It is fluid rather than rigid, with nations moving up or down, depending on foreign influence and domestic conditions.

9. *Why do functionalists think that social stratification is useful for society to have?* Because stratification ensures that relatively important jobs are performed by competent people. *How do conflict theorists view stratification?* As harmful to society—limiting opportunities for those not in the privileged class, preserving the status quo of injustices, and producing social unrest. *How do symbolic interactionists view stratification?* Stratification influences how higher-status people show off their power in social interaction.

10. *Is it possible to achieve social equality?* Yes, according to Kaus. It involves the government encouraging citizens of all classes to mingle in public spheres of life.

Absolute poverty   The lack of minimum food and shelter necessary for maintaining life. (p. 150)

Core countries   The world's upper class, the most industrialized and richest societies; popularly known as industrialized or developed countries. (p. 158)

Deindustrialization   The loss of numerous factory jobs as a result of relocating a massive number of manufacturing plants to peripheral countries. (p. 162)

Feminization of poverty   A huge number of women bearing the burden of poverty, mostly as single mothers or heads of families. (p. 151)

Horizontal mobility   Movement from one job to another within the same status category. (p. 156)

Individual mobility   Social mobility related to an individual's personal achievement and characteristics. (p. 158)

Intergenerational mobility   A change in social standing from one generation to the next. (p. 156)

Intragenerational mobility   A change in an individual's social standing. (p. 156)

Life chances   The likelihood of living a good, long, or successful life in a society. (p. 149)

Lifestyles   Tastes, preferences, and ways of living. (p. 150)

Objective method   The method of identifying social classes by using occupation, income, and education to rank people. (p. 147)

Peripheral countries   The world's lower class, relatively poor societies; popularly known as developing countries. (p. 159)

Power   The ability to control the behavior of others, even against their will. (p. 145)

Power elite   A small group of individuals who hold top positions in the federal government, military, and corporations and have similar backgrounds, values, and interests. (p. 145)

Reindustrialization   The proliferation of unstable, low-skilled, or low-paying jobs. (p. 162)

Relative poverty   A state of deprivation resulting from having less than what the majority of the people have. (p. 151)

Reputational method   The method of identifying social classes by selecting a group of people and asking them to rank others. (p. 146)

Semiperipheral countries   The world's middle class, relatively affluent societies in the middle of global stratification; also known as newly industrialized countries. (p. 159)

Social class   A category of people who have about the same amount of income, power, and prestige. (p. 146)

Social mobility   Movement from one social standing to another. (p. 156)

Social stratification   The division of society in such a way that some people get more rewards than others. (p. 144)

Status inconsistency   The condition in which the same individual is given different status rankings, such as being high in occupation but low in ethnicity. (p. 146)

Status system   A system in which people are stratified according to their social prestige. (p. 146)

Structural mobility   Social mobility related to changes in society. (p. 157)

Subjective method   The method of identifying social classes by asking people to rank themselves. (p. 146)

Vertical mobility   Moving up or down the status ladder. (p. 156)

World system   A network of commercial and other relationships among all the members of the world's community. (p. 158)

SUGGESTED **R**EADINGS

Bane, Mary Jo, and David T. Ellwood. 1994. *Welfare Realities: From Rhetoric to Reform.* Cambridge, Mass.: Harvard University Press. A collection of the authors' articles describing and explaining various aspects of the welfare problem.

Gans, Herbert J. 1995. *The War Against the Poor: The Underclass and Antipoverty Policy.* New York: Basic Books. Analyzes how poverty can be reduced without hurting the poor.

Jencks, Christopher. 1994. *The Homeless.* Cambridge, Mass.: Harvard University Press. A careful, objective analysis of homelessness in the United States.

Luttwak, Edward N. 1994. *The Endangered American Dream.* New York: Simon & Schuster/Touchstone. An examination of how the United States has begun to develop such conditions as the declining earnings for the majority, the spectacular enrichment of the few, and the increasingly violent desperation of the poor.

Wolff, Edward N. 1994. *Top Heavy: A Study of the Increasing Inequality of Wealth in America.* New York: Twentieth Century Fund Press. Shows how the gap between wealth and poverty has widened in the midst of economic growth.

RACE AND ETHNICITY

Myths and Realities

MYTH: *When people move from one country to another their racial characteristics, such as skin color and facial features, do not change. Therefore, if African Americans go to another country, they will be considered blacks there, as in the United States.*
REALITY: It is true that people's physical features do not change when they move to another country. But their racial identification as blacks or whites may change. Most African Americans in the United States, for example, would be considered whites in some Latin American countries. (p. 169)

MYTH: *As "model Americans," Asian Americans are more economically successful than other groups, including whites.*
REALITY: The family income is higher for Asians than whites, but this is because the average Asian family is larger and more members of the family work, compared with the average white family. Individual income is lower for Asians than for whites. (p. 176)

MYTH: *Since Jewish Americans as a whole are prosperous, they tend to be conservative or to vote Republican, like other prosperous U.S. citizens.*
REALITY: On the contrary, they tend more to be liberal, supporting welfare, civil rights, women's rights, and the like. They are also more likely to vote Democratic. (p. 177)

MYTH: *If a white person discriminates against blacks, he or she must be prejudiced.*
REALITY: Not necessarily. Many whites discriminate without being prejudiced, primarily because of social pressure. Unprejudiced whites, for example, may not sell their houses to blacks for fear of offending the neighbors. (p. 183)

In the summer of 1992 a deluge of horror stories about human cruelties shocked the world. The reports poured out of newly independent Bosnia, the most ethnically diverse republic of what used to be Yugoslavia. The Serbs were reported to be carrying out an "ethnic cleansing" campaign, driving Muslims and Croats from their homes, torturing and killing some, and abusing and terrorizing the rest. In a northern Bosnian town, armed Serbs, rounding up 100 prisoners for a move from one detention camp to another, pulled out about 30 prisoners and shot them. At one camp, the family of one starving prisoner tried to bring him some food, but the guards took it away and then beat the prisoner in front of his relatives. Near Tuzla in eastern Bosnia, three Muslim girls were stripped and chained to a fence "for all to use." After being raped for three days, they were doused with gasoline and set on fire. Other Muslim and Croatian girls were used as sex slaves for months, and if they became pregnant they were set free to "have Serbian babies." While most reports focused on Serbian cruelties, some Muslims and Croats struck back with atrocities of their own in areas where they predominate (Watson, 1992).

Mistreatment of minorities is not limited to Bosnia. It occurs in other parts of Eastern Europe and Russia as well. In Western Europe, Pakistanis, Turks, Algerians, and other non-European minorities are often subjected to random insults and hostile stares, which sometimes escalate into gang attacks or firebombs thrown from the streets. In Japan, the Koreans, Burakumin, and Konketsuji (born of American and Japanese parents) are targets of considerable prejudice and discrimination. In the United States, African Americans are given poor service in stores or restaurants, have racial epithets hurled at them, are harassed by white police, and are attacked by white supremacists (Feagin, 1995b). These are only a few of the countless cases of mistreatment minorities suffer.

SOCIOLOGICAL DEFINITIONS

People are accustomed to thinking of a minority as a category of people who are physically different and who make up a small percentage of the population. But this is not the way sociologists define a minority. Consider the Jews in China and the United States and the blacks in South Africa. The Jews in China do not "look Jewish"—they look like other Chinese. Similarly, the Jews in the United States do not "look Jewish"— they look like other white Americans. Jews cannot be differentiated from the dominant group on the basis of their physical characteristics, but they are sociologically considered a minority. In South Africa, blacks are also sociologically a minority, although they make up a majority of the population. Neither physical traits nor numbers alone determines whether people constitute a minority. To understand the sociological idea of minority, we need first to look at race and ethnicity.

Race

As a biological concept, race refers to a large category of people who share certain inherited physical characteristics. These may include a particular skin color, nasal shape, or lip form. The popular classification of human races recognizes three groups: Caucasoid, Mongoloid, and Negroid. Caucasoids have light skin, Mongoloids yellowish skin, and Negroids dark skin—and other physical differences exist among the three groups.

There are at least two problems with this classification of races. First, some groups fit into none of these categories. Natives of India and Pakistan have Caucasoid

A minority is characterized by its experiences of prejudice and discrimination at the hands of the dominant group. Oppressed blacks in South Africa have been considered a minority even though they greatly outnumber whites in the country.

facial features but dark skin. The Ainu of Japan have Mongoloid faces but white skin. The Vogul of Siberia have Caucasoid faces but yellowish skin. Some aboriginal groups in Australia have dark skin and other Negroid features but blond hair. The Polynesians of the Pacific Islands have a mixture of Caucasoid, Mongoloid, and Negroid characteristics (Jacquard, 1983).

Another problem with the biological classification of races is that there are no "pure" races. People in these groups have been interbreeding for centuries. In the United States, for example, about 70 percent of blacks have some white ancestry and approximately 20 percent of whites have at least one black ancestor (Sowell, 1983; Davis, 1991; Kilker, 1993). Biologists have also determined that all current populations originate from one common genetic pool—one single group of humans that evolved about 30,000 years ago, most likely in Africa. Today, about 95 to 99 percent of the DNA molecules (which make up the gene) are the same for all humans, and only the remaining 1 to 5 percent are responsible for all the differences in appearance (Vora, 1981; Shipman, 1994). Even these outward differences are meaningless because the differences among members of the same "race" are greater than the average differences between two racial groups. Some American blacks, for example, have lighter skin than many whites, and some whites are darker than many blacks.

Since there are no clear-cut biological distinctions—in physical characteristics or genetic make-up—between racial groups, sociologists define race as a social rather than biological phenomenon. Defined sociologically, a **race** is a group of people who are *perceived* by a given society to be biologically different from others. People are assigned to one race or another, not necessarily on the basis of logic or fact but by public opinion, which, in turn, is molded by society's dominant group. Consider a boy in the United States whose father has 100 percent white ancestry and whose mother is the daughter of a white man and black woman. This youngster is considered "black" in our society, although he is actually more white than black because 75 percent of his ancestry is white. In many Latin American countries, however, this same child would be considered "white." In fact, according to Brazil's popular perception of a black as a person of African descent who has no white ancestry at all, about three-fourths of all U.S. blacks would *not* be considered blacks (Denton and Massey, 1989; Fish, 1995). The definition of race, then, varies from one society to another. Sociologists use this societal definition to identify "races" because it is the racial status to which people are assigned by their society—rather than their real biological characteristics—that has profound significance for their social lives.

Ethnicity

Jews have often been called a race. But they have the same racial origins as Arabs—both are Semites—and through the centuries Jews and non-Jews have interbred extensively. As a result, as noted earlier, Jews are often physically indistinguishable from non-Jews. Besides, a person can become a Jew by conversion to Judaism. Jews do not constitute a race, but are instead a religious group or, more broadly, an ethnic group.

Whereas race is based on popularly perceived physical traits, ethnicity is based on cultural characteristics. An **ethnic group,** then, is a collection of people who share a distinctive cultural heritage. Members of an ethnic group may share a language, religion, history, or national origin. They always share a feeling that they are a distinct people. In the United States, members of an ethnic group typically have the same national origin. As a result, they are named after the countries from which they or their ancestors came. Examples are Polish Americans, Italian Americans, or Irish Americans.

For the most part, ethnicity is culturally learned. People learn the language, values, and other characteristics of their ethnic group. Members of an ethnic group are usually born into it, but the cultural traits of the group are passed from one generation to the next.

Minority

A **minority** is a racial or ethnic group that is subjected to prejudice and discrimination. **Prejudice** is a negative attitude toward a certain category of people. It includes ideas and beliefs, feelings, and predispositions to act in a certain way. For example, whites prejudiced against blacks might fear meeting a black man on the street at night. They might resent blacks who are successful. They might plan to sell their houses if a black family moves into the neighborhood.

Whereas prejudice is an attitude, discrimination is an act. More specifically, **discrimination** is an unfavorable action against individuals that is taken because they are members of a certain category. It is discrimination, for instance, when a landlord will not rent an apartment to a family because they are African American or Hispanic.

A minority is not necessarily a small percentage of the population. Blacks are considered a minority in South Africa, even though they make up about 70 percent of the population, because they are the subordinate group. Similarly, the dominant group need not make up a large part of the population. People of English descent in the United States today constitute only about 13 percent of the population. But because of their continuing social and cultural influence, they are still considered the dominant group—as they were more than 200 years ago.

Questions for Discussion and Review

1. Why do sociologists define race as a social rather than a physical phenomenon?
2. When does a racial or ethnic group become a minority group?

RACE AND ETHNICITY IN THE UNITED STATES

The United States is a nation of immigrants, as Figure 8.1 shows. The earliest immigrants were the American Indians, who arrived from Asia more than 20,000 years ago. Long after the Indians settled as Native Americans, other immigrants began to pour in from Europe and later from Africa, Asia, and Latin America. They came as explorers, adventurers, slaves, or refugees—most hoping to fulfill a dream of success and happiness. The English were the earliest of these immigrants and, on the whole, the most successful in fulfilling that dream. They became the dominant group. Eventually, they founded a government dedicated to the democratic ideal of equality, but they kept African Americans as slaves and discriminated against other racial and ethnic groups. This "American dilemma"—the discrepancy between the ideal of equality and the reality of discrimination—still exists, though to a

FIGURE 8.1
Ancestry of U.S. Population

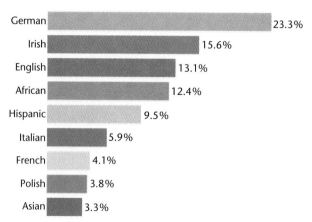

All other Europeans 19.5% Southwest Asian 0.6% West Indian 0.4%

(Figures add up to more than 100% because some people reported multiple ancestries.)

Source: Data from *Statistical Abstract of the United States, 1994.*

lesser degree than in the past. Let us look at how the major minority groups have fared under the burden of the American dilemma.

Native Americans

Native Americans have long been called Indians—one result of Columbus's mistaken belief that he had landed in India. The explorer's successors passed down many other distorted descriptions of the Native Americans. They were described as savages, although it was whites who slaughtered hundreds of thousands of them. They were portrayed as scalp hunters, although it was the white government that offered large sums to whites for the scalps of Indians. They were stereotyped as lazy, although it was whites who forced them to give up their traditional occupations. These false conceptions of Native Americans were reinforced by the contrasting pictures whites painted of themselves. The white settlers were known as pioneers rather than invaders and marauders; their conquest of the Native Americans' land was called homesteading, not robbery.

When Columbus "discovered" what would later become the United States, there were more than 300 native American tribes with a total population of over a million. Of the natives he encountered around the Caribbean, Columbus wrote: "Of anything they have, if it be asked for, they never say no, but do rather invite the person to accept it, and show as much lovingness as though they would give their hearts" (Hraba, 1979). In North America, too, the earliest white settlers were often aided by friendly Native Americans.

As the white settlers increased in numbers and moved westward, however, Native Americans resisted them. But the native population was decimated by outright killing, by destruction of their food sources, and by diseases brought by whites, such as smallpox and influenza. With their greater numbers and superior military technology, the whites prevailed. Sometimes they took land by treaty rather than by outright force. The treaties required the U.S. government to provide Native Americans with "foreign aid," such as helping them maintain a reasonable level of education and health and protecting their resources. But the treaties have often been violated even to this day (Van Biema, 1995).

By 1995, there were about two million Native Americans. Slightly more than half lived on 278 reservations, mostly in the Southwest, the rest in urban areas. After more than two centuries of colonial subjugation, Native Americans today find themselves at the bottom of the socioeconomic ladder—the poorest

More than 200 years after Europeans arrived in North America, Native Americans today find themselves at the bottom of the socioeconomic ladder in the United States. Many live without electricity, heat, or plumbing.

minority in the United States. Their unemployment and poverty rates are much higher than those among other Americans, and their family income is also considerably lower (see Figure 8.2). Moreover, they suffer from much higher rates of pneumonia, influenza, diabetes, tuberculosis, suicide, alcoholism, and car accidents, compared with the general U.S. population.

Under constant pressure by Native Americans, the U.S. government has since 1988 instituted a policy "to promote tribal economic development, tribal self-sufficiency, and strong tribal government." Today, on some reservations Native Americans are exempted from paying taxes and, further, are allowed to sell gasoline,

FIGURE 8.2
Native Americans: the Poorest Minority

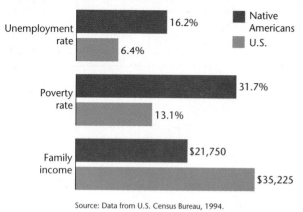

Source: Data from U.S. Census Bureau, 1994.

cigarettes, and other items tax-free to non-Indians. About 59 percent of the reservations are also permitted to run highly profitable gambling operations that cater to non-Indians. At least seven tribes have recently been allowed to govern themselves virtually as sovereign nations. These tribes may set their own budgets, run their own programs, and negotiate directly with the federal government for services, functions that have long been performed by the U.S. Bureau of Indian Affairs (Gartner, 1990; Verhovek, 1990; Egan, 1991).

All this has sparked a national movement to recapture traditions, to make Native Americans feel proud of their cultural heritage. Virtually every tribe places a heavy emphasis on teaching the younger generation its native language, crafts, tribal history, and religious ceremonies. There used to be a lack of unity among the 300 tribes, but today intertribal visiting and marriage are common occurrences. Moreover, in the last 15 years, many Native American men and women have successfully established themselves in business, law, and other professions. Of course, the majority of Native Americans still have a long way to go. Without a viable economic base to draw on, they still find themselves powerless, mired in high unemployment, deep poverty, and other problems. The last 15 years have not been long enough to overcome two centuries of government oppression.

African Americans

There are more than 31 million African Americans, constituting about 12 percent of the U.S. population. They are the largest minority in the nation. In fact, there are more blacks in the United States than in any single African nation except Nigeria.

Their ancestors first came from Africa to North America as indentured servants in 1619. Soon after that they were brought here as slaves. Most lived in the South, where they worked on cotton, tobacco, or sugar-cane plantations. Slavery ended during the Civil War in 1865. But soon after federal troops withdrew from the South, white supremacy returned. Many **Jim Crow laws** were enacted to segregate blacks from whites in all kinds of public and private facilities—from restrooms to schools. A more basic tactic to control blacks was terror. If an African American man was suspected of killing a white or of raping a white woman, he might be lynched, beaten to death, or burned at the stake.

Lynchings occurred in the North, too. Still, the North did offer more opportunities to African Americans. Since the early 1900s, as southern farms were mechanized and as the demand for workers in northern industrial centers rose during the two World Wars, many southern African Americans migrated north. When the wars ended and the demand for workers decreased, however, they were often the first to be fired. Even in the North, where there were no Jim Crow laws, African Americans faced discrimination and segregation.

A turning point in U.S. race relations came in 1954 when the U.S. Supreme Court ordered that public schools be desegregated. The order gave momentum to the long-standing campaign against racial discrimination. In the late 1950s and 1960s, the civil rights movement launched marches, sit-ins, and boycotts. The price was high: many civil rights workers were beaten and jailed; some were killed. Eventually Congress passed the landmark Civil Rights Act of 1964, prohibiting segregation and discrimination in virtually all areas of social life, such as public facilities, schools, housing, and employment.

In the last 30 years, the Civil Rights Act has put an end to many forms of segregation and paved the way for some improvement in the position of African Americans. Various studies have shown a significant decline in white opposition to such issues as school integration, integrated housing, interracial marriage, and voting for an African American president. The number of African Americans elected to various public offices has sharply increased since 1980. The proportion of African Americans with college degrees has also grown significantly. An affluent middle class has emerged among African Americans.

Full equality, however, is still far from being achieved. Most evident is the continuing large economic gap between blacks and whites. The latest figures on median family income are $21,161 for blacks and $38,909 for whites—with blacks earning only about 54 percent of the amount made by whites, a decline from 57 percent in 1980. Over 33 percent of blacks live in poverty, compared with less than 12 percent of whites (U.S. Census Bureau, 1994). More glaring racial inequality shows up in housing. Over the last decade there has been some decline in residential segregation, especially in relatively small metropolitan areas with active housing construction in the South and West, as Figure 8.3 shows. But the decline has been very modest; most blacks continue to reside in segregated neighborhoods and are more likely than whites with similar incomes to live in overcrowded and substandard housing (Hacker, 1992; Massey and Denton, 1993).

In sum, progress has been significant in education and politics, but not in housing and economic conditions. The economic situation is a little complicated, though. Unemployment and poverty have soared in the black working class, primarily because of numerous plant shutdowns caused by the shift from a manufacturing to a service economy in the face of increased global competition. On the other hand, the black middle class has become more prosperous, largely because of their advanced education and skills required by the technological changes in the U.S. economy (Takaki, 1993). Still, it is difficult for middle-class blacks to enjoy the rewards of their success. They are often outraged at being treated like the "black underclass," which involves being stopped and questioned as crime suspects by police, getting bad—or no—service in shops and restaurants, having difficulty flagging down a taxi, or being falsely charged with shoplifting (Feagin, 1995b; Close, 1993).

The Civil Rights Act of 1964 paved the way for improvement in the position of African Americans in the United States. The proportion of African Americans with college degrees has grown significantly, an affluent middle class has emerged, and the number of African Americans elected to public office has increased sharply in recent years. The personal achievements and character of retired-General Colin Powell vaulted him into the limelight and a lead in many public opinion polls as a presidential contender before he decided not to run in the 1996 contest.

Hispanic Americans

In 1848 the United States either won in war or bought from Mexico land that would become Texas, California, Nevada, Utah, Arizona, New Mexico, and Colorado. Many Mexicans consequently found themselves living in U.S. territories as U.S. citizens. The vast majority of today's Mexican Americans, however, are the result of immigration from Mexico since the turn of the century. At first immigrants came largely to work in the farmlands of California and to build the railroads of the Southwest. Later a steady stream of Mexicans began to pour into the United States, driven by Mexico's population pressures and economic problems and attracted by U.S. industry's need for low-paid, unskilled labor.

In 1898 the United States added Puerto Rico to its territory by defeating Spain in the Spanish-American War. In 1917 Congress granted all Puerto Ricans citizenship, but they may not vote in presidential elections and are not represented in Congress. Over the years, especially since the early 1950s, many Puerto Ricans, lured by job opportunities and the cheap plane service between New York City and San Juan, have migrated to the mainland. In the last two decades, though, more have returned to Puerto Rico than have come here.

Thus, a new minority group has emerged in the United States—Hispanic Americans, also called Latinos. Today the category actually includes several groups. Besides Mexican Americans and Puerto Ricans, there are Cuban immigrants who began to flock to the Miami area when their country became communist in 1959. There are also the "other Hispanics"—immigrants from other Central and South American countries who have come here as political refugees and job seekers. By 1992, the members of all these groups totaled about 24 million, constituting over 9 percent of the U.S. population, the second largest minority. Because of high birth rates and the continuing influx of immigrants, Hispanic Americans may outnumber African Americans in the next decade (U.S. Census Bureau, 1994).

The Spanish language is the unifying force among Hispanic Americans. Another source of common identity is religion: at least 85 percent are Roman Catholic. There are, however, significant differences within the Hispanic community. Mexican Americans are by far the largest group, accounting for 64 percent of Hispanics. They are heavily concentrated in the Southwest and West. Puerto Ricans make up 11 percent and live mostly in the Northeast, especially in New York City. As a group, they are the poorest

FIGURE 8.3
Residential Integration

Out of 232 cities, 194 have shown a modest decline in residential segregation since 1980. The largest decrease in segregation took place in small southern and western metropolitan areas with significant housing construction. Here are the most and least segregated cities.

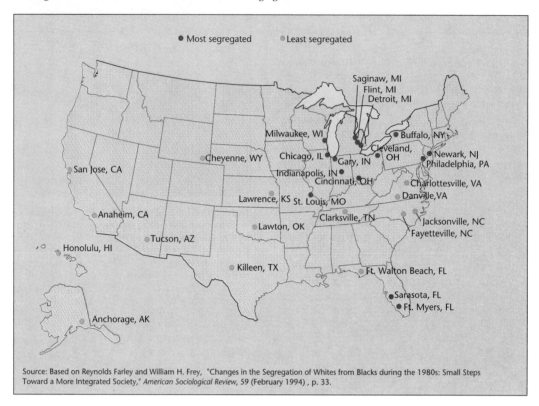

Source: Based on Reynolds Farley and William H. Frey, "Changes in the Segregation of Whites from Blacks during the 1980s: Small Steps Toward a More Integrated Society," *American Sociological Review*, 59 (February 1994), p. 33.

among the Hispanics (Figure 8.4), which may explain why many have gone back to Puerto Rico. The Cubans, who constitute 5 percent of the Hispanic population, are the most affluent and therefore have the greatest tendency toward integration with "Anglos" (white Americans). The remaining Hispanics are a diverse group, ranging from uneducated, unskilled laborers to highly trained professionals (U.S. Census Bureau, 1994).

Hispanics in general lag behind both whites and blacks in educational attainment. Among those age 25 or older, only 9 percent have completed college, compared with 23 percent for whites and 12 percent for blacks. But some Hispanic groups are more educated than others. Cubans are the best educated, primarily because most of the early refugees fleeing communist Cuba were middle-class and professional people. Mexican Americans and Puerto Ricans are less educated because they consist of many recent immigrants with much less schooling. The young, U.S.-born Hispanics usually have more education. Lack of profi-

ciency in English has slowed the recent Hispanic immigrants' educational progress. As many as 25 percent of Hispanics in public schools speak little or no English, which has resulted in higher dropout rates than those for non-Hispanic students (Bernstein, 1990; U.S. Census Bureau, 1994).

Hispanics are primarily clustered in lower-paying jobs. They earn about 60 percent of the amount made by Anglos. They also have a higher rate of unemployment and poverty. However, the higher educational achievement of young Hispanics provides hope that more Hispanics will be joining the higher paid white-collar work force in the future. Research has shown that if Hispanics speak English fluently and have at least graduated from high school, their occupational achievement is close to that of non-Hispanics with similar English fluency and schooling (Stolzenberg, 1990). Nationwide, Hispanics are also already a growing force in politics, with an increasing number of members of Congress, state governors, and mayors of large cities.

FIGURE 8.4
Poverty Rates Among Hispanic Groups

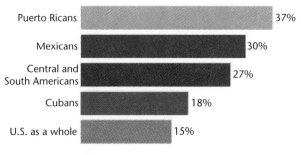

Puerto Ricans	37%
Mexicans	30%
Central and South Americans	27%
Cubans	18%
U.S. as a whole	15%

Source: Data from U.S. Census Bureau, 1994.

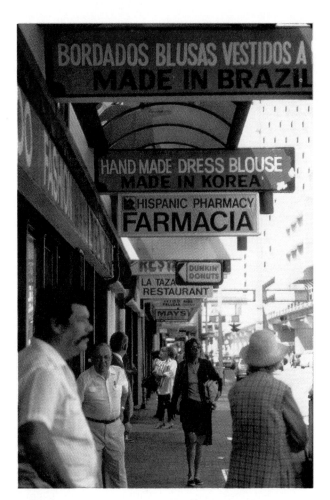

Hispanic Americans make up the second largest minority group in the United States, and due to high birth rates and continuing immigration, they may outnumber African Americans within the next decade. The Spanish language is the unifying force among Hispanic Americans, who come from many countries—Mexico, Cuba, Puerto Rico, and Central and South American countries.

Asian Americans

Since 1980, Asian Americans have been the fastest growing minority, although they remain a much smaller minority—about 3 percent of the U.S. population—than Hispanics and African Americans. There is tremendous diversity among Asian Americans, whose ancestry can be traced to over 20 different countries. The larger groups are Chinese, Japanese, Filipinos, Koreans, and Vietnamese. The first two have the longest history in the United States.

The Chinese first came in 1849 during the gold rush on the West Coast, pulled by better economic condi-

tions in the United States and pushed by economic problems and local rebellions in China. Soon huge numbers of Chinese were imported to work for low wages, digging mines and building railroads. After these projects were completed, jobs became scarce, and white workers feared competition from the Chinese. As a result, special taxes were imposed on the Chinese, and they were prohibited from attending school, seeking employment, owning property, and bearing witness in court. In 1882 the Chinese Exclusion Act restricted immigration to the United States, and it stopped all Chinese immigration from 1904 to 1943. Many returned to their homeland (Kitano, 1981; Henry, 1990).

Immigrants from Japan met with similar hostility. They began to come to the West Coast somewhat later than the Chinese, also in search of better economic opportunities. At first they were welcomed as a source of cheap labor. But soon they began to operate small shops, and anti-Japanese activity grew. In 1906 San Francisco forbade Asian children to attend white schools. In response, the Japanese government negotiated an agreement whereby the Japanese agreed to stop emigration to the United States, and President Theodore Roosevelt agreed to end harassment of the Japanese who were already here. But when the Japanese began to buy their own farms, they met new opposition. In 1913 California prohibited foreign-born Japanese from owning or leasing lands; other Western states followed suit. In 1922 the U.S. Supreme Court ruled that foreign-born Japanese could not become U.S. citizens.

Worse events occurred during World War II. All the Japanese—both aliens and U.S. citizens—were rounded up from the West Coast and confined in concentration camps in isolated areas. They were forced to sell their homes and properties. The action was condoned even by the Supreme Court as a legitimate way of ensuring that the Japanese Americans would not

Many Asian Americans have become successful in education, business, and the professions. However, Korean storeowners in large cities shown here, as well as other Asian Americans, can attest to continuing prejudice and discrimination against them in the United States.

help Japan defeat the United States. Racism, however, was the real source of such treatment. There was no evidence of any espionage or sabotage by a Japanese American. Besides, German Americans were not sent to concentration camps, although Germany was at war with the United States and there were instances of subversion by German Americans. In 1987, when the survivors sued the U.S. government for billions of dollars in compensation, the solicitor general acknowledged that the detention was "frankly racist" and "deplorable." And in 1988 the Senate voted overwhelmingly to give $20,000 and an apology to each of the surviving internees (Molotsky, 1988).

Despite this history of discrimination, the Asians *seem* to be educationally and economically among the most successful minorities in the United States today. As Figure 8.5 shows, a higher percentage of Asians than whites have college degrees and annual family incomes of $50,000 or more. But the same figure indicates more poverty among Asians than whites. Moreover, the Asians' higher family income is misleading for two reasons: First, the average Asian family is larger and more members of the family work, compared with the average white family. *Individual* income is actually lower for Asians than for whites. Second, most Asians live in California, Hawaii, and New York, where the cost of living is higher than the national average (Takaki, 1993). Contrary to popular belief, then, Asian Americans still have not attained real income equality with whites, even though they have more education.

Discrimination against Asians is subtle. Many well-educated Asian Americans can get work as profes-

sionals and technicians, but they rarely become officials and managers. White bosses often cite language deficiencies as an excuse for denying promotions. Privately, they stereotype the Asians as weak and incapable of handling people, although Japanese-managed companies are well known for outperforming U.S. companies. It is assumed that Asian talent can flourish in the classroom or laboratory but not in senior management. The Asians are in effect victims of the **glass ceiling,** the prejudiced belief that keeps minority professionals from holding high, leadership positions in organizations. Thus, many Asian professionals are prevented from joining the top ranks of corporations.

The stereotype of Asians as a "model minority" also hurts. It implies that virtually all Asians do well, which of course is not true because there is still much poverty among, for example, Filipinos and Chinatown residents. By suggesting that Asian Americans are not victims of discrimination, the model-minority stereotype further shuts Asians out of affirmative action programs. The stereotype is similarly used against Hispanics and African Americans. They are told directly or indirectly that they do not need racial preferences because "the Asians have made it, so why can't you?" This provokes resentment and even hostility against Asians, as blacks have shown against Korean stores in some cities. Finally, the model-minority stereotype puts undue pressure on young Asian Americans to succeed in school, particularly in mathematics and science classes, which may lead to mental health problems and even teen suicide (U.S. Commission on Civil Rights, 1992).

FIGURE 8.5
How Asian Americans Fare

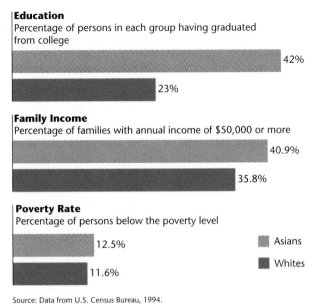

|Education
Percentage of persons in each group having graduated from college

- 42%
- 23%

|Family Income
Percentage of families with annual income of $50,000 or more

- 40.9%
- 35.8%

|Poverty Rate
Percentage of persons below the poverty level

- 12.5%
- 11.6%

▨ Asians
■ Whites

Source: Data from U.S. Census Bureau, 1994.

Jewish Americans

The first Jews came here from Brazil in 1654; their ancestors had been expelled from Spain and Portugal. Then other Jews arrived directly from Europe. Their numbers were very small, however, until the 1880s, when large numbers of Jewish immigrants began to arrive, first from Germany, then from Russia and other Eastern European countries. Here they were safe from the *pogroms* (massacres) they had faced in Europe, but not from prejudice and discrimination.

During the 1870s, many colleges in the United States refused to admit Jewish Americans. At the turn of the century, Jews often encountered discrimination when they applied for white-collar jobs. During the 1920s and 1930s, they were accused of being part of an international conspiracy to take over U.S. business and government, and **anti-Semitism**—prejudice or discrimination against Jews—became more widespread and overt. The president of Harvard University proposed restrictive quotas for Jewish Americans. Large real estate companies in New Jersey, New York, Georgia, and Florida refused to sell property to Jews. The Chamber of Commerce of St. Petersburg, Florida, announced its intention to make St. Petersburg "a 100 percent American gentile city" (McWilliams, 1948). Many country clubs and other social and business organizations barred Jewish Americans from membership.

But since the 1960s anti-Semitism has declined sharply. Today Jewish Americans are widely recognized as hard-working, family-oriented, religious, and

Physicist Albert Einstein was one of the large number of Jewish immigrants who left Germany with the rise of fascism in that country in the 1930s. Today, many Jews have become successfully integrated into U.S. society.

friendly. Their contributions to U.S. cultural life are appreciated. Vandalism and violence against Jewish Americans are rare; the membership of anti-Semitic hate groups is extremely small; economic and social discrimination against Jews has practically disappeared; and non-Jews have elected a growing number of Jews to high public office (Lipset, 1987).

Jewish Americans are so highly regarded largely because they have become the most successful minority. Their levels of education, occupation, and income are higher than those of any other group. Their success may stem from the emphasis Jewish culture gives to education, from a self-image as God's chosen people, and from parental pressure to succeed. Not all Jews are successful, though. There is still significant poverty in their midst. Being rich or poor has much to do with the recentness of arrival to the United States. Most of the poor Jews are Orthodox, the most recent immigrants in the United States. The more successful are Conservative Jews, who have been in this country longer. The wealthiest are Reform Jews, who have been here the longest.

Although Jewish Americans as a whole are prosperous, they are not conservative or inclined to vote Republican, as other prosperous U.S. citizens are. Instead, they tend more to be liberal—supporting welfare, civil rights, women's rights, civil liberties, and the like—and to vote Democratic. Perhaps this reflects their ability to identify with the dispossessed and oppressed. It also reflects the impact of Jewish norms underlying *tzedakah* (pronounced si-DOCK-ah, meaning "righteousness"), which requires the fortunate and the well-to-do to help individuals and communities in difficulty (Lipset, 1990a).

Jewish Americans, however, are in danger of losing their traditional identity. Today, about half of all Jewish Americans are not affiliated with a synagogue, and only a small minority (about 20 percent) attend synagogue regularly. Marriage with non-Jews has increased greatly; over half of all Jewish marriages involve a non-Jew, and most children from such marriages are brought up as non-Jews. The Jewish birth rate has also declined. All this has caused consternation among some rabbis and Jewish communal workers. But Jewish sociologists point out that, despite all those changes in their lives, Jews "have been able to maintain a stronger sense of group identity than most other ethnic groups" in the United States (Waxman, 1990). A major reason is that Jewish cohesion does not derive from traditional Jewish values but rather from occupational and residential concentration. By sharing similar neighborhoods, schools, occupations, organizations, and friends, Jewish Americans have been and continue to be able to maintain the highest level of cohesion (Zenner, 1985; Waxman, 1990).

European Americans

The majority of the U.S. population is descended from immigrants from Europe.

WASPs and Other Western and Northern European Americans   Western and northern European Americans make up the dominant group in the United States. This group includes WASPs (white Anglo-Saxon Protestants), Germans, Irish, and others whose ancestors came from western and northern Europe. Most WASPs are English, and a few are Scottish and Welsh. With the exception of Native Americans, WASPs have a longer history in the United States than any other racial or ethnic group. However, since 1990 WASPS have been outnumbered by Germans and Irish.

Still, WASPs continue to dominate U.S. society with their English language, English laws, and Protestant religion. WASPs also continue to control U.S. political and economic institutions, since most high government officials, large business owners, and corporate executives are WASPs. WASP dominance has faced vigorous challenges from other European Americans, such as the Irish, Germans, and Italians, who have rapidly moved up the success ladder in education, the professions, politics, and business. The WASP culture, into which various minorities have long been forced to assimilate, has also been under siege by multiculturalism, which emphasizes the equal importance of various minority ways of life. Many average, middle-class WASPs, along with other European Americans, now feel that minorities are getting special advantages in jobs and education at their expense (Brookhiser, 1991; Baltzell, 1991; Baltzell, 1994).

White Ethnics: Southern and Eastern European Americans   Toward the end of the nineteenth century a new wave of immigrants came from southern and eastern Europe. Many native-born citizens thought these new immigrants to be inferior people and treated them as such. This belief was reflected in the National Origins Act of 1924, which set quotas that greatly restricted immigration from southern and eastern Europe—a policy that was not altered until 1965.

Today, the descendants of those immigrants are called **white ethnics,** Americans of eastern and southern European origins. Although they have made their mark in education, business, profession, and politics, they are often stereotyped as ultraconservative, uneducated blue-collar workers. In fact, there are more middle-class people among white ethnics than other minorities, and about half have attended college, the same proportion as other European Americans. According to several surveys, white ethnics largely favor liberal policies, such as welfare programs, antipollution laws, and guaranteed wages. They are also relatively free of racial prejudice, perhaps because they can easily identify with African Americans since, like blacks, many have held low-paying manual jobs and been subjected to discrimination (Feagin, 1995a; Farley, 1995).

White ethnics by and large no longer speak their immigrant parents' language, no longer live in ethnic neighborhoods, and routinely marry into the dominant group. They have become such an integral part of mainstream U.S. society that it is difficult to tell them apart. Traces of prejudice toward some white ethnics still exist, though. Italian Americans, for example, continue to be associated with organized crime, although people of Italian background make up less than 1 percent of the 500,000 individuals involved in such activities. In general, the young and

White ethnics, including the owners of this Greek restaurant in Chicago, are the descendants of immigrants from eastern and southern Europe who arrived in the United States at the end of the nineteenth century. Though they have worked at low-paying manual jobs and have been subjected to discrimination, many have worked their way into the middle class and have become an integral part of mainstream U.S. society.

highly educated white ethnics are particularly sensitive to ethnic stereotypes, because they identify themselves strongly with their ethnicity (Giordano, 1987; Alba, 1990).

Putting It All Together

Put in perspective, the status of all the minorities is generally better today than before. Getting closest to the American dream of success are Jews, Asians, and white ethnics, followed by blacks and Hispanics. Ironically, the original owners of this land—Native Americans—have experienced the least improvement in their lives. Of course, we still have considerable prejudice and discrimination. But it is less than before, especially less than in a country like South Africa, where racism has until recently been an official policy (see Figure 8.6). It is also less serious than in Bosnia, Rwanda, and other countries, where a single incident of ethnic conflict often takes hundreds or thousands of lives. Therefore, as black sociologist Orlando Patterson (1991) notes, "The sociological truths are that America, while still flawed in its race relations, is now the least racist white-majority society in the world; has a better record of legal protection of minorities than any other society, white or black; offers more opportunities to a greater number of black persons than any other society, including all those of Africa; and has gone through a dramatic change in its attitude toward miscegenation [interracial marriage or sexual relations] over the last 25 years."

However, we tend to focus on our own current racial problems, without comparing them with how things were in the past or with similar problems in other societies. Interestingly, although the lack of historical and cross-cultural concern may limit our understanding of race relations, it can intensify our impatience with our own racial inequality. This may be good for our society

FIGURE 8.6
Disparity Between Blacks and Whites

In the U.S. and South Africa, whites are better off than blacks by the following percentages.

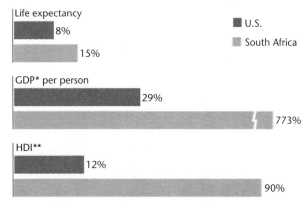

*GDP(Gross Domestic Product) is the total amount of goods and services produced.

**HDI (Human Development Index) is a combined measure of longevity, adult literacy, years of schooling, and standard of living.

Source: Based on United Nations, *Human Development Report 1994* (New York: Oxford University Press, 1994).

because it compels us—especially the minorities among us—to keep pushing for racial equality. On the other hand, the historical and cross-societal analysis in this chapter, which does reveal improvement in our race relations, is also useful. It counsels against despair, encouraging us to be hopeful that racial equality can be achieved.

Questions for Discussion and Review

1. Why have Native Americans become the poorest minority in their own land?
2. What is the social condition of African Americans today?
3. Who are the different groups of Hispanic Americans, and what factors unify all of them?
4. What is the nature of prejudice and discrimination against Asian Americans?
5. How have the experiences of Jewish Americans differed from those of other white ethnic groups?
6. Are European Americans a homogeneous group?
7. What is the status of U.S. minorities as whole?

RACIAL AND ETHNIC RELATIONS

Racial and ethnic relations appear in different forms, from violent conflict to peaceful coexistence. The functionalist perspective emphasizes peaceful coexistence and other positive forms of intergroup relations because they are functional to society, contributing to social order and stability. In contrast, the conflict perspective focuses on violent conflict and other negative aspects of intergroup relations, in which the powerful, dominant group mistreats powerless minorities. Alternatively, the symbolic interactionist perspective focuses on how perceptions influence intergroup interactions and vice versa.

Functionalist Perspective

According to the functionalist perspective, various racial and ethnic groups contribute to social order through assimilation, amalgamation, or cultural pluralism. **Assimilation** is the process by which a minority adopts the dominant group's culture as the culture of the larger society. **Amalgamation** is the process by which the subcultures of various groups are blended together, forming a new culture. **Cultural pluralism** is the peaceful coexistence of various racial and ethnic groups, each retaining its own subculture.

Assimilation   Assimilation can be expressed as A + B + C = A, where minorities B and C lose their subcultural traits and become indistinguishable from the dominant group A (Newman, 1973). There are two kinds of assimilation: The first is **behavioral assimilation,** the social situation in which the minority adopts the dominant group's language, values, and behavioral patterns. Behavioral assimilation, however, does not guarantee **structural assimilation**, the social condition in which the minority is accepted on equal terms with the rest of society. A white Russian immigrant who speaks halting English may find it relatively easy to get structurally assimilated in the United States, but this is less the case with a black middle-class American. Nevertheless, most members of the disadvantaged minorities look upon assimilation as necessary to get ahead—economically and socially—in the United States (Hirschman, 1983).

Amalgamation   In a society that encourages assimilation, there is little respect for the distinctive traits of minority groups. By contrast, a society that seeks amalgamation as an ideal has a greater appreciation for the equal worth of various subcultures. Amalgamation is popularly compared to a "melting pot," in which many subcultures are blended together to produce a new culture, one that differs from any of its components. It can be described as A + B + C = D, where A, B, and C represent different groups jointly producing a new culture—D—unlike any of its original components (Newman, 1973).

More than 80 years ago, a British-Jewish dramatist portrayed the United States as an amalgamation of subcultures. "There she lies," he wrote, "the great melting pot—listen! . . . Ah, what a stirring and seething—Celt and Latin, Slav and Teuton, Greek and Syrian, Black and Yellow—Jew and Gentile" (Zangwill, 1909). Indeed, to some extent the United States is a melting pot. In popular music and slang you can find elements of many subcultures. And there has been considerable intermarriage among some groups, particularly among those of English, German, Irish, Italian, and other European backgrounds. But such amalgamation is less likely to involve white and non-white groups.

Cultural Pluralism   Switzerland provides an example of yet a third way in which ethnic groups may live together. In Switzerland, three major groups—Germans, French, and Italians—retain their own languages while living together in peace. They are neither assimilated nor amalgamated. Instead, these diverse groups retain their distinctive subcultures while coexisting peacefully. Unlike either assimilation or amalgamation, cultural pluralism encourages each group to take pride in its distinctiveness, to be con-

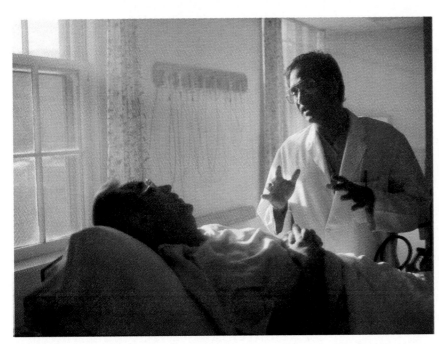

According to the functionalist perspective, various racial and ethnic groups contribute to social order through assimilation, amalgamation, or cultural pluralism. Through assimilation, a minority adopts the dominant group's culture, whereas through amalgamation, the subcultures of various groups are blended, forming a new culture. Cultural pluralism encourages minority groups to retain their cultural identity in the midst of the mainstream culture. Immigrants from the Asian subcontinent demonstrate these processes: they have become assimilated into the economic and educational systems in the United States and join other groups in contributing to the development of the uniquely American culture, while maintaining their own cultural and religious identities.

scious of its heritage, and to retain its identity. Such pluralism can be shown as A + B + C = A + B + C, where various groups continue to keep their subcultures while living together in the same society (Newman, 1973). To some extent, the United States has long been marked by cultural pluralism. This can be seen in the Chinatowns, Little Italies, and Polish neighborhoods of many U.S. cities.

Conflict Perspective

To conflict theorists, racial and ethnic relations can be negative, marked by **racism,** the belief that one's own race or ethnicity is superior to that of others. Racism tends to cause the dominating group to *segregate, expel,* and *exterminate* minorities.

Segregation   Segregation means more than spatial and social separation of the dominant and minority groups. It means that minority groups, because they are believed inferior, are compelled to live separately, and in inferior conditions. The neighborhoods, schools, and other public facilities for the dominant group are both separate from and superior to those of the minorities.

The compulsion that underlies segregation is not necessarily official, or acknowledged. In the United States, for example, segregation is officially outlawed, yet it persists. In other words, **de jure segregation**—segregation sanctioned by law—is gone, but **de facto segregation**—segregation resulting from tradition and custom—remains. This is particularly the case with regard to housing for African Americans. Like the United States, most nations no longer practice de jure

segregation. Even South Africa finally ended its official policy of *apartheid*—racial separation in housing, jobs, and political opportunities—in 1992. But apartheid has become so entrenched that it will continue in the form of de facto segregation for many years to come.

Expulsion   In some cases, the dominant group has expelled a minority from certain areas or even out of the country entirely. During the nineteenth century, Czarist Russia drove out millions of Jews, and the U.S. government forced the Cherokee to travel from their homes in Georgia and the Carolinas to reservations in Oklahoma. About 4000 Cherokee died on this "Trail of Tears." During the 1970s, Uganda expelled more than 40,000 Asians—many of them Ugandan citizens—and Vietnam forced 700,000 Chinese to leave the country (Schaefer, 1988).

Extermination   The most drastic action against minorities is to kill them. **Genocide,** the wholesale killing of a racial or ethnic group, has been attempted in various countries. During the nineteenth century, Dutch settlers in South Africa exterminated the native Khoikhoin, or "Hottentots." During the pioneer days of the United States, white settlers slaughtered Native Americans. On the island of Tasmania, near Australia, British settlers killed the entire native population, whom they hunted like wild animals. Between 1933 and 1945, the Nazis systematically murdered six million Jews. More recently, in 1992, the Serbs in Bosnia killed and tortured numerous Muslims and Croats as part of their campaign of "ethnic cleansing." In 1993 and 1994, thousands of minority members were massacred in the African country of Rwanda.

Symbolic Interactionist Perspective

According to this perspective, if the dominant group defines a minority as inferior, undesirable, or dangerous, interaction between them will be greatly affected. There is likely to be segregated interaction, with members of each group interacting mostly with others of the same group (Charon, 1992). If dominant-group members do interact with minority-group members, the interaction will likely be tense or superficial. The nature of intergroup interaction, then, can be determined by the dominant group's definition of minorities.

That definition is seldom based on reality. Instead, it is a **stereotype,** an oversimplified, inaccurate mental picture of others. Consider the stereotype of blacks as dangerous. Many whites seem to carry this picture in their minds, after having been repeatedly fed by the media with images of black violence and criminality. The reality is that the vast majority of blacks are law-abiding, middle-class people. The remaining minority fall below the poverty line, but most are far from being violent criminals; rather they are young children and single mothers. The small minority that commit violence rarely target whites; most of their victims are fellow blacks. Still, many whites are fearful of blacks.

The stereotype of blacks as dangerous often causes African Americans—including highly successful middle-class blacks—to suffer legal harassment in the hands of white police officers as well as other indignities, as suggested earlier. The stereotype can also bring about grotesque consequences for whites themselves. As a white man said:

> My wife was driving down the street in a black neighborhood. The people at the corners were all gesticulating at her. She was very frightened, turned up the windows, and drove determinedly. She discovered, after several blocks, she was going the wrong way on a one-way street and they were trying to help her. Her assumption was they were blacks and were out to get her. Mind you, she's a very enlightened person. You'd never associate her with racism, yet her first reaction was that they were dangerous (Terkel, 1992).

While stereotypic definitions can shape intergroup interaction, the interaction can also change the definitions. If the interaction is *cooperative*, in which two groups work or play together, negative definitions may dissolve into positive definitions, such as definitions of African Americans as helpful and friendly. Similar positive definitions are also likely to emerge if the interactants from different groups are of *equal status*, such as being equally well-educated (See and Wilson, 1988). Although cooperative and equal-status interactions may improve the dominant group's definition of

minorities, they may have little impact, for example, on African American's distrust of whites. In recent decades, many blacks have studied, worked, and lived in predominantly white settings, but they still feel that many whites they interact with do not accept them as equals (Jones, 1994). In other words, such whites are defined by many blacks as prejudiced although they may interact respectfully with blacks.

Questions for Discussion and Review

1. What kinds of racial and ethnic relations can we see better through the functionalist and conflict perspectives?
2. How is intergroup interaction related to the dominant group's definition of a minority?

PREJUDICE AND DISCRIMINATION

Is it possible for a prejudiced person to act in a respectable, nondiscriminatory way toward a minority person? Don't prejudiced people always discriminate? In this section we will find answers to these and other similar questions by analyzing the characteristics, causes, and consequences of prejudice and discrimination as well as attempted solutions to the problem.

Characteristics

Prejudice and discrimination can be the characteristics of both individual persons and social institutions.

Individual Responses to Minorities   As we have said, prejudice is an attitude; discrimination is an act. Robert Merton (1976) found that the two do not necessarily go hand in hand. Analyzing the possible combinations of prejudice and discrimination, Merton developed a typology of four dominant-group members on the basis of their responses to minorities (see Table 8.1).

First are the *unprejudiced nondiscriminators*. These people believe in the U.S. creed of equality and put their belief into action—their attitudes and behavior are consistent. Merton also calls them *all-weather liberals* because they are likely to abide by their beliefs regardless of where they are—even if their friends and neighbors are bigots.

The second type of dominant-group member in Merton's analysis is the *unprejudiced discriminator*. These people's discriminatory behavior is inconsistent with their unprejudicial attitude. Although free from

TABLE 8.1
A Typology of Dominant-Group Members

	Nondiscriminator	Discriminator
Unprejudiced	1. Unprejudiced nondiscriminator (all-weather liberal)—is not prejudiced and does not discriminate, whatever the social pressure might be.	2. Unprejudiced discriminator (fair-weather liberal)—is not prejudiced but, because of social pressure, does discriminate.
Prejudiced	3. Prejudiced nondiscriminator (fair-weather illiberal)—is prejudiced but, because of social pressure, does not discriminate.	4. Prejudiced discriminator (all-weather illiberal)—is prejudiced and does discriminate, whatever the social pressure might be.

SOURCE: Data from Robert K. Merton, *Sociological Ambivalence and Other Essays* (New York: Free Press, 1976).

prejudice themselves, they practice discrimination because of social pressure. Hence, they are also called *fair-weather liberals.* Unprejudiced homeowners are fair-weather liberals if they refuse to sell their house to a minority family for fear of offending the neighbors. An unprejudiced executive may also hesitate to promote minority employees to managers lest other employees be resentful.

Merton's third category is the *prejudiced nondiscriminator,* the prejudiced person who is afraid to express his or her prejudice through discrimination. Like the fair-weather liberals, these people do not practice what they believe in. They allow social pressure to keep them from doing what they want to do. But, since they are prejudiced despite their nondiscriminatory behavior, they are called *fair-weather illiberals* rather than liberals. Under the pressure of antidiscrimination laws, prejudiced people will hire or work with minorities.

Finally there is the *prejudiced discriminator* who is deeply prejudiced against minorities and practices discrimination. Like all-weather liberals, these *all-weather illiberals* are consistent: their actions match their beliefs. Examples include members of the Ku Klux Klan or neo-Nazis.

Institutionalized Discrimination   Even if every single white were no longer prejudiced and discriminating, discrimination would still exist for some time. Over the years it has been built into various social institutions, so that discrimination can occur even when no one is aware of it. When blacks and whites have long lived in separate neighborhoods, neighborhood schools will remain segregated, even though no

one tries to discriminate against blacks. If employers prefer to hire people who graduated from their own universities that have long denied entrance to blacks, then blacks will not have much chance of being hired. When fire and police departments continue to use the height requirements in hiring that were originally intended for evaluating white applicants, then many otherwise qualified Mexican and Asian Americans—who are generally shorter than whites—will not get the jobs (Kimmel, 1986).

These are all cases of **institutionalized discrimination,** the persistence of discrimination in social institutions, not necessarily recognized by everybody as discrimination. They are traceable to the long history of discrimination by educational, economic, and other social institutions, not to individual prejudice. African Americans suffer the most from institutionalized discrimination. Long victimized by racial oppression, many African Americans lack adequate education and job skills. Many colleges and companies, then, have unintentionally practiced discrimination by denying them college admission and professional or managerial positions only because of their inadequate scholastic and occupational performance, failing to recognize that these are largely the effects of the long history of slavery and discrimination.

Causes

Prejudice and discrimination are far from unique to the United States. They are found throughout the world and there are many causes.

One cause is *social-psychological*. It involves **scape-goating,** blaming others for one's own failure. Through prejudice and discrimination, dominant-group members who have suffered failures in life make themselves feel superior to minorities and so build up their self-image. Hostility against minorities is likely to mount when many dominant-group members are beset with unemployment, poverty, and other problems, which threaten to deflate their self-image. In the last century, antiblack mob violence usually increased in the Deep South during an economic downturn. In the Middle Ages, when thousands of Europeans died in a plague, "rioters stormed Jewish ghettos and burned them down, believing that Jews were somehow responsible for the epidemic" (Beck and Tolnay, 1990; Coleman and Cressey, 1993).

A second cause is *sociological*. It involves socialization. If our parents, teachers, and peers are prejudiced, we are likely to follow their lead. If minorities are often portrayed in the media as inferior or violent, we are likely to be prejudiced and to discriminate against them. Even parents opposed to racism may unknowingly plant seeds of racist thought when they select for their children popular books, such as *The Story of Little Black Sambo,* that contain disparaging images of African Americans (Madsen, 1982).

A third cause is *economic*. It involves the desire for job security and business profit. Historically, given widespread prejudice and discrimination, minorities were prevented from competing for employment, thereby helping to ensure job security for the dominant group's middle and working classes. Prejudice and discrimination also brought profits to the dominant group's upper class. Racism created a huge supply of cheap labor from among oppressed minorities, and prevented much competition from minority businesses.

A fourth cause is *political*. It involves maintaining governmental power. This is why for so many years the white regime in extremely racist South Africa denied black people the right to vote. In the United States in the past, many state and local governments used various means to keep minorities out of the political process, primarily to prevent blacks from voting. When these efforts became unconstitutional, some states continued to discourage minorities from political participation by charging a poll tax, by requiring a literacy test, or by printing ballots only in English in areas where many minority people did not know the language.

Consequences

Prejudice and discrimination have costly consequences for minorities.

First, minorities generally have a lower quality of life than the dominant group. As we have observed, Native Americans, African Americans, and Hispanics

Prejudice is a preconceived negative attitude toward members of a group. These attitudes are seldom critically examined. As a result, they are easily passed to children from parents, as well as from teachers and peers.

have lower income, more unemployment and poverty, fewer years of schooling, and lower life expectancy than whites. There are exceptions. West Indian blacks—immigrants or descendants of immigrants from the Caribbean, such as Colin Powell—have suffered discrimination, but they have achieved higher educational and economic levels than the national average (Harrison, 1992; Sowell, 1994).

Second, partly because of prejudice and discrimination, the black lower class has grown larger and more desperate. Deep poverty persists from generation to generation; the rate of unemployment continues to remain distressingly high among young people; and the number of poor female-headed families is soaring. All this has in turn generated a dramatic rise in violent crime, especially among the youth (as discussed in Chapter 6: Deviance and Control). Occasionally, riots erupt, as they did in South-Central Los Angeles in 1992. In many other cities the rage of the "underclass" simmers just below the surface.

Third, young victims of prejudice and discrimination tend to develop a negative self-image. In 1947, Kenneth and Mamie Clark did a study that helped influence the Supreme Court to desegregate schools in 1954. In the study, 253 black children were asked to choose between four dolls, two black and two white. Two-thirds of the children chose white dolls. In 1985, Darlene Powell-Hopson updated the Clarks' experiment and found essentially the same result: about 65 percent of the black children preferred white dolls. Powell-Hopson believes that the result would likely be the same if the study were repeated today. One reason is the pervasive real-life reminders that blacks are still regarded less highly than whites. Another reason is that television, movies, and children's books seem to link everything beautiful with whiteness. But most black parents try to shield their children from this racial bias and instill ethnic pride (White, 1993).

Attempted Solutions

Under the pressure of the civil rights movement, the Supreme Court first outlawed school segregation in 1954. To achieve school integration, students were bused from predominantly black to white schools. But mandatory busing provoked strong protests from white parents and some "white flight" from cities to suburbs. As a result, mandatory busing programs have largely been dismantled. Today most of the busing programs are voluntary. In addition, the schools that need to be desegregated are turned into "magnet schools." Since these schools offer better education, many white parents are eager to have their children bused to them.

Also under the pressure of the civil rights movement, federal legislators passed a series of antidiscrimination laws in the 1960s. But because of institutionalized discrimination, Congress instituted a policy of **affirmative action,** a policy that requires employers and colleges to make special efforts to recruit qualified minorities and women for jobs, promotions, and educational opportunities. Given equal qualifications, the opportunity must be given to the minority or woman. Sometimes, a less qualified black may have to be chosen over a more qualified white. President Lyndon Johnson summarized the reasoning behind special opportunities for African Americans in a 1965 speech: "You do not take a person who for years has been hobbled by chains, and liberate him, bring him up to the starting line, and then say, 'You are free to compete with all the others'" (Hacker, 1992). Since then the affirmative action has enabled middle-class African Americans to enter higher education and gain professional and managerial positions. But it has failed to help the masses of poor African Americans, who have instead become poorer (Wilson, 1990).

Affirmative action has also aggravated racial tensions because many whites see it as "reverse discrimination" against them. They demand that opportunities be open without regard to race or ethnicity. Conservative African Americans are also opposed to racial preference. They view it as contrary to Dr. Martin Luther King, Jr.'s belief that people should be judged by the content of their character, not the color of their skin. They further observe that affirmative action revives the old racist belief about blacks being inferior by suggesting to whites that blacks are incapable of competing for college admission or jobs unless they are given preference (Wilson, 1990; Steele, 1990). As a consequence, there has been a growing attempt to abolish affirmative action. But, according to a 1995 poll, a majority—65 percent—of U.S. citizens agree with President Clinton that affirmative action should be "mended" rather than "ended" (Carney, 1995). The mending involves avoiding reverse discrimination and rigid quotas while considering only qualified minorities or women for college admission, employment, or promotion.

Questions for Discussion and Review

1. How do dominant-group members react to minorities?
2. What is institutionalized discrimination?
3. What causes prejudice and discrimination?
4. What consequences do prejudice and discrimination have for minorities?
5. How have the attempts to end discrimination turned out?

A GLOBAL ANALYSIS OF RACE AND ETHNICITY

For more than 200 years, the United States has faced the "American dilemma," proclaiming equality yet practicing discrimination. As we have observed, government efforts have not put an end to discrimination. Nevertheless, the problem seems much more severe in other parts of the world. In the 1992 Los Angeles race riot, one of the most destructive in recent U.S. history, about 44 people died, but some 250,000 were killed in the ethnic conflict in Rwanda in 1994 (Rosenblatt, 1994).

Why the difference? As a democratic state, our nation at least officially encourages respect for ethnic differences while providing aggrieved minorities with legal recourse. But many other countries with more severe ethnic problems are mostly authoritarian states that outlaw diverse ethnic expressions. In such societies, the state is defined as the preserve of only one ethnic group, with other groups made to feel like outsiders (Maybury-Lewis, 1994). Thus, numerous members of these other groups have in recent years been attacked or killed, not only in Africa, but also in many countries that had been part of the former Soviet Union.

There are at least three other reasons why ethnic conflict is so fierce in some countries. First, the hostile group has an excessive ethnic identity (Williams, 1994). The strength of this identity usually comes from a shared history of victimization. In Rwanda, for example, the Hutus who slaughtered the Tutsis in 1994 had kept alive the memory of how Tutsis had killed some 100,000 Hutus in 1972. Second, those countries are experiencing enormous political and economic problems, especially high rates of inflation, unemploy-ment, and poverty. Third, politicians seek power by blaming the problems on minorities and inciting destructive action against them (Lemarchand, 1994).

Question for Discussion and Review

1. Why is ethnic conflict more deadly in countries outside of the United States?

CHAPTER REVIEW

1. *Do racial classifications mean anything?* Biologically, they have little significance. They do not correspond to genetically distinct groups. Socially, however, racial classifications have profound meaning, because people often think of themselves and respond to others in terms of race. *How does an ethnic group differ from a race?* People are categorized into races on the basis of their popularly perceived physical characteris-tics, but ethnic groups are based on shared cultural characteristics. *How do racial and ethnic groups become minorities?* They become minorities when subjected to prejudice and discrimination by the dominant group.

2. *Are there indications that Native Americans still experi-ence discrimination?* Their income and health fall below the national average, while their unemployment and poverty are higher. But they have been recapturing their proud traditions.

3. *Have the civil rights laws of the 1960s made a differ-ence?* Yes, but they did not end inequality. They have helped African Americans make significant strides in education and politics, but not in housing and eco-nomic conditions.

4. *What are the origins of Hispanic Americans?* The cate-gory lumps many people together—from the descen-dants of Mexicans and Puerto Ricans who became citizens because the United States took their lands in wars, to recent immigrants from Cuba and other Central and South American countries. *What are their current social conditions?* Hispanics find their common identity in the Spanish language and Roman Catholicism. They generally lag behind whites in edu-cational and economic achievement, but they have become a significant political force in the nation.

5. *How do Asian Americans fare today?* They seem to have achieved more than other groups in education and family income. But they have a relatively high poverty rate and continue to face discrimination.

6. *What is the position of Jewish Americans today?* Their educational, occupational, and economic status is very high. Their affluence, however, has not weak-ened their traditionally liberal stand on social and political issues.

7. *Who are European Americans?* Most have their national origins in western and northern Europe, among whom WASPs are the dominant group. A much smaller group of European Americans are white ethnics, whose ancestors immigrated from southern and eastern Europe. Though successful in various arenas of U.S. life, white ethnics still encounter traces of prejudice.

8. *How is the status of U.S. minorities today?* Though still experiencing prejudice and discrimination, the minorities are faring better today than before and better in the United States than in other countries.

9. *What do racial and ethnic relations look like from the three sociological perspectives?* Seen from the function-alist perspective, intergroup relations appear in the form of assimilation, amalgamation, and cultural plu-ralism, all of which contribute to social order. Viewed from the conflict perspective, intergroup relations appear in the form of segregation, expulsion, and extermination, all of which harm society. According to symbolic interactionists, intergroup relations and defi-nitions influence each other.

10. *Can a person be prejudiced without being discrimi-natory or be discriminatory without being prejudiced?* Yes, because prejudice and discrimination are not the same—the first is an attitude and the second an act. Although the two are related, they do not always go together. *What is institutionalized discrimination?* It is the practice of discrimination in social institutions that is not necessarily recognized by everybody as discrimination. *What causes prejudice and discrimina-tion?* Scapegoating, socialization, and desire for jobs,

profits, or power. *What are the consequences of prejudice and discrimination?* Lower quality of life for minorities, a larger and more desperate "black underclass," and a negative self-image among black children. *What official efforts have been made to combat prejudice and discrimination?* School segregation has been outlawed and antidiscrimination laws have been enacted, with some but not complete success.

11. *How are the racial problems in other parts of the world?* Racial problems tend to cause more deaths in other countries than in the United States. Reasons include excessive group identity, enormous political and economic problems, and power-hungry politicians blaming the problems on minorities.

KEY TERMS

Affirmative action A policy that requires employers and colleges to make special efforts to recruit qualified minorities for jobs, promotions, and educational opportunities. (p. 185)

Amalgamation The process by which the subcultures of various groups are blended together, forming a new culture. (p. 180)

Anti-Semitism Prejudice or discrimination against Jews. (p. 177)

Assimilation The process by which a minority adopts the dominant group's culture as the culture of the larger society. (p. 180)

Behavioral assimilation The social situation in which the minority adopts the dominant group's language, values, and behavioral patterns. (p. 180)

Cultural pluralism The peaceful coexistence of various racial and ethnic groups, each retaining its own subculture. (p. 180)

De facto segregation Segregation resulting from tradition and custom. (p. 181)

De jure segregation Segregation sanctioned by law. (p. 181)

Discrimination An unfavorable action against individuals that is taken because they are members of a certain category. (p. 170)

Ethnic group A collection of people who share a distinctive cultural heritage. (p. 170)

Genocide Wholesale killing of a racial or ethnic group. (p. 181)

Glass ceiling The prejudiced belief that keeps minority professionals from holding high, leadership positions in organizations. (p. 176)

Institutionalized discrimination The persistence of discrimination in social institutions, not necessarily recognized by everybody as discrimination. (p. 183)

Jim Crow laws A set of laws that segregates blacks from whites in all kinds of public and private facilities. (p. 172)

Minority A racial or ethnic group that is subjected to prejudice and discrimination. (p. 170)

Prejudice A negative attitude toward a certain category of people. (p. 170)

Race A group of people who are perceived by a given society to be biologically different from others. (p. 169)

Racism The belief that one's own race or ethnicity is superior to that of others. (p. 181)

Scapegoating Blaming others for one's own failure. (p. 184)

Stereotype An oversimplified, inaccurate mental picture of others. (p. 182)

Structural assimilation The social condition in which the minority is accepted on equal terms with the rest of society. (p. 180)

White ethnics Americans of eastern and southern European origins. (p. 178)

SUGGESTED READINGS

Kotkin, Joel. 1993. *Tribes: How Race, Religion and Identity Determine Success in the New Global Economy.* New York: Random House. How Jews, Britons, Japanese, Chinese, and Indians have prospered in countries far away from their ancestral homes.

Dinnerstein, Leonard. 1994. *Anti-Semitism in America.* New York: Oxford University Press. An account of anti-Semitism from its colonial origins to the present.

Massey, Douglas S., and Nancy A. Denton. 1993. *American Apartheid.* Cambridge, Mass.: Harvard University Press. A study of the continuing segregation of African Americans from mainstream U.S. society.

Nabokov, Peter (ed.). 1992. *Native American Testimony: A Chronicle of Indian-White Relations from Prophecy to the Present, 1492—1992.* New York: Penguin. Includes hundreds of stories about the relations between Native and white Americans, told by the Indians themselves.

Sowell, Thomas. 1994. *Race and Culture: A World View.* New York: Basic Books. A controversial analysis of the differences among racial and ethnic groups.

GENDER AND AGE

Myths and Realities

MYTH: *Physicians are among the highest paid professionals solely because of the importance of their work to society.*

REALITY: There is an additional reason: Most doctors in the United States are men. In the former Soviet Union, where medicine was considered a "feminine" occupation because most physicians were women, they were paid less than skilled blue-collar workers. (pp. 192–193)

MYTH: *Nowadays, with the women's movement influencing most aspects of U.S. life, parents usually bring up their sons and daughters in the same way.*

REALITY: Girls and boys are still treated differently. Usually, girls are given dolls and boys are given action figures. Mothers also tend to fuss about how pretty their little girls look, but are less concerned about their little boys' appearance. (p. 193)

MYTH: *Women receive lower pay than men simply because their jobs typically require fewer skills and less training.*

REALITY: Sexism is also a factor, because, even when women hold the same jobs as men, they tend to earn less. (p. 198)

MYTH: *A highly democratic society, the United States has proportionately more female political leaders than other nations.*

REALITY: The U.S. lags behind most other industrial nations in female political leadership. (p. 199)

MYTH: *It is natural for old people to be senile.*

REALITY: Old age does not inevitably lead to senility. Senility is an abnormal condition, not a natural result of aging. The large majority of old people are not senile. (p. 205)

In 1991, a plane packed with businesspeople and tourists took off from a southern city in India to the country's capital, New Delhi. On that flight a 10-year-old Indian girl named Ameena sat sobbing, her hands covering her tears. Beside her was a 60-year-old Arab man staring blankly out of the window. A flight attendant came over and asked her what was wrong. Appearing afraid of the man, she did not answer and kept on weeping. After the attendant and several passengers ushered her away from him, she said, "This man came to our house. He found my elder sister dark and ugly. My father, who drives an autorickshaw, made me marry this man. He is taking me to Saudi Arabia. I don't want to go with him." When the plane landed in New Delhi, the police arrested the man and took the girl into protective custody. It turned out that the man had been bride shopping in southern India, buying the girl from her poor father for 6000 rupees ($240). Selling young daughters into marriage is common among lower-class Indians, though against the law (Gargan, 1991).

In the same year, a shocking event of a different kind involved an old woman in the United States. When 70-year-old Margaret Embrey was brought into the emergency room of a hospital in Houston, her condition appalled the doctors and nurses. She was covered with bedsores, some as large as a hand. Maggots were gnawing at her wounds, which had cut into her bones. She also suffered from dehydration and malnutrition. Five-foot-seven tall, she weighed only 95 pounds, having lost 40 pounds over the previous six months. The old woman's 19-year-old granddaughter and her husband, aged 22, were later charged with criminal abuse. Such abuse is not uncommon. It happens to as many as 1.5 million elderly Americans—about 5 percent of the elderly population (Rosado, 1991).

These two cases of human abuse are part of the larger, common problem of prejudice and discrimination against females and older people. In this chapter, we will first discuss gender roles and inequalities and then the experience of growing old.

GENDER ROLES

Societies expect different things of women and men. These differences are made explicit in **gender roles:** patterns of attitude and behavior that a society expects of its members because of their being female or male. What is the nature of these gender roles? Are they the same in other societies? Where do the roles come from? Let us analyze each of these issues.

Gender Roles in the United States

In the United States women have traditionally been assigned the role of homemaker and men the role of breadwinner. The "woman's world" was the home; her job was to comfort and care for husband and chil- dren, maintain harmony, and teach her children to conform to society's norms. The man was expected to work out in the world, competing with other men in order to provide for his family. The "man's world" outside the home was viewed as a harsh and heartless jungle in which men needed to be strong, ambitious, and aggressive.

This basic division of labor has been accompanied by many popular *stereotypes*—oversimplified mental images—of what women and men are supposed to be, and to some extent these stereotypes persist. Women are supposed to be shy, easily intimidated, and passive; men, bold, ambitious, and aggressive. Women should be weak and dainty; men, strong and athletic. It is not bad form for women, but it is for men, to worry about their appearance and aging. Women are expected to be emotional, even to cry easily, but men should hold back their emotions and must not cry. Women are expected to be sexually passive and naive; men, aggressive and experienced. Women are believed to be dependent, in need of male protection; men are supposed to be independent, fit to be leaders. Women are expected to be intuitive and inconsistent; men, logical, rational, and objective.

These are the traits that have long been associated with each gender in the United States. They represent both *stereotypes* about how men and women behave and *expectations* about how they should behave. Today, some groups are more likely than others to hold or reject them. Among women, those who are relatively young, unmarried, well educated, gainfully employed, or who have strong feelings of personal competence tend to reject the traditional gender-role attitudes. Among men, the working and lower classes are more traditional in gender-role outlook than are the middle and upper classes.

Although people may consciously reject the traditional gender roles, they tend to behave otherwise. Research has shown that women are more likely to be passive and men aggressive in a number of ways. In interactions between the sexes, the male is more likely to initiate interactions and the female to respond. During a conversation, men tend more to touch women than vice versa. When a man opens the door for women, women tend to say "thank you" or smile their appreciation. But men tend to look confused if a woman opens the door for them, because they are not accustomed to being women's passive beneficiaries. Women are also more likely than men to express feelings of sympathy, sadness, and distress, but are more inhibited with regard to anger and sexual desire

(Tannen, 1990; Campbell, 1993). All these behaviors reflect the powerful influence of traditional gender roles, which make men and women behave differently.

Gender Roles in Other Societies

The traditional gender roles in the United States are not necessarily the same in all societies. Many years ago, anthropologist Margaret Mead (1935) found striking differences among three tribes in the southwest Pacific island of New Guinea. Among one of them, the Arapesh, *both* women and men behaved in what many North Americans would consider a *feminine* way. They were passive, gentle, and home-loving. The men were just as enthusiastic as the women about taking care of babies and bringing up children. The second tribe, the Mundugumor, were just the opposite: *both* sexes showed what many in our society would consider *masculine* traits. Both women and men were competitive, aggressive, and violent. In the third tribe, the Tchambuli, the female and male roles were sharply different, and they were the *opposite* of those traditional in the West: Tchambuli women were the bosses at home; they were the economic providers, doing the hunting, farming, and fishing. Tchambuli men were emotional, passive, and dependent; they took care of children, did housework, and used cosmetics. But the traditional U.S. gender roles can be found in most societies, with men assigned the primary role of breadwinner and women the secondary role of homemaker. The public world is considered a man's domain and the private world a woman's. "Men's work" is more highly valued than "women's work." Even in most of

The basic division of labor in society has been influenced by gender stereotypes about how men and women should behave and therefore what work they are best suited to do. These stereotypes gradually are giving way in our society, especially among the better-educated and those in the middle and upper classes. Only in the last decade or so, for example, would we not be surprised to find a female flight engineer in the cockpit.

the egalitarian hunting-gathering societies, where women often contribute more than half the food supply by gathering nuts, fruits, and plants, men may dominate women. Thus, male dominance over females is nearly universal. As anthropologists Kay Martin and Barbara Voorhies (1975) have observed, "A survey of human societies shows that positions of authority are almost always occupied by males." Since this gender difference appears to be universal, is it biologically determined?

Biological Constraints

What makes one person female and another person male has to do with their **chromosomes,** the materials in a cell that transmit hereditary traits to the carrier from the carrier's parents. Females have two similar chromosomes, XX, one inherited from each parent. Men have two different chromosomes, XY, the X inherited from the mother and the Y from the father.

Whether a person will develop the appropriate sex characteristics—say, breasts or facial hair—depends on the proportion of female and male sex **hormones,** chemical substances that stimulate or inhibit vital biological processes. If a woman has more male than female hormones, she will have facial hair rather than breasts. If a man has more female than male hormones, he will end up with breasts instead. But in most females the proportion of female hormones is greater, and in most men the proportion of male hormones is greater. It is clear that women and men differ both chromosomally and hormonally.

The chromosomal and hormonal differences underlie other biological differences between the sexes. Stimulated by the greater amount of male sex hormones, men are on average bigger and stronger than women. Yet due to their lack of a second X chromosome, men are less healthy. Men are susceptible to more than 30 types of genetic defects, such as hemophilia and color blindness, which are very rare in women. At birth, males are more likely to die. Throughout life, males tend to mature more slowly. They are more physiologically vulnerable to stress. They are stricken with heart disease at a younger age. And they die sooner (Stoll, 1978; Gorman, 1992).

There are also sex differences in brain structure. Neuroscience research has long established that the left hemisphere, or half, of the brain controls speech, and the right hemisphere directs spatial tasks such as object manipulation. There is less specialization in the female's brain, so that she tends to use both hemispheres for a given task at the same time, whereas the male tends to use only one hemisphere. For example, women are more likely to listen with both ears and men with the right ear. Moreover, the female experi-

ences greater cell growth in her language-dominated hemisphere, while the male's greater growth is in his spatial perception-dominated hemisphere (Restak, 1979; Goy and McEwen, 1980; Gorman, 1992).

The differences in brain structure and hormonal production may have contributed to some behavioral differences between the sexes. Thus, female babies are more sensitive than males to certain sounds, particularly their mother's voices, and are more easily startled by loud noises. Female infants are also more quiet, and males are more vigorous and inclined to explore, shout, and bang in their play. Female infants talk sooner, have larger vocabularies, and are less likely to develop speech problems. Stuttering, for example, is several times more prevalent among males. Girls are superior not only in verbal abilities but also in overall intelligence, while boys excel in spatial performances such as mental manipulation of objects and map reading. When asked how they have mentally folded an object, boys tend to say simply "I folded it in my mind," but girls are more likely to produce elaborate verbal descriptions. Women are more sensitive to touch, odor, and sound. They show greater skill in picking up peripheral information as well as nuances of facial expression and voice. They are six times more likely than men to sing in tune (Rossi, 1984; Trotter, 1987). In sum, nature makes women and men different, but these differences do not add up to female inferiority or male superiority. On some measures—such as physical health and early verbal ability—females as a group seem superior to males, and by other measures—especially size and strength—males as a group are superior.

The Role of Culture

The biological differences between males and females seem logically related to the division of labor between the sexes. If men are bigger and stronger, then it makes sense for them to do the work that requires strength. Likewise, assigning women the care of the home and children may be a logical extension of their biological ability to bear and nurse children.

However, there are limitations to biological constraints on gender roles. Since women generally have smaller hands and greater finger agility than men, they are logically more fit to be dentists and neurosurgeons. Yet men dominate these high-paying professions because our culture has long defined them as "men's work." Indeed, the cultural definition of gender roles exercises awesome power. Because U.S. culture has defined being a physician as men's work, the majority of our doctors are males, and they are among the highest paid professionals. By contrast, in the former Soviet Union, where medicine was a "feminine" profession, most of the doctors were women, and they were generally paid "women's wages"—less than what skilled blue-collar workers made.

Undeniably, biology sets females and males apart. But it can only predispose—not force—us to behave in certain ways. Society does much to accentuate gender differences. As Alice Rossi (1984) points out, women may have the natural tendency to handle an infant with tactile gentleness and soothing voice and men may have the natural tendency to play with an older child in a rough-and-tumble way, but these tendencies are often exaggerated through socialization—under the guidance of culture. Also, boys may have been born with a *slightly* greater spatial ability than girls. But as adults, males can perform *much* better on spatial tasks, largely due to socialization. As Beryl Benderly (1989) explains: "Most boys, but few girls, grow up throwing baseballs, passing footballs, building models, breaking down engines—activities that teach about space." Thus, we are born female or male, but we learn to become women or men. We will take a closer look at this learning process in the next section.

Questions for Discussion and Review

1. What are gender roles, and what traits does U.S. society associate with them?
2. How are gender roles different or similar in various societies?
3. How do biology and culture influence the development of gender roles?

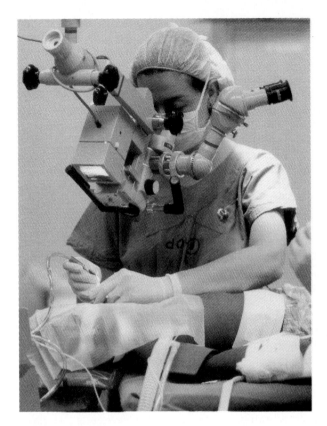

There are limits to the biological constraints on gender roles. For example, since women generally have smaller hands and greater dexterity than men, they are logically more fit—in terms of biology—to be dentists and neurosurgeons, yet men dominate these high-paying professions because they have been deemed "men's work."

GENDER SOCIALIZATION

However a society defines gender roles, its socializing agents pass that definition from generation to generation. The family, peer group, school, and mass media all teach important lessons about these roles.

The Family

Newborn babies do not even know their gender, much less how to behave like girls or boys. Influenced by parents, children quickly develop their sexual identity and learn their gender roles. Right from birth, babies are usually treated according to their gender. At birth, girls tend to be wrapped in pink blankets and boys in blue. Baby girls are handled more gently than boys; girls are cuddled and cooed over but boys are bounced around and lifted high in the air. Girls are given dolls, whereas boys are given action figures. Mothers tend to fuss about how pretty their little girls should look, but they are less concerned about their little boys' appearance.

When they learn to talk, children become more aware of the gender difference. They are taught to differentiate "he" and "his" from "she" and "hers." Gender cues are also available. Both parents use more words about feelings and emotions with girls than with boys, so that by age 2, girls use more emotion words than boys do. Mothers further tend to talk more politely ("Could you turn off the TV, please?"), but fathers use more commanding or threatening language ("Turn off the TV"). By age four, girls and boys have learned to imitate those conversational styles: talking among themselves, girls emphasize agreement and mutuality, and boys use more threatening, dominating language (Shapiro, 1990).

Girls are taught to be "ladylike," polite, gentle, and to rely on others—especially males—for help. They are allowed to express their emotions freely. Observing their mothers' focus on fashion and cosmetics, they learn the importance of being pretty, and they may even learn that they must rely more on their beauty than on intelligence to attract men. On the other hand, boys are taught to behave "like men," to avoid being "sissies." They are told that boys don't cry. If they put on makeup and wear dresses, though in play, their parents are horrified. Growing up with a fear of being feminine, young men learn to maintain a macho image as well as an exploitative attitude toward women. Boys are also encouraged to be self-reliant and assertive, to avoid being "mama's boys" (Elkin and Handel, 1988; Power and Shanks, 1989).

In recent years, though, there has been a trend toward more gender-neutral socialization. Young parents, female professionals, and well-educated parents are particularly inclined to socialize their children into egalitarian gender roles.

The Peer Group

The socialization of girls and boys into their gender roles gets a boost from their same-sex peers, as Barrie Thorne (1993) found in her research. First, girls engage more often in cooperative kinds of play. They jump rope and count in unison, swing around "jungle gym" bars one after another, or practice dance steps in a synchronized fashion. Girls further tend more to say "Let's . . ." or "We gotta . . ." to generate collaborative action. By contrast, boys engage more in competitive rough-and-tumble play and physical fighting. Older boys like to play competitive sports. Boys also like to appear tough by issuing verbal threats: "Shut up or I'll bust your head" or "I'm gonna punch you." Such threats are sometimes made in annoyance or anger, but also in a spirit of play.

Second, girls like to spend time with only one or two best friends, whereas boys tend more to hang around with a larger group of casual friends. With best friends, girls often show gestures of intimacy, such as combing each other's hair or borrowing each other's sweaters. By contrast, boys express their solidarity in a rough way, with, for example, "giving five" handslaps, friendly teasing, or mock violence such as pushing or poking.

Third, far from being "sugar and spice and everything nice," girls do occasionally suffer a breakdown in group harmony, experiencing considerable tension and conflict. But girls are not as direct and confrontational as boys in expressing their conflict. The offenses of others are usually talked about behind their backs rather than to their faces. A dispute among girls is consequently more protracted, much of if carried out through reports to and by third parties (Thorne, 1993).

In short, girls are more likely than boys to learn cooperation, intimacy, and indirectness in dealing with conflict. But, as Thorne cautions, these gender differences should not be exaggerated. Not all of the youngsters show the same gendered characteristics. Those traits are less common among nonwhite and working-class youth. For example, African American girls are just as skilled in direct verbal conflict as boys, and white working-class girls value "being tough" as much as boys do.

The School

Until recently, schools usually segregated courses and sports on the basis of gender. Secretarial courses and home economics were for girls; business and mechanics courses, for boys. Girls played softball; boys, hardball. High school counselors were less likely to encourage girls to go on to college, because they were expected to get married and stay home to raise children. If a girl was going to college, counselors tended to steer her toward traditionally feminine careers, such as teaching, nursing, and social work. While these overtly differential treatments are no longer prevalent, more subtle lessons of gender-role differences are still common. Consider the two examples that follow:

Girls are often led to believe that they are not as proficient in mathematics as boys. If a gifted female student builds a robot, her achievement may be trivialized with questions like "Did you build it to do housework?" Since math is stereotyped as a male domain, boys benefit more than girls from math classes: They are spoken to more, are called on more, and receive more corrective feedback, social interaction, individual instruction, and encouragement. They learn more than what is in the textbook. By contrast, girls are mostly consigned to learning by rote the math in the text, with little exposure to extracurricular math and science. Not surprisingly, girls usually end up scoring lower on standardized math tests, though they may receive better grades on classroom exams—which largely require memorization of course material (Kimball, 1989).

Another subtle lesson of gender-role differences is inherent in the structure of the school. In virtually all elementary and secondary schools, men hold positions of authority (principals and superintendents), and women are in positions of subservience (teachers and aides). In such a male-dominant atmosphere, children are led to believe that women are subordinate, needing the leadership of men. As Laurel Richardson (1988) observes, "Children learn that although their teacher, usually a female, is in charge of the room, the school is run by a male without whose strength she could not cope; the principal's office is where the incorrigibles are sent."

The Mass Media

The media are pervasive sources of gender-role socialization. In such traditional magazines as *Good Housekeeping* and *Family Circle,* until recently the tendency has been to talk down to women as if they were children needing endless reiterations of basics on how to take care of the family. Today, the publications are more sophisticated, but they still tend to define the female role in terms of homemaking and motherhood, and to offer numerous beauty tips to help attract men or please husbands. There are now relatively new, less traditional magazines, such as *New Woman* and *Working Woman,* which show fewer gender stereotypes. But they are dwarfed in circulation by the traditional "seven sisters"—*Better Homes and Gardens, Family Circle, Woman's Day, McCall's, Ladies' Home Journal, Good Housekeeping,* and *Redbook.* These traditional magazines have a combined circulation of 37 million, compared with only three million for the new magazines (Carmody, 1990; Peirce, 1990).

Women's magazines are not alone in perpetuating gender stereotypes. Television commercials have until recently presented women as sex objects and as dedicated housewives. Young sexy women were shown admiring an old cigar smoker who used an air freshener. Housewives were shown in ecstasy over their shiny waxed floors or stricken with guilt for not using the right detergent to rid their husbands' shirts of "ring around the collar." Prime-time television programs also often typecast women as lovers, as mothers, or as weak, passive sidekicks to powerful, effective men. Today, the media are more likely to present women as successful and able to support themselves and their families, but the traditional stereotypes of women are still there. On television and in movies, women are still too often depicted as sex objects, even when they are successful professionals. In men's as well as general-interest magazines, women are told that it's all right to be successful in the workplace but they shouldn't forget that they must also be sexy because "looks are crucial" (Sidel, 1990).

The Learning Process

We may know much about what a socializing agent teaches, but we still need to understand how the child learns the gender role in the first place. According to social learning theory, such social-psychological factors as *conditioning* and *imitation* lie in the process of learning gender roles. Children are rewarded for behaving in ways that parents and others consider appropriate for their gender—and punished for not doing so—so they eventually conform to their society's gender roles. A little boy, for example, learns to hide his fears or pain because he has been praised for being brave and scolded for crying. Children also learn by imitation. They tend to imitate their same-sex parent and other adult models because these adults are powerful, nurturant, and able to reward or punish them. Through reinforcement and imitation, children engage in certain gender-typed activities, which lead to the development of a stable gender identity—"I do girl things. Therefore I must be a girl."

According to social learning theory, children learn gender roles by imitating older people of the same sex: "I do boy things like mow the lawn; therefore I must be a boy." Parents serve as models of gender-typed behavior.

But according to cognitive development theory, gender *identification* is the cause rather than the product of gender-role learning. Children first learn to identify themselves as a male or female from what they observe and what they are told. Then they seek to act and feel like one: "I am a boy, therefore I want to do boy things." Thus, children are not passive objects in the acquisition of gender roles. They are active actors developing their gender identities and performing their gender roles. How clear their identities are and how well they perform their gender roles depend significantly on their *cognitive skills* as, for example, fast or slow learners. Apparently, all the processes discussed here—conditioning, imitation, identification, and cognition—play a part in the learning of gender roles. They are also interrelated. Children cannot rely on their cognition alone to distinguish what is masculine from what is feminine. They have to depend on their parents to serve as models of masculinity and femininity. In serving as models, the parents are likely to reinforce specific gender-typed behavior. Identification with the same-sex parent may also result from—as well as influence—the parents' tendency to reinforce certain gender-typed behavior (Basow, 1986).

According to cognitive development theory, gender identity is the cause of gender-role learning. Children identify themselves as male or female, and then seek to act accordingly: "I am a girl, therefore I want to use makeup." Parents tend to reinforce gender-acceptable behaviors. A young boy wanting to put on lipstick would most likely be discouraged from doing so in our society.

Questions for Discussion and Review

1. How do the family, peer group, school, and mass media contribute to gender-role socialization?
2. How do girls and boys learn gender roles through the processes of conditioning, imitation, identification, and cognition?

GENDER INEQUALITY

At one time or another, laws have denied women "the right to hold property, to vote, to go to school, to travel, to borrow money, and to enter certain occupations" (Epstein, 1976). In recent years, there has been significant movement toward gender equality, but large inequalities remain, even in the United States. They are evident in education, in the workplace, in politics, and in religion. Underlying these inequalities is **sexism**—prejudice and discrimination based on the victim's gender. Sexism also involves sexual abuses against women, of which the most common is sexual harassment.

Sexism

A fundamental characteristic of sexism is the belief that women are inferior to men. Even when a male and a female have the same personalities or are equally competent in performing the same task, the woman is still likely to be considered inferior to the man. We can see this sexist attitude even in psychiatry, a profession that is supposed to be scientific and objective in analyzing human traits. Psychiatrists tend to describe normal men positively—as independent, courageous, and the like—but are more likely to describe normal women negatively, as having "sexual timidity" and "social anxiety." What if women lose their sexual timidity and become sexually active—a trait typically considered normal for men? Then they are likely to be diagnosed as abnormal (Goleman, 1990).

Such a "damned if you do, damned if you don't" attitude toward women is revealed in a study of college students asked to evaluate the social desirability of men and women with various characteristics. Women with "feminine" traits, such as compassion and sensitivity to others' needs, were rated more poorly than men with "masculine" characteristics, such as assertiveness. But women with the "masculine" traits were also rated less favorably than men with the "feminine" traits (Gerber, 1989).

Sexism has long exerted a negative impact on women, making them believe they were inferior to men. In a classic study by Matina Horner (1969), most college women were afraid to pursue successful careers because sexism had caused them to believe that success would ruin their lives—making them unpopular, unmarriageable, lonely, or otherwise miserable. This "fear of success" is far less common among educated women today, a consequence of the women's movement, which vigorously attacked sexism in the 1970s and 1980s. Nevertheless, sexism is still powerful enough to make some women reluctant to pursue careers as men do. According to Susan Faludi (1991), over the last ten years many women have become less willing to pursue careers and more willing to stay home to care for the family. A major reason, Faludi contends, is the exaggerated, negative portrayal of career women in the mass media: suffering depression and burnout from the "rat race," being confronted with fewer opportunities for marriage, and running up against infertility from postponing childbearing.

Sexism may produce inequality between the sexes in two ways. When sexism takes the active form of discrimination against women, it obviously creates inequality. At each level of occupational skill, for example, men receive higher pay than women. Sexism may also foster inequality in a less direct way.

If women have been socialized to feel inferior or abnormal, they may lower their expectations, aiming to achieve less than they otherwise might. Whether through overt discrimination or traditional gender-role socialization, sexism has brought gender inequalities in education, employment, politics, and religion.

Education

Before the turn of this century it was widely believed that "schoolwork would make women sick, diverting blood from their wombs to their brains" (Manegold, 1994). Thus women were long deprived of the opportunities for higher education. They were barred from many colleges and universities, especially graduate and professional schools, far into the 1960s. In general, the more prestigious the educational institutions, the more strongly they discriminated against women. Harvard, for example, was one of the last to give up sex discrimination. It began to admit women to its graduate business program only in 1963.

In 1973, the federal government, under pressure from the women's movement, began to pass laws against sex discrimination in schools. As a result, women have made impressive gains in education. As Figure 9.1 shows, more women than men are now attending and graduating from college. Although still fewer women than men receive medical and law degrees, the proportion of women earning these degrees has increased enormously since 1970. Women are expected to achieve parity with men in receiving these and other advanced degrees in the near future. Apparently, education has become the institution in the United States with most equal opportunity for both sexes.

But there is still substantial inequality in other aspects of education. First, from preschool through high school, girls are given less attention than boys. Teachers call on boys more often, offer boys more detailed and constructive criticism, and allow boys to shout out answers but reprimand girls for doing so, especially in math and science classes. Receiving less attention from teachers, girls further suffer a drop in self-esteem when reaching high school. At age 9 a majority of girls are confident, assertive, and feel positive about themselves, but by age 14 less than one-third feel that way (Sadker and Sadker, 1994). As a result, high school girls score lower on most subjects on standardized tests (see Figure 9.2).

Significant inequalities also persist on the faculties of numerous colleges and universities. As anthropologist Judith Shapiro (1994) points out, women make up less than 30 percent of full-time college faculty. The figures are even lower in the higher ranks of faculty

FIGURE 9.1
Progress Toward Equality in Education

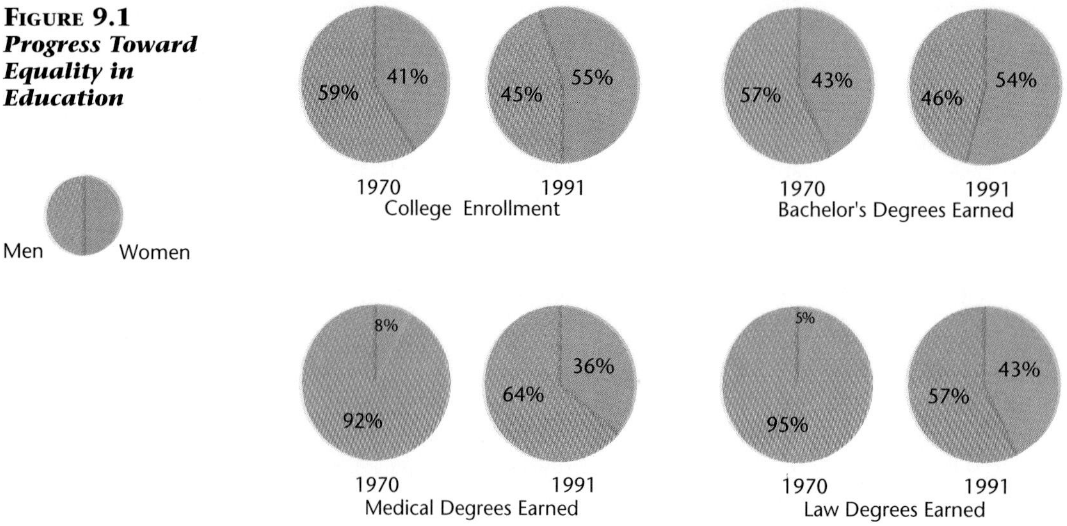

Men | Women

59% | 41%
1970

45% | 55%
1991

College Enrollment

57% | 43%
1970

46% | 54%
1991

Bachelor's Degrees Earned

8%
92%
1970

36%
64%
1991

Medical Degrees Earned

5%
95%
1970

43%
57%
1991

Law Degrees Earned

Source: Data from *Statistical Abstract of the United States*, 1994, pp. 180, 188, 191.

FIGURE 9.2
The Gender Gap in Academic Achievement
The difference in points between men's and women's average scores on standardized tests given to college-bound high school students in 1993 are shown below.

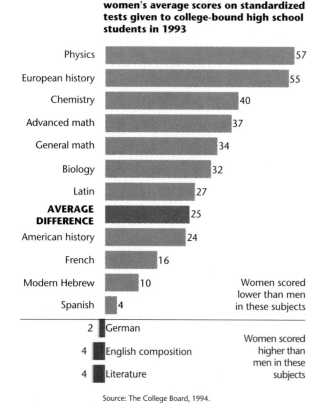

Difference in points between men's and women's average scores on standardized tests given to college-bound high school students in 1993

Physics — 57
European history — 55
Chemistry — 40
Advanced math — 37
General math — 34
Biology — 32
Latin — 27
AVERAGE DIFFERENCE — 25
American history — 24
French — 16
Modern Hebrew — 10
Spanish — 4

Women scored lower than men in these subjects

German — 2
English composition — 4
Literature — 4

Women scored higher than men in these subjects

Source: The College Board, 1994.

and at prestigious universities. Various studies have consistently shown that, compared with their male colleagues, female academics are less likely to be hired, less likely to be promoted, and more concentrated in the lower ranks of institutions. They are also paid substantially less. This treatment is attributed to gender discrimination because there is no evidence that women faculty are less competent in teaching or research.

Employment

Since laws were passed to prohibit sex discrimination in employment more than 30 years ago, women have made some gains in the workplace. More women are gainfully employed than before, and their pay is also higher. Still, women are far from economically equal to men.

Women typically hold lower-status, lower-paying jobs, such as nursing, public school teaching, and secretarial work (see Table 9.1). These traditionally female occupations, known in sociology as **women's ghettos,** are subordinate to positions usually held by men. Thus, nurses are subordinate to doctors, schoolteachers to principals, and secretaries to executives.

Even when women hold the same jobs as men or have comparable skills, training, and education, they tend to earn less. Among industrial nations, the United States has nearly the worst record in women's earnings, as Figure 9.3 shows. The state of Washington has tried to solve this problem by instituting a policy of *comparable worth*, which pays women the same as men for doing different but

TABLE 9.1
The Women's Ghettos

Percent of women in lower-status, lower-paying positions.

	Percent of women
Secretaries	99
Dental hygienists	99
Receptionists	97
Childcare workers	97
Cleaners and servants	94
Registered nurses	94
Bank tellers	88
Librarians	88
Billing clerks	86
Elementary school teachers	86
Waiters	80

SOURCE: *Statistical Abstract of the United States, 1994,*
pp. 407–409.

FIGURE 9.3
The Gender Gap in Earnings: A Global View

Female wages as percentages of male wages

Sweden	90%
Denmark	83%
France	81%
Italy	80%
Germany	78%
Ireland	71%
Spain	70%
Britain	70%
Canada	63%
U.S.	59%
Japan	51%

Source: Data from United Nations, *Human Development Report 1994.*

equally demanding work, such as office cleaning as compared to truck driving. Some other states have followed Washington's lead by developing similar programs (Kilborn, 1990). But the gap in earnings continues to be large. The gap is even more striking when it comes to higher-management positions. As Rochelle Sharpe (1994) found, women make up about 24 percent of officials and managers in various industries as a whole. At the higher, vice-presidential level, women make up an even smaller proportion—less than 5 percent (Reskin and Padavic, 1994; Kilborn, 1995).

Politics

Theoretically, women can easily acquire more political power than men. After all, women voters outnumber men, and most of the volunteer workers in political campaigns are women. Yet, until recently, most women felt that politics was a male activity and that women should not plunge into the dirty world of politics. Sexism also tended to trap women in a double bind to squash their political ambition: If a woman campaigned vigorously, she would likely be regarded as a neglectful wife and mother. If she was an attentive wife and mother, she was apt to be judged incapable of devoting energy to public office. But in a man comparable qualities—a vigorous campaigner or a devoted husband and father—are considered to be great political assets.

In recent years, more and more women have assumed political leadership, but they still have a long way to go. Although they make up over 50 percent of the voting population, women capture no more than 5 percent of all public offices. As Figure 9.4 shows, even in 1993, the year of "genderquake" when a greatly increased number of women were elected to the U.S. Congress, women occupied only 47 House seats (10.8 percent) and seven Senate seats (7 percent). Globally, as Figure 9.5 shows, the United States also lags behind most other industrial nations in female political leadership. Why don't U.S. women recognize their power as a majority of the voting population and use it to elect more women candidates? A major reason, Naomi Wolf (1993) suggests, is lack of unity. According to Wolf, many women wrongly assume that in order to be feminists they must be liberal feminists and promote abortion rights. Wolf therefore calls for a broadly inclusive "power feminism" that helps all kinds of women, whether liberal or conservative, to win more political offices.

FIGURE 9.4
The Gender Gap in the U.S. Congress

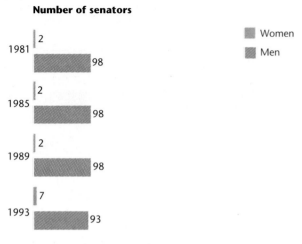

Number of senators

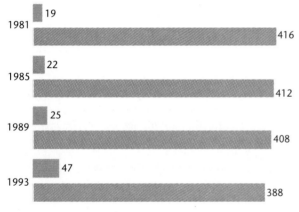

Number of representatives

Source: Data from *Statistical Abstract of the United States,* 1994.

FIGURE 9.5
The Gender Gap in Politics: A Global View

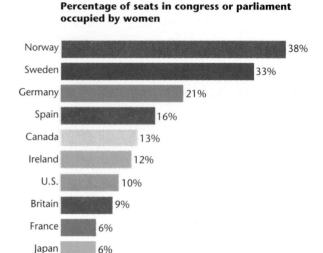

Percentage of seats in congress or parliament occupied by women

Source: Data from United Nations, *Human Development Report 1994.*

Religion

Long used to justify male dominance, the sexist notion of female inferiority can be found in the sacred texts of all the world's major religions. Buddhism and Confucianism instruct wives to obey their husbands. The Muslim Koran states, "Men are superior to women on account of the qualities in which God has given them preeminence." The Christian Bible says that after Eve ate the forbidden fruit and gave it to Adam, God told her: "In pain you shall bring forth children, yet your desire shall be for your husband, and he shall rule over you" (Genesis 3:16). The daily Orthodox Jewish prayer for men includes this sentence: "I thank Thee, O Lord, that Thou has not made me a woman."

All this should *not* be taken to suggest that religion *always* puts down women. In the four Gospels of the

New Testament, for example, "there is a total of 633 verses in which Jesus refers to women, and almost none of these is negative in tone" (van Leeuwen, 1990). But sexist ideas can be found in other parts of the Bible. Even the most central concept of religion—God—is spoken and thought of as being male. To some feminists, the notion of the Supreme Being as male is the quintessence of sexism. Because of this, some liberal church leaders have begun purging hymnals and liturgies of references to God as male (such as "God the Father") and preaching about a genderless deity (called the Creator or Great Spirit). But many bishops, pastors, and laypeople have resisted the changes (Niebuhr, 1992).

Sexism is hardly confined to sacred, historical texts. It also shapes contemporary religious organizations and practices. For the past 20 years in the United States, under the increasing influence of the women's movement, more women have been enrolling in theological seminaries and becoming ordained ministers. But they are still a small minority and have limited career opportunities. Compared with their male counterparts, women clergy are more likely to be underemployed, to be paid low salaries, to serve merely as assistant or associate pastors, or to be relegated to small congregations. Moreover, Conservative and Orthodox Judaism and the Missouri Synod Lutherans are still opposed to ordaining women. The Roman Catholic and Eastern Orthodox churches, which represent over half of all Christians, also continue to pro-

Over the past decade, sexism in religion has been unraveling as women have questioned gender inequalities both in sacred texts and in religious organizations and practices. During this time, more women have been enrolling in seminaries and becoming ordained clergy, but they are still a small minority and have limited career opportunities.

hibit ordination for women (Andersen, 1993; Cowell, 1994). These church hierarchies are at odds with the rank-and-file, though. Two-thirds of lay Catholics, for example, favor opening the priesthood to women (Goldman, 1992).

In sum, gender inequalities in religion can be found both in the sacred texts and the contemporary practices. These two subjects will continue to be a focus of debate as the world's religions confront gender-related issues.

Sexual Harassment

Most sociologists define **sexual harassment** as an unwelcome act of a sexual nature. In 1993 the Supreme Court provided a more precise, legal definition: Sexual harassment is any sexual conduct that makes the workplace environment so hostile or abusive to the victims that they find it hard to perform their job. This definition came with the Court's ruling on the suit that Teresa Harris filed against her former boss, Charles Hardy. In 1987 Harris quit her job in despair because she felt she had been sexually harassed

by Hardy. According to Harris, Hardy often asked her—and other female employees—to retrieve coins from the front pockets of his pants. He once asked Harris to go with him to a hotel room to negotiate her raise. And he routinely made such remarks to her as "You're a woman; what do you know?" She spent six years trying to convince judges that she was sexually harassed in violation of federal law, but to no avail. The judges found Hardy's conduct not severe enough to "seriously affect her psychological well-being." But Harris persisted, and finally the Supreme Court ruled that sexual harassment does not have to inflict "severe psychological injury" on the victim. As the Court says, federal law "comes into play before the harassing conduct leads to a nervous breakdown" (Sachs, 1993).

The Harris case was the second on sexual harassment to reach the Supreme Court. In the first, in 1986, the Court ruled that sexual harassment was a form of gender discrimination prohibited by the Civil Rights Act of 1964. Since that first ruling, the number of harassment charges has increased substantially. In 1992 alone the figure was about 13,000, nearly double the previous year. To avoid being sued, many companies as well as universities and colleges have instituted antiharassment policies, guidelines, or educational programs (Sachs, 1993).

But the problem is too prevalent to go away soon. About half of all working women have been sexually harassed at some point in their careers. One study shows that on college campuses some 28 percent of female graduate students and 40 percent of undergraduate women say they have been harassed. Examples of harassment are, in descending order of frequency, unwanted sexual remarks, leers and suggestive looks, deliberate touching, pressure for dates, pressure for sexual favors, and attempted or actual rape. According to another study, among high school and junior high students, more than two-thirds of girls and 42 percent of boys have been touched, groped, or pinched on school grounds (Kantrowitz, 1991; Henneberger and Marriott, 1993).

Generally, sexual harassment reflects men's attempt to preserve their traditional dominance over women. Men are therefore more likely to harass a woman if they feel threatened by her "invasion" into their male-dominated world. This may explain why sexual harassment seems to occur most frequently in heavily male-dominated occupations such as surgery, investment banking, and the U.S. Navy (Goleman, 1991b). At bottom, sexual harassment is an expression of power, involving a more powerful person victimizing the less powerful. It is possible, for example, for a female boss to sexually harass a male employee. But, given the prevalence of men in positions of power over women, men are the offenders in most cases.

Questions for Discussion and Review

1. What are the characteristics and consequences of sexism?
2. What is the current status of women in educational institutions?
3. Why have jobs traditionally reserved for women led to the creation of women's employment ghettos?
4. How have women fared in politics in recent years?
5. What impact does sexism have on religion?
6. How did the Supreme Court define sexual harassment, and why is sexual harassment so common?

Perspectives on Gender Inequality

We have just seen how gender inequality is manifested in various aspects of society. But why the inequality in the first place? Functionalists and conflict theorists provide different answers. For their part, symbolic interactionists are not interested in the origin of gender inequality but are more concerned with how gender inequality influences the interaction between men and women and vice versa.

Functionalist Perspective

According to functionalists, it is functional for society to assign different tasks to men and women. This division of labor was originally based on the physical differences between the sexes. For thousands of years, when hunting-gathering societies predominated, men were more likely to roam far from home to hunt animals because men were larger and stronger, and women were more likely to stay near home base to gather plant foods, cook, and take care of children because only women could become pregnant, bear and nurse babies. Today, in industrial societies, muscle power is not as important as brain and machine power. Contraceptives, baby formula, childcare centers, and convenience foods further weaken the constraints that the childbearing role places on women. Yet traditional gender roles persist.

The reason for this persistence, functionalists assume, is that these roles continue to be functional to modern societies. How? Talcott Parsons and Robert Bales (1953) argued that two basic roles must be fulfilled in any group. One is the **instrumental role,** which requires performance of a task. The other is the **expressive role,** which requires taking care of personal relationships. In the modern family, the instrumental role is fulfilled by making money; playing this role well requires competence, assertiveness, dominance. The expressive role requires offering love and affection, and it is best filled by someone warm, emotional, nonassertive. When men are socialized to have the traits appropriate for the instrumental role and women are socialized to have the traits suitable for the expressive role, then the family is likely to function smoothly. Each person fits into a part, and the parts fit together.

This role differentiation may have worked well for many traditional families, especially in traditional societies in Asia, as suggested by their lower rates of divorce. But functionalists may exaggerate the role differentiation because women do perform the instrumental role to a large degree. In the United States, every day, many women still spend hours on such instrumental tasks as cooking, housecleaning, laundering, and shopping—and, in many cases, after a full day's work outside the home. Even in many highly sex-segregated preindustrial societies, women perform a significant instrumental role. As Joel Aronoff and William Crano's (1975) research shows, in nearly half the preindustrial societies women contributed at least 40 percent of their societies' food supply. If women perform at least some of the instrumental tasks that men do, it is not role differentiation alone that determines gender inequality. There must be something else that also contributes to gender inequality. That something else has been found in the conflict perspective.

Conflict Perspective

Conflict theorists argue that gender inequality arose because men were able to exploit women. According to the classic Marxist view, gender inequality is part of the larger economic stratification. By restricting women to childbearing and household chores, men ensured their own freedom to acquire property and amass wealth. They also used their power over women to obtain heirs and thus guarantee their continued hold on economic power. Moreover, men have directly exploited women by getting them to do much work with little or no pay. Thus, married women are not paid for doing housework and child care, which would cost about half of most husbands' income if those tasks had to be purchased from others. Gainfully employed wives also do most of the housework and child care, although they work as much as their husbands outside the home. In addition, as we have seen, they are usually paid less than men for their work outside the home (Hochschild 1989; Shellenbarger, 1991; Ingrassia and Wingert, 1995). In short, according to the conflict perspective, the economic exploitation of women helps bring about gender inequality.

Conflict theorists argue that men have directly exploited women by getting them to do much work for little or no pay. The tasks of housework and child care would cost about half of most husbands' incomes if that work had to be purchased from others.

Some conflict theorists give greater weight to sexual exploitation as the source of gender inequality. Randall Collins (1975) argues that "the fundamental motive is the desire for sexual gratification, rather than for labor per se; men have appropriated women primarily for their beds rather than their kitchens and fields, although they could certainly be pressed into service in the daytime too." More recently, according to some feminists, surrogate motherhood has emerged as the ultimate exploitation of women by men because it turns women into mere breeding machines. To conflict theorists, female exploitation of one type or another contributes greatly to the development of gender inequality.

Symbolic Interactionist Perspective

According to symbolic interactionists, interaction between the sexes reflects as well as reinforces gender inequality.

When women interact with men, the interaction tends to reflect their inequality. Suppose a group of women and men discuss some issues at a meeting. Men usually talk more often than women, and they tend to interrupt women more than the other way around. Men are also more likely to boast about their accomplishments and take credit for those of others. On the other hand, women tend to speak more softly and politely and to say more often "please," "thank you," and "I'm sorry." Such interaction between men and women, while reflecting gender inequality, also reinforces it. Because of their verbal aggressions men

are more likely to end up being considered highly competent, having their arguments and decisions accepted, and getting promotions or larger salary raises. By contrast, the less verbally aggressive women tend to lose out, even if they may really be more competent, be the ones who actually get the job done, or contribute more to the company (Tannen, 1994b).

Nonverbal interactions between the sexes also reflect and reinforce gender inequality. Women talking to a man typically give such low-status signals as smiling, nodding, holding their arms to their bodies, or keeping their legs together. Men are more likely to use high-status gestures by smiling only occasionally, holding their heads still, and sprawling out with legs spread apart, taking up substantial space around them (as noted in Chapter 4: Social Interaction in Everyday Life). Because of such an unequal interaction, a mutually aggravated spiral is likely to occur: the woman's conciliatory and nonaggressive gestures lead the man to see her as weak, which makes him more overbearing and aggressive, which intimidates her so as to make her more conciliatory (Cory, 1979; Tannen, 1994a). Ultimately, gender inequality is reinforced, with the man's power enhanced at the woman's expense.

Questions for Discussion and Review

1. According to the functionalist and conflict perspectives, what is the origin of gender inequality?
2. What insight about gender inequality can be learned from the symbolic interactionist perspective?

A GLOBAL ANALYSIS OF GENDER INEQUALITY

While the women's rights movement has produced significant gains in the United States, discrimination against women is still rampant in many developing countries. The abuse of women is by no means unique to developing countries. As the United Nations (1994) found, every single country in the world today still treats its women less well than its men. The problem is more serious and widespread in developing countries than in industrial societies. More specifically, the gender gap in literacy, education, employment, income, and health is significantly larger in developing than in industrial countries.

But some forms of gender discrimination appear unique to certain countries. As the U.S. State Department reported in 1994, many women in China are forced to undergo sterilization and abortion so that they will not have more than one child; young village girls in Burma and Thailand are sold by their parents to brothel owners; maids are beaten in Saudi Arabia; and girls in the Sudan and Somalia are ritually subjected to "female circumcision," during which the clitoris is cut off (Greenhouse, 1994). In China and India the tradition of female infanticide continues in small pockets of the huge countries, and the availability of ultrasound machines that can detect the sex of a fetus has resulted in widespread abortions of females. In India, every year over one thousand young wives are burned to death by their husbands or in-laws because their parents cannot pay any more dowries. In Russia, business etiquette often calls for female secretaries to sleep with their bosses (MacFarquhar, 1994; Pope, 1994).

Question for Discussion and Review

1. In what ways is gender discrimination similar around the globe? In what ways is it different around the globe?

THE AGING PROCESS

The Heinz ketchup company once tried to market dietetic food to older people under the name "Senior Foods." It turned out to be a flop. A perceptive observer explained, "People didn't want to be seen eating the stuff. It was labeling them as old—and in our society, it is still an embarrassment to be old."

Another company, Johnson & Johnson, made a similar mistake when it introduced Affinity shampoo. Its first TV commercial featured a chance meeting between a middle-aged woman and an old boyfriend. He says, "You still look great." By emphasizing age, the commercial failed to sell the product and was soon pulled off the air (Gilman, 1986). The bottom line is that our culture is youth-oriented. Growing old bothers many people. This feeling has much to do with the biological and psychological effects of aging. But social forces, such as our society's tendency to define older persons as a national burden rather than a national treasure, also play an important role. These social forces can aggravate or diminish the biological and psychological effects of aging.

Biological Consequences of Aging

Sooner or later, we all gradually lose our energies and our ability to fight off diseases. This natural physical process of aging is called **senescence.** Biologists have been trying to crack the mystery of why it occurs, but without much success. Some believe that humans are genetically programmed to age; others point to the breakdown of the body's immune system, cells, or endocrine and nervous systems. In any event, it is clear that senescence involves a decline in the body's functioning, which increases the vulnerability to death. It is a gradual process in which the changes come from within the individual, not from the environment. It is also both natural and universal, occurring in all people.

Old age has many biological consequences. The skin becomes wrinkled, rough, dry, and vulnerable to malignancies, bruises, and loss of hair. Because aging also causes the spinal disks to compress, most older persons lose 1 to 3 inches in height. Another result of aging is a loss of muscular strength. More important, blood vessels harden as we age, creating circulatory problems in the brain and heart, problems that raise the incidence of stroke and heart disease among older people. Functioning of the kidneys shows the greatest decline with advancing age. Although aging has all these deteriorative effects, they do not cause disability in most older persons.

Aging also affects sensory perceptions. By age 65, more than 50 percent of men and 30 percent of women in the United States suffer hearing losses severe enough to hinder social interaction. Visual acuity also declines with age: 87 percent of those over age 45 wear glasses, compared with only 30 percent of those under 45. For most people, though, hearing and visual problems are generally inconveniences, not disabilities (Butler, 1984; Kart, 1990).

Aging varies from one person to another; in most older people, it does not cause disability. Being physically and socially active can slow down the aging process, making older people feel healthy and look young longer.

Psychological Consequences of Aging

Aging affects such psychological processes as psychomotor responses, memory, and personality. Older persons tend to have slower, though more accurate, psychomotor responses—such as being able to type at lower speeds but with fewer errors—than young people. Short-term memory—recall of recent events for a brief time—seems to decline with age, although memory of remote events does not. Old age, however, does not inevitably lead to **senility,** an abnormal condition characterized by serious memory loss, confusion, and loss of the ability to reason. Nor does aging necessarily lead to a decline in intellectual performance. In fact, **crystalline intelligence**—wisdom and insight into the human condition, as shown by one's skills in language, philosophy, music, or painting—continues to

grow with age. Only **fluid intelligence**—the ability to grasp abstract relationships as in mathematics, physics, or some other science—tends to stabilize or decline with age (Butler, 1984; Kart, 1990).

Much of the decline in psychomotor and intellectual performance amounts to only a slowing in work, not a falling off in quality. Older people may lose some mental speed, but their accumulated experience more than compensates for the loss of quickness. In fact, compared with youngsters, elders may take longer to make a decision, but it is usually a better one. Therefore, contrary to the stereotyped assumption about the aged automatically experiencing mental deterioration, many studies have shown the quality of job performance to improve with age. With advancing age, people also tend to change from an active to a passive orientation to their environment, becoming less inclined to bend the world to their own wishes and more likely to conform and accommodate to it (Butler, 1984).

Social Effects on Aging

Biological aging does not affect all people in the same way. The speed of aging, for example, varies greatly from one individual to another. Some people at age 75 look 60, and others who are 60 look 75. A number of social factors may determine the disparities. The older look, characterized by the sagging and wrinkling of the skin, may stem from too much sun exposure in earlier years, a legacy of an active, outdoorsy lifestyle. Lack of exercise, another lifestyle, may also speed up the aging process. Thus, those who sit in a rocking chair waiting for the Grim Reaper usually look and feel older than those who are physically active. Social isolation and powerlessness further enhance aging. These largely social, environmental factors suggest that if aging can be accelerated, it can also be retarded (Gelman, 1986; Begley, 1990).

Psychological aging does not affect all people in the same way, either, because of the intervention of social factors. Elderly persons who are well educated, and thus presumably accustomed to flexing their minds, maintain strong mental abilities. So do those older people who have a complex and stimulating lifestyle. By contrast, deterioration of the intellect is more likely to occur among those whose lifestyle is marked by a lack of mental activity, a rigid adherence to routine, and a low satisfaction with life.

Societal definition of aging also influences the impact of aging on mental ability. In their cross-societal study, Becca Levy and Ellen Langer (1994) gave a memory test to comparable samples of young and old people in the United States and China. They found that the U.S. youth turned in a slightly better performance

FIGURE 9.6
Societal Impact on Older Persons' Memories

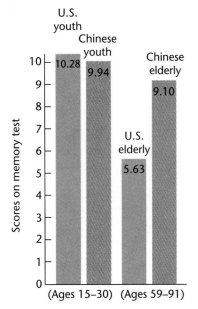

Source: Data from Becca Levy and Ellen Langer, "Aging Free from Negative Stereotypes", *Journal of Personality and Social Psychology*, Vol. 66 (June 1994), p. 994.

than the Chinese youth. But the elderly in China were found to have a sharper memory than their U.S. counterparts (see Figure 9.6). A self-fulfilling prophecy is apparently at work here: widely respected in Chinese society for being wise, elders are often asked for advice, thus creating considerable opportunities for keeping the aging mind active and sharp. But the elderly in U.S. society are less respected and less often given those opportunities.

Question for Discussion and Review

1. What are some of the biological and psychological consequences of aging?
2. How do social factors blunt or worsen the biological and psychological effects of aging?

PERSPECTIVES ON AGING

There are different views on the later stages of a person's life, represented in, among others, disengagement theory, minority theory, activity theory, and sub-culture theory. These theories appear related to the three major perspectives in sociology.

Functionalist Perspective

According to **disengagement theory**, aging causes people to disengage from society. Although elders do not withdraw like hermits, their social interaction does decline. The disengagement is mutual—both aged and younger members of society withdraw from each other. As Elaine Cumming (1963) explains: "The disengagement theory postulates that society withdraws from the aging person to the same extent as the person withdraws from society . . . the process is normatively governed and in a sense *agreed upon by all concerned.*" In other words, social consensus, as the functionalist perspective emphasizes, is crucial; otherwise, disengagement cannot take place. Thus, disengagement occurs when older people retire; when their grown children leave home; when their spouses, friends, and relatives die; when they lose contact with friends and fellow workers; and when they turn their attention to personal rather than societal concerns.

Disengagement theory further holds, as the functionalist perspective suggests, that this mutual withdrawal serves useful functions for society. It is as if two friends, knowing that separation is imminent, gradually drift apart, easing the pain of separation. Society benefits in at least two ways: disengagement renders the eventual death of the elderly less disruptive to the lives of friends and relatives, and it precludes harmful economic effects of the older workers' increasing incompetence or sudden death, because younger people have already replaced them in the workplace. The elderly themselves also benefit because disengagement relieves them of responsibilities, making their lives easier, and encourages them to begin preparing for their own inevitable death. Being "well adjusted" to old age, then, means accepting that one is outside the mainstream of life and coming to terms with one's mortality. Therefore, according to the theory, disengaged elders tend to be happier and healthier than those who try to ignore their age and remain as active as before (Cumming and Henry, 1961; Cumming, 1963).

Critics, however, have challenged the assumption that disengagement is universal or inevitable. They point, for example, to many older members of the U.S. Congress who are far from disengaged from society. Critics also contend that disengagement may be harmful to both society and the individual: it may mean losing the talent, energy, and expertise of the disengaged elders, and, among some, it could contribute to poor health, poverty, and loneliness (Levin and Levin, 1980).

Conflict Perspective

Derived from the conflict perspective, **minority theory** suggests that older people are treated in society as an oppressed minority. In other words, they are victims of **ageism,** prejudice and discrimination against the aged. Like race and gender, age can be used as the basis for judging and reacting to people, regardless of their individual characteristics.

Prejudice against older people is often expressed in various ways. When an 82-year-old man went to visit a doctor with the complaint that his left knee was stiff and painful, the physician examined it. Then he said, "Well, what do you expect? After all, it's an 82-year-old knee." The patient retorted, "Sure it is. But my right knee is also 82, and it's not bothering me a bit" (Dychtwald, 1989). In fact, age prejudice with its underlying stereotype of the elderly as frail or weak, as shown by that doctor, has become so ingrained in many people that they are unaware of its existence. Consider the popular AT&T commercial in which the elderly woman's son calls "just to say I love you, Ma." It won the hearts of many television viewers because they were apparently touched by how sweet the son was to his mother. But they did not realize that it also implied that older people waste their time doing nothing. As one older person says about the commercial, "What do you think we do—just sit around waiting for someone to call?" (Beck, 1990b).

Prejudice is also evident in the common belief that old people are set in their ways, old-fashioned, forgetful, or spend their days dozing in a rocking chair. Some of these ageist beliefs are expressed in jokes such as "Old college presidents never die; they just lose their faculties." Prejudice can further be found in mass communication: in prime-time television shows, the aged tend to be depicted as evil, unsuccessful, or unhappy. Stereotypes about the aged being accident-prone, rigid, dogmatic, and unproductive are often used to justify firing older workers, pressuring them to retire, or refusing to hire them (Levin and Levin, 1980; Meer, 1986).

Discrimination against elders can be seen in mandatory retirement laws, substandard nursing homes, and the domestic neglect and abuse of elders. Even well-intentioned people may unconsciously practice discrimination by patronizing the elderly, treating them like children. As the famous psychologist B. F. Skinner (1983) observed from his perspective as a 79-year-old: "Beware of those who are trying to be helpful and too readily flatter you. Second childishness brings you back within range of those kindergarten teachers who exclaim, 'But *that* is very *good!*' Except that now, instead of saying, 'My, you are really growing up!' they will say, 'You are not really getting old!'"

But in some respects the elderly are far from oppressed. Especially in government and politics, many leaders are aged 65 or older. And older people are such a powerful political force that many elected officials are afraid to anger them by cutting Social Security payments.

Symbolic Interactionist Perspective

In direct opposition to functionalists' disengagement theory is **activity theory**, which suggests that most elders maintain a great deal of interaction with others, even in vigorous physical activities. People do lose certain roles when they retire or when their children leave home. But, according to activity theory, this loss does not necessarily produce disengagement. Instead, the elderly can invest more of their energies in the roles they retain, or in new activities. They may, for example, deepen relationships with grandchildren, make new friends, or join volunteer organizations. By keeping socially active, say activity theorists, older people remain physically and psychologically fit—healthy, happy, and able to live a long life (Havighurst, 1963; Lemon, Bengtson, and Peterson, 1972).

But, according to **subculture theory,** elders interact primarily with one another, sharing interests and experiences with members of the same age group. Several factors increase interaction among the elderly. First are social and demographic trends, including the increasing size of the elderly population, the growing concentration of older people in areas such as retirement communities and public housing for the elderly, and the proliferation of social services for the aged. Second, because of widespread prejudice against the aged and discomfort with aging, elders may find it difficult to interact with younger persons. For example, when older people want to talk about their impending death, their 40-year-old children are likely to change the conversation. The result, according to subculture theory, is that elders interact with their peers more than with younger people (Rose, 1965).

Critics have argued that activity theory presents elders with an often unattainable goal by urging them to cling to an active role in life. Because their activities may not seem meaningful in comparison to their previous roles as workers or parents, older people are likely to feel like failures, useless, and worthless (Atchley, 1988). However, because of increased longevity, elders are becoming more and more active than their counterparts of the past. Not surprisingly, many today engage in a wide variety of activities, even as strenuous as marathon running, that two decades ago would have been considered beyond their reach. As for subculture theory, it is not clear whether there is truly an elderly

The symbolic interactionist perspective suggests that most elders maintain a good deal of interaction with others, even in vigorous physical activities, though they tend to interact primarily with members of their same age group. The popularity of Elderhostel programs—travel and educational activities for elders, such as this hiking trip in Northern California—bears this out.

subculture with values, beliefs, and lifestyles different from the rest of society.

Questions for Discussion and Review

1. What is disengagement theory, and why has it been criticized?
2. What is ageism, and how does it support the theory that the elderly are an oppressed minority?
3. According to activity and subculture theories, how do elders live their lives?

A GLOBAL ANALYSIS OF AGING

Elders generally enjoy higher status in traditional societies than in modern industrialized societies. Part of the reason is that it is no mean feat to grow into old age in traditional societies, which typically have far fewer elderly than modern societies, as Figure 9.7 shows. Thus, by merely living to be old at a time when few survive past middle age, elders earn a certain respect. In addition, because traditional societies change slowly, the knowledge and skills of the aged remain useful. Their experience is greatly valued. They are the community's "experts." Not surprisingly, throughout Africa, growing old results in rising status and increased respect. For example, among the Igbo of northwestern Africa, old people are widely regarded as wise, consulted for their wisdom, and accorded great respect. In central and southern Africa, the male Bantu elder is known as "the Father of His People" and revered as such. In Samoa, too, old age is considered "the best time of life," and elders are highly respected. Similar respect for older people has also been observed in various other countries, from Thailand to rural Mexico (Cowgill, 1974).

In many societies, however, the norm changed with the arrival of industrialization. Older people lost their previous role and status. No longer were they the storehouses of a community's knowledge or the guardians of its traditions, because the knowledge important to the community was changing and traditions were losing their hold. Thus, in many modern societies today, elders lose status because their skills have become obsolete. The loss of status can also be found in rural areas that have been touched by modernization. In a remote community in the Nepal Himalayas, for example, the elderly are unhappy with their lot, wishing that they were dead, complaining that their children have abandoned them, and trying to drown their sorrows in home-brewed liquor every day. The reason is that many of their young men have gone to India to work on construction projects and brought back ideas and attitudes that have no room for the traditional value of filial devotion (Goldstein and Beall, 1982; Gilleard and Gurkan, 1987).

Modernization does not always have such adverse effects on the elderly, though. Faced with an extremely high level of industrialization, Japan nonetheless continues to embrace its long-standing tradition of respect for old people. This tradition is derived from the Confucian principle of filial duty, which requires children to repay their parents a debt of gratitude for bringing them up. It is further supported by a sharply inegalitarian social structure, which requires inferiors, like servants, students, and

FIGURE 9.7
Fewer Elderly in Traditional Societies

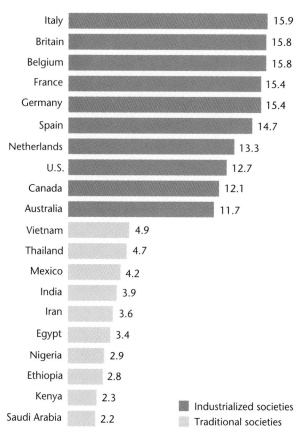

Percentage of each country's population age 65 and older

Italy	15.9
Britain	15.8
Belgium	15.8
France	15.4
Germany	15.4
Spain	14.7
Netherlands	13.3
U.S.	12.7
Canada	12.1
Australia	11.7
Vietnam	4.9
Thailand	4.7
Mexico	4.2
India	3.9
Iran	3.6
Egypt	3.4
Nigeria	2.9
Ethiopia	2.8
Kenya	2.3
Saudi Arabia	2.2

■ Industrialized societies
▨ Traditional societies

Source: Data from U.S. Census Bureau, 1994.

children, to respect superiors, like masters, teachers, and parents (Palmore and Maeda, 1985). Nevertheless, the case of Japan is only an exception to the rule that modernization reduces the elder's status.

In contrast to Japan, the United States is founded on the ideology of equality and individualism. With egalitarianism opposing the traditional inequality between old and young, the elderly began to lose their privileged status when independence was declared in 1776. The emphasis on individualism also helped loosen the sense of obligation between young and old (Fischer, 1977). Assisted by this ideological background, extreme industrialization has decisively brought down the status of elderly. Today, it sometimes seems as if the elderly are expected to do nothing but wait to die. The elderly can be imprisoned in a **roleless role**—being assigned no role in society's division of labor, a predicament of the elderly in industrial society.

Questions for Discussion and Review

1. Why are elders more respected in traditional societies?
2. Why has there been a shift in this respect in modern societies?

---

1. *What are the traditional gender roles of men and women in the United States?* Men are expected to be breadwinners, aggressive, and ambitious. Women are expected to be homemakers, passive, and dependent. Consequently, the sexes tend to behave differently. *Are these gender roles the same all over the world?* No. They are different in some societies, though similar in most other societies. *Do biological differences between the sexes make women inferior to men?* No. In some ways women seem biologically superior and in other ways inferior. *How does culture influence gender-role differences?* Culture

defines what the gender differences should be, and through socialization we develop those differences.

2. *How do we learn our gender roles?* Through socialization by the family, peer group, school, and media. *What is the process by which children learn gender roles?* Gender roles are learned through conditioning, imitation, identification, and cognition.

3. *What is sexism?* It involves prejudice and discrimination against women, based on the belief that women are inferior to men. *Do women today match men*

in educational attainment? Yes in attending and graduating from college. But high school girls still score lower than boys on most subjects. *Have women in the workplace achieved equality with men?* No. Women still tend to hold lower-status jobs and to be paid less than men. *How have U.S. women fared in politics?* They are better off than before, but are still far from achieving political parity with men. *What is the impact of sexism on women in religion?* Women are generally accorded low status and are refused ordination in conservative churches. *What is the sociological nature of sexual harassment?* It reflects an attempt by the powerful to put the less powerful in their place.

4. *According to functionalists, why are gender roles still functional in industrial societies?* With men playing the instrumental role and women the expressive role, the family's smooth functioning can be ensured. *How do conflict theorists explain gender inequality?* It stems from the economic or sexual exploitation of women. *How does symbolic interactionism enhance our understanding of gender inequality?* By showing how interaction between women and men reflects as well as reinforces gender inequality.

5. *How prevalent is gender inequality around the world?* Gender inequality exists in all countries, except that the problem seems more serious and widespread in developing countries. Some forms of female abuse also appear unique to some societies.

6. *What are the biological and psychological consequences of aging?* With age, people become more vulnerable to disease. There are many more specific changes that typically accompany old age—from wrinkled skin to declining visual acuity and slowing of psychomotor responses. *How do social forces influence aging?* By slowing down or speeding up the biological and psychological processes of aging.

7. *Generally, what is the life of the elderly like?* According to disengagement theory, which is influenced by the functionalist perspective, the elderly and society withdraw from each other. Influenced by the conflict perspective, minority theory suggests that the elderly are an oppressed minority victimized by ageism. Influenced by symbolic interactionism, activity theorists argue that, instead of withdrawing from society, the elderly continue to interact with others, although mostly with one another, as members of a subculture.

8. *Why are the elderly in traditional societies more respected than their peers in modern societies?* Because few can survive into old age and society changes slowly, the elderly are admired and their knowledge and skills remain useful.

KEY TERMS

Activity theory The theory that most elders maintain a great deal of interaction with others, even when it requires vigorous physical activities. (p. 207)

Ageism Prejudice and discrimination against the aged. (p. 207)

Chromosomes The materials in a cell that transmit hereditary traits to the carrier from the carrier's parents. (p. 192)

Crystalline intelligence Wisdom and insight into the human condition, as shown by one's skills in language, philosophy, music, or painting. (p. 205)

Disengagement theory The theory that aging causes people to disengage from society. (p. 206)

Expressive role A role that requires taking care of personal relationships. (p. 202)

Fluid intelligence The ability to grasp abstract relationships, as in mathematics, physics, or some other science. (p. 205)

Gender role The pattern of attitudes and behaviors that a society expects of its members because of their being female or male. (p. 190)

Hormones Chemical substances that stimulate or inhibit vital biological processes. (p. 192)

Instrumental role A role that requires performance of a task. (p. 202)

Minority theory The theory that older people are treated in society as an oppressed minority. (p. 207)

Roleless role Being assigned no role in society's division of labor, a predicament of the elderly in industrial society. (p. 209)

Senescence The natural physical process of aging. (p. 204)

Senility An abnormal condition characterized by serious memory loss, confusion, and loss of the ability to reason. (p. 205)

Sexism Prejudice and discrimination based on the victim's gender. (p. 196)

Sexual harassment An unwelcome act of a sexual nature. (p. 201)

Subculture theory The theory that the elderly interact mostly with one another, sharing interests and experiences with members of the same age group. (p. 207)

Women's ghettos Traditionally female occupations that are subordinate to positions usually held by men. (p. 198)

SUGGESTED READINGS

Friedan, Betty. 1993. *The Fountain of Age*. New York: Simon & Schuster. Analyzes the often unrecognized positive side of aging among business and professional people.

Gerson, Kathleen. 1993. *No Man's Land: Men's Changing Commitments to Family and Work*. New York: HarperCollins. An empirical analysis of how traditional and nontraditional men respond to gender equality.

Reskin, Barbara, and Irene Padavic. 1994. *Women and Men at Work*. Thousand Oaks, Calif.: Pine Forge. Analyzes various aspects of gender inequality at work.

Sadker, Myra, and David Sadker. 1994. *Failing at Fairness: How America's Schools Cheat Girls*. New York: Scribner's. Shows the gender discrimination that girls encounter throughout their education, from preschool to college.

Wolf, Naomi. 1993. *Fire with Fire*. New York: Random House. Presents the concept of "power feminism," showing how women achieve more by recognizing their power as a majority in society.

FAMILIES

Myths and Realities

MYTH: The popularity of romantic love in the United States causes young people to choose their mates emotionally and thus irrationally.
REALITY: U.S. youths do not irrationally fall in love with undesirable characters. Most make sound choices, using their heads more than their hearts in choosing whom to love. (p. 219)

MYTH: There is no difference between dating and marriage in the choice of mates. In both cases people are equally likely to choose someone close to their own level of attractiveness.
REALITY: The similarity in attractiveness is greater among married couples than dates. In marriage people usually choose someone whose looks match theirs, but this is less true in dating. (p. 220)

MYTH: High divorce rates in the United States mean that fewer people want to get married.
REALITY: Despite high divorce rates, marriage remains popular. The United States has the highest marriage rate in the industrial world. (p. 223)

MYTH: The traditional U.S. family, which consists of a breadwinner father and a homemaker mother, has been around for hundreds of years. Its existence can be traced all the way to the colonial period.
REALITY: On the farms of colonial days, the family was, in effect, a two-career family, with the wife working side by side with her husband. Only toward the end of the last century, when industrialization was in full swing, did the wife lose her status as her husband's economic partner and acquire the subordinate position as homemaker. (pp. 224–225)

Driving home from work, Janice Edwards, a 27-year-old single mother, tells a journalist interviewing her how she felt when her husband left her five years ago, just after their second child was born: "I thought we'd fall apart with no man there. There was a time I had no money for formula, no gas, no water, no electricity, and I didn't know what in the world we would do." But she has managed for all those years to work at least two jobs at a time to keep her family going. She has most often had an office job during the day and another job at Kmart in the evening. At one point, she even delivered newspapers from 2 to 5 in the morning. She says proudly, "I'm going to work 17 jobs if I have to, but I'm going to take care of my children. I'm not going to listen to people who tell me single mothers are bad. I'm not single by choice; I'm single by force, and I'm not going to listen to those negative things." Like many single mothers, Ms. Edwards is indeed doing reasonably well for her family (Lewin, 1992).

The traditional image of the average U.S. family shows Mom tending her two kids and a house in the suburb while Dad drives off to work. In fact, such a family is relatively rare today. Meanwhile, new forms of the family unit, such as single-parent families like the one just described, have become increasingly common. In this chapter, we discuss various forms of family not only in the United States, but around the world.

FAMILIES: A GLOBAL ANALYSIS

People who marry have, in effect, two families. One is the **family of orientation,** the family in which one grows up, made up of oneself and one's parents and siblings. The other is the **family of procreation,** the family that one establishes through marriage, consisting of oneself and one's spouse and children. As the abundance of jokes about mothers-in-law illustrates, the relationships between these two families can be complicated. Societies need norms that govern this relationship as well as norms that assign roles within each family. Societies must offer the answers to questions like these: Who is part of my family? Who lives with whom? Who is an acceptable spouse? Who makes that decision?

All over the world, societies have given varied answers to these and other questions. The responses have much to do with family composition, norms of mate selection, rules of residence and descent, and rules of authority.

Family Composition

Who makes up a family? Societies' definitions of a family can be classified into two basic types. In the United States, a "family" has long been defined as a **nuclear family,** consisting of two parents and their unmarried children. It is also called a *conjugal family,* because its members are related by virtue of the marriage between the parents. This type of family is quite common in Western industrial societies.

Another type of family is more prevalent in less industrialized societies. It includes not only the nuclear family, but grandparents, uncles, aunts, and cousins. When a nuclear family lives in close proximity to other relatives, interacting with them frequently and acting together as a unit for some purposes, it becomes an **extended family,** consisting of two parents, their unmarried children, and other relatives. This kind of family is also called a *consanguine family,* because the blood tie among relatives is considered more important than the marital bond. In traditional Chinese and Japanese extended families, for example, the tie between a married man and his mother is much stronger than his bond to his wife. In fact, if a mother does not like her son's wife, she can force him to divorce the wife.

Mate Selection

Societies differ, too, in their norms specifying who selects the marriage partner and who is an appropriate partner. In many traditional societies, **arranged**

The selection of a partner depends, too, on the society's norms regarding which partners are appropriate. In most societies, people are required to practice **exogamy** (literally, "marrying outward"), the act of marrying someone from outside one's group—such as the clan, tribe, or village. Contrasted with exogamy is **endogamy** ("marrying within"), the act of marrying someone from one's own group. Endogamy, however, stops short of violating the incest taboo, because endogamous societies do not encourage marriage between close relatives.

There are also norms governing the number of spouses a person may have. **Monogamy**—the marriage of one man to one woman—is the most common form in the world. But many societies, especially small, preindustrial ones, approve of **polygamy,** marriage of one person to two or more people of the opposite sex. It is rare for a society to allow the practice of **polyandry,** marriage of one woman to two or more men. But many societies permit **polygyny,** marriage of one man to two or more women. A new variant of polygamy has become increasingly common in the United States. Rather than having several spouses at the same time, many have one spouse at a time, going through a succession of marriage, divorce, and remarriage. Such practice is not really polygamy, but **serial monogamy,** the marriage of one person to two or more people but only one at a time.

Residence and Descent

In the United States, when most couples marry, they establish a home of their own, away from both families of orientation. They have what is called a **neolocal residence,** a home where the married couple live by themselves, away from both husband's and wife's families. Although this is the most common rule of residence in the United States, it is the least common in the world. People in most societies have a **patrilocal residence,** a home where the married couple live with the husband's family. People in other societies have a **matrilocal residence,** a home where the married couple live with the wife's family.

There are similar rules about who are considered close relatives. The most common of such rules in the world is **patrilineal descent,** the norm that recognizes only the father's family as a child's close relatives. The children belong to their father's family of orientation, not that of their mother, and they adopt their father's family name. But daughters lose their family name when they marry, and their tie to their father's family is not permanent. Only sons, not daughters, may inherit property from the father in patrilineal societies.

The family's functions include sexual regulation, reproduction, socialization, emotional security, and economic cooperation. Family members cooperate as an economic unit, working to earn income or doing household chores to minimize expenses.

marriages—marriages in which partners are selected by the couple's parents—are the rule. The young couple may not even know each other until the wedding day, but they are expected to learn to love each other during the marriage. They are considered too emotional to choose the "right" compatible mates. Usually the parents base their choice of a spouse on how financially secure the other family is, how agreeable the prospective daughter-in-law is to the young man's mother, and how compatible the couple's personalities are.

Much less common is **matrilineal descent,** the norm that recognizes only the mother's family as a child's close relatives. Even in matrilineal societies, however, daughters rarely have the right to inherit property. Usually, sons inherit property from their mother's brother.

The influence of patrilineal traditions seems to exist in U.S. society. Wives and children mostly adopt only the husband's family name. But there is an observance of **bilateral descent,** the norm that recognizes both parents' families as the child's close relatives. Children feel closely related to both their father's and their mother's kin, and both sons and daughters may inherit property from their mother's and their father's families.

Authority

Societies differ in defining who has authority in the family. In most societies, authority rests with the eldest male. Thus, the **patriarchal family,** in which the dominant figure is the eldest male, is the most prevalent around the world. In such a family, the eldest male dominates everyone else. He allocates tasks, settles disputes, and makes other important decisions that affect family members.

Other options are a **matriarchal family,** in which the dominant figure is the eldest female, and an **egalitarian family,** in which authority is equally distributed between husband and wife. Globally, these two types of family are rare. A variant of the matriarchal family, however, has appeared in many industrial countries. In the United States, for example, many poor families are matriarchal by default. Either the father is not present, or he has lost his dominant status because of chronic unemployment. Many other U.S. families, though still dominated by husbands, are also becoming increasingly egalitarian, due to the women's movement.

Questions for Discussion and Review

1. How do family composition and mate selection differ from society to society?
2. How do the world's families differ in regard to residence, descent, and authority?

PERSPECTIVES ON THE FAMILY

The three perspectives in sociology shed light on different aspects of the family. Together, they can give

us a deeper understanding of the family than each alone can.

Functionalist Perspective

According to the functionalist perspective, the family performs certain functions for virtually all societies. The more important functions include sexual regulation, reproduction, socialization, economic cooperation, and emotional security.

Sexual Regulation No society advocates total sexual freedom. Although societies have different sexual norms, all impose some control on who may have sex with whom. Even societies that encourage premarital and extramarital sex restrict and channel these activities so that they reinforce the social order. The Trobrianders of the South Pacific, for example, use premarital sex to determine whether a girl is fertile and to prepare adolescents for marriage. Traditional Inuit society condones extramarital sex, but under conditions that do not disrupt family stability: as a gesture of hospitality, husbands offer their wives to overnight guests.

Traditionally, Western sexual norms have been relatively restrictive, demanding that people engage in sex only with their spouses. Tying sex to marriage seems to serve several functions. First, it helps minimize sexual competition, thereby contributing to social stability. Second, it gives people an incentive to marry. Even today, most young adults eventually feel dissatisfied with unstable, temporary sexual liaisons and find the prospect of a regular, secure sexual relationship in marriage attractive. Even most of the divorced, who usually find their postmarital sex lives pleasurable, eventually remarry because sex with commitment is available in marriage. Finally, encouraging people to marry and confining sexual intercourse to those who are married tends to ensure that children will be well cared for.

Reproduction In order to survive, a society must produce children to replace older adults who die, and practically all societies depend on the family to produce these new members. In some traditional societies, such as the Baganda in the African nation of Uganda, children are considered so precious that a marriage must be dissolved if the wife turns out to be barren. In many industrial nations like the United States, families with children are rewarded with tax deductions.

Socialization To replace members who pass away, a society needs not only biological reproduction, but "sociological reproduction." It needs, in other words, to transmit its values to the new generation, to socialize them. As we saw in Chapter 3 (Socialization), the family is the most important agent of socialization. Because parents are likely to be deeply interested in their own children, they are generally more effective socializing agents than other adults.

Economic Cooperation   Besides socialization, children also need physical care—food, clothing, and shelter. Fulfilling these needs is the core of the family's economic function, and it can facilitate effective socialization. Generally, however, the family's economic role goes beyond care for children and embraces the whole family. Family members cooperate as an economic unit, working to earn income or doing household chores to minimize expenditure. Each person's economic fate rises and falls with that of the family as a whole.

Emotional Security   Finally, the family is the center of emotional life. As we saw in Chapter 3 (Socialization), the relationships we form in our families as children shape our personalities and create hard-to-break patterns for all our relationships. Throughout life, the family is the most important source of primary relationships, the most likely place for us to turn to when we need comfort or reassurance.

Conflict Perspective

Through the functionalist perspective, we see the bright side of the family. But the family also has a dark side, which the conflict perspective reveals.

First of all, the family, because of the strong feelings it generates, is a powerful source not just of love and care but also of pain and conflict. According to a major study, the family is the most violent institution in U.S. society, except the military in time of war (Gelles and Cornell, 1990). In most families, there are instances of conflict and violence, such as anger, physical punishment of children, or spouses poking and slapping each other. In fact, the family is one of the few groups in society empowered by law or tradition to hit its members. It is, for example, legal for parents to spank their children as a form of punishment. Moreover, many husbands who strike their wives to "keep them in line" are not arrested, prosecuted, or imprisoned.

From the conflict perspective, we can also see the family as a mechanism for men's exploitation of women (Delphy and Leonard, 1992). Homemakers and mothers have greatly contributed to the rise and maintenance of capitalism with such forms of labor as reproduction and care of children, food preparation, daily health care, and emotional support. Without this "household production," men would not be free to go out to work. Yet, while men are paid for their jobs outside the home, women are not paid wages for their work in the home. Ironically, women's household work is on the average worth more than men's paid employment. If a woman were paid for services as mother and homemaker according to the wage scale for chauffeurs, baby-sitters, cooks, and therapists, she would earn more than most men do. By demeaning women's housework, however, the family serves the interests of male domination. Even in families where both spouses are gainfully employed, wives generally do most of the housework (Hochschild, 1989; Ingrassia and Wingert, 1995).

In short, according to the conflict perspective, the family is far from "a haven in a heartless world." It is seen as an extension of that world, full of violence and exploitation of women.

Symbolic Interactionist Perspective

Both the functionalist and conflict perspectives deal with the larger issue of what the family is like as a social institution. The symbolic interactionist perspective focuses on more immediate issues, such as how the interaction between husband and wife can bring marital happiness or unhappiness.

In a family, symbolic interaction occurs between husband and wife, between parent and child, between one sibling and another, or among all these individuals. Using the symbolic interactionist perspective as a guide, researchers can focus on any of these interactions and find how the interaction affects the group. Let us see what John Gottman (1994) finds out in his study of marital interaction.

Gottman has observed many couples interact in his lab, concentrating not only on what the spouses say to each other but also on the tone of their voices. He finds three different types of interaction. One is *validating* interaction, in which the partners compromise, showing mutual respect and accepting their differences. The second is *volatile* interaction, in which conflict erupts, resulting in a vehement, loud dispute. The third is *conflict-avoiding* interaction, in which the partners agree to disagree, making light of their differences rather than trying to confront and resolve them. But these three interacting styles do not by themselves determine marital happiness or unhappiness. What is conducive to happiness, Gottman found, is an *excess of positive interactions over negative interactions*. Positive interactions involve touching, smiling, paying compliments, and other acts of thoughtful friendliness. Negative interactions involve ignoring, criticizing, calling names, and other acts of thoughtless nastiness. Gottman discovered that among happy couples there are at least five positive interactions for every one negative interaction, but among unhappy couples the ratio is less than 5 to 1.

Questions for Discussion and Review

1. What functions does the family perform for society?
2. How does the family appear from the conflict perspective?
3. How can the symbolic interactionist perspective be used to understand the quality of family life?

PATTERNS OF U.S. MARRIAGES

In the United States the family is by and large nuclear and monogamous and increasingly egalitarian. Its cornerstone is the relationship between husband and wife. In this section, we discuss how people prepare for marriage, how they choose a spouse, and how most U.S. couples achieve marital success.

Preparing for Marriage

Most people do not consciously prepare themselves for marriage or diligently seek a person to marry. Instead, they engage in activities that gradually build up a momentum that launches them into marriage. They date, they fall in love, and in each of these steps they usually follow patterns set by society.

The Dating Ritual Developed largely after World War I came to an end in 1918, the U.S. custom of dating has spread to many industrial countries. It has also changed in the United States in the last two decades. Before the 1970s, dating was more formal. Males had to ask for a date at least several days in advance. It was usually the male who decided where to go, paid for the date, opened doors, and was supposed to be chivalrous. The couple often went to an event, such as a movie, dance, concert, or ball game.

Today, dating has become more casual. In fact, the word "date" now sounds a bit old-fashioned to many young people. Usually you do not have to call somebody and ask for a date. "Getting together" or "hanging around" is more likely. Spontaneity is the name of the game. A young man may meet a young woman at a snack bar and strike up a brief conversation with her. If he bumps into her a day or two later, he may ask if she wants to go along to the beach, to the library, or to have a hamburger. Males and females are also more likely today than in the past to hang around—get involved in a group activity—rather than pair off for some seclusive intimacy. Neither has the responsibility to ask the other out, which spares them much of the anxiety of formal dating. Getting together

For most people, dating provides opportunities for learning to get along with members of the opposite sex. It also offers the opportunity for falling in love with one's future spouse.

has also become less dominated by males. Females are more likely than before to ask a male out, to suggest activities, pay the expenses, or initiate sexual intimacies. Premarital sex has also increased, but it tends to reflect true feelings and desires rather than the need for the male to prove himself or for the female to show gratitude (Strong and DeVault, 1992).

The functions of dating, however, have remained pretty constant. It is still a form of entertainment. More important, dating provides opportunities for learning to get along with members of the opposite sex—to develop companionship, friendship, and intimacy. Finally, it offers opportunities for courting, for falling in love with one's future spouse. "Playing the field" does not lead to a higher probability of marital success, though. Those who have married their first and only sweetheart are just as likely to have an enduring and satisfying marriage as those who have married only after dating many people (Whyte, 1992).

Romantic Love Asked why they want to get married, Americans usually say, "Because I am in love." In U.S. society, love between husband and wife is the foundation of the nuclear family. In fact, young people are most reluctant to marry someone if they do not love the person even though the person has all the right qualities they desire (see Figure 10.1). Many people in traditional societies, though, believe that love is too irrational to form the basis for a marriage and that intense love between husband and wife may even threaten the stability of the extended family. To them, it is more rational to marry for such pragmatic considerations as economic security and good character.

But does romantic love really cause people to choose their mates irrationally? Many studies have suggested that the irrationality of love has been greatly exaggerated. An analysis of these studies has led William Kephart and Davor Jedlicka (1988) to reach this conclusion: "Movies and television to the contrary, U.S. youth do not habitually fall in love with unworthy or undesirable characters. In fact, [they] normally make rather sound choices." In one study, when people in love were asked, "Does your head rule your heart, or does your heart rule your head?" 60 percent answered, "The head rules." Apparently, romantic love is not the same as infatuation, which involves physical attraction to a person and a tendency to idealize that person. Romantic love is less emotionalized, but it is expected to provide intrinsic satisfactions, such as happiness, closeness, personal growth, and sexual satisfaction. These differ from the extrinsic rewards offered by a pragmatic loveless marriage—rewards such as good earnings, a nice house, well-prepared meals, and overt respect.

In the United States over the last 30 years, the belief in romantic love as the basis for marriage has grown more fervent than before. In several studies in the 1960s, 1970s, and 1980s, college men and women were asked, "If a person had all the other qualities you desired, would you marry this person if you were not in love with him/her?" Today, as opposed to earlier decades, a greater proportion of young people say no (Simpson, Campbell, and Berscheid, 1986).

Marriage Choices

Romantic love is far from blind, but it also does not develop in a social vacuum. It depends heavily on the partners' support from others, particularly family and friends. Such support is usually available if the couple believes in **homogamy,** marrying someone with social characteristics similar to one's own.

Most marriages occur within the same social class because of shared values, expectations, tastes, goals, and occupations. People also tend to choose mates of the same religious faith. The more cohesive and smaller the group is in a community, the more homogamous the group. Jews are therefore more likely to marry Jews than Catholics are to marry Catholics. Most marriages further involve members of the same race.

There is also a tendency to marry people very close to one's own age. Most couples are only two years apart. But most men who marry at 25 have a wife who is three years younger; at 37, most men marry a

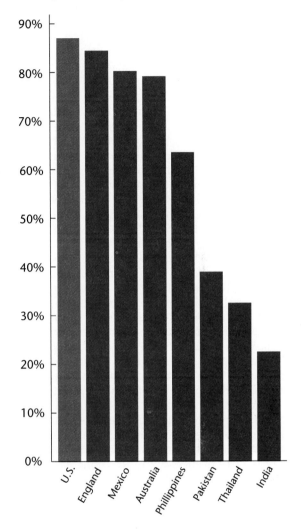

Percentage of college students who say they would *not* marry someone with all the right qualities if they didn't love the person

Source: Data from Robert Levine et al., "Love and Marriage in Eleven Cultures," *Journal of Cross-Cultural Psychology*, Vol. 26 (September, 1995), pp. 554–71.

FIGURE 10.1
No Love, No Marriage

woman six years younger. A major reason that older men tend to marry much younger women is that men generally place greater importance on physical attractiveness than women. But the age difference between brides and grooms increases only until the men reach age 50. After this, most men marry women close to their own age again (Schulz, 1982; Mensch, 1986).

Since people of similar race, religion, and class are likely to live close to one another, there is a strong tendency to marry someone who lives nearby. This tendency may be weakening as cars and airplanes continue to increase mobility, yet most couples still come from the same city, town, or even neighborhood. According to many studies, there is more than a 50–50 chance that one's future spouse lives within walking distance (Kephart and Jedlicka, 1988). As James Bossard (1932) said, "Cupid may have wings, but apparently they are not adapted for long flights."

We have seen how homogamy applies to the *social* characteristics of couples. What about their individual characteristics, such as aggressive personalities and talkativeness? Do they also follow the same pattern? The answer is no, according to Robert Winch's (1971) well-known theory of complementary needs. Winch argues that people with *different* personality traits are attracted to each other if these traits complement each other. This theory resembles the popular belief that "opposites attract." Thus, aggressive men tend to marry passive women; weak men like strong women; talkative women go for quiet men; emotional men find rational women attractive; and so on. Winch's own research has supported this theory, but more recent studies by other investigators have backed the social psychological version of homogamy—the theory that people with *similar* traits are attracted to each other, much as "birds of a feather flock together" (Wilson, 1989; Morell et al., 1989). Perhaps, given increasing gender equality in recent decades, the sexes may have become more alike. For example, men now seem more sensitive than before and women more assertive.

Homogamy also reigns in regard to physical attractiveness. Everybody prefers the person of their dreams, but most people end up marrying someone close to their own level of attractiveness. Interestingly, the similarity in attractiveness is greater among deeply committed couples than among casual ones. When people are playing the field, their looks may not match their dates'. But they are more likely to get serious with the dates who have about the same level of attractiveness (Kalick and Hamilton, 1986; Stevens et al., 1990).

Marital Happiness

With time, both the physical attraction and the idealization of romantic love are likely to fade, so that marital love involves mostly commitment. Love may be less exciting after marriage, but, as William Kephart and Devor Jedlicka (1988) observe, it "provides the individual with an emotional insight and a sense of self-sacrifice not otherwise attainable," qualities that may be keys to marital success.

How successful are U.S. marriages? The answer obviously depends on how we define "successful." Gerald Leslie and Sheila Korman (1989) suggest that in a successful marriage the couple have few conflicts,

basically agree on major issues, enjoy the same interests during their leisure time, and show confidence in and affection for each other. To others, this sounds like a static, spiritless relationship. Instead, some argue, a successful marriage is one that is zestful and provides opportunity for personal growth. Such disagreement among scholars suggests that a "successful marriage" is basically a value judgment, not an objective fact (Strong and DeVault, 1992).

It is, therefore, best to simply look at whether people consider their own marriages successful, however experts might judge them. By this standard, most U.S. marriages are a success. Several studies have shown that the overwhelming majority (over 90 percent) of people say they are either "very happy" or "pretty happy" with their marriages. In fact, married

The success of marriages depends on how we define "successful." If the criterion is how people themselves rate their own marriages, then most U.S. marriages can be judged successful. Studies have shown that the majority of people say they are either "very happy" or "pretty happy" in their marriages. Regarding one's spouse as a friend is one of the characteristics found to be associated with happy marriages.

couples are much more likely than single people to say that they are happy, whether it is about love, personal growth, or even job satisfaction (Strong and DeVault, 1992; NORC, 1994). Marriage, however, rather than parenthood, is the focal point of marital happiness. As research has suggested, the presence of children often detracts from marital happiness because the couple see their relationship less as a romance and more as a working partnership. In fact, these working partners often find parenting so stressful that they feel relieved or happy after their children reach adulthood and leave home (White and Edwards, 1990).

What makes for marital happiness? By comparing happily married with unhappily married couples, researchers have come up with a long list of characteristics associated with happy marriages. Among these are having happily married parents; knowing the prospective spouse for at least two years; being engaged for at least two years; getting married at an age above the national average (about 25 for men and 23 for women); being religious or adhering to traditional values; regarding one's spouse as a friend; being of the same religion and race; having the same level of education; and having good health, a happy childhood, emotional stability, parental approval of the marriage, and an adaptable personality (Kephart and Jedlicka, 1988; Hatch, James, and Schumm, 1986). But why are couples with these characteristics likely to be happy? Perhaps they engage in positive interactions far more frequently than negative interactions (Gottman, 1994) as discussed earlier.

Questions for Discussion and Review

1. What roles do dating and romantic love play in preparing individuals for marriage?
2. What are the distinguishing characteristics of homogamy?
3. What accounts for marital happiness?

FAMILY PROBLEMS

While most couples are happy with their marriages, many do have serious problems. One example is family violence. Another is divorce, the culmination of marital problems.

Violence

Family violence is relatively common in the United States. Its exact incidence is hard to pin down, because various researchers do not define family violence in the

same way. There is, of course, little disagreement about extreme cases, in which a family member is killed or seriously injured by another. But there is disagreement over what kinds of behavior are acceptable for disciplining children or dealing with spousal conflict. Some researchers consider spanking, for example, an act of violence, whereas others do not (Klaus and Rand, 1984; Dobash et al., 1992). Thus, there have been different estimates of the extent of family violence in the United States. The estimates on the proportion of families in which violence occurs at least once in a year range from 10 to 20 percent, and anywhere between 25 and 50 percent of all couples have been estimated to suffer serious family violence at least once during the course of their marriage (Straus et al., 1988; Gelles and Cornell, 1990). All this may make family violence appear to be an enormous problem because the family is supposed to be "home sweet home."

Why does family violence occur? A major reason is stress. Research shows that the incidence of violence is highest among groups most likely to feel under stress, such as the urban poor, families with a jobless husband, and those with four to six children (Straus et al., 1988). Stress by itself, however, does not necessarily cause violence. People would not resort to violence as a way of relieving stress if they were not culturally encouraged to do so. There seems to be a "culturally recognized script for behavior under stress" in U.S. society (Straus et al., 1988). The violence on television, corporal punishment in schools, and the death penalty, for example, convey the idea that violence is an acceptable solution to problems. Research further suggests that the tendency for marital violence is transmitted from one generation to another. It has been found that most of the violent married individuals have, as children, seen their parents hit each other (Kalmuss, 1984).

Ironically, though, as many as half of the battered women do not leave their husbands who continue to abuse them. Why? Most do not have money and do not believe they can earn enough to support themselves or their children. Moreover, they fear that if they leave, their husbands may stalk them to inflict more serious violence. These reasons, along with repeated abuse, cause the victims to feel helpless, which forces them to survive in the same way as hostages, prisoners of war, or concentration camp victims do: by accommodating their captors and focusing on just living from hour to hour (Brody, 1992).

Divorce

Divorce is common in the United States. About half of the people who marry for the first time will eventually get a divorce. Although the divorce rate has begun to

Family violence is a continuing problem because research shows it tends to be transmitted from one generation to the next. Many battered women stay in abusive situations because they do not have the economic or social resources to leave, and many stay for fear that their abusers will stalk them to inflict more violence. Many social programs have been established to help and protect battered women; the photo here is part of Liz Claiborne, Inc.'s Women's Work program.

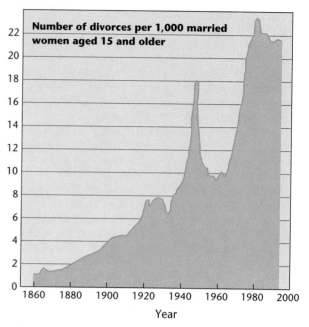

Source: Data from Census Bureau, 1994; Andrew J. Cherlin, *Marriage, Divorce, Remarriage* (Cambridge, Mass.: Harvard University Press, 1992).

FIGURE 10.2
U.S. Divorce Rate

dip slightly since 1980, it is still more than twice as high as it was in 1960—the year when the rate began to rise (see Figure 10.2). It is also the highest in the world (U.S. Census Bureau, 1994).

Why do so many marriages end in divorce? Numerous studies have compared divorced couples with nondivorced couples and found a number of personal problems and social characteristics to be associated with divorce. They include infidelity, incompatibility, financial difficulties, lower socioeconomic status, and marrying too young (Strong and DeVault, 1992; Goode, 1982, 1993). But these data cannot explain why industrial Western societies have higher divorce rates than traditional Eastern societies, or why the U.S. divorce rate today is far higher than it was a century ago. A cross-cultural analysis suggests at least five larger social forces behind the current high divorce rate in U.S. society:

1. *Decreased social disapproval of divorce.* In many traditional societies, unhappily married couples stay married because of the stigma attached to divorce. In the United States, there is virtually no stigma. Divorce has gained wide acceptance as a solution to marital unhap-

piness, and it has become easier to obtain from the courts.

2. *Greater availability of services and opportunities for the divorced.* In traditional societies, men depend heavily on marriage for sexual gratification and housekeeping, and women look to it for financial security. Such services and opportunities are more easily available to U.S. adults without the need for marriage. For example, men can find sexual gratification outside marriage, and women can become financially independent without husbands. In addition, the high divorce rate today has expanded the pool of eligible new partners. All this can make divorce more attractive to unhappily married couples.

3. *The family's increased specialization in providing love and affection.* In U.S. society, the family has become specialized in offering love and affection, while the importance of its other functions has declined. When love and affection are gone, a couple are likely to break up their "empty shell" marriage. By contrast, in traditional societies with low divorce rates, the family's other functions—especially socializing children and providing economic security—remain highly important. Thus, even when love has disappeared from marriage, there are still other reasons for keeping the family together.

4. *High expectations about the quality of marital relationship.* Young people in traditional societies do not expect an exciting romantic experience with their spouses, especially if their marriages are arranged by their parents. But young people in the United States expect a lot, including an intense love relationship. These expectations are difficult to fulfill year after year, and the chances of disillusionment with the partner are therefore great. Since young people have higher expectations than older ones, it is not surprising that most divorces occur within the first four years of marriage (Cherlin, 1992).

5. *Increased individualism.* The rights of the individuals are considered far more important in the United States than in traditional societies. Individualism encourages people to put their own needs and privileges ahead of those of others, including their spouse, and to feel that if they want a divorce, they are entitled to get one. In traditional societies, people are more likely to subordinate their needs to those of the kinship group and thus to feel they have no right to seek a divorce.

The current high divorce rate in the United States does not mean, as common sense would suggest, that the institution of marriage is very unpopular. On the contrary, people seem to love marriage too much, as suggested by several pieces of evidence: First, our society has the highest rate of marriage in the industrial world despite having the highest rate of divorce (U.S. Census Bureau, 1994). Second, in the United States, as shown in Figure 10.3, most of the southeastern, southwestern, and western states have higher divorce rates than the national average but also have higher marriage rates. Third, the majority of those who are divorced eventually remarry (Cherlin, 1992). Why don't they behave like Mark Twain's cat, who after having been burned by a hot stove would not go near *any* stove? Apparently, divorce in U.S. society does not represent a rejection of marriage but only of a specific partner.

Questions for Discussion and Review

1. What causes family violence?
2. What are the social causes of divorce?

Figure 10.3
How Divorce and Marriage Go Together in the United States

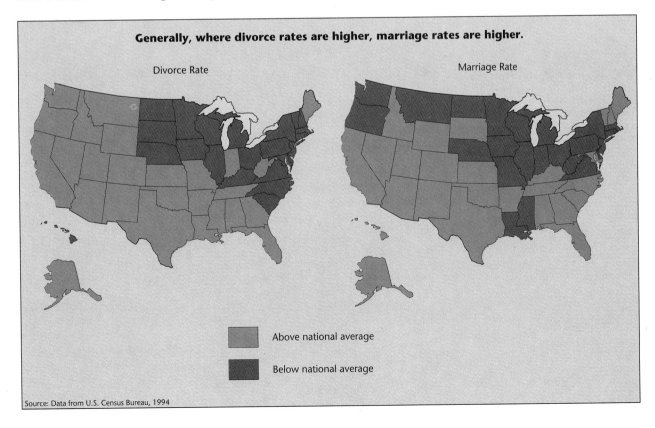

Generally, where divorce rates are higher, marriage rates are higher.

Divorce Rate   Marriage Rate

Above national average

Below national average

Source: Data from U.S. Census Bureau, 1994

CHANGES IN THE U.S. FAMILY

The traditional nuclear family, which consists of two parents living with children, is no longer the typical U.S. family. As far back as 1970, the proportion of traditional families had already declined to 40 percent. By 1993 it was only 26 percent (see Figure 10.4). Increasingly, people are choosing new patterns of family life. To see how much the family has changed, let us first take a quick tour of its past.

Historical Background

Before the industrialization of this country in the last century, the family had long consisted of husband, wife, and children, with no other relatives. One reason for the popularity of the nuclear family in those days is that few people lived long enough to form an extended, three-generation family. Another reason is that *impartible* inheritance practices—which allow for only one heir to inherit all the property—forced sons who did not inherit the farm to leave and set up their own households (Cherlin, 1983).

On colonial farms, men, women, and children helped produce the family's livelihood. The wife was typically an essential economic partner to the husband. If her husband was a farmer, she would run the household; make the clothes; raise cows, pigs, and poultry; tend a garden; and sell milk, vegetables, chickens, and eggs. If the husband was a skilled craftsman, she would work with him. Thus, weavers' wives spun yarn, cutlers' wives polished metal, tailors' wives sewed buttonholes, and shoemakers' wives waxed shoes (Tilly and Scott, 1978).

But, as the United States became industrialized in the nineteenth century, the "household ceased to be a center of production and devoted itself to child rearing instead" (Lasch, 1979). Industrialization took production out of the home. Initially husbands, wives, and children worked for wages in factories and workshops to contribute to the common family budget. But, due to the difficulty of combining paid employment with the domestic tasks imposed on them, married women tended to work for wages irregularly. As wages rose, growing numbers of families could earn enough without the wife's paid work. Then, increasingly, the home was seen as the emotional center of life and a private refuge from the competitive public world. The woman's role became emotional and moral rather than economic. Women were expected to rear their children and comfort their husbands. This became the stereotype of a typical and ideal U.S. family.

Thus, after industrialization was in full swing, women lost their status as their husbands' economic partners and acquired a subordinate status as housewives (Cherlin, 1983). But over the last few decades there have been significant increases in gender equality, female independence through paid employment, and personal freedom for everybody. As a result, a diversity

In colonial America, the wife was typically an essential economic partner with her husband. If they had a craft, she would work with her husband as a skilled craftsperson. In the case of the husband being a weaver, for instance, the wife would shear the sheep and spin and dye the yarn.

Percentage of married couples with children under age 18

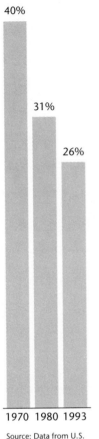

1970 1980 1993

Source: Data from U.S.
Census Bureau, 1994.

FIGURE 10.4
Traditional Nuclear Families: A Shrinking Minority

Percentage of married women in the labor force

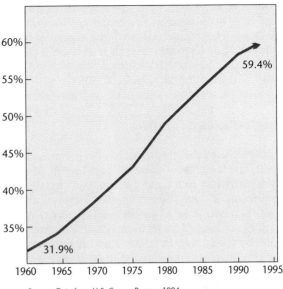

Source: Data from U.S. Census Bureau, 1994.

FIGURE 10.5
The Surge of Employment Among Married Women

of family types has emerged, causing the traditional nuclear family to become less common. Some of these new family types are discussed in the following sections.

Two-Career Families

In the last 30 years, there has been a tremendous surge of married women into the labor force. As Figure 10.5 shows, the proportion of gainfully employed wives shot up from only 31.9 percent in 1960 to about 59.4 percent in 1993. Their employment has increased family income significantly. In 1993 the median income of two-career families ($56,000) was more than 34 percent higher than the income for one-career families ($37,000). At the low end of the income scale, the wife's contribution is so great that relatively few dual-earner families fall below the poverty line (U.S. Census Bureau, 1994).

Does this economic gain bring marital happiness? Apparently it does for *most* two-career couples. But research comparing them with one-career families has produced conflicting results. Some studies found that the wife's employment benefited her but not her husband. In one such study, employed wives reported more marital happiness, more communication with husbands, fewer worries, and better health, while their husbands were less content with their marriage and in poorer health (Burke and Weir, 1976). But other studies found more strain in two-career marriages because the wife was still expected to be a homemaker rather than a career seeker (Skinner, 1980). The strain is much heavier for the employed wife than for her husband, because she does most of the housework, as already observed.

The effect of a wife's employment seems to depend on how much support she gets from her husband. Many husbands still find it difficult to render total support to their wives' careers, particularly if their wives earn more than they do. Consequently, in cases where the wife outperforms the husband in earnings, sex lives are more likely to suffer, feelings of love are more likely to diminish, and marriages are more likely to end in divorce. Lack of support for the wife's career may also explain why premature death from heart disease is 11 times more frequent among husbands whose wives outshine them professionally (Rubenstein, 1982).

On the other hand, in cases where the husbands fully support their wives' employment by doing their share of house cleaning and child care, the couples do head off marital stress and achieve marital happiness (Cooper et al., 1986). Generally, supportive husbands have long been exposed to egalitarian ideologies and lifestyles. They have accepted the value of gender equality. They have also seen their mothers as competent and influential individuals who shared equal status with their fathers (Rosin, 1990).

Single-Parent Families

With increased divorce, there has been a phenomenal rise in the number of children growing up in households with just one parent. From 1970 to 1993, the proportion of single-parent families increased from 13 to 30 percent. A large majority (80 percent) of such families are headed by women. About a quarter of the children today live for some time in female-headed families. It has been estimated that more than half of all children born in the 1990s will live with their mothers alone before they reach age 18 (Strong and DeVault, 1992; U.S. Census Bureau, 1995).

Most (about 70 percent) single mothers today are women who have been divorced, separated, widowed, or abandoned by their husbands (Lewin, 1992). Most of these families live below or near the poverty level. Even women of higher-income groups tend to suffer a sharp drop in household income as a result of marital breakup. African American mothers are more likely to reside with the children's grandmothers, who provide free child care. But they are far from well prepared to cope with the challenges of single parenthood (Hogan et al., 1990).

Since the early 1980s there has been a significant increase in *never-married* women having children. As shown in Figure 10.6, 23.7 percent of all never-married women had children in 1992, a 57 percent increase over the 15.1 percent of just ten years earlier. Figure 10.6 also shows that the most dramatic increase is among women in managerial and professional jobs, whites, and college graduates. This increase may be attributed to growing middle-class acceptance of unwed motherhood, women's rising earning power, and women's higher standards for choosing husbands (Seligmann, 1993). Nevertheless, the number of these more affluent unwed mothers is still much smaller than that of other groups.

Compared with two-parent families, female-headed families are more likely to experience social and psychological stress, such as unemployment, job change, lack of social support, negative self-image, and pessimism about the future (McLanahan, 1983). Children from single-parent families also have a larger share of such problems as juvenile delinquency, truancy, and poor school work. Whatever problems these children may have, however, they do not result directly from

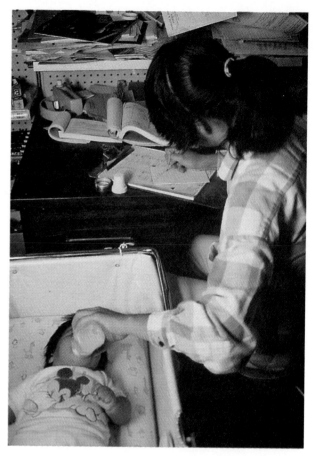

Compared with two-parent families, single mothers are more likely to experience social and psychological stress because their financial resources are more often severely limited.

the absence of a father in a female-headed home, as popularly believed, but from factors that can also be found in a two-parent family, such as low income, poor living conditions, and lack of parental supervision (Cherlin and Furstenberg, 1983; Cherlin, 1992).

Stepfamilies

Given the high rates of divorce and remarriage, stepfamilies have become quite common. They number some 7.3 million and account for 16 percent of all married couples with children under age 18. Because women usually win custody of children in divorce cases, most stepfamilies—also called *blended families*—consist of mothers, their biological children, and stepfathers. Nine out of ten stepchildren live with their biological mothers and stepfathers (U.S. Census Bureau, 1994).

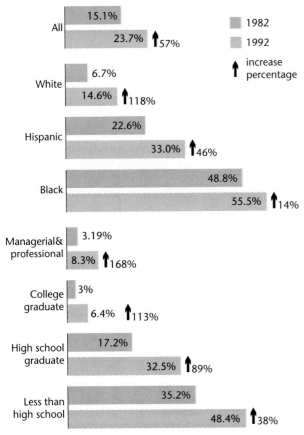

Percentage of never-married women aged 18 to 44 who have children

	1982	1992	increase percentage
All	15.1%	23.7%	↑57%
White	6.7%	14.6%	↑118%
Hispanic	22.6%	33.0%	↑46%
Black	48.8%	55.5%	↑14%
Managerial & professional	3.19%	8.3%	↑168%
College graduate	3%	6.4%	↑113%
High school graduate	17.2%	32.5%	↑89%
Less than high school	35.2%	48.4%	↑38%

Source: Data from U.S. Census Bureau, 1993

FIGURE 10.6
Never-Married Women with Children

The happiness of stepfamilies depends largely on how well the stepfather gets along with the children. It is tough to be a stepfather. Society has not yet provided a script for performing that role as it does for the father role. Thus, it is much more difficult for stepfathers to develop intimate and durable bonds with their stepchildren than for other fathers to do so with their biological children (Cherlin and Furstenberg, 1994).

Accustomed to living with their biological fathers, children tend to regard their stepfathers as interlopers or as distant, unwanted relatives overstaying their visits. They may resent having to change their lifestyle, as a 15-year-old girl sobs to her mother, "I can't stand it. I have to put on my bathrobe at 10 o'clock at night in 'our' own house to go downstairs to get an apple from the refrigerator because he's there in 'our' living room." Aside from running into such conflicts over territoriality, stepfathers are likely to have

problems with discipline. If they tell a 13-year-old stepson that he should not watch an R-rated cable movie, he may retort: "My dad lets me watch them. Besides, it's Mom's television set" (Nordheimer, 1990).

Conflicts over territoriality and discipline are most likely to erupt with teenagers. Young children can quickly accept their stepfathers' love and discipline because of their physical and emotional dependence on adults. But teenagers are striving to break free of adult authority, as they are preoccupied with schoolwork, friends, sports, and their developing sexuality. They accept parental discipline only out of love and respect, which the stepfather initially does not or may never have. During an argument, teenagers are likely to shout at their stepfathers: "You're not my real father!" Not surprisingly, the presence of stepchildren has been found to be a major reason why second marriages fail at a higher rate than first marriages. Nevertheless, most stepfamilies are relatively free of serious trouble and conflict (Nordheimer, 1990; Strong and DeVault, 1992).

Questions for Discussion and Review

1. Why did the traditional nuclear family made up of the breadwinner husband and homemaker wife emerge in the last century?
2. How has the entry of large numbers of married women into the labor force changed the family?
3. What special problems do single mothers and stepfathers face in raising children?

ALTERNATIVE LIFESTYLES

There are always people who reject conventional family life and pursue different lifestyles. Some of these lifestyles have in recent decades become more popular.

Staying Single

Of various alternatives to marriage, staying single is by far the most common. In 1990 about 10 percent of people lived alone, accounting for 24 percent of all U.S. households. This represents an increase of more than 112 percent over the last 20 years, from just fewer than 11 million singles in 1970 to 23 million today, many in their thirties and forties. But most are younger adults, who postpone marriage into their late twenties. More significant, a growing number of young adults live with their parents and will also stay single for some time (Crispell, 1990; Nemy, 1991; Gross, 1991).

Most singles are not actually opposed to marriage and do expect to be married sooner or later. One reason they often give for their current singlehood is that they have not met the right person. But increasing numbers of men and women choose to stay single. Some studies have found them to be happier than their married counterparts. They are also more likely to see themselves as very romantic. If asked why they are single, they are likely to say that "marriage entails too much commitment and responsibility" or "I prefer the lifestyle" (Simenauer and Carroll, 1982; Harayda, 1986; Janus and Janus, 1993). There are, however, two sociological reasons for the increase in committed singlehood.

First, the social pressure to get married has declined. This is particularly true for city dwellers, who face far less pressure to marry than small town residents. Second, the opportunity for singles to have a good life has expanded. This is especially true for women. As educational and career opportunities open up for them, along with the freedom to choose to be a single mother, marriage is no longer the only avenue to economic security, emotional support, social respectability, and meaningful work. Although singles are generally happy and respected, our society, like most others, still relegates them to a diminished status, treating their way of life as less desirable than that of married couples (Nemy, 1991).

Living Together

In the past, very few couples lived together without a formal wedding ceremony or marriage license. These couples were said to be "living in sin." They were mostly the very rich, who could afford to ignore society's rules, and the very poor, who had little to lose by ignoring them. Today, cohabitation has spread to other sectors of U.S. society, including college students and young working adults. The result is a dramatic rise in cohabitation. In 1970, the number of unmarried couples living together was only slightly over half a million, but since then it has soared to 3.5 million (U.S. Census Bureau, 1994). Social disapproval has vastly diminished, and courts have stepped in to protect couples' rights as if they were legally married (Lewin, 1982; Bumpass and Sweet, 1989; Steinhauer, 1995).

Because the incidence of cohabitation continues to rise, some fear that it may undermine the institution of marriage. In Sweden, where cohabitation is already four times as prevalent as in the United States, living together does not pose a threat to marriage at all. Most cohabitants live like married couples and intend to marry eventually. The situation in the United States is similar. Often called common-law marriage, cohabitation as a permanent alternative to marriage is relatively rare today; it occurs mostly among the very poor. For most cohabitants, living together is a temporary arrangement, which usually lasts for fewer than two years. Although it does not imply a commitment to marry later, cohabitation often leads to marriage. It is a modern extension of the courtship process, comparable to the traditional custom of "going steady" (Spanier, 1983; Gwartney-Gibbs, 1986; Tanfer, 1987).

Does living together lead to more marital happiness than traditional courtship? Couples who live together often argue that cohabitation works like a trial marriage, preparing them for marital success. But research has mostly shown less marital satisfaction or more divorces among couples who have cohabited than among those who have not. The reason for marital failure, however, is not the prior experience of cohabitation. It is the lack of strong commitment to marriage, which often exists among couples who have lived together (Watson and DeMeo, 1987; Barringer, 1989; Trussell and Rao, 1989; Whyte, 1992).

Gay and Lesbian Marriages

More gay men and lesbians live together today than before. Same-sex couples now number over 1.6 million in the United States (Seligmann, 1992). Gay marriages have recently been legalized in only a few countries such as Denmark, Norway, and Sweden. But they are not legally recognized in the United States, where gay couples do not have the same legal protections and financial benefits as "straight" couples, such as tax exemptions and deductions or Social Security survivor's benefits. In recent years, though, a number of cities have granted unmarried couples, both gay and straight, a legal document called a "domestic partnership agreement." Some gay couples have used it to gain family benefits from employers, insurance companies, health clubs, and other commercial establishments. Also, in 1993 the Supreme Court of Hawaii ruled that the ban on same-sex marriages violates the state constitution's ban against sex discrimination. Hawaii could well be the first state in the United States to legalize gay marriages.

Like heterosexuals, most gay men and lesbians want to get married when they are in love. Though denied the legal right to marry, they tie the knot in about the same way as their "straight" counterparts. Gay weddings range from simply exchanging rings in private to "pulling out all the stops"—such as having "the church ceremony, matching tuxedos or dresses, traditional vows, formal reception for two hundred, and a four-tiered wedding cake topped with two

Most singles are not opposed to marriage; they expect to be married eventually. They remain single because they have not met the "right person." But increasing numbers of men and women choose to stay single. The reasons include a decline in social pressure to get married and an expanded opportunity for singles to have a good life.

grooms or two brides" (Marcus, 1993). Sociologically, the wedding serves to strengthen the couple's relationship. By expressing their vows and love for each other in the presence of their significant others, the same-sex couple tend to feel a stronger sense of commitment and security.

Also like their heterosexual counterparts, many gay and lesbian couples have children. Most of these children come from earlier, heterosexual relationships. But an increasing number of the children are adopted or born through artificial insemination.

Gay couples are far more egalitarian in their relationship than heterosexual couples. Heterosexual men and women usually have been socialized to play different gender roles, with the husband expected to do "masculine" things such as fixing the family car and the wife "feminine" things such as preparing the family meals. Such gender-role differences often make men dominant over women. By contrast, gay partners have been socialized to the same gender role, so that they tend to have an egalitarian relationship. If a gay couple works—as most do—both partners do about the same amount of housework. One does not do more housework than the other, as is often the case with heterosexual couples (see Chapter 9: Gender and Age).

Questions for Discussion and Review

1. Why do some people stay single?
2. Does the great increase in cohabitation threaten the institution of marriage? Why or why not?
3. In what ways are gay and lesbian families similar to and different from conventional families?

ETHNIC DIVERSITY OF U.S. FAMILIES

The discussion so far is mostly based on studies of European American families. Here we focus on families of other ethnicities.

Native American Families

Before the emergence of the United States as a nation, some Native American tribes were patrilineal, but most were matrilineal, including the better known tribes like the Zuni and Hopi in the Southwest and the Iroquois in the Northeast. Despite their tribal differences, various Native American families shared certain characteristics. Infants were born in special birth huts. During the years of breastfeeding, mothers refrained from sex. Physical punishment was rarely used to discipline children, who were taught instead by example. Children learned adult roles at an early age, so that most girls were married between ages 12 and 15 and boys between ages 15 and 20. Most tribes were monogamous. Only a few allowed men to have two wives or engage in extramarital sex when their wives were pregnant or breastfeeding. Extended family networks predominated, and kinship ties and obligations to relatives flourished (Strong and DeVault, 1992; Wilkinson, 1993).

Today this traditional family life has disappeared among many Native Americans. Between 1870 and 1930 the U.S. government embarked on a program of destroying the Native American culture. It involved assimilating Native Americans into the white culture by, among other things, sending their children to white-run boarding schools. Today only a small minority of Native Americans have successfully resisted assimilation and kept alive their traditional values, particularly the importance of kinship ties and obligations. The rest, including the third of all Native Americans who marry outside their race, have either adopted white values completely or a mixture of white and Indian values. Compared with other ethnic groups, Native Americans suffer from higher rates of poverty, alcoholism, suicide, and other problems, all of which create severe difficulties for many Native American families (Strong and DeVault, 1992; Harjo, 1993).

Hispanic American Families

Most Hispanic families are nuclear, with only parents and children living together, but they do have the characteristics of an extended family. There exist strong kinship ties, as various relatives live close to one another and often exchange visits, emotional support, and economic assistance (Vega, 1992).

Hispanic families tend to have large numbers of children, generally more than families of other ethnicities. Children typically occupy the center of family life. They are taught to respect the elders, to appreciate family unity, and to assume family responsibilities. The father tends to be very affectionate and easygoing toward younger children, but becomes more authoritarian and strict as they get older. His role as the head of the family is often described as *machismo,* being manly in protecting and providing for the family, exercising authority fairly, and respecting the role of the wife (Becerra, 1988). The wife is in charge of the day-to-day matters of child rearing and homemaking. Gender equality increases with the length of residence in the United States; families started by younger generations tend to be more egalitarian than families of older generations (Wilkinson, 1993; Chilman, 1993).

Imbued with strong family values, Hispanics generally have lower divorce rates compared with Anglos. The exception is Puerto Ricans, who have a much higher rate as a result of a greater prevalence of poverty. Hispanics are also likely to marry outside their group, especially among those with a higher socioeconomic status. Generally, the longer their families have been in the United States, the higher their rates of interethnic marriage (Wilkinson, 1993).

African American Families

When they were slaves, African Americans were prohibited from marrying. They created their own marriages, developing strong family ties similar to those in the traditional African extended family. These emotional bonds helped African Americans cope with the daily indignities of servitude. Still, slavery made it difficult for many African American families to be stable, because family members were often sold. After slavery was abolished, African Americans continued to suffer, this time as victims of racism and poverty. Throughout their travails, the mutual aid and emotional support that characterized the early family system has survived (Strong and DeVault, 1992; Wilkinson, 1993).

Since the early 1970s many African American families have been dealt a devastating blow from deindustrialization and the resulting massive loss of blue-collar jobs from many U.S. cities to labor-cheap countries. One consequence has been rampant unemployment among African Americans in inner cities. As their poverty rate soared, the traditional African American family declined sharply. Today about 52 percent of African American families have only one parent, mostly a single mother, and 67 percent of African American babies are born to unmarried women under age 35 (Chideya et al., 1993; U.S. Census Bureau, 1994).

It has been observed that ironically "the traditional family system that slavery could not destroy during 200 years may be dismantled in a few short years by the modern industrial transition" (Billingsley, 1993). Still, the African American family is most likely to survive, because it continues to draw its strength from the legacy of mutual assistance among relatives, friends, neighbors, and church members (Taylor et al., 1993).

Asian American Families

Compared with other U.S. families, Asian American families—particularly Chinese, Japanese, Korean, and Vietnamese—generally are more stable, having lower divorce rates, fewer female-headed households, fewer problems with child rearing, greater familial solidarity, and stronger kinship associations (Wilkinson, 1993). These are often attributed to the Asians' Buddhist or Confucian culture, which emphasizes the subordination of the individual to the family.

Instead of stressing the importance of the individual's independence and autonomy, Confucianism emphasizes the individual's obligation to the family. The nature of the obligation varies with the status of each family member. The father is the head of the family, and thus must provide for the economic welfare of his family. The mother is expected to be the nurturant caretaker of both her husband and children. And the children are supposed to practice *hsiao,* or filial piety. This essentially involves showing gratitude toward parents by performing two tasks: (1) providing parents with economic and emotional support, such as

Asian cultures, particularly Buddhist and Confucian cultures, typically emphasize subordination of the individual to the kinship group. Although such traditions decline over succeeding generations of Asian Americans, the residual effect is to make their families more stable than many U.S. families from other backgrounds.

aid, comfort, or affection, especially in their old age, and (2) bringing parents reflected glory by achieving success in educational and occupational activities (Shon and Ja, 1992; Lin and Liu, 1993).

The influence of this traditional culture declines with succeeding generations of Asian Americans. Thus, among the third or fourth generations, the family has fewer children, the father is less authoritarian, the mother is more likely to be gainfully employed, interracial marriage has increased significantly, and divorce is more common. But the Confucian culture still has a residual effect on many Asian American families, making them more stable than other U.S. families (Lin and Liu, 1993; Wilkinson, 1993).

Questions for Discussion and Review

1. What are the similarities among Native American, Hispanic American, African American, and Asian American families?

2. What are the differences among these groups?

THE FUTURE OF THE FAMILY

The death of the family has been predicted for decades. In 1949 Carle Zimmerman concluded from his study on the family that "We must look upon the present confusion of family values as the beginning of violent breaking up of a system." By the "confusion of family values," Zimmerman (1949) referred to the threat that individualism presented to the tradition of paternalistic authority and filial duty. He assumed that individualism would eventually do the family in. Today, many continue to predict the demise of the family, pointing out as evidence the increases in divorce, out-of-wedlock births, cohabitation, and singlehood.

However, the family is alive and well. The flaw in the gloomy forecast is that it confuses change with breakdown. Many of the traditional families—hubands as breadwinners and wives as homemakers—have merely changed into two-career families, which still hang together as nuclear families rather than disintegrate. Despite the increased number of people staying single, an overwhelming majority of those who now live alone will eventually marry. Although divorce rates have doubled over the last two decades, three out of four divorced people remarry, most doing so within three years of their marital breakup. Most of the young adults who live together before marriage will also marry eventually. It is true that being part of a single-parent family, especially from an out-of-wedlock birth, is a problem for many mothers and their children. But the problem stems more from economic deprivation than from single parenthood as a new form of family.

Evidence from public opinion polls also points to the basic health of the U.S. family. Asked to describe their marriages in a recent national survey, 60 percent of married individuals said "very happy," 36 percent said "pretty happy," and only 3 percent said "not too happy" (NORC, 1994).

What will the U.S. family be like in the next 20 years? Most likely it will be much the same as it is today: manifesting *diversity* without destroying the basic family values. The continuing acceptance of these values comes through clearly in two studies. One shows that, compared with Europeans, people in the United States are more likely to marry, to do so at an earlier age, and to have slightly larger families, despite the higher incidence of divorce and single-parent families (Sorrentino, 1990). Another study, which has tracked changes in family attitudes and values from the 1960s to the 1980s, shows that the vast majority of young people in the United States still value marriage, parenthood, and family life. They plan to marry, have children, and be successful in marriage (Thornton, 1989).

1. What will the family be like in the future?

___

CHAPTER REVIEW

1. *In what ways does the family vary from one society to another?* Key variations occur in the definition of who makes up the family, in norms regarding who selects a marriage partner and who is an appropriate partner, and in rules of residence, descent, inheritance, and authority.

2. *What is the family like as seen through the three sociological perspectives?* Seen through the functionalist perspective, the family is functional to society for providing sexual regulation, reproduction, socialization, economic cooperation, and emotional security. Seen through the conflict theory, the family is full of violence and female exploitation. Symbolic interactionism focuses on how certain interactions between a couple lead to marital happiness.

3. *How do people in the U.S. prepare for marriage?* Usually, they do not prepare for marriage intentionally, but dating and falling in love are the traditional preparatory steps in the United States. *Is there any truth to the saying that opposites attract?* Winch believes so, but most studies support the contrary view, saying that "birds of a feather flock together." The theory that people of similar personality traits are attracted to each other gains further support from the norm of homogamy, namely, that a person is likely to marry someone of the same class, race, religion, and other social characteristics. *Are most marriages successful?* An overwhelming majority of individuals say they are very or pretty happy with their marriages.

4. *What causes family violence?* One reason is the popular acceptance of violence as a solution to problems. Another reason is the history of violence in the offender's family of orientation. *Why is the divorce rate so high?* Among the likely social causes are (1) decreased social disapproval of divorce, (2) greater availability of services and opportunities for the divorced, (3) increased specialization of the family in providing love and affection, (4) higher expectations about the quality of marital relationships, and (5) increased individualism.

5. *What changes have taken place in the U.S. family in recent decades?* The family has taken on diverse forms, such as two-career families, single-parent families, stepfamilies, cohabitation, singlehood, and gay or lesbian families. *How is ethnic diversity revealed among U.S. families?* The families of Native Americans, Hispanic Americans, African Americans, and Asian Americans are basically alike in emphasizing the importance of kinship ties, which contrasts with European American families' emphasis on the individual's independence. But differences in history and culture bring about different types of family life.

6. *What is the future of the U.S. family?* The diversity of family forms will continue while the basic family values, such as marrying and having children, will remain very much alive.

KEY TERMS

Arranged marriage   A marriage in which partners are selected by the couple's parents. (p. 214)

Bilateral descent   The norm that recognizes both parents' families as the child's close relatives. (p. 216)

Egalitarian family   The family in which authority is equally distributed between husband and wife. (p. 216)

Endogamy   Literally, "marrying within," the act of marrying someone from one's own group. (p. 215)

Exogamy   Literally, "marrying outward," the act of marrying someone from outside one's group—such as the clan, tribe, or village. (p. 215)

Extended family   The family that consists of two parents, their unmarried children, and other relatives. (p. 214)

Family of orientation   The family in which one grows up, made up of oneself and one's parents and siblings. (p. 214)

Family of procreation   The family that one establishes through marriage, consisting of oneself and one's spouse and children. (p. 214)

Homogamy   Marrying someone with social characteristics similar to one's own. (p. 219)

Matriarchal family   The family in which the dominant figure is the eldest female. (p. 216)

Matrilineal descent   The norm that recognizes only the mother's family as a child's close relatives. (p. 216)

Matrilocal residence   The home where the married couple live with the wife's family. (p. 215)

Monogamy   The marriage of one man to one woman. (p. 215).

Neolocal residence   The home where the married couple live by themselves, away from both husband's and wife's families. (p. 215)

Nuclear family   The family that consists of two parents and their unmarried children. (p. 214)

Patriarchal family   The family in which the dominant figure is the eldest male. (p. 216)

Patrilineal descent   The norm that recognizes only the father's family as a child's close relatives. (p. 215)

Patrilocal residence   The home where the married couple live with the husband's family. (p 215)

Polyandry   The marriage of one woman to two or more men. (p. 215)

Polygamy   The marriage of one person to two or more people of the opposite sex. (p. 215)

Polygyny   The marriage of one man to two or more women. (p. 215)

Serial monogamy   The marriage of one person to two or more people but one at a time. (p. 215)

SUGGESTED READINGS

Billingsley, Andrew. 1993. *Climbing Jacob's Ladder: The Enduring Legacy of African-American Families*. New York: Simon & Schuster. A rare analysis of the resourcefulness and resilience of African American families.

Cherlin, Andrew J. 1992. *Marriage, Divorce, Remarriage*. Cambridge, Mass.: Harvard University Press. Analyzes the trends, explanations, and consequences of divorce and remarriage.

McAdoo, Harriette Pipes (ed.). 1993. *Family Ethnicity: Strength in Diversity*. Newbury Park, Calif.: Sage. A collection of articles offering insight into families of various ethnic minorities.

Schwartz, Pepper. 1994. *Love Between Equals: How Peer Marriage Really Works*. New York: Free Press. Analyzes how modern couples combine equality and intimacy to achieve marital happiness.

Stacey, Judith. 1991. *Brave New Families: Stories of Domestic Upheaval in Late Twentieth Century America*. New York: Basic Books. Provides an intimate look into the lives of people confronted with changes in their traditional nuclear family.

EDUCATION AND RELIGION

Myths and Realities

MYTH: *Because college education provides abstract knowledge rather than practical training, college graduates find it increasingly difficult to find well-paid work in today's highly competitive economy.*
REALITY: Due to the increasing reliance of modern industries on highly educated workers, the value of college education has risen dramatically. In 1980 college graduates earned about 32 percent more than high school graduates, but ten years later the earnings difference had increased to 61 percent. (p. 236)

MYTH: *A major function of schools is to teach children nothing but the truth about their country.*
REALITY: A major function of schools is to foster national unity. Therefore, the nation's glorious achievements are played up, but its shameful acts are often watered down or left out. (p. 237)

MYTH: *Japanese schools are so much better than ours that U.S. society will benefit if our educators emulate the Japanese.*
REALITY: Japanese schools are not necessarily better. They might even be worse: by emphasizing extreme conformity, they tend to stifle individuality and creativity, qualities that U.S. schools cultivate. (p. 241)

MYTH: *A belief in God is present in all religions.*
REALITY: A belief in God is present in some religions, such as Christianity, but not in others, such as Buddhism. (p. 253)

Barbara Donovan, a mother of three school-age children, considers herself moderately conservative, like most residents of the southern California community where she lives. She was therefore not alarmed when Christian conservatives won control of the school board in her district. But she became greatly concerned when the board began to push an ultraconservative religious agenda: proposing the teaching of creationism in science classes, rejecting as too intrusive federal lunch programs for low-income students, and attempting to replace the sex education curriculum with "Sex Respect"—a program that avoids discussing safe sex and birth control and condemns homosexuality and abortion. Donovan started meeting with other concerned parents, and they eventually launched a successful campaign to replace the religious-right trustees with moderates. However, religious-right organizations, such as Citizens for Excellence in Education, have in recent years elected many school board members throughout the nation and will continue to do so (Impoco, 1995). Given the increasing influence of religion on education, we will analyze these two social institutions in this chapter.

SOCIOLOGICAL PERSPECTIVES ON EDUCATION

From the three sociological perspectives we can see various aspects of education. One is the positive side of education, another is the negative side, and the third is the teacher-student interaction.

Functionalist Perspective

According to the functionalist perspective, education performs many functions for society. Here we discuss only the most important functions: teaching knowledge and skills, enhancing social mobility, promoting national unity, and providing custodial care.

Teaching Knowledge and Skills The most obvious function of education is to provide a new generation with the knowledge and skills necessary to maintain the society. Of course, family background does have an impact on student learning. Given their greater learning resources—such as a daily newspaper, dictionary, and encyclopedia in their homes—upper- and middle-class students do have higher educational attainment than their lower-class peers (Teachman, 1987). Nevertheless, when researchers take family background into account, they still find that schools make a difference in how much their students learn.

Students from lower-income families attending "good" high schools, for example, have been found to learn more and have a better chance of going to college than other lower-income students attending "bad" schools. Moreover, studies conducted during summer months and teacher strikes have shown that inner-city and minority youngsters are most likely to suffer sharp drops in learning skills and knowledge when not in school. Studies in developing countries, where schooling is not available to all children, have also shown that whether or not children attend school has a significant impact on their cognitive development. In fact, an extensive review of relevant studies concludes that schools can and do make a big difference in transmitting knowledge and skills to students (Rutter, 1983; Heyneman and Loxley, 1983; Mortimore, 1988; Griffith et al., 1989).

Enhancing Social Mobility Most people value the knowledge and skills transmitted by the schools because they hope to translate those skills into good jobs and money. Does education really enhance the opportunity for social mobility? The answer is apparently yes. As Figure 11.1 shows, the more education people get, the higher their incomes are. Today, due to the increasing reliance of modern industries on highly educated workers, the value of a college education has risen dramatically. In 1980 college graduates earned about 32 percent more than high school graduates, but 10 years later the earnings difference had gone up to 61 percent (Kosters, 1990).

Education also makes social mobility available throughout the society by stimulating economic growth. Pamela Walters and Richard Rubinson (1983) have found that the expansion of education in the United States since 1933 has boosted the nation's economy by increasing worker productivity, developing more productive or labor-saving technology, and creating a stable political climate. Studies in other industrial societies as well as developing countries have further shown that mass schooling contributes to modernization (Ramirez and Meyer, 1980).

Promoting National Unity To foster national unity, schools—chiefly primary and secondary schools rather than colleges and universities—play an important role in transmitting the culture to a new generation. Students are taught to become good citizens, to love their country, to cherish their cultural values, and to be proud of their nation—Mexico, Japan, Nigeria, Russia, or whatever it may be. Teaching good citizenship may involve the performance of rituals. In the United States, for example, schoolchildren are taught to recite the Pledge of Allegiance to the flag and to stand at attention for the playing of "The Star-Spangled Banner" before a ball game.

Schools also plant seeds of patriotism in their young charges by teaching civics, history, and other social studies. In these courses, the glorious national achievements are played up but often the shameful acts are watered down or left out for fear of a negative effect on children. Thus, U.S. children are taught that their European ancestors came to this country as heroic pioneers; less frequently taught is that those pioneers slaughtered massive numbers of Native Americans and stole their lands. In Japan, school textbooks do not contain information or pictures showing Japanese wartime atrocities in China, such as massacring 200,000 Chinese civilians in the city of Nanjing, bayoneting Chinese civilians for practice, or burying Chinese civilians alive (Sayle, 1982; Kristof, 1995a).

Providing Custodial Care Another major but latent function of schooling is to offer custodial care of children—providing a place to put them and having someone to watch them. Schools keep children off the streets, and presumably out of trouble. The importance of this function has increased, as the number of two-career and single-parent households has grown. Schools have traditionally been effective in performing their custodial role. In the past many schools were run under strict discipline, with teachers diligently enforcing rules and regulations and students obeying without question. But since the middle of this century a growing number of schools seem to have turned into "blackboard jungles," where violence and drugs are rampant. Nevertheless, an orderly routine still prevails in most schools.

The custodial function of schools is important for yet another reason: it keeps the young out of the job market. The nation's unemployment rate would shoot up dangerously if there was no compulsory school

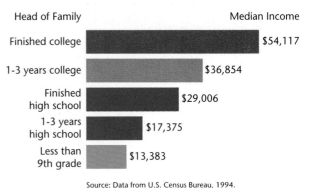

The more education people have, the bigger their earnings

Head of Family		Median Income
Finished college		$54,117
1-3 years college		$36,854
Finished high school		$29,006
1-3 years high school		$17,375
Less than 9th grade		$13,383

Source: Data from U.S. Census Bureau, 1994.

FIGURE 11.1
Level of Education Raises Income

attendance. The need to keep young people out of the job market, though, requires that they spend more years in school than are necessary for acquiring basic knowledge and skills. Thus, most students take 12 years—from grades 1 through 12—to acquire basic reading and mathematical skills that could be achieved in about three years of intensive training between ages 15 and 18 (White, 1977). Given the enormous bulk of time left over from learning those basic skills, how can students be kept so long in school without getting too restless? They are given ample opportunities for recreational, extracurricular, or nonacademic activities. In fact, the schools play their custodial role so well that many students end up considering games, sports, and friends—not books, classes, and teachers—the most important features of their school experience (Goodlad, 1984).

Conflict Perspective

While the functionalist perspective focuses on how education benefits society, the conflict perspective sheds light on how education can harm society.

Education as Cultural Imperialism Like other societies, the United States has long recognized the importance of using education to unify its people by teaching history from its own viewpoint. Schoolchildren can therefore be "Americanized," thinking of themselves as U.S. citizens, supporting the American democratic idea, and becoming assimilated into the mainstream of U.S. culture.

Seen from the functionalist perspective, Americanization is not only necessary for the nation as a whole,

To functionalists, schools play an important role in the Americanization of young people, enabling the nation to enhance its unity and helping minorities to improve their life chances. But conflict theorists see the so-called Americanization as a threat to the cultural heritage of minorities.

but is also useful to immigrants and minorities. It enables minorities to improve their life chances and the nation to enhance its unity. Viewed from the conflict perspective, however, Americanization looks like **cultural imperialism,** the practice of making minorities accept the dominant group's culture. It involves forcibly imposing much of the WASP (White Anglo-Saxon Protestant) culture on U.S. citizens of other cultural backgrounds. The typical U.S. history textbook is written from the WASP's point of view so that it presents mostly whites as heroes—and very few heroes from minority groups. Americanization also forces minority children to give up their cultural heritage, such the Spanish language, and to be taught in English only. Thus, the so-called Americanization not only threatens to destroy minority cultures but also encourages teachers to stereotype minority students as "culturally deprived."

Reinforcing Social Inequality Functionalists assume that schools serve to reduce social inequality in the larger society by improving the life chances of the poor and minorities. But conflict theorists argue just the opposite—that schools reinforce the existing social structure of inequality.

Education in the United States is therefore seen as supporting the capitalist system by producing an array of skills and attitudes appropriate for maintaining social inequality. In elementary and secondary schools, lower-class children are trained to respect authority and obey orders—characteristics that employers like in manual laborers. In high school, higher-income youths are usually channeled

into college preparatory courses, and thus eventually into higher-status jobs, while lower-income students are typically guided into vocational courses, which lead to lower-status jobs. After graduating from high school, higher-income students are more likely to attend college than are lower-income students. Those in elite universities learn independent thinking and decision-making skills, which are useful for leadership positions. Meanwhile, in average universities and colleges, middle-class youth are taught responsibility, dependability, and the ability to work without close supervision—qualities needed for middle-level professions and occupations. In short, according to the conflict perspective, education teaches youth to know their place and to fill it (Bowles and Gintis, 1976; Carnoy and Levin, 1985; Weis, 1988).

There is evidence to support the conflict argument. In the United States, a majority of elementary and secondary schools practice **tracking,** the system of sorting students into different groups according to ability (Strum, 1993). In his study of nearly 900 high school classes throughout the United States, John Goodlad (1984) found that higher-income students tend to be in higher-track (higher-ability) classes and lower-class and minority students in lower-track classes. Goodlad further discovered that higher-track students were taught "a more independent type of thinking— self-direction, creativity, critical thinking, pursuing individual assignments, and active involvement in the process of learning." By contrast, lower-track students were taught "a more conforming type of classroom behavior—working quietly, punctuality, cooperation, improving study habits, conforming to rules and expectations, and getting along with others." Higher-income students were, in effect, taught to be high-paid professionals, while lower-class and minority students were taught to become low-paid manual workers.

Symbolic Interactionist Perspective

According to a key tenet of symbolic interactionism, in social interaction we tend to behave in accordance with how we think others see us. Thus, in classroom interaction, how the teacher defines a student can have powerful consequences for the student's academic performance. If a student is viewed as intelligent, the student will likely perform well. If another student is considered less intelligent, that student will likely perform less well. Such power held by the teacher reflects the **Pygmalion effect,** the impact of a teacher's expectations on student performance.

The Pygmalion Effect In Greek mythology, Pygmalion is a sculptor who created Galatea, an ivory statue of a beautiful woman. Pygmalion fell in love with his creation and prayed to the goddess of love, who brought the statue of Galatea to life. In a sense, teachers can be compared to Pygmalion and their students to Galatea: teachers can bring their expectations to life. If a teacher expects certain students to fail, they are likely to do so. If a teacher expects them to succeed, then they are likely to succeed. Thus, the Pygmalion effect is an example of a *self-fulfilling prophecy*. Robert Rosenthal and numerous other researchers have demonstrated the Pygmalion effect in a series of experiments, one of which was described briefly in Chapter 1 (The Essence of Sociology).

How does the Pygmalion effect work? The teachers' expectations do not affect the students' performance directly, but they do influence the teachers' behavior, which in turn directly affects students. Teachers tend to give attention, praise, and encouragement to students they consider bright. If the students fail to perform as well as expected, the teachers work extra hard to help them live up to expectations. But teachers tend to be uninterested in, critical toward, or impatient with those they expect to do poorly in school. When these students have difficulty, teachers are likely to think it is a waste of time trying to help them. As a result of this differential treatment, the differences in students' performances tend to match teachers' expectations: the "bright" students do better than the "poor" ones (Rosenthal, 1973; Harris and Rosenthal, 1985).

Pygmalion and Tracking In view of the Pygmalion effect, it is not surprising that school tracking generally benefits higher-track students more than lower-track students. Tracking raises teacher

In high school, youths from the upper and middle classes are usually channeled into college-preparatory courses, but students from lower classes are more likely to end up in vocational courses, which lead to lower-status jobs.

expectations for higher-track students and lowers teacher expectations for lower-track students.

This may explain why, as research by John Goodlad (1984) indicates, teachers in higher-track classes spend more time on instruction, expect students to study more at home, and are seen by students as more enthusiastic in teaching, more concerned about them, and less punitive toward them, when compared with teachers in lower-track classes. Thus, the good students tend to get better and the poor students poorer. As many studies have shown, higher-track students are more likely to go to college, and lower-track students are more likely to have low self-esteem, drop out of school, or become delinquents (Alexander and Cook, 1982; Goodlad, 1984; Strum, 1993).

Questions for Discussion and Review

1. How does education promote social mobility and national unity?
2. What benefits does society gain from having the schools provide custodial care?
3. How does the conflict perspective on education differ specifically from the functionalist perspective?
4. What is the Pygmalion effect?
5. What is the connection between the Pygmalion effect and school tracking?

EDUCATION IN THE UNITED STATES

For some time now, many critiques of education in the United States have documented a decline in educational standards and achievement compared with the past and with other countries. Specifically, scores on Scholastic Aptitude Tests (SAT) taken by college-bound high school seniors fell continuously from 1963 to 1980. Although the SAT scores have inched upward since 1980, they still appear inadequate. Compared with their counterparts in other countries, U.S. high school students also score lower on math tests (see Figure 11.2). As a result, the media as well as many national task forces on education have raised the alarm about a crisis in U.S. schools said to threaten our very future as a nation and a people (Lord and Horn, 1987; Gleick, 1995). Is U.S. education really in a state of crisis? If we put the discouraging data in proper perspective, the answer is probably no.

Problems in Perspective

First, the decline of SAT scores may have partly resulted from the increasing democratization of U.S. education. In contrast to the continued elitism of foreign educational systems, the U.S. system has included growing numbers of poor, minority, and immigrant students.

FIGURE 11.2
Comparative Math Test Scores of High School Students

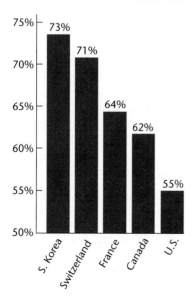

Percent correct on math test

Source: Data from National Center for Education Statistics, 1991

Because of inadequate academic preparation or the tests' cultural bias or both, the socially disadvantaged students do not do as well on the SAT as the socially advantaged, helping to bring down the average score for the entire group. But the investment in equal education has begun to pay off. Since 1980 the national SAT averages have begun to level off or pick up, partly as a result of the steady improvement in test scores among African American, Hispanic, and other minority students. On other standardized tests, minorities have even shown greater gains in scores than whites (Grissmer, 1994).

Second, the United States is not alone in having educational problems. Japan, which is often touted as being a world leader in science and technology, has serious problems with its higher education. Although Japanese schoolchildren are under enormous pressure to study hard, university students are allowed to take it easy, as if in reward for having worked so hard before college. As Robert Christopher (1983) observes, "the great majority of Japanese universities are extraordinarily permissive: once you get into one, it takes real effort to get kicked out . . . Japanese university authorities do not regard a student's failure to attend classes or even to pass courses as a ground for dismissal." Moreover, Japanese leaders have grown concerned that their schools' emphasis on conformity, such as finding the "single right answer" to a problem, is depriving their society of much needed creativity, especially in the current age of rapid change (Fiske, 1987).

Third, U.S. schools are not entirely to blame for the lower achievement of their students compared with the Japanese. For one thing, our schools are expected to dilute their teaching resources by dealing with such social problems as alcohol and drug abuse and teenage pregnancy, which Japanese schools do not. Given the high rates of divorce, single parenthood, and two-career couples, U.S. parents are often too stressed, tired, or self-absorbed to do what Japanese mothers do—help with their children's homework and make sure they study three or four hours a night. Moreover, many U.S. teenagers hold part-time jobs, significantly reducing their ability to hit the books after school. By contrast, working during the school year is virtually unheard of in Japan. Finally, U.S. teenagers are under great pressure from their peers to look good, drink, socialize, date, or even have sex. In contrast, the Japanese adolescent peer culture pressures teenagers to study hard. Japanese students like to say, though a little facetiously, "Four you score; five you die," meaning "If you sleep five hours a night instead of four, you won't pass the exams" (Steinberg, 1987). In short, it is largely social problems, the lack of support from parents, and the adolescent subculture that make it hard for U.S. schools to compete with their Japanese counterparts.

Finally, while many problems can be found in U.S. schools, there is a lot of good in them, particularly in

Japanese society offers a setting for schoolchildren that is different from that in the United States. Unlike U.S. schools, Japanese schools do not spend time dealing with such problems as alcohol and drug abuse or teenage pregnancy. Japanese mothers make sure their children study three to four hours a night, and Japanese adolescent peer culture pressures teenagers to study hard.

their mission of providing quality with equality (Goodlad, 1984). Although education researcher and reformer Theodore Sizer (1984) criticizes the nation's high schools for being rigid and impersonal, he still finds that "they are, on the whole, happy places, settings that most adolescents find inviting, staffed by adults who genuinely care for youngsters." In contrast, most Japanese students do not enjoy their school experience, because they feel like robots or prisoners in a rigidly controlled environment. Moreover, some Japanese professors who have taught in the United States have observed that U.S. students are more creative than their Japanese counterparts (Tharp, 1987). Japanese schools, like their society, stress extreme conformity, pressuring students to do what everybody else is doing while discouraging them from sticking out by taking risks. In contrast, U.S. schools, like U.S. society, place a high premium on individuality, prodding students to think for themselves.

Nonetheless, there are always efforts to improve U.S. schools. Among the main reforms that have emerged over the last three decades and still continue today are Head Start, school choice, and lifelong learning.

Head Start

Sociologists in the 1960s often found that trying to equalize the quality of the nation's schools and educational opportunities did not produce educational equality, because some children's family backgrounds handicapped them even from the start of school. Some youngsters never see a book at home and are never encouraged to do well at school. There seemed to be a need for **compensatory education,** a school program intended to improve the academic performance of socially and educationally disadvantaged children. So in the mid–1960s the federal government began funding Head Start, a compensatory education program for disadvantaged preschoolers across the nation. It was not run by public school administrators, but rather mostly by pediatricians and child psychologists working for poverty agencies. The aim was to prepare poor children aged 3 and 4 for kindergarten. These children were taught the skills and vocabulary that many of their middle-class peers absorb at home. Their parents were also brought in to learn child care, health care, and nutrition.

Early studies of the results were not encouraging. They showed that, although the training did raise children's I.Q. scores and scholastic achievement, the benefits were temporary. In the first grade, disadvantaged pupils who had had preschool training might perform better than those who had not, but by the third grade this difference tended to disappear, and both disadvantaged groups were equally likely to fall behind their grade level (Stearns, 1971). This is the kind of evidence that conservative politicians in the 1990s often point to in their call for the elimination of Head Start. Why did the benefits disappear, and why did students not respond better to remedial programs? In the 1970s, researchers were not able to find a definitive answer. Most argued that the continuing influence of a poor family environment was the cause—it simply overwhelmed the influence of any educational program. Others contended that the preschool programs had been doomed to failure because of inadequate funding. A few argued that they had been unfairly evaluated before they had time to prove their effectiveness. The last argument turns out to be the one that hit the nail on the head. In the 1980s and 1990s, many studies showed that the preschool programs do benefit low-income students in the long run. When poor youngsters who were in the preschool programs reach ages 9 to 19, they do better in school than peers who were not. They are also more likely to graduate from high school, attend college, and have higher rates of employment (Celis, 1993b).

Head Start is still far from being fully funded, though. Only about half of eligible children can enroll. The quality of the staff—teachers, nutritionists, social workers, and psychologists—is not uniformly adequate in all Head Start programs. The average staff salary is only $12,000 a year, compared with about $30,000 for an average public school teacher. Low salaries have led to shortages of well-trained staff at some places. President Clinton and other liberal politicians want to increase government support for Head Start, but conservatives want to abolish it (Schweinhart and Weikert, 1990; Kantrowitz and Wingert, 1993).

School Choice

In the late 1960s, a new idea began to receive considerable publicity. It was vintage USA: If there were more competition among schools, perhaps schools would be better. After all, people were entitled to more freedom in choosing where their children would be educated. This idea inspired proposals for voucher plans. Public schools have a virtual monopoly on public funds for education, and children attend schools depending, for the most part, on where they live. A voucher plan can change this situation. In a sense, parents, not schools, receive public money. They receive it in the form of a *voucher*, which they use to pay for their children's attendance at the schools of their choice. The schools receive money from the government in return for the vouchers. The greater the number of parents who choose a particular school, the more money it receives. The idea is to force the public schools to compete with each other, and with private and parochial schools, for "customers." Presumably, good schools would attract plenty of students, and poor schools would be forced either to improve or to close. But the majority of teachers and

their unions, along with some civil rights groups, opposed vouchers for several reasons: Vouchers would encourage white parents to choose schools on the basis of racial or ethnic prejudice. They would promote economic and racial segregation and, eventually, greater divisiveness in U.S. society generally. If vouchers stimulated competition, they would probably also stimulate hucksterism, such as offering field trips to Disneyland. Moreover, because a voucher plan would mean giving government money to religious schools, many worried that it would violate the separation of church and state required by the Constitution (Hegedus, 1976). In any event, the voucher plan never caught on, and finally the government let it die in the late 1970s.

In the 1990s, however, popular support for vouchers has grown significantly because many schools continue to have such problems as overcrowding, violence, and poor test scores. The federal government has considered providing vouchers in the form of tuition tax credits for enrolling children in any schools, including private or parochial schools. A number of states have already started "school choice" programs. One immediate impact has been the proliferation of TV commercials and other ads promoting various schools (Newman, 1994). But will school choice greatly improve poor schools, as its advocates believe? It is still too early to tell.

Lifelong Learning

Yet another trend in education has involved not children and adolescents but adults who have been out of school for some time. The appeal of "lifelong learning" has led many adults to return to the classroom, often for formal college credits. Most of these lifelong learners are enrolled in two-year community colleges. But seeing the popularity of adult education in community colleges and facing declining enrollments of traditional students, many four-year colleges and universities have offered their own continuing education programs. Today, adults aged 35 and older make up over 16 percent of total enrollment, nearly twice the figure of 20 years ago (Figure 11.3). Adults older than 24 account for about 44 percent of total enrollment and are expected to represent half of all undergraduates by the year 2000 (Levine, 1993).

The remarkable growth of continuing education owes much to changing economic forces: corporate downsizing, the loss of blue-collar jobs that paid middle-class wages, and the demands imposed on workers by new technology. Not surprisingly, many nontraditional students are adult workers seeking retraining, additional training, or new careers. But there

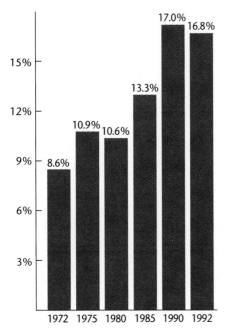

Percentage of college students aged 35 and older

Source: Data from U.S. Census Bureau, 1994.

FIGURE **11.3**
Older Students on Campus

are others: homemakers preparing to enter the job market at middle age; retired people seeking to pursue interests postponed or dormant during their working years; and people who want to enrich the quality of their personal, family, and social lives. Most of these adults are serious students; 60 percent are enrolled in a degree program (Cohen and Brawer, 1982; *Futurist*, 1989; Johnson, 1995). To accommodate their students' diverse responsibilities and interests, continuing education courses tend to be flexible. The courses are usually offered in the evenings or on weekends, and sometimes outside conventional classrooms, in various community facilities such as libraries. Their requirements are flexible, too. Some programs allow students to earn college credits without taking a course, by passing an examination, or by proving their competency through their job, hobby, writing, and so on. In the future, students will also take courses by audiocassette, videocassette, CD-ROM, and independent study. Many courses offered on the campus will be shorter and more focused than typical college courses. Since most of the students will be over age 25 and working full time, most of the courses currently designed for lifelong learners may well become the standard curricula at most colleges and universities (Johnson, 1995).

Questions for Discussion and Review

1. What is the nature of our educational problems?
2. How can Head Start improve academic performance?
3. What is school choice, and why do many teachers and some civil rights groups oppose this kind of educational reform?
4. How have community college and continuing education programs tried to meet the educational needs of adults?

A GLOBAL ANALYSIS OF EDUCATION

To understand the U.S. educational system better, we can compare it with schools in other industrial societies. Let us take a quick tour of the schools in four countries, focusing on their most distinctive features (see Figure 11.4). We will see that, given different social environments, the schools in various societies produce different results.

Schools in Belgium

The Belgian educational system is unique for having proportionately larger numbers of schoolteachers than virtually all other countries in the world. School teachers make up 5.3 percent of Belgium's work force, compared with, for example, 2.6 percent for the United States and 2.4 percent for Britain. As a consequence, the average class size in Belgian schools is the smallest in the world. Belgium's student-teacher ratio is only 9.3 primary students and 6.8 secondary students per teacher, compared with 15.5 and 15.9 for the United States. But Belgian teachers' salaries are relatively low, as the country spends less per student than the United States and other industrial societies. Still, parents generally give high marks to the Belgian schools.

One major reason for the huge teacher population in Belgium is growing unemployment, which now reaches about 10 percent. This has caused the government to raise the age of compulsory education to 18, as well as to allow children to start school as young as age two-and-a-half. If the older teenagers in Belgium were not forced to stay in school longer than their U.S. counterparts, many would wind up on the unemployment rolls, pushing the nation's jobless rate even higher. In addition, increased student enrollment helps reduce the unemployment rate by producing jobs for teachers (Brock, 1993).

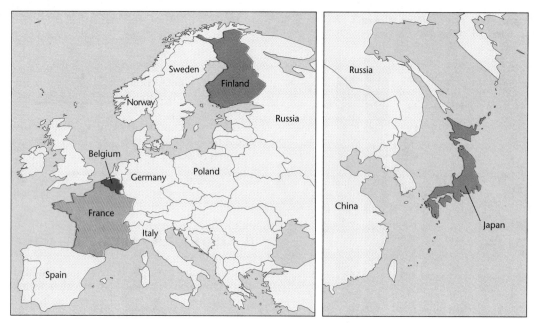

FIGURE 11.4
Countries in the Global Analysis: Belgium, Finland, France, and Japan

Schools in Finland

Finland is the world's most educated society. Forty percent of Finns aged 24 to 65 have a college degree, compared with 12 percent in the United States. Understandably, Finns are, per capita, the greatest consumers of literature in the world. School attendance is compulsory up to age 16. Schooling is rigorous. High school students attend classes 38 hours a week, compared with about 25 hours in the United States. Finnish students are also required to take more courses, including two foreign languages. All higher education is free, with most financial support coming from the state and the rest from private industries (Peltonen, 1993).

Schools in France

As suggested, the educational bureaucracy in the United States does not give teachers the freedom to teach the way they see fit, such as choosing their own textbooks rather than having the school board do it. By contrast, French teachers are free to do their job in virtually any way they want. The French government only offers *general* guidelines, such as suggesting that 5-year-olds be given some reading instruction so that they can handle primary-school lessons after their year of preschool games. But the teachers are free, for example, to pick the books for their classes or even

not to use any books. The teachers are given so much freedom because their government assumes that they know their job better than anybody else. The assumption turns out to be correct: 14-year-olds in France, along with those in Finland, are the most proficient readers, compared with their peers in other industrial countries (Riding, 1993).

Schools in Japan

Japanese schools are world-famous for producing high achievers. According to researcher Thomas Rohlen (1983), the average high school graduate in Japan has learned as much basic knowledge in all fields, especially math and science, as the average college graduate in the United States. A major reason is that school occupies a much larger place in Japanese teenagers' lives. They spend far more hours in education-related activities in school and at home, which leaves much less free time for play, when compared with U.S. teenagers. The very intensity of the educational experience, however, has increased school violence and truancy. Moreover, Japanese schooling emphasizes memorized learning far more than original thinking, while the reverse is more common with U.S. schools (Kristof, 1995b).

Japanese youngsters' academic excellence cannot be attributed to the schools alone. Japanese mothers play a crucial role in their children's education, not only constantly encouraging hard work but also rendering help with homework. After-school classes, called *jukus* ("cram shops"), also contribute substantially; they are attended by more than one-quarter of all primary pupils and more than one-half of all secondary students. Since so many students are involved in this supplementary learning, Francis McKenna (1993) concludes that the quality of Japanese schooling is actually lower than popularly believed.

Questions for Discussion and Review

1. How do the schools in Belgium, Finland, France, and Japan differ from one another?
2. How are those schools different from U.S. schools?

SOCIOLOGICAL PERSPECTIVES ON RELIGION

Like education, religion is an important social institution. Not surprisingly, some form of religious belief exists all over the world. Some people may see religion as a carryover from the superstitious past, hence highly important only for "primitive" or "backward" societies. Actually, religion is also very much a part of modern social life. Although the United States is one of the world's most scientifically and technologically advanced societies, it is also one of the most religious (Woodward, 1992). Why does religion seem so important to many people? What can religion do for society? Various answers to such questions can be found in the three sociological perspectives.

Functionalist Perspective

According to the functionalist perspective, religion is of immense importance to society as well as to individuals. Exactly why is religion so important? One answer can be found in Durkheim's classical functionalist theory, another in modern sociologists' functionalist analyses.

Society as Representation of God   Emile Durkheim presented his functionalist view of religion in *The Elementary Forms of Religious Life,* first published in 1912. It was Durkheim's aim to refute the popular view that God—or whatever is worshipped as sacred—is merely an illusion, a figment of human imagination. According to Durkheim, if religion were an illusion, it would have disappeared in rational

The functionalist perspective of religion was set forth by Emile Durkheim, who argued that because God is a symbolic representation of society, religion functions to preserve social order. One of the functions of religion is supportive—consoling, reconciling, and providing relief from anxiety through worship in a community of fellow believers.

modern societies. But it has not. "It is inadmissible," said Durkheim, "that systems of ideas like religion, which have held so considerable a place in history, and to which people have turned in all ages for the energy they need to live, should be mere tissues of illusion." If God were merely a product of the individual's imagination, Durkheim also argued, God would occupy the same status as any other idea—a part of the profane world incapable of inspiring reverence, awe, and worship. Instead, God must be sacred and far above humans, as demonstrated by the fact that the deity is widely worshipped.

If this revered entity is both real and superior to us, then what is God? Durkheim's answer: society. Society is more powerful than any of us and beyond our personal control. It is separate from us, yet we are part of it, and it is part of our consciousness. It outlives each of us, and even our children. We are dependent on it, and it demands our obedience. It is neither a person nor a thing, yet we feel and know its reality. These attributes of society are also characteristics of the sacred—in Western religions, of God. In short, the sacred, according to Durkheim, is the symbolic representation of society. By worshiping God, we in effect are worshiping society.

Such a view of religion led Durkheim to emphasize that religion functions to preserve social order. Every religion, he argued, possesses both rituals and moral norms. Through their religion's rituals, people sanctify and renew their bonds to one another. Their belief in the sacred and their acceptance of common norms are strengthened. Thus, religion binds the society and helps maintain it.

While Durkheim made the general statement that religion helps to preserve social order, today's functionalist sociologists are more specific on the functions of religion. They also find a paradox in each of these functions: if religion is too successful in carrying out a positive function, it may become a negative force in society (O'Dea and Aviad, 1983).

Supportive Function Religion often performs a supportive function by providing consolation, reconciliation, and relief from anxiety. By praying, believers may become less anxious about losing their jobs or about old age and death. Faith may console those who have lost a loved one or are beset by illness, loneliness, disappointment, frustration, or sorrow. Religion can reconcile people to the sinfulness of others, the hostility of enemies, the injustices of society, or other unpleasant aspects of this world. Not surprisingly, as research has shown, religiously active people are healthier and happier than those who are not religious (Myers, 1993).

However, if religion offers *too much* support and consolation, it can impede useful social change. Many religions urge their believers to see all worldly things as trivial compared with the life of the spirit. Others perceive this world as a mere way station, or a "vale of tears" that is meant to be a test of love and faith, or even as an illusion. All these beliefs can encourage the faithful, not only to be consoled but also to endure their suffering docilely. Thus, religions can discourage people from confronting the sources of their suffering, or from joining a social or revolutionary movement that may help to alleviate their suffering.

Social Control Function Religion performs a social control function by strengthening conformity to society's norms in at least two ways: First, religion helps to *sacralize* (make sacred) the norms and values of established society with such commandments as "Thou shalt not kill" and "Thou shalt not steal." Thus, religious people are less likely to violate the laws of the state because these laws are taken to be the laws of God. Not surprisingly, as over 50 research studies have shown, religious participation inhibits crime, delinquency, and deviant behavior in general (Ellis, 1985; Peek, Curry, and Chalfant, 1985). Second, religion encourages good, friendly, or cooperative behavior, illustrated through the story of the Good Samaritan, the maxim "Do unto others as you would have others do unto you," and other such teachings. As a result, as research has indicated, more-religious people seem more friendly and cooperative—more likely to stop and comfort a crying child, to be good listeners, and even to get along with loud-mouthed, obnoxious people (Morgan, 1983, 1984).

However, religion's power to reinforce social control may set up yet another roadblock to useful change. Some of the state's laws and values sacralized by religion are unjust and harmful, such as those supporting racial or gender inequality. But the extremely faithful may consider them too sacred to question or change, perhaps saying, for example, "It is God's will that women should stay home and be only wives and mothers."

Prophetic Function Acting as a source of social change, religion may perform a prophetic function. It does this through some leaders who, like the ancient Jewish prophets, challenge the unjust political authorities of their day in order to bring a better life to the people. In the 1950s and 1960s, for example, Dr. Martin Luther King, Jr., led the fight against racial discrimination in the United States. During the 1980s, Anglican Archbishop Desmond Tutu played an important role in blacks' struggle against the white racist government in South Africa. Similarly, the leader of the Philippines' Roman Catholic church, Jaime Cardinal Sin, helped bring down President Marcos' repressive government.

Sometimes, however, prophetic calls for reform may produce violent fanaticism. During the seventeenth century, some 20,000 peasants in Russia were inspired to burn themselves as a way of protesting liturgical reforms in the Russian Orthodox Church. In 1420 the Adamites, a religious cult of Bohemians in Europe, set about making holy war to kill the unholy. They believed that they had to continue killing until they could make the blood fill the world to "the height of a horse's head" (Morrow, 1978). Today, Muslim terrorists in the Middle East who try to kill their enemies welcome death as God's blessing for themselves.

Religion can act as a source of social change through prophets who challenge unjust political conditions of the day, as did Reverend Martin Luther King, Jr., in his fight against racial discrimination in the 1950s and 1960s.

Identity Function   Religion may perform the identity function by enabling individuals to know who they are, what they are, and what the purpose of their lives is. In modern societies marked by impersonal relations and a confusing variety of values and norms, this function of providing self-identity may be especially important to individuals. Without an identity, people may fall into an existential vacuum, finding life meaningless and merely muddling through.

Intense social conflict, however, is likely to erupt if people identify too strongly with their own religion. Such people tend to believe that there is only one true

religion—their own—and become intolerant of all other "false" religions. Indeed, history is filled with persecutions and wars related to religious differences. Consider the medieval Christian Crusades against Muslim "heathens," the Thirty Years' War between Catholics and Protestants in seventeenth-century Europe, the persecution and slaughter of Mormons in the United States during the last century, the Hindu-Muslim conflicts that resulted in the creation of mostly Hindu India and a separate Islamic Republic of Pakistan in 1947, the strife between Protestants and Catholics in Northern Ireland, and the clash between Buddhists and Hindus that plagues the Asian nation of Sri Lanka today.

Conflict Perspective

Unlike Durkheim, Karl Marx considered religious beliefs to be mere illusions. Nevertheless, Marx believed those illusions to be a powerful force in society.

A Supporter of the Ruling Class   Marx presented the conflict theory that, in a society divided into classes, the dominant religion usually represents the interests of the ruling class. The religion disguises and justifies the power of that class, though the deception is not deliberate. The ruling class is not conscious of the true state of things. Yet religion, argued Marx, is nonetheless a real and an oppressive illusion, one that helps the ruling class perpetuate its domination of the masses. In medieval Europe, the Roman Catholic Church bolstered the feudal system by promoting the notion that kings ruled by divine right. In India the Hindu religion for thousands of years has provided religious justification for the caste system. Religion supports the ruling class by justifying existing inequalities.

The Opium of the Masses   If religion is merely an oppressive illusion, why would the masses support and even cling to it? The reason, according to Marx, is the prevailing social inequality and oppression, which drive the masses to seek solace somewhere. "Religion," Marx declared, "is the sigh of the oppressed creature, the heart of a heartless world, the soul of soulless circumstances. It is the opium of the people" (Acton, 1967). Opium offers relief and escape, and it drains one's will to find the source of problems. Similarly, religion brings relief to oppressed workers, dulls their sensitivity to suffering, and diverts them from attacking the root of their pain—their exploitation by the wealthy and powerful. Religion accomplishes all this, argued Marx, by emphasizing the superiority of spiritual over earthly matters or promising eternal bliss in the afterlife with such doctrines as

"Blessed are the poor." As a result, religion ends up "alienating" workers from themselves by acquiring a harmful power over them—causing them to develop a "false consciousness," an acceptance of the dominance of their oppressors.

Many studies have supported Marx's assumption that poverty or oppression tends to make people embrace religion for consolation (Wimberley, 1984). This serves as a useful counterbalance against the functionalist analysis. But at the same time it should be noted, as discussed earlier, that sometimes religion does fight oppression through its prophetic function.

Symbolic Interactionist Perspective

Marx's analysis suggests that religion in general induces a passive resignation to poverty. But Max Weber saw that at least one religion—Protestantism—promoted an active pursuit of wealth.

An Interpretation of the World   As a symbolic interactionist, Weber regarded religion as an interpretation of the world around us that powerfully influences our behavior toward that world. He noticed that the early Protestants in Europe, especially those of the Calvinist sect, had a unique belief. The belief was that long before they were born, God had predestined them to either salvation in heaven or damnation in hell. But they could not know which would be their eternal destiny. This generated a great deal of anxiety. To relieve anxiety, the Calvinists turned to constant self-control and work. They further believed that, whether saved or damned, the faithful must work hard for the glory of God so as to establish God's kingdom on earth. Work came to be seen as a "calling" from God, and the worldly success that work brought came to be interpreted as a sign of election to heaven. Inevitably, the Calvinists worked extremely hard.

The Rise of Capitalism   But the Calvinists also had a unique definition of hard work. To them, the purpose of hard work was to glorify God, not to produce wealth that would enable people to indulge in their own pleasures. Thus the Calvinists believed that they should not spend their wealth on worldly pleasures. Instead, they invested and reinvested their profits to make their businesses grow. The constant accumulation of wealth—the continual investment of profit—lay a foundation on which capitalism could emerge in Protestant societies.

Weber further argued that capitalism did not emerge in predominantly Catholic countries or China or India because their world views differed from what he called the *Protestant ethic.* Catholicism does not teach predestination. It encourages people to seek their rewards in heaven, and it does not view earthly success as a sign of God's favor. Confucianism values social harmony, not individualistic strivings. Taoism teaches acceptance of the world as it is and withdrawal from it. Buddhism views worldly things as illusory and encourages escape from them through meditation. Hinduism requires its believers to endure the hardships of life and fulfill the obligations of their respective castes. These religions, Weber argued, did not offer ideas and habits favorable to the development of capitalist industrialism, as Calvinist Protestantism did.

But it is difficult to see how Weber's theory can be valid today. Catholics in the United States are now economically better off than many Protestants, such as Methodists and Baptists (see Figure 11.5). Capitalism is also booming in such non-Protestant countries as Japan, South Korea, and Taiwan. Nevertheless, Weber's theory sounds convincing in explaining the *emergence* of capitalism in Europe.

Questions for Discussion and Review

1. Why did Emile Durkheim argue that society is a representation of God?
2. How can positive functions of religion turn into negative forces in society?
3. According to Karl Marx, how does religion support the ruling class?
4. What did Marx mean when he wrote that religion is the opium of the people?
5. How did the early Protestants in Europe interpret the world, and how did this interpretation help develop capitalism?

FIGURE 11.5
How Religions in the U.S. Rank in Income

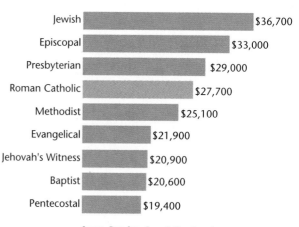

Median annual household income

Jewish	$36,700
Episcopal	$33,000
Presbyterian	$29,000
Roman Catholic	$27,700
Methodist	$25,100
Evangelical	$21,900
Jehovah's Witness	$20,900
Baptist	$20,600
Pentecostal	$19,400

Source: Data from Barry A. Kosmin and Seymour P. Lachman, *One Nation Under God* (New York: Harmony Books, 1993).

RELIGION IN THE UNITED STATES

As early as 1835, French historian and political philosopher Alexis de Tocqueville observed that "there is no country in the world in which the Christian religion retains a greater influence over the souls of men" than in the United States. Even today, religion is pervasive in our society. According to several surveys, about 95 percent of U.S. adults believe in God, 90 percent pray, and 88 percent believe that God loves them. Some 56 percent also consider religion "very important" in their lives (Gallup and Castelli, 1989; NORC, 1994). But religion in the United States is highly diverse, reflecting different religious affiliations, the faithful's differences in social characteristics, and different beliefs and practices.

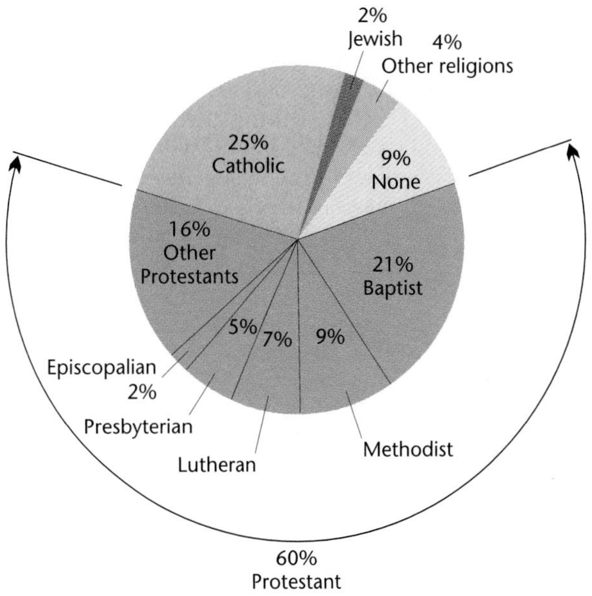

Religious Affiliation

There are more than 280 religious denominations in the country, but a few large churches have the allegiance of most people. Protestants constitute the largest group, although Catholics outnumber the largest Protestant denomination—the Baptists. According to the latest survey, 92 percent of the U.S. adult population have a specific religious preference, with 60 percent saying they are Protestants, 25 percent Catholics, and 2 percent Jews (see Figure 11.6).

The correlation between affiliation with an organized religion and religious belief and practice is far from perfect. Although 91 percent of the U.S. population claim to have a religious preference, only a small minority (about 20 percent of Protestants and 28 percent of Catholics) attend religious services regularly (Hadaway et al., 1993). Among those who do go to church, very few do so for strictly religious reasons. As a survey of Minnesota Christians has shown, less than 10 percent cited worship as the primary reason they attend church (Bilheimer, 1983). Apparently, religious affiliation reflects something besides religious belief and practice. Belonging to a church can also afford a way of conforming to social norms or a way of enjoying fellowship.

The Class Factor

Although they may consider themselves equal before God, various religious groups are far from equal socioeconomically. They have different statuses, and they tend to attract people from different educational and income levels. Usually, Jews, Episcopalians, and Presbyterians top the status hierarchy. They are followed by Catholics and Methodists, and trailed by

Source: Data from National Opinion Research Center, 1994.

FIGURE 11.6
Religious Affiliations in the United States

Baptists and Pentecostals (see, again, Figure 11.5, p. 248).

Social class also influences people's religious participation. In general, the higher their classes, the more likely people are to attend church regularly, join Bible study groups, and provide their children with religious education. Moreover, people of higher classes hold most of the leadership positions, such as membership on a church's board of trustees. But these facts do not mean that higher-income people are more religious. In fact, belief in God is more widespread among the poor than among the rich. The lower classes are also more likely to believe in a literal interpretation of the Bible, to believe in a personal God, and to be emotionally involved in religion. The higher rate of participation by higher-income people seems to reflect a greater inclination to participate in *all* kinds of voluntary organizations. For many higher-income people, religious participation appears to be a public activity required for social respectability.

The Age Factor

Adults above age 24 are also more active in their church than younger people. Religious involvement normally begins to escalate by age 25, first with marriage and then with parenthood. Adults are also more involved in a variety of social, political, and charitable activities—more likely, for example, to be registered to vote. Church involvement, then, reflects a broader pattern of social involvement (Gallup and Castelli, 1989).

The same age factor in religious involvement emerges in a study of baby boomers, who are now in their thirties and forties. During their teens or early twenties, two-thirds dropped out of their churches and synagogues. Now older in the 1990s, nearly 40 percent of these dropouts have returned to religious practice. Why do they return to organized religion? One reason is their feeling that religion is important for bringing up children. Another is their personal quest for meaning, triggered by feelings of emptiness and loneliness. A third reason is their need to belong to a community—to be with others, share faith, and do things together (Roof, 1993). In short, religious involvement tends to increase with age.

The Fundamentalist Revival

Although religious membership throughout the United States remains high, the growth in church membership has not kept pace with the growth of the general population. Since the early 1970s, the U.S. population has grown by over 12 percent, but religious institutions

have expanded by only 4 percent. Some churches have actually lost members. Others, however, have gained many members (Naisbitt and Aburdene, 1990).

Generally, the large mainline churches—Episcopal, Methodist, Presbyterian, and Congregational—have lost many members. Those churches that have registered large gains tend to be smaller, less established religious groups. They are also the more conservative groups. Among them are various fundamentalists (see Table 11.1). In contrast to mainline Protestants, fundamentalists emphasize a literal interpretation of the Bible. Evangelical, "born again" Christians also stress emotional demonstrativeness rather than quiet devotion at church services. Through the experience of being "born again," they believe that their lives have been dramatically changed. Some of these groups, known as charismatics or pentecostals, also speak in tongues, utter prophecies, and heal the sick.

Southern Baptists, Jehovah's Witnesses, Mormons, members of the Church of God, and Catholic Pentecostals are among the groups participating in this revival. In the past, fundamentalist and evangelical Christianity was associated with the poor and uneducated. Today, however, its appeal has spread, and business executives and prominent politicians can be found among its advocates. The revival has also spawned most

TABLE 11.1
Growth and Decline in Church Membership

	1970	Latest	Change
Over the last two decades, fundamentalist churches have gained members:			
Southern Baptist Convention	11,628,032	15,359,000	Up 32%
Church of Jesus Christ of Latter-Day Saints (Mormons)	2,073,146	4,430,000	Up 113%
Assemblies of God	625,027	2,258,000	Up 261%
Seventh-Day Adventists	420,419	749,000	Up 78%
Church of the Nazarene	383,284	574,000	Up 49%
In that same period, many mainline churches have declined:			
United Methodist Church	10,509,198	8,780,000	Down 16%
Presbyterian Church (U.S.A.)	4,045,408	3,758,000	Down 7%
Episcopal Church	3,285,826	2,472,000	Down 25%
Lutheran Church in America	2,788,536	2,610,000	Down 6%
Christian Church (Disciples of Christ)	1,424,479	1,012,000	Down 29%

SOURCE: Data from U.S. Census Bureau, 1995.

While large mainline Protestant churches have lost many members in the last decade, fundamentalists (who emphasize a literal interpretation of the Bible) and evangelicals (who preach the return of the flesh-and-blood Jesus) have seen their congregations blossom. One of the most famous evangelists is Billy Graham, who here gives a benediction at a California ceremony. He had conducted evangelical campaigns around the globe for nearly 50 years.

of the 43 new superchurches, each accommodating 5000 or more worshippers every Sunday. The growing strength of fundamentalism has further helped many African American churches to hold their own in the midst of various social ills, such as rising drug use, unemployment, crime, and family disintegration. Like white fundamentalism and evangelicalism, black Christianity preaches the reality of the flesh-and-blood Jesus and the urgency of spiritual rebirth. But it also includes social and economic liberation in its gospel (Lincoln and Mamiya, 1990; Ostling, 1991).

The fundamentalist revival is a reflection of the conservative trend in society. It is also a culmination of a number of factors. First is the aggressive, skillful use of television, as illustrated by the popularity of such fundamentalist preachers as Jerry Falwell and Pat Robertson. A second factor is the social changes of the last two decades that have driven many conservative people into fundamentalist churches. These social changes have involved the women's movement, gay rights movement, unmarried mothers, legalization of abortion, and court decisions against school prayer. And a third factor is the highly personal style of worship in fundamentalist churches, which tends to attract the casualties of this fast-changing, high-tech age—individuals who are socially isolated, alienated, and dehumanized by modern society (Moberg, 1984; Hammond, 1985; Marty and Appleby, 1992).

The Rise of Islam

Islam in the United States has considerably more adherents than most people might suspect. The number is estimated to be anywhere between 3 million and 6 million. However, this figure includes virtually all immigrants from predominantly Muslim Arab countries, and most of these Arab Americans are Christians rather than Muslims. Actually, only about 1.4 million U.S. adults identify themselves as Muslims (Goldman, 1991). Still, U.S. Muslims are one of our fastest-growing religious groups.

Slightly over half of all Muslims are immigrants, a number that has doubled in the past two decades. A steadily increasing number of native-born U.S. citizens are converts. Many of them are African Americans who used to espouse a militant, antiwhite, and separatist philosophy, but now embrace orthodox, mainstream Islam. African Americans make up about 40 percent of the U.S. Muslim population (Sheler, 1990).

Muslims must follow a strict code of ethics and diet. They must not consume alcohol, illicit drugs, or pork. They must refrain from premarital and extramarital sex and dating. They are forbidden to gamble or to pay or accept interest on loans or savings accounts. These religious rules bring Muslims into conflict with the dominant U.S. culture, which is based so much on credit purchases and payment of interest for such activities as buying homes and cars. Devout Muslims find U.S. society shockingly permissive, riddled with what they consider moral problems, such as sexual freedom, drug use, crime, and lack of respect for authority. Immigrant parents often clash with their teenage children over dating and drinking (Ostling, 1988; Sheler, 1990).

The conflict between Islamic and Western cultures may ultimately produce a distinctively American brand of Islam. In many ways, some U.S. mosques already function more like Christian churches than traditional mosques in Islamic countries. The Toledo center—the largest U.S. mosque, located in Perrysburg, Ohio—has 22 nationality groups among its members. Weddings and funerals are held in the mosque. There are Sunday classes for children and teenagers as well as "lectures" for adults. After the afternoon prayer service, the faithful get together for a meal in a lower-level dining room. The problem is that there is still a lack of Western-trained *imams* (Muslim prayer leaders, comparable to Christian pastors or Jewish rabbis) and Islam scholars. Nearly all imams come from the Middle East with little firsthand experience of Western culture. There are also no Islamic "divinity schools" in North America (Sheler, 1990).

Questions for Discussion and Review

1. What are the traditional religious affiliations in the United States?
2. How do social class and age relate to religion?
3. What is the nature of the current fundamentalist religious revival?
4. Who are the Muslims in the United States? What is the nature of their religion?

A Global Analysis of Religion

There are various forms of religion around the world, as shown in Figure 11.7. They can classified into three broad categories: **theism,** the type of religion that centers on the worship of a god or gods; **ethicalism,** the type of religion that emphasizes moral principles as guides for living a righteous life; and **animism,** the belief in spirits capable of helping or harming people.

Theism

Theistic religions define the sacred as one or more supernatural beings. These religions center on the worship of a god or gods. There are two subtypes of theism: **monotheism,** or belief in one god, and **polytheism,** belief in more than one god.

Christianity, Judaism, Islam, and Zoroastrianism are all monotheistic. With over a billion followers, Christianity is the world's largest religion. It is split into three principal groups—Roman Catholic, Protestant, and Eastern Orthodox—but these groups share a belief in God as the creator of the world and in Jesus as its savior. Judaism worships Yahweh, the God of the Old Testament, as the creator of the universe and teaches that He chose the people of Israel as witness to His presence. Islam, the world's second-largest religion, was established by the prophet Muhammad in the seventh century A.D. It emphasizes that believers must surrender totally to the will of Allah (God), the creator, sustainer, and restorer of the world. Zoroastrianism is an ancient, pre-Christian religion, which still has a quarter of a million followers, known as Parsees, in India. Parsees believe in one supreme God whose omnipotence is temporarily limited by an ongoing battle with evil—although God

Like Judaism, Christianity, and Zoroastrianism, Islam is a monotheistic religion. It is one of the fastest-growing religions in the United States, whose adherents follow a strict code of ethics and diet. Many Islamic centers in the United States provide both worship and education, to foster the growth of Islam among families.

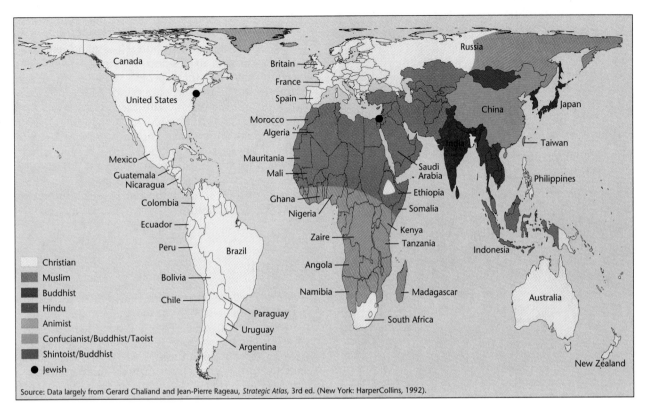

Source: Data largely from Gerard Chaliand and Jean-Pierre Rageau, *Strategic Atlas*, 3rd ed. (New York: HarperCollins, 1992).

FIGURE 11.7
Religions Around the Globe

is ensured of eventual victory. The faithful join forces with God by keeping themselves pure through ablution, penance, and prayers.

The best-known polytheistic faith is Hinduism. The great majority of Hindus live in India. In small villages throughout India, countless gods are worshipped, each believed to have a specific sphere of influence, such as childbirth, sickness, the harvest, or rain. These local deities are often looked on as manifestations of higher gods. Hinduism also teaches that we are *reincarnated*— born and reborn again and again—into new human or animal bodies. People may escape the cycle of reincarnation and achieve salvation by practicing mystical contemplation and steadfast endurance and by following traditional rules of conduct for their castes, families, and occupations.

Ethicalism

Some religions do not focus on supernatural beings. Instead, these *ethicalist religions* ascribe sacredness to moral principles. The heart of these religions is a set of

principles that serve as guides for a righteous life. The best examples are Buddhism, Confucianism, Taoism, and Shintoism.

Buddhism was founded in India in the sixth century B.C. by Gautama, who is known as the Buddha ("enlightened one"). It is today the largest ethical religion. According to Buddhism, there is no independent, unchanging "self" and no physical world— both are illusions. Belief in their reality, attachment to them, and the craving for human pleasures are, according to Buddhism, the source of human misery. To escape this misery is to attain *nirvana* (salvation). It requires meditation—freeing one's mind from all worldly desires and ideas—and right thinking, right speech, right action, and the right mode of living. Buddhism is widely practiced in many Asian societies.

Confucianism was founded by Confucius (551–479 B.C.) in China. For well over 2000 years, it was practically the state religion of China. Confucianism stresses personal cultivation through learning and self-examination, so that the individual becomes imbued with confidence and serenity. It also urges harmony between individuals. Confucius described

Buddhism is considered an ethicalist religion, focusing on moral principles that serve as guideposts for a righteous life. Other ethicalist religions are Confucianism, Taoism, and Shintoism. The term Buddha means the enlightened one, and enlightenment is the goal of the many Buddhists around the world, who meditate to free their minds from worldly desires and ideas.

proper social conduct as "reciprocity," which means, in his words, "Do not do to others what you would not want others to do to you."

Like Confucianism, Taoism has shaped the Chinese character for more than 2000 years, but today has a much smaller following. Whereas Confucianism compels its adherents to be austere and duty-conscious, Taoism encourages joyful, carefree quietism, nonintervention, or "not overdoing." According to Taoism, every deliberate intervention in the natural course of events sooner or later turns into the opposite of what was intended. In essence, in a mystical manner, Taoism tells people to yield totally to the *Tao* ("the Way"), accepting what is natural and spontaneous in people. Actually, Taoism and Confucianism pursue the same goal—the subordination of individuals to groups, such as families and society. They differ only in the means of achieving that goal. While Confucianism urges *activism* through performance of one's social duties, such as

obeying one's parents and being polite to others, Taoism teaches *passivity* through avoidance of self-indulgence, power seeking, and self-aggrandizement.

Shintoism has always been a part of Japanese culture. It teaches that people should strive for *magokoro*—a "bright and pure mind" or "truthfulness, sincerity, or uprightness." This means that individuals must be sincerely interested in doing their best in whatever work they have chosen, and they must be truthful in their relationships with others. Purification, physical and spiritual, is the path to these goals. To remove the "dust" of humans' wickedness believed to cover their divine nature, purification rites are performed at Shinto shrines.

Animism

Animists believe that spirits, whether helpful or harmful to people, may reside in humans, animals, plants, rivers, or winds. They are not gods to be worshipped, but supernatural forces that can be manipulated to serve human ends. Rituals such as feasting, dancing, fasting, and cleansing are often performed to appease the spirits so that crops can be harvested, fish caught, illness cured, or danger averted. Animism is prevalent in sub-Saharan Africa.

Among indigenous peoples in North and South America, a common type of animism is called **shamanism,** the belief that a spiritual leader can communicate with the spirits by acting as their mouthpiece or letting the soul leave the leader's body and enter the spiritual world. The spirits, in effect, live in the shaman ("one who knows"). By communicating with them, the shaman heals the sick, discovers lost animals, sees events in distant places, foresees those in the future, and forecasts prospects for farming, fishing, and hunting.

Another form of animism, popular among native peoples of Australia and some Pacific islands, is **totemism,** the belief that a kinship exists between humans and an animal (or, less commonly, a plant). The animal, called a *totem,* represents a human family, a clan, or a group of ancestors. It is thought of as a person—but a person with superhuman power—and it must be treated with respect, awe, and fear. Killing, eating, touching, and even seeing the animal are often prohibited. The totem is relied on as a helper and protector, but it also punishes those who breach a taboo.

Question for Discussion and Review

1. What are the differences among theism, ethicalism, and animism?

Among Native Americans, a common type of animism is called Shamanism, the belief that a spiritual leader can communicate with the spirits by acting as their mouthpiece or letting the soul leave the leader's body and enter the spiritual world. Here, a shaman performs at a Ute ceremony in Utah.

CHAPTER REVIEW

1. *According to the functionalist perspective, what are the functions of education?* The main functions are teaching knowledge and skills, enhancing social mobility, promoting national unity, and providing custodial care.

2. *According to the conflict perspective, what does "Americanization" mean?* It means that much of the dominant WASP culture is imposed on U.S. minorities.

Does education reduce social inequality? According to the conflict perspective, education does the opposite, reinforcing inequality by channeling students of different socioeconomic backgrounds into different classes and colleges.

3. *According to symbolic interactionism, how does the Pygmalion effect work?* Certain expectations about students lead teachers to behave in a particular way that

causes the students to live up to what the teachers expect of them. *What does the Pygmalion effect have to do with school tracking?* Because of tracking, students who are perceived positively or negatively are treated accordingly, and they thus end up doing well or poorly in school.

4. *Does the decline in standardized test scores mean that there is a crisis in U.S. education?* Not necessarily. The drop in test scores may reflect the opening up of educational opportunities for the poor and minorities. Lower achievement scores in the United States compared to other industrialized countries may also reflect the impact of democratization. The United States is not the only country having some problems with its schools. Thus, U.S. education is not as bad as it appears, though it always needs improvement.

5. *What are Head Start, school choice, and lifelong learning?* Head Start is designed to help young disadvantaged children become better students. School choice reflects an effort to improve schools by establishing competition among them for students. Lifelong learning involves adults who want to continue their education by attending college.

6. *How do schools in some societies vary from one another?* In Belgium, there are proportionately more teachers than in virtually all other countries. In Finland, schooling is rigorous and all higher education is free, making the nation the most educated in the world. In France, teachers are allowed to teach in any way, without interference from bureaucrats. In Japan, schooling is intense and pervasive so as to produce a high-achieving society, but it has also generated student violence and truancy.

7. *According to Durkheim, what is God?* Durkheim argued that God is a symbolic representation of society. By their worship, members of society strengthen their bonds to each other and their acceptance of the society's norms. Thus, religion helps preserve social order. *What other functions does religion serve?* Religion supports people, provides social control, stimulates social change, and provides individuals with a sense of identity. If these functions are carried too far, however, religion can become dysfunctional. *How did Marx view religion?* To Marx, religion is an oppressive illusion, which helps the rich and powerful to perpetuate their domination of the masses. He argued that religion justifies society's inequalities and gives solace to the masses, diverting their attention from the source of their oppression. *According to Weber, how did Calvinist*

Protestantism help develop capitalism? It helped by encouraging believers to work hard and accumulate money.

8. *What are some distinguishing characteristics of religion in the United States?* There is great diversity in U.S. religion, reflecting different religious affiliations, the faithful's differences in class and age, and different beliefs and practices. The two fastest-growing religious movements in the United States are fundamentalist groups and Islam.

9. *What are the world's religions like?* They appear in three different forms: theism, which worships a god or gods; ethicalism, which provides a guide for living a righteous life; and animism, which believes in spirits capable of helping or harming people.

KEY TERMS

Animism   The belief in spirits capable of helping or harming people. (p. 252)

Compensatory education   A school program intended to improve the academic performance of socially and educationally disadvantaged children. (p. 241)

Cultural imperialism   The practice of making minorities accept the dominant group's culture. (p. 238)

Ethicalism   The type of religion that emphasizes moral principles as guides for living a righteous life. (p. 252)

Monotheism   The belief in one god. (p. 252)

Polytheism   The belief in more than one god. (p. 252)

Pygmalion effect   The impact of a teacher's expectations on student performance. (p. 239)

Shamanism   The belief that a spiritual leader can communicate with the spirits, by acting as their mouthpiece or letting the soul leave the leader's body and enter the spiritual world. (p. 254)

Theism   The type of religion that centers on the worship of a god or gods. (p. 252)

Totemism   The belief that a kinship exists between humans and an animal—or, less commonly, a plant. (p. 254)

Tracking   The system of sorting students into different groups according to ability. (p. 238)

Suggested Readings

Bloom, Harold. 1992. *The American Religion: The Emergence of the Post-Christian Nation.* New York: Simon & Schuster. An analysis of how the Mormons, the Southern Baptists, and other made-in-America religions reflect the U.S. preoccupation with the self.

Chubb, John E., and Terry M. Moe. 1990. *Politics, Markets, and America's Schools.* Washington, D.C.: Brookings Institute. Shows how excessive bureaucracy has ruined public education, and proposes that schools be run entirely by teachers and that parents be allowed to choose schools for their children.

Greeley, Andrew M. 1989. *Religious Change in America.* Cambridge, Mass.: Harvard University Press. A data-packed analysis of how people continue to be as religious as ever despite all the social changes around them.

McKenna, Francis R. 1993. *Schooling in America.* Dubuque, Iowa: Kendall/Hunt. A collection of articles dealing with reform, power, and equity in the U.S. educational system.

Roof, Wade Clark. 1993. *A Generation of Seekers: The Spiritual Journeys of the Baby Boom Generation.* New York: HarperCollins. An analysis of how the baby boomers, who are now in their thirties and forties, feel about religion.

ECONOMY AND POLITICS

Myths and Realities

MYTH: *Industrialization can be a boon to the world by helping all nations prosper, so that international peace can be achieved.*
REALITY: According to a 50-nation study, industrialization creates global inequality, with highly industrialized nations enjoying higher status and more power than the less industrialized nations, and this inequality threatens world peace. (p. 262)

MYTH: *Most U.S. adults work for huge companies, such as GM and IBM, which have more than 1000 employees each.*
REALITY: Most adults work in relatively small firms, which have fewer than 100 employees. (p. 268)

MYTH: *In the United States most workers would rather pursue leisure than work.*
REALITY: Most workers are satisfied with their jobs. Even if they inherited enough money to live comfortably without having to lift a finger, most say they would still want to work. (p. 268)

MYTH: *Many conservatives dislike "big government," wanting to "get government off our backs" in all aspects of our lives.*
REALITY: Many conservatives are ideologically opposed to government intervention in people's private lives, but at the same time support school prayer and antiabortion laws, which, in effect, represent government intervention in private lives. (p. 272)

MYTH: *Poverty is the breeding ground for revolution and terrorism. Revolutionary leaders and terrorists are therefore mostly poor.*
REALITY: Most of the revolutionary leaders and terrorists come from relatively affluent families. (p. 275)

In 1981, after Morris Shanks left the navy at age 37, he could find no work except a low-wage job as a security guard. At that time the U.S. economy was in deep recession and had a very high rate of unemployment. Besides, Shanks only had a high school equivalency diploma and had been trained to fix fighter planes with hand tools, a skill that does not pay well in an increasingly high-tech society. But today the economy has slowly turned around, with more "Help Wanted" signs than before. Over the last 14 years, Shanks has obtained more education, which includes completion of several computer courses. He now works as a maintenance technician earning a middle-class salary and living a middle-class life (Levinson, 1995).

Like Shanks, people everywhere are affected by their nation's economy as they work to fulfill even their simplest needs. Beyond basic needs of survival, we have developed countless others—needs for clothing, housing, schooling, medical care, entertainment, and innumerable other goods and services. To meet these needs, societies develop an **economic institution,** a system for producing and distributing goods and services. In studying this institution, economists tend to focus on impersonal things such as productivity, wages, prices, and profits. Sociologists are more interested in people, such as Shanks, and how they work or how their occupations affect their lives. Sociologists are further interested in how the economy relates to other aspects of society, especially **politics**—the type of human interaction that involves some people acquiring and exercising power over others. We will therefore analyze both the economic and political institutions in this chapter.

THE ECONOMY IN PERSPECTIVE

To understand the economic world today, we need to look back at least to the eighteenth century, when a momentous event took hold in England. It was the **Industrial Revolution,** the drastic economic change brought about by the introduction of machines into the work process about 200 years ago. The revolution transformed the world's economies and its societies. The revolution also made possible the emergence of **capitalism,** an economic system based on private ownership of property and competition in producing and selling goods and services.

The Industrial Revolution

For 98 percent of the last 10,000 years, the pattern of economic life changed rather little. Practically all our ancestors eked out a mere subsistence living from relatively simple economies such as hunting and gathering (see Chapter 2: Society and Culture). During all those years, as sociologists Raymond Mack and Calvin

Bradford (1979) pointed out, "the whole economic process was wrapped up in the individual." This was especially true for craftsworkers: They owned their own tools, secured their own raw materials, worked in their own homes, set their own working hours, and found their own markets for finished products.

But gradually, as the population grew and the demand for goods increased, individual craftsworkers became more and more dependent on intermediaries to find raw materials and to sell their finished products. Some of these intermediaries took over the economic process, telling craftsworkers what and how much to produce. In essence, these intermediaries became capitalists, and the formerly independent craftsworkers became employees. Craftsworkers, however, still worked separately in their own homes, forming what is called a *cottage industry*.

Characteristics   As the Industrial Revolution was about to dawn in England, cottage industry began to give way to a *factory system*. Capitalists found it more economical to hire people to work together in one building than to collect goods from many scattered

Sparked by the invention of spinning jennies and other machines, which made mass production possible, the Industrial Revolution began in England around 1760. It later brought tremendous wealth to the West, while changing work patterns, the distribution of population, human relations, and social values. But it has also brought about global inequality.

cottages. They began to own every part of the manufacturing process: the factory, the tools, the raw materials, and the finished products. In effect, they even owned the landless workers, who had only their labor to sell in order to survive. To make the process more efficient, capitalists increased the division of labor. Some individuals were hired to spin thread, others to weave cloth, and one person to oversee all the workers as their supervisor.

Then, with the invention of steam engines, spinning jennies, and other machines, mass production became possible, and the Industrial Revolution was underway. It began in England around 1760, and during the following century profoundly changed the economic structure of Western Europe and North America. The Industrial Revolution substituted machines for human labor to perform many tasks, greatly improved the getting and working of raw materials, developed widespread railroad and steamship systems to transport huge quantities of raw materials and manufactured goods, and moved labor and resources from agriculture to industry. All this created tremendous wealth. At the same time, small machines were replaced by large ones, little mills became giant factories, and modest partnerships changed into large corporations.

Consequences Industrialization has far-reaching results. *First, it changes the nature of work.* The mechanization of agriculture calls for few operators, leading most farmers into industrial work. Bigger and better machines in the factory, in the mines, and at construction sites also require fewer workers, reducing the number of blue-collar jobs. But, because technology is highly productive, it brings prosperity, which increases the demand for all kinds of services, from education and health to entertainment and money management. Thus, white-collar occupations proliferate. Even in manufacturing companies, white-collar workers outnumber blue collars. The General Electric Company, for example, produces numerous different items from turbines to light bulbs, but the majority of its employees are engaged in white-collar services, from accounting to marketing.

Second, industrialization brings about demographic changes—changes in the characteristics of a population. In general, as a society industrializes, cities grow, and fewer people live on farms, but the population as a whole increases. Once a society has developed an industrialized economy, population growth tends to slow, and the percentage of elderly people in the population rises.

Third, industrialization changes human relations. In industrial societies, people usually spend much of their time in huge, bureaucratic organizations. They interact with a broad range of people, but their relationships with these people tend to be formal, fragmentary, and superficial. Ties to primary groups loosen. Industrialization alters other institutions as well: Formal schooling tends to become more important, and functions once served by the family are taken over by other institutions, such as business and government. According to a study of 50 countries, industrialization also creates global inequality, with highly industrialized nations enjoying higher status and more power than the less industrialized, thereby threatening world peace (Rau and Roncek, 1987).

Fourth, industrialization changes the values of a society. Traditional values and ways of living are discredited. People learn to view change as natural and to hope for a better future. Thus, industrialization brings a dynamism into society. It produces greater energy and open-mindedness but also restlessness and discontent. Social and political conflict often follow.

Toward a Postindustrial World   Many developing countries have been trying to achieve in a few years the industrialization that took the West over 200 years to develop. Thus they can realize modernization only partially. These countries have imported Western technology that has lowered death rates but not birth rates, with the result that population growth has eaten up or outstripped any gains in income. They have instituted Western-style education, enough to let people dream of a better life but not enough to create and operate a modern economy. They have seen the rewards of an industrial technology—and developed a craving for what they believe to be a material paradise—but they do not have the means to satisfy that appetite. As a result, widespread poverty, high rates of unemployment, and other social problems tend to ensue.

Meanwhile, the developed countries continue to industrialize and to take the process a step further. During industrialization, machines take over tasks from humans and people control the machines. Increasingly, the task of controlling the machines is given over to computers. A growing number of factory workers sit at computer terminals in clean, quiet offices, monitoring tireless, precise robots doing the kind of work that assembly-line workers used to do with dirty, noisy machines. Along with computers, other related technological breakthroughs, such as electronics, microchips, and integrated circuits, are ushering in a postindustrial age.

Postindustrialism has brought many developed countries a high degree of affluence and leisure. It has also made it possible for anyone on the globe to be in instant communication with anyone else. Consequently, the spread of high technology throughout the world will likely mean greater output per worker and a higher standard of living in more and more societies. Instant communication may further undermine authoritarian

controls, as it has in Eastern Europe, and keep democratic governments on their toes with a new degree of scrutiny. In short, we are likely to see more economic wealth and political freedom in the postindustrial world (Bartley, 1991).

Sociological Perspectives on Capitalism

No factory functions on its own. It must buy raw materials and sell its products. It is enmeshed in a complicated network of exchanges. This network must be organized in some way. One way is through markets. A market economy is driven by the countless decisions individuals make to buy and sell. This is how *capitalism* works. To functionalists, capitalism can bring about a prosperous and stable social order. But to conflict theorists, capitalism threatens society by allowing a powerful wealthy class to exploit a weak poor class. On the other hand, symbolic interactionists focus on how people's definition of their world creates or supports capitalism.

Functionalist Perspective   The functionalist ideas about the contributions of capitalism to a prosperous society can be traced to Adam Smith (1732–1790). Although Smith was an economist, his theory of capitalism has become a part of economic sociology. At the core of the theory lies a belief about the psychology of human beings: we are inherently selfish and act to serve our own interests. Capitalism works by allowing this pursuit of self-interest to flourish. It does so through two key characteristics: (1) *private ownership* of property and (2) *free competition* in buying and selling goods and services. Without these, capitalism does not exist.

Private ownership is considered functional for society's economic health because it motivates people to be efficient and productive. This may explain why Federal Express and other private companies in the United States are generally more financially successful than the U.S. Postal Service and other government agencies. Private ownership may also explain why private lands in China are far more productive than state-owned farms. In that country, the private plots once constituted only 4 percent of all cultivated land but produced some 33 percent of the country's meat and dairy products and 50 percent of its potatoes (Naisbitt and Aburdene, 1990).

Free competition is also considered beneficial to society's economic health because it compels businesses to make the most efficient use of resources, to produce the best possible goods and services, and to sell them at the lowest price possible. Only by doing so can they expect to beat their competitors. Competition, then, acts—in Smith's terminology—as an "invisible hand," bringing profits to the efficient producers and putting the inefficient ones out of business.

Doesn't the pursuit of self-interest reduce society to a jungle and harm the public good? On the contrary, Adam Smith argued that because of free competition the self-serving decisions of individuals to buy and sell end up promoting the public good. Competition forces people to take account of others' interests in order to serve their own. If Apple Computer does not meet your needs, you can buy a product from Texas Instruments or IBM—and Apple knows it. It is in their interest to serve your interests. Since many businesses strive to serve their own interests by serving those of the public, the whole society will benefit. There will be an abundance of high-quality, low-priced goods and services, which will entice many people to buy. Businesses will then produce more to meet consumers' increased demand, which will create more jobs and raise wages. The result is a prosperous economy for the society as a whole.

Conflict Perspective   The conflict ideas about the harmfulness of capitalism can be traced to Karl Marx (1818–1883). He saw as inevitable private property owners' exploitation of their laborers by paying them as little as possible. Marx also disagreed with Smith on the specialized division of labor in industrial capitalism. To Smith, specialization *enhances efficiency* in the generation of wealth. But when Marx looked at specialization, he saw **alienation of labor,** laborers' loss of control over their work process. Because workers own neither their tools nor the products they make and because they cannot exercise all their capacities as they choose but are forced to perform an isolated, specific task, their work is no longer their own. Instead, Marx contended, it becomes a separate, alien thing.

Marx further saw severe contradictions within the capitalist system, contradictions that would serve as "its own gravediggers." One contradiction grows from capitalism's devotion to individualism. As Heilbroner (1972) said, "*capitalism* had become so complex that it needed direction, but *capitalists* insisted on a ruinous freedom." Marx saw another contradiction as well: Capitalists depend on profit, but their profit comes from the fact that workers put more value into products than they are given in the form of wages. To increase their profits, capitalists often hold down wages, and, whenever possible, substitute machines for human labor as well. As a result, the poor get poorer from lower wages or job loss. This, in turn, reduces the demand for the capitalists' products, thereby decreasing their profits. The economy can work itself out of this crisis, but such crises will recur, argued Marx, with each one getting worse until the workers revolt.

Ultimately, Marx believed, the contradictions of capitalism would lead to **communism,** a classless society that operates on the principle of "from each according to his ability, to each according to his needs." In this society, the state would wither away. First, however, the destruction of capitalism would be followed by a temporary era of **socialism,** an economic system based on public ownership and government control of the economy.

No state, including the so-called communist countries such as the former Soviet Union and China, has ever reached full-blown communism, but many have tried socialism. In a socialist economy, the state owns and operates the means of production and distribution, such as land, factories, railroads, airlines, banks, and stores. It determines what the nation's economic needs are and develops plans to meet those goals. It sets wages and prices. Individual interests are subordinate to those of society.

Symbolic Interactionist Perspective   As a symbolic interactionist, Max Weber (1864–1920) concentrated on how subjective meanings affect economic action. To Weber, subjective meanings involve "taking into account the behavior of others," which in turn leads the individual to engage in certain activities (Weber, 1968). As suggested in Chapter 11 (Education and Religion), Weber saw how the early Protestants in Europe acquired from their interactions with each other some shared beliefs that gave rise to capitalism.

First, the Protestants defined hard work as a sign that God would send them to heaven rather than hell. They in effect equated toil with God's work. By working hard, they were able to produce wealth. Second, they defined play as the devil's temptation. They were thus afraid to spend the fruit of their labor on amusements and other worldly pleasures (Biggart, 1994). The wealth, then, was used as capital to be put into business. The continuing accumulation of capital and growth of business led to the development of capitalism.

After capitalism emerged, it continued to operate for a long time because the early Protestants learned to behave in a rational and systematic manner. The early Protestantism helped discipline an unruly working class, restraining its members from consuming alcohol, from engaging in disorderly conduct, and even from taking breaks or walking off their jobs, thus turning them into a docile labor force (Wuthnow, 1994). Simultaneously, the same religion encouraged the capitalist class to run its businesses rationally. As a result, these capitalists developed bureaucracy as the most rational form of organization to perpetuate capitalism.

Questions for Discussion and Review

1. What impact did the Industrial Revolution have on societies?

2. What is the nature of capitalism as seen from the functionalist and conflict perspectives?
3. According to the symbolic interactionist perspective, how did early Protestantism produce and support capitalism?

THE WORLD'S ECONOMIC SYSTEMS

Economic systems vary from one society to another. Some are mainly capitalist and others socialist, but they all are mixed economies, having elements of both capitalism and socialism. They differ only in degree, ranging on a continuum from the most capitalist to the most socialist.

The Economic Continuum

The United States and Japan are among the most capitalist societies. Yet, the U.S. government manages the economy by, for example, levying taxes and controlling the supply of money. In Japan the government takes a leading role in planning investment for the future, in turning corporations toward industries that are likely to grow.

Ranging along the middle of the continuum are the European democracies. From time to time, several of these democracies have had socialist governments. In general, these nations have combined capitalist enterprise with wide-ranging government control—and high taxes. They tend to establish stricter controls on business and offer more extensive social services than the United States. All these countries, for example, provide a national system of health insurance. Over the years, their governments have owned and managed many industries. Great Britain, for example, has had the coal, steel, automobile, and television industries under government control at various times. Even before France elected a socialist government in 1981, its government had created subway and aerospace industries. Nevertheless, these European democracies are so much more capitalist than socialist that they are usually considered capitalist.

At the socialist end of the continuum we find countries such as North Korea, Vietnam, China, and Cuba. Their governments largely control their economies. But some have recently tried to introduce a new economic arrangement in which centralized direction of the economy by the government is reduced. China has adopted some free enterprise practices. It has abolished most rural communes, restored family farms, estab-

At the socialist end of the economic continuum are countries such as Vietnam, North Korea, China, and Cuba, whose governments largely control their economies. But some have recently reduced government control by allowing citizens to practice free enterprise to some degree. Here, Vietnamese women work in a market stall in Ho Chi Minh City.

lished a free market for agricultural and consumer goods, granted state-owned enterprises wide autonomy in running their businesses, and opened up its coastal regions to foreign investors. This free enterprise, however, is still more limited than in other countries.

The U.S. Economy Today

There are both bright and dark spots in the current U.S. economic picture. Over the last decade, the U.S. economy has been producing an abundance of jobs. Massive numbers of women and immigrants have joined the baby-boom generation in entering the labor force without causing a bulge in unemployment. Throughout most of the 1980s, only about 5 percent of our workforce was unemployed. This was a remarkable achievement. By contrast, in Europe, few new jobs have been generated, so that unemployment there has increased sharply. During the 1992 recession the U.S. jobless rate went up to 7.6 percent, causing profound distress and fear among millions of unemployed and employed workers. But that rate was still far lower than the 10.8 percent of a decade before, and now (in 1995), with the recession over, it has come down to about 5 percent again. Inflation has also gone down to a level that generates only little discomfort—from 12 percent in 1980 to about 5 percent today (Krugman, 1990; Gwynne, 1992; Hershey, 1995).

Despite lower unemployment and lower inflation over the last 10 years, our living standard has mostly failed to improve. Income has remained relatively stagnant for most people. Significantly more workers have to moonlight to meet regular household expenses or to pay off debts. Low-income people have suffered more, with real incomes falling, more people dropping below the poverty line, and homelessness rising. A key reason is that since 1970 we have suffered a slowdown in productivity growth. Although the U.S. economy has grown significantly since 1983, its growth is still much smaller today than 30 and 40 years ago. Since 1970 U.S. output per worker has risen an average of only 1.2 percent a year, compared with 2.8 percent in the 1950s and 1960s. This has made it impossible for most people to improve their living standard. If the productivity growth continues to remain low, today's young families will live no better than their parents (Krugman, 1990).

Related to our slowdown in productivity growth is the large U.S. **trade deficit**—buying more goods and services from foreign countries than selling to them. Before 1984 we had a **trade surplus**—selling more goods and services to foreign countries than buying from them. But since 1984 we have annually spent over $100 billion more on foreign imports than we earned from our exports abroad. As a result, foreign companies have been using the dollars we pay them to buy a steady stream of U.S. assets, such as stocks, bonds, real estate, and whole corporations. This further causes a drain on our national income, because the United States has to pay interest to foreign bondholders, dividends to foreign stockholders, and rents to foreign landowners. We are also running the risk that foreigners will precipitate an economic crisis here by liquidating their U.S. assets and taking their profits home. This is likely to occur if their confidence in the U.S. economy wavers or their own economies worsen considerably.

Another economic problem is the huge federal **budget deficit**—spending more than we take in. Many fear that the government may someday be unable to pay the accumulated *national debt* and become as bankrupt as many Latin American countries were in the 1980s. Traditionally, most Democrats have wanted to reduce the budget deficit by raising taxes but have failed to take the lead for fear of alienating voters. Most Republicans have wanted to eliminate the deficit by cutting government spending but have feared alienating voters by cutting popular social insurance programs (primarily Social Security), which account for 40 percent of the federal expenditure. Today the Republican-controlled Congress may pass the balanced-budget amendment, but it will require ratification by at least 38 states, a process that can take years (Alter, 1995).

The Economies in Other Countries

The health of the U.S. economy, like a pebble thrown into a pool of water, has an effect on the economies of other nations. We now live in a global economy, with the economies of different countries affecting one another. We can see this in the current economic trends around the world. As the U.S. economy, the most powerful in the world, started to climb out of the worldwide recession in 1992, the economies in many other countries followed suit, producing significant growth in 1994. Today's hottest economies—in Southeast Asia and Latin America—have attracted considerable foreign investment. Free from domination by the former Soviet Union, Eastern Europeans have in recent years been heavily influenced by capitalist nations. They not only have received a great deal of foreign investment but also have gotten rid of many government-controlled industries. Being part of the same global economy, various nations have also experienced problems similar to ours, such as the budget deficit, inflation, or unemployment. But the economies in most countries are now doing better than they were several years ago. Let's look at several important economies other than our own.

Canada Canada has become the most successful exporting country in the industrial world. Along with sharply increasing exports, surging corporate investment and job growth have significantly pushed down its unusually high unemployment. But consumer spending cannot go up much because of both tax increases and higher borrowing costs. The government plans to raise taxes, as well as reduce spending, to tackle a huge budget deficit, the second highest among industrialized countries (Farnsworth, 1995).

Contrast this photo of the interior of "Nevsky Passage," a leading department store in St. Petersburg, Russia, with the department stores you are familiar with in your hometown. Although market reforms are under way in Eastern Europe and Russia, there still are many shortages of goods. The situation is not likely to improve until the political situation stabilizes and the government addresses the problems of inflation and high unemployment.

Latin America With runaway inflation under control and foreign investors pouring in capital, Latin America is likely to maintain its position as the world's second fastest-growing region—after Southeast Asia. Traditional export commodities, from coffee to copper, are also expected to bring in higher profits because of improved prices. To stimulate their economies, most Latin American countries are removing trade barriers and using private capital to build roads and power plants. The region's exception is Venezuela, whose gross national product fell 3 percent and where annual inflation hovered around 70 percent in 1994, while for the region as a whole the GNP (Gross National Product, the total value of all goods and services) went up 4 percent and inflation was 10 percent (Brooke, 1995).

Western Europe Economies from Italy to Scandinavia have just passed through their worst recession since the end of the Second World War in the 1940s. Growth has picked up and is expected to be 3 percent or higher for 1995 and 1996. Inflation remains low—less than 3 percent. Corporate profits have gone up more than 50 percent. Confident of further successes, companies have begun to increase their capital investments by building more factories. All these signs of recovery since 1993 have largely resulted from a surge in demand for European goods from rapidly growing economies such as those of Asia and North America (Nash, 1995).

Eastern Europe and Russia In their transition from socialist to capitalist economies, most Eastern European nations have shown significant growth, with their GNPs increasing over 4 percent. Foreign investment is expected to continue expanding, but the extent of the increase will depend on how fast and how extensively the state industries are privatized. Foreign investors are wary of Poland, for example, because its government, dominated by two parties with past communist influence, has been reluctant to implement mass privatization. But foreign investors are more interested in the Czech Republic, which has forged ahead with its privatization program by selling state industries cheaply to Czech citizens. While Eastern Europe is improving economically, Russia continues to suffer high unemployment and inflation because of political instability (Perlez, 1995; Erlanger, 1995).

South Africa With apartheid legally dead, South Africa is actively involved in the economies of various African nations. South African companies can be found building railroads, digging mines, and building hotels. South Africans further provide the entire continent with enough jets and telephone lines to help revitalize its sagging economy. South African trade with the rest of Africa is booming, displacing much of the economic influence long held by Western Europe and the United States (French, 1995).

China and Southeast Asia Since 1992 China has turned in an extraordinary economic performance, with annual growth rates of over 13 percent, by far the highest in the world. The growth has partly been fueled by foreign investment, which continues to flood into the country. But the economy remains mostly socialist. State-owned factories continue to soak up most of the capital (investment and bank loans) in China, although they contribute only a small percentage to the nation's industrial output (Tyler, 1995).

As a region, Southeast Asia (especially Indonesia, Malaysia, Singapore, and Thailand) continues to have the world's most vibrant economy as it has had in the last several years, boasting an annual growth rate of 7 percent or more. This remarkable growth has largely been attributed to the region's large numbers of low-wage but relatively well-educated workers. Huge foreign investment, notably from Japan, has also been an important factor. But with the unrestrained economic boom, many cities are now overbuilt, congested, and polluted. The vast disparity between rich and poor has also become a common sight (Shenon, 1995).

Questions for Discussion and Review

1. How can the world's economies be classified?
2. What is the condition of the U.S. economy today?
3. What is the current status of various economies in the world?

WORK IN THE UNITED STATES

When we meet strangers, one of our first questions is likely to be, "What do you do?" They might answer, "I am a salesperson" or "I am a cabdriver" or a doctor or lawyer, or whatever. Work is not just a way to make enough money to pay the bills. For many of us, work helps define our identity and our sense of self-worth. Just what it is that we are able to do for a living, however, depends to a great extent on the economic institutions we have described. As we see in the following sections, the kinds of workers needed by our complex economy have implications for job satisfaction and the workplace.

Occupations

With the industrialization of the farm—a process that accelerated greatly after World War II—the stage was set for the appearance of today's labor force. Thanks to technological innovations ranging from new machinery to new fertilizers to new breeding techniques, agricultural productivity has soared during this century. In 1900 one U.S. farmer on average produced enough food to support seven other people. Today, one farmer produces enough for more than 60 people.

This increasing agricultural productivity pushed many workers off the farm. Now only about 1 percent of the U.S. labor force works on the farm, compared with nearly 60 percent in 1870 and 30.2 percent in 1920. The continuing exodus also reflects the failure of many small family farms to survive. Government subsidies and other "save the family farm" programs, such as crop insurance and production control, have largely come to naught. What remains is an increasingly smaller number of highly efficient farms that need only a few workers to produce enough food for the whole nation. In fact, these farms are capable of producing so much food that the federal government pays them about $10 billion a year *not* to produce more than necessary—in order to support prices of farm commodities (Robbins, 1990).

Many of those who left the farm in earlier decades went to work in manufacturing industries, producing clothes, furniture, or cars. But major changes were under way in manufacturing as well. Just as in agriculture, new machines decreased the number of people needed to produce things. Since World War II, the share of *jobs in manufacturing held by white-collar workers*—managers, professionals, clerical workers, salespersons— has increased greatly. Before 1945, blue-collar workers had long outnumbered white-collar workers, but then white collars began to grow so fast in numbers that today they are three times as numerous as blue collars in manufacturing companies. At General Motors Corporation, for example, 77.5 percent of the workforce is white-collar, compared with 22.5 percent blue-collar (Rosecrance, 1990).

Meanwhile, the growth in jobs in manufacturing and other goods-producing industries has slowed, but *jobs in service industries*—education, health care, banking, real estate, insurance—have increased. In 1900 about 75 percent of the labor force was employed in production and fewer than 25 percent in service. By 1982 the situation was reversed—74 percent in service and 26 percent in production. In the 1990s, the largest job growth in service industries will be among retail salespeople, janitors and maids, waiters and waitresses, and registered nurses, along with doctors, lawyers, teachers, accountants, and other professionals (Crispell, 1990). The rapid growth in the service sector as a whole results largely from an increased demand for health care, entertainment, and business and financial services.

The Workers

The composition of the U.S. labor force has changed, too. The most publicized change has occurred in gender. In 1984 the U.S. Department of Labor announced that since 1960 the number of women in the labor force had nearly doubled. Today, about 58 percent of women are in the labor force, compared with just 38 percent in 1960. The number of women workers will continue to rise, and women are projected to account for about two-thirds of the entire labor force *growth* between 1982 and 1995 (U.S. Census Bureau, 1994). By publicizing and legitimizing the rights and needs of women to earn enough money to support themselves and contribute to total family income, the feminist movement has largely aided the increase.

Important changes have also occurred in the age and racial composition of the work force. In the last two decades, the employment rate for men older than 65 declined significantly. Age discrimination

In the U.S. economy, the growth in manufacturing jobs has slowed, while the growth in service-industry jobs has increased. For example, demand for workers in health care, such as registered nurses, is expected to remain strong over the next decade.

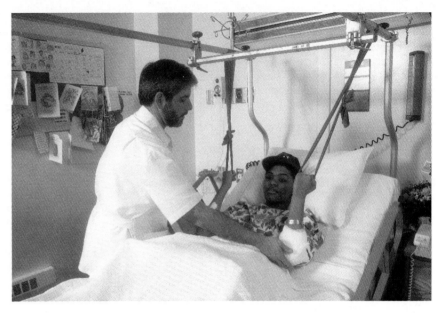

and retirement programs, such as Social Security and private pension plans, have probably played a part in this decline. But in recent years, a growing industrial demand for cheaper labor—stimulated by global competition—has fueled a dramatic increase in labor-force participation among minorities and immigrants. These groups will account for 88 percent of work-force *growth* between 1989 and 1999. Meanwhile, there will be proportionately fewer white men in the labor force (Solomon, 1989).

These breakdowns by gender, race, and age do not tell us much about what is actually going on in the U.S. economy. We have a **dual economy,** an economy that comprises a *core* of large corporations dominating the market and a *periphery* of small firms competing for the remaining, smaller shares of business. In addition, there is a *third sector*, consisting of various government agencies. About 30 percent of the U.S. labor force work in the third, state sector, and the rest are employed in the private core and peripheral sector. Contrary to popular belief, most of the privately employed individuals do not work in the core's large companies (with more than 1000 employees each). Only 30 to 40 percent do so. Most work in the peripheral sector, especially in small firms with fewer than 100 employees (Granovetter, 1984).

Whatever sector they work in, U.S. workers are now better educated than before. In 1940 most workers had just slightly more than a grade school education. Today, more than half have some college and three out of four are high school graduates (Granovetter, 1984; U.S. Census Bureau, 1995). Unfortunately, they are faced with problems that did not exist before.

In today's fiercely competitive global economy, many U.S. companies have begun to minimize produc-

tion costs by paying their employees low wages, comparable to those received by skilled but low-paid workers in the fast developing economies of Asia and Eastern Europe. A popular way to keep payroll costs low involves hiring temporary, contingent, part-time, or contract workers. In fact, since 1982 temporary employment has soared by nearly 250 percent, compared with a less than 20 percent increase in all employment. Temporary workers now compose one-third of the U.S. labor force, and their ranks are growing so fast that they are expected to outnumber permanent full-time workers by the end of this decade (Castro, 1993).

Job Satisfaction

It may be extremely important to have a job, but does it bring happiness? Are U.S. workers really happy with their jobs? In many studies during the last two decades, representative samples of workers have been asked whether they would continue to work if they inherited enough money to live comfortably without working. More than 70 percent replied that they would. Asked how satisfied they were with their jobs, even more—from 80 to 90 percent—replied that they were very or moderately satisfied. But asked whether they would choose the same line of work if they could begin all over again, most said no. Only 43 percent of white-collar workers and 24 percent of blue-collar workers said yes. And when asked, "Do you enjoy your work so much that you have a hard time putting it aside?" only 34 percent of men and 32 percent of women answered affirmatively (Glenn and Weaver, 1982; Burtless, 1990; Lipset, 1990b; NORC, 1994). In short, most people seem to like their jobs but are not too excited about them.

Job satisfaction does not depend solely on economic rewards. Workers who do strenuous physical labor or repetitive tasks, as shown here, may find their jobs worthwhile if they are paid adequate wages. But white-collar workers generally like their jobs because they can enjoy a great deal of autonomy or self-management.

Job satisfaction varies from one group to another. Generally, older workers are more satisfied than younger ones. One reason is that older workers, being more advanced in their careers, have better jobs. Another is that younger workers are more likely to expect their jobs to be highly interesting and stimulating, hence are more likely to be disillusioned because of the difficulty in realizing their high aspirations. White-collar workers, especially professionals and businesspeople, are also more likely than blue collars to feel genuinely satisfied with their jobs. Among blue-collar workers, union members report significantly *less* job satisfaction than nonmembers, which may reflect job dissatisfaction as the primary reason for joining unions in the first place (Schwochau, 1987).

Generally paid less and having less prestigious jobs than men, women may be expected to be less satisfied with their work. But research has shown just the opposite: women are equally or more satisfied when compared with men. Why? One reason is that, because of gender discrimination, women expect less than men from the job market and so can more easily fulfill their lower expectations. If they get jobs that are as good as men's, going beyond their expectation, they are likely to express more satisfaction than men (Hodson, 1989; Weaver and Matthews, 1990).

The Changing Workplace

The traditional work ethic among U.S. workers has been imbued with the early Protestant belief in work as a moral duty—a way of sacrificing for others. Thus, until recently, most have believed that "a man with a family has a responsibility to choose the job that pays the most, rather than one that is more satisfying but pays less." They worked hard to support their families, disregarding how unpleasant and boring their work might be. But today a majority reject that view and attitude. Most are more interested in jobs that allow for personal growth, self-fulfillment, and other post-materialist values. There is, then, a shift in the work ethic, from an emphasis on self-sacrifice to a stress on self-development as the primary motive for hard work (Cramer, 1989; Schor, 1991).

How has this new ethic come about? As we have observed, the number of white-collar workers and the amount of average workers' education have increased substantially over the last several decades. It is these white-collar and better-educated workers who value autonomy and personal growth in the workplace. As a result, attempts have been made to reorganize the workplace. They usually include offering workers more interesting jobs, more autonomy, and increased participation in decision making. A growing number of companies give workers some freedom to set their own working hours within specified limits. Some have introduced mechanisms that allow workers to take part in decisions about production methods, promotions, hiring, and firing. Some companies have even raised wages by sharing profits with workers. These efforts have boosted productivity by 5 to 40 percent. Apparently, workers are more productive when management treats them as equal partners (Yankelovich and Immerwahr, 1984; Gwynne, 1992; Wartzman, 1992).

Questions for Discussion and Review

1. What occupations make up the U.S. labor force today, and what kinds of people fill these positions?
2. What kinds of people are more satisfied with their jobs and why?
3. How and why has the U.S. work ethic changed?

POWER AND AUTHORITY

People everywhere are "political animals." Because valued resources such as jobs and money are scarce, people feel compelled to play politics to determine who gets what, when, and how. Politics is the type of human interaction that involves some people acquiring and exercising power over others. In most societies, the government steps in to regulate conflict and allocate resources among the citizens, because it has a tremendous amount of power and authority.

The Nature of Power

In some societies, the government has the power to tell citizens what work they will do and what god, if any, they can worship. Governments take their citizens' money and spend it to educate children or to overthrow a foreign government or to do many other things. What, then, is power?

Power is the ability to control the behavior of others, even against their will. If a robber forces us to hand over our wallets, that is an example of power. If our friends convince us to cancel a dinner and help them move, that is power. Power is at work when we pay taxes. Power is an aspect of all kinds of social interaction, but obviously there are important differences in the types of power people can exercise.

The most basic difference is between illegitimate and legitimate power. *Illegitimate power* is control that is exercised over people who do not recognize the right of those exercising the power to do so. Weber referred to the use of such power as **coercion,** the illegitimate use of force or threat of force to compel obedience. In contrast, *legitimate power* is control that is exercised over people with their consent; they believe that those exercising power have the right to do so.

Exercising power through coercion requires constant vigilance. If this is their only source of power, leaders are not likely to be able to sustain their power for long. In contrast, legitimate power can often be exercised with little effort, and it can be very stable. Employers, for example, often need do little more than circulate a memo in order to control their employees' behavior. A memo goes out telling workers to stop making personal telephone calls or to request vacations in writing a month in advance, and, at least for a while, workers are likely to obey.

There are at least two kinds of legitimate power. One is **influence,** the ability to control others' behavior through persuasion rather than coercion or authority. Frequently, those who wield other types of power also exercise influence. They may acquire influence because of wealth, fame, charm, knowledge, persuasiveness, or any other admired quality. Business executives may use their wealth to achieve influence over politicians through campaign contributions. Television reporters may acquire the ability to influence public opinion because of their personal attractiveness or journalistic skill. In general, influence is less formal and direct, and more subtle, than other forms of power. A second type of legitimate power is **authority,** which is institutionalized in organizations. When authority exists, people grant others the right to power because they believe that those in power have the right to command and that they themselves have a duty to obey. Authority is essential to the government.

Types of Authority

What is the source of the government's authority? For an answer, we turn to Weber (1957). He described three possible sources of the right to command, which produce what he called *traditional* authority, *charismatic* authority, and *legal* authority.

Traditional Authority   In many societies, people have obeyed those in power because, in essence, "that is the way it has always been." Thus, kings, queens, feudal lords, and tribal chiefs did not need written rules in order to govern. Their authority was based on tradition, on long-standing customs, and it was handed down from parent to child, maintaining traditional authority from one generation to the next. Often, traditional authority has been justified by religious tradition. For example, medieval European kings were said to rule by divine right, and Japanese emperors were considered the embodiment of heaven.

Charismatic Authority   People may also submit to authority because of the extraordinary attraction of an individual. Napoleon, Gandhi, and Mao Zedong all illustrate authority that derives its legitimacy from **charisma**—an exceptional personal quality popularly attributed to certain individuals. Their followers see charismatic leaders as persons of destiny endowed with remarkable vision, the power of a savior, or God's grace. Charismatic authority is inherently unstable; it

 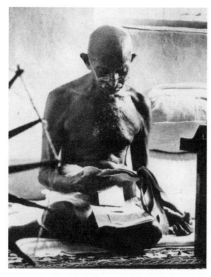 

There are three types of authority. Traditional authority, as usually held by African chiefs, derives from long-standing customs and is handed down from parent to child. Charismatic authority, as illustrated by the Indian nationalistic leader Mahatma Gandhi, is based on an exceptional personal quality popularly attributed to certain individuals. Legal authority, as held by U.S. presidents such as John F. Kennedy, comes from explicit rules and procedures that spell out the leader's rights and duties, although Kennedy is often said to have possessed charisma as well.

cannot be transferred to another person. If a political system is based on charismatic authority, it will collapse when the leader dies. Otherwise, it will go through a process of *routinization*, in which the followers switch from "personal attachment" to "organizational commitment," with their personal devotion to a leader being replaced by formal commitment to a political system (Madsen and Snow, 1983). In essence, charismatic authority is thus transformed into legal authority.

Legal Authority   The political systems of industrial states are based largely on a third type of authority: legal authority, which Weber also called *rational authority*. These systems derive legitimacy from a set of explicit rules and procedures that spell out the ruler's rights and duties. Typically, the rules and procedures are put in writing. The people grant their obedience to "the law." It specifies procedures by which certain individuals hold offices of power, such as governor or president or prime minister. But the authority is vested in those offices, not in the individuals who temporarily hold the offices. Thus, a political system based on legal authority is often called a "government of laws, not of men." Individuals come and go, as U.S. presidents have come and gone, but the office, the

presidency, remains. If individual officeholders overstep their authority, they may be forced out of office and replaced.

In practice, these three types of authority occur in combinations. The U.S. presidency, for example, is based on legal authority, but the office also has considerable traditional authority. Executive privilege, whereby a president can keep certain documents secret, even from Congress, acquired its force from tradition, not through the Constitution or laws. Some presidents, like Abraham Lincoln, Franklin Roosevelt, and John F. Kennedy, have also possessed charismatic authority. Still, the primary basis of the power of the president is legal authority. In general, when societies industrialize, traditional and charismatic authority tend to give way and legal authority becomes dominant, as in the United States.

Citizens' Attitudes Toward Government

Legal authority does not guarantee citizen support for all the things the government does. In the United States, as surveys have shown, there is wide support among all social classes for government spending to clean up the environment, improve the nation's health, combat crime, strengthen the educational system, improve the situation of minorities, and provide medical care and legal assistance for the poor. But while citizens support all these government services, they are highly critical of the government itself, which they believe has become too powerful, too intrusive, and too wasteful—spending too much taxpayers' money (Lipset and Schneider, 1983; NORC, 1994).

In short, most citizens are angry over "big government," yet they support big government by demanding more services. This inconsistency reflects a uniquely U.S. political character. There is a strong tendency to be **ideological conservatives,** who, in theory, are opposed to big government because of their belief in free enterprise, rugged individualism, and capitalism. Simultaneously, the same individuals tend to be **operational liberals,** who, in effect, support big government by backing government programs that render services to the public. Such mixed, ambivalent attitudes pertain not only to economic issues but also to social issues: Many conservatives, for example, want to "get government off our backs," but at the same time support school prayer and antiabortion laws, which, in effect, represent government intervention in private lives (Ladd, 1983).

Questions for Discussion and Review

1. How does legitimate power differ from illegitimate power?
2. What is the difference between influence and authority?
3. What are the differences among traditional, charismatic, and legal authority?
4. What is U.S. citizens' reaction to their government?

WHO REALLY GOVERNS IN U.S. SOCIETY?

The emergence of political parties and interest groups in the United States has brought us a long way from the government envisioned by James Madison, the fourth U.S. president from 1809 to 1817. It was his hope to exclude "interests" and "factions" from the government. Legislators were to represent and vote for the public good, not one interest or the other. Where has this evolution brought us? Are the interest groups and political parties mechanisms through which the people gain more effective control of government, or have the people lost control? Who in fact has **political power,** the capacity to use the government to make decisions that affect the whole society?

The Pluralist View

A pluralist looking at the U.S. government sees many centers of power and many competing interest groups. Government reflects the outcome of their conflict. In this view, the interest groups are central to U.S. democracy. Together they create a mutually restraining influence. No one group can always prevail. Thus, through their competition the interests of the public are reflected in government policy.

But, as we have seen in Chapter 7 (U.S. and Global Stratification), there are large inequalities of wealth, power, and prestige. How, in the face of such inequality, can pluralism be maintained? Cannot one group marshal its resources to dominate others? *Why* doesn't one group or one coalition of groups gradually achieve a concentration of power?

The reason, according to Robert Dahl (1981), is that inequalities are *dispersed,* not cumulative. Inequalities would be cumulative if a group rich in one resource (wealth, for example) were also better off than other groups in almost every other resource—political power, social standing, prestige, legitimacy, knowledge, and control over religious, educational, and other institutions. In the United States, however, one group may hold most of one of these resources, but other groups may have the lion's share of others. What the upper middle class lacks in wealth, for example, it makes up for in knowledge and legitimacy. Power over economic institutions may be concentrated in the hands of corporations, but U.S. religious institutions elude their grasp.

This dispersal of power in society is reflected in a dispersal of political clout. The country's many competing groups vie for control over government policy and end up dominating different spheres. Corporations may dominate the government's decisions on taxes but not on crime. Even tax policy is not dictated solely by corporations, because labor unions and other groups fight with the corporations for influence on politicians and voters. The structure of the government, with its separation of powers, promotes this pluralism. What civil rights groups could not win in Congress in the 1950s, they sometimes won in the courts. Corporations that have lost a battle in Congress may win the war by influencing regulations issued by the executive branch. In the end, in Dahl's view, competing groups usually compromise and share power. Thus, there is no ruling group in the United States. It is instead a pluralist democracy dominated by many different sets of leaders.

David Riesman (1950) and Arnold Rose (1967) have developed a somewhat different analysis. In their view, the United States has become so pluralistic that various interest groups constitute *veto groups,*

According to the pluralist view, various interest groups constitute veto groups that have enough power to block each other's actions. In order to get anything done, these groups must seek support from the unorganized public. Thus we see much lobbying and jockeying for positions among various veto groups, such as the American Association of Retired Persons (AARP) and the National Rifle Association (NRA).

which are powerful enough to block each other's actions. To get anything done, the veto groups must seek support from the unorganized public. The masses, then, have the ultimate power to ensure that their interests and concerns are protected. The bottom line is that the overall leadership is weak, stalemate is frequent, and no single elite can emerge to dominate the others.

The "Elitist" View

It is true that there are many competing groups in the United States. But does their competition actually determine how policy is made? Is the government merely the neutral arbitrator among these conflicting interests? According to power-elite theorists, the answer is no.

Many years ago, Italian sociologists Vilfredo Pareto (1848–1923) and Gaetano Mosca (1858–1941) argued that a small elite has governed the masses in all societies. Why should this be so? If a nation is set up along truly democratic lines, isn't control by an elite avoidable? According to German sociologist Robert Michels (1915), there is an "iron law of oligarchy" by which even a democracy inevitably degenerates into an *oligarchy*—rule by a few. A democracy is an organization,

and according to Michels, "whoever says organization says oligarchy."

In Michels' view, three characteristics of organizations eventually produce rule by the elite. First, to work efficiently, even a democratic organization must allow a few leaders to make the decisions. Second, through their positions of leadership, the leaders accumulate skills and knowledge that make them indispensable to the rank-and-file. Third, the rank-and-file lack the time, inclination, or knowledge to master the complex tasks of government, and they become politically apathetic. Thus, in time, even a democracy yields to rule by an elite.

How does this view apply to the United States? According to C. Wright Mills (1916–1962), there are three levels of power in this country. At the bottom are ordinary people—powerless, unorganized, fragmented, and manipulated by the mass media into believing in democracy. In the middle are Congress, the political parties, interest groups, and most political leaders. At this level, pluralism reigns. The middle groups form "a drifting set of stalemated, balancing forces" (Mills, 1959a). Above them, however, ignored by pluralist theorists, is an elite—what Mills called the *power elite*—that makes the most important decisions. This elite consists of the top leaders in three institutions—the federal government, the military, and the large corporations. These leaders cooperate with one another in controlling the nation. Government leaders can allocate billions to defense to strengthen the military and enrich the corporations from which the weapons are purchased. Big business can support political leaders with campaign money. The politicians can aid business with favorable legislation.

If Mills is correct, all the hoopla of political campaigns and debates is but so much sound and fury because the power elite determines who gets elected and how the government is run. There is some evidence to support Mills' view that a cohesive elite exists. Time and again researchers have found, for example, that top officials in both Democratic and Republican administrations previously held high positions in corporations, that they return to corporations after leaving the government, and that leaders come disproportionately from upper-class backgrounds (Domhoff, 1978, 1983; Barlett and Steele, 1992).

The Marxist View

According to the Marxist view, Mills's analysis confuses the issue. Marxists argue that his political and military elites are not free to act in their own interests—they are merely agents of the corporate elite. What we have are not three elites that come together but one ruling class.

Marxist sociologist Albert Szymanski (1978) provides an example of this approach. According to Szymanski, there are four classes in the United States: The first is the *capitalist class*, which owns and controls the major means of production and is commonly known as big business. The second is the *petty bourgeoisie*, which includes professionals, small-business people, and independent farmers. Some of these people own the "means of production," but they must work with it themselves. The third class is the *working class*, including industrial, white-collar, and rural workers; they must sell their physical or mental labor to live. The fourth is the *lumpenproletariat*, which consists of the unemployed, welfare recipients, criminals, and down-and-outs. Szymanski argues that the capitalist class uses the state as an instrument for exploiting the other three economically subordinate classes.

To control the state, capitalists may use the same methods employed by interest groups, such as lobbying and supporting sympathetic candidates. In using these tools, however, the capitalist class has a big advantage over the run-of-the-mill interest group: it has more money. The capitalist class also uses the media, schools, churches, and other institutions to permeate society with its values, such as free enterprise, economic growth, and competition. Violations of these capitalist values are often taken to be "un-American," giving capitalist interests a potent weapon against unsympathetic politicians. Understandably, few U.S. politicians want to be branded as antigrowth, antibusiness, or socialist. In addition, if the government acts against the capitalists' interests, big business can refuse to put its capital to work. The corporations may close plants or stop investing or send their money abroad (Greider, 1992). As a result, "business can extort favors, virtually without limit, from the political authorities" (Walzer, 1978).

Thus, politicians of all stripes have often talked about molding an economic policy that would "send a message" to "reassure Wall Street." In state after state in recent years, gubernatorial and mayoral campaigns have been fought over the issue of whether a particular candidate will create a good or bad "business climate," over which candidate has the best plan of subsidies and tax breaks to lure business into the city or state. The public interest is identified with business interests, and political choices thus become hostages to the decisions of capitalists.

The issue of who really governs in U.S. society boils down to three questions: Which group holds the most power? Where does it get the power? And what role do the masses play in the government? The three views that we have discussed are different in some respects and similar in others. Both elitists and Marxists see power concentrated in the hands of a small group and hardly any influence by the masses on the government. These theorists differ, however, in regard to the key source of power. To elitists, the ruling elite's power comes from its leadership in business, government, and the military, whereas to Marxists, the ruling class gets its power from controlling the economy. On the other hand, pluralists disagree with both. They argue that political leaders ultimately derive their power from the citizenry, and they must compete among themselves to stay at the top. Table 12.1 summarizes these three views of power.

Which view, then, most accurately represents the reality of the U.S. government? It is difficult, if not impossible, to answer the question because relevant data are unavailable. But it seems obvious that each of the three views captures only a small portion, rather than the complex whole, of the political reality. Pluralists are most likely to hit the bull's eye in regard to most domestic issues, such as jobs and inflation, about which the public feels strongly. In these cases the government tries to do what the people want. Elitists and Marxists are more likely to be correct on most foreign and military policy matters, about which the masses are less concerned and

TABLE 12.1
Who Really Governs?

	Pluralist View	Elitist View	Marxist View
1. Who holds the most power?	Various competing groups.	Top leaders in business, government, and military.	Capitalists; top leaders of the corporate world.
2. Where does the power come from?	The authority vested in elected officials.	Key positions in business, government, and military.	The control of the nation's economy.
3. What role do the masses play?	Choose political leaders in competitive elections.	Are exploited or manipulated by the power elite.	Are exploited or manipulated by the capitalists.

knowledgeable. This explains why defense contractors are able to sell the U.S. government far more arms than are needed (Page, 1983). The three views may be oversimplistic and one-sided, but they are basically complementary, helping to enlarge our understanding of the complex, shifting nature of political power.

Questions for Discussion and Review

1. How does the elitist view of who exercises political power differ from the pluralist view?
2. According to the Marxist view, which elite makes the most important decisions, and how does this elite exercise power?

POLITICAL VIOLENCE: A GLOBAL ANALYSIS

Throughout U.S. history, various groups that believed the government would not respond to their needs have resorted to one form of violence or another. Analyzing 53 U.S. protest movements, William Gamson (1975) found that 75 percent of those groups that used violence got what they wanted, compared with only 53 percent of those that were nonviolent. Violence, it seems, can pay off.

But much of the violence in U.S. history has taken the form of riots, or brief seizures of property for limited aims, inspired by specific grievances. Violent as our history is, we have seen rather little of the two forms of political violence—revolution and terrorism—both more broadly aimed at overthrowing the government.

Causes of Revolution

If a protest movement turns to violence, it may produce a **revolution**—the movement aimed at the violent overthrow of the existing government. Numerous studies on revolutions in many different societies differ in explaining the causes of revolution, but they all suggest in one way or another that a revolution is likely to occur if the following conditions are met (Goldstone, 1982):

1. *A group of rather well-off and well-educated individuals is extremely dissatisfied with the society.* They may be intellectuals or opinion leaders such as journalists, poets, playwrights, teachers, clergy, and lawyers. These people would withdraw support from the government, criticize it, and demand reforms. Discontent may also exist within such elites as wealthy landowners, industrialists, leading bureaucrats, and military officials. It is from among all these people that most revolutionary leaders emerge.

2. *Revolutionary leaders rely on the masses' rising expectation to convince them that they can end their oppression by bringing down the existing government.* By itself, poverty does not produce revolution. Most of the world, after all, is poor. When people have long lived with misery, they may become fatalists, resigned to their suffering. They may starve without raising a fist or even uttering a whimper against the government. But, if their living conditions improve, then fatalism may give way to hope. They may expect a better life. It is in times of such a *rising expectation* that revolutionary leaders may succeed in attracting mass support.

3. *A deepening economic crisis triggers peasant revolts and urban uprisings.* In a social climate of rising expectations, large masses of peasants and workers tend to

respond explosively to serious economic problems. When the state raises taxes too high, and landlords, in turn, jack up the dues of tenant farmers or take over their lands, the peasants are likely to revolt. When the cost of food and the rate of unemployment soar, food riots and large-scale antigovernment protests tend to erupt in the cities.

4. *The existing government is weak.* Usually, before a government is overthrown, it has failed to resolve one problem after another and has gradually lost legitimacy. As the crisis mounts, the government often tries to initiate reforms, but usually too little or too late. This only reinforces people's conviction that the regime is flawed, and encourages demands for even bigger reforms. All this can quicken the government's downfall. As Machiavelli (1469–1527) said in his warning to rulers, "If the necessity for [reforms] comes in troubled times, you are too late for harsh measures. Mild ones will not help you, for they will be considered as forced from you, and no one will be under obligation to you" (Goldstone, 1982).

Revolution in Eastern Europe

The four conditions described above can be found in the revolution that brought down the communist governments, one after another, in Eastern Europe in late 1989 (Echikson, 1990).

1. *Most of the revolutionary leaders were well educated.* They included writers, professors, journalists, and college students. The most famous was playwright Vaclav Havel, who later became president of Czechoslovakia. An exception was electrician Lech Walesa, who organized his fellow workers into a politically powerful force in Poland. This was extraordinary because "everywhere else the initial pressure for revolution came from intellectuals, with workers providing back-up support." Nevertheless, Walesa felt it necessary to have intellectuals as his advisors. As he told them, "We are only workers. These government negotiators are educated men; we need someone to help us" (Echikson, 1990).

2. *Expectations of freedom rose significantly after 1985.* Before Mikhail Gorbachev became the Soviet leader in 1985, Eastern Europeans had long lived in fear under communism. They knew that if they spoke out against the communist rule, they could lose their jobs, cars, and homes, even face prison or death. The 1956 Soviet invasion of Hungary, the 1968 invasion of Czechoslovakia, and the 1981 suppression of Solidarity in Poland further showed how dangerous it was to question the status quo. Soon after 1985, however, Gorbachev removed this fear. He refused to interfere with the internal affairs of Eastern European

nations, and even thinned out Soviet forces in those countries. Consequently, the masses of Eastern Europe were no longer afraid. Their expectation for freedom rose, and they took to the streets to demonstrate against their repressive governments.

3. *Economic crisis added impetus to the revolution.* After Eastern Europe turned communist in 1945, its traditionally impoverished, rural societies underwent significant modernization. A whole generation of workers, who were mostly peasants' children, could live in apartments with running water and toilets. But beginning in the early 1980s, incomes and living standards plummeted, inflation and foreign debt accelerated, and economic growth and innovation went downhill. Even worse, after 1985, Eastern Europe began to lose the subsidy of vital resources such as oil and gas that it had long received from the former Soviet Union. Beset by his own country's economic problems, Gorbachev refused to supply the precious raw materials to Eastern Europe in exchange for its low-quality and obsolete products that could not be sold on the world market. The worsening economic crisis provoked many antigovernment strikes and protests, especially among the workers in Poland.

4. *The communist governments in Eastern Europe became weak.* For a long time, those governments had largely been controlled by the Soviet Union. They were able to rule with an iron hand because of the tremendous military force that the Soviet Union used to prop them up. But after 1985 the Soviet Union, under Gorbachev, decided that it would no longer use its troops to squash any uprising in Eastern Europe. Without the Soviet support, the Eastern European regimes became weak, which encouraged a fast-growing number of people to join the revolution.

The Collapse of the Soviet Union

The forces that had caused the revolution in Eastern Europe finally toppled the Soviet government itself in late August 1991:

1. Boris Yeltsin and other revolutionary leaders are all well-educated people who chafed at the slowness of the liberal reforms started by Gorbachev.

2. Under Gorbachev's liberal leadership, the expectation for freedom soared throughout the Soviet Union.

3. Like the Eastern Europeans, the Soviets were hit with a worsening economic crisis.

4. The Soviet government, which had long derived its power from the Communist Party, had become increasingly weak. Not surprisingly, when the Party's hard-liners staged a coup to take over the government, they failed quickly after only two days of resistance by

the people. With the collapse of the Communist Party, the Soviet Union disintegrated, and all 15 of its republics declared independence one after another.

Most of the U.S. media have regarded the collapse of communism in the Soviet Union—as well as in Eastern Europe—as the failures of socialism. But the socialism that has been practiced in the Soviet Union was not the real socialism expounded in Marxist theory. According to Marx, a socialist state is supposed to reduce social inequality by freeing the poor masses from exploitation by the rich. But the communist regimes have merely turned this Marxist idea into slogans such as "All power to the people," while creating a privileged elite to exercise absolute power over the masses. It is true that the capitalist practices of private ownership and enterprise were eliminated to end the exploitation of the poor by the rich. But the communist rulers took over the exploitation themselves, causing even more misery to the masses than in capitalist countries. In fact, there is arguably more socialism in the United States today than there ever was in the Soviet Union, as there is more power for ordinary people, who have more opportunity to influence U.S. government and economy.

The Nature of Terrorism

What if the masses do not support a revolutionary movement and the government is not vulnerable? In that case, a violent protest is likely to produce not revolution but **terrorism**—the use of violence to express dissatisfaction with a government. The would-be leaders of a revolution become terrorists, trying on their own to destabilize, if not to topple, the government through violence. Their methods include bombing, kidnapping, airplane hijacking, and armed assault. Terrorist groups include Palestinian extremists in Israel, neo-Nazi extremists in Germany, and right-wing extremists in the United States. Most terrorists are in their early twenties and have attended college. They usually come from middle-class rather than poor families. In short, their background resembles that of leaders of revolutions—but the terrorists are self-styled leaders without followers.

These terrorists are basically powerless individuals futilely fighting a government. Some are international terrorists, who leave their country to attack a foreign government. An example is the Islamic radicals from the Middle East who bombed New York's World Trade Center in 1993 because of U.S. support for Israel. Other international terrorists, however, carry out policies of their own governments. Examples of such governments are the militant

Some terrorists may be powerless individuals who are fighting their own government, while others are international terrorists who carry out their government's policies against foreign governments. The United States has in recent years suffered attacks by both types—domestic terrorists blew up the federal office building in Oklahoma City and international terrorists attacked the World Trade Center in New York City.

regimes in Libya, Syria, and Iran—known to the U.S. State Department as the "League of Terror"—which have sent terrorists to foreign countries to assassinate their opponents. Other terrorists fight their own governments. Examples of these domestic terrorists include Timothy McVeigh and his associates, who were accused of bombing the federal office building in Oklahoma City in 1995.

Responses to Terrorism

U.S. and European governments have generally adopted hard-line, "no ransom, no concessions" policies on international terrorism. Since 1986, they have also stepped up their cooperative efforts against terrorism. They have imposed arms embargoes, improved extradition procedures, reduced the size of diplomatic missions of terrorism-supporting countries, and refused to admit any person expelled from another country because of suspected involvement in terrorist activities.

But it has been difficult to implement the "get tough" policies against terrorists who hold hostages.

Before 1986 the Reagan administration declared a no-concessions all-out war against terrorists. But in 1986 the plight of the U.S. hostages held in the Middle East and the appeals of their families finally compelled the Reagan administration to secretly swap arms with Iran for the hostages. The Iranians got the weapons but most of the hostages were not released. Finally, toward the end of 1991, all the hostages were released. A major reason was the conciliatory stance expressed by the Bush administration, telling the terrorist governments that "good will begets good will" (Dowell, 1991). In early 1986, the prime minister of France also compromised his strong public position against concessions to terrorists. He secured the release of French hostages by agreeing to return to Iran the late Shah's billion-dollar investment in France (Oakley, 1987).

The response to home-grown terrorism has been different. In countries where incidents of terrorism are relatively common, law enforcers are given considerable powers to prevent terrorist acts. In Britain, for example, the police have the legal authority to detain suspects for seven days without charge, which would probably violate U.S. law. But similar authority may be given to U.S. law enforcement agencies because the 1995 Oklahoma bombing has heightened concern for domestic security. In fact, the Clinton administration proposed that the F.B.I. be granted more power in dealing with suspected terrorists, such as monitoring their telephone calls or infiltrating their organizations. But this has caused concern that it may unintentionally end up infringing the civil liberties of innocent citizens (Lewis, 1995; Lacayo, 1995).

Questions for Discussion and Review

1. What social conditions usually exist before a revolution occurs?
2. Who are terrorists, and how have Western governments responded to them?

SOCIOLOGICAL PERSPECTIVES ON WAR

Insight into the nature of war can be gained from the three major sociological perspectives. According to the functionalist perspective, war occurs because it serves some useful functions for society. According to the conflict perspective, war reflects an exploitation of the masses by the ruling elite. According to the symbolic interactionist perspective, war is the culmination of a series of interpretations that the leaders of two hostile nations impute to each other's actions.

Functionalist Perspective

To functionalists, war serves a number of functions. First, it enhances social solidarity by focusing people's attention on fighting a common enemy. Consider the 1991 Persian Gulf War between Iraq and the United States and its allies, which resulted in Iraq being driven out of Kuwait. Arabs in the Middle East who supported Iraq felt strongly united against the United States and its allies. The United States, in turn, joined forces with various nations, including traditionally anti-U.S. Russia and Syria.

Second, war stimulates scientific and technological development. The Gulf War in effect served as a live laboratory for testing new high-tech weapons. Before the war, it was uncertain, for example, whether Tomahawk cruise missiles and stealth fighter-bombers could fly undetected and hit their targets with pinpoint accuracy. Because the high-tech weapons were guided by computer systems, knowledge gained from their use in the war also benefited the computer industry.

Third, war tends to bring about positive changes in society. The Gulf War brought pressures for democratic reforms in Kuwait, Saudi Arabia, and other Gulf states that had long been governed by kings or sheiks with an iron hand. After the war, Kuwait's autocratic ruler, for example, promised democratic reforms. He acknowledged that without popular support from his subjects in exile as well as military help from the United States and other democratic countries, his tiny nation could still be under Iraq's thumb.

Conflict Perspective

The conflict perspective suggests that war often involves the ruling elite exploiting the masses. Political leaders have been known to whip up a war frenzy against some foreign enemy as a way of regaining popular support or diverting the citizenry's attention from domestic problems. Other members of the power elite also benefit, as the military brass become heroes and business tycoons reap profits from sales of military hardware. More important, members of the ruling elite do not have to suffer the heartrending familial consequences of war. During the Gulf War, for example, no one in the president's cab-

Insight into the nature of war can be gained from the three sociological perspectives. Seen from the functionalist perspective, war occurs because it serves some useful functions for society. Viewed from the conflict perspective, war reflects an exploitation of the masses by the ruling elite. According to the symbolic interactionist perspective, war is a culmination of a series of interpretations imputed by the leaders of hostile nations to each other's actions.

inet had a son or daughter being sent to the front line. Of the 535 members of Congress, only two had sons involved in the war against Iraq (Lacayo, 1990). It is mostly poor, working-class, and minority families whose children do the fighting and dying.

Symbolic Interactionist Perspective

According to symbolic interactionism, the way the leaders of two hostile nations interpret each other's actions may lead to war. A good example is how George Bush and Saddam Hussein interpreted each other's actions leading to the Gulf War.

Before the Iraqi invasion of Kuwait, Bush regarded Saddam as a potential force for stability in the Middle East. Bush therefore refrained from strongly criticizing Saddam for using chemical weapons against Iran or for spreading poison gas on Iraq's Kurdish minority. A week before the Iraqi invasion of Kuwait, the U.S. ambassador in Iraq assured Saddam that President Bush wanted to seek better relations with Iraq and that the United States would not intervene in Saddam's border dispute with Kuwait, though it urged that violence not be used. All this, however, was taken by Saddam as a green light to invade Kuwait.

The invasion outraged Bush, who threatened Saddam with war if he did not withdraw from Kuwait. But Saddam shrugged off the threat, apparently believing that the U.S. experience of losing the Vietnam war in the 1960s would deter it from going to war against Iraq. Even when he finally realized that Bush would carry out his threat, Saddam did not pull out of Kuwait. He was hoping for a "victorious defeat." As an Arab diplomat who had dealt personally with the Iraqi dictator on numerous occasions explained, "If there is no war and Saddam withdraws, then he looks like a coward, an idiot, who's lost everything. He is thinking, 'If I go to war, there is a chance that I will survive it, and at least I will be looked on by the Arabs as a hero who went against the whole world because of right and justice'" (Dickey, 1991). Saddam expected to lose the war and be forced out of Kuwait, but he still considered the war his triumph for having fought and survived against the mighty United States and its allies. Thinking that Saddam did not appreciate the awesomeness of the military power arrayed against him, Bush finally decided to show it to him by starting the war.

In short, a sequence of interpretations by two national leaders of each other's actions may culminate in the outbreak of a war.

Questions for Discussion and Review

1. How do the three sociological perspectives differ in explaining the occurrence of war?
2. How can the Gulf War be explained from the symbolic interactionist perspective?

CHAPTER REVIEW

1. *How did the Industrial Revolution change the economic process?* Machines replaced much human labor, mass production in factories displaced cottage industry, and agriculture lost ground to industry. *What are some effects of industrialization?* Industrialization speeds up production, shrinking blue-collar employment and enlarging white-collar work. It further changes demographic features, human relations, and the values of society.

2. *What are the major sociological perspectives on capitalism as an economic system?* To functionalists, capitalism serves a useful function by bringing about a prosperous and stable society. To conflict theorists, capitalism threatens society by allowing the rich to exploit the poor. Symbolic interactionists focus on how people's definition of their world creates or supports capitalism.

3. *What kinds of economic systems exist around the globe?* Some are primarily capitalist and others socialist, but they all are mixed economies, with elements of both capitalism and socialism. They differ only in degree, ranging on a continuum from the most capitalist to the most socialist. *What is the current condition of the U.S. economy?* The rates of unemployment and inflation are relatively low, but the productivity growth and living standard are largely at a standstill, while the trade and budget deficits remain high. *What is the status of the economies in other countries today?* Most economies have started to recover from the worldwide recession of several years ago, with some showing greater growth than others. One of the major forces behind this growth is foreign investment.

4. *How has the U.S. labor force changed in recent years?* The number of jobs in agriculture has dropped sharply, the number in service industries has risen, and the population of white-collar workers has expanded. Meanwhile, the employment rate for women, blacks, and other minorities has increased, while the rate for older men has declined significantly. At the same time, temporary employment has increased sharply. *Who are more likely to be satisfied with their work?* Older and white-collar workers are more likely to be satisfied. Given the same kinds of jobs, women are happier than men. *How has the U.S. workplace changed?* Workers are less willing to accept unpleasant jobs and more likely to expect meaningful ones. Thus efforts have been made to give employees more interesting jobs, more freedom, and more power in the workplace.

5. *How is legitimate power different from illegitimate power?* When power is exercised over people with their consent, the power is called legitimate; otherwise it is illegitimate. The legitimate power institutionalized in the state is called authority. *Where does authority come from?* It may be derived from tradition, from the charisma of a leader, or from a set of legal rules. *How do U.S. citizens react to their government?* They tend to be ideological conservatives but operational liberals.

6. *According to pluralist theory, who really governs in the U.S.?* Diverse interest groups share power. *Who controls the government according to C. Wright Mills?* Control is held by a power elite made up of those who hold top positions in the federal government, the military, and corporations. *According to Marxists, what is wrong with Mills's power-elite theory?* It does not recognize that the power elite serves as the agent for the capitalist class. In Marxists' view, capitalists use the state to maintain their dominance over the other classes.

7. *What conditions make revolution likely?* There are four: (1) some disgruntled, well-off, and well-educated individuals; (2) the masses' rising expectations; (3) a sudden economic crisis; and (4) weak government. These four conditions can be found in the 1989 revolution in Eastern Europe and the 1991 collapse of the Soviet Union. *When is terrorism likely to occur?* When the would-be leader of a revolution does not have the support of the masses against a strong government. *How do Western governments respond to terrorism?* By adopting hard-line policies against international terrorists while being willing to compromise to save the lives of hostages. But the response to domestic terrorists is tougher.

8. *What is the nature of war as seen through the major sociological perspectives?* To functionalists, war can be useful for society. To conflict analysts, war reflects an exploitation of the masses by the ruling elite, and to symbolic interactionists, war culminates a series of interpretations the leaders of two hostile nations impute to each other's actions.

KEY TERMS

Alienation of labor Marx's term for laborers' loss of control over their work process. (p. 263)

Authority Legitimate power institutionalized in organizations. (p. 270)

Budget deficit   Spending more than we take in. (p. 265)

Capitalism   An economic system based on private ownership of property and competition in producing and selling goods and services. (p. 260)

Charisma   An exceptional personal quality popularly attributed to certain individuals. (p. 270)

Coercion   The illegitimate use of force or threat of force to compel obedience. (p. 270)

Communism   A classless society that operates on the principle of "from each according to his ability, to each according to his needs." (p. 263)

Dual economy   An economy that comprises a *core* of giant corporations dominating the market and a *periphery* of small firms competing for the remaining, smaller shares of business. (p. 268)

Economic institution   A system for producing and distributing goods and services. (p. 260)

Ideological conservatives   U.S. citizens who, in theory, are opposed to big government because of their belief in free enterprise, rugged individualism, and capitalism. (p. 272)

Industrial Revolution   The dramatic economic change brought about by the introduction of machines into the work process about 200 years ago. (p. 260)

Influence   The ability to control others' behavior through persuasion rather than coercion or authority. (p. 270)

Operational liberals   U.S. citizens who, in effect, support big government by backing government programs that render services to the public. (p. 272)

Political power   The capacity to use the government to make decisions that affect the whole society. (p. 272)

Politics   The type of human interaction that involves some people acquiring and exercising power over others. (p. 260)

Power   The ability to control the behavior of others, even against their will. (p. 270)

Revolution   The movement aimed at the violent overthrow of the existing government. (p. 275)

Socialism   An economic system based on public ownership and government control of the economy. (p. 263)

Terrorism   The use of violence to express dissatisfaction with a government (p. 277)

Trade deficit   Buying more goods and services from foreign countries than selling to them. (p. 265)

Trade surplus   Selling more goods and services to foreign countries than buying from them. (p. 265)

SUGGESTED READINGS

Beck, Nuala. 1995. *Shifting Gears: Thriving in the New Economy.* New York: HarperCollins. An analysis of how we can benefit from the new U.S. economy that is increasingly dominated by knowledge-intensive industries such as health care, telecommunication, computers, and semiconductors.

Granovetter, Mark. 1992. *The Sociology of Economic Life.* Boulder, Co.: Westview. A collection of articles on the sociological study of the economy.

Osborne, David, and Ted Gaebler. 1992. *Reinventing Government: How the Entrepreneurial Spirit Is Transforming the Public Sector.* Reading, Mass.: Addison-Wesley. Shows how government can serve its citizens better by decentralizing authority, reducing bureaucracy, and promoting competition.

Schwartz, Barry. 1994. *The Costs of Living: How Market Freedom Erodes the Best Things in Life.* New York: Norton. A critical analysis of how the pursuit of wealth weakens the bonds of religion, family, friendship, and other aspects of human life.

Witt, Linda, Karen M. Paget, and Glenna Matthews. 1993. *Running As a Woman: Gender and Power in American Politics.* New York: Free Press. An analysis of the inroads women are making in U.S. politics.

HEALTH AND POPULATION

Myths and Realities

MYTH: *Being frail, older people are more likely than young people to fall victim to virtually all kinds of illness.*
REALITY: While they are more likely to suffer from such chronic illnesses as arthritis, heart disease, and cancer, older people are less susceptible to acute and infectious illnesses, such as measles and pneumonia. (p. 284)

MYTH: *Compassionate and sensitive, most doctors listen to their patients' complaints with great attentiveness and understanding.*
REALITY: Most doctors tend to interact poorly with patients. Consequently, about 60 percent of patients fail to understand adequately the instructions about their medications. (p. 294)

MYTH: *The world's total population has become very large today, because of steady growth over many thousands of years.*
REALITY: Most of the world's population growth has occurred in relatively recent years. Before the modern era began (in 1600), the global population had reached only about half a billion in more than 500,000 years. Since then, in less than 400 years, the world population has skyrocketed to more than 5.6 billion today. (p. 296)

MYTH: *The poor countries' high birth rates are virtually the only reason for their tremendous population growth.*
REALITY: The introduction of modern medicine, along with better hygiene and sanitation, also contributes significantly to population growth, by sharply reducing death rates. (p. 299)

It was a hot day in Bardera, a small town in southern Somalia in Africa. A crowd of starving, emaciated people gathered at a United Nations feeding center. They were waiting for a meal of brown gruel. A 5-year-old boy passed out. Two relief workers rushed over, picked him up, and put him down under a shade tree. The child was suffering from severe dehydration. A nurse quickly inserted an intravenous tube, hooking the bottle to a branch. But it was too late. The boy's eyes rolled back beneath quivering eyelids, which an older woman gently shut with her fingers. The boy had come from a village 34 miles away, where both his parents and eight brothers and sisters had also died from starvation in the past six months. Weak and hungry, the boy had walked for four days to this town with his last relative, an elder brother. Now his sibling was rocking and weeping quietly by his lifeless body (Purvis, 1992).

The mass starvation in Somalia and other African countries can be traced partly to population explosion. Even hard-won advances in food production cannot catch up with the continuing enormous growth in population. Increased population pressure has made many of Africa's farms and fields barren through overuse. In addition, demands for heating and cooking fuel have run so high that woodlands—Africa's chief source of energy—have virtually disappeared. The resulting deforestation has damaged flood control, sped up erosion, and increased the hardship of simply staying alive. All this inevitably threatens human health. In this chapter we first discuss various social aspects of health and then population.

HEALTH AND SOCIETY

As a social phenomenon, health varies from one society to another and from one group to another within the same society. From these variations, we can see how social factors affect health and what consequences an outbreak of illness has for society. We can also track down the origin of a disease by examining all its victims for something that they have in common as a social group.

Social Factors

In the United States older people are less likely than young people to suffer from acute and infectious illnesses such as measles and pneumonia. But they are more susceptible to chronic illnesses such as arthritis, heart disease, and cancer. Cancer deaths, in particular, have been climbing steeply and steadily among people aged 55 and older (U.S. Census Bureau, 1994).

Health also varies with gender. Women have higher rates of both chronic and acute illnesses than men of the same age, yet women live longer than men. Why? One reason is biological superiority. Women are more able to endure sickness and survive. They also are less likely to develop hemophilia and other diseases linked to the X chromosome. Their sex hormones further protect them from risk of cardiovascular disease, up to the time of menopause. A second reason is that women maintain stronger emotional ties with others than men do. By offering social support and deterring loneliness, intimate human relationships can reduce the severity and duration of illness. A third reason is the greater tendency of men to smoke, drink, and drive. Such behaviors increase the risk of serious chronic diseases and physical injuries (Verbrugge, 1985).

Race and ethnicity are also correlated with health. African Americans, Hispanic Americans, and Native Americans all have shorter life expectancies than do Anglo-Americans. Minorities are far more likely to suffer or die from many diseases such as influenza, pneumonia, and AIDS. Both Hispanics and Native Americans, however, are less likely than Anglos to die from heart disease and cancer, partly because Anglos live longer and those chronic illnesses typically increase with age (Johnson et al., 1991; Cockerham, 1995).

These racial and ethnic differences may reflect another social factor that influences health: social class. The diseases that hit minority groups the hardest are those associated with poverty. In particular, acute and infectious diseases, such as influenza and tuberculosis, are more prevalent among the lower social classes. Researchers have attributed the higher rates of disease among the lower classes to several related factors: toxic, hazardous, and unhygienic environments; stress resulting from life changes, such as job loss and divorce; and inadequate medical care (Syme and

Berkman, 1987). More recent research has found another problem: unhealthy eating habits. Poor people are much more likely than others to eat high-sugar, high-salt, and high-fat food (Freedman, 1990). Poverty can also aggravate the problem of hypertension suffered by minorities. Because they may be less able to deal with the sociopsychological stress induced by racism in the United States, poor African Americans are significantly more likely than middle-class blacks to have high blood pressure (Klag et al., 1991).

Epidemiology

In analyzing the social forces behind illness, sociologists can help physicians and public health workers track down the cause of a disease. This task requires a kind of detective work called **epidemiology,** the study of the origin and spread of disease in a given population. As epidemiologists, sociologists and medical scientists first hunt down all the people who already have the disease. Then they ask the victims

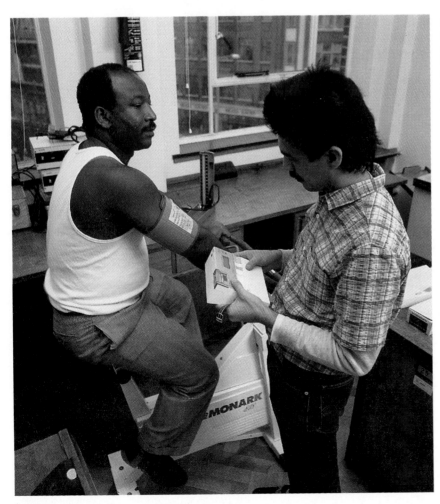

Social factors figure strongly in health. For example, poverty can aggravate the problem of hypertension suffered by minorities, and various other acute and infectious diseases are more common among the poor and those in the lower social classes.

where they were and what they did before they got sick. Epidemiologists also collect data on the victims' age, gender, marital status, occupation, and other characteristics. The aim is to find out what all the victims have in common besides the disease so that its cause can be identified and eliminated. Usually, the common factor that ties all the victims together provides the essential clue.

Epidemiology emerged as an applied science in 1854, when the English physician John Snow discovered the source of one of London's periodic cholera epidemics. He had gone to the neighborhoods where the victims lived and asked them what they did every day, where they worked, what they ate and drank, and many other questions about their lives and activities. Finally, after sifting through a huge pile of information, Snow hit upon the clue to the origin of the disease. He found that all the victims had one thing in common: they had drunk water from a particular pump on Broad Street. Snow simply shut off the pump and, with that single act, stopped the epidemic in its tracks. Not until many years later, with the discovery of germs, could anyone explain why shutting down the pump was effective: Dr. Snow had removed the source of the cholera bacteria (Cockerham, 1995).

Since then, epidemiology has been used to trace the origins of many different diseases such as cancer and heart disease. In investigating heart disease, for example, epidemiologists have discovered that the majority of victims have eaten high-cholesterol foods, smoked or drunk heavily, and failed to get enough exercise. Avoiding these habits can reduce the risk of heart disease.

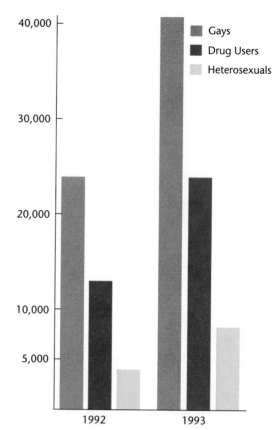

FIGURE 13.1
The AIDS Epidemic in the United States

Source: Data from Centers for Disease Control and Prevention, 1994.

AIDS

Directly caused by a virus called HIV, AIDS is a deadly disease that destroys the body's immune system, leaving the victim defenseless against other diseases. The disease first came to the attention of U.S. physicians in early 1981. Since then, it has spread rapidly.

Social Causes   In searching for the cause of the AIDS virus, epidemiologists have found clues in the social characteristics and behaviors of the victims. So far, in the United States, most of the victims have been gay or bisexual men. The second largest group has been intravenous drug users. The rest are non-drug-using heterosexuals, of whom most have caught the AIDS virus through sex and a few have been infected through blood transfusions or being born to mothers with AIDS (see Figure 13.1).

New cases of AIDS among gay men declined or leveled off in the late 1980s and early 1990s because of the increasing practice of safer sex. But now the dis-

ease among gay men is on the rise again, a result of the return to unsafe sex (Signorile, 1995). AIDS has also increased among non-drug-using heterosexuals. But new infection among intravenous drug users has increased the most. These people are mostly poor, African American, and Hispanic heterosexuals in the inner city. They often share contaminated needles when shooting drugs, thus passing the AIDS virus from one to another.

All these epidemiological facts clearly suggest that AIDS spreads mostly through sexual intercourse with an infected person and through the sharing of a hypodermic needle that has been contaminated with the virus. Studies in other societies can also be useful. For example, epidemiologists have discovered some similarities and differences between African AIDS victims and their U.S. counterparts. Unlike the U.S. victims, the African patients do not have histories of intravenous drug use, homosexuality, or blood transfusion. But like U.S. gays with AIDS, African heterosexuals with the disease mostly live in large cities and have had sex with many different partners. Thus, AIDS has spread among Africans in the same way as it has among gays in the United States: through sex with multiple partners. By itself, though, promiscuity is not the source of the AIDS virus. It is unprotected sex that increases the risk of infection.

Social Consequences   Unlike such familiar killers as cancer and heart disease, AIDS is mysterious and has had an unusual impact on our society. As we have seen, the disease is not only lethal but can be transmitted through life's most basic human interaction—sex and procreation. Understandably, the general public is gripped with the fear of contagion. The initial appearance of AIDS among two groups of which the larger society disapproves—gays and drug addicts—has added to the fear, because prejudice discourages understanding of "their" disease.

According to a series of surveys by the U.S. Public Health Service, a growing number of people have quickly learned the risk factors for AIDS, but misinformation about the disease's transmission remains a problem. Many still fear that they can get AIDS by donating blood or through casual contact with an infected person. Though such fears are groundless, they have spawned strange, sad, or hostile actions against AIDS victims.

In 1987, for example, the school board in Arcadia, Florida, barred three hemophiliac brothers—Richard, Robert, and Randy Ray—who had been infected with the virus through blood transfusions. When the boys were ordered admitted to class by a court, many parents boycotted the school. The Ray family received telephone threats and lost their home to arson, forcing them to leave the town. Parents in many other places have also demanded mandatory testing of all school-children and segregation of those with AIDS. The parents are not the only ones that discriminate against AIDS victims. There are many instances where people with AIDS are prevented from keeping jobs or getting housing, insurance coverage, or medical care. Such acts of discrimination sometimes are directed against those who are not already infected with AIDS but are only perceived to be at risk for the disease. Those who care for AIDS patients are also likely to encounter discrimination (Hilts, 1990).

A Global Analysis of Health

People in the United States are much healthier than ever before. Since 1900 our life expectancy has increased by more than 50 percent, from about 49 years in 1900 to 75 today. At birth we can expect to live 26 more years than did our counterparts in 1900—more than one-and-a-half times as long as they did then. Another indicator of our health, the infant mortality rate, has shown even more dramatic improvement: about 15 percent of all U.S. babies died during the first year of life at the turn of this century, compared with only 1 percent today (U.S. Census Bureau, 1994). All this can be chalked up to healthier living conditions, better diet, immunization against various diseases, and penicillin and other antibiotics.

But our increased life expectancy loses its impressiveness when compared with that of other industrial countries. As Table 13.1 shows, people in other industrialized countries live longer than we do. Our standing in regard to infant mortality is the same: Proportionately more babies die in the United States. This seems ironic, because we spend more money on health care than any of these nations. But the problem cannot be attributed

TABLE 13.1
Health Among Industrial Countries
The United States has the lowest life expectancy and highest infant mortality in the industrial world. This seems ironic because we spend more money on health care than does any of the other countries.

Country	Life Expectancy	Country	Infant Mortality Rate
Japan	79.3	Japan	4.3
Sweden	78.3	Sweden	5.7
France	78.2	Netherlands	6.1
Canada	78.1	Germany	6.5
Netherlands	77.8	France	6.6
Australia	77.6	Canada	6.9
Italy	77.6	Britain	7.2
Britain	76.8	Australia	7.3
Germany	76.3	Italy	7.6
U.S.	75.9	U.S.	8.1

SOURCE: Data from U.S. Census Bureau, 1994.

totally to the lack of efficiency in our health care system. Unhealthy lifestyles, such as eating high-cholesterol food and smoking, may also be a contributing factor (Grubaugh and Santerre, 1994). Only when compared with poor, developing countries does the United States have a much higher life expectancy and a considerably lower infant mortality rate.

Questions for Discussion and Review

1. How do social factors like age, gender, ethnicity, and class influence a person's health?
2. What is epidemiology, and how does it help doctors locate the causes of disease?
3. How have epidemiologists discovered the sources of the AIDS virus?
4. What are the social consequences of the AIDS epidemic?
5. What is the status of health in the United States today?

MEDICAL CARE

Before 1870, doctoring was a lowly profession. Many of the doctors were more like quacks than true medical scientists. They had little knowledge of how the various body systems worked or of how diseases developed. In the face of such ignorance, doctors could be a menace. For numerous ailments, they bled patients profusely; evacuated their bowels, often until they passed out; stuffed them with dangerous drugs; and tormented them with various ghastly appliances. One treatment for syphilis involved roasting the patient in an oven. Sometimes the patients survived despite all this assistance, but more often they died. Either way, the doctors learned a great deal from them. In time, they developed a store of knowledge that eventually enabled them to practice a highly respectable profession (Blundell, 1987).

The Changing Medical Profession

Over the last ten years, there have been significant changes in the medical profession. Today, doctors often find their autonomy eroded, their prestige reduced, and their competence challenged by everyone from insurance companies to patients.

Before 1980 most doctors practiced alone. Today more than half are salaried employees, working in group practices or health maintenance organizations (HMOs). One reason is that the cost of starting a pri-

vate practice is too high for most young doctors, whose medical training has left them deeply in debt. Another reason is that doctors get most of their payments from the government and insurance companies, not from patients, as they did in the past. To be paid, doctors must fill out numerous forms to justify their fees, which often proves too burdensome for a private doctor to handle (Altman, 1990).

Efforts by employers, insurance companies, and the government to control costs have caused many doctors to complain about losing their professional autonomy. Physicians must seek permission from outside regulators—government agencies or insurance companies—for major but nonemergency hospitalization and surgeries. If the regulators do not approve a case in advance, they will not pay. They occasionally refuse to authorize a treatment that they consider too costly or unnecessary (Kramon, 1991). While chafing at these outside regulators, doctors also complain of internal controls from their employers. HMOs routinely pass around lists ranking their physicians on the time spent with patients. This is intended to give the doctors the subtle but clear message that those highest on the list cause a financial drain on the organization (Belkin, 1990).

The general public also seems to hold less esteem for doctors than before. According to a Gallup poll, 57 percent of the people questioned agreed that "doctors don't care about people as much as they used to." Sixty-seven percent said that doctors are too interested in making money. Seventy-five percent complained that "doctors keep patients waiting too long." And 26 percent said that they have less respect for doctors than they did ten years ago (Kolata, 1990). Many patients do not fully trust their doctors, and the better educated often feel obliged to make themselves as informed as possible about their illness so that they can get the best treatment. This has led many doctors to complain that some patients challenge their expertise after learning about medical advances only from television or newspapers and magazines (Altman, 1990).

The growing discontent among doctors for a while discouraged many college students from pursuing a medical career, but today numerous students are eager to become doctors. The number of applicants to medical school fell from 35,944 in 1984 to only 26,915 in 1990 but rebounded to 45,365 in 1995. Most of the recent increase in applications came from women and minority-group members. These demographic changes will make the medical profession more representative of U.S. society. Moreover, today's medical students of diverse backgrounds have a lower income expectation and a greater sense of public duty than their elders, which should more effectively meet the increasingly cost-conscious needs for health care in the near future (Altman, 1990; Rosenthal, 1995).

Sexism in Medical Research

With more women entering the medical profession, more attention is being given to women's health. Indeed, researchers have found that some well-accepted treatments may actually be dangerous to women patients, because they are based on men-only research.

In 1988 the medical profession, along with the general public, was informed that aspirin reduces the risk of heart attacks. This conclusion was based on a study of 22,071 men. Because the study did not include women, nobody knows whether aspirin also benefits women. If it does not, women with heart disease who rely on aspirin for treatment could be in trouble. In 1990 a similar study showed that heavy coffee intake did not increase the risk of heart attacks or strokes. Is it safe, then, for women with a heart problem to drink coffee heavily? Not necessarily, because the 45,589 subjects of the study, aged 40 to 75, were all men (Ames, 1990; Purvis, 1990).

It is not necessary to include women in a study on heart disease if their hearts do not differ from men's. But they do. For one thing, cardiovascular disease strikes women later in life, and women are much more likely to die after undergoing heart-bypass surgery. Another thing is that blood cholesterol levels seem to affect female patients differently. Women seem less vulnerable than men to high levels of LDL (the so-called bad cholesterol) but more vulnerable to low levels of HDL (the "good" cholesterol). Diets that reduce *both* levels, as promoted by the American Heart Association, may end up harming women (Ames, 1990; Purvis, 1990).

The bias against women further shows up in the lack of research on health problems that affect women only. The medical profession therefore knows very little about how any of the 19 million women with osteoporosis could have prevented the bone-breaking condition. Doctors also do not know for sure whether it is wise to supply women with replacement hormones when they go through menopause. There is also a serious lack of knowledge about breast cancer, which kills about 44,000 women *every year* (for comparison, the Vietnam War, which lasted *more than 10 years*, took 58,000 U.S. lives). Still, research institutes have not studied these female diseases as much as they have studied diseases that also afflict men (Silberner, 1990; Beck, 1990a).

However, increased awareness of the medical research bias against women, coupled with mounting pressure from various women's health groups, has begun to produce positive results. The National Institutes of Health, for example, has issued new guidelines that applications for research grants should include women as subjects. At least 20 bills have also been introduced in Congress to fund projects that are aimed at improving women's health (Silberner, 1990).

Social Diversity in Using Health Care

When people feel sick, they obviously want to get well again, but not everyone automatically goes to see a doctor. Some may simply shrug off their illness, feeling that it is not serious enough. But more than the

Gender bias in medical research has resulted in lack of research on women's health problems. However, mounting pressure from women's groups has helped bring this research bias into the open and has begun to increase the amount of research money devoted to women's health issues.

severity of illness motivates people to seek medical care. Social factors such as age, gender, ethnicity, and class, which reflect the social diversity in the United States, are also involved. They help determine who is likely to visit a doctor and who is not.

It is common knowledge that the elderly are more often ill than are younger people. It is, therefore, not surprising that they are most likely of all age groups to seek medical care.

Women are more likely than men to use health services. But women are less likely to obtain proper care. Under the influence of sexual prejudice, doctors tend to dismiss women's complaints with such terms as "overstress," "back strain," "could be just the heat," or "nothing to worry about." Even when a patient complains of chest pains and other symptoms of heart disease, the doctor is less likely to take the complaints seriously when they come from a woman than from a man. As Jonathan Tobin and his colleagues (1987) found, doctors are twice as likely to label women's chest pains as a psychiatric complaint or something other than a sign of heart disease. Among those who suffer from kidney failures, women are also less likely than men to receive kidney transplants (Blakeslee, 1989). Nevertheless, when they feel ill, women are still more likely than men to consult doctors.

Some ethnic groups tend less to visit doctors. When ill, Mexican Americans tend more to see the doctor as a last resort, preferring to try Mexican folk medicine first. Their relatives, friends, neighbors, or *curanderos* (folk healers) are generally ready to provide certain patent medicines, herbs, and teas along with the performance of religious rituals. Native Americans also have a similar system of folk medicine, which they believe to be capable of restoring health by restoring a harmonious balance among various biological and spiritual forces in the sick person's life. Similar principles of harmonious balance can be found in traditional Chinese medicine, which is popular with residents in America's Chinatowns. According to the Chinese, illness results from an imbalance between *yin* (the female, "cold" force) and *yang* (the male, "hot" force). If illness results from an excess of (cold) yin over (hot) yang, certain herbs and foods that are classified as hot should be taken to bring back the balance between yin and yang—and hence health. If illness results from too much (hot) yang, "cold" herbs and foods should be taken (Cockerham, 1995).

African Americans, without the system of folk medicine available to other minorities, are nearly as likely as whites to visit physicians. But blacks are more likely than whites to receive treatment in hospital outpatient clinics or emergency rooms, which are more often public than private. Whites are more likely to go to a private doctor's office. This is largely because a greater proportion of blacks than whites are poor. The poor are indeed more likely than the rich to get medical treatment in public clinics and emergency rooms (Dutton, 1978; Cockerham, 1995).

Some ethnic groups turn first for medical care to ancient systems of herbal or folk medicine. Such systems of alternative medicine have worked for thousands of years, yet are largely unknown in Western medical systems. Here, an "herbolaria" in a Mexican American community sells traditional herbal medicines and potions.

Health Care Delivery

One major problem with the health care system in the United States is unequal access. There is no scarcity of medical resources. In fact, we have more doctors per person than many other industrial countries, as well as an abundance of medical technology and hospitals. But the distribution of these resources is very unequal. Doctors are plentiful in affluent areas but often scarce in poverty-stricken parts of the inner cities and countryside.

Another problem with our health care system is soaring costs. In the last 20 years, medical costs have gone up faster than the rate of inflation for other goods and services. According to a 1994 government report, the cost of health care in 1993 came to $884 billion (or $3,299 for every person), compared with $75 billion in 1970. Our yearly medical expenditure amounts to over 10 percent of our gross national product—a higher percentage than any other nation spends on medical care (Toufexis, 1990; Cockerham, 1995).

Why have health care costs escalated so rapidly? The aging of the U.S. population may be one contributing factor. The proliferation of expensive medical technology may be another. There have also been significant advances in keeping coma and stroke victims alive—but these patients may then require extremely expensive medical care for years.

There are also other reasons for rising costs. The medical establishment has emphasized curing illness rather than preventing it and maintaining health. This may explain why the United States does not do as good a job as most other industrial countries in low-cost preventive medicine, such as providing free prenatal care, free infant care, and free exams for the middle-aged and elderly. Most significant, medical care in the United States is organized as a business, but it is quite different from other businesses. Medical "customers" do not have much say about what they buy because they usually cannot judge what they need. They rely on doctors to tell them what they need and how much they must pay. Meanwhile, consumers have few incentives to keep prices down. They pay only a small share (about a third) of the cost directly. Most of it is passed on to third parties—insurance companies, employers, and the government.

The Right to Die

Advanced medical technology can prolong life. But, ironically, the same technology can also prolong the agony of dying for the hopelessly ill—and the suffering of the families who have to live with their loved one's living death. Today, about 10,000 patients lie irreversibly comatose in hospital beds across the United

"I don't use chemical anesthetics anymore. I just give them an estimate of their hospital bill."

States, kept alive by machines such as respirators and feeding tubes. Many have been living in a vegetative, semi-death state for years. Most of their loved ones would like to let them die with dignity. But they cannot have the treatment halted unless they first get authorization from a court. The problem is that the court is likely to deny them the right to let the patient die.

Usually, a physician is required to obtain *informed consent* from the patient (or the patient's parent or guardian) before carrying out surgery or some other important treatment. **Informed consent** is the approval that a patient gives to the doctor for a treatment after receiving adequate information on it. This clearly implies that the patient has the right to *refuse* treatment. Formally, courts support the principle of informed refusal. But since comatose patients cannot possibly provide informed refusal, the courts have to determine the patient's fate. Normally, they will not let the patient die if the doctor or prosecutor wants the patient kept alive, as they often do (Capron, 1990).

But in 1990 the U.S. Supreme Court ruled that a person has a constitutional right to die but only if the wish to die is clearly known. This has stirred a great deal of interest in **living wills**—advance instructions on what people want their doctors to do in the event of a terminal illness. Still, only the rich and well educated are likely to draw up a living will. Even among this group, young people are the least interested in living wills. They are unlikely to anticipate suffering major brain damage, although they are the most likely of all age groups to be involved in automobile accidents (Davis, 1990). In view of these factors, many hopelessly ill patients can expect to be unable to exercise their right to die.

Questions for Discussion and Review

1. What are some recent changes in the medical profession?
2. How is sexism reflected in medical research?
3. How do social factors determine who might seek medical care?
4. Why has the cost of health care risen so dramatically over the last 20 years?
5. Is it easy for hopelessly ill patients to die? Why or why not?

PERSPECTIVES ON HEALTH AND MEDICAL CARE

From the functionalist perspective, we can see the positive aspects of medical care and even the positive functions of sickness for society. In contrast, the conflict perspective directs our attention to the negative side of health and medical care. While these two perspectives deal with the larger issues of health, symbolic interactionism focuses on the direct interaction between doctor and patient.

Functionalist Perspective

According to functionalists, both physicians and patients play roles that contribute to social order. Patients must play the **sick role,** a set of social expectations regarding how an ill person should behave. As discussed in Chapter 2 (Society and Culture), role is associated with status, which in turn presents the person with a set of rights and obligations. In his classic definition of the sick role, Talcott Parsons (1951) essentially laid out what rights the sick can claim and what obligations the sick should discharge.

First their rights: (1) The sick have the right to be taken care of by others, because they do not choose to be sick and thus should not be blamed for their illness. (2) They have the right to be exempted from certain social duties. They should not be forced to go to work. In the case of students, they should be allowed to miss an exam and take it later. Then their obligations: (1) They are obligated to want to get well. They should not expect to remain ill and use the illness to take advantage of others' love, concern, and care for them or to shirk their work and other social responsibilities. (2) They are obligated to seek technically competent help. In seeing a doctor, they must cooperate to help ensure their recovery.

On the other hand, doctors have their own rights and obligations in playing the **healing role,** a set of social expectations regarding how a doctor should behave. Basically, doctors are obligated to help the sick get well, as required by the Hippocratic oath, which they take when embarking on their medical careers. At the same time, they have the right to receive appropriate compensation for their work. Because their work is widely regarded as highly important, they may expect to make a great deal of money and enjoy considerable prestige.

Seen from the functionalist perspective, both the sick and the healing roles serve a social control function. They help to prevent illnesses from disrupting economic production, family relations, and social activities. Moreover, the functionalist perspective suggests that the system of medical care helps maintain the health of society. Thus functionalists tend to attribute an improvement in the nation's health to medicine, the physician, the medical profession, or some new technology of treatment. Such medical discoveries as the germ theory and such medical interventions as vaccines and drugs are credited for our great victory over infectious diseases. All this, however, is a myth to conflict theorists.

Conflict Perspective

According to conflict theorists, improvements in the social environment contribute far more than medical interventions to the reduction of illness and mortality. As one study shows, only about 3.5 percent of the total decline in mortality from five infectious diseases (influenza, pneumonia, diphtheria, whooping cough, and poliomyelitis) since 1900 can be attributed to medical measures. In many instances, the new measures to combat those diseases were introduced several decades *after* a substantial decline in mortality from the diseases had set in (McKinlay and McKinlay, 1987). According to the conflict perspective, this decline in mortality has been brought about mostly by several social and environmental factors: (1) a rising standard of living, (2) better sanitation and hygiene, and (3) improved housing and nutrition (Conrad and Kern, 1994).

Conflict theorists, however, do not mean to suggest that modern clinical medicine does not alleviate pain or cure disease in *some individuals*. Their point is that the medical institution fails to bring about significant improvements in the health of *the population as a whole*. Why, then, does our society continue to spend such vast sums of money on medical care? This, according to conflict theorists, has much to do with the pursuit of private profit in our capitalist society.

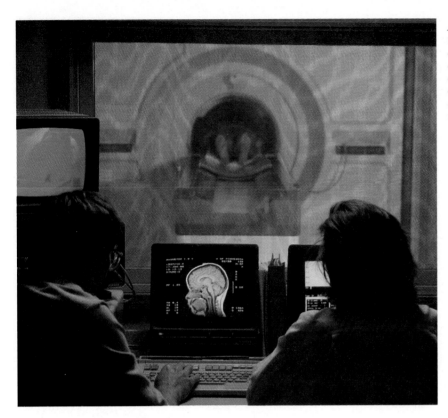

According to the conflict perspective, the profit motive has driven corporations to oversell many expensive technological advances, even though they have benefited only a limited number of patients and have not significantly improved the nation's health.

In his Marxist analysis of coronary-care technology, for example, Howard Waitzkin (1987) found that, since its introduction in the 1960s, the expensive coronary care units have become so popular that today they can be found in half of all the acute-care hospitals in the United States. But the intensive care provided by that medical technology has not been proven more effective than simple rest at home. Waitzkin argues that the proliferation of this expensive but relatively ineffective form of treatment can be traced to the profit motive. He finds that corporations such as Warner-Lambert Pharmaceutical Company and the Hewlett-Packard Company have participated in every phase of the research, development, promotion, and dissemination of today's coronary care technology, which produces huge profits for them. Waitzkin also points out that the same profit motive has driven corporations to oversell many other expensive technological advances, such as computerized axial tomography and fetal monitoring, even though these devices have not significantly improved the nation's health; they have benefited only a limited number of patients.

The conflict perspective further suggests that the unequal distribution of health and medical care reflects the larger social inequality. The poor suffer from higher rates of most diseases than do the rich. The poor are also more likely to receive inadequate or no medical care.

Symbolic Interactionist Perspective

An important aspect of medical practice is the symbolic interaction between doctor and patient. As suggested by research, patients tend to evaluate warm, friendly doctors favorably even when these doctors have not provided successful treatment. By contrast, patients are most likely to sue for malpractice those physicians who are the most highly trained and who practice in the most sophisticated hospitals. Although these physicians are not intentionally negligent, they are most likely to be viewed by their patients—not just the ones who sue them—as cold and bureaucratic (Twaddle and Hessler, 1987). It is the friendly doctor's "affiliative style" of communication that enhances patient satisfaction, and it is the highly competent but bureaucratic doctor's "dominant style" that alienates patients. "Affiliative style" involves behaviors that communicate honesty, compassion, humor, and a nonjudgmental attitude. "Dominant style" involves the manifestation of power, authority, professional detachment, and status in the physician's interaction with the patient (Buller and Buller, 1987).

Why does the doctor's communication style affect patient satisfaction? From the symbolic interactionist perspective, we can assume that, in interacting with patients, friendly doctors are more likely than dominant doctors to take into account the views, feelings, and expectations held by the patients about themselves, their illnesses, and their doctors. To the patients, the illness is unusual, as it does not happen to them every day, and their suffering is a highly intimate, emotional reality. Thus, they expect their doctors to show a great deal of concern. They obviously want a cure, but they also crave emotional support. If doctors attune themselves to these expectations, they can develop a warm relationship with their patients. But this is no easy task because physicians have been trained to take an objective, dispassionate approach to disease. They have learned to view patients unemotionally, especially when performing surgeries, which involves sticking their hands inside diseased strangers without flinching or losing their nerve (Easterbrook, 1987).

Such emotional detachment often intrudes into the medical interview as well. According to the National Task Force on Medical Interviews, "In the typical doctor-patient encounter, all too often the doctor dominates with questions based on his technical understanding of the cause and treatment of the illness, while the patient, often in vain, tries to get the doctor to pay attention to his very personal sense of the illness" (Goleman, 1988). In one study, average patients were found to have three different problems on their minds when they went to see their doctors, but their efforts to tell their stories were cut off by the doctors within the first 18 seconds of the interview. In fact, most patients never got beyond the first question. In cases where patients were allowed to talk, the physician often responded only with an "um hum." Such a response is noncommittal and indicates only minimal interest (Goleman, 1988). Detached professionalism tends to exact a price by alienating patients, making them feel that they are being treated as mere diseases rather than as people. Such patients are also likely to suffer other consequences. As one study shows, about 60 percent of patients leave their doctors' offices confused about medication instructions, and more than half of new prescriptions are taken improperly or not at all (Winslow, 1989; Nazario, 1992).

Questions for Discussion and Review

1. How do the roles played by patients and physicians contribute to the social order?
2. What facts about U.S. health care do conflict theorists emphasize?
3. What is the nature of the doctor-patient relationship?

THE STUDY OF POPULATION

The scientific study of population is called **demography.** More than any other area of sociology, demography is based on a large body of reasonably accurate data. Most of these data come from vital statistics and censuses. **Vital statistics** consists of information about births, marriages, deaths, and migrations into and out of a country. Since 1933, the U.S. government has required all states to record these data. The other source of population information, the **census,** is a periodic head count of the entire population of a country. It includes a wealth of data, such as age, sex, education, occupation, and residence.

How the Census Is Taken

Census taking has been with us for a long time. As early as 3000 B.C., China conducted a census in some parts of the country for tax purposes. In biblical times, after the Israelites escaped from Egypt, they listed all men aged 20 and older to assess their military strength. These and other ancient censuses were intended to control particular categories of people—to identify who should be taxed, drafted into military service, or forced to work on certain government projects, such as building the Great Wall in China. Early censuses did not seek to count the entire population—only such categories of people as family heads or males of military age.

By contrast, the modern census, which began to develop in the seventeenth century, is designed to count all people within a country for governmental, scientific, and commercial purposes. A good example is the U.S. census, which has been taken every ten years since 1790. It is used for determining the number of congressional seats for each state and allocating federal and state funds to local governments. It is also used for scientific analyses of the nation's demographic traits and trends, economic development, and business cycles. Moreover, businesses find useful information in the census data. Orthodontists, for example, could learn where there are a lot of teenagers in high-income households.

But how does one take a census in a huge, complex society like the United States? Taking the latest U.S. census in 1990 was a massive task. It required the orchestration of some 500,000 workers and the delivery of 106 million forms to people throughout the United States, Puerto Rico, Guam, the U.S. Virgin Islands, Samoa, and other U.S.-held Pacific locales. Using a decentralized approach, the U.S. Bureau of the Census, which is part of the Department of Commerce, set up about 484 computer-equipped district offices, hiring mainly local people from a wide variety of backgrounds.

The latest, 1990 census made the first-ever attempts to count the nation's homeless. Census takers fanned out to such places as heating grates, where the homeless were known or suspected to stay.

Most of the census takers worked part-time only, but they all had received special training. Their jobs ranged from office managers, data-entry people, and payroll clerks to regular enumerators and Special Place enumerators (who went to such places as bus depots and abandoned buildings to count the homeless). They compiled and checked address lists, marked census questionnaires, followed up on nonrespondents, and reported results (Roberts, 1990; Little, 1991).

Problems appeared in all these operations, but in most cases the Census Bureau had anticipated them and had developed solutions from six years of planning the project. The most common problem was the public's fear that personal data would fall into the hands of the Internal Revenue Service, Immigration, and other government agencies. Thus, the Census Bureau waged massive national and local public relations campaigns via television, radio, newspapers, fliers, and posters. It repeatedly conveyed the message that strict confidentiality had been ensured by law for 72 years, with census workers being sworn to secrecy. But some 10 percent of the potential respondents remained skeptical. They were typically minorities—the poor and nonwhites—ironically, the very people who, if they are counted, stand to benefit the most from government funds.

The Census Bureau tried to solve the nonresponse problem by door-to-door canvassing, with enumerators making three or more personal visits. As Barbara Bryant, the Census Bureau's director, said, "Eighty or 90 percent of our effort is targeted at the 10 percent we're most likely to miss" (Little, 1991). The effort included the first-ever attempt to count the homeless. Special Place enumerators fanned out to where the homeless were known or suspected to stay. In addition to established shelters, the places included rail, bus, and air depots; hidden spots under viaducts; abandoned buildings; laundromats; heating grates; and shanties.

The census put the 1990 U.S. population at 249,632,692—an increase of more than 23 million people, or 10.2 percent, over the 1980 total. Is this number, and the numbers for various subgroups, accurate? Probably not; the census could not be perfect. Some African American leaders have already accused the Census Bureau of undercounting minorities. Cities that were shown to have suffered population decline have also complained of an undercount. But, given the extraordinary efforts to enumerate the population accurately, the 1990 census must be more accurate than any of the past censuses: In the 1890 census, families were asked if they had any "idiots" and whether their heads were larger or smaller than average. The 1910 census missed most of the numerous immigrants in Chicago who hid from the counters for fear of being deported. And the 1960 and 1970 censuses seriously undercounted people in many cities despite the great migration from rural to urban areas that had begun 20 and 30 years earlier (Roberts, 1990).

From today's considerably more accurate census, demographers can tell a great deal about population characteristics and changes. These variables are greatly influenced by social factors, and they vary from one society to another.

Population Growth

The world's population increases enormously. About 94 million new babies are added every year, a number equal to the size of Mexico's population (Elliott and Dickey, 1994). Moreover, given the same yearly growth rate, population does not increase linearly, with the *same* number of people added annually. Instead, it grows exponentially, with an *increasingly larger* number of new people appearing in each succeeding year. It works like your savings account, which earns increasingly more interest, rather than the same interest, in each succeeding year because it builds on a larger base each year.

Increases in population are therefore far more dramatic in modern times of large populations than in ancient times of small populations. Before the year 1600, it took more than 500,000 years for the human population to reach about half a billion. Thereafter, the population skyrocketed to 5.4 billion in less than 400 years. Today it takes only 5 or 6 years (in contrast to the 500,000 years before 1600) for the world to produce 500 million people. Figure 13.2 shows the

remarkable rate of population growth in the modern era.

In general, populations are growing much faster in poor, developing countries than in rich, developed ones. As Figure 13.3 shows, rich nations generally have an annual growth rate of less than 1 percent, but poor nations typically grow at a rate of above 2 percent. The growth of a nation's population is determined by the number of births minus the number of deaths plus the *net immigration rate*—the excess of people moving into a country (*immigrants*) over those leaving it (*emigrants*). Let us take a closer look at these three determinants of population growth.

Birth Rates

The **birth rate** is the number of babies born in a year for every 1000 members of a population:

$$\frac{\text{Births}}{\text{Total population}} \times 1000$$

For many years the birth rates of most industrialized nations have been far lower than 20 per 1000 population, whereas those of most agricultural countries have far exceeded 30 per 1000.

Indeed, people in poor countries do tend to have larger families—an average of four or more children—than people in rich countries, who have an average of about two children per family. Because of high birth rates in past years, poor countries also have a very large number of women entering their childbearing years. As a result, even if these women average fewer children than their mothers did, their nations' birth rates will remain high. Meanwhile, developed countries are close to or already experiencing *zero population growth*, a situation in which the population stops growing. Consequently, well over 90 percent of the world's population increase in coming decades will occur in the poorest nations. By the year 2000, the United States will probably account for only about 4 percent of the total population (U.S. Census Bureau, 1994).

Why do people in rich nations have fewer babies? One reason is access to effective and convenient methods of birth control. Another is the nuclear family system. Unlike a married couple in an extended family, who have many relatives to help raise their children, couples in nuclear families must assume all the responsibility for their children's care. More fundamental than these two reasons is a third—industrialization. In agricultural societies, children are economic assets; they can help with the farmwork. In industrialized societies, however, children have become economic liabilities.

FIGURE 13.2
How the World's Population Grows
In recent history, the world's population has experienced exponential growth. Before the modern era began in A.D. 1600, it took more than 500,000 years for global population to reach only about half a billion. But since then it has taken less than 400 years for the population to skyrocket to more than 5.6 billion today.

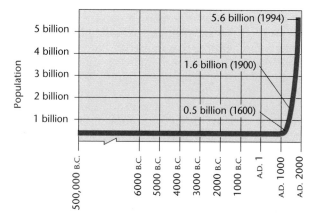

Source: Population Reference Bureau, "How Many People Have Ever Lived on Earth?" *Population Bulletin.* Feb. 1962. p. 5., *The Statistical Abstract of the United States,*1994. p. 850.

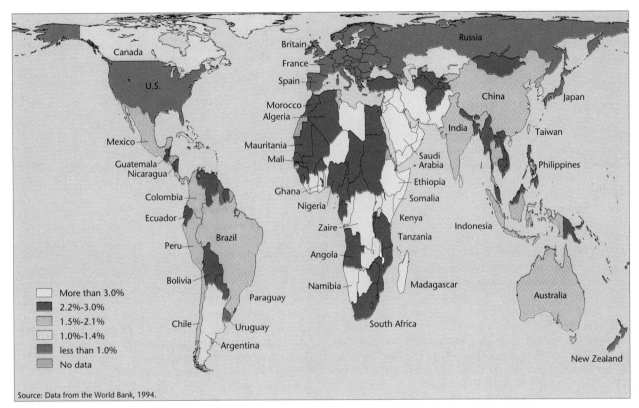

FIGURE 13.3
Population Growth Around the Globe

They depend on their families for financial support, but they cannot contribute significantly to the family's income. Industrialization is in turn associated with two other related factors that hold down fertility: the entrance of women into the work force, and a preference for small families. If women join the labor force outside the home, they may find the prospect of raising children too difficult. A preference for small families is then more likely to take hold.

Death Rates

The **death rate** is the number of deaths in a year for every 1000 members of a population. Rich nations have an average of 10 deaths per 1000 population, and the poor nations have 13. The difference is surprisingly small. In fact, death rates obscure the large gap between rich and poor nations in health and living conditions. Because the percentage of young people is much higher in developing countries than in developed ones and the percentage of old people much lower, the death rates in these two kinds of nations are more similar than we might expect.

To compare the health and living conditions of nations, demographers therefore use refined rates, especially the **infant mortality rate,** which shows the number of deaths among infants less than one year old for every 1000 live births. In many developed countries, the infant mortality rate is far lower than 20. In many developing countries, it is far higher than 30 (U.S. Census Bureau, 1994). Another indicator of health conditions is **life expectancy,** the average number of years that a group of people can expect to live. If the group being considered is a nation's newborn infants, then the average life expectancy in developing nations is 63, compared with 75 for industrialized nations (United Nations, 1994).

At least two factors shape death rates or life expectancies. One is medical practice. Immunization of children, for example, has greatly reduced the number of deaths resulting from infectious diseases, and death rates in many poor nations today are being reduced because modern medical practices have been brought into these countries. But early in this century the U.S. life expectancy improved *before* modern medicine could make a substantial contribution to health. The improvement came about because of a second factor that often leads to better health: wealth. As living standards rose, nutrition and sanitation improved, and the life expectancy in the United States rose as a result.

International Migration

International migration—movement of people from one country to another—obviously does not increase or decrease the world's population, but it may greatly alter the population of a specific country. Israel is a case in point. For several years after it was established in 1948, Israel experienced a tremendous annual population growth of 24 percent. Ninety percent of this growth was a result of immigration by European Jews. Another notable example is the United States. Between 1880 and 1910, more than 28 million European immigrants settled in the United States. In the last 20 years the United States further attracted millions of immigrants from Latin America and Asia (Wrong, 1990).

The effect of immigration goes beyond the immediate addition to the population. Most immigrants are young adults from lower-class families—categories with relatively high fertility rates. As a result, through their children and grandchildren the immigrants multiply population growth, producing an effect that echoes through the years.

Both "pushes" and "pulls" stimulate international migrations. The "push" typically comes from economic hardship, which compels people to leave their country; the "pull" comes from economic opportunity elsewhere. A hundred years ago, nearly half of Ireland's population was "pushed" out of the country by its great potato famine and "pulled" into the United States by its reputation for providing economic opportunity. Nowadays, there is a worldwide mass movement of people from various poor countries to more prosperous ones. Why is this happening now? After all, poverty has been around from time immemorial. The answer is that we have had two revolutions: One is the information revolution, which enables people, even the very poor, to know what life is like in other parts of the world. Another is the transportation revolution, which makes it much easier than before for people to travel long distances.

Economics, however, does not motivate all migrations. Political and religious oppression has pushed many people to brave the uncertainties of a new land. Some 50 years ago, millions of Jews fled persecution in Nazi Germany. More recently, hundreds of thousands of Vietnamese and Cubans escaped communist oppression in their homelands. In the last decade, many Jews left behind their oppressive lives in the former Soviet Union, immigrating to Israel and the United States. Similarly, since 1990 hostility toward ethnic minorities throughout Eastern Europe has spurred migration, with, for example, Romania's ethnic Hungarians fleeing to Hungary and Bulgaria's ethnic Turks going to Turkey.

Age, Gender, and Marriage

Other characteristics of a population also influence its growth. Among the most important are the age structure, sex ratio, and marriage rate.

The **age structure**—the pattern of the proportions of different age groups within a population—shapes birth rates. Compared with industrialized countries, developing countries generally have a very low percentage of old people and a high percentage of children. Since the current large numbers of children will grow up to produce children themselves, future birth rates in these nations are likely to be high. The age structure also affects death rates. If two nations have equally healthy populations and living conditions, the country with the higher percentage of older people will have a higher death rate.

The **sex ratio** indicates the number of males per 100 females. A sex ratio of more than 100 means there are more males than females. If the sex ratio is 100, the number of males equals the number of females. In most societies, slightly more boys are born than girls, but males have higher death rates. As a result, females outnumber males in the population as a whole. The sex ratio for young adults is about even in normal times, but it falls in wartime because wars are waged mainly by men. In the United States, about 105 males are born for every 100 females each year (representing a sex ratio of 105), but because males die sooner than females, the sex ratio for the entire population is 95 (U.S. Census Bureau, 1994).

If the sex ratio is close to 100, then the **marriage rate**—the number of marriages in a given year for every 1000 people—is likely to be high. Because most babies are born to married rather than unmarried couples, a high marriage rate will likely bring a high birth rate. When soldiers came home from World War II, for example, the U.S. marriage rate went up, and the "baby boom" followed. Since 1960 the numbers of unmarried adults, late marriages, and divorces in the United States have all increased, partly helping to bring down our birth rates.

Questions for Discussion and Review

1. What is demography?
2. How are demographic data collected?

3. What influences birth rates, death rates, and international migration?
4. What are the age structure, sex ratio, and marriage rate of a population?

PATTERNS OF POPULATION CHANGE

Demographers can tell us a great deal about how populations are changing. The most influential explanations of population change are the Malthusian theory and the theory of demographic transition. Demographers also can offer insight into the consequences of population change.

Malthusian Theory

In 1798 the English clergyman and economist Thomas Malthus (1766–1834) published a truly dismal portrait of population dynamics in *An Essay on the Principles of Population*. He argued that population grows much faster than the production of food supplies, because a population *multiplies* itself but food production increases only by *addition*—through the cultivation of land. Thus, population typically increases geometrically (2, 4, 8, 16, . . .), but food supplies increase only arithmetically (2, 3, 4, 5, . . .). As a population outstrips food supplies, it will be afflicted by war, disease, and poverty. Eventually, population growth will stop.

People might halt this growth through what Malthus called "preventive checks," by which he meant late marriage and sexual restraint, which would reduce birth rates. But Malthus doubted that people, especially the lower classes, had the will to exercise such restraint. Instead, he argued, population growth would eventually be stopped by nature. Its tools would be what Malthus called "positive checks"—disease and famine.

Malthus failed to foresee three revolutions that undermined his theory: the revolutions in contraception, agricultural technology, and medicine. He did not anticipate the development of effective and convenient contraceptives such as the pill and the IUD (intrauterine contraceptive device). He did not expect that birth control would become widespread. Especially in the West, the use of contraceptives has helped bring birth rates down to a point lower than Malthus thought possible. Meanwhile, the technological revolution has allowed farmers to increase production by raising the yield of their land, not just by adding farmland. Finally, medical advances have

given us an arsenal of effective weapons against the contagious diseases that Malthus expected would devastate overpopulated nations. As a result, instead of being reduced by disease, overpopulated nations continue to grow more crowded. Thus, the awful fate Malthus predicted has not come to pass. His theory, however, is still valuable because it has served as a warning to nations that populations cannot expand indefinitely, because natural resources are finite.

The Demographic Transition

Most demographers subscribe to the **demographic transition** theory, namely, that human populations tend to go through specific demographic stages and that these stages are tied to a society's economic development. This theory is based on the population changes that have occurred in Western Europe during the past 200 years. According to the theory, there are four demographic stages, shown in Figure 13.4.

In the first stage, both birth rates and death rates are high. Because the two rates more or less balance each other, the population is fairly stable, neither growing nor declining rapidly. This was the stage of the populations in Western Europe in 1650, before industrialization.

During the second stage, the birth rate remains high but the death rate declines sharply. This stage occurred in Western Europe after it became industrialized, and it is occurring today in many developing nations. The introduction of modern medicine, along with better hygiene and sanitation, has decreased death rates in developing countries. But economies and values in these countries are still essentially traditional, so their birth rates remain high. As a result, their populations grow rapidly.

During the third stage, both birth rates and death rates decline. Western countries found themselves in this stage after they reached a rather high level of

FIGURE 13.4
The Demographic Transition

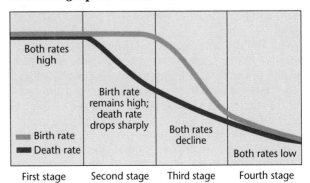

Both rates high	Birth rate remains high; death rate drops sharply	Both rates decline	Both rates low
▬ Birth rate ▬ Death rate			
First stage	Second stage	Third stage	Fourth stage

industrialization. Today, Taiwan, South Korea, and Argentina are among the developing nations that have reached this stage. Their birth rates have declined significantly. The population still grows because the birth rate continues to exceed the death rate, but growth is slower than during the second stage.

The fourth stage is marked by a low birth rate and a low death rate. Only the most industrialized nations of Western Europe, the United States, and Japan have reached this stage. They have fairly stable populations and are moving close to zero population growth. Some countries, such as Japan, France, and Italy, have fallen below zero growth, with birth rates lower than death rates.

To proponents of the demographic transition theory, the future of human populations looks bright. They believe that developing countries will eventually join the industrialized world and have stable populations. To critics of the theory, the future is far less certain. There is at least one major difference between the developing countries of today and the European nations of 200 years ago: Thanks to modern medicine, death rates in developing countries have declined far more rapidly than they did in nineteenth-century Europe. While it took Europe 200 years to lower its mortality, it takes developing countries today only a year or so to lower theirs. At the same time, their birth rates remain high. As a result, the population is exploding in the developing world today, a condition that did not occur in nineteenth-century Europe.

Demographic "Fallout"

The fallout from the population explosion can be seen in the oppressive poverty of many of the developing nations. Their cities are filled with people who live in overcrowded shacks, and others who must live on the streets, sidewalks, vacant lots, rooftops, and cemeteries. In these poor countries, most are undernourished, and malnutrition is devastating 200 million children under age 5, weakening their bodies and their minds. Some 15 million children die of starvation every year (Ehrlich, 1984; United Nations, 1994).

The rapidly growing populations of developing nations greatly complicate their efforts to fight poverty. Instead of climbing up the economic ladder, these nations find themselves on a treadmill, constantly in danger of slipping backward to the Malthusian famine. Economic investment can barely keep up with the rapid population growth. More than half of Africa's economic expansion, for example, has been used just to maintain the expanding population at a subsistence level. More

than 40 percent of Africa's population are already living below the region's poverty line. Some African countries, such as Ethiopia, Somalia, and the Sudan, have experienced and will continue to face massive starvation. Other developing countries in Asia and Latin America, though, have made significant progress against poverty by slowing population growth and hastening economic growth. Indonesia, for example, over the last two decades has reduced its poverty rate from nearly 60 percent to less than 20 percent today (Farnsworth, 1990).

Questions for Discussion and Review

1. How would a Malthusian theorist's view of current world population patterns differ from that of a demographic transitionist?
2. What is the demographic "fallout" of population explosion?

COMBATING POPULATION GROWTH

For thousands of years, there have been individuals who practiced birth control, but many nations at various times in their histories have sought to *increase* their population because they associated a large population with great military power and national security. Religious, medical, and political authorities have often argued against birth control. For more than a century, the United States even had laws that prohibited the mailing of birth control information and devices. During the 1950s and 1960s, however, many governments began to see population growth as a social problem. By 1984 most countries, representing about 95 percent of the world's population, had formulated official policies to combat population growth (Davis, 1976; Russell, 1984). These policies can be classified into two types: encouragement of voluntary family planning and compulsory population control.

Voluntary Family Planning

A number of governments make contraceptives available to anyone who wants them. They encourage birth control, but they do not try to impose a limit on how many children a couple may have. For this voluntary family planning to work, however, people must *prefer small families* to large ones—otherwise they will not use birth control.

This is the heart of the problem with family planning. Family planning programs have reduced birth rates significantly in advanced developing countries such as Taiwan and South Korea, because these societies value small families. Family planning is even more successful in the more industrialized nations of the West, where the preference for small families is strong. However, many less advanced developing countries retain the preference for the large families typical of agricultural societies. In these societies, having many children is a status enhancer, particularly for the less educated. Children are also considered a form of old-age pension because there are no social welfare systems like the ones we have in the United States. Because many children die early, parents are even more anxious to have a large family to increase their chances of being looked after in their senior years (Francis, 1987).

As a result, voluntary planning programs in these poor societies have failed to reduce birth rates significantly. This has led the governments of some of these countries to resort to compulsory programs.

Compulsory Population Control

In the early 1970s, India forced government employees who had more than two children to undergo sterilization. With the encouragement of the central government, some states in India also forced men to be sterilized after their second child was born. If the men refused, they could be fined $250 and imprisoned for up to a year. In some villages, overzealous government officials rounded up and sterilized all the men, without checking how many children they had. The program stirred up widespread opposition. Demographer Frank Notestein predicted in 1971 that if a developing country tried to force its people to practice birth control, it "would be more likely to bring down the government than the birth rate." Indeed, the sterilization program apparently contributed to the fall of Prime Minister Indira Gandhi's government in 1977. Since then, India has returned to a voluntary program. But it has been difficult to control the relentless population growth because of low literacy and a dearth of sustained family planning information and services. India now has a fertility rate of four children per woman (compared with two in the United States), and it will become the world's most populous nation by about 2045 (Crossette, 1990; World Bank, 1994).

China has had more success with a program that combines rewards and punishments. For a couple with only one child, the rewards are substantial. The parents get a salary bonus, and the child receives free schooling, priority in medical care, admission to the best schools and universities, and preference in employment. By contrast, multichild parents are severely penalized. They must pay all costs for each

India has failed to control its relentless population growth because of relatively low literacy and a dearth of sustained family-planning information and services. Shown here is an attempt to promote family planning on a placard on the back of a bus in India.

additional child, are taxed about 10 percent of their income, and are often denied job promotion for two years. Since starting this "one-child family" campaign in 1979, China has halved its birth rate, a record unmatched by any other developing nation.

Beginning in 1986, though, the birth rate began to rise again because the government relaxed its one-child policy—by allowing rural couples to have a second baby if their firstborn was a girl. One reason for the relaxation has been the increasing prosperity among the Chinese, many of whom are willing to pay the fines for having more than one child. Another reason is the international criticism that China has received for pressuring women to abort fetuses even late in pregnancy. A third reason is that the one-child policy has encouraged, albeit unintentionally, the killing of female infants by parents who hope to have sons. Nevertheless, China continues to exhort couples to have only one child, though it now focuses on persuasion, education, and publicity campaigns rather than coercion and penalties. All this has been quite successful with urban couples, though it tends to fall on deaf ears in the countryside (Kristof, 1990).

U.S. Population Policy

In the 1960s, the U.S. government began to recognize global population growth as a potential problem; by 1968 it had spent several hundred million dollars to help developing countries. During the conservative Reagan and Bush administrations in the 1980s and early 1990s, however, the U.S. government suspended aid to countries that advocated abortion as a family planning operation. More liberal, the Clinton administration has restored the aid. Similar assistance is given to family planning in the United States.

The federal government has been spending over $100 million a year to assist family planning centers. But our population growth has slowed primarily because of social and economic factors, not government action. In fact, family planning has become the norm rather than the exception. Even the majority of U.S. Catholics practice forms of birth control forbidden by their church. Today, sterilization is the most popular type of birth control in the United States, followed by the pill and the condom (see Figure 13.5). The use of sterilization and the condom has increased faster than most other methods, because of concern and controversy over the side effects of the pill and the IUD (Ingrassia, 1995).

But all these contraceptives are antiquated; the pill and the IUD, for example, were introduced 30 years ago. They are also less convenient and less effective than the ones coming out in Western Europe. In 1990 the innovative Norplant device—introduced in Europe 20 years earlier—was approved for use in the United States. Norplant, when properly implanted in a woman's upper arm, can protect against pregnancy for five years. But, since it is very expensive, it will be of little use to the poor, who have the highest incidence of unwanted pregnancy. Owing to the lack of modern and inexpensive contraceptives, more than half of all U.S. pregnancies every year are accidents or unwanted—more than in Western Europe. This may explain why our rate of abortion as a form of birth control is among the highest in the industrialized

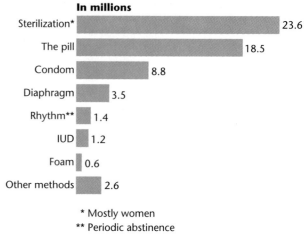

FIGURE 13.5
Contraceptive Choices in the United States

In millions

Sterilization*	23.6
The pill	18.5
Condom	8.8
Diaphragm	3.5
Rhythm**	1.4
IUD	1.2
Foam	0.6
Other methods	2.6

* Mostly women
** Periodic abstinence

Source: Data from the U.S. Census Bureau, 1994.

world, despite restrictions by the federal government and many state governments on the use of public funds for abortions (Elmer-DeWitt, 1991).

Nevertheless, the use of contraception is prevalent enough. And given the added prevalence of abortion, the U.S. Census Bureau (1994) believes that within 15 years U.S. women in their childbearing years will average just 1.8 births—less than the replacement rate of 2.1. (Demographers determine the *replacement rate* at 2.1 rather than 2.0 to take into account young people who die before reaching their reproductive age.) It seems inevitable that if the "birth dearth" continues, the United States will rely increasingly on immigration to stop its population from declining.

Questions for Discussion and Review

1. How does family planning differ from population control?
2. What has been the result of compulsory birth control programs in overpopulated countries like India and China?
3. What kinds of contraceptives are commonly used to keep birth rates low in the United States?

CHAPTER REVIEW

1. *What social factors influence our health?* One factor is age: old people are more likely to suffer chronic illnesses. Another factor is gender: women are more likely than men to experience chronic and acute ill-

nesses, though they do live longer. African, Hispanic, and Native Americans also have lower life expectancies and higher illness rates than whites. Poor people, too, are more likely than higher-income groups to become ill. *Can epidemiology track down the social causes of diseases?* Yes. It can do so by finding out who has the disease and what all the victims have in common. *How has AIDS spread?* It has spread mostly through unprotected sex and intravenous drug use. *What social consequences have ensued from the AIDS epidemic?* There is a lot of fear about the disease and discrimination against AIDS victims. *How does the health in the U.S. compare with that in other industrial nations?* We have lower life expectancy and higher infant mortality.

2. *How has the medical profession changed over the last decade?* Doctors' autonomy has eroded, their prestige has declined, and their competence is more open to challenge by laypersons. *How does gender bias in medical research affect women?* Because it produces medical knowledge from studying men only, the treatment based on this knowledge can be inappropriate and dangerous to women. The lack of research on women's diseases further prolongs their suffering.

3. *Who is likely to seek medical care when ill?* Those who visit physicians more often are the elderly, women, African Americans, and whites. Mexican Americans, Native Americans, and the residents of Chinatowns are more likely to rely on folk medicine and less likely to visit physicians. The poor are more likely than others to go to public clinics and emergency rooms. *What is wrong with the health-care system?* One problem is unequal access to medical care, with the poor receiving inadequate and poor-quality care and the affluent getting better care. Another problem is the soaring cost of health care. *Do terminally ill patients have the right to die?* In principle, they do. But in reality, it is difficult to exercise that right, because the courts will not let the patients die if the doctor or prosecutor wants to keep them alive.

4. *How do functionalists and conflict theorists view health and medical care?* To functionalists, the sick role and the healing role contribute to social order, and the system of medical care significantly maintains health or reduces illness. But to conflict theorists, a better social environment reduces mortality from diseases much more than medicine does. In this view, medical care and technology reflect the pursuit of private profit in our capitalist society. *How can symbolic interactionism shed light on the doctor-patient relationship?* If doctors take into account the patients' own views about themselves, their illnesses, and their doctors, patients are likely to be happy with the medical treatment they receive.

5. *Why is the modern census better than the earlier ones?* The modern census seeks to achieve its governmental, scientific, and commercial objectives by employing an enormous number of trained census takers and by making extra efforts to reach the typically hard-to-reach people, such as the poor.

6. *What determines a nation's growth rate?* It is the birth rate plus the net immigration rate minus the death rate. *What social factors hold down birth rates?* Access to effective birth control methods, substitution of nuclear for extended families, industrialization, movement of women into the labor force, and a preference for small families are all significant factors. *What social factors lower death rates?* The availability of modern medicine and wealth or high living standards lower the death rate. *What motivates migrations?* The "push" of deprivation and oppression and the "pull" of opportunity and freedom elsewhere are often the key motives. *What other factors influence population growth?* They are the age structure, sex ratio, and marriage rate.

7. *What are two prominent theories regarding population patterns?* According to the Malthusian theory, human populations tend to grow faster than food supplies. As a population outstrips its supply of food, it is afflicted by war, disease, poverty, and even famine, which eventually stop population growth. Malthus's predictions have been derailed by contraceptive, technological, and medical revolutions. According to the theory of demographic transition, human populations go through four specific stages, which are tied to economic development.

8. *How can governments control population growth?* They can do so by encouraging voluntary family planning and setting up compulsory population programs. But family-planning programs work only if people prefer to have small families, and compulsory programs may meet stiff opposition. China, however, has reduced its birth rate through a basically compulsory program that combines rewards for small families and punishments for large families. *Does the U.S. government control population growth?* No, but it does give some aid to family-planning centers. Social and economic factors, not government action, keep birth rates low.

KEY TERMS

Age structure   The pattern of the proportions of different age groups within a population. (p. 298)

Birth rate   The number of babies born in a year for every 1000 members of a given population. (p. 296)

Census   A periodic head count of the entire population of a country. (p. 294)

Death rate   The number of deaths in a year for every 1000 members of a population. (p. 297)

Demographic transition   The theory that human populations tend to go through specific, demographic stages and that these stages are tied to a society's economic development. (p. 299)

Demography   The scientific study of population. (p. 294)

Epidemiology   The study of the origin and spread of disease within a population. (p. 285)

Healing role   A set of social expectations regarding how a doctor should behave. (p. 292)

Infant mortality rate   The number of deaths among infants less than one year old for every 1000 live births. (p. 297)

Informed consent   The approval that a patient gives to a doctor for a treatment after receiving adequate information on it. (p. 291)

Life expectancy   The average number of years that a group of people can expect to live. (p. 297)

Living will   Advance instructions on what people want their doctors to do in the event of a terminal illness. (p. 291)

Marriage rate   The number of marriages in a given year for every 1000 people. (p. 298)

Sex ratio   The number of males per 100 females. (p. 298)

Sick role   A set of social expectations regarding how an ill person should behave. (p. 292)

Vital statistics   Information about births, marriages, deaths, and migrations into and out of a country. (p. 294)

SUGGESTED READINGS

Feinsilver, Julie M., and David E. Apter. 1993. *Healing the Masses: Cuban Health Politics at Home and Abroad.* Berkeley, Calif.: University of California Press. An analysis of the free health care system in Cuba and its political significance.

Ginzberg, Eli, and Miriam Ostow. 1994. *The Road to Reform: The Future of Health Care in America.* New York: Free Press. Discusses various problems of the U.S. health care system and offers suggestions for dealing with them.

Polednak, Anthony P. 1989. *Racial and Ethnic Differences in Disease.* New York: Oxford University Press. An extensive review of the data on the influences of race and ethnicity on various diseases, such as cancer, heart disease, infectious diseases, and chronic disorders.

Ratcliff, Kathryn Strother (ed.). 1989. *Healing Technology: Feminist Perspectives.* Ann Arbor: University of Michigan. A collection of articles about how health care, environmental, and occupational technologies affect women's health.

Simon, Julian L. 1990. *Population Matters: People, Resources, Environment, and Immigration.* New Brunswick, N.J.: Transaction. A collection of controversial articles about population and the environment, presenting an optimist view of the issue.

14

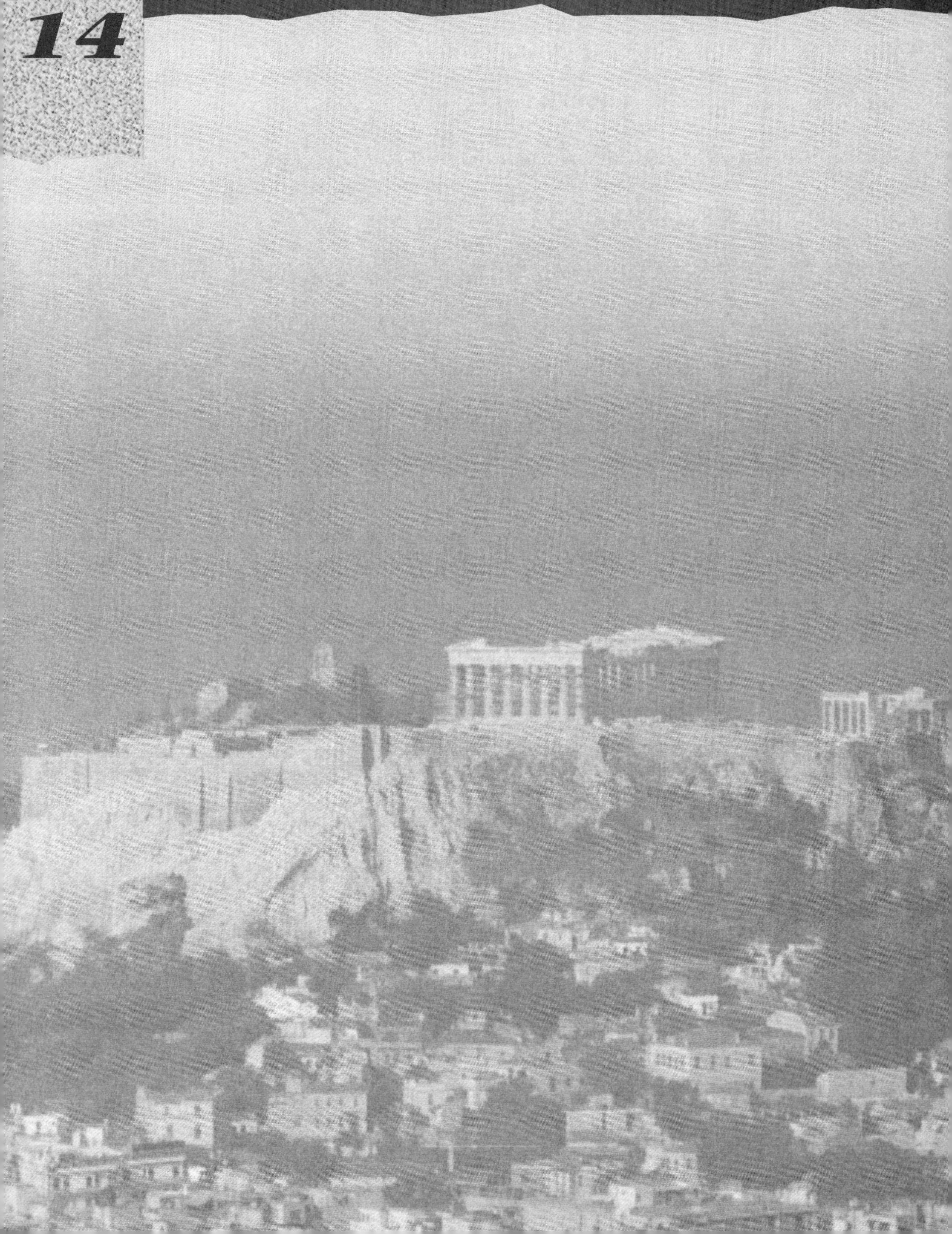

ENVIRONMENT AND URBANIZATION

Myths and Realities

MYTH: *Since they have a far larger population than rich countries, poor countries must be contributing more to the world's environmental pollution.*

REALITY: Despite their smaller population, rich countries consume more resources than poor countries and thereby contribute more to environmental pollution. For instance, by burning far more fuel than the average Brazilian, the average U.S. resident contributes five times as much to the greenhouse effect. (pp. 309–310)

MYTH: *Most of the world's large cities—like New York or Tokyo—are in prosperous, industrialized countries.*

REALITY: Generally, the poorer the country, the faster its urban growth. As a result, more than half of the world's megacities are now in developing countries. (p. 314)

MYTH: *Living in an impersonal world of strangers, city dwellers are more lonely than rural and small town people.*

REALITY: Those who live in the city are no more lonely than those who live in small towns and rural areas. Urbanites visit friends and relatives as often as do rural people. (p. 320)

MYTH: *New York City is well known for its crime, poverty, homelessness, racial tension, exorbitant rents, and official corruption. It is no wonder that most New Yorkers dislike living in this city.*

REALITY: Most New Yorkers are ambivalent about their city. On the one hand, they tend to consider their city an urban hellhole; on the other hand, they very much like living in "the Big Apple." (p. 321)

Seven years ago farmer Yang Yufu left his village to find work in a large city in China. Unable to get a job, he has eked out a living by repairing shoes, fixing appliances, and selling glasses and plastic buckets. The most he can earn in a month is only $100. Yet he has to support his mother, brother, and sister, who live with him in two rented rooms. His father is left in the village to farm the tiny family plot (Tefft, 1993).

Like Yang, millions of poor rural Chinese as well as their counterparts in many developing countries are moving into cities. What we have here is **urbanization,** the migration of people from the countryside to the city, increasing the percentage of the population that lives in the city. It began to transform many societies a hundred years ago. Today most people in the developed world already live in urban areas, and within a decade most of the developing world will also be urbanized. But urbanization often leads to industrial pollution of the environment.

ENVIRONMENT

To understand how urbanization can damage the environment and thus endanger life on earth, we look to **ecology,** a study of the interactions among organisms and between organisms and their physical environment.

Elements of Ecology

Like all organisms, humans exist within the **biosphere**—a thin layer of air, soil, and water surrounding the earth. Within the biosphere we can isolate countless **ecosystems,** self-sufficient communities of organisms depending for survival on one another and on the environment. An ecosystem may be as small as a puddle in a forest or as large as the biosphere itself. But whatever ecosystem we choose to look at, we find that the organisms within it depend on one another and on the physical environment for their survival. They are bound together by mutual interdependence. Energy and matter are constantly being transformed and transferred by the components of an ecosystem, providing the organisms with the essentials of life. Plants, for example, take in carbon dioxide and give off oxygen, which humans and other animals require for survival, and animals exhale carbon dioxide. Plants, in turn, use carbon dioxide in photosynthesis, the process by which they convert solar energy into carbohydrates and become food for animals. When animals die, their decomposed bodies provide nutrients to the soil, which plants then use.

From analyzing ecosystems we can isolate two simple ecological principles. First, natural resources are finite. Every ecosystem therefore has a limited *carrying capacity,* a limited number of living things that it can support. Second, all our actions have related consequences. If we try to alter one aspect of an ecosystem, we end up changing others as well. When farmers used DDT, a toxic pesticide, for example, they meant merely to kill pests. But DDT also got into the soil and water, from there into plankton, into fish that ate plankton, and into birds that ate the fish. The chemical also found its way into our food.

Despite all the amazing things humans have managed to do, we are still limited by these ecological principles. We are still living organisms, dependent like other organisms on ecosystems. However, we have tried to ignore that dependence and act in defiance of nature's limits. Two environmental problems result: a depletion of natural resources and environmental pollution.

Diminishing Resources

Although they make up less than 6 percent of the world's population, each year people in the United States consume about 30 percent of the world's energy and raw materials. If this high level of consumption continues, the world will soon run out of resources. According to some estimates, the world's reserves of lead, silver, tungsten, mercury, and other precious resources will be depleted within 40 years. Even if new discoveries increase oil reserves fivefold, the global supply of oil will last only 50 years. Poor nations fear that by the time they become fully industrialized, the resources they hope to enjoy will be gone. In the meantime, their cropland is literally disappearing—running down the rivers or blowing away with the wind (Wald, 1990).

Closer to home, we are endangering our own supplies of arable land and water. We are losing topsoil to erosion at an alarming rate. In the worst cases, an inch of topsoil, which nature takes 100 to 1500 years to form, is being destroyed in 10 to 20 years. At the same time, homes and stores and businesses are taking over millions of acres of farmland each year. Meanwhile, in the western United States, underground water reservoirs are being depleted. In the East, thousands of gallons of water are wasted because of leaking city pipes. Even wetlands and marshes, which help control shoreline erosion and act as filtering systems to purify water, are disappearing at a rate of 450,000 acres a year (Carpenter, 1990).

In short, we are fast running out of natural resources. "Barring revolutionary advances in technology," concludes the *Global 2000 Report,* "life for most people on earth will be more precarious in 2000 than it is now." Economist Julian Simon (1990), however, disagrees. He argues that the future is likely to be better "because our powers to manage our environment have been increasing throughout human history." To Simon, if nonrenewable resources such as mineral, metals, coal, or oil are used up, substitutes will be found through technology. Solar energy can be captured to replace coal and oil. We can also find substitutes for metals, such as plastics and aluminum for tin cans, and we can use satellites and fiber-optic lines instead of copper telephone wires. But to produce substitutes may require the use of materials that will themselves eventually run out. More ominous, the production process for the substitutes may contribute to the pollution of the environment.

Environmental Pollution

To consume more, we must produce more and thereby create more wastes. These by-products of our consumption must go somewhere. Nature has many cycles for transforming wastes to be used in some other form, but we are overtaxing nature's recycling capacity. We put too much waste, such as automobile emissions, in one place at the same time, and we have created new toxic substances, such as dioxin, that cannot be recycled safely. The result is pollution.

Pollution of the air has many sources. Throughout the world, power-generating plants, oil refineries, chemical plants, steel mills, and the like spew about 140 million tons of pollutants into the air every year. The heaviest polluter is the automobile, which accounts for at least 80 percent of air pollution. The pollutants irritate our eyes, noses, and throats; damage buildings; lower the productivity of the soil; and may cause serious illnesses, such as bronchitis, emphysema, and lung cancer. Air pollution is especially bad in Eastern Europe. As many as 10 percent of the deaths in Hungary are attributed directly to air pollution; the problem is even worse in parts of the former Czechoslovakia, Poland, and the former East Germany (Nelson, 1990).

Throughout the world, the constant burning of coal, oil, and wood is releasing more and more industrial gases (such as carbon dioxide) into the atmosphere, which in turn trap an increasing amount of heat from the sun. A United Nations panel of 2500 scientists from around world have predicted that this trapped heat will substantially raise the temperature of the earth's surface in the next century. The scientists expect this *global warming* to cause worldwide flooding, climatic change, and social disruption (Stevens, 1995; Lemonick, 1995). Some of the industrial gases—especially chlorofluoro-carbons, used in refrigeration and air conditioning—have already weakened the ozone layer in many areas of the globe, thereby letting in more of the sun's ultraviolet light, which may cause skin cancer, harm the human immune system, and damage some crops and wild plants (Lemonick, 1992).

Another kind of air pollution, called *acid rain,* has also aroused concern. When sulfur and nitrogen compounds are emitted by factories and automobiles, chemical reactions in the atmosphere may convert them to acidic compounds that can be carried hundreds of miles and then fall to the earth in rain and snow. Rain as acidic as vinegar has been recorded. This acid rain can kill fish and aquatic vegetation. It damages forests, crops, and soils. It corrodes buildings and water pipes and tanks because it can erode limestone, marble, and even metal surfaces. Because of acid rain, thousands of lakes and rivers in North America and Europe are now "dead," unable to support fish and plant life. Worst is the acid rain in Russia's Siberia, which has ruined more than 1500 square miles of timber, an area half as large as Rhode Island (Feshbach and Friendly, 1992).

A Primary Cause

Polluting our environment and depleting its resources may amount to a slow form of suicide. Sometimes the cause is ignorance; sometimes it is poverty. In many developing nations, rivers and streams are polluted by human wastes. Poor people desperate for fuel in developing countries have stripped mountainsides of trees, clearing the way for massive erosion. Overgrazing is expanding the deserts of Africa.

Neither ignorance nor poverty, however, can explain much of the environmental damage now being done

We have created new toxic substances, such as dioxin, that cannot be recycled safely. The result is pollution, as shown here at a site in North Carolina that has been polluted by dioxin from a paper mill.

around the world. After all, affluent societies consume many more resources. Although U.S. inhabitants make up only about 6 percent of the world's population, they consume more than 30 percent of the world's energy and raw material. By burning far more fossil fuel in power plants, factories, and family cars, each U.S. resident contributes to air pollution five times as much as does the average Brazilian (Easterbrook, 1989; U.S. Census Bureau, 1994).

A primary source of environmental problems is the fact that clean air, clean rivers, and other environmental resources are *public*, not private, *goods*. In Aristotle's words, "What is common to the greatest number gets the least amount of care." Garrett Hardin (1993) has used a parable called the "Tragedy of the Commons" to illustrate why this is so and how damage to the environment results. Suppose you are raising sheep, and you and your neighbors share a commons, a common piece of land for grazing. To increase your income, you want to raise more sheep and graze them on the commons. If you do, you may damage the commons by overgrazing, but you will gain the entire bene-

efit of raising additional sheep and share only part of the cost of the damage done to the commons. So you add another sheep to your herd, and then perhaps another. Everyone else using the commons makes the same calculation, however, and in their own self-interest, they add to their herds. Eventually, overgrazing is severe enough to destroy the commons.

Without government intervention, the physical environment is much like this grazing commons. Individuals gain by using it, even polluting it, but society as a whole bears the cost of the damage. When people act on the basis of their individual self-interests, they end up degrading the environment. How, then, can the environment be saved?

Saving the Environment

Since 1970 a number of methods have been used to bring environmental problems under control.

First, various *antipollution laws* have been passed. Initially, industry tended to resist them because of their expense. Unions sometimes opposed them because of fear that jobs would be lost as a result of the cost to industry. Some consumers objected to the laws because they feared prices would rise too high if industry was forced to reduce pollution. Therefore, state governments were often reluctant to make or enforce their own pollution-control laws for fear that companies would move their businesses elsewhere. But as pollution has continued to worsen, popular support for the laws has increased significantly (Wald, 1990).

Conservation provides a second method of reducing our negative impact on the environment. During the late 1970s, the federal and state governments took many steps to encourage the conservation of energy. People were urged to insulate their homes, turn down the thermostat in cold months, drive smaller cars at lower speeds, and ride buses and trains. The government began to offer tax credits and direct subsidies to encourage energy conservation. We were reminded that most European countries use far less energy than the United States while maintaining a high standard of living. Conservation efforts combined with rising energy prices and economic recession to produce a drop in our energy use from 1979 to 1982 that was greater than experts had thought possible. Recycling, aside from combating pollution, provided another means of conserving energy and raw materials. Today, conservation has become popular. According to one poll, for example, more than 80 percent of people are willing to separate their trash for recycling, to give up plastic containers and superfluous packaging to reduce waste, and to favor a ban on disposable diapers (Rosewicz, 1990).

A third approach to dealing with environmental problems focuses on the development of *new, alternative technology* that is efficient, safe, and clean. Changes in automobiles illustrate this approach. Since the early 1970s, the fuel efficiency of cars has been increased and their polluting emissions have been reduced. Especially in the last ten years, the widespread use of catalytic converters in cars has greatly reduced two types of pollutants emitted by tailpipes: carbon monoxide and nitrogen oxide. Industrial scrubbers have also been used to remove much of the sulfur dioxide—the major ingredient of acid rain—from the process of producing energy from coal. More recently, scientists have been trying to develop photovoltaic cells to produce electricity directly from the sun, without releasing any pollutants into the air. The solar cells are expected to be in widespread use in the sunny Southwest later this decade, when they become cheaper than conventional power sources. By using energy more efficiently and at less cost, the new technology would make the U.S. economy more productive and more competitive internationally (Wald, 1990; Stevens, 1992)

Limiting both population and economic growth is a fourth way of solving environmental problems. As

Recycling provides a means of conserving energy and raw materials and of combating pollution. In 1993, the Illinois Power Company began to burn 7.5 million used tires a year as a source of fuel. Tires are cheaper to burn and produce lower sulfur emissions than the coal used in Illinois.

John Firor (1990) observes, nearly every environmental problem, be it acid rain, global warming, or ozone depletion, is first driven and then made worse by growth in the world's population. By stemming population growth, we will go a long way toward reducing environmental pollution and resource depletion. As we saw in Chapter 13 (Health and Population), rich countries have done much better than poor countries in curbing population growth. This is achieved primarily by abandoning the traditional value that favors having many children.

But most countries, rich or poor, have not abandoned the traditional value that favors economic growth with little regard to its *environmental* cost. Gross national product (GNP) is still measured the old-fashioned way: by adding the total value of goods and services *without* subtracting the value of clean air, water, ground, trees, fish, animals, human health, and other ecological elements that have been harmed by the production process—as if these were free goods rather than assets that are being lost. Thus, without taking into account the environmental impact of economic production, a large economic growth measured as a great increase in GNP does not *truly* represent a country's wealth, the welfare of its citizens, or the value of its goods and services. Environmentalists have therefore called on governments and industries to stop pursuing this old kind of economic growth, which harms the environment, and to start seeking a "green," ecologically safe economic growth (Simon, 1990; Commoner, 1990).

Questions for Discussion and Review

1. What major environmental problems now challenge the ecosystems of modern industrial societies?
2. Why can't technology solve all the problems of diminishing resources and environmental pollution?
3. How does the "Tragedy of the Commons" help explain environmental destruction?
4. How can environmental destruction be brought under control?

A GLOBAL ANALYSIS OF URBANIZATION

In 1693, William Penn wrote that "the country life is to be preferred for there we see the works of God, but in cities little else than the work of man." Most people at the time probably agreed with him. Less than 2 percent of the world's population then were urban dwellers. But, today, about 39 percent of the world's population lives in urban areas, and more than 50 percent will do so by the end of the century (Fischer, 1984; Linden, 1993).

While urban populations have grown, cities themselves have changed. We can identify three periods in their history: the preindustrial, industrial, and metropolitan-megalopolitan stages.

The Preindustrial City

For more than 99 percent of the time since human beings appeared on earth, our ancestors roamed about in search of food. They hunted, fished, and gathered edible plants, but they could never find enough food in one place to sustain them for very long. They had to move on, traveling in small bands from one place to another.

Then, about 10,000 years ago, technological advances allowed people to stop their wandering. This was the dawn of what is called the *Neolithic period*. People now had the simple tools and the know-how to cultivate plants and domesticate animals. They could produce their food supplies in one locale, and they settled down and built villages. The villages were very small—only about 200 to 400 residents each. For the next 5000 years, villagers produced just enough food to feed themselves.

By about 5000 years ago, humans had developed more powerful technologies. Thanks to innovations like the ox-drawn plow, irrigation, and metallurgy, farmers could produce more food than they needed to sustain themselves and their families. Because of this food surplus, some people abandoned agriculture and made their living by weaving, making pottery, and practicing other specialized crafts. Methods of transporting and storing food were also improved. The result was the emergence of cities (Childe, 1952).

Cities first arose on the fertile banks of such rivers as the Nile of Egypt, the Euphrates and Tigris in the Middle East, the Indus in Pakistan, and the Yellow River in China. Similar urban settlements later appeared in other parts of the world. These *preindustrial cities* were small compared with the cities of today. Most had populations of 5000 to 10,000 people. Only a few cities had more than 100,000 people, and even Rome never had more than several hundred thousand.

Several factors prevented expansion of the preindustrial city. By modern standards, agricultural techniques were still primitive. It took at least 75 farmers to produce enough of a surplus to support just one city dweller. For transportation, people had to depend on their own muscle power or that of animals. It was difficult to carry food supplies from farms to cities, and even more difficult to transport heavy materials for construction in the cities. Poor sanitation, lack of sewer facilities, and ineffective medicine kept death rates high. Epidemics regularly killed as much as half of a city's population. Moreover, families still had a strong attachment to the land, which discouraged immigration to the cities. All these characteristics of preindustrial society kept the cities small (Davis, 1955).

The Industrial City

For almost 5000 years, cities changed little. Then their growth, in size and number, was so rapid it has been called an urban revolution or urban explosion. In 1700 less than 2 percent of the population in Great Britain lived in cities, but by 1900 the majority of the British did so. Other European countries and the United States soon achieved the same level of urbanization in an even shorter period.

The major stimulus to this urban explosion was the Industrial Revolution. It triggered a series of related events, identified by sociologist Philip Hauser (1981) as population explosion, followed by population displosion and population implosion, and then by technoplosion. Industrialization first causes a rise in production growth, and the mechanization of agriculture brings about a farm surplus. Fewer farmers can support more people—and thus larger urban pop-

Above: Food surpluses, which enabled some people to abandon agriculture and practice specialized crafts, as well as improved methods of transporting and storing food, allowed for the emergence of the preindustrial city, represented here by the Aztec's capital city of Tenochtitlán. Left: The emergence of the industrial city came about largely as a result of changes begun by the Industrial Revolution.

ulations *(population explosion).* Workers no longer needed on the farms move to the city. There is, then, displacement of people from rural to urban areas *(population displosion)* and a greater concentration of people in a limited area *(population implosion).* The development of other new technologies (a *technoplosion*) spurs urbanization on. Improved transportation, for example, speeds the movement of food and other materials to urban centers.

The outcome of these events was the *industrial city.* Compared with the preindustrial city, the industrial city was larger, more densely settled, and more diverse. It was a place where large numbers of people—with different skills, interests, and cultural backgrounds—could live and work together in a limited space. Also, unlike the preindustrial city, which had served primarily as a religious or governmental center, the industrial city was a commercial hub. In fact, its abundant job opportunities attracted so many rural migrants that migration accounted for the largest share of its population growth. Without these migrants, cities would not have grown at all, because

of the high mortality rate brought about by extremely poor sanitary conditions.

Metropolis and Megalopolis

Early in this century, the large cities of the industrialized nations began to spread outward. They formed **metropolises,** large urban areas that include a city and its surrounding suburbs. Some of these suburbs are politically separate from their central cities, but socially, economically, and geographically, the suburbs and city are tied together. The U.S. Census Bureau recognizes this unity by defining what is called a *Standard Metropolitan Statistical Area,* which cuts across political boundaries. Since 1990 most U.S. residents have been living in metropolitan areas with a million residents or more (Suro, 1991).

In the United States, the upper and middle classes have usually sparked the expansion of cities outward. Typically, as migrants from rural areas moved into the central city, the better-off classes moved to the suburbs. The automobile greatly facilitated this development. It encouraged people to leave the crowded inner city for the more comfortable life of the suburbs, if they could afford it. As the number of cars increased, so did the size of suburbs and metropolises. In 1900 there were only 8000 cars in the United States; by 1930 the number had soared to more than 26 million. Meanwhile, the proportion of the U.S. population living in the suburbs grew from only 15.7 percent in 1910 to 48.6 percent in 1950 (Glaab and Brown, 1983).

Since 1950, virtually all the growth in metropolitan areas has occurred in the suburbs. During the 1960s, U.S. suburbs grew four times faster than inner cities, and stores and entertainment facilities followed the people there. Suburban jobs increased 44 percent, while inner-city employment dropped 7 percent. This pattern of suburban growth at the expense of the urban core continued in the 1970s and 1980s. Today, suburbanites outnumber city residents three to two (Jaret, 1983; Gottdiener, 1983; U.S. Census Bureau, 1994).

As suburbs expand, they sometimes combine with the suburbs of adjacent metropolitan areas to form a **megalopolis,** a vast area in which many metropolises merge. For hundreds of miles from one major city to the next, suburbs and cities have merged with one another to form a continuous region in which distinctions between suburban, urban, and rural areas are blurred. The hundreds of miles from Boston to Washington, D.C. form one such megalopolis, another stretches from Detroit through Chicago to Milwaukee in the Midwest, and another goes from San Francisco to San Diego.

The World's Megacities

The world's urban population has grown so fast that today there are about 40 **megacities**—cities with populations of 5 million or more. Generally, the poorer the country, the faster its urban growth. Thus, today, only three of the world's megacities are in the United States, and more than half are in developing countries (see Figure 14.1). Many more in the developing world will soon become megacities.

Since the emergence of the preindustrial city 5000 years ago, great cities have risen and fallen. The same is true today. One city that is collapsing is Kinshasa, the capital of Zaire (see Figure 14.1). Although the country is endowed with abundant natural resources such as gold, diamonds, copper, and rich agricultural land, Kinshasa has produced massive miseries under the corrupt 27-year reign of President Mobutu. Government officials have routinely looted fuel, manufactured goods, food, and medical supplies, even most of the emergency food aid sent by foreign countries. As a result, the annual inflation rate often goes up more than 3000 percent and the jobless rate stands

FIGURE 14.1
Megacities Around the World
Generally, the poorer the country, the faster its urban growth. Today more than half of the world's megacities (cities with 5 million or more people) are in developing countries.

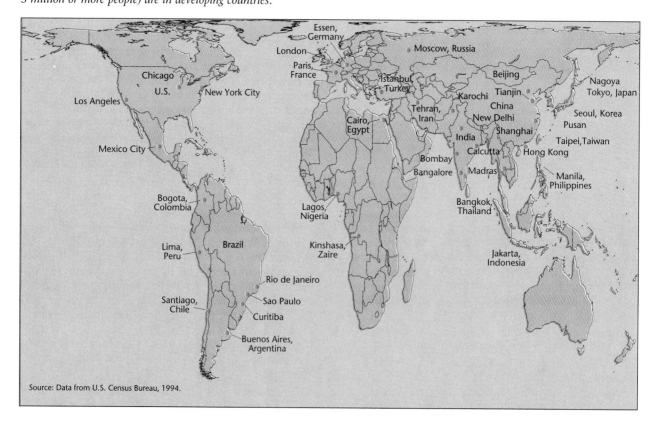

Source: Data from U.S. Census Bureau, 1994.

at 80 percent, posing serious threats of starvation and epidemics. In contrast, the city of Curitiba in Brazil is a success story. The city is not rich, but its government makes the most of its resources. One example is recycling: parks are lit with lamps made from soda bottles, and some government offices were built in part with old telephone poles. The city further delivers excellent services, including a highly efficient bus system and well-constructed housing projects for the poor (Linden, 1993).

In between those two contrasting types, most megacities are saddled with serious problems but manage to cope reasonably well, usually in ways that reflect the nature of their societies. Consider three cities:

1. Tokyo, the world's largest city, with 28.4 million people, faces such enormous problems as traffic-choked streets, sky-high housing costs, and over-whelming waste. But the technologically advanced Japanese have, among other things, developed the "Urban Heat System" to extract heat from sewage, which is then used to regulate temperatures in several of Tokyo's buildings.

2. Mexico City, the world's second largest city, has grown so fast that air pollution is a severe problem. But the Mexican devotion to community will likely solve the problem, just as it saved the city from collapse after the 1985 earthquake.

3. New York City, the world's fifth largest, is full of poverty, crime, and other signs of urban decay. But the city is likely to survive because it has a history of rising from its ashes. After losing its pre-eminence as a port and a manufacturing center, New York City has now become a leader in finance, the media, design, advertising, and the arts (Linden, 1993).

Questions for Discussion and Review

1. What accounted for the emergence of the preindustrial city?
2. How does the industrial city differ from the preindustrial city?
3. What forces have led to the development of suburbs, metropolises, and, finally, megalopolises?
4. What problems do megacities have and how can the problems be tackled?

CITIES IN THE UNITED STATES

Cities around the world are similar in some ways, such as being overcrowded, polluted, and in need of ways to solve their problems. But cities also vary from one society to another. Here we focus on the cities in the United States.

A Demographic Profile

In general, the poor and minority groups concentrate in the inner cities and more affluent people live in the suburbs. A closer look, however, led sociologist Herbert Gans (1968) to find five types of people in many cities:

1. Cosmopolites—artists, intellectuals, professionals
2. Unmarried individuals and childless couples
3. "Ethnic villagers"—immigrants from other countries
4. The deprived—the poor, including many African Americans and other minorities
5. The trapped—poor elderly people

These groups are not likely to feel strong ties to each other or to the city as a whole. The deprived and the trapped are too poor to move—they live in the city by necessity, not by choice. The ethnic villagers are likely to be strongly tied only to fellow immigrants in their neighborhoods. The unmarried and childless have ties mostly to those who share their lifestyle. Cosmopolites associate primarily with those who share their interests.

The movement of African Americans into the central city has been especially striking. Just 50 years ago, less than half of the black population was urban. Today, a large majority live in urban areas, and most of these in the inner cities. Several large cities are already predominantly black. For years African Americans entering the city came from the rural South, but now most of these migrants come from other urban areas. Compared with the inner-city natives, these later migrants rank higher in education and employment and have lower rates of crime. Some middle-class African Americans have joined the exodus to the suburbs, but they move mostly to black suburbs.

The number of cosmopolites, young professionals, adult singles, and childless couples in the inner city has also grown significantly. Increasing numbers of these affluent people now choose to remain in the inner city. They buy run-down buildings and renovate them into elegant townhouses and expensive condominiums. This urban revival is called **gentrification,** the movement of affluent people into poor urban neighborhoods. It has transformed poor neighborhoods into such stylish enclaves as Capitol Hill in Washington, Philadelphia's Queen Village, Boston's South End, Cincinnati's Mount Adams, and Chicago's New Town. To a large extent, urban rehabilitation programs have stimulated gentrification by selling abandoned homes and stores for the price of a few dollars and offering low-interest mortgage loans. Ironically, though, gentrification tends to drive up rents and property taxes, forcing poor and elderly residents to give up their homes to the well-off gentrifiers. However, gentrification has not been extensive enough to transform most of the city. In the last decade, nearly twice as many people have been moving from central cities to suburbs as those moving in the opposite direction. Central cities continue to lose residents, a trend that began in the early 1970s.

Edge Cities

Most suburbs still offer better schools, more living space, less pollution, and less crime than the central city, so people continue to "vote with their feet" and head for suburbia. More than a decade ago, most suburbs were largely bedroom communities: their residents commuted to the nearby cities to work. But in the last ten years, a new kind of suburbanization has taken place—involving not only people and homes but also offices and jobs—that has transformed many suburbs into economic centers.

In these suburbs, new office buildings, factories, and warehouses have sprung up alongside the housing subdivisions and shopping malls. Developers have already created vast clusters of big buildings, people, and cars. Thus, many suburbs, in effect, have become cities in their own right. Unlike the traditional U.S. city, where diverse businesses operate, the new suburban cities, also popularly called *edge cities*, are typically focused on a principal activity, such as a collection of computer companies, a large regional medical center, or a sports or recreation complex. The growth of edge cities, therefore, has taken away many jobs from the urban cores. Despite the arrival of some nonwhite residents, the edge cities are generally "whiter" than the inner cities (Suro, 1991).

Recent Trends

The latest U.S. census reveals a number of significant changes in U.S. cities over the last decade. As long expected by sociologists, many cities in the West and Southwest, particularly California, have grown significantly larger, while many northeastern and midwestern cities have experienced population declines. However, some changes have largely gone unnoticed.

First, older industrial cities in the South have fallen into the same cycle of decline as their northern counterparts. These cities include Atlanta, Georgia;

Birmingham, Alabama; and Chattanooga, Tennessee. They represent half of all the big U.S. cities that have lost population since 1980.

Second, immigration has served as a brake against population decline in major cities such as New York, Miami, and New Jersey's Elizabeth and Jersey City. With a large influx of immigrants from countries such as India, China, the Philippines, and the Dominican Republic, these cities have registered some population gain rather than decline (Salins, 1991).

Third, although California's population growth was expected to be significant, it has turned out to be astonishing. Of the 29 U.S. cities that have surpassed the population mark of 100,000, most are in California. Seven of the ten fastest-growing, large U.S.

A recent trend observed in U.S. cities has been an influx of immigrants. New residents from such countries as India, China, the Philippines, and the Dominican Republic have enabled some major U.S. cities to record modest population gains, rather than declines.

cities are in Southern California: Bakersfield, Irvine, and Escondido, for example.

Fourth, a large majority (two-thirds) of state capitals have gained population, even though the states themselves have stagnated. North Dakota, for example, lost 1.7 percent of its population, but its capital, Bismarck, had a gain of 10.7 percent. Most cities that are within a declining state but that have a college or university have also grown larger. Examples are Lawrence, Kansas, home of the University of Kansas, and West Lafayette, Indiana, the site of Purdue University (Barringer, 1991b).

Questions for Discussion and Review

1. What kinds of people are most likely to live in U.S. cities?
2. How do today's edge cities differ from traditional suburbs?
3. How have U.S. cities changed over the last decade?

THE URBAN ENVIRONMENT

As we observed earlier, ecologists study the natural world to see how everything in it is related to everything else. Organisms affect other organisms and they all affect the environment, which in turn affects them. During the 1920s and 1930s, some sociologists at the University of Chicago began to look at the urban world in a similar way. They initiated a new approach to the study of cities called **urban ecology,** the study of the relationship between people and their urban environment.

Spatial Patterns

Like a natural environment, the urban environment is not a random arrangement of elements. Walking around a city, we rarely see a mansion next to a poor neighborhood, or an apartment next to a factory. Different areas tend to be used for different purposes. As a result, the people, activities, and buildings within a city are distributed in certain patterns. The urban ecologists tried to describe these patterns and how they arose. Three prominent theories came out of their efforts, as shown in Figure 14.2.

Concentric-Zone Theory In the 1920s, Ernest Burgess presented the **concentric-zone theory,** the model of land use in which the city spreads out from the center in a series of concentric zones, each used for a particular kind of activity. The heart of the city is the

central business district. This innermost zone is occupied by shops, banks, offices, hotels, and government buildings. The next zone is the transition zone, characterized by shabby rooming houses, deteriorating apartments, and high crime rates. The third zone is in better shape. It is made up of working people's homes. Beyond it is a zone that houses mostly middle-class people, and beyond that is the commuters' zone, with large homes and plenty of open space. The rich live here, and commute to the city to work (Burgess, 1925).

According to this theory, social class has a lot to do with spatial distribution: the farther a piece of land is from the center of the city, the higher the status of those using it. However, land values tend to *drop* with distance from the center of the city. Thus, the pattern of land use has a rather perverse result: the poor live on expensive land and the rich on relatively cheap land (Alonso, 1964).

The concentric-zone theory describes some U.S. cities fairly well, especially those such as Chicago and St. Louis that grew rapidly early in this century under the stimulus of intense industrialization and the automobile. But many cities do not have concentric zones.

Sector Theory Henry Hoyt in the late 1930s proposed the **sector theory,** the model of land use in which a city grows outward in wedge-shaped sectors from the center. Hoyt agreed with concentric-zone theorists that a city grows outward from the center, and that the center is occupied by the central business district. But, Hoyt said, growth occurs in wedge-shaped sectors that extend outward from the city, not in concentric circles. As a result, low-class housing occurs not just close to the business district but in a band extending from the center outward, perhaps to the rim of the city. The key to the extension of a sector is transportation. If, say, warehouses are built along a railroad, they tend to expand along the length of the railroad toward the periphery of the city. Similarly, a retail district might expand along a highway. The poor tend to live along transportation lines near factories, whereas the rich tend to choose areas that are on the fastest lines of transportation and occupy high ground, safe from floods and offering beautiful views (Hoyt, 1943). San Francisco and Minneapolis illustrate the sector pattern.

Multiple-Nuclei Theory Boston is one of many cities that do not show either wedge-shaped sectors or concentric zones. It seems to be described better by yet a third theory, which was proposed by Chauncy Harris and Edward Ullman in the 1940s. Unlike the concentric and sector theories, which suggest that each city is built around one center, Harris and Ullman's **multiple-nuclei theory** describes a model of land use in which a city is built around

FIGURE 14.2
Cities' Spatial Patterns
A diagram of the three theories about the shapes and locations of various districts within a typical U.S. city.

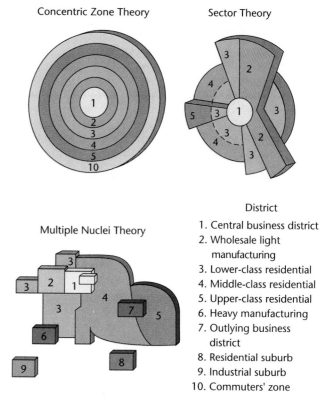

Concentric Zone Theory

Sector Theory

Multiple Nuclei Theory

District

1. Central business district
2. Wholesale light manufacturing
3. Lower-class residential
4. Middle-class residential
5. Upper-class residential
6. Heavy manufacturing
7. Outlying business district
8. Residential suburb
9. Industrial suburb
10. Commuters' zone

Source: Reprinted from "The Nature of Cities," by Chauncy D. Harris and Edward L. Ullman, in *Annals of the American Academy of Political and Social Sciences*, Nov. 1945, p. 13.

many discrete nuclei, each being the center of some specialized activity. There are centers of finance and commerce, which are separate from the political center, which in turn is separate from the center of heavy industries, and so on.

These separate nuclei, according to Harris and Ullman, arise as a result of at least three factors. First, some activities require specialized facilities. Manufacturing districts must be located on large blocks of land with easy connections to railroads or water transportation; a port district must be attached to a suitable waterfront. Second, similar activities often profit from being grouped together. If retail stores are concentrated in one district, they all profit from an increased number of potential customers, who are usually attracted by the chance to compare the offerings of various stores. Third, putting dissimilar activities together in one location often harms them. Factories and homes do not mix well. Wholesale districts, which require street loading and rail facilities, stay away from retail districts, which need many pedestrians, cars, and buses (Harris and Ullman, 1945).

These three theories are largely valuable for depicting the major patterns of some of our cities, such as Chicago, San Francisco, and Boston. But because the theories were based on studies of U.S. cities, they are less applicable to land-use patterns in other countries, where, for example, upper-class residences are close to the center of the city rather than far away from it. The theories are also less accurate in describing many U.S. cities today. Most of the middle and white working classes no longer live in inner cities but in edge cities. Many factories, office complexes, wholesale and retail trade, and jobs involving people (retail sales, medical services, food service) have further moved out of the urban center.

Ecological Processes

How do these urban spatial patterns come about? Nowadays, city governments often use zoning laws and building codes to determine the patterns of land use and to segregate activities. But many patterns arose without anyone planning them, forming what are called *natural areas* of segregated activities. Urban ecologists believed that two forms of human behavior are most important in shaping the urban environment: dominance and competition. A group of people typically concentrate in a particular area of the city for a specific purpose, dominating that area. Businesses, for example, usually dominate the center of U.S. cities. Sometimes, a group achieves dominance only after competing with others to determine how the land will be used. Businesses and residents often clash over land use in a city. Businesses can usually win by buying out the land at a high price, forcing residents to move. Universities often engage in a similar competition with residents. Thus, the use of land in a city is determined directly by *dominance* and indirectly by *competition*.

The city, however, is not static. Instead, over time a new group or type of land use will move into an established area, a process called *invasion*. If the new group forces others out, *succession* has occurred. The process of gentrification discussed earlier is an example: Young professionals invade an urban neighborhood, raising land values and rents, and eventually they push out its lower-income residents, who can no longer afford the neighborhood. This reverses the traditional pattern of succession that shaped many U.S. cities. As industries, immigrants, and minorities moved into the cities, those who were better off moved out to the suburbs, and their neighborhoods "filtered down" to the lower class.

Dominance, competition, invasion, and succession constitute what are called the **urban ecological processes,** processes in which people compete for certain land use, one group dominates another, and a particular group moves into an area and takes it over from others.

Questions for Discussion and Review

1. According to the three theories of land use, what do cities look like?
2. How do urban ecological processes shape a city?

THE NATURE OF CITY LIFE

In 1964 people were horrified by a story that many took as typical of life in New York City—or any large city. A young woman named Kitty Genovese was walking home from work in the early morning hours when she was attacked. Her murderer stabbed her repeatedly for more than half an hour. Thirty-eight neighbors heard her screams or witnessed the attack. But no one helped or even called the police. Most of the neighbors later explained that they did not want to "get involved." A

TABLE 14.1
The Nature of City Life

Urban anomie theory	City people have a unique way of life, characterized by alienation, impersonal relations, and stress.
Compositional theory	City dwellers are as involved with small groups of friends, relatives, and neighbors as are noncity people.
Subcultural theory	The city enriches people's lives by offering diverse opportunities and developing various subcultures.

similar incident took place in Detroit in 1995: Dozens of bystanders did nothing to prevent a young woman from being violently assaulted by a man, and some onlookers even cheered as the woman jumped off a bridge to escape her attacker and fell to her death (Stokes, 1995).

What could cause such cold-bloodedness? Many commentators blamed the city. Living in a city, they believed, changes people for the worse. This charge echoed what some sociologists had long been saying. Louis Wirth, for example, contended in the 1930s that the conditions of the city produce a distinctive way of life, *urbanism,* and that the urban environment harms the people who live there. His analysis represented the ecological approach of the Chicago school. Since Wirth's time, some sociologists have supported his view. Richard Sennett (1991), for example, criticizes city life for insulating people from others who are racially, socially, or economically different. But many other sociologists have rejected Wirth's view. Some have argued that the city does not make much difference in people's lives, and others contend that the urban environment enriches people's lives by creating and strengthening subcultures. These three theories about the nature of urban life, summarized in Table 14.1, are called urban anomie theory, compositional theory, and subcultural theory.

Urban Anomie Theory

In 1938 Louis Wirth presented his **urban anomie theory,** arguing that city people have a unique way of life, characterized by alienation, impersonal relations, and stress. According to Wirth, the urban environment has three distinctive features: huge population size, high population density, and great social diversity. These characteristics, Wirth argued, have both a sociological and a psychological impact, producing social and personality disorders.

In the city, people are physically close but socially distant. Every day they encounter strangers. They become accustomed to dealing with people only in terms of their roles. Their relationships tend to be impersonal. In other words, much of their lives are filled, not with primary relations with neighbors, who are also relatives and friends, but with secondary relations. Moreover, these people are separated by diverse religious, ethnic, and racial backgrounds. It is difficult, argued Wirth, for people in the city to form friendships across these lines or to develop a moral consensus. Under these circumstances, people can no longer ensure social order by relying on informal controls such as tradition and gossip. Instead, they turn to formal controls, such as the police. Rather than talking to a young troublemaker's parents, they call the police. But formal controls, Wirth contended, are less effective than informal controls, so crimes and other forms of deviance are more frequent in the city than in the countryside.

The size, density, and diversity of the city, according to Wirth, also damage the psychological health of its residents by making life stressful. Much of the stress comes from being bombarded with various kinds of stimuli. Sights, sounds, and smells assault urbanites virtually every minute of their waking hours. Wherever they turn, they must contend with the actions of others. They are jostled on the street and in the elevator. They wake to the sound of their neighbor's radio and fall asleep despite screaming sirens. Panhandlers, staggering inebriates, and soliloquizing mental patients are a common sight. All may make people feel irritable, nervous, anxious. The result, Wirth claimed, is that mental disorders are more common in the city than in rural areas.

Compositional Theory

Wirth's description of the urban environment and its effects sounds reasonable. But is it accurate? Many empirical studies of cities have shown that his portrait amounts to an overdrawn stereotype. Some sociologists have instead proposed a **compositional theory,** arguing that city dwellers are as involved with small groups of friends, relatives, and neighbors as are noncity people.

Perhaps the crucial difference between the urban anomie and compositional theorists concerns the influence of the urban environment on primary relations. Wirth argued that city life is impersonal, that the city erodes primary relations. But compositional theorists contend that no matter how big, how dense, how diverse the city is, people continue to be deeply involved with a small circle of friends and relatives and others who have similar lifestyles, backgrounds, or personalities. In this small social world, they find protection from the harsher, impersonal world of strangers.

Many studies show that there is indeed a significant amount of social cohesion within cities, as compositional theorists contend. Herbert Gans (1982a), for example, has found that people in ethnic neighborhoods of large cities have a strong sense of community loyalty. He found the solidarity in these neighborhoods impressive enough to call them "ethnic villages." Other researchers have also found that city residents carry on their personal lives much as people in rural areas do, such as visiting relatives at least once a week (Palisi and Canning, 1983). What about studies that show higher rates of crime and mental illness in urban than in rural areas? According to compositional theorists, these disorders are not *created* by the urban environment itself. Instead, they result from the *demographic makeup* of the city—from the fact that the urban population includes a high percentage of those categories of people likely to suffer from social and mental disorders. Examples are young unmarried individuals and the lower classes.

Subcultural Theory

Claude Fischer (1984) presented a **subcultural theory** of urban life, arguing that the city enriches people's lives by offering diverse opportunities and developing various subcultures. While urban anomie theorists emphasize the negative impact of city life, Fischer stresses the positive. In his view, the urban environment creates and strengthens various groups of people. These groups are, in effect, *subcultures*—culturally distinctive groups, such as college students, African Americans, artists, corporate executives, and so forth. These subcultures are able to emerge because of the great population size, density, and diversity of the city, and the clash of subcultures within a city may strengthen each of them. When people come in contact with individuals from other subcultures, Fischer (1984) wrote, they "sometimes rub against one another only to recoil, with sparks flying.... People from one subculture often find people in another subculture threatening, offensive, or both. A common reaction is to embrace one's own social world all the more firmly, thus contributing to its further intensification."

Fischer has also argued that the urban experience brings some personal benefits to city dwellers. For example, urban housing, when compared to rural housing, generally has better plumbing facilities and is

People in ethnic neighborhoods in large cities have a strong sense of community loyalty. Sociologist Herbert Gans has found the solidarity in these neighborhoods impressive enough to call them "ethnic villages."

less crowded. Compared with people in the country, city people have access to far more facilities, services, and opportunities. As Harvey Cox (1966) noted, "Residents of a city of 10,000 may be limited to one or two theaters, while people who live in a city of a million can choose among perhaps 50 films on a given night. The same principle holds for restaurants, schools, and even in some measure for job opportunities or prospective marriage partners."

Each of the three theories presents only a partial truth about city life. As urban anomie theory suggests, residents of large cities are usually much less satisfied with their neighborhoods than are their counterparts in small towns (Lee and Guest, 1983). At the same time, city life is not as bad as popularly believed. People do lead normal, pleasant lives in the city with friends and subcultural groups, as compositional and subcultural theories suggest. But all the theories fail to capture the ambivalence people feel toward cities. According to a survey, most New Yorkers consider their city an urban hellhole, with all its crime, poverty, homelessness, racial tension, heavy taxes, high rents, filth, and official corruption. Still, they very much like living in "the Big Apple." To them, "the pulse and pace and convenient, go-all-night action of the city, its rich ethnic and cultural stew, still outweigh its horrors" (Blundell, 1986). Indeed, many urbanites throughout the United States seem to consider the horrors a fair price for the freedom of expression they enjoy in the city. Those who find the price too high generally choose to leave the city for the suburb (Lapham, 1992).

Questions for Discussion and Review

1. According to urban anomie theory, how does the city affect people's life?
2. In what ways are compositional and subcultural theories similar and in what ways are they different?

CAUSES OF URBAN PROBLEMS

Almost every problem in U.S. society—drug abuse and crime, racism and poverty, poor education and environmental pollution—seems more severe in the cities, particularly in the older and more congested ones. Even as newer cities grow and age, their problems will probably become more severe. The difficulties that cities face and their ability to deal with them are shaped to a great extent by the intertwining effects of various social forces. We discuss some of them here.

Population Decline

In the last ten years Detroit, Cleveland, Pittsburgh, St. Louis, and other big cities have lost more than 10 percent of their populations. In fact, most of the cities that have more than 200,000 people have suffered population declines (U.S. Census Bureau, 1994). On the face of it, this may look like good news for the cities' finances:

Fewer people should mean less demand for, and less spending on, police protection, fire protection, education, and other public services. In reality, however, population decreases have created serious problems.

As the years go by, a city must spend more on maintaining its road, sewer, and water networks, even if it has fewer residents to pay for those services. Similarly, when families abandon the central city, the need for police and fire protection increases, because abandoned homes can become magnets for vandalism and crime. They become fire hazards and finally must be torn down at the city's expense. Furthermore, behind the statistics of declining populations lies the fact that those who move out of the cities are largely middle-class whites, and with them go many businesses. Thus, the cities have fewer private-sector jobs and declining revenues. Those left behind in the city are typically less educated, poorer, and older—the people most in need of government spending for education, housing, health services, and welfare.

Fiscal Squeeze

In large part, urban problems stem from the city government's inability to generate sufficient income to provide various kinds of service to the public. Cities get most of their revenues from taxes on property, income, sales, and corporations. Some money can come from charging fees for services. But all these revenues have shrunk over the last decade: the suburbs have drained off much of the cities' tax base by attracting industries and stores and middle-class and upper-class people.

There are other potential sources of revenue, but cities generally cannot tap these sources. In many states, cities are prohibited from raising as much in taxes as they wish. Cities are also deprived of other revenue-producing opportunities: When federal and state governments use city property, they are exempted from paying city taxes worth billions of dollars. Suburbanites come into town, adding to traffic congestion, garbage, and wear and tear on roads and parks, while benefiting from police protection and other urban resources, but they pay no taxes to the city for these services. Consequently, since the 1960s cities have come to depend increasingly on the state and federal governments to help pay their bills. Since the late 1980s, however, the federal government has been forced by its huge budget deficit to end its revenue-sharing program.

Political Dilemma

Part of the cities' fiscal problem originates with elected officials' unwillingness to raise taxes even if they have the power to do so and their citizens have the ability to pay. Given the unpopularity of tax increases, politicians tend to avoid risking taxpayers' anger even when taxes are low and necessary. But this political dilemma seems to have forced the cities to rely increasingly on private enterprise to tackle urban problems.

With their eyes on economic development, cities compete with one another to keep or attract businesses and industries. Low taxes and tax exemptions are used as lures. Although this may undermine the current tax base, the cities hope to build a larger tax base, through an increase in jobs, for the future.

Cities also set up **enterprise zones,** economically depressed urban areas that businesses, with the help of generous tax credits, try to revive by creating jobs. In the late 1980s the U.S. Congress voted against a bill designed to create 75 enterprise zones around the country. A majority of states have nonetheless proceeded on their own, creating thousands of jobs for the poor residents of the special zones (Carlson, 1991). A similar effort to solve public ills with private cures has appeared. Grass-roots entrepreneurs known as CDCs—community development corporations—have rehabilitated abandoned homes, created commercial enterprises, and organized social services in various large cities. Their objective is to succeed where governments have failed—by reclaiming city streets from crime and economic decline (*New York Times,* 1991).

Housing Segregation

Every year billions of dollars are spent on housing in the United States. The government helps out by granting billions in tax deductions to landlords and homeowners. As a result, we are among the best-housed people in the world, with most of the nation's families owning their own homes. But it has become more difficult financially to own or rent a home. Housing problems are most severe for the nation's minorities. For one thing, minorities, especially African Americans, make up a high percentage of the population of the inner cities, where good housing at reasonable prices is increasingly scarce. While most blacks living in metropolitan areas are concentrated in the inner cities, most of the metropolitan whites are spread out in the surrounding suburbs. In both the inner cities and in the suburbs, blacks are frequently segregated from whites, with the housing of blacks being inferior to that of whites.

Economics may be a factor in the segregation. Because African Americans tend to have lower incomes, they often cannot afford to move into more expensive white neighborhoods. But racial discrimination is an even bigger factor. Real estate agents tend to steer potential black buyers and renters away from white neighborhoods, perpetuating segregation. Banks are often more cautious in granting loans to blacks than to whites, making it difficult for blacks to own or rehabilitate homes and thus encouraging the deterioration of black neighborhoods. Many blacks will not move into white neighborhoods because they wish to avoid rejection by whites (Hayes, 1990).

Questions for Discussion and Review

1. What impact does population decline have on a city?
2. Why do many cities have serious financial problems?
3. How have cities dealt with the political dilemma of raising taxes?
4. What factors contribute to housing segregation?

PERSPECTIVES ON URBANIZATION

Both the functionalist and conflict perspectives have been used to explain the forces behind the urbanization of U.S. society. To functionalists, the masses of ordinary people seek, and benefit from, urbanization as a way of adapting to their changing environment. To conflict theorists, the real driving force and beneficiary of urbanization is big business. Symbolic interactionists, however, are more interested in explaining how strangers interact with each other in the city.

Functionalist Perspective

A key concept in the functionalist perspective is interdependence. Thus the nature of a city can be said to depend on a set of interrelationships among its different parts. If a city is modern, its most important parts may be people, organization, environment, and technology. Consider how these different parts are interrelated (Palen, 1992):

> In Los Angeles a favorable natural environment was conducive to large-scale population growth, which brought with it organizational problems (civic and governmental) and technological changes (freeways and factories). These in turn led to environmental changes (smog), which resulted in organizational changes (new pollution laws), which in turn resulted in technological changes (antipollution devices on automobiles).

The same concept of interdependence can also explain the process of urbanization in the United States as a whole. First, technology increased agricultural production so much that considerably fewer people were

Both economics and racial discrimination are factors in housing segregation. Because African Americans tend to have lower incomes, they often do not move into more expensive white neighborhoods. Though it is illegal to do so, some realtors also tend to steer potential black buyers away from white neighborhoods, further perpetuating segregation.

needed to work on farms. Second, seeking better job opportunities, throngs of people left farms for the cities, which led to their explosive growth. Third, since these former farmers were mostly manual laborers, their huge numbers in cities helped expand the manufacturing industry, mass-producing everything from shoes to clothes to cars. Fourth, as cities became crowded, increasing numbers of people moved to the outskirts to live while continuing to work in the inner cities, thanks to the mass production of cars. Fifth, as suburbs became increasingly populated, various businesses emerged to cater to the shopping needs of suburbanites, eventually leading to the proliferation of shopping malls. Finally, a cornucopia of jobs was created in the suburbs, so that suburbanites did not need to commute to the inner cities. At this late stage of urbanization, metropolises and megalopolises began to emerge. Functionalists assume that all these social changes benefit the masses by raising their standard of living.

Conflict Perspective

The conflict perspective provides a different picture of urbanization. This perspective stresses the role played by big business in the growth and expansion of cities (Gottdiener, 1985, 1994).

First, in the pursuit of profit, large corporations are said to have bought up huge farmlands and mass-produced food, driving many small family farms into bankruptcy and forcing huge numbers of farmers to leave for the city. In doing so, big business has received considerable assistance from big government as a partner of the ruling elite. The assistance included direct subsidies to business, grants for research and development, low-interest loans, and support of farm-related education.

Second, the expansion of cities into suburbs has resulted from big business "making a killing" in the real estate, construction, and banking industries. Again, with considerable government subsidies and tax deductions, numerous single-family homes were built in the suburbs in the 1950s and 1960s. To induce people to buy these houses, the government guaranteed mortgages as well as providing tax deductions for interest payments. The result was massive suburbanization.

Third, from the 1970s to today, large corporations have helped turn many suburbs into edge cities by moving their businesses and factories there from central cities. This move has been motivated by profit. By building new plants in the suburbs, corporations have intended to avoid problems in central cities such as labor unrest, high city taxes, and other financial costs—or have expected to receive such benefits from the suburbs as cheap land, lower taxes, a local industry-friendly government, and the lack of organized labor.

Symbolic Interactionist Perspective

We can learn much from symbolic interactionists about how strangers interact in cities (Karp, Stone, and Yoels, 1991).

First, city people tend to interact with one another in a superficial, impersonal way. Given the density of the urban population and hence the huge number of potential interpersonal contacts, urbanites have learned to protect themselves from "psychic overload" by shutting out as many sensations as possible, sometimes even the call of a neighbor for help. Thus most interactions with strangers are brief. An example is one person asking another for a street direction and the other person responding by pointing at a street and saying "over there."

Second, city people tend to interact through "civil inattention" as a way of respecting others' desire for privacy in public places. This involves avoiding eye or physical contact in an elevator, a bus, or some other public place. But conversations with strangers do occur under unusual circumstances, as when people are stuck in a stalled elevator or a traffic jam.

Third, city people tend to be tolerant of others' alternative lifestyles, such as different sexual orientations or religious practices. When such people interact, they usually refrain from imposing their values on others or showing disapproval of others' behavior.

Questions for Discussion and Review

1. How do the functionalist and conflict perspectives differ in explaining urbanization?
2. According to symbolic interactionism, how do strangers in the city interact?

THE FUTURE OF U.S. CITIES

Most cities, particularly those in the Northeast and Midwest, will continue to lose population to the suburbs and the country. Most migrants from the city are white and middle class, leaving behind in inner cities a large concentration of black, poor, and elderly people. The trend is toward racially separate communities. Gentrification will continue, but it will not be enough to revive the decaying inner cities. The gentrifiers will create only small enclaves of residential wealth—luxury apartments, townhouses, and condominiums—segregated from the urban poor.

Central cities will suffer more than just the loss of population. As the nation's economy shifts from manufacturing to service, informational, and high-technology industries, businesses will build their plants in edge cities, where most white-collar workers live. But if enterprise zones and other similar programs in inner cities succeed, the loss of blue-collar jobs will stop, and unemployment and poverty will decline.

Finally, the federal government will continue to cut its financial support for the cities. Especially if the federal budget deficit remains enormous, the government can hardly be expected to pump much money into urban programs. On the other hand, the federal government cannot leave the cities out in the cold. There will always be a tension between the conservative impulse toward local control and the liberal tendency toward federal intervention. The federal government will probably continue to tackle problems that are essentially national in scope, such as welfare, Medicaid, and long-term health care, though to a reduced degree. Programs that are local in nature will probably be returned to state and local governments. Such programs may include community-development block grants, mass transit, rural wastewater grants, and vocational education.

Question for Discussion and Review

1. What does the future hold for U.S. cities?

CHAPTER REVIEW

1. *Why are sociologists interested in ecology?* Humans, like other organisms, live within ecosystems, dependent on other organisms and on the physical environment. Thus, we are limited by two ecological principles: One, natural resources are finite. Two, if we alter one aspect of our environment, we end up changing others as well. *What are our basic environmental problems?* They are the depletion of natural resources and pollution. *How is pollution related to consumption?* To consume we must produce, and both production and consumption create waste materials that must go somewhere. When our creation of wastes exceeds nature's capacity to recycle the material, pollution results. *What are the main causes of environmental problems?* Poverty, ignorance, and overconsumption are among the causes. *What are the main methods of saving the environment?* They are antipollution laws, conservation, development of more efficient, less polluting technology, and a slowing of traditional economic and population growth.

2. *What are the main stages in the history of cities?* They are preindustrial, industrial, and metropolitan-megalopolitan. Preindustrial cities began developing about 5000 years ago. They were very small, and people lived where they worked. The industrial city developed when the Industrial Revolution triggered urbanization. During the twentieth century the industrial city spread outward, and the city and its suburbs became interdependent, forming a metropolis and megalopolis. *What is the condition of megacities around the globe?* Megacities have grown faster in the developing world than in the developed world. All are faced with problems, but most are able to solve the problems in ways that reflect the nature of their societies.

3. *Who usually lives in the city, and who lives in the suburbs?* Generally, more affluent people live in the suburbs. The poor and minority groups tend to concentrate in central cities. But typical urban residents also include immigrants, professionals, unmarried individuals, and childless couples. *How have suburbs changed over the last decade?* Many suburbs that used to be residential communities have turned into edge cities, economic centers like central cities. *What changes have occurred in U.S. cities over the last ten years?* Many western and southwestern cities have grown larger, while many northeastern, midwestern, and southern cities have lost population. Some large cities have been rescued from decline by substantial immigration from foreign countries. Most state capitals and college towns have grown larger, even in the midst of their states' decline.

4. *Is there a pattern behind land use in a city?* Yes, but no one pattern characterizes all cities. Three theories explain the patterns found in many U.S. cities. According to concentric-zone theory, cities spread outward from a central business district, forming a series of concentric zones. According to sector theory, cities expand from a central business district, not in concentric circles, but in wedge-shaped sectors. By contrast, multiple-nuclei theory holds that a city is not built around one center but around discrete nuclei, each of which is the center of specialized activities. *What determines the spatial pattern of a city?* Dominance, competition, invasion, and succession.

5. *Does the urban environment make city people different from other people?* Three theories offer different answers: According to urban anomie theory, city life is filled with alienation, impersonal relations, and reliance on formal social control as well as emotional stress and mental disorders. By contrast, compositional theorists argue that city dwellers' social lives, centered in small groups of friends, relatives, and neighbors, are much like those of people outside the city. Subcultural theorists contend that the city enriches people's lives

by offering them diverse opportunities and by promoting the development of subcultures.

6. *If large U.S. cities have been losing populations, why have their budgets increased?* The costs of maintaining streets, sewers, public buildings, and so on have risen as the cities age. Many of those who remain in the city are the ones who depend most on its services to survive. *Why is it difficult for a city to be financially independent?* One reason is that a city often receives no tax revenues from suburbanites and other nonresidents who use its services. *What is the political dilemma in running a city?* Elected officials are not willing to raise taxes for fear of antagonizing voters. *Why has housing remained segregated?* Reasons include lower minority income, racial prejudice in white neighborhoods, and racial discrimination among real estate agents and banks.

7. *What insight do the three sociological perspectives provide about urban growth and city life?* According to functionalists, ordinary people contribute to and benefit from urbanization. But to conflict theorists, big business, with help from big government, is the driving force behind urban expansion. Symbolic interactionists focus on how strangers interact in the city.

8. *What is the future of U.S. cities?* Separation between whites and minorities and between rich and poor will continue within cities. Population and job loss will also continue. The federal government will expect cities to solve more of their own problems by themselves.

KEY TERMS

Biosphere A thin layer of air, water, and soil surrounding the earth. (p. 308)

Compositional theory The theory that city dwellers are as involved with small groups of friends, relatives, and neighbors as are noncity people. (p. 320)

Concentric-zone theory The model of land use in which the city spreads out from the center in a series of concentric zones, each used for a particular kind of activity. (p. 317)

Ecology A study of the interactions among organisms and between organisms and their physical environment. (p. 308)

Ecosystem A self-sufficient community of organisms depending for survival on one another and on the environment. (p. 308)

Enterprise zone The economically depressed urban area that businesses, with the help of generous tax credits, try to revive by creating jobs. (p. 322)

Gentrification The movement of affluent people into poor urban neighborhoods. (p. 315)

Megacity A city with a population of 5 million or more. (p. 314)

Megalopolis A vast area in which many metropolises merge. (p. 314)

Metropolis A large urban area that includes a city and its surrounding suburbs. (p. 313)

Multiple-nuclei theory The model of land use in which a city is built around many discrete nuclei, each being the center of some specialized activity. (p. 317)

Sector theory The model of land use in which a city grows outward in wedge-shaped sectors from the center. (p. 317)

Subcultural theory The theory that the city enriches people's lives by offering diverse opportunities and developing various subcultures. (p. 320)

Urban anomie theory The theory that city people have a unique way of life, characterized by alienation, impersonal relations, and stress. (p. 319)

Urban ecological processes Processes in which people compete for certain land use, one group dominates another, and a particular group moves into an area and takes it over from others. (p. 319)

Urban ecology The study of the relationship between people and their urban environment. (p. 317)

Urbanization Migration of people from the countryside to city, increasing the proportion of the population that lives in the city. (p. 308)

SUGGESTED READINGS

Commoner, Barry. 1990. *Making Peace with the Planet.* New York: Pantheon. Shows the importance of harmonizing our technologies with our environment to prevent pollution.

D'Antonio, William V., Masamichi Sasaki, and Yoshio Yonebayashi (eds.). 1994. *Ecology, Society and the Quality of Social Life.* New Brunswick, N.J.: Transaction. A collection of articles on how the way a society handles its environment affects the quality of life.

Gottdiener, Mark. 1994. *The New Urban Sociology.* New York: McGraw-Hill. A text on urban sociology discussing such topics as metropolitan areas, urbanization, suburbs and suburban lives.

Hardin, Garrett. 1993. *Living Within Limits: Ecology, Economics, and Population Taboos.* New York: Oxford University Press. A collection of essays discussing the dangers of population growth and environmental destruction while suggesting solutions to the problems.

Peirce, Neal R. 1993. *Citistates: How Urban America Can Prosper in a Competitive World.* Washington, D.C.: Seven Locks Press. Analyzes how U.S. cities deal with their problems in the new world economy.

15

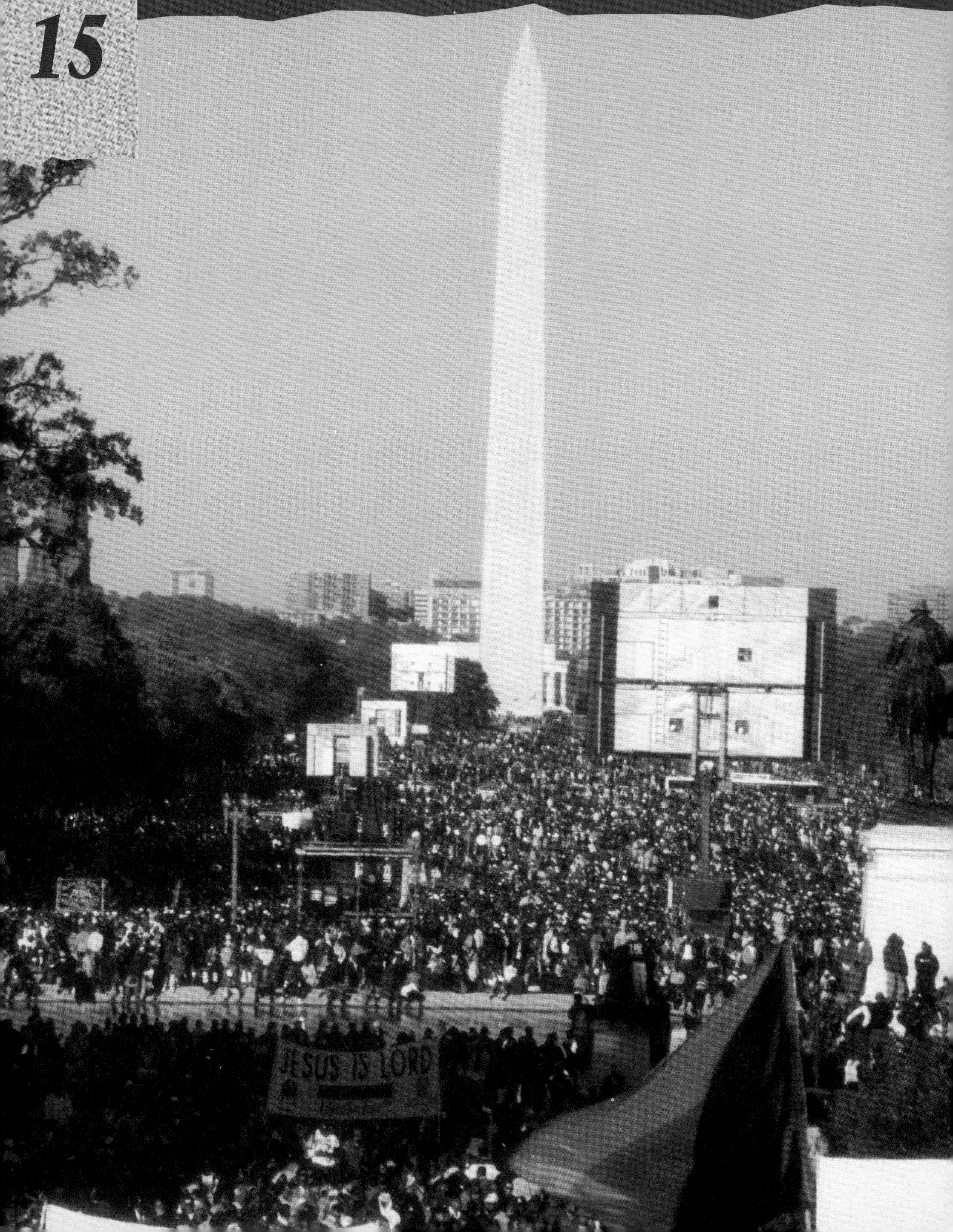

COLLECTIVE BEHAVIOR AND SOCIAL CHANGE

Myths and Realities

MYTH: *If you are watching a humorous movie in a theater, how often you laugh depends solely on how funny you think the movie is.*
REALITY: The size of the audience also has a significant impact. The larger the audience, the more frequent your laughter will be. (p. 334)

MYTH: *Violence in most riots is contagious—virtually all participants are involved.*
REALITY: Not all participants in riots engage in violence. Many simply watch others commit the violence. (p. 335)

MYTH: *It's better not to listen to rumors, because they are always false.*
REALITY: Rumors are not necessarily false; they may turn out to be true. They are merely unverified stories spread from one person to another—unverified because people do not bother to check them against facts. (p. 336)

MYTH: *Discontent, if deep enough, can by itself bring about a social movement.*
REALITY: Discontent alone does not spark a movement; there also must be resources available for mobilization, such as strong organization, effective leadership, money, and media access. (pp. 339–340)

MYTH: *Modernization always threatens or destroys tradition.*
REALITY: Tradition and modernization can co-exist or even reinforce each other, as evidenced by the continuing traditional practices among India's Westernized elites or by the positive impact of group-oriented culture on modernization in Japan. (p. 340)

The long ideological conflict between the United States and the former Soviet Union is finally over. But, like many people of his generation, 45-year-old John Driscoll still holds many Cold War memories. One of his most vivid memories is the fear that came with the air-raid drills at school. All the students learned to crawl under their desks, practicing for the day when the Soviet hydrogen bombs were expected to fall. "It seems surreal now," he said soon after the Soviet Union formally announced its end as a nation in 1991. "Every summer, when I heard lightning over the city and the sky would light up, I was convinced it was over. My whole childhood was built on the notion that the Soviets were a real threat." Today, Driscoll teaches economics and government at a high school just outside Washington, D.C. He is helping an organization to coordinate food shipments to Moscow, the capital of the "evil empire" that terrified him as a child. He found on a recent visit to Moscow that "these folks have absolutely no confidence in themselves" (Brinkley, 1992).

Like Driscoll, we can expect to witness great changes in our lives. The reason is that **social change**—the alteration of society over time—is nothing new. We can see it in the emergence of space travel, heart transplants, computers, fax machines, cellular phones, large shopping malls, the increased gap between rich and poor, widespread homelessness, and the many great events that make our society different from what it was a decade or two ago. Where will all this social change take us? Is there some general pattern behind the way societies change? Where can we expect future changes to come from, and do we have any control over them?

To understand these issues better, we look in this chapter at several theories of social change. We will also examine *modernization*—a particular type of social change that shaped many features of our society and is now reshaping societies around the world. But let us first take a look at collective behavior, which can be an impetus to social change.

THE STUDY OF COLLECTIVE BEHAVIOR

Collective behavior is relatively spontaneous, unorganized, and unpredictable social behavior. It contrasts with *institutionalized behavior*, which occurs in a well-organized, rather predictable way. Institutionalized behavior is frequent and routine. Every weekday, masses of people hurry to work. On every campus, groups of students walk to classes. These predictable patterns of group action are basically governed by social norms and are the bedrock of social order. Collective behavior, however, operates largely outside the confines of these conventional norms.

General Characteristics

Sociologists who study collective behavior face a problem: Whereas scientific analysis seeks out predictable, regular patterns, collective behavior is relatively unstructured, spontaneous, and unpredictable. Nevertheless, sociological analysis of collective behavior has been fruitful. Although collective behavior is relatively unstructured, it does have a structure that sociologists have been able to illuminate. Even rumor, for example, includes a structural division of labor: some people are messengers, others interpreters, skeptics, or merely an audience.

The difference between institutionalized and collective behavior is not absolute. Instead, the behaviors can

FIGURE 15.1
A Continuum of Normative Regulation
There are two kinds of social behavior—collective and institutionalized. The difference is not absolute, but relative to normative regulation. Collective behavior is less strongly controlled by traditional norms. Collective behavior may be further divided into different forms, which vary from one another in the degree to which they are regulated by traditional norms.

Degrees of normative regulation

Collective behavior						Institutionalized behavior	
Panics	Crowds	Fashions	Rumors	Public opinion	Social movements	Small groups	Large organizations
Behavior less regulated by traditional norms						Behavior more regulated by traditional norms	

be classified according to the relative degree of control exercised by traditional norms. Thus, we can arrange social behaviors on a continuum like that shown in Figure 15.1. As we move from left to right in the figure, the behavior noted is increasingly subject to traditional norms. Thus, institutionalized behavior is at the far right of the continuum and collective behavior lies to the left.

Only the main forms of collective behavior are shown on the continuum. At the far left, for example, is *panic*, the least structured, most transitory, and rarest form of mass action. When people in a burning theater rush to the same exit, losing their capacity to cooperate and reducing their chance of escape, that is a panic. Next on the continuum are *crowds*, somewhat more structured than panics and more subject to the influence of social norms. As a result, members of a crowd can be persuaded to work toward a common goal. Moving further to the right on the continuum, we see that *social movements* are even more structured than crowds; their members consciously work together to achieve a common objective.

Social Factors

Despite their diversity, all forms of collective behavior are basically an attempt to deal with a stressful situation, such as danger to life, threat of loss of money, social injustice, or an unacceptable status quo. The specific form such behavior takes depends largely on how the people involved define the problem. If they see it as a simple matter, they are likely to engage in such "clumsy" or "primitive" behavior as a panic or riot. If they believe the problem is complex enough to require an elaborate analysis, they are more prone to respond through a social movement. Thus, the more complex the situation of strain is believed to be, the more structured the collective behavior.

Whatever the form of the collective behavior, according to Neil Smelser (1962), six factors are necessary to produce the behavior. By itself, no one of these factors can generate collective behavior. Only the *combination of all six factors*, occurring *in sequence*, creates the conditions necessary for any kind of collective behavior to occur. Let us examine these six factors, illustrated by some facts about the 1992 riot in South-Central Los Angeles:

1. *Structural conduciveness.* Individuals by themselves cannot start a collective action; some aspect of social organization permits collective action to occur. Before people can take part in collective behavior, some condition, such as living in the same neighborhood, must exist in order for them to assemble and communicate with each other. In South-Central Los Angeles, the African American residents who joined the riot were brought together by media reports that a nearly all-white jury had found four white policemen not guilty of savagely beating black motorist Rodney King.

2. *Social strain.* The strain may arise from a conflict between different groups, from the failure of a government to meet citizens' needs, or from the society's inability to solve a social problem. The strain that existed in the black community stemmed from many cases of police brutality against blacks.

3. *The growth and spread of a generalized belief.* Participants in a collective action come to share some belief about the social strain. The rioters in South-Central Los Angeles shared the belief that the local police had often brutalized and mistreated blacks.

4. *A precipitating factor.* Some event brings the social strain to a high pitch and confirms the generalized belief about it. The King verdict clearly touched off the riot.

In 1984 the Indian Army attacked the Sikh's holiest Golden Temple, shown here. The conflict that existed between the Hindu majority and the Sikh minority was one of the preconditions that led to the anti-Sikh riots, which resulted in the destruction of many Sikh homes and lives, as well as Hindu lives.

5. *The mobilization of participants for action.* Leaders emerge to move people to take a specific action. Some leaders in the Los Angeles riot urged people on the street to follow them, saying something like "Come with us. Let's burn." Others set an example for the crowd by initiating the burning or looting of stores.

6. *Inadequate social control.* Agents of control such as the police fail to prevent the collective action. The Los Angeles police department was slow to respond to the riot. The police were virtually absent in the early hours of rioting, allowing many looters to smash storefronts and burn buildings with impunity.

If we look at other riots, such as those in the Liberty City section of Miami in 1980 and in the Overtown section in 1982, we find a similar sequence of events (Porter and Dunn, 1984).

Questions for Discussion and Review

1. What makes collective behavior different from institutionalized behavior, and why is it difficult to study?
2. According to Smelser, what six factors together generate collective behavior?

FORMS OF COLLECTIVE BEHAVIOR

The *general* analyses of collective behavior that we have just discussed assume that all forms of collective behavior are in some way similar to one another. But each form is also *unique* in some other ways, as we will see in this section.

Panics

On a December afternoon in 1903, a fire broke out in Chicago's Iroquois Theater. According to an eyewitness,

Somebody had yelled "Fire!" . . . The horror in the auditorium was beyond all description. . . . The fire-escape ladders could not accommodate the crowd, and many fell or jumped to death on the pavement below. Some were not killed only because they landed on the cushion of bodies of those who had gone before. But it was inside the house that the greatest loss of life occurred, especially on the stairways. Here most of the dead were trampled or smothered, though many jumped or fell to the floor. In places on the stairways, particularly where a turn caused a jam, bodies were piled seven or eight feet deep. . . . An occasional living person was found in the heap, but most of these were terribly injured. The heel prints on the dead faces mutely testified to the cruel fact that human animals stricken by terror are as mad and ruthless as stampeding cattle (Schultz, 1964).

The theater did not burn down. Firefighters arrived quickly after the alarm and extinguished the flames so promptly that no more than the seats' upholstery was burned. But 602 people died, and many more were injured. Panic, not the fire itself, largely accounted for the tragedy. Similarly, on a July morning in 1990 in the holy city of Mecca, Saudi Arabia, when the lights accidentally went out in a 600-yard-long tunnel through which thousands of Muslim pilgrims were walking, panic triggered a stampede, killing 1426 people.

The people in the Iroquois Theater and the Mecca tunnel behaved as people often do when faced with unexpected threats such as fires, earthquakes, floods, and other disasters: they exhibited panic behavior. A **panic** is a type of collective behavior characterized by a maladaptive, fruitless response to a serious threat. That response generally involves flight, but it is a special kind of flight. In many situations, flight is a rational, adaptive response: it is perfectly sensible to flee a burning house or an oncoming car. In these cases, flight is the only appropriate way of achieving a goal—successful escape from danger. In panic behavior, however, the flight is irrational and uncooperative. It follows a loss of self-control, and it increases, rather than reduces, danger to oneself and others. If people in a burning theater panic, they stampede each other, rather than filing out in an orderly way, and produce the kind of unnecessary loss of life that occurred in the Iroquois Theater or the Mecca tunnel.

Preconditions   When five knife-wielding hijackers took over a Chinese airplane bound for Shanghai in 1982, the passengers did not panic. Instead, they cooperated and, with mop handles, soda bottles, and other objects, overpowered the hijackers. About 20 years earlier, during a performance of the play *Long Day's Journey into Night* in Boston, word spread through the audience that there was a fire. But the audience did not stampede to the exits. One of the actors "stepped to the footlights and calmly said, 'Please be seated, ladies and gentlemen, nothing serious has happened. Just a little accident with a cigarette. . . . The fire is out now and if you will sit down again we can resume.'" The audience laughed and sat down (Brown, 1965). In this case, as in the Iroquois fire, the audience had an impulse to flee for their lives. But, because the crisis was defused, a contradictory impulse—to follow the norms of polite society and remain calm and quiet—won out.

In short, the existence of a crowd and a threat does not ensure that people will panic. There are several

social-psychological preconditions for the development of a panic. First, there must be a *perception* that a crisis exists. Second, there must be *intense fear* of the perceived danger. This fear is typically compounded by a feeling of *possible* entrapment. If people believed they were *certainly* trapped, as in the case of prisoners who are about to be executed by a firing squad, they would give in to calm resignation rather than wild panic. Third, there must be some *panic-prone individuals.* Typically, they are overly self-centered persons whose frantic desire to save themselves makes them oblivious to the fate of others and to the self-destructive consequences of their panic. Fourth, there must be *mutual emotional facilitation.* The people in the crowd must spread and enhance each other's terror. Finally, there must be a *lack of cooperation* among people. Cooperation typically breaks down in a panic because no norms exist to tell people how to behave appropriately in an unusual, unanticipated situation. But most crowds are made up of many small, primary groups of relatives or friends rather than strangers. Constrained by the bonds of these primary groups, members of crowds usually do not panic and stampede each other to death (Schultz, 1964; Johnson, 1987).

Mass Hysteria   Panic sometimes takes the form of **mass hysteria,** in which numerous people engage in frenzied activity without bothering to check the source of their fear. A classic case occurred in 1938, when the play *War of the Worlds* was broadcast on the radio. Many people thought that they were hearing a news report. Tuned in to music on the radio, they suddenly heard an announcement that Martians had invaded the earth:

> Ladies and gentlemen, I have a grave announcement to make. Incredible as it may seem, both the observations of science and the evidence of our eyes lead to the inescapable assumption that those strange beings who landed in the New Jersey farmlands tonight are the vanguard of an invading army from the planet Mars. The battle which took place tonight . . . has ended in one of the most startling defeats ever suffered by an army in modern times; seven thousand men armed with rifles and machine guns pitted against a single fighting machine of the invaders from Mars. One hundred and twenty known survivors. The rest strewn over the battle area . . . and trampled to death under the metal feet of the monster, or burned to cinders by its heat ray (Cantril, 1940).

Long before the broadcast ended, at least a million of the 6 million listeners were swept away by panic. Many prayed, cried, or fled, frantic to escape death from the Martians. Some hid in cellars. Young men tried to rescue girlfriends. Parents woke their sleeping children. People telephoned friends to share the bad news or to say goodbye. Many called hospitals for ambulances; others tried to summon police cars.

But not everyone panicked. Hadley Cantril directed a study to find out who panicked, who didn't, and why. Those who did not were found to have what Cantril called *critical ability*. Some of these people found the broadcast simply too fantastic to believe. As one of them reported, "I heard the announcer say that he saw a Martian standing in the middle of Times Square and he was as tall as a skyscraper. *That's all I had to hear*—just the word Martian was enough even without the fantastic and incredible description." Others with critical ability had sufficient specific knowledge to recognize the broadcast as a play. They were familiar with Orson Welles's story or recognized that he was acting the role of Professor Pierson. Still others tried to check the accuracy of the broadcast by looking up newspaper listings of radio schedules and programs. These people, on the whole, had more years of education than those who did panic. The less educated, aside from lacking critical ability, were found to have a feeling of personal inadequacy and emotional insecurity (Cantril, 1940).

Questions for Discussion and Review

1. What preconditions usually exist before a panic occurs?
2. Why are some people more vulnerable than others to mass hysteria?

———————

Crowds

A **crowd** is a collection of people temporarily doing something while in proximity to one another. They may be gathered on a street corner, watching a fire. They may be in a theater, watching an opera. They may be on a street, throwing rocks at police.

Traits and Types Nearly all crowds share a few traits. One is *uncertainty*: the participants do not share clear expectations about how to behave or about the outcome of their collective behavior. Another element common to most crowds is a *sense of urgency*. The people in the crowd feel that something must be done right away to solve a common problem. The third characteristic of crowds is the *communication* of mood, attitude, and idea among the members, which pressures them to conform. Crowds are also marked by *heightened suggestibility*. Those in a crowd tend to respond uncritically to the suggestions of others and to go along impulsively with their actions. Finally, crowds are characterized by *permissiveness*, freedom from the constraint of conventional norms. Thus, people tend to express feelings and take actions that they would suppress under ordinary circumstances (Turner and Killian, 1987).

Beyond these similarities, there are significant differences. Sociologist Herbert Blumer (1978) has classified crowds into four types: casual, conventional, acting, and expressive. The *casual crowd* is the type with the shortest existence and loosest organization. It emerges spontaneously. People collecting at a street corner to watch a burning building, a traffic accident, or a street musician constitute a casual crowd. The *conventional crowd,* unlike the casual crowd, occurs in a planned, regularized manner. Examples include the audience in a theater and the spectators at a football game. Whereas the conventional crowd assembles to observe some activity, the *acting crowd* is involved in an activity that enables its members to focus their energy on one particular goal. Rioters, a lynch mob, and a revolutionary crowd are all acting crowds. The *expressive crowd* has no goal. Its members plunge themselves into some unrestrained activity, releasing emotions and tensions. Examples include people at a rock concert or at a religious revival.

Social Contagion Some acting and expressive crowds are irrational or destructive. Consider the lynch mobs in the United States before 1900. Thousands of whites and blacks were lynched. The number of lynchings dropped during this century, but still, between 1900 and 1950 there were more than 3000 victims, nearly all of them black. The alleged crimes of the black victims were often trivial, such as trying to act like a white man, making boastful remarks, winking at a white man's wife, or being too ambitious (Raper, 1970). Why did the members of lynch mobs behave so irrationally and destructively? In particular, why did otherwise civilized whites act like beasts as members of a lynch mob?

According to French social psychologist Gustave Le Bon (1841–1931), a crowd is homogeneous in thought and action. All the people in a crowd think, feel, and act alike. As a crowd, they possess a "collective mind." This mind is emotional and irrational, stripped bare of all civilizing restraints. Beneath those restraints, Le Bon believed, hides a barbarian. All the members of a crowd bring to the situation this hiding barbarian with its primitive instincts. Normally, they suppress these instincts, wearing the mask of civilized behavior. But a crowd provides them with a different sort of mask: the large number of people gives individuals a cloak of anonymity that weakens their restraining sense of responsibility and releases primitive emotions.

But why do individuals give up their individuality and let themselves become part of a collective mind? The reason, in Le Bon's view, is **social contagion**—the spreading of a certain emotion and action from one member of the crowd to another. Research has uncovered factors that can facilitate contagion. Among these factors are *crowd size* and *noise*. When people are viewing a humorous movie in a theater, the larger the audience, the more frequent the laughter. If a person coughs in a room full of people, others are more likely to cough than if there were only a few people around. Watching a videotaped arm-wrestling match, the subjects' tendency to imitate the wrestlers increases with higher levels of audience noise (Levy and Fenley, 1979; Pennebaker, 1980; Markovsky and Berger, 1983).

The Emergent Norm   To most sociologists today, Le Bon's notion of a collective mind is valid only as a loose metaphor for what happens in crowds. Members of a crowd may appear homogeneous. They may seem to have given up their individuality and become absorbed in a "collective mind." But beneath these appearances, the members of a crowd are basically just individuals engaged in a particular kind of interaction. Whereas Le Bon set the behavior of crowds apart from normal social interaction as a sort of bizarre regression to almost subhuman behavior, other sociologists have found that routine and orderly behavior prevails in most crowds (McPhail and Wohlstein, 1983).

Two U.S. sociologists, Ralph Turner and Lewis Killian (1987), for example, accept Le Bon's fundamental idea that a crowd appears to act as a homogeneous group, but they have argued that Le Bon exaggerated its homogeneity. In a lynch mob, for example, not all the members think or act in the same way. Some individuals storm the jail, others drag out the prisoner, others bring ropes, others hang the victim, and some just stand by and watch. Even those engaged in the same act may have different feelings, attitudes, or beliefs, and they participate because of diverse motives. How, then, does the apparent unanimity among the participants develop?

The answer can be found in Turner and Killian's **emergent-norm theory,** the theory that members of a crowd develop, through interaction, a new norm to deal with the unconventional situation facing them. Because of the norm, people feel pressed to conform with the crowd's outward behavior, even if they disagree with the action. The result is the *appearance* of unanimity, which may be more illusion than reality. Indeed, many studies have found the "illusion of unanimity" in most crowds (McPhail and Wohlstein, 1983).

Questions for Discussion and Review

1. What are the traits and types of a crowd?
2. Why do individuals in a crowd tend to lose their individuality and act irrationally?

Most fashions, which are a great but brief enthusiasm among a large number of people for a particular innovation, are related to clothes. But any artifact that strikes people's fancy can become a fashion.

Fashions

Compared with crowds, fashions are more subject to traditional norms. Practically all aspects of human life—clothes, hairstyles, architecture, philosophy, and the arts—are influenced by fashions. A **fashion** is a great though brief enthusiasm among a relatively large number of people for a particular innovation. Because their novelty wears off quickly, fashions are very short-lived. Most are related to "the latest" in clothes, but as long as there is something new about any artifact that strikes many people's fancy, it can become a fashion.

Sources of Fashions   Why do fashions occur in the first place? One reason is that some cultures, like ours, *value change*: what is new is good. Thus, in many modern societies clothing styles change yearly, while people in traditional societies may wear the same style for generations. A second reason is that many industries *promote* quick changes in fashions to increase sales. A third reason is that fashions usually *trickle down from the top*. A new style may occasionally originate from lower-status groups, as blue jeans did. But most fashions come from upper-class people, who like to adopt some style or artifact as a badge of their status. But they cannot monopolize most status symbols for long. Their style is adopted by the middle class, and maybe copied or modified for use by lower-status groups, offering many people the prestige of possessing a high-status symbol (Turner and Killian, 1987).

Fads and Crazes   Similar to fashions but less predictable and shorter-lived are fads and crazes. A **fad** is a temporary enthusiasm for an innovation less respectable than a fashion, while a **craze** is a fad with serious consequences. Examples of fads include hula hoops, goldfish-swallowing, telephone booth–stuffing, streaking, pet rocks, yo-yos, and Air Jordans. (If these mean nothing to you, it is testimony to how fast the magic of fads can fade.) Fads are basically trivial, but they can be a source of status to some people. Carrying a beeper, for example, is a status symbol for teenagers in some U.S. cities. Certain individuals get a sense of being part of an in-group by wearing ripped jeans.

More bizarre and harmful than fads, crazes are a kind of contagious folly with serious consequences. Usually crazes are economic in nature, including a *boom,* in which many people frantically try to buy something of wildly exaggerated value, and a *bust,* in which many frantically try to sell a worthless thing. The most famous craze is probably the tulip mania that swept Holland in 1634. For some unknown reason, the Dutch developed a passion for tulips. Eventually, one bulb cost as much as a large house. Soon the Dutch were more interested in making a fortune out of tulips than in growing them. People bought bulbs only to sell them for a huge profit. They were astonished when people who returned from long trips abroad did not share this appreciation of the bulbs at all. It was widely known that a sailor mistook a valuable bulb for an onion and ate it with his herring. Eventually, people began to realize that the price of tulips could not keep rising forever. Thus, the boom was broken, and the price of tulips fell sharply, bankrupting thousands.

Questions for Discussion and Review

1. Where do fashions come from?
2. What is the nature of fads and crazes?

Rumor

On the face of it, rumor may appear as unreal as a craze. But it is not necessarily false.

Characteristics   A **rumor** is an unverified story that is spread from one person to another. As the story circulates, each person distorts the account by dropping some items and adding his or her own interpretation. But a rumor is not necessarily false: it may turn out to be true. It is unverified *not* because it is necessarily a distortion but because people do not bother to check it against facts.

Everyday we all act on the basis of unverified reports. Sociologists therefore view rumors as a normal form of communication. According to Tamotsu Shibutani (1966), for example, rumor is a communication people use in an effort to comprehend what is going on in a situation where information is lacking. Rumor, then, is a process in which many individuals try together to construct a definition of an ambiguous situation.

Contributing Factors   A rumor is likely to develop and circulate if people's demand for news about an ambiguous situation is not met by institutionalized channels of communication, such as newspapers, government announcements, and television and radio newscasts. The more *ambiguous* a situation, the greater the chance a rumor will develop. Thus, rumor is much more a part of interpersonal communications in police states and totalitarian societies where people do not trust the media because it is controlled by the government.

Anxiety also plays a significant role. Not long ago, widespread anxiety over economic problems made the United States ripe for the rumor mill. People who had lost or were afraid of losing their jobs were especially likely to believe or pass on damaging rumors about big companies. Seeing a corporate giant in trouble seemed to make them feel better. All this provided fertile ground for the growth of the rumor in 1978 that McDonald's added earthworms to its hamburgers. In 1982 another rumor had it that Procter & Gamble's logo, showing 13 stars and a man in the moon, was a sign of devil worship. In 1991 it was rumored that Liz Claiborne, the clothing company, gave 30 percent of its profits to the Church of Satan. In that same year, Tropical Fantasy—a soft drink marketed to minorities in Northeastern cities, became the target of a rumor that the Ku Klux Klan owned the company and that they added to the drink an ingredient that would make black men sterile (Koenig, 1982; Goleman, 1991a). Although *all these rumors were false,* they spread like prairie fires.

Questions for Discussion and Review

1. What is the nature of rumor?
2. What causes rumor to emerge?

Public Opinion

When we talk about "the public," we usually mean the population at large. In sociology, however, the term is more precise: a **public** is a dispersed collection of people who share a particular interest or concern. The interest may involve environmental issues, or civil rights, or outlawing pornography. Thus, there are a great many publics within the population at large.

Whenever a public comes into being, it forms an opinion. **Public opinion** is the collection of ideas and attitudes shared by the members of a particular public. As measured by polls and surveys, public opinion often seems fickle, changing easily even while values appear constant. This fickleness may reflect the difference between private and public opinion. "What a person says only to his wife, himself, or in his sleep," wrote Turner and Killian (1987), "constitutes his private opinion. What he will say to a stranger is public opinion." In private, many people will express doubts about an opinion. In public, they might state an opinion shared by others.

Propaganda   Politicians want to win our hearts and minds, and businesses want to win our dollars. Both use the media to try to gain mass support by manipulating public opinion. In other words, they generate **propaganda**—communication tailored to influence opinion. Propaganda may be true or false. What sets it apart from other communications is the intent to change opinion. Alfred and Elizabeth Lee (1979) have identified seven methods that are frequently used to sway public opinion:

1. *Name calling,* or giving something a negative label. This method is designed to make the audience reject an idea, person, or product without analysis. If a candidate is "ultraconservative," "ultraliberal," "flaky," or

a "big spender," why bother to consider his or her qualifications seriously? If abortion is "murder," who can support its legalization?

2. *Glittering generality,* the opposite of name calling. An idea or product is associated with a general, ambiguous, but extremely popular concept or belief. If a war represents the defense of democracy and freedom, who can oppose it?

3. *Transfer,* or associating an idea or product with something else that is widely respected, admired, or desired. Beautiful, scantily clad actresses sell cars and mattresses on television commercials. Presidents give television speeches with the U.S. flag prominently displayed behind them.

4. *Testimonial,* or having a famous person endorse or oppose some idea or product. Top athletes tell us to use a certain shampoo or shaving cream. Famous politicians travel to towns they never heard of to urge people to vote for obscure candidates.

5. *Plain folks,* or identifying the propagandist with the average person. While president, Jimmy Carter made sure people saw him playing softball and going fishing—doing what ordinary people do. He frequently presented himself as a mere peanut farmer, not much different from an average-income person, even though he was a wealthy man.

6. *Card stacking,* in which one fact or falsehood supporting a point of view is piled on top of another. Commercials do not tell us both the strengths and the weaknesses of a product or a candidate. Instead, we read that a brand-new car, for example, is "Quiet. Smooth riding. Full size. With comfort and luxury for six passengers. . . . Rich velour fabrics, thick carpeting and warm woodtones. . . . A truly fine automobile."

7. *Bandwagon,* creating the impression that everyone is using a product or supporting an idea or person. Soft-drink companies use commercials to show a horde of young, happy people drinking their product and singing its praises. Political candidates are usually quick to announce favorable poll results. Thus, the propagandist creates pressure to conform to a real or illusory norm.

Media Influence   Despite those manipulations, the effect of propaganda, like the effect of any communication, is limited. Because we are not computers to be programmed or clay to be molded, neither propagandists nor the media can simply insert opinions into our heads or erase previously held beliefs.

The power of the media to influence public opinion comes largely from the media's role as gatekeepers–determining what information will be passed on to large numbers of readers and listeners.

In general, at least three factors limit the influence of the media on public opinion. First, a multitude of independent organizations *present diverse viewpoints*, canceling each other's impact on the audience. Second, because most of the media are interested in making a profit, they often *present what the audience wants to see or hear*. Third, communication frequently occurs through the *two-step flow* of influence: We may hear an analysis of an issue on television ("the first step"), but we often accept or reject it after *being influenced by our* **opinion leaders** ("the second step"), individuals whose opinion is respected by others and influences them (Turner and Killian, 1987).

The media do influence public opinion to some degree. Their power comes largely from their role as gatekeepers—determining what information will be passed on to large numbers of people. There are at least five ways in which the media affect opinion. First, they *authenticate* information, making it more credible to the audience. A news item reported in the mass media often seems more believable than one passed by word of mouth. Second, the media *validate* private opinions, preferences, and values. If a famous commentator offers a view similar to our own, we are likely to feel more confident of our own opinion. Third, the media *legitimize* unconventional viewpoints. The wildest idea may eventually sound reasonable, or at least worth considering, if we read it repeatedly on the editorial pages of newspapers or hear it on the evening news. Fourth, the mass media *concretize* free-floating anxieties and ill-defined preferences. By supplying such labels as "population explosion," "the crime wave," and "the great racial

divide," the media in effect create a world of objects against which feelings can be specifically expressed. Fifth, the mass media help *establish a hierarchy* of importance and prestige among persons, objects, and opinions. If the national media never interview the senators from your state, the public is not likely to consider them important, even if they are very influential among their colleagues in the Senate (Turner and Killian, 1987).

Questions for Discussion and Review

1. How do people use propaganda and the media to mold public opinion?
2. How can the media influence public opinion and what is the limitation of their influence?

Social Movements

A hundred years ago, women in the United States could not vote. Fifty years ago, paid vacations for workers were almost unheard of. A little more than two decades ago, George Wallace took office as governor of Alabama, declaring "segregation now, segregation tomorrow, segregation forever." These features of U.S. society were transformed through **social movements,** conscious efforts to bring about or prevent change.

Compared with the forms of collective behavior we have so far discussed, social movements are far more purposive. A stock market crash, for example, unfolds without plan, but a social movement develops as a

A resistance movement is a type of social movement that cherishes an existing system and tries to reverse trends that threaten to change the system. Antiabortion groups have tried to resist the legalization of abortion.

result of purposeful effort. Social movements are also far more structured than other forms of collective behavior, even if they are not centrally coordinated. A lynch mob may develop a division of labor, but it is an informal division with a very short life. By contrast, the civil rights movement has within it numerous organizations, recognized leaders, and sets of roles and statuses. Finally, a social movement is also more enduring than other forms of collective behavior. A crowd may stay together for a few hours, but a movement may endure for years. These characteristics give social movements the potential to build a membership in the thousands or even millions.

Types   Most social movements aim to change society, but they seek varying degrees of change. They can be classified into four types on the basis of their goals.

1. *Revolutionary movements* seek total, radical change in society. Their goal is to overthrow the existing form of government and replace it with a new one. Revolutionary movements typically resort to violence or some other illegal action. Examples include the revolution for independence in the United States, the Bolshevik revolution in Russia, the Chinese Communist revolution, and the Castro-led revolution in Cuba.

2. *Reform movements* seek only a partial change in society. They support the existing social system as a whole and want to preserve it, but they aim to improve it by removing its blemishes, typically through legal methods. Each reform movement usually focuses on just one issue. The civil rights movement seeks to rid society of racial discrimination. The

women's movement seeks to eliminate gender inequality. The ecology movement seeks to put a stop to environmental pollution.

3. *Resistance movements* seek to preserve an existing system by resisting social change. The Ku Klux Klan and the U.S. Nazi party, for example, try to stop racial integration. In Muslim countries, the Islamic revolution seeks to protect the traditional Islamic ways of life against Western influences.

4. *Expressive movements* seek to change the individual, not society. Many are religious, aimed at converting individuals to a particular faith. These movements enable their members to express their sense of guilt, their joy of redemption, and their devotion to their religion. Examples include the "Moonies," Hare Krishnas, and other sects.

Causes   There are so many things to do in this world: We can spend our time making money, or fishing, or whatever. Why would people instead spend their time pushing a social movement? According to Eric Hoffer (1966), those who participate in social movements are frustrated and troubled. They use social movements as a diversion, enabling them to hide from themselves their personal problems, such as a sense of inadequacy and inferiority. Furthermore, through a social movement they can gain a sense of being noble and magnanimous, as they fight a good cause beyond their own self-interest. A social movement can also provide a sense of belonging and a way of identifying oneself. Members are therefore, in Hoffer's view, strongly dedicated to their movement's objective, following their leaders blindly as "true believers."

There are, however, some holes in Hoffer's psychological theory. For one thing, he blames movement participants rather than society for their frustration. It is often the unpleasant social conditions, such as social injustice or racial discrimination, that have brought about the discontent in the first place, as is obvious in the case of the civil rights movement. Another problem with Hoffer's view is that, although frustration may motivate people to join a social movement, it cannot explain why some participate in the *pro*-abortion rights movement, while others take part in the *anti*-abortion movement. Nevertheless, some sociologists have argued that frustration among masses of people may be the first condition necessary for the emergence of a movement. But other social factors are also considered important, such as discontented individuals identifying a common frustration, working out a plan to change the offending conditions, and banding together to carry out that plan (Turner and Killian, 1987).

Other sociologists have proposed the **resource mobilization theory,** arguing that social movements result from the availability of resources for mobilization. According to this theory, what sparks a movement is not discontent but the availability of such mobilization resources as strong organization, effective leadership, money, and media access. But these theorists have in turn been criticized for virtually ignoring the place of discontent in social movements.

In fact, both resource mobilization and discontent can be found in practically all social movements. The importance of each varies from one movement to another. As Harold Kerbo (1982) notes, discontent plays a larger role in "crisis movements" involving African Americans, the unemployed, or poor people, while resource mobilization figures more in "affluence movements," such as environmental movements and abortion-rights movements, which involve mostly affluent Americans.

Questions for Discussion and Review

1. How do sociologists define and categorize social movements?
2. What causes social movements?

A GLOBAL ANALYSIS OF SOCIAL CHANGE

Social change takes place around the world. In some respects, social change differs from one society to another, and in other respects, it does not.

Sociologists therefore question whether diverse societies are converging into one world or diverging into separate worlds.

Tradition and Modernization

Modernization is the form of social change that involves the transformation of an agricultural society into an industrial one. Contrary to popular belief, such social change does not inevitably destroy tradition. In many instances, modernization reinforces tradition, or the other way around.

In India, for example, modernization reinforces tradition. When Indians of middle and lower levels seek upward mobility, they do so by "becoming more devoutly Hinduistic," by being as traditionally Indian as possible. Even among very Westernized elites, the native culture still exerts a powerful influence. Nearly all highly modernized Indian intellectuals speak a regional language as their mother tongue, are steeped in classical Sanskrit literature, are strongly tied to an extended family, and are likely to find a spouse through parental arrangements.

We can also see the positive impact of tradition on modernization in Japan. Without its traditional culture, Japan would not have become an industrial giant. The Japanese culture emphasizes the importance of social relations and collective welfare. It encourages consensus rather than conflict, deference to rather than disrespect for authority, and paternalism rather than indifference by those in authority. These cultural values saturate Japan's economic system. A business enterprise, no matter how large, is run like a household, with the accompanying interdependence and loyalty characteristic of the family. Since the company takes care of its workers by giving them lifetime employment, employees tend to identify strongly with employers and work as hard as they can. Moreover, the traditional emphasis on collective welfare does more than enhance productivity through cooperation between managers and workers: It further causes society to favor business and industry at the expense of individuals, transferring funds and wealth from individuals to industries. This can be seen in the fact that factories and company apartments are mostly grand and imposing, whereas private homes are cramped though highly expensive.

Convergence and Divergence

Through modernization, many non-Western societies such as India and Japan are becoming technologically more like Western societies. At the same time, though,

According to convergence theory, modernization will bring Western and non–Western countries together and cause the spread of Western values and ways. Here, Russian entrepreneurs show off the "first American pizza in Moscow."

both types of societies are growing apart culturally, with one valuing tradition more than the other. These opposite trends have led to the development of two contrasting theories about the changing global society.

According to **convergence theory,** modernization will bring the West and non-West together by breaking down cultural barriers to produce a global society. The assumption is that exposure to supersonic aircraft, satellite communication, the information superhighway, and multinational companies will cause non-Western societies to adopt Western ways of living and virtually all the Western values. Under the influence of modernization, technocrats and leaders in Asia, Africa, and South America will become a "cos-

mopolitan elite." They will abandon their own traditional cultures, thereby dissolving the cultural differences between their countries and the West.

Countering this view is **divergence theory,** which emphasizes the growing separation between Western and non-Western cultures. Especially in many Asian and Muslim societies, the tides of cultural nationalism are rising, rejecting Western culture. Saudi Arabia and other Middle Eastern countries, for example, preserve their traditional Islamic way of life despite their embrace of modernization. Thus, in Saudi Arabia, gambling, movies, and dancing are forbidden, and Western videos, books, and publications are heavily censored. Islamic laws are also strictly enforced: thieves' hands are chopped off, adulterers are stoned to death, murderers and rapists are beheaded, and lesser offenders are flogged; all such punishments are carried out in the city squares for the public to see (Beyer, 1990).

Is the United States in Decline?

The convergence and divergence theories essentially deal with the issue of whether non-Western societies are more like or unlike the West. Now let us examine the same issue from the standpoint of the West: Is the United States, widely seen as the epitome of all that is Western, becoming more like the developing countries by losing its status as the world's leader?

According to Paul Kennedy, the United States has not actually suffered a serious decline. But he warns that "if the trends in national indebtedness, inadequate productivity increases, mediocre educational performance, and decaying social fabric in the United States are allowed to continue at the same time that massive U.S. commitments of men, money and materials are made in different parts of the globe" in order to maintain our international status as a foremost military power, we will lose that very power in a decade or so (Kennedy, 1988, 1991). Kennedy is concerned that the United States does not have the financial resources to solve its economic problems, improve its public education, and eliminate its social problems, such as crime, drugs, and homelessness. He believes that all these problems are capable of turning the United States into a poor developing nation.

Other social scientists are more optimistic. Joseph Nye (1990) agrees with Kennedy that U.S. decline will occur if its domestic issues are not soundly addressed, but Nye has faith in the U.S. ability to deal with those problems. One reason is that the United States, for all its problems, continues to be the world's largest economy and has the highest level of absolute productivity. Another reason is that the United States still has a great deal of what Nye calls "hard" and "soft" power to lead the world. *Hard power* is economic and military strength. *Soft power* is the ability to persuade rather than command, which comes from intangible sources, such as the worldwide popularity of U.S. movies and the admiration and goodwill that U.S. citizens often enjoy abroad.

The 1991 Gulf War showed that the United States possesses those two kinds of power. It succeeded in using its military's hard power to defeat Iraq swiftly and with remarkably few U.S. casualties. It succeeded in using its soft power to persuade the United Nations to pass resolutions demanding that Iraq withdraw from Kuwait, and it further used its soft power to mobilize an international coalition to wage war against Iraq. Increasingly, the soft, noncoercive power will be more effective than the hard, military power in leading the world, and here Nye believes the United States has a clear edge over any other nation.

Questions for Discussion and Review

1. How are tradition and modernization related in India and Japan?
2. Are various societies converging into one world?
3. Is the United States in danger of joining the developing world?

FUNCTIONALIST PERSPECTIVE

Modern sociology was born in a period of great social tumult, and its founding fathers developed many of their ideas as a result of trying to understand the vast social changes of their time. Anthropologists and historians, too, were intrigued by the question of how societies change. Most of them were basically functionalists. To some, human society seemed like a well-functioning one-way train, headed toward eventual Utopia. To others, it was like a healthy human body, growing from innocent childhood to old age. To yet others, it was rather like an ocean tide, rising and falling and then rising again. To more recent sociologists, it was a social system, with its different parts cooperating to make it function properly. All these social scientists seemed to consider society a harmonious, peaceful system.

Evolutionary Theory

Human horizons expanded greatly during the nineteenth century, as Europeans "discovered" and studied peoples of other lands and of the distant past. The early anthropologists believed that these peoples offered a portrait of their own ancestors. Most agreed that all societies progressed, or evolved, through three stages of development: savagery, barbarism, and civilization. Western societies, of course, were deemed civilized; all other peoples were considered savages or barbarians.

This was the origin of **evolutionary theory,** the theory that societies change gradually from simple to complex forms. One of its early exponents was functionalist Herbert Spencer (1820—1903). He believed that all societies followed uniform, natural laws of evolution. These laws decreed "survival of the fittest": those aspects of society that worked well would survive; those that did not would die out. Thus, over time, societies would naturally and inevitably improve. Behind this old theory were several questionable assumptions, including the extremely ethnocentric belief that Western culture represents the height of human civilization.

Modern evolutionary theorists have discarded several of these assumptions. In general, they argue that societies tend to change gradually from simple to complex forms. Pastoral societies may be considered simple; modern industrial societies, complex. But evolutionary theorists no longer imply that the change represents an improvement (Lenski, Lenski, and Nolan, 1995). Evolving complexity can be seen in the change Durkheim described from mechanical solidarity to organic solidarity (see Chapter 2: Society and Culture). But organic solidarity is not necessarily "better" than mechanical solidarity. A modern lifestyle is not always an improvement over a traditional one.

Cyclical Theory

Evolutionists assume that social change has only one direction. They believe that when societies change they, in effect, burn their bridges behind them—they cannot return to their previous states. In contrast, proponents of **cyclical theory** believe that societies move forward and backward, up and down, in an endless series of cycles.

Spengler's "Majestic Cycles" German historian Oswald Spengler (1880–1936) was the first to make the cyclical assumption explicit. He wrote in 1918 that Western civilization was headed downhill and would soon die out, just as the Greek and Egyptian civilizations had. "The great cultures," he explained, "accomplish their majestic wave cycles. They appear suddenly, swell in splendid lines, flatten again, and vanish, and the face of the waters is once more a sleeping waste." More often, Spengler likened a culture to an organism. Like any living thing, a culture, he believed, went through a life cycle of birth, youth, maturity, old age, and death. Western civilization, as he saw it, had reached old age and was tottering toward death.

Spengler's theory was very popular for a time. But to modern sociologists, there is too much poetry and too little science in his argument, and the analogy between societies and biological organisms is more misleading than useful. Nevertheless, Spengler's basic idea that social change is cyclical has influenced social science. Arnold Toynbee and Pitirim Sorokin, for example, offered famous theories based on this view.

Toynbee's "Challenge" and "Response" Like Spengler, British historian Arnold Toynbee (1889–1975) believed that all civilizations rise and fall. But in his view, the rise and fall do not result from some inevitable, biologically determined life cycle. Instead, they depend both on human beings and on their environments. Environments present "challenges," and humans choose "responses" to those challenges. The fate of a civilization, according to Toynbee, depends on both the challenges presented to a civilization and the responses it devises.

The challenge may come from the natural environment or from human sources. Barren land, a frigid climate, and war, for example, all represent "challenges." A civilization declines if the challenge it faces is either too weak or too severe. Suppose food is extremely abundant; people may become lazy, and their civilization will decline. But if food is very scarce, starvation may kill the people, and their civilization as well. A moderate challenge is likely to stimulate a civilization to grow and flourish. The relatively large population and relatively scarce natural resources of Japan, for example, might represent a "moderate" challenge.

The fate of a civilization, however, depends not just on the challenge from the environment but also on the people's response. Whether a successful response comes about usually hinges on the actions of a creative minority, which involve developing new ideas and leading the masses to meet the challenge. Without such leaders, the civilization will decline.

Toynbee's theory provides an interesting way of looking at the history of civilizations, but it does not give us a means of predicting how societies will change. What, after all, is a "severe" challenge? Will the depletion of oil and minerals represent a "moderate" or an overly "severe" challenge for Western civilization? We know the answer *only after the fact*. If a civilization falls, we may assume that the challenge was too severe and the response was inadequate. *Before* a civilization rises or falls, we have no way of testing

Toynbee's theory. But it still can be considered a useful theory. According to French sociologist Raymond Boudon (1983a, 1983b), social change is so complex that the best we can expect from a theory is whether it can help us understand what has happened rather than predict what will happen. That's what Toynbee's theory does.

Sorokin's Principle of Immanent Change According to Pitirim Sorokin (1889–1968), a Russian American sociologist, societies fluctuate between two extreme forms of culture, which he called ideational and sensate. **Ideational culture** emphasizes faith or religion as the key to knowledge and encourages people to value spiritual life. **Sensate culture** stresses empirical evidence or science as the path to knowledge and urges people to favor a practical, materialistic, and hedonistic way of life.

External forces such as international conflict or contact with another culture may force change on a society, but Sorokin believed in the **principle of immanent change,** the notion that social change is the product of the social forces that exist *within* a society. When the time has come for a society's "inwardly ordained change," all the main aspects of the culture change. Thus, society eventually reacts against one extreme form of culture and swings to the other extreme. Sorokin regarded the Western culture of his time, for example, as sensate, and, like Spengler, thought it was declining. In the widespread pursuit of pleasure, proliferation of fraud and crime, and deterioration of the family, Sorokin saw signs that Western culture was "overripe" and ready to swing to the other extreme—ideational culture.

To most sociologists today, Sorokin's theory is too speculative, impossible to test scientifically. Although Sorokin supported his theory with a mountain of historical data, he seems to have selected those facts that supported his view and ignored those that did not. Nevertheless, Sorokin's theory, like Toynbee's, can help us understand some of the changes in our history, such as the rise of fundamentalist religion in the last decade (see Chapter 11: Education and Religion). Changes in our society today can be interpreted as a reflection of the shift from a sensate to an ideational culture.

Equilibrium Theory

U.S. sociologist Talcott Parsons (1902–1979) developed yet another theory of social change, one that remains influential today. According to his **equilibrium theory,** all the parts of society serve some function and are interdependent. As a result, a change in one part produces compensatory changes elsewhere. It has recently become necessary, for example, for both parents to work in order to earn enough income to support a family. But if both parents must leave the home, who will care for their children? Society has responded with the increased availability of day-care services. Such changes keep the various parts of the social system in balance, ensuring social order and stability.

In this view of society, social change triggers the social system to make adjustments. If there is a change in one part of society, other parts will change to keep society functioning smoothly. To Parsons, social change is not the overthrow of the old and the creation of something wholly new. Instead, new elements are integrated with aspects of the old society through a "moving equilibrium," or movement toward a new harmonious system.

Parsons's theory is useful for describing gradual change. According to its critics, though, it fails to explain *why* social change occurs, does not deal with *revolutionary* change, and portrays societies as far more stable and harmonious than they are.

Questions for Discussion and Review

1. How does today's evolutionary theory differ from the older one?
2. How do the separate versions of cyclical theory differ from each other, and how does each contribute to sociology's understanding of social change?
3. What is the equilibrium theory of social change?

CONFLICT PERSPECTIVE

According to the **conflict theory** of social change, societies are always marked by conflict and that conflict is the key to change. Karl Marx (1818–1883) is the father of this theory. We have discussed aspects of his work in previous chapters, especially his prediction of the downfall of capitalism.

According to Marx, a capitalist society includes two classes: the owners of the means of production (the bourgeoisie or capitalists) and those who must sell their labor (the proletariat or workers). These classes are in constant conflict with each other. The capitalists want to keep wages low in order to maximize their profits, and the workers resist this exploitation. The capitalists have the upper hand, Marx argued, but they unwittingly sow the seeds of their own destruction. By exploiting workers, capi-

talists fuel rage and resentment among workers and lead them to feel that they have nothing to gain from the present system. Through factories and improved transportation and communication, the capitalist society brings workers together. As they share their sufferings with one another, the workers develop a consciousness of themselves as a class. According to Marx, the alienation, resentment, and class consciousness eventually lead workers to revolt against capitalist society.

History has not fulfilled these predictions. Marx failed to anticipate the emergence of a large middle class, made up largely of white-collar workers. He also failed to see that governments might respond to social conflict by improving the condition of workers. In fact, Marx's dire predictions about the future of capitalism helped spur governments to ease the suffering of workers. In a sense, by predicting that capitalism carried the seeds of its destruction, Marx sowed seeds that would help destroy his own prediction. Through the emergence of the welfare state as well as the growth of the middle class, workers in capitalist societies have grown richer, not poorer as Marx predicted. They have thus gained a stake in the system and are not likely to overthrow it by supporting revolution.

Other aspects of Marx's work have stood up better against the test of time. Marx did accurately predict the rise of large-scale industry, the emergence of multinational corporations, and the continuous squeeze of technology on employees. His analysis further predicted the concentration of capital in a few giant corporations, which is evident today. Moreover, many social scientists agree with Marx that material conditions—economic production in particular—shape intellectual, political, and social life. They also accept his view that "the innermost nature of things" is dynamic and filled with conflict (Heilbroner, 1980).

Question for Discussion and Review

1. What are the strengths and weaknesses of Marx's approach to social change?

SYMBOLIC INTERACTIONIST PERSPECTIVE

According to symbolic interactionism, human beings actively interpret the world around them and then act—or interact with others—in accordance with the interpretation. Imbedded in this interpretation is how the individuals see themselves and want others to see them, which itself also influences the social interaction. Thus, when society changes to create a new social life, people will define their world differently than they have in the past. If the individuals are young and therefore familiar only with the current world, their worldview will differ from their parents' view of the earlier world. Therefore, through the symbolic interactionist perspective, we can gain insight into how social change shapes our definition of the world, our selves, and our interactions with others.

There seem to be two major types of social change around the globe today. In most societies the change has involved modernization, transforming society *from agricultural to industrial*. In industrial societies, the modernization has transformed society *from industrial to postindustrial*. Both types of social change have a great impact on the individual's worldview, self-perception, and social interactions. This point can be illustrated with just two examples.

First, people in relatively traditional societies have a relatively clear concept of who they are because their social statuses have been familiar to them since childhood. They thus know themselves as farmers, carpenters, and the like—just like their parents—which determines how they interact with others. By contrast, people in more modern societies tend to achieve their statuses as teachers, lawyers, businesspersons, and so on, which they have not learned to live with since childhood. As a result, people in modern societies tend to be less self-confident, more anxious, and more inclined to ask who they are.

Second, people in traditional societies tend to define themselves as an integral part of a group and seek happiness from developing close relationships with others. By contrast, people in modern societies tend to define themselves as being free and independent of others, with the result that they are more likely to engage in superficial interactions.

Question for Discussion and Review

1. According to symbolic interactionism, how does social change influence our personal life?

MAJOR CHANGES IN OUR FUTURE

What is in store for us in the remainder of this century? Demographic changes should have a marked impact on U.S. society. Working adults and the elderly will each make up a larger share of the population, while the young will constitute a smaller share. With fewer youth, we can expect crime and competition for entry-level jobs to decrease. With more working and elderly adults, productivity and political conservatism will increase. The conservatism may find expression in toughness toward criminals, in heartlessness toward the poor, and in resistance to efforts by women and minorities to achieve social and economic equality. Brought up in such an environment, the young may also become more conservative. Political conflict between the young and the old may increase, as the interests of those receiving Social Security and those paying to support it clash.

Technology will continue to stimulate change. We are now entering the postindustrial age, which seems as momentous as the Industrial Revolution. A postindustrial society is largely based on services, particularly information-related services. Today, more than two-thirds of the U.S. labor force already work in information-related service industries, such as health care, retail trade, and financial services.

Computer-driven technologies have also begun to dismantle the traditional industrial principle of mass production aimed at a mass society. By using computers, companies are increasingly customizing their goods and services for niche markets. The new technologies are also making local production as competitive as national mass production. Many supermarkets, in addition to selling national brands of bread, have begun to bake their own. Photos, which used to be sent to Rochester, New York, to be processed centrally by Kodak, can now be developed and printed anywhere in the United States. The same demassification process has taken away much of the audience from the three giant TV networks, as cable and other media have proliferated to serve new niche markets. Similar changes have also weakened the mass-production labor unions (Toffler, 1990).

With *demassification*, however, our society will become more individualistic, more fragmented, and less cohesive. There are already signs of how demassification has made us more aware of our individual rights. Our society has become awash with almost as many different rights as there are different individuals. There are criminal rights, victim rights, animal rights, pro-abortion rights, anti-abortion rights, housing rights, privacy rights, the right to own AK-47s (powerful assault rifles) for hunting purposes, a damaged fetus's right not to be born, and airline pilots' right not to be randomly tested for alcohol, which presumably leaves passengers the right to crash every now and then (Leo, 1991). With many different groups demanding that only *their* rights be protected, social responsibility or civic obligation will decline, and national consensus will be harder to sustain. Thus, more social conflict will occur.

Finally, the end of the Cold War may temporarily make us less interested in foreign affairs because the Soviet threat to our national security no longer exists. But new international problems will goad our nation into action. The United States will help to contain the inter-ethnic conflict unleashed by the disintegra-tion of the Soviet empire. Our nation will try to con-trol the spread of missiles and nuclear technology, which the former members of the Soviet Union are eager to sell to developing countries. And our gov-ernment will try to make sure that U.S. companies can more easily sell their products in foreign coun-tries, in order to promote economic well-being at home (Friedman, 1992).

CHAPTER REVIEW

1. *According to Smelser, what are the preconditions for the appearance of collective behavior?* Six conditions must appear, in this sequence: (1) structural con-duciveness, (2) social strain, (3) the spread of a gen-eralized belief, (4) a precipitating factor, (5) mobilization of participants, and (6) inadequate social control.

2. *What conditions create a panic?* There must be a per-ception of a crisis, intense fear of possible entrapment, some panic-prone individuals, mutual emotional facil-itation, and a lack of cooperation among people. *What type of people are most likely to succumb to mass hysteria?* People with little critical ability and little education are most likely to succumb.

3. *Why do crowds sometimes act irrationally, even vio-lently?* Le Bon argued that as a result of the anonymity of a crowd, people give up their individuality and release their primitive instincts. Then as a result of social contagion, they become part of a collective mind that is irrational. Many sociologists today believe that Le Bon's "collective mind" is a fiction and that crowds are not as homogeneous as they appear. Instead, as Turner and Killian have argued, crowds appear homogeneous because they conform to a new norm that emerges to deal with the unconventional situation in which the crowd finds itself.

4. *How do fashions, fads, and crazes differ?* Fashions occur more predictably, last longer, and are more socially respectable than fads and crazes. Fads are less outrageous and less harmful than crazes.

5. *Are rumors always distortions?* No. They are merely unverified. They, or parts of them, may turn out to be true. *When are rumors likely to develop?* If a situation is ambiguous and institutionalized channels of commu-nication do not satisfy the demand for news about it, then a rumor is likely to emerge.

6. *How can propaganda influence opinion?* Seven methods can be used to achieve the objective of pro-paganda: name calling, glittering generality, transfer, testimonial, plain folks, card stacking, and bandwagon. *Why is the influence of the U.S. media limited?* There are several reasons: the multitude of viewpoints the media present; the tendency to tell people what they want to hear; and the frequency with which communication occurs by a two-step flow—from the media to opinion leaders and only then to the public. *What influence do the media have?* They frequently authenticate informa-tion; validate private opinions, preferences, and values; legitimize unconventional viewpoints and behavior; concretize ill-defined anxieties and preferences; and establish a hierarchy of importance and prestige among people, objects, or ideas.

7. *What are the aims of social movements?* In general, they seek some sort of change. Revolutionary move-ments seek total, radical change of society. Reform movements seek a partial change. Resistance move-ments try to turn back some ongoing social change. Expressive movements seek to change individuals, not society. *What are the social causes of social move-ments?* According to the traditional perspective, social conditions must first frustrate masses of people; then people must identify a common frus-tration and work out a plan and band together to change the offending conditions. But resource mobi-lization theory emphasizes the importance of the availability of certain resources more than discon-tent as the cause.

8. *Does modernization necessarily destroy tradition?* No. It may even reinforce tradition. *Will modernization produce a global society?* Not necessarily. Modern-ization of non-Western countries may increase increase their cultural differences with the West. *Is the United States really in decline?* Not really, but if its various problems remain unsolved, decline can be expected.

9. *How do modern evolutionary theorists describe social change?* They argue that societies tend to change grad-ually from simple to complex forms. *What is a primary*

difference between evolutionary and cyclical theorists? Evolutionary theorists see social change as moving in one principal direction: toward increased complexity. Cyclical theorists portray social change as reversible: societies may move "forward" and "backward," they may rise and fall, in cycles. *What is equilibrium theory?* It holds that the various parts of society are all interdependent and that a change in any one part stimulates compensatory changes in other parts of the system. *What does conflict theory say about social change?* Social change stems from conflict, which always characterizes societies. *What does symbolic interactionism reveal about social change?* Social change shapes the individual's self-perception and interactions with others.

10. *What effects are demographic changes in the United States likely to produce in the near future?* The aging of the population seems likely to lead to lower crime rates and increased productivity and conservatism. Political conflict between racial and ethnic groups, sexes, and generations may increase. *How is technology changing society?* It is carrying us into the postindustrial age in which information is the most important product. Computer technology will produce goods and services more efficiently, but its tendency to demassify production for individual needs will encourage more social conflict.

KEY TERMS

Collective behavior Relatively spontaneous, unorganized, and unpredictable social behavior. (p. 330)

Conflict theory The theory that societies are always marked by conflict and that conflict is the key to change. (p. 344)

Convergence theory The theory that modernization will bring the West and non-West together by breaking down cultural barriers to produce a global society. (p. 341)

Craze A fad with serious consequences. (p. 336)

Crowd A collection of people temporarily doing something while in proximity to one another. (p. 334)

Cyclical theory The theory that societies move forward and backward, up and down, in an endless series of cycles. (p. 342)

Divergence theory The theory that emphasizes the growing separation between Western and non-Western cultures. (p. 341)

Emergent-norm theory The theory that members of a crowd develop, through interaction, a new norm

to deal with the unconventional situation facing them. (p. 335)

Equilibrium theory The theory that all the parts of society serve some function and are interdependent. (p. 343)

Evolutionary theory The theory that societies change gradually from simple to complex forms. (p. 342)

Fad A temporary enthusiasm for an innovation less respectable than a fashion. (p. 336)

Fashion A great though brief enthusiasm among a relatively large number of people for a particular innovation. (p. 335)

Ideational culture Sorokin's term for the culture that emphasizes faith or religion as the key to knowledge and encourages people to value spiritual life. (p. 343)

Mass hysteria A form of collective behavior in which numerous people engage in a frenzied activity without checking the source of their fear. (p. 333)

Modernization The form of social changes that involves the transformation of an agricultural society into an industrial one. (p. 340)

Opinion leader A person whose opinion is respected by others and influences them. (p. 338)

Panic A type of collective behavior characterized by a maladaptive, fruitless response to a serious threat. (p. 333)

Principle of immanent change The notion that social change is the product of the social forces that exist within a society. (p. 343)

Propaganda Communication tailored to influence opinion. (p. 337)

Public A dispersed collection of people who share a particular interest or concern. (p. 337)

Public opinion The collection of ideas and attitudes shared by the members of a particular public. (p. 337)

Resource mobilization theory The theory that social movements result from the availability of resources for mobilization. (p. 340)

Rumor An unverified story that is spread from one person to another. (p. 336)

Sensate culture Sorokin's term for the culture that stresses empirical evidence or science as the key to knowledge and urges people to favor a practical, materialistic, and hedonistic way of life. (p. 343)

Social change The alteration of society over time. (p. 330)

Social contagion   The spreading of a certain emotion and action from one member of a crowd to another. (p. 334)

Social movement   A conscious effort to bring about or prevent change. (p. 338)

Suggested Readings

Inkeles, Alex. 1983. *Exploring Individual Modernity*. New York: Columbia University Press. A well-integrated collection of articles that reports and analyzes findings from the author's famous studies on becoming modern in developing countries.

Kennedy, Paul M. 1988. *The Rise and Fall of the Great Powers*. New York: Random House. A Spenglerian, cyclical analysis of how past great powers such as Spain and Britain eventually declined, spiced with a controversial comparison between those former superpowers and the United States of today.

Morris, Aldon D., and Carol McClurg Mueller, eds. 1992. *Frontiers in Social Movement Theory*. New Haven, Conn.: Yale University Press. A collection of articles by eminent scholars about their new theories of social movements.

Nye, Joseph, Jr. 1990. *Bound to Lead: The Changing Nature of American Power*. New York: Basic Books. An anticyclical analysis of how in the new international order the United States will lead the world with its social and cultural resources more than with its military power.

Toffler, Alvin, and Heidi Toffler. 1995. *Creating a New Civilization*. Atlanta: Turner Publishing. Discusses how our world is becoming information-driven and globally integrated, with great impact on everything from family life to the political institution.

Glossary

Absolute poverty   The lack of minimum food and shelter necessary for maintaining life.

Achieved status   A status that is attained through an individual's own actions.

Activity theory   The theory that most elders maintain a great deal of interaction with others, even when it requires vigorous physical activities.

Affirmative action   A policy that requires employers and colleges to make special efforts to recruit qualified minorities for jobs, promotions, and educational opportunities.

Afrocentrism   The view of the world from the standpoint of African culture.

Age structure   The pattern of the proportions of different age groups within a population.

Ageism   Prejudice and discrimination against the aged.

Agricultural society   A society that produces food primarily by using plows and draft animals on the farm.

Alienation of labor   Marx's term for laborers' loss of control over their work process.

Amalgamation   The process by which the subcultures of various groups are blended together, forming a new culture.

Animism   The belief in spirits capable of helping or harming people.

Anticipatory socialization   The process by which people learn to assume a role in the future.

Anti-Semitism   Prejudice or discrimination against Jews.

Aptitude   The capacity for developing physical or social skills.

Arranged marriage   A marriage in which partners are selected by the couple's parents.

Ascribed status   A status that one has no control over, such as status based on race, gender, or age.

Assimilation   The process by which a minority adopts the dominant group's culture as the culture of the larger society.

Authority   Legitimate power institutionalized in organizations.

Behavioral assimilation   The social situation in which the minority adopts the dominant group's language, values, and behavioral patterns.

Belief   An idea that is relatively subjective, unreliable, or unverifiable.

Bilateral descent   The norm that recognizes both parents' families as the child's close relatives.

Biosphere   A thin layer of air, water, and soil surrounding the earth.

Birth rate   The number of babies born in a year for every 1000 members of a given population.

Budget deficit   Spending more than we take in.

Bureaucracy   A modern Western organization defined by Max Weber as being rational in achieving its goal efficiently.

Capitalism   An economic system based on private ownership of property and competition in producing and selling goods and services.

Census   A periodic head count of the entire population of a country.

Charisma   An exceptional personal quality popularly attributed to certain individuals.

Chromosomes   The materials in a cell that transmit hereditary traits to the carrier from the carrier's parents.

Class conflict   Marx's term for the struggle between capitalists, who own the means of production, and the proletariat, who do not.

Coercion   The illegitimate use of force or threat of force to compel obedience.

Collective behavior   Relatively spontaneous, unorganized, and unpredictable social behavior.

Communism   A classless society that operates on the principle of "from each according to his ability, to each according to his needs."

Compensatory education   A school program intended to improve the academic performance of socially and educationally disadvantaged children.

Competition   An interaction in which two individuals follow mutually accepted rules in trying to achieve the same goal before the other does.

Compositional theory   The theory that city dwellers are as involved with small groups of friends, relatives, and neighbors as are noncity people.

Concentric-zone theory   The model of land use in which the city spreads out from the center in a series of concentric zones, each used for a particular kind of activity.

Conflict   An interaction in which two individuals disregard any rules in trying to achieve their own goal by defeating each other.

Conflict perspective   A theoretical perspective that

portrays society as always changing and always marked by conflict.

Conflict theory The theory that societies are always marked by conflict and that conflict is the key to change.

Content analysis Searching for specific words or ideas and then turning them into numbers.

Control group The subjects in an experiment who are not exposed to the independent variable.

Conventional morality Kohlberg's term for the practice of defining right and wrong according to the *motive* of the action being judged.

Convergence theory The theory that modernization will bring the West and non-West together by breaking down cultural barriers to produce a global society.

Cooperation An interaction in which two or more individuals work together to achieve a common goal.

Core countries The world's upper class, the most industrialized and richest societies; popularly known as industrial or developed countries.

Craze A fad with serious consequences.

Crowd A collection of people temporarily doing something while in proximity to one another.

Crystalline intelligence Wisdom and insight into the human condition, as shown by one's skills in language, philosophy, music, or painting.

Cultural imperialism The practice of making minorities accept the dominant group's culture.

Cultural integration The joining of various values into a coherent whole.

Cultural pluralism The peaceful coexistence of various racial and ethnic groups, each retaining its own subculture.

Cultural relativism The belief that a culture must be understood on its own terms.

Cultural universals Practices found in all cultures as the means for meeting the same human needs.

Culture A design for living or a complex whole consisting of objects, values, and other characteristics that people acquire as members of society.

Cyclical theory The theory that societies move forward and backward, up and down, in an endless series of cycles.

De facto segregation Segregation resulting from tradition and custom.

De jure segregation Segregation sanctioned by law.

Death rate The number of deaths in a year for every 1000 members of a population.

Deindustrialization The loss of numerous factory jobs as a result of relocating a massive number of manufacturing plants to peripheral countries.

Demographic transition The theory that human populations tend to go through specific, demographic stages and that these stages are tied to a society's economic development.

Demography The scientific study of population.

Detached observation A method of observation in which the researcher observes as an outsider, from a distance, without getting involved.

Developmental socialization The process by which people learn to be more competent in playing their currently assumed role.

Deviance An act that is considered by public consensus or by the powerful at a given place and time to be a violation of some social rule.

Differential association The process of acquiring through interaction with others "an *excess* of definitions favorable to violation of law over definitions unfavorable to violation of law."

Discrimination An unfavorable action against individuals that is taken because they are members of a certain category.

Disengagement theory The theory that aging causes people to disengage from society.

Disintegrative shaming The process by which the wrongdoer is punished in such a way as to be stigmatized, rejected, or ostracized.

Divergence theory The theory that emphasizes the growing separation between Western and non-Western cultures.

Dramaturgy A method of analyzing social interaction as if the participants were performing on a stage.

Dual economy An economy that comprises a *core* of giant corporations dominating the market and a *periphery* of small firms competing for the remaining, smaller shares of business.

Ecology A study of the interactions among organisms and between organisms and their physical environment.

Economic globalization The interrelationship of the world's economies.

Economic institution A system for producing and distributing goods and services.

Ecosystem A self-sufficient community of organisms depending for survival on one another and on the environment.

Egalitarian family The family in which authority is equally distributed between husband and wife.

Ego Freud's term for the part of personality that is rational, dealing with the world logically and realistically.

Emergent-norm theory The theory that members of a crowd develop, through interaction, a new norm to deal with the unconventional situation facing them.

Emotional intelligence The ability to identify and manage one's own *affect* (feelings).

Endogamy Literally, "marrying within," the act of marrying someone from one's own group.

Enterprise zone The economically depressed urban area that businesses, with the help of generous tax credits, try to revive by creating jobs.

Epidemiology The study of the origin and spread of disease within a population.

Equilibrium theory The theory that all the parts of society serve some function and are interdependent.

Ethicalism The type of religion that emphasizes moral principles as guides for living a righteous life.

Ethnic group A collection of people who share a distinctive cultural heritage.

Ethnocentrism The attitude that one's own culture is superior to those of others.

Ethnomethodology The analysis of how people define the world in which they live.

Eurocentrism The view of the world from the standpoint of European culture.

Evolutionary theory The theory that societies change gradually from simple to complex forms.

Exchange An interaction in which two individuals offer each other something in order to obtain a reward in return.

Exogamy Literally, "marrying outward," the act of marrying someone from outside one's group—such as the clan, tribe, or village.

Experiment A research operation in which the researcher manipulates variables so that their influence can be determined.

Experimental group The subjects in an experiment who are exposed to the independent variable.

Expressive leaders Leaders who achieve group harmony by making others feel good.

Expressive role A role that requires taking care of personal relationships.

Extended family The family that consists of two parents, their unmarried children, and other relatives.

Fad A temporary enthusiasm for an innovation less respectable than a fashion.

Family of orientation The family in which one grows up, made up of oneself and one's parents and siblings.

Family of procreation The family that one establishes through marriage, consisting of oneself and one's spouse and children.

Fashion A great though brief enthusiasm among a relatively large number of people for a particular innovation.

Feminist theory A form of conflict theory that explains human life from the experiences of women.

Feminization of poverty A huge number of women bearing the burden of poverty, mostly as single mothers or heads of families.

Fluid intelligence The ability to grasp abstract relationships, as in mathematics, physics, or some other science.

Folkways Weak norms that specify expectations about proper behavior.

Formal organization A group whose activities are rationally designed to achieve specific goals.

Functionalist perspective A theoretical perspective that focuses on social order.

Gender identity People's image of what they are socially expected to be and do on the basis of their sex.

Gender role The pattern of attitudes and behaviors that a society expects of its members because of their being female or male.

Genderlects Linguistic styles that reflect the different worlds of women and men.

Generalized others Mead's term for people who do not have close ties to a child but do influence the child's internalization of the values of society.

Genocide Wholesale killing of a racial or ethnic group.

Gentrification The movement of affluent people into poor urban neighborhoods.

Glass ceiling The prejudiced belief that keeps minority professionals from holding high, leadership positions in organizations.

Global village A closely knit community of all the societies in the world.

Groupthink The tendency for members of a cohesive group to maintain consensus to the extent of ignoring the truth.

Healing role A set of social expectations regarding how a doctor should behave.

Homogamy Marrying someone with social characteristics similar to one's own.

Horizontal mobility Movement from one job to another within the same status category.

Hormones Chemical substances that stimulate or inhibit vital biological processes.

Horticultural society A society that produces food primarily by growing plants in small gardens.

Humorology The study or practice of humor.

Hunting-gathering society A society that hunts animals and gathers plants as its primary means for survival.

Hypothesis A tentative statement about how various events are related to one another.

Id Freud's term for the part of personality that is irrational, concerned only with seeking pleasure.

Ideational culture Sorokin's term for the culture that emphasizes faith or religion as the key to knowledge and encourages people to value spiritual life.

Ideological conservatives U.S. citizens who, in theory, are opposed to big government because of their belief in free enterprise, rugged individualism, and capitalism.

Idiosyncrasy credit The privilege that allows leaders to deviate from their group's norms.

Individual mobility Social mobility related to an individual's personal achievement and characteristics.

Industrial Revolution The dramatic economic change brought about by the introduction of machines into the work process about 200 years ago.

Industrial society A society that produces food for its subsistence primarily by using machinery.

Infant mortality rate The number of deaths among infants less than 1 year old for every 1000 live births.

Influence The ability to control others' behavior through persuasion rather than coercion or authority.

Informal organization A group formed by the informal relations among members of an organization—based on personal interactions, not on any plan by the organization.

Informed consent The approval that a patient gives to a doctor for a treatment after receiving adequate information on it.

In-group The group to which an individual is strongly tied as a member.

Instincts Biologically inherited capacities for performing relatively complex tasks.

Institutionalized discrimination The persistence of discrimination in social institutions, not necessarily recognized by everybody as discrimination.

Instrumental leaders Leaders who achieve their group's goal by getting others to focus on task performance.

Instrumental role A role that requires performance of a task.

Intelligence The capacity for mental or intellectual achievement.

Interaction ritual The form of interaction in which the participants perform certain acts to show reverence to the other.

Intergenerational mobility A change in social standing from one generation to the next.

Intragenerational mobility A change in an individual's social standing.

Jim Crow laws A set of laws that segregates blacks from whites in all kinds of public and private facilities.

Kinesics The use of body movements as a means of communication; also called body language.

Knowledge A collection of relatively objective ideas and facts about the physical and social worlds.

Latent function A function that is unintended and often unrecognized.

Laws Norms that are specified formally in writing and backed by the power of the state.

Life chances The likelihood of living a good, long, or successful life in a society.

Life expectancy The average number of years that a group of people can expect to live.

Lifestyles Tastes, preferences, and ways of living.

Living will Advance instructions on what people want their doctors to do in the event of a terminal illness.

Looking-glass self Cooley's term for the self-image that we develop from the way others treat us.

Macro view A view that focuses on the large social phenomena of society, such as social institutions and inequality.

Manifest function A function that is intended and seems obvious.

Marginal surplus population Marxist term for unemployed workers who are superfluous or useless to the economy.

Marriage rate The number of marriages in a given year for every 1000 people.

Mass hysteria A form of collective behavior in which numerous people engage in a frenzied activity without checking the source of their fear.

Master status A status that dominates a relationship.

Material culture Every conceivable kind of physical object produced by humans.

Matriarchal family The family in which the dominant figure is the eldest female.

Matrilineal descent The norm that recognizes only the mother's family as a child's close relatives.

Matrilocal residence The home where the married couple live with the wife's family.

Mechanical solidarity A form of social cohesion that develops when people do similar work and have similar beliefs and values.

Megacity A city with a population of 5 million or more.

Megalopolis A vast area in which many metropolises merge.

Metropolis A large urban area that includes a city and its surrounding suburbs.

Micro view A view that focuses on the immediate social situations where people interact with one another.

Minority A racial or ethnic group that is subjected to prejudice and discrimination.

Minority theory The theory that older people are treated in society as an oppressed minority.

Modernization The form of social changes that involves the transformation of an agricultural society into an industrial one.

Monogamy The marriage of one man to one woman.

Monotheism The belief in one god.

Mores Strong norms that specify normal behavior and constitute demands, not just expectations.

Multiculturalism A state in which all subcultures are equal to one another in the same society.

Multiple-nuclei theory The model of land use in which a city is built around many discrete nuclei, each being the center of some specialized activity.

Neolocal residence The home where the married couple live by themselves, away from both husband's and wife's families.

Neurosis The mental disorder characterized by a persistent fear, anxiety, or worry about trivial matters.

Nonmaterial culture The intangible aspect of culture.

Normative theories Theories that suggest what we *should* do to achieve our goals.

Norms Social rules that specify how people should behave.

Nuclear family The family that consists of two parents and their unmarried children.

Objective method The method of identifying social classes by using occupation, income, and education to rank people.

Operational liberals U.S. citizens who, in effect, support big government by backing government programs that render services to the public.

Opinion leader A person whose opinion is respected by others and influences them.

Oppositional interaction The interaction in which the participants treat each other as competitors or enemies.

Organic solidarity A type of social cohesion that arises when people in a society perform a wide variety of specialized jobs and therefore have to depend on one another.

Out-group The group of which an individual is not a member.

Panic A type of collective behavior characterized by a maladaptive, fruitless response to a serious threat.

Parkinson's Law The observation that "work expands to fill the time available for its completion."

Participant observation A method of observa-tion in which the researcher takes part in the activities of the group being studied.

Pastoral society A society that domesticates and herds animals as its primary source of food.

Patriarchal family The family in which the dominant figure is the eldest male.

Patriarchy A system of domination in which men exercise power over women.

Patrilineal descent The norm that recognizes only the father's family as a child's close relatives.

Patrilocal residence The home where the married couple live with the husband's family.

Peer group A group whose members are about the same age and have similar interests.

Peripheral countries The world's lower class, relatively poor societies; popularly known as developing countries.

Personality A fairly stable configuration of feelings, attitudes, ideas, and behaviors that characterizes an individual.

Peter Principle The observation that "in every hierarchy every employee tends to rise to their level of incompetence."

Political power The capacity to use the government to make decisions that affect the whole society.

Politics The type of human interaction that involves some people acquiring and exercising power over others.

Polyandry The marriage of one woman to two or more men.

Polygamy The marriage of one person to two or more people of the opposite sex.

Polygyny The marriage of one man to two or more women.

Polytheism The belief in more than one god.

Popular culture A collection of relatively unso-phisticated artistic creations that appeal to a mass audience.

Population The entire group of people to be studied.

Postconventional morality Kohlberg's term for the practice of judging actions by taking into account the importance of *conflicting norms*.

Postindustrial society A society that produces food for subsistence primarily by using high technology.

Power The ability to control the behavior of others, even against their will.

Power elite A small group of individuals who hold top positions in the federal government, military, and corporations and have similar backgrounds, values, and interests.

Preconventional morality Kohlberg's term for the practice of defining right and wrong according to the *consequence* of the action being judged.

Prejudice A negative attitude toward a certain cate-gory of people.

Prescribed role A set of expectations held by society regarding how an individual with a particular status should behave.

Primary deviance Norm violations that a person commits for the first time and without considering them deviant.

Primary group A group whose members interact informally, relate to each other as whole persons, and enjoy their relationship for its own sake.

Principle of immanent change The notion that social change is the product of the social forces that exist within a society.

Propaganda Communication tailored to influence opinion.

Proxemics The use of space as a means of communication.

Psychosis The mental disorder typified by loss of touch with reality.

Public A dispersed collection of people who share a particular interest or concern.

Public opinion The collection of ideas and attitudes shared by the members of a particular public.

Pygmalion effect The impact of a teacher's expectations on student performance.

Race A group of people who are perceived by a given society to be biologically different from others.

Racism The belief that one's own race or ethnicity is superior to that of others.

Random sample A sample drawn in such a way that all members of the population have an equal chance of being selected.

Rape The use of force to get someone to do something sexual against their will.

Rationalization Max Weber's term for the process of replacing the subjective, spontaneous, informal, or diverse ways of doing things with a planned, formally unified method based on abstract rules.

Recidivism Repeated commission of crimes.

Reference group A group that is used as the frame of reference for evaluating one's own behavior.

Reindustrialization The proliferation of unstable, low-skilled, or low-paying jobs.

Reintegrative shaming Making wrongdoers feel guilty while showing them understanding, forgiveness, or even respect.

Relative deprivation Feeling unable to achieve a relatively high aspiration.

Relative poverty A state of deprivation resulting from having less than what the majority of the people has.

Reputational method The method of identifying social classes by selecting a group of people and asking them to rank others.

Resocialization The process by which people are forced to abandon their old self and to develop a new self in its place.

Resource mobilization theory The theory that social movements result from the availability of resources for mobilization.

Revolution The movement aimed at the violent overthrow of the existing government.

Role A set of expectations of what individuals should do in accordance with a particular status of theirs.

Role conflict Conflict between two roles being played simultaneously.

Role distance Separating the role-playing as outward performance from the inner self.

Role performance Actual performance of a role.

Role strain Stress caused by incompatible demands built into a role.

Roleless role Being assigned no role in society's division of labor, a predicament of the elderly in industrial society.

Rumor An unverified story that is spread from one person to another.

Sample A relatively small number of people selected from a larger population.

Sanction A reward for conformity to norms, or punishment for violation of norms.

Scapegoating Blaming others for one's own failure.

Secondary analysis Searching for new knowledge in the data collected earlier by another researcher.

Secondary deviance Repeated norm violations that the violators themselves recognize as deviant.

Secondary group A group whose members interact formally, relate to each other as players of particular roles, and expect to profit from each other.

Sector theory The model of land use in which a city grows outward in wedge-shaped sectors from the center.

Semiperipheral countries The world's middle class, relatively affluent societies in the middle of global stratification; also known as newly industrialized countries.

Senescence The natural physical process of aging.

Senility An abnormal condition characterized by serious memory loss, confusion, and loss of the ability to reason.

Sensate culture Sorokin's term for the culture that stresses empirical evidence or science as the key to knowledge and urges people to favor a practical, materialistic, and hedonistic way of life.

Serial monogamy The marriage of one person to two or more people but one at a time.

Sex ratio The number of males per 100 females.

Sexism Prejudice and discrimination based on the victim's gender.

Sexual harassment An unwelcome act of a sexual nature.

Shamanism The belief that a spiritual leader can communicate with the spirits, by acting as their mouthpiece or letting the soul leave the leader's body and enter the spiritual world.

Sick role A set of social expectations regarding how an ill person should behave.

Significant others Mead's term for people who have close ties to a child and exert a strong influence on the child.

Social aggregate A number of people who happen to be in one place but do not interact with one another.

Social category A number of people who have something in common but neither interact with one another nor gather in one place.

Social change The alteration of society over time.

Social class A category of people who have about the same amount of income, power, and prestige.

Social consensus Condition in which most members of society agree on what is good for everybody to have and cooperate to achieve it.

Social construction of reality The process by which people create through social interaction a certain idea, feeling, or belief about their environment.

Social contagion The spreading of a certain emotion and action from one member of a crowd to another.

Social control The process by which individuals are pressured by society to conform to social norms.

Social forces Forces that arise from the society of which we are a part.

Social group A collection of people who interact with one another and have a certain feeling of unity.

Social institution A set of widely shared beliefs, norms, or procedures necessary for meeting the basic needs of a society.

Social integration The degree to which people are tied to a social group.

Social interaction The process by which individuals act toward and react to others.

Social marginality Being excluded from mainstream society.

Social mobility Movement from one social standing to another.

Social movement A conscious effort to bring about or prevent change.

Social network A web of social relationships that link individuals or groups to one another.

Social stratification The division of society in such a way that some people get more rewards than others.

Socialism An economic system based on public ownership and government control of the economy.

Socialization The process by which a society transmits its cultural values to its members.

Society A collection of interacting individuals sharing the same way of life and living in the same territory.

Sociobiology A new Darwinian theory that human behavior is genetically determined.

Sociocultural evolution The process of changing from a technologically simple society to a more complex one with significant consequences for social and cultural life.

Sociological imagination C. Wright Mills's term for the ability to see the impact of social forces on individuals, especially on their private lives.

Sociology The systematic, scientific study of human society.

Status A position in a group or society.

Status inconsistency The condition in which the same individual is given different status rankings, such as being high in occupation but low in ethnicity.

Status system A system in which people are stratified according to their social prestige.

Stereotype An oversimplified, inaccurate mental picture of others.

Stratified sampling The process of drawing a random sample in which various categories of people are represented in proportions equal to their presence in the population.

Structural assimilation The social condition in which the minority is accepted on equal terms with the rest of society.

Structural mobility Social mobility related to changes in society.

Subcultural theory The theory that the city enriches people's lives by offering diverse opportunities and developing various subcultures.

Subculture theory The theory that the elderly interact mostly with one another, sharing interests and experiences with members of the same age group.

Subjective method The method of identifying social classes by asking people to rank themselves.

Subordinate status A status that does not dominate a relationship; the opposite of master status.

Superego Freud's term for the part of personality that is moral; popularly known as conscience.

Supportive interaction The interaction in which the participants treat each other as supporters or friends.

Survey A research method that involves asking questions about opinions, beliefs, or behavior.

Symbol A word, gesture, music, or anything that stands for some other thing.

Symbolic interactionist perspective A theoretical perspective that directs our attention to the details of a specific situation and of the interaction between individuals in that situation.

Systematic sampling The process of drawing a random sample systematically, rather than haphazardly.

Terrorism The use of violence to express dissatisfaction with a government.

Theism The type of religion that centers on the worship of a god or gods.

Theoretical perspective A set of general assumptions about the nature of society.

Theory A set of logically related hypotheses that explains the relationship among various phenomena.

Thomas theorem Sociologist W. I. Thomas's famous pronouncement that "If people define situations as real, they are real in their consequences."

Total institutions Places where people are not only cut off from the larger society but also rigidly controlled by the administrators.

Totemism The belief that a kinship exists between humans and an animal—or, less commonly, a plant.

Tracking The system of sorting students into different groups according to ability.

Trade deficit Buying more goods and services from foreign countries than selling to them.

Trade surplus Selling more goods and services to foreign countries than buying from them.

Urban anomie theory The theory that city people have a unique way of life, characterized by alienation, impersonal relations, and stress.

Urban ecological processes Processes in which people compete for certain land use, one group dominates another, and a particular group moves into an area and takes it over from others.

Urban ecology The study of the relationship between people and their urban environment.

Urbanization Migration of people from the countryside to city, increasing the proportion of the population that lives in the city.

Value A socially shared idea about what is good, desirable, or important.

Verstehen Weber's term for empathetic understanding of the subjects studied by sociologists.

Vertical mobility Moving up or down the status ladder.

Vital statistics Information about births, marriages, deaths, and migrations into and out of a country.

White ethnics Americans of eastern and southern European origins.

Women's ghettos Traditionally female occupations that are subordinate to positions usually held by men.

World system A network of commercial and other relationships among all the members of the world's community.

References

Abbott, Pamela, and Claire Wallace. 1990. *An Introduction to Sociology: Feminist Perspectives*. London: Routledge.

Abramovitz, Mimi, and Frances Fox Piven. 1994. "Scapegoating women on welfare." *New York Times*, September 2, p. A13.

Acton, H. B. 1967. *What Marx Really Said*. New York: Schocken.

Alba, Richard D. 1990. *Ethnic Identity: The Transformation of White America*. New Haven, Conn.: Yale University Press.

Aldrich, Howard E. 1992. "Incommensurable paradigms? Vital signs from three perspectives." In Michael Reed and Michael Hughes (eds.), *Rethinking Organization: New Directions in Organization Theory and Analysis*. Newbury Park, Calif.: Sage.

Alexander, Karl L., and Martha A. Cook. 1982. "Curricula and coursework: A surprise ending to a familiar story." *American Sociological Review*, 47, pp. 626–40.

Alonso, William. 1964. "The historic and the structural theories of urban form: Their implications for urban renewal." *Journal of Land Economics*, 40, pp. 227–31.

Alter, Jonathan. 1995. "Decoding the contract." *Newsweek*, January 9, pp. 26–27.

Altman, Lawrence K. 1990. "Changes in medicine bring pain to healing profession." *New York Times*, February 18, pp. 1, 20–21.

Ames, Katrine. 1990. "Our bodies, their selves." *Newsweek*, December 17, p. 60.

Andersen, Margaret L. 1993. *Thinking About Women*, 3rd ed. New York: Macmillan.

Anderson, David C. 1994. "The crime funnel." *New York Times Magazine*, June 12, pp. 57 –58.

Archer, Margaret S. 1985. "The myth of cultural integration." *British Journal of Sociology*, 36, pp. 333–53.

Aronoff, Joel, and William D. Crano. 1975. "A re-examination of the cross-cultural principles of task segregation and sex role differentiation in the family." *American Sociological Review*, 40, pp. 12–20.

Asch, Solomon E. 1955. "Opinions and social pressure." *Scientific American*, 193, pp. 31–35.

Ashe, Arthur. 1977. "An open letter to black parents: Send your children to the libraries." *New York Times*, February 6, section 5, p. 2.

———. 1992. "A zero-sum game that hurts blacks." *New York Times*, February 27, p. A10.

Atchley, Robert C. 1988. *Social Forces and Aging*, 5th ed. Belmont, Calif.: Wadsworth.

Azmitia, Margarita. 1988. "Peer interaction and problem solving: When are two hands better than one?" *Child Development*, 59, pp. 87–96.

Babbie, Earl R. 1995. *The Practice of Social Research*, 7th ed. Belmont, Calif.: Wadsworth.

Bailey, J. Michael, and Richard C. Pillard. 1991. "A genetic study of male sexual orientation." *Archives of General Psychiatry*, 48, pp. 1089–96.

Bailey, Kenneth D. 1994. *Methods of Social Research*, 4th ed. New York: Free Press.

Balkan, Sheila, Ronald J. Berger, and Janet Schmidt. 1980. *Crime and Deviance in America: A Critical Approach*. Belmont, Calif.: Wadsworth.

Baltzell, E. Digby. 1991. *The Protestant Establishment Revisited*. New Brunswick, N.J.: Transaction.

———. 1994. *Judgment and Sensibility: Religion and Stratification*. New Brunswick, N.J.: Transaction.

Bane, Mary Jo, and David T. Ellwood. 1994. *Welfare Realities: From Rhetoric to Reform*. Cambridge, Mass.: Harvard University Press.

Banfield, Edward C. 1974. *The Unheavenly City Revisited*. Boston: Little, Brown.

Barlett, Donald L., and James B. Steele. 1992. *America: What Went Wrong?* Kansas City: Andrews and McMeel.

Barringer, Felicity. 1989. "Doubt on 'trial marriage' raised by divorce rates." *New York Times*, June 9, pp. 1, 23.

———. 1991. "Population grows in state capitals." *New York Times*, January 26, pp. 1, 10.

Bart, Pauline B. 1991. "Feminist theories." In Henry Etzkowitz and Ronald M. Glassman (eds.), *The Renascence of Sociological Theory*, pp. 249–65. Itasca, Ill.: Peacock.

Bartley, Robert L. 1991. "Beyond the recession." *Wall Street Journal,* January 2, p. A6.

Basow, Susan A. 1986. *Sex-Role Stereotypes.* Monterey, Calif.: Brooks/Cole.

Baum, Alice S., and Donald W. Burnes. 1993. *A Nation in Denial: The Truth About Homelessness.* Boulder, Colo.: Westview.

Becerra, Rosina. 1988. "The Mexican American family." In Charles Mindel et al. (eds.), *Ethnic Families in America: Patterns and Variations,* 3rd ed. New York: Elsevier.

Beck, E. M., and Stewart E. Tolnay. 1990. "The killing fields of the deep South: The market for cotton and the lynching of blacks, 1882–1930." *American Sociological Review,* 55, pp. 526–39.

Beck, Melinda. 1990a. "The politics of cancer." *Newsweek,* December 10, pp. 62–65.

———. 1990b. "Trading places." *Newsweek,* July 16, pp. 48–54.

Becker, Howard S. 1963. *Outsiders: Studies in the Sociology of Deviance.* New York: Free Press.

———. 1982. "Culture: A sociological view." *The Yale Review,* 71, pp. 513–27.

Begley, Sharon. 1990. "The search for the fountain of youth." *Newsweek,* March 5, pp. 44–48.

Beirne, Piers, and James Messerschmidt. 1995. *Criminology,* 2nd ed. San Diego: Harcourt Brace Jovanovich.

Belkin, Lisa. 1990. "Many in medicine are calling rules a professional malaise." *New York Times,* February 19, pp. A1, A9.

Bellah, Robert N., et al. 1986. *Habits of the Heart: Individualism and Commitment in American Life.* New York: Harper & Row.

Benderly, Beryl Lieff. 1989. "Don't believe everything you read . . . " *Psychology Today,* November, pp. 67–69.

Bendix, Reinhard. 1962. *Max Weber: An Intellectual Portrait.* Garden City, N.Y.: Anchor.

Bennett, William J. 1989. "A response to Milton Friedman." *Wall Street Journal,* September 19, p. A32.

Bennis, Warren. 1989. "The dilemma at the top." *New York Times,* December 31, p. F3.

Benson, Michael L. 1985. "Denying the guilty mind: Accounting for involvement in a white-collar crime." *Criminology,* 23, p. 594.

Berger, Peter L. 1992. "Sociology: A disinvitation?" *Society,* November/December, pp. 12–18.

Bernstein, Richard. 1990. "In U.S. schools a war of words." *New York Times Magazine,* October 14, pp. 34, 48–52.

Berreby, David. 1995. "Unabsolute truths: Clifford Geertz." *New York Times Magazine,* April 9, pp. 44–47.

Beyer, Lisa. 1990. "Lifting the veil." *Time,* September 24, pp. 38–44.

Biggart, Nicole Woolsey. 1994. "Labor and leisure." In Neil J. Smelser and Richard Swedberg (eds.), *The Handbook of Economic Sociology.* Princeton, N.J.: Princeton University Press.

Bilheimer, Robert S. 1983. *Faith and Ferment: An Interdisciplinary Study of Christian Beliefs and Practices.* Minneapolis, Minn.: Augsburg.

Billingsley, Andrew. 1993. *Climbing Jacob's Ladder: The Enduring Legacy of African-American Families.* New York: Simon & Schuster.

Black, Donald. 1983. "Crime as social control." *American Sociological Review,* 48, pp. 34–45.

Blakeslee, Sandra. 1989. "Race and sex are found to affect access to kidney transplants." *New York Times,* January 24, pp. 19, 23.

Blalock, Hubert M., Jr. 1984. *Basic Dilemmas in the Social Sciences.* Beverly Hills, Calif.: Sage.

Blau, Peter M., and Otis Dudley Duncan. 1967. *The American Occupational Structure.* New York: Wiley.

Blumer, Herbert. 1978. "Elementary collective groupings." In Louis E. Genevie (ed.), *Collective Behavior and Social Movements.* Itasca, Ill.: Peacock.

Blumstein, Alfred. 1995. "Violence by young people: Why the deadly nexus?" *National Institute of Justice Journal,* August, pp. 2–9.

Blundell, William E. 1986. "Gripe session." *Wall Street Journal,* May 9, pp. 1, 9.

———. 1987. "When the patient takes charge." *Wall Street Journal,* April 24, pp. D5–D6.

Bohannan, Paul. 1995. *How Culture Works.* New York: Free Press.

Bornstein, Marc H. et al. 1991. "Parenting in cross-cultural perspective: The United States, France, and Japan." In Marc H. Bornstein (ed.), *Cultural Approaches to Parenting,* pp. 69–90. Hillsdale, N.J.: Lawrence Erlbaum Associates.

Bossard, James. 1932. "Residential propinquity as a factor in marriage selection." *American Journal of Sociology,* 38, pp. 219–44.

Boudon, Raymond. 1983a. "Individual action and social change: A no-theory of social change." *British Journal of Sociology,* 34, pp. 1–18.

———. 1983b. "Why theories of social change fail: Some methodological thoughts." *Public Opinion Quarterly*, 47, pp. 143–60.

Bowles, Samuel, and Herbert Gintis. 1976. *Schooling in Capitalist America*. New York: Basic Books.

Box, Steven. 1983. *Power, Crime, and Mystification*. London: Tavistock.

Bradburd, Daniel. 1982. "Volatility of animal wealth among Southwest Asian pastoralists." *Human Ecology*, 10, pp. 85–106.

Bradsher, Keith. 1995. "More on the wealth of nations." *New York Times*, August 20, p. E6.

Braithwaite, John. 1989. *Crime, Shame and Reintegration*. New York: Cambridge University Press.

Bridges, William P., and Wayne J. Villemez. 1986. "Informal hiring and income in the labor market." *American Sociological Review*, 51, pp. 574–82.

Brinkley, Joel. 1992. "U.S. looking for a new path as superpower conflict ends." *New York Times*, February 2, pp. 1, 8.

Brinson, Susan L. 1992. "The use and opposition of rape myths in prime-time television dramas." *Sex Roles*, 27, pp. 359–75.

Brock, Fred. 1993. "Belgium: Keeping spending high and guaranteeing jobs." *New York Times*, December 9, p. A8.

Brody, Jane E. 1992. "Personal health." *New York Times*, March 18, p. B8.

Brooke, James. 1995. "Higher growth seen for Latin America." *New York Times*, January 3, p. C10.

Brookhiser, Richard. 1991. *The Way of the WASP: How It Made America, and How It Can Save It, So to Speak*. New York: Free Press.

Brown, Roger. 1965. *Social Psychology*. New York: Free Press.

Buford, Bill. 1992. *Among the Thugs*. New York: Norton.

Buller, Mary Klein, and David B. Buller. 1987. "Physicians' communication style and patient satisfaction." *Journal of Health and Social Behavior*, 28, pp. 275–88.

Bumpass, Larry, and James Sweet. 1989. "National estimates of cohabitation." *Demography*, 26, pp. 615–25.

Burgess, Ernest W. 1925/1967. "The growth of the city: An introduction to a research project." In R. E. Park, E. W. Burgess, and R. D. McKenzie (eds.), *The City*. Chicago: University of Chicago Press.

Burke, Ronald J., and Tamara Weir. 1976. "Relationship of wives' employment status to husband, wife, and pair satisfaction and performance." *Journal of Marriage and the Family*, 38, pp. 279–87.

Burtless, Gary. 1990. "It's better than watching Oprah." *Wall Street Journal*, January 4, p. A14.

Butler, Robert. 1984. Interviewed in *U.S. News & World Report*, July 2, pp. 51–52.

Campbell, Anne. 1993. *Men, Women, and Aggression*. New York: Basic Books.

Cantril, Hadley, with Hazel Gaudet and Herta Herzog. 1940/1982. *The Invasion from Mars*. Princeton, N.J.: Princeton University Press.

Capron, Alexander Morgan. 1990. "The burden of decision." *Hastings Center Report*, May/June, pp. 36–41.

Carlson, Eugene. 1991. "Impact of zones for enterprise is ambiguous." *Wall Street Journal*, April 1, pp. B1, B2.

Carmody, Deirdre. 1990. "Identity crisis for 'Seven Sisters.'" *New York Times*, August 6, p. C1.

Carney, James. 1995. "Mend it, don't end it." *Time*, July 31, p. 35.

Carnoy, Martin, and Henry M. Levin. 1985. *Schooling and Work in the Democratic State*. Stanford, Calif.: Stanford University Press.

Carpenter, Betsy. 1990. "Living with our legacy." *U.S. News & World Report*, April 23, pp. 60–65.

Casper, Lynne M., Sara S. McLanahan, and Irwin Garfinkel. 1994. "The gender-gap: What we can learn from other countries." *American Sociological Review*, 59, pp. 594–605.

Castro, Janice. 1993. "Disposable workers." *Time*, March 29, pp. 43–47.

Celis, William 3rd. 1993a. "International report card shows U.S. schools work." *New York Times*, December 9, pp. A1, A8.

———. 1993b. "Study suggests Head Start helps beyond school." *New York Times*, April 30, p. A11.

Chambliss, William J. 1969. *Crime and the Legal Process*. New York: McGraw-Hill.

Charon, Joel M. 1992. *Symbolic Interactionism*, 4th ed. Englewood Cliffs, N.J.: Prentice-Hall.

Cherlin, Andrew J. 1983. "Changing family and household: Contemporary lessons from historical research." *Annual Review of Sociology*, 9, pp. 51–66.

———. 1992. *Marriage, Divorce, Remarriage*. Cambridge, Mass: Harvard University Press.

————, and Frank F. Furstenberg, Jr. 1983. "The American family in the year 2000." *Futurist,* 18, June, pp. 7–14.

————. 1994. "Stepfamilies in the United States: A reconsideration." *Annual Review of Sociology,* 20, pp. 359–81.

Chideya, Faria, et al. 1993. "Endangered family." *Newsweek,* August 30, pp. 17–27.

Childe, Gordon. 1952. *Man Makes Himself.* New York: New American Library.

Chilman, Catherine Street. 1993. "Hispanic families in the United States: Research perspectives." In Harriette Pipes McAdoo (ed.), *Family Ethnicity: Strength in Diversity.* Newbury Park, Calif.: Sage.

Chomsky, Noam. 1993. *The Prosperous Few and the Restless Many.* Berkely, Calif.: Odonian.

Christopher, Robert C. 1983. *The Japanese Mind: The Goliath Explained.* New York: Linden/Simon & Schuster.

Church, George J. 1993. "Gorezilla zips the system." *Time,* September 13, pp. 25–28.

Clark, Charles S. 1993. *TV Violence.* Washington, D.C.: Congressional Quarterly, Inc.

Close, Ellis. 1993. *The Rage of a Privileged Class.* New York: HarperCollins.

Cockerham, William C. 1995. *Medical Sociology,* 6th ed. Englewood Cliffs, N.J.: Prentice-Hall.

Cohen, Arthur M., and Florence B. Brawer. 1982. "The community college as college." *Change,* March, pp. 39–42.

Cohen, Albert K. 1966. *Deviance and Control.* Englewood Cliffs, N.J.: Prentice-Hall.

Coleman, James William, and Donald R. Cressey. 1993. *Social Problems,* 5th ed. New York: HarperCollins.

Collins, Randall. 1975. *Conflict Sociology.* New York: Academic Press.

————. 1986. "Is 1980s sociology in the doldrums?" *American Journal of Sociology,* 91, pp. 1336–55.

Commoner, Barry. 1990. *Making Peace with the Planet.* New York: Pantheon.

Conrad, Peter, and Rochelle Kern (eds.). 1994. *Sociology of Health and Illness: Critical Perspectives,* 4th ed. New York: St. Martin's.

Cooley, Charles H. 1909. *Social Organization.* New York: Scribner's.

Cooper, Kristina, et al. 1986. "Correlates of mood and marital satisfaction among dual-worker and single-worker couples." *Social Psychology Quarterly,* 49, pp. 322–29.

Corliss, Richard. 1993. "A few good women." *Time,* April 15, pp. 58–59.

Corsaro, William A., and Donna Eder. 1990. "Children's peer cultures." *Annual Review of Sociology,* 16, pp. 197–220.

Corsaro, William A., and Tomas A. Rizzo. 1988. "*Discussione* and friendship: Socialization processes in the peer culture of Italian nursery school children." *American Sociological Review,* 53, pp. 879–94.

Cory, Christopher T. 1979. "Women smile less for success." *Psychology Today,* March, p. 16.

Cose, Ellis. 1995. "The silly season." *Newsweek,* October 16, pp. 63–65.

Coverman, Shelley. 1989. "Role overload, role conflict, and stress: Addressing consequences of multiple role demands." *Social Forces,* 67, pp. 965–82.

Cowell, Alan. 1994. "Pope rules out debate on women as priests." *New York Times,* May 31, pp. A1, A4.

Cowgill, Donald O. 1974. "Aging and modernization: A revision of the theory." In J. F. Gubrium (ed.), *Late Life: Communities and Environmental Policy.* Springfield, Ill.: Thomas.

Cowley, Geoffrey. 1988. "The wisdom of animals." *Newsweek,* May 23, pp. 52–59.

Cox, Harvey. 1966. *The Secular City.* New York: Macmillan.

Cramer, Jerome. 1989. "Where did the gung-ho go?" *Time,* September 11, pp. 52–56.

Crispell, Diane. 1990. "Workers in 2000." *American Demographics,* March, pp. 36–40.

Crossen, Cynthia. 1991. "Kids acting up? Don't yell, validate their tiny feelings." *Wall Street Journal,* December 10, pp. A1, A4.

Crossette, Barbara. 1990. "India to shake up birth-control bureaucracy." *New York Times,* March 14, p. A4.

Cullingford, Cedric. 1993. "Children's social and moral claims." *Society,* November/December, pp. 52–54.

Cumming, Elaine. 1963. "Further thoughts on the theory of disengagement." *International Social Science,* 15, pp. 377–93.

————, and William E. Henry. 1961. *Growing Old: The Process of Disengagement.* New York: Basic Books.

Currie, Elliott. 1993. *Reckoning: Drugs, the Cities, and the American Future.* New York: Hill and Wang.

Dahl, Robert A. 1981. *Democracy in the United States: Promise and Performance,* 4th ed. Boston: Houghton Mifflin.

Davis, Bernard D. 1990. "Right to die: Living wills are inadequate." *Wall Street Journal,* July 31, p. A12.

Davis, James. 1982. "Up and down opportunity's ladder." *Public Opinion,* June/July, pp. 11–15, 48–51.

Davis, James F. 1991. *Who Is Black?: One Nation's Definition.* University Park, Pa: Pennsylvania State University Press.

Davis, Kingsley. 1947. "Final note on a case of extreme isolation." *American Journal of Sociology,* 52, pp. 432–37.

———. 1955. "The origin and growth of urbanization in the world." *American Journal of Sociology,* 60, pp. 429–37.

———. 1976. "The world's population crises." In Robert K. Merton and Robert Nisbet (eds.), *Contemporary Social Problems,* 4th ed. New York: Harcourt Brace Jovanovich.

———, and Wilbert E. Moore. 1945. "Some principles of stratification." *American Sociological Review,* 10, pp. 242–49.

Davis, Murray S. 1993. *What's So Funny? The Comic Conception of Culture and Society.* Chicago: University of Chicago Press.

Day, Kathleen, and Meda Chesney-Lind. 1988. "Feminism and criminology." *Justice Quarterly,* 5, pp. 101–43.

Deegan, Mary Jo. 1988. *Jane Addams and the Men of Chicago School.* New Brunswick, N.J.: Transaction.

Delphy, Christine, and Diana Leonard. 1992. *Familiar Exploitation: A New Analysis of Marriage in Contemporary Western Societies.* Cambridge, U.K.: Polity Press.

Denton, Nancy A., and Douglas S. Massey. 1989. "Racial identity among Caribbean Hispanics: The effect of double minority status on residential segregation." *American Sociological Review,* 54, pp. 790–808.

DeParle, Jason. 1994. "Report to Clinton sees vast extent of homelessness." *New York Times,* February 17, pp. A1, A10.

Dickey, Christopher. 1991. "Not just a case of trying to save face." *Newsweek,* January 21, p. 22.

Diesenhouse, Susan. 1990. "More women are playing, but fewer call the shots." *New York Times,* December 11, pp. B11–B12.

Dobash, Russell P., et al. 1992. "The myth of sexual symmetry in marital violence." *Social Problems,* 39, pp. 71–91.

Domhoff, G. William. 1978. *The Powers That Be: Processes of Ruling-Class Domination in America.* New York: Random House.

———. 1983. *Who Rules America Now? A View for the Eighties.* Englewood Cliffs, N.J.: Prentice-Hall.

Dowd, Maureen. 1994. "Americans like G.O.P. agenda but split on how to reach goals." *New York Times,* December 15, pp. A1, A14.

Dowell, William. 1991. "Freedom is the best revenge." *Time,* December 16, pp. 24–29.

Durkheim, Emile. 1897/1951. *Suicide.* New York: Free Press.

———. 1915/1966. *The Elementary Forms of the Religious Life.* New York: Free Press.

Dutton, Diana B. 1978. "Explaining the low use of health services by the poor: Costs, attitudes, or delivery system?" *American Sociological Review,* 43, pp. 348–68.

Dychtwald, Ken. 1989. *Age Wave: The Challenges and Opportunities of an Aging America.* Los Angeles: Jeremy Tarcher.

Easterbrook, Gregg. 1987. "The revolution in medicine." *Newsweek,* January 26, pp. 40–74.

———. 1989. "Cleaning up." *Newsweek,* July 24, pp. 26–42.

Echikson, William. 1990. *Lighting the Night: Revolution in Eastern Europe.* New York: Morrow.

Egan, Timothy. 1991. "7 Indian tribes seeking end to shackles of dependency." *New York Times,* January 16, pp. A1, A11.

Ehrlich, Anne. 1984. "Critical masses: World population 1984." *Sierra,* July/August, pp. 36–40.

Elkin, Frederick, and Gerald Handel. 1988. *The Child and Society,* 5th ed. New York: Random House.

Elkind, David. 1992. "The future of childhood." *Psychology Today,* May/June, pp. 38–81.

Elliott, Michael, and Christopher Dickey. 1994. "Body politics: Population wars." *Newsweek,* September 12, pp. 22–27.

Ellis, Lee. 1985. "Religiosity and criminality." *Sociological Perspectives,* 28, pp. 501–20.

Elmer-DeWitt, Philip. 1991. "Why isn't our birth control better?" *Time*, August 12, pp. 52–53.

Epstein, Cynthia Fuchs. 1976. "Sex roles." In Robert K. Merton and Robert Nisbet (eds.), *Contemporary Social Problems*. New York: Harcourt Brace Jovanovich.

Erlanger, Steven. 1995. "Russia faces plenty of disappointment." *New York Times*, January 3, p. C10.

Espinosa, P. K. 1992. "Life in these United States." *Reader's Digest*, January, p. 68.

Etzioni, Amitai. 1975. *A Comparative Analysis of Complex Organizations*, rev. ed. New York: Free Press.

———. 1993. *The Spirit of Community: Rights, Responsibilities and the Communitarian Agenda*. New York: Crown.

Faludi, Susan. 1991. *Backlash: The Undeclared War Against American Women*. New York: Crown.

Farley, John E. 1995. *Majority-Minority Relations*, 3rd ed. Englewood Cliffs, N.J.: Prentice-Hall.

Farnsworth, Clyde H. 1990. "Report by World Bank sees poverty lessening by 2000 except in Africa." *New York Times*, July 16, p. A3.

———. 1995. "Canada's momentum expected to continue." *New York Times*, January 3, p. C10.

Farran, D. C., and R. Haskins. 1980. "Reciprocal influence in the social interactions of mothers and three-year-old children from different socioeconomic backgrounds." *Child Development*, 51, pp. 780–91.

Feagin, Joe R. 1995a. *Racial and Ethnic Relations*, 5th ed. Englewood Cliffs, N.J.: Prentice-Hall.

———. 1995b. *White Racism: The Basics*. New York: Routledge.

Featherman, David L., and Robert M. Hauser. 1978. *Opportunity and Change*. New York: Academic Press.

Felson, Richard B., and Mark D. Reed. 1986. "Reference groups and self-appraisals of academic ability and performance." *Social Psychology Quarterly*, 49, pp. 103–9.

Feshbach, Murray, and Alfred Friendly Jr. 1992. *Ecocide in the U.S.S.R.* New York: Basic Books.

Filer, Randall K. 1990. "What we really know about the homeless." *Wall Street Journal*, April 10, p. 22.

Firor, John. 1990. *The Changing Atmosphere: A Global Challenge*. New Haven, Conn.: Yale University Press.

Fischer, Claude. 1984. *The Urban Experience*, 2nd ed. San Diego: Harcourt Brace Jovanovich.

Fischer, David Hackett. 1977. *Growing Old in America*. New York: Oxford University Press.

Fischman, Joshua. 1986. "What are friends for?" *Psychology Today*, September, pp. 70–71.

Fish, Jefferson M. 1995. "Mixed blood." *Psychology Today*, November/December, pp. 55–61, 76, 80.

Fiske, Edward B. 1987. "Global focus on quality in education." *New York Times*, June 1, pp. 19, 23.

Florida, Richard, and Martin Kenney. 1991. "Transplanted organizations: The transfer of Japanese industrial organization to the U.S." *American Sociological Review*, 56, pp. 381–98.

Fox, James Alan. 1994. "American killers are getting younger." *USA Today*, January, pp. 24–26.

Fox, John W. 1993. "The conceptualization and measurement of social mobility differences: A brief reply to Rogers and Mann." *Journal of Health and Social Behavior*, 34, pp. 173–77.

Francis, David R. 1987. "Despite concern, black Africa's population picture grows worse." *Christian Science Monitor*, November 7, p. 22.

Frank, Robert H., and Philip J. Cook. 1995. *The Winner-Take-All Society*. New York: Free Press.

Freedman, Alix M. 1990. "Deadly diet." *Wall Street Journal*, December 18, pp. A1, A4.

Freedman, Jonathan L. 1986. "Television violence and aggression: A rejoinder." *Psychological Bulletin*, 100, pp. 372–78.

French, Howard W. 1995. "Out of South Africa, progress." *New York Times*, July 6, pp. C1, C5.

Friedman, Thomas L. 1992. "Rethinking foreign affairs: Are they still a U.S. affair?" *New York Times*, February 7, pp. A1, A7.

Fussell, Paul. 1992. *Class: A Guide Through the American Status System*. New York: Touchstone.

Futurist. 1989. "Adult education: Beyond 'night school.'" January/February, pp. 43–44.

Galles, Gary M. 1989. "What colleges really teach." *New York Times*, June 8, p. 23.

Gallup, George, Jr., and Jim Castelli. 1989. *The People's Religion: American Faith in the '90s*. New York: Macmillan.

Gamson, William A. 1975. *The Strategy of Social Protest*. Homewood, Ill.: Dorsey.

Gans, Herbert J. 1968. *People and Plans.* New York: Basic Books.

———. 1971. "The uses of poverty: The poor pay all." *Social Policy,* 2, pp. 20–24.

———. 1982. *The Urban Villagers.* New York: Free Press.

———. 1989. "Sociology in America: The discipline and the public." *American Sociological Review,* 54, pp. 1–16.

Gardner, Howard. 1993. *Creating Minds: An Anatomy of Creativity Seen Through the Lives of Freud, Einstein, Picasso, Stravinsky, Eliot, Graham, and Gandhi.* New York: Basic Books.

Garfinkel, Harold. 1967. *Studies in Ethnomethodology.* Englewood Cliffs, N.J.: Prentice-Hall.

Gargan, Edward A. 1991. "Tearful bride, just 10, touches India." *New York Times,* October 21, p. A7.

Gartner, Michael. 1990. "Indian tribes shouldn't bet their future on casinos." *Wall Street Journal,* June 28, p. A15.

Gecas, Viktor. 1981. "Contexts of Socialization." In Morris Rosenberg and Ralph H. Turner (eds.), *Social Psychology: Sociological Perspectives.* New York: Basic Books.

Gelles, Richard J., and Claire Pedrick Cornell. 1990. *Intimate Violence in Families,* 2nd ed. Beverly Hills, Calif.: Sage.

Gelman, David. 1986. "Why we age differently." *Newsweek,* October 20, pp. 60–61.

Gerber, Gwendolyn L. 1989. "The more positive evaluation of men than women on the gender-stereotyped traits." *Psychological Reports,* 65, pp. 275–86.

Gilbert, Dennis, and Joseph A. Kahl. 1993. *The American Class Structure,* 4th ed. Belmont, Calif.: Wadsworth.

Gilleard, Christopher John, and Ali Aslan Gurkan. 1987. "Socioeconomic development and the status of elderly men in Turkey: A test of modernization theory." *Journal of Gerontology,* 42, pp. 353–57.

Gilligan, Carol. 1982. *In a Different Voice: Psychological Theory and Women's Development.* Cambridge: Harvard University Press.

Gilman, Hank. 1986. "Marketers court older consumers as balance of buying power shifts." *Wall Street Journal,* April 23, p. 37.

Gimenez, Martha E. 1990. "The feminization of poverty: Myth or reality?" *Social Justice,* 17, pp. 43–69.

Giordano, Joseph. 1987. "The Mafia mystique." *U.S. News & World Report,* February 16, p. 6.

Glaab, Charles N., and A. Theodore Brown. 1983. *A History of Urban America,* 3rd ed. New York: Macmillan.

Gleick, Elizabeth. 1995. "The costly crisis in our schools." *Time,* January 30, pp. 67–68.

Glenn, Norval D., and Charles N. Weaver. 1982. "Enjoyment of work by full-time workers in U.S., 1955 and 1980." *Public Opinion Quarterly,* 46, pp. 459–70.

Goffman, Erving. 1967. *Interaction Ritual.* New York: Random House.

———. 1971. *Relations in Public: Microstudies of the Public Order.* New York: Basic Books.

Goldman, Ari L. 1991. "Portrait of religion in U.S. holds dozens of surprises." *New York Times,* April 10, pp. A1, A11.

———. 1992. "Catholics are at odds with bishops." *New York Times,* June 19, p. A8.

Goldstein, Melvyn C., and Cynthia M. Beall. 1982. "Indirect modernization and the status of the elderly in a rural third-world setting." *Journal of Gerontology,* 37, pp. 743–48.

Goldstone, Jack A. 1982. "The comparative and historical study of revolutions." *Annual Review of Sociology,* 8, pp. 187–207.

Goleman, Daniel. 1988. "Physicians may bungle part of treatment: Medical interview." *New York Times,* January 21, p. 12.

———. 1990. "Stereotypes of the sexes said to persist in therapy." *New York Times,* April 10, pp. B1, B7.

———. 1991a. "Anatomy of a rumor: Fear feeds it." *New York Times,* June 4, pp. B1, B7.

———. 1991b. "Sexual harassment: About power, not sex." *New York Times,* October 22, 1991, p. C12.

———. 1995. *Emotional Intelligence.* New York: Bantam Books.

Goode, Erich. 1989. *Drugs in American Society,* 3rd ed. New York: Knopf.

Goode, William J. 1982. *The Family,* 2nd ed. Englewood Cliffs, N.J.: Prentice-Hall.

———. 1993. *World Changes in Divorce Patterns.* New Haven, Conn.: Yale University Press.

Goodlad, John I. 1984. *A Place Called School: Prospects for the Future.* New York: McGraw-Hill.

Gorman, Christine. 1992. "Sizing up the sexes." *Time,* January 20, pp. 42–51.

Gottdiener, Mark. 1983. "Understanding metropolitan

deconcentration: A clash of paradigms." *Social Science Quarterly,* 64, pp. 227–46.

———. 1985. *The Social Production of Urban Space.* Austin: University of Texas Press.

———. 1994. *The New Urban Sociology.* New York: McGraw-Hill.

Gottman, John. 1994. *Why Marriages Succeed or Fail.* New York: Simon & Schuster.

Goy, R. W., and B. S. McEwen. 1980. *Sexual Differentiation of the Brain.* Cambridge, Mass.: MIT Press.

Granovetter, Mark. 1983. "The strength of weak ties: A network theory revisited." In Randall Collins (ed.), *Sociological Theory 1983.* San Francisco: Jossey-Bass.

———. 1984. "Small is bountiful: Labor markets and establishment size." *American Sociological Review,* 49, 323–34.

Gray, John. 1992. *Men Are From Mars, Women Are From Venus.* New York: HarperCollins Publishers.

Greenberg, David. 1981. *Crime and Capitalism: Readings in Marxist Criminology.* Palo Alto, Calif.: Mayfield.

Greenberger, Ellen, and Wendy A. Goldberg. 1989. "Work, parenting, and the socialization of children." *Developmental Psychology,* 25, pp. 22–35.

Greenhouse, Steven. 1994. "State dept. finds widespread abuse of world's women." *New York Times,* February 3, pp. A1, A6.

Greider, William. 1992. *Who Will Tell the People?: The Betrayal of American Democracy.* New York: Simon & Schuster.

Griffith, Jeanne E., et al. 1989. "American education: The challenge of change." *Population Bulletin,* December, pp. 2–39.

Grissmer, David W. 1994. *Student Achievement and The Changing American Family: An Executive Summary.* Santa Monica, Calif.: Rand Corp.

Gross, Jane. 1991. "More young single men clinging to apron strings." *New York Times,* June 16, pp. 1, 10.

Grubaugh, Stephen G., and Rexford E. Santerre. 1994. "Comparing the performance of health care systems: An alternative approach." *Southern Economic Journal,* 60, pp. 1030–42.

Gwartney-Gibbs, Patricia A. 1986. "The institutionalization of premarital cohabitation: Estimates from marriage license applications, 1970 and 1980." *Journal of Marriage and the Family,* 48, pp. 423–34.

Gwynne, S. C. 1992. "The long haul." *Time,* September 28, pp. 34–38.

Hacker, Andrew. 1983. "What the very rich really think." *Forbes,* Fall, pp. 66–70.

———. 1992. *Two Nations: Black and White, Separate, Hostile, Unequal.* New York: Scribner's

Hadaway, C. Kirk, et al. 1993. "What the polls don't show: A closer look at U.S. church attendance." *American Sociological Review,* 58, pp. 741–52.

Hall, Wayne. 1986. "Social class and survival on the *S.S. Titanic." Social Science and Medicine,* 22, pp. 687–90.

Hammond, Phillip E. 1985. "The curious path of conservative Protestantism." *Annals of the American Academy of Political and Social Science,* 480, July, pp. 53–62.

Hancock, LynNell. 1994. "Red, white—and blue." *Newsweek,* November 7, p. 54.

Harayda, Janice. 1986. *The Joy of Being Single.* Garden City, N.Y.: Doubleday.

Hardin, Garrett. 1993. *Living Within Limits: Ecology, Economics, and Population Taboos.* New York: Oxford University Press.

Hare, A. Paul. 1962. *Handbook of Small Group Research.* Glencoe, Ill.: Free Press.

Harjo, Suzan Shown. 1993. "The American Indian experience." In Harriette Pipes McAdoo (ed.), *Family Ethnicity: Strength in Diversity.* Newbury Park, Calif.: Sage.

Harper, Lucinda. 1993. "Good looks can mean a pretty penny on the job . . ." *Wall Street Journal,* November 23, p. B1.

Harris, Chauncy D., and Edward L. Ullman. 1945. "The nature of cities." *Annals of the American Academy of Political and Social Science,* 242, pp. 7–17.

Harris, Marvin. 1985. *Good to Eat: Riddles of Foods and Culture.* New York: Simon & Schuster.

———. 1995. *Cultural Anthropology,* 4th ed. New York: HarperCollins.

Harris, Monica J., and Robert Rosenthal. 1985. "Mediation of interpersonal expectancy effects: 31 meta-analyses." *Psychological Bulletin,* 97, pp. 363–86.

Harrison, Lawrence E. 1992. *Who Prospers? How Cultural Values Shape Economic and Political Success.* New York: Basic Books.

Hatch, Ruth C., Dorothy E. James, and Walter R. Schumm. 1986. "Spiritual intimacy and marital satisfaction." *Family Relations,* 35, pp. 539–45.

Hauser, Philip M. 1981. "Chicago—urban crisis exemplar." In J. John Palen (ed.), *City Scenes,* 2nd ed. Boston: Little, Brown.

Havighurst, Robert J. 1963. "Successful aging." In Richard H. Williams, Clark Tibbitts, and William Donahue (eds.), *Processes of Aging,* vol. 1. New York: Atherton.

Hawkes, Kristen, and James F. O'Connell. 1981. "Affluent hunters? Some comments in light of the Alyawara case." *American Anthropologist,* 83, pp. 622–26.

Hawkins, Dana. 1992. "A very rich dessert." *U.S. News & World Report,* March 23, pp. 52–53.

Hayes, Arthur S. 1990. "Suburban dilemma." *Wall Street Journal,* October 4, pp. A1, A16.

Headland, Thomas N., and Lawrence A. Reid. 1989. "Hunter-gatherers and their neighbors from prehistory to the present." *Current Anthropology,* 30, pp. 43–51.

Hegedus, Rita. 1976. "Voucher plans." In Steven E. Goodman (ed.), *Handbook on Contemporary Education.* New York: Bowker.

Heilbroner, Robert L. 1972. *The Worldly Philosophers: The Lives, Times, and Ideas of the Great Economic Thinkers,* 4th ed. New York: Simon & Schuster.

———. 1980. *Marxism: For and Against.* New York: Norton.

Heim, Pat, and Susan Golant. 1993. *Hardball for Women.* New York: Plume.

Henneberger, Melinda, and Michel Marriott. 1993. "For some, youthful courting has become a game of abuse." *New York Times,* July 11, pp. 1, 14.

Henry, William A., III. 1990. "Beyond the melting pot." *Time,* April 9, pp. 28–31.

Henslin, James M., and Mae A. Biggs. 1971. "Dramaturgical desexualization: The sociology of the vaginal examination." In James M. Henslin (ed.), *Studies in the Sociology of Sex.* New York: Appleton-Century-Crofts.

Herrnstein, Richard J., and Charles Murray. 1994. *The Bell Curve: Intelligence and Class Structure in American Life.* New York: Free Press.

Hershey, Robert D., Jr. 1995. "U.S. closed year with employment growing sharply." *New York Times,* January 7, pp. 1, 29.

Heyneman, Stephen P., and William A. Loxley. 1983. "The effect of primary-school quality on academic achievement across twenty-nine high- and low-income countries." *American Journal of Sociology,* 88, pp. 1162–94.

Hilts, Philip J. 1990. "AIDS bias grows faster than disease, study says." *New York Times,* July 17, pp. 1, 14.

Hirschi, Travis. 1969. *Causes of Delinquency.* Berkeley and Los Angeles: University of California Press.

Hirschman, Charles. 1983. "America's melting pot reconsidered." *Annual Review of Sociology,* 9, pp. 397–423.

Hochschild, Arlie R. 1989. *The Second Shift.* New York: Viking.

Hodge, Robert W., Paul M. Siegel, and Peter H. Rossi. 1964. "Occupational prestige in the United States: 1925–1963." *American Journal of Sociology,* 70, pp. 286–302.

Hodson, Randy. 1989. "Gender differences in job satisfaction: Why aren't women more dissatisfied?" *Sociological Quarterly,* 30, pp. 385–99.

Hoecker-Drysdale, Susan. 1992. *Harriet Martineau: First Woman Sociologist.* Oxford, UK: Berg.

Hoffer, Eric. 1966. *The True Believer: Thoughts on the Nature of Mass Movements.* New York: Harper & Row.

Hogan, Dennis P., et al. 1990. "Race, kin networks, and assistance to mother-headed families." *Social Forces,* 68, pp. 797–812.

Horn, Thelma Sternberg, and Curt Lox. 1993. "The self-fulfilling prophecy theory: When coaches' expectations become reality." In Jean M. Williams (ed.), *Applied Sport Psychology: Personal Growth to Peak Performance,* pp. 68–81. Mountain View, Calif.: Mayfield.

Horner, Matina S. 1969. "Fail: Bright women." *Psychology Today,* November, pp. 36–38.

Hoult, Thomas Ford. 1979. *Sociology for a New Day,* 2nd ed. New York: Random House.

House, James S., et al. 1988. "Social relationships and health." *Science,* 241, pp. 540–45.

Hoyt, Homer. 1943. "The structure of American cities in the post-war era." *American Journal of Sociology,* 48, pp. 475–92.

Hraba, Joseph. 1979. *American Ethnicity.* Itasca, Ill.: Peacock.

Humphreys, Laud. 1970. *Tearoom Trade: Impersonal Sex in Public Places.* Chicago: Aldine.

Huntington, Samuel P. 1993. "The clash of civilizations?" *Foreign Affairs,* Summer, pp. 22–49.

Impoco, Jim. 1995. "Separating church and school." *U.S. News & World Report,* April 24, p. 30.

Ingrassia, Michele. 1995. "Still fumbling in the dark." *Newsweek,* March 13, pp. 60–62.

———, and Pat Wingert. 1995. "The new providers." *Newsweek,* May 22, pp. 36–38.

Jackson, Linda A., John E. Hunter, and Carole N. Hodge. 1995. "Physical attractiveness and intellectual competence: A meta-analytic review." *Social Psychology Quarterly,* 58, pp. 108–22

Jacquard, Albert. 1983. "Myths under the microscope." *UNESCO Courier,* 36, November, pp. 25–27.

Janis, Irving L. 1982. *Groupthink: Psychological Studies of Policy Decisions and Fiascos.* Boston: Houghton Mifflin.

Janus, Samuel S., and Cynthia L. Janus. 1993. *The Janus Report on Sexual Behavior.* New York: John Wiley & Sons.

Jaret, Charles. 1983. "Recent neo-Marxist urban analysis." *Annual Review of Sociology,* 9, pp. 499–525.

Jencks, Christopher. 1994. *The Homeless.* Cambridge, Mass.: Harvard University Press.

Johnson, Julie, et al. 1991. "Why do blacks die young?" *Time,* September 16, pp. 50–52.

Johnson, Sally. 1995. "Continuing education: college a la carte." *New York Times: Education Life,* August 6, pp. 22–24.

Johnson, Sterling, Jr. 1987. "This is the wrong message to give." *New York Times,* December 20, p. E20.

Jones, Charisse. 1994. "Years on integration road: New views of an old goal." *New York Times,* April 10, pp. 1, 15.

Jones, Peter, et al. 1993. "Premorbid social under-achievement in schizophrenia: Results from the Camberwell collaborative psychosis study." *British Journal of Psychiatry,* 162, pp. 65–71.

Josephson, Wendy L. 1987. "Television violence and children's aggression: Testing the priming, social script, and disinhibition predictions." *Journal of Personality and Social Psychology,* 53, pp. 882–90.

Kalick, S. Michael, and Thomas E. Hamilton III. 1986. "The matching hypothesis reexamined." *Journal of Personality and Social Psychology,* 51, pp. 673–82.

Kalmuss, Debra. 1984. "The intergenerational transmission of marital aggression." *Journal of Marriage and the Family,* 46, pp. 11–19.

Kanin, Eugene J. 1983. "Rape as a function of relative sexual frustration." *Psychological Reports,* 52, pp. 133–34.

Kantrowitz, Barbara. 1991. "Striking a nerve." *Newsweek,* October 21, pp. 38, 40.

———, and Pat Wingert. 1993. "No longer a sacred cow." *Newsweek,* April 12, p. 57.

Karp, David A., and William C. Yoels. 1993. *Sociology in Everyday Life.* Itasca, Ill.: Peacock.

Karp, David A., Gregory P. Stone, and William C. Yoels. 1991. *Being Urban: A Sociology of City Life.* New York: Praeger.

Kart, Gary S. 1990. *The Realities of Aging,* 3rd ed. Boston: Allyn and Bacon.

Katz, Jack. 1988. *Seductions of Crime.* New York: Basic Books.

Kaus, Mickey. 1992. *The End of Equality.* New York: Basic Books.

Keller, Helen. 1954. *The Story of My Life.* Garden City, N.Y.: Doubleday.

Kennedy, Paul M. 1988. *The Rise and Fall of the Great Powers.* New York: Random House.

———. 1991. "A declining empire goes to war." *Wall Street Journal,* January 24, p. A10.

Kephart, William M., and Davor Jedlicka. 1988. *The Family, Society, and the Individual,* 6th ed. New York: Harper & Row.

Kerbo, Harold R. 1982. "Movements of 'crisis' and movements of 'affluence': A critique of deprivation and resource mobilization theories." *Journal of Conflict Resolution,* 26, pp. 645–63.

Kerckhoff, Alan C., Richard T. Campbell, and Idee Winfield-Laird. 1985. "Social mobility in Great Britain and the United States." *American Journal of Sociology,* 91, pp. 281–308.

Kessler, Ronald C., Richard H. Price, and Camille B. Wortman. 1985. "Social factors in psychopathology: Stress, social support, and coping processes." *Annual Review of Psychology,* 36, pp. 560–61.

Kilborn, Peter T. 1990. "Wage gap between sexes is cut in test, but at a price." *New York Times,* May 31, pp. A1, A12.

———. 1995. "Women and minorities still face 'glass ceiling.'" *New York Times,* March 16, p. C22.

Kilker, Ernest Evans. 1993. "Black and white in America: The culture and politics of racial classification." *International Journal of Politics, Culture and Society,* 7, pp. 229–58.

Kimball, Meredith M. 1989. "A new perspective on women's math achievement." *Psychological Bulletin,* 105, pp. 198–214.

Kimmel, Michael S. 1986. "A prejudice against prejudice." *Psychology Today,* December, pp. 47–52.

————. 1992. "Reading men: Men, masculinity, and publishing." *Contemporary Sociology*, 21, March, pp. 162–71.

Kitahara, Michio. 1982. "Menstrual taboos and the importance of hunting." *American Anthropologist,* 84, pp. 901–3.

Kitano, Harry H. L. 1981. "Asian-Americans: The Chinese, Japanese, Koreans, Filipinos, and Southeast Asians." *Annals,* 454, March, pp. 125–49.

Klag, Michael J., et al. 1991. "The association of skin color with blood pressure in U.S. blacks with low socioeconomic status." *Journal of the American Medical Association,* 265, pp. 599–640.

Klaus, Patsy A., and Michael R. Rand. 1984. "Family violence." *Bureau of Justice Statistics Special Report.* U.S. Department of Justice.

Koenig, Fredrick. 1982. "Today's conditions make U.S. 'ripe for the rumor mill.'" *U.S. News & World Report,* December 6, p. 42.

Kohlberg, Lawrence. 1981. *The Philosophy of Moral Development: Moral Stages and the Idea of Justice.* New York: Harper & Row.

Kohn, Alfie. 1986. *No Contest: The Case Against Competition.* Boston: Houghton Mifflin.

————. 1988. "You know what they say . . . " *Psychology Today,* April, pp. 36–41.

Kohn, Melvin L. 1980. "Job complexity and adult personality." In Neal Smelser and Erik Erikson (eds.), *Themes of Love and Work in Adulthood.* Cambridge, Mass.: Harvard University Press.

————. 1983. "The benefits of bureaucracy." In Melvin L. Kohn and Schooler (eds.), *Occupational Structure and Personality.* Norwood, N.J.: Ablex.

Kolata, Gina. 1990. "Wariness is replacing trust between physician and patient." *New York Times,* February 20, pp. A1, A10.

Kolbert, Elizabeth. 1994. "Television gets closer look as a factor in real violence." *New York Times,* December 14, pp. A1, A13.

Kosters, Marvin H. 1990. "Be cool, stay in school." *The American Enterprise,* March/April, pp. 60–67.

Kramon, Glenn. 1991. "Medical second-guessing—in advance." *New York Times,* February 24, p. F12.

Kristof, Nicholas D. 1990. "More in China willingly rear one child." *New York Times,* May 9, pp. 1, B9.

————. 1995a. "Japan confronting gruesome war atrocity." *New York Times,* March 17, pp. A1, A4.

————. 1995b. "Japan's schools: safe, clean, not much fun." *New York Times,* July 18, pp. A1, A4.

Krugman, Paul. 1990. *The Age of Diminished Expectations: U.S. Economic Policy in the 1990s.* Cambridge, Mass.: MIT Press.

Kübler-Ross, Elisabeth. 1969. *On Death and Dying.* New York: Macmillan.

Lacayo, Richard. 1987. "Whose trial is it anyway?" *Time,* May 25, p. 62.

————. 1990. "Why no blue blood will flow." *Time,* November 26, p. 34.

————. 1995. "How safe is safe?" *Time,* May 1, pp. 68–72.

Ladd, Everett Carll. 1983. "Politics in the 80's: An electorate at odds with itself." *Public Opinion,* December/January, pp. 2–5.

Lane, Harlan. 1976. *The Wild Boy of Aveyron.* Cambridge, Mass.: Harvard University Press.

Lapham, Lewis H. 1992. "Fear of freedom." *New York Times,* June 6, p. 15.

Larsen, Otto. 1981. "Need for continuing support for social sciences." *ASA Footnotes,* March, p. 8.

Larson, Reed. 1994. *Divergent Realities: The Emotional Lives of Mothers, Fathers, and Adolescents.* New York: Basic Books.

Lasch, Christopher. 1979. *The Culture of Narcissism: American Life in an Age of Diminishing Expectations.* New York: Norton.

Latané, Bibb, and Steve Nida. 1981. "Ten years of research on group size and helping." *Psychological Bulletin,* 89, pp. 308–24.

Leach, Penelope. 1994. *Children First.* New York: Knopf.

Lee, Alfred McClung, and Elizabeth Briant Lee. 1979. *The Fine Art of Propaganda.* San Francisco: International Society for General Semantics.

Lee, Barrett A., and Avery M. Guest. 1983. "Determinants of neighborhood satisfaction: A metropolitan-level analysis." *Sociological Quarterly,* 24, pp. 287–303.

Lemarchand, Rene. 1994. "The apocalypse in Rwanda." *Cultural Survival Quarterly,* 18, pp. 29–33.

Lemert, Edwin M. 1951. *Social Pathology.* New York: McGraw-Hill.

Lemon, B. W., K. L. Bengston, and J. A. Peterson. 1972.

"An exploration of the activity theory of aging: Activity types and life satisfaction among in-movers to a retirement community." *Journal of Gerontology,* 27, pp. 511–23.

Lemonick, Michael D. 1992. "The ozone vanishes." *Time,* February 17, pp. 60–63.

———. 1995. "Heading for apocalypse?" *Time,* October 2, pp. 54–55.

Lengermann, Patricia Madoo, and Jill Niebrugge-Brantley. 1992. "Contemporary feminist theory." In George Ritzer, *Sociological Theory,* 3rd ed., pp. 447–96. New York: McGraw-Hill.

Lenski, Gerhard, Jean Lenski, and Patrick Nolan. 1995. *Human Societies,* 7th ed. New York: McGraw-Hill.

Leo, John. 1991. "Community and personal duty." *U.S. News & World Report,* January 28, p. 17.

Leslie, Gerald R., and Sheila K. Korman. 1989. *The Family in Social Context,* 7th ed. New York: Oxford University Press.

Levin, Jack, and William C. Levin. 1980. *Ageism: Prejudice and Discrimination Against the Elderly.* Belmont, Calif.: Wadsworth.

Levine, Daniel S. 1993. "Adult students, adult needs." *New York Times,* April 4, Section 4A, pp. 32–33.

Levine, John M., and Richard L. Moreland. 1990. "Progress in small group research." *Annual Review of Psychology,* 14, pp. 585–634.

Levinson, Marc. 1995. "Hey, you're doing great." *Newsweek,* January 30, pp. 42–44.

Levy, Becca, and Ellen Langer. 1994. "Aging free from negative stereotypes: Successful memory in China and among the American deaf." *Journal of Personality and Social Psychology,* 66, pp. 989–97.

Levy, S. G., and W. F. Fenley, Jr. 1979. "Audience size and likelihood and intensity of response during a humorous movie." *Bulletin of Psychonomic Society,* 13, pp. 409–12.

Lewin, Bo. 1982. "Unmarried cohabitation: A marriage form in a changing society." *Journal of Marriage and the Family,* 44, pp. 763–73.

Lewin, Tamar. 1992. "Rise in single parenthood is reshaping U.S." *New York Times,* October 5, pp. A1, A16.

Lewinsolhn, Peter M., et al. 1993. "Adolescent psychopathology: I. Prevalence and incidence of depression and other DSM-III-R disorders in high school students." *Journal of Abnormal Psychology,* 102, pp. 133–44.

Lewis, Neil A. 1995. "Clinton plan would let FBI infiltrate menacing groups." *New York Times,* April 25, p. A9.

Lewis, Oscar. 1961. *The Children of Sanchez.* New York: Random House.

Liebow, Elliot. 1993. *Tell Them Who I Am: The Lives of Homeless Women.* New York: Free Press.

Lin, Chien, and William T. Liu. 1993. "Intergenerational relationships among Chinese immigrant families from Taiwan." In Harriette Pipes McAdoo (ed.), *Family Ethnicity: Strength in Diversity.* Newbury Park, Calif.: Sage.

Lin, Nan. 1982. "Social resources and instrumental action." In Peter V. Marsden and Nan Lin (eds.), *Social Structure and Network Analysis,* pp. 131–45. Beverly Hills, Calif.: Sage.

Lincoln, C. Eric, and Lawrence H. Mamiya. 1990. *The Black Church in African American Experience.* Durham, N.C.: Duke University Press.

Lind, Michael. 1995. *The Next American Nation: The Nationalism and the Fourth American Revolution.* New York: Free Press.

Linden, Eugene. 1993. "Megacities." *Time,* January 11, pp. 28–38.

Link, Bruce G., Mary Clare Lennon, and Bruce P. Dohrenwend. 1993. "Socioeconomic status and depression: The role of occupations involving direction, control, and planning." *American Journal of Sociology,* 98, pp. 1351–87.

Lipset, Seymour Martin. 1987. "Blacks and Jews: How much bias?" *Public Opinion,* July/August, pp. 4–5, 57–58.

———. 1990a. "A unique people in an exceptional country." In S. M. Lipset (ed.), *American Pluralism and the Jewish Community,* pp. 3–29. New Brunswick, N.J.: Transaction.

———. 1990b. "The work ethic—then and now." *Public Interest,* Winter, pp. 61–69.

———, and William Schneider. 1983. *The Confidence Gap: Business, Labor, and Government in the Public Mind.* New York: Free Press.

Little, Stratton. 1991. "The 1990 U.S. census." *Encyclopaedia Britannica: 1991 Book of the Year,* pp. 279–80.

Lord, Lewis J., and Miriam Horn. 1987. "The brain battle." *U.S. News & World Report,* January 19, pp. 58–64.

Lord, Walter. 1981. *A Night to Remember.* New York: Penguin.

Luttwak, Edward N. 1994. *The Endangered American Dream.* New York: Touchstone/Simon & Schuster.

McCormick, John. 1994. "Why parents kill." *Newsweek,* November 14, pp. 31–34.

MacFarquhar, Emily. 1994. "The war against women." *U.S. News & World Report,* March 28, pp. 42–48.

Mack, Raymond W., and Calvin P. Bradford. 1979. *Transforming America.* New York: Random House.

McKenna, Francis R. 1993. *Schooling in America.* Dubuque, Iowa: Kendall/Hunt.

McKinlay, John B., and Sonja M. McKinlay. 1987. "Medical measures and the decline of mortality." In Howard D. Schwartz (ed.), *Dominant Issues in Medical Sociology,* 2nd ed. New York: Random House.

McLanahan, Sara S. 1983. "Family structure and stress: A longitudinal comparison of two-parent and female-headed families." *Journal of Marriage and the Family,* 45, pp. 347–57.

McPhail, Clark, and Ronald T. Wohlstein. 1983. "Individual and collective behaviors within gatherings, demonstrations, and riots." *Annual Review of Sociology,* 9, pp. 579–600.

McWilliams, Carey. 1948. *A Mask for Privilege.* Boston: Little, Brown.

Madsen, Douglas, and Peter G. Snow. 1983. "The dispersion of charisma." *Comparative Political Studies,* 16, pp. 337–62.

Madsen, Jane M. 1982. "Racist images." *USA Today,* 111, p. 14.

Malson, Lucien. 1972. *Wolf Children and the Problem of Human Nature.* New York: Monthly Review.

Manegold, Catherine S. 1994. "Bill seeks equality of sexes in school." *New York Times,* February 13, p. 14.

Marcus, Eric. 1993. *Is It a Choice?* New York: HarperSanFrancisco.

Markides, Kyriacos C., and Steven F. Cohn. 1982. "External conflict/internal cohesion: A reevaluation of an old theory." *American Sociological Review,* 47, pp. 88–98.

Markovsky, Barry, and Seymour M. Berger. 1983. "Crowd noise and mimicry." *Personality and Social Psychology Bulletin,* 9, pp. 90–96.

Martin, M. Kay, and Barbara Voorhies. 1975. *Female of the Species.* New York: Columbia University Press.

Marty, Martin E., and R. Scott Appleby (eds.). 1992. *Fundamentalisms Observed.* Chicago: University of Chicago Press.

Marx, Karl. 1866/1967. *Capital,* Vol. 1. New York: International Publishers.

Massey, Douglas S., and Nancy A. Denton. 1993. *American Apartheid.* Cambridge, Mass.: Harvard University Press.

Massing, Michael. 1993. "The rehabbing of America." *New York Times Book Review,* January 24, p. 10.

Matthews, Tom. 1992. "Secrets of a serial killer." *Newsweek,* February 3, pp. 44–49.

Maybury-Lewis, David. 1994. "What is the future and will it work?" *Cultural Survival Quarterly,* Summer/Fall, p. 1.

Mayo, Elton. 1933. *The Human Problems of Industrial Civilization.* New York: Macmillan.

Mazur, Allan. 1986. "U.S. trends in feminine beauty and over-adaptation." *Journal of Sex Research,* 22, pp. 281–303.

Mead, Lawrence M. 1992. *The New Politics of Poverty: The Nonworking Poor in America.* New York: Basic Books.

Mead, Margaret. 1935. *Sex and Temperament in Three Primitive Societies.* Garden City, N.Y.: Mentor.

Meer, Jeff. 1986. "The reason of age." *Psychology Today,* June, pp. 60–64.

Mensch, Barbara. 1986. "Age differences between spouses in first marriages." *Social Biology,* 33, pp. 229–40.

Merton, Robert K. 1957. *Social Theory and Social Structure.* New York: Free Press.

———. 1976. *Sociological Ambivalence and Other Essays.* New York: Free Press.

Michael, Robert T. et al. 1994. *Sex in America: A Definitive Survey.* Boston: Little, Brown.

Michels, Robert. 1915. *Political Parties.* Glencoe, Ill.: Free Press.

Milgram, Stanley. 1967. "The small-world problem." *Psychology Today,* 1, pp. 61–67.

Miller, Jody. 1995. "Feminist theory." In Alex Thio and Thomas Calhoun (eds.), *Readings in Deviant Behavior,* pp. 54–62. New York: HarperCollins.

Mills, C. Wright. 1959a. *The Power Elite.* New York: Oxford University Press.

———. 1959b. *The Sociological Imagination.* New York: Grove.

Moberg, David O. 1984. "Review of James Hunter's *American Evangelicalism.*" *Contemporary Sociology,* 13, pp. 371, 372.

Molotsky, Irvin. 1988. "Senate votes to compensate Japanese-American internees." *New York Times,* April 21, pp. 1, 9.

Morell, Marie A., et al. 1989. "Would a Type A date another Type A?: Influence of behavior type and personal attributes in the selection of dating partners." *Journal of Applied Social Psychology,* 19, pp. 918–31.

Morelli, Gilda A., and Edward Z. Tronick. 1991. "Parenting and child development in the Efe foragers and Lese farmers of Zaire." In Marc H. Bornstein (ed.), *Cultural Approaches to Parenting,* pp. 91–113. Hillsdale, N.J.: Lawrence Erlbaum Associates.

Morgan, Gareth. 1989. *Creative Organization Theory: A Resourcebook.* Newbury Park, Calif.: Sage.

Morgan, S. Philip. 1983. "A research note on religion and morality: Are religious people nice people?" *Social Forces,* 61, pp. 683–92.

———. 1984. "Reply to King and Hunt." *Social Forces,* 62, pp. 1089–90.

Morgen, Sandra. 1994. "Personalizing personnel decisions in feminist organizational theory and practice." *Human Relations,* 47, pp. 665–84.

Morrow, Lance. 1978. "The lure of doomsday." *Time,* December 4, p. 30.

Mortimore, Peter. 1988. *School Matters.* Berkeley: University of California Press.

Mullen, Brian, et al. 1989. "Group size, leadership behavior, and subordinate satisfaction." *Journal of General Psychology,* 116, pp. 155–69.

Mulvihill, Donald J., and Melvin M. Tumin, with Lynn A. Curtis. 1969. *Crimes of Violence,* vol. 11. Washington, D.C.: U.S. Government Printing Office.

Murdock, George Peter. 1945. "The common denominator of cultures." In Ralph Linton (ed.), *The Science of Man in World Crisis.* New York: Columbia University Press.

Myers, David G. 1993. *The Pursuit of Happiness.* New York: Avon Books.

Myers, Jerome K., et al. 1984. "Six-month prevalence of psychiatric disorders in three communities." *Archives of General Psychiatry.* 41, pp. 959–67.

Naisbitt, John, and Patricia Aburdene. 1990. *Megatrends 2000.* New York: Morrow.

Nanda, Serena. 1994. *Cultural Anthropology,* 5th ed. Belmont, Calif.: Wadsworth.

Nash, Nathaniel C. 1995. "Europe's economies are in an upswing." *New York Times,* January 3, p. C10.

Nazario, Sonia L. 1992. "Medical science seeks a cure for doctors suffering from boorish bedside manner." *Wall Street Journal,* March 17, pp. B1, B8.

Nelson, Mariah Burton. 1994. *The Stronger Women Get, The More Men Love Football: Sexism and the American Culture of Sports.* New York: Harcourt Brace.

Nelson, Mark M. 1990. "Darkness at noon." *Wall Street Journal,* March 1, pp. A1, A13.

Nemy, Enid. 1991. "Numbers are up, status down for the family of one." *New York Times,* February 28, pp. B1, B5.

New York Times. 1991. "Private cures for public ills." February 28, p. A18.

New York Times/CBS News. 1994. *New York Times,* December 15, pp. A1, A14.

Newcomb, Theodore. 1958. "Attitude development as a function of reference group: The Bennington study." In Guy E. Swanson et al. (eds.), *Readings in Social Psychology.* New York: Holt, Rinehart and Winston.

Newman, Maria. 1992. "Charismatic movement gains among Catholics." *New York Times,* March 1, p. 17.

———. 1994. "California schools compete for pupils in an open market." *New York Times,* May 25, pp. A1, B8.

Newman, William M. 1973. *American Pluralism: A Study of Minority Groups and Social Theory.* New York: Harper & Row.

Niebuhr, Gustav. 1992. "The lord's name." *Wall Street Journal,* April 27, pp. A1, A4.

Nisbet, Robert A. 1977. *The Social Bond,* 2nd ed. New York: Knopf.

NORC (National Opinion Research Center). 1994. *General Social Surveys, 1972–1994: Cumulative Codebook.* Storrs, Conn.: Roper Center for Public Opinion Research.

Nordheimer, Jon. 1990. "Stepfathers: The shoes rarely fit." *New York Times,* October 18, p. B6.

Nuland, Sherwin B. 1994. *How We Die: Reflections on Life's Final Chapter.* New York: Knopf.

Nye, Joseph, Jr. 1990. *Bound to Lead: The Changing Nature of American Power.* New York: Basic Books.

Oakley, Robert. 1987. "International terrorism." *Foreign Affairs,* 65, pp. 611–29.

Ochse, Rhona, and Cornelis Plug. 1986. "Cross-cultural investigation of the validity of Erikson's theory of personality development." *Journal of Personality and Social Psychology,* 50, pp. 1240–52.

O'Dea, Thomas F., and Janet O'Dea Aviad. 1983. *The Sociology of Religion,* 2nd ed. Englewood Cliffs, N.J.: Prentice-Hall.

Orwell, George. 1949. *1984.* New York: Signet.

Ostling, George. 1988. "Americans facing toward Mecca." *Time,* May 23, pp. 49–50.

———. 1991. "Superchurches and how they grow." *Time,* August 5, pp. 62–63.

Page, Benjamin I. 1983. *Who Gets What from Government.* Berkeley: University of California Press.

Palen, J. John. 1992. *The Urban World,* 4th ed. New York: McGraw-Hill.

Palisi, Bartolomeo J., and Claire Canning. 1983. "Urbanism and social psychological well-being: A cross-cultural test of three theories." *Sociological Quarterly,* 24, pp. 527–43.

Palmore, Erdman, and Daisaku Maeda. 1985. *The Honorable Elders Revisited: A Revised Cross-Cultural Analysis of Aging in Japan.* Durham, N.C.: Duke University Press.

Papousek, Hanus, and Mechthild Papousek. 1991. "Innate and cultural guidance of infants' integrative competencies: China, the United States, and Germany." In Marc H. Bornstein (ed.), *Cultural Approaches to Parenting,* pp. 23–44. Hillsdale, N.J.: Lawrence Erlbaum Associates.

Pareles, Jon. 1994. "You call that music?" *New York Times Book Review,* August 14, pp. 10–11.

Parker, Robert Nash. 1989. "Poverty, subculture of violence, and types of homicide." *Social Forces,* 67, pp. 983–1005.

Parkes, Peter. 1987. "Livestock symbolism and pastoral ideology among the Kafirs of the Hindu Kush." *Man,* 22, pp. 637–60.

Parsons, Talcott. 1951/1964. *The Social System.* Glencoe, Ill.: Free Press.

———, and Robert F. Bales. 1953. *Family, Socialization, and Interaction Process.* Glencoe, Ill.: Free Press.

Patterson, Orlando. 1991. "Race, gender, and liberal fallacies." *Black Scholar,* 22, pp. 77–80.

———. 1994. "Ecumenical America: Global culture and the American cosmos." *World Policy Journal,* 11, pp. 103–17.

Pear, Robert. 1995a. "Proposed defintion of indigence could expand number of poor." *New York Times,* April 30, pp. 1, 15.

———. 1995b. "A welfare revolution hits home, but quietly." *New York Times,* August 13, Section 4, pp. 1, 5.

Pearce, Diana M. 1993. "The feminization of poverty: Update." In Alison M. Jaggar and Paula S. Rothenberg (eds.), *Feminist Frameworks,* 3rd ed., pp. 290–96. New York: McGraw-Hill.

Peek, Charles W., Evans W. Curry, and H. Paul Chalfant. 1985. "Religiosity and delinquency over time: Deviance deterrence and deviance amplification." *Social Science Quarterly,* 66, pp. 120–31.

Peirce, Kate. 1990. "A feminist theoretical perspective on the socialization of teenage girls through *Seventeen* magazine." *Sex Roles,* 23, pp. 491–500.

Peltonen, Anita. 1993. "Finland: A free school system with very few cracks." *New York Times,* December 9, p. A8.

Pennebaker, J. W. 1980. "Perceptual and environmental determinants of coughing." *Basic Applied Social Psychology,* 1, pp. 83–91.

Perlez, Jane. 1992. "For bedouins of Africa, sands are running out." *New York Times,* March 5, 1992, p. A4.

———. 1995. "East Europe looks to union with West." *New York Times,* January 3, p. C10.

Pescosolido, Bernice A., and Sharon Georgianna. 1989. "Durkheim, suicide, and religion: Toward a network theory of suicide." *American Sociological Review,* 54, pp. 33–48.

Pines, Maya. 1981. "The civilizing of Genie." *Psychology Today,* September, pp. 28–34.

Pizzo, Stephen P., and Paul Muolo. 1993. "Take the money and run." *New York Times Magazine,* May 9, p. 26.

Pollak, Lauren Harte, and Peggy A. Thoits. 1989. "Processes in emotional socialization." *Social Psychology Quarterly,* 52, pp. 22–34.

Pope, Victoria. 1994. "To be young and pretty in Moscow." *U.S. News & World Report,* March 28, p. 56.

Porter, Bruce, and Marvin Dunn. 1984. *The Miami Riot of 1980.* Lexington, Mass.: Lexington Books.

Power, Thomas G., and Josephine A. Shanks. 1989. "Parents and socializers: Maternal and paternal views." *Journal of Youth and Adolescence,* 18, pp. 203–17.

Prerost, Frank J., and Robert E. Brewer. 1980. "The appreciation of humor by males and females during conditions of crowding experimentally induced." *Psychology,* 17, pp. 15–17.

Purvis, Andrew. 1990. "A perilous gap." *Time,* Fall, pp. 66–67.

———. 1992. "A day in the death of Somalia." *Time,* September 21, pp. 32–40.

Quinney, Richard. 1974. *Critique of Legal Order.* Boston: Little, Brown.

Radford, John. 1990. *Child Prodigies and Exceptional Early Achievers.* New York: Free Press.

Ramirez, Francisco O., and John W. Meyer. 1980. "Comparative education: The social construction of the modern world system." *Annual Review of Sociology,* 6, pp. 369–99.

Raper, Arthur F. 1970. *The Tragedy of Lynching.* New York: Dover.

Rau, William, and Dennis W. Roncek. 1987. "Industrialization and world inequality: The transformation of the division of labor in 59 nations, 1960–1981." *American Sociological Review,* 52, pp. 359–69.

Regier, Darrel A., et al. 1993. "The de facto US mental and addictive disorders service system: Epidemiologic catchment area prospective 1-year prevalence rates of disorders and services." *Archives of General Psychiatry,* 50, pp. 85–94.

Reich, Robert B. 1994. "The fracturing of the middle class." *New York Times,* August 31, p. A13.

Reskin, Barbara F., and Irene Padavic. 1994. *Women and Men at Work.* Thousand Oaks, Calif.: Pine Forge.

Restak, Richard M. 1979. *The Brain: The Last Frontier.* Garden City, N.Y.: Doubleday.

Rice, Mabel L., et al. 1990. "Words from 'Sesame Street': Learning vocabulary while viewing." *Developmental Psychology,* 26, pp. 421–28.

Richardson, Laurel. 1988. *The Dynamics of Sex and Gender: A Sociological Perspective.* New York: Harper & Row.

Riding, Alan. 1993. "France: A method of teaching that produces readers." *New York Times,* December 9, p. A8.

Riesman, David. 1950. *The Lonely Crowd.* New Haven, Conn.: Yale University Press.

Robbins, William. 1990. "New decade finds new hope on the farm." *New York Times,* May 18, pp. A1, A10.

Roberts, Sam. 1993. *Who We Are: A Portrait of America Based on the Latest U.S. Census.* New York: Times Books.

Roberts, Steven. 1990. "An all-American snapshot: How we count and why." *U.S. News & World Report,* April 2, p. 10.

Robins, Lee N., et al. 1984. "Lifetime prevalence of specific psychiatric disorders in three sites." *Archives of General Psychiatry,* 41, pp. 949–958.

Rockwell, John. 1994. "The new colossus: American culture as power export." *New York Times,* January 30, Section 2, pp. 1, 30.

Rodgers, Bryan, and Susan L. Mann. 1993. "Re-thinking the analysis of intergenerational social mobility: A comment on John W. Fox's "Social class, mental illness, and social mobility." *Journal of Health and Social Behavior,* 34, pp. 165–172.

Roethlisberger, Fritz J., and William J. Dickson. 1939. *Management and the Worker.* Cambridge, Mass.: Harvard University Press.

Rohlen, Thomas P. 1983. *Japan's High Schools.* Berkeley: University of California Press.

Roof, Wade Clark. 1993. *A Generation of Seekers.* New York: HarperCollins.

Rosado, Lourdes. 1991. "Who's caring for grandma?" *Newsweek,* July 29, p. 47.

Rose, Arnold M. 1965. "The subculture of aging." In Arnold M. Rose and Warren A. Peterson (eds.), *Older People and Their Social World.* Philadelphia: F. A. Davis.

———. 1967. *The Power Structure.* New York: Oxford University Press.

Rosecrance, Richard. 1990. "Too many bosses, too few workers." *New York Times,* July 15, p. F11.

Rosenberg, Morris. 1990. "Reflexivity and emotions." *Social Psychology Quarterly,* 53, pp. 3–12.

Rosenblatt, Roger. 1994. "A killer in the eye." *New York Times Magazine,* June 5, pp. 38–47.

Rosener, Judy B. 1990. "Ways women lead." *Harvard Business Review,* 68, pp. 119–25.

Rosenthal, Elisabeth. 1995. "Rejecting elders' pessimism, students jam medical school." *New York Times,* October 15, pp. 1, 15.

Rosenthal, Robert. 1973. "The Pygmalion effect lives." *Psychology Today,* pp. 56–63.

Rosewicz, Barbara. 1990. "Friends of the earth." *Wall Street Journal,* April 20, pp. A1, A12.

Rosin, Hazel M. 1990. "The effects of dual career participation on men: Some determinants of variation in career and personal satisfaction." *Human Relations*, 43, pp. 169–82.

Ross, Dorothy. 1991. *The Origins of American Social Science*. New York: Cambridge University Press.

Rossi, Alice S. 1984. "Gender and parenthood." *American Sociological Review*, 49, pp. 1–19.

Rossi, Peter H. 1989. *Down and Out in America: The Origins of Homelessness*. Chicago: University of Chicago Press.

Rothschild, Joyce, and Celia Davies. 1994. "Organizations through the lens of gender: Introduction to the special issue." *Human Relations*, 47, pp. 583–90.

Rothschild, Joyce, and Raymond Russell. 1986. "Alternatives to bureaucracy: Democratic participation in the economy." *Annual Review of Sociology*, 12, pp. 307–28.

Rubenstein, Carin. 1982. "Real men don't earn less than their wives." *Psychology Today*, November, pp. 36–41.

Rubin, Lillian Breslow. 1976. *Worlds of Pain: Life in the Working-Class Family*. New York: Basic Books.

Russell, George. 1984. "People, people, people." *Time*, August 6, pp. 24–25.

Rutter, Michael. 1983. "School effects on pupil progress: Research findings and policy implications." *Child Development*, 54, pp. 1–29.

Rymer, Russ. 1993. *Genie: An Abused Child's Flight From Silence*. New York: HarperCollins.

Sachs, Andrea. 1993. "9-Zip! I Love It!" *Time*, November 22, pp. 44–45.

Sadker, Myra, and David Sadker. 1994. *Failing at Fairness: How America's Schools Cheat Girls*. New York: Scribners.

Sahlins, Marshall. 1972. *Stone Age Economics*. Chicago: Aldine.

Salins, Peter D. 1991. "In living colors," *The New Republic*, January 21, pp. 14–15.

Sapir, Edward. 1929. "The status of linguistics as a science." *Language*, 5, pp. 207–14.

Sayle, Murray. 1982. "A textbook case of aggression." *Far Eastern Economic Review*, 117, August 20, pp. 36–38.

Schaefer, Richard T. 1988. *Racial and Ethnic Groups*, 3rd ed. Boston: Little, Brown.

Schor, Juliet B. 1991. *The Overworked American: The Unexpected Decline of Leisure*. New York: Basic Books.

Schultz, Duane P. 1964. *Panic Behavior*. New York: Random House.

Schulz, David A. 1982. *The Changing Family*, 3rd ed. Englewood Cliffs, N.J.: Prentice-Hall.

Schur, Edwin M. 1984. *Labeling Women Deviant: Gender, Stigma, and Social Control*. New York: Random House.

Schweinhart, Lawrence J., and David P. Weikrt. 1990. "A fresh start for Head Start?" *New York Times*, May 13, p. E19.

Schwochau, Susan. 1987. "Union effects on job attitudes." *Industrial and Labor Relations Review*, 40, pp. 209–24.

Scott, David Clark. 1986. "How 'quality circles' move from the assembly line to the office." *Christian Science Monitor*, August 4, p. 18.

Scully, Diana, and Joseph Marolla. 1984. "Convicted rapists' vocabulary of motive: Excuses and justifications." *Social Problems*, 31, pp. 530–44.

Sebald, Hans. 1986. "Adolescents' shifting orientation toward parents and peers: A curvilinear trend over recent decades." *Journal of Marriage and the Family*, 48, pp. 5–13.

See, Katherine O'Sullivan, and William J. Wilson. 1988. "Race and ethnicity." In Neil J. Smelser (ed.), *Handbook of Sociology*, pp. 223–42. Newbury Park, Calif.: Sage.

Seligmann, Jean. 1992. "Variations on a theme." In Arlene S. Skolnick and Jerome H. Skolnick (eds.), *Family in Transition*, 7th ed. New York: HarperCollins.

———. 1993. "Husbands no, babies yes." *Newsweek*, July 26, p. 53.

Sennett, Richard. 1991. *The Conscience of the Eye: The Design and Social Life of Cities*. New York: Alfred A. Knopf.

Shapiro, Judith. 1994. "What women can teach men." *New York Times*, November 23, p. A15.

Shapiro, Laura. 1990. "Guns and dolls." *Newsweek*, May 28, pp. 56–65.

Sharpe, Rochelle. 1994. "The waiting game." *Wall Street Journal*, March 29, p. A8.

Sheler, Jeffery L. 1990. "Islam in America." *U.S. News & World Report*, October 8, pp. 69–71.

Shellenbarger, Sue. 1991. "Work and family." *Wall Street Journal*, December 11, p. B1.

Shenon, Philip. 1995. "Continued vitality for Southeast Asia." *New York Times*, January 3, p. C10.

Sherif, Muzafer. 1956. "Experiments in group conflict." *Scientific American,* 195, pp. 54–58.

Shibutani, Tamotsu. 1966. *Improvised News.* Indianapolis: Bobbs-Merrill.

Shipman, Pat. 1994. *The Evolution of Racism: Human Differences and the Use and Abuse of Science.* New York: Simon & Schuster.

Shon, Steven P., and Davis Y. Ja. 1992. "Asian families." In Arlene S. Skolnick and Jerome H. Skolnick (eds.), *Family in Transition,* 7th ed. New York: HarperCollins.

Sidel, Ruth. 1990. *On Her Own: Growing Up in the Shadow of the American Dream.* New York: Viking.

Signorile, Michelangelo. 1995. "H.I.V. positive, and careless." *New York Times,* February 26, p. 15.

Silberner, Joanne. 1990. "Health: Another gender gap." *U.S. News & World Report,* September 24, pp. 54–55.

Simenauer, Jacqueline, and David Carroll. 1982. *Singles: The New Americans.* New York: Simon & Schuster.

Simon, Julian L. 1990. *Population Matters: People, Resources, Environment, and Immigration.* New Brunswick, N.J.: Transaction.

Simpson, Jeffry A., Bruce Campbell, and Ellen Berscheid. 1986. "The association between romantic love and marriage: Kephart (1967) twice revisited." *Personality and Social Psychology Bulletin,* 12, pp. 363–72.

Sizer, Theodore R. 1984. *Horace's Compromise: The Dilemma of the American High School.* Boston: Houghton Mifflin.

Skinner, B. F. 1983. "Creativity in old age." *Psychology Today,* September, pp. 28, 29.

Skinner, Denise. 1980. "Dual-career family stress and coping: A literature review." *Family Relations,* 29, pp. 473–80.

Smelser, Neil J. 1962/1971. *Theory of Collective Behavior.* New York: Free Press.

Smith, Garry J. 1993. "The noble sports fan." In D. Stanley Eitzen (ed.), *Sport in Contemporary Society: An Anthology,* 4th ed., pp. 3–14. New York: St. Martin's Press.

Snow, David A., and Leon Anderson. 1993. *Down on Their Luck: A Study of Homeless Street People.* Berkeley: University of California Press.

So, Alvin Y. 1990. *Social Change and Development: Modernization, Dependency, and World-System Theories.* Newbury Park, Calif.: Sage.

Solomon, Jolie. 1989. "Firms grapple with language barriers." *Wall Street Journal,* November 7, pp. B1, B4.

Sorrentino, Constance. 1990. "The changing family in international perspective." *Monthly Labor Review,* March, pp. 41–55.

Sowell, Thomas. 1983. *The Economics and Politics of Race: An International Perspective.* New York: Morrow.

———. 1994. *Race and Culture: A World View.* New York: Basic Books.

Spanier, Graham B. 1983. "Married and unmarried cohabitation in the United States: 1980." *Journal of Marriage and the Family,* 45, pp. 277–88.

Spates, James L. 1983. "The sociology of values." *Annual Review of Sociology,* 9, pp. 27–49.

Spitz, Rene A. 1945. "Hospitalism." *Psychoanalytic Study of the Child,* 1, pp. 53–72.

Stearns, Marion S. 1971. *Report on Preschool Programs.* Washington, D.C.: U.S. Government Printing Office.

Steele, Shelby. 1990. *The Content of Our Character: A New Vision of Race in America.* New York: St. Martin's.

Steinberg, Laurence. 1987. "Why Japan's students outdo ours." *New York Times,* April 25, p. 15.

———. 1994. *Crossing Paths: How Your Child's Adolescence Triggers Your Own Crisis.* New York: Simon & Schuster.

Steinhauer, Jennifer. 1995. "Living together without marriage or apologies." *New York Times,* July 6, p. A9.

Stevens, Gillian, et al. 1990. "Education and attractiveness in marriage choices." *Social Psychology Quarterly,* 53, pp. 62–72.

Stevens, William K. 1992. "New studies predict profits in heading off warming." *New York Times,* March 17, pp. B5, B9.

———. 1995. "Scientists say earth's warming could set off wide disruptions." *New York Times,* September 18, pp. A1, A5.

Stokes, Myron. 1995. "The shame of the city." *Newsweek,* September 4, p. 26.

Stoll, Clarice Stasz. 1978. *Female & Male.* Dubuque, Iowa: Brown.

Stolzenberg, Ross M. 1990. "Ethnicity, geography, and occupational achievement of Hispanic men in the United States." *American Sociological Review,* 55, pp. 143–54.

Straus, Murray A., et al. 1988. *Behind Closed Doors: Violence in the American Family.* Newbury Park, Calif.: Sage.

Strong, Bryan, and Christine DeVault. 1992. *The Marriage and Family Experience,* 5th ed. St. Paul, Minn.: West.

Strum, Charles. 1993. "School tracking: Efficiency or elitism?" *New York Times,* April 1, p. B5.

Suro, Roberto. 1991. "Where America is growing: The suburban cities." *New York Times,* February 23, pp. 1, 10.

Sutherland, Edwin H. 1939. *Principles of Criminology.* Philadelphia: Lippincott.

Suttles, Gerald. 1970. *The Social Order of the Slum.* Chicago: University of Chicago Press.

Syme, S. Leonard, and Lisa F. Berkman. 1987. "Social class, susceptibility, and sickness." In Howard D. Schwartz (ed.), *Dominant Issues in Medical Sociology,* 2nd ed. New York: Random House.

Szymanski, Albert. 1978. *The Capitalist State and the Politics of Class.* Cambridge, Mass.: Winthrop.

Takaki, Ronald. 1993. *A Different Mirror: A History of Multicultural America.* Boston: Little, Brown.

Tanfer, Koray. 1987. "Patterns of premarital cohabitation among never-married women in the United States." *Journal of Marriage and the Family,* 49, pp. 483–97.

Tannen, Deborah. 1986. *That's Not What I Meant!* New York: William Morrow.

———. 1990. *You Just Don't Understand: Women and Men in Conversation.* New York: Ballantine Books.

———. 1994a. *Gender and Discourse.* New York: Oxford University Press.

———. 1994b. *Talking from 9 to 5.* New York: William Morrow.

Tannenbaum, Frank. 1938. *Crime and the Community.* New York: Columbia University Press.

Taylor, Frederick W. 1911. *Scientific Management.* New York: Harper.

Taylor, Robert Joseph, et al. 1993. "Developments in research on black families: A decade review." In Harriette Pipes McAdoo (ed.), *Family Ethnicity: Strength in Diversity.* Newbury Park, Calif.: Sage.

Teachman, Jay D. 1987. "Family background, educational resources, and educational attainment." *American Sociological Review,* 52, pp. 548–57.

Tefft, Sheila. 1993. "Rural laborers seek fortunes in burgeoning Chinese cities." *Christian Science Monitor,* May 25, pp. 1, 4.

Terkel, Studs. 1992. *Race: How Blacks and Whites Think and Feel About the American Obsession.* New York: The New Press.

Tharp, Mike. 1987. "Academic debate." *Wall Street Journal,* March 10, p. 1.

Thio, Alex. 1995. *Deviant Behavior,* 4th ed. New York: HarperCollins.

Thorne, Barrie. 1993. *Gender Play: Girls and Boys in School.* New Brunswick, N.J.: Rutgers University Press.

Thornton, Arland. 1989. "Changing attitudes toward family issues in the United States." *Journal of Marriage and the Family,* 51, pp. 873–93.

Tilly, Louise A., and Joan W. Scott. 1978. *Women, Work, and the Family.* New York: Holt, Rinehart and Winston.

Tobin, Jonathan N., et al. 1987. "Sex bias in considering coronary bypass surgery." *Annals of Internal Medicine,* 107, pp. 19–25.

Toffler, Alvin. 1990. *Powershift.* New York: Bantam Books.

Toner, Robin. 1992. "Politics of welfare: Focusing on the problem." *New York Times,* July 5, pp. 1, 13.

Toufexis, Anastasia. 1990. "A call for radical surgery." *Time,* May 7, p. 50.

Travers, Jeffrey, and Stanley Milgram. 1969. "An experimental study of the small world problem." *Sociometry,* 32, pp. 425–43.

Treiman, Donald J. 1977. *Occupational Prestige in Comparative Perspective.* New York: Academic Press.

Triandis, Harry C. 1989. "Cross-cultural studies of individualism and collectivism." *Nebraska Symposium on Motivation,* vol. 37, pp. 41–133.

Trotter, Robert J. 1987. "Mathematics: A male advantage?" *Psychology Today,* January, pp. 66–67.

Trussell, James, and K. Vaninadha Rao. 1989. "Premarital cohabitation and marital stability: A reassessment of the Canadian evidence." *Journal of Marriage and the Family,* 51, pp. 535–40.

Tumin, Melvin M. 1953. "Some principles of stratification: A critical analysis." *American Sociological Review,* 18, pp. 387–93.

Turner, Barry A. 1992. "The symbolic understanding of organizations." In Michael Reed and Michael Hughes (eds.), *Rethinking Organization: New Directions in Organization Theory and Analysis.* Newbury Park, Calif.: Sage.

Turner, Ralph H., and Lewis M. Killian. 1987. *Collective Behavior,* 4th ed. Englewood Cliffs, N.J.: Prentice-Hall.

Turner, Ronny E., and Charles Edgley. 1990. "Death as

theater: A dramaturgical analysis of the American funeral." In Dennis Brissett and Charles Edgley, (eds.), *Life as Theater: A Dramaturgical Sourcebook,* pp. 285–98. New York: Aldine de Gruyter.

Twaddle, Andrew, and Richard Hessler. 1987. *A Sociology of Health,* 2nd ed. New York: Macmillan.

Tyler, Patrick E. 1995. "Daunting challenges for China's leaders." *New York Times,* January 3, p. C10.

Tyree, Andrea, et al. 1979. "Gaps and glissandos: Inequality, economic development, and social mobility in 24 countries." *American Sociological Review,* 44, pp. 410–24.

Tyree, Andrea, and Moshe Semyonov. 1983. "Social mobility and immigrants or immigrants and social mobility." *American Sociological Review,* 48, pp. 583–84.

United Nations. 1994. *Human Development Report 1994.* New York: Oxford University Press.

U.S. Census Bureau. 1994. *Statistical Abstract of the United States.* Washington, D.C.: U.S. Government Printing Office.

U.S. Commission on Civil Rights. 1992. *Civil Rights Issues Facing Asian Americans in the 1990s.* Washington, D.C.: U.S. Government Printing Office.

Van Biema, David. 1995. "Bury my heart in committee." *Time,* September 18, pp. 48–51.

van Leeuwen, Mary Stewart. 1990. "Life after Eden." *Christianity Today,* July 16, pp. 19–21.

Varghese, Raju. 1981. "An empirical analysis of the Eriksonian bipolar theory of personality." *Psychological Reports,* 49, pp. 819–22.

Vealey, Robin S., and Susan M. Walter. 1993. "Imagery training for performance enhancement and personal development." In Jean M. Williams (ed.), *Applied Sport Psychology: Personal Growth to Peak Performance,* pp. 200–24. Mountain View, Calif.: Mayfield.

Vega, William A. 1992. "Hispanic families in the 1980s: A decade of research." In Arlene S. Skolnick and Jerome H. Skolnick (eds.), *Family in Transition,* 7th ed. New York: HarperCollins.

Verbrugge, Lois M. 1985. "Gender and health: An update on hypotheses and evidence." *Journal of Health and Social Behavior,* 26, pp. 156–82.

Verhovek, Sam Howe. 1990. "Whose law applies when lawlessness rules on Indian land?" *New York Times,* May 6, p. E6.

Vora, Erika. 1981. "Evolution of race: A synthesis of social and biological concepts." *Journal of Black Studies,* 12, pp. 182–92.

Voydanoff, Patricia, and Brenda W. Donnelly. 1989. "Work and family roles and psychological distress." *Journal of Marriage and the Family,* 51, pp. 923–32.

Waitzkin, Howard. 1987. "A Marxian interpretation of the growth and development of coronary care technology." In Howard D. Schwartz (ed.), *Dominant Issues in Medical Sociology,* 2nd ed. New York: Random House.

Wald, Matthew L. 1990. "Guarding environment: A world of challenges." *New York Times,* April 22, pp. 1, 16–17.

Wallerstein, Immanuel. 1987. "World-system analysis." In Anthony Giddens and Jonathan H. Turner (eds.), *Social Theory Today,* pp. 309–24. Stanford, Calif.: Stanford University Press.

Wallis, Claudia. 1994. "A class of their own." *Time,* October 31, pp. 53–61.

Walters, Pamela Barnhouse, and Richard Rubinson. 1983. "Educational expansion and economic output in the United States, 1890–1969: A production function analysis." *American Sociological Review,* 48, pp. 480–93.

Walters, Suzanna Danuta. 1995. *Material Girls: Making Sense of Feminist Cultural Theory.* Berkely: University of California Press.

Walzer, Michael. 1978. "Must democracy be capitalist?" *New York Review of Books,* July 20, p. 41.

Wartzman, Rick. 1992. "Sharing gains." *Wall Street Journal,* May 4, pp. A1, A4.

Watson, Roy E. L., and Peter W. DeMeo. 1987. "Premarital cohabitation vs. traditional courtship and subsequent marital adjustment: A replication and follow-up." *Family Relations,* 36, pp. 193–97.

Watson, Russell. 1992. "Ethnic cleansing." *Newsweek,* August 17, pp. 16–20.

———. 1995. "When words are the best weapon." *Newsweek,* February 27, pp. 36–40.

Waxman, Chaim I. 1990. "Is the cup half-full or half-empty?: Perspectives on the future of the American Jewish community." In Seymour Martin Lipset (ed.), *American Pluralism and the Jewish Community,* pp. 71–85. New Brunswick, N.J.: Transaction.

Weaver, Charles N., and Michael D. Matthews. 1990. "Work satisfaction of females with full-time employment and full-time housekeeping: 15 years later." *Psychological Reports,* 66, pp. 1248–50.

Weber, Max. 1946. *From Max Weber: Essays in Sociology,* translated and edited by H. H. Gerth and C. Wright Mills. New York: Oxford University Press.

——. 1957. *The Theory of Social and Economic Organization.* New York: Free Press.

——. 1968. *Economy and Society: An Outline of Interpretive Sociology,* Volume 1. Edited by Guenther Roth and Claus Wittich. New York: Bedminster Press.

Weinraub, Bernard. 1995. "An angry chorus in Hollywood . . . " *New York Times,* June 2, pp. A1, A10.

Weis, Lois (ed.). 1988. *Class, Race, and Gender in American Education.* Albany: State University of New York Press.

Weisheit, Ralph. 1992. "Patterns of female crime." In Robert G. Culbertson and Ralph Weisheit (eds.), *Order Under Law,* 4th ed. Prospect Heights, Ill.: Waveland.

White, Jack E. 1993. "Growing up in black and white." *Time,* May 17, pp. 48–49.

White, Lynn K., and John N. Edwards. 1990. "Emptying the nest and parental well-being: An analysis of national panel data." *American Sociological Review,* 55, pp. 235–42.

White, Sheldon H. 1977. "The paradox of American education." *National Elementary Principal,* 56, May/June, pp. 9, 10.

Whiteford, Michael B., and John Friedl. 1992. *The Human Portrait,* 3rd ed. Englewood Cliffs, N.J.: Prentice-Hall.

Whorf, Benjamin. 1956. *Language, Thought, and Reality.* New York: Wiley.

Whyte, Martin King. 1992. "Choosing mates—The American way." *Society,* March/April, pp. 71–77.

Wiley, Norbert. 1979. "Notes on self genesis: From me to we to I." *Studies in Symbolic Interaction,* 2, pp. 87–105.

Wilkinson, Doris. 1993. "Family ethnicity in America." In Harriette Pipes McAdoo (ed.), *Family Ethnicity: Strength in Diversity.* Newbury Park, Calif.: Sage.

Williams, Robin M., Jr. 1970. *American Society: A Sociological Interpretation,* 3rd ed. New York: Knopf.

——. 1994. "The sociology of ethnic conflicts: Comparative international perspectives." *Annual Review of Sociology,* 20, pp. 49–79.

Wilson, Edward O. 1980. *Sociobiology: The Abridged Edition.* Cambridge, Mass.: Harvard University Press.

Wilson, Warner. 1989. "Brief resolution of the issue of similarity versus complementary in mate selection using height preferences as a model." *Psychological Reports,* 65, pp. 387–93.

Wilson, William Julius. 1990. "Race-neutral programs and the Democratic coalition." *The American Prospect,* 1, pp. 75–81.

Wimberley, Dale W. 1984. "Socioeconomic deprivation and religious salience: A cognitive behavioral approach." *Sociological Quarterly,* 25, pp. 223–238.

Winch, Robert F. 1971. *The Modern Family.* New York: Holt, Rinehart and Winston.

Winslow, Ron. 1989. "Sometimes, talk is the best medicine." *Wall Street Journal,* October 5, p. B1.

Wolf, Naomi. 1993. *Fire with Fire.* New York: Random House.

Wood, Julia T. 1994. *Gendered Lives: Communication, Gender, and Culture.* Belmont, Calif.: Wadsworth.

Woodburn, James. 1982. "Egalitarian societies." *Man,* 17, pp. 431–51.

Woodward, Kenneth L. 1992. "Talking to God." *Newsweek,* January 6, pp. 39–44.

World Bank. 1994. *World Development Report 1994.* New York: Oxford University Press.

Wright, Robert. 1995. "Who's really to blame?" *Time,* November 6, pp. 33–37.

Wrong, Dennis H. 1961. "The oversocialized conception of man in modern sociology." *American Sociological Review,* 26, pp. 183–93.

——. 1990. *Population and Society,* 4th ed. New York: Random House.

Wuthnow, Robert. 1994. "Religion and economic life." In Neil J. Smelser and Richard Swedberg (eds.), *The Handbook of Economic Sociology.* Princeton, N.J.: Princeton University Press.

Yankelovich, Daniel, and John Immerwahr. 1984. "Putting the work ethic to work." *Society,* 21, January/February, pp. 58–76.

Zangwill, Israel. 1909. *The Melting Pot.* New York: Macmillan.

Zenner, Walter P. 1985. "Jewishness in America: Ascription and choice." *Ethnic and Racial Studies,* 8, pp. 117–33.

Zimmerman, Carle C. 1949. *The Family of Tomorrow.* New York: Harper & Brothers.

Zoglin, Richard. 1990. "Is TV ruining our children?" *Time,* October 15, pp. 75–76.

Credits

Unless otherwise acknowledged, all photographs are the property of Scott, Foresman and Company. Page abbreviations are as follows: (T) top, (C) center, (L) left, (R) right.

Chapter 1

Page 2 © David Madison/Tony Stone Images; p. 6 © Lee Snider/The Image Works; p. 8 © The Bettmann Archive; p. 9 © The Bettmann Archive; p. 10 © The University Library/University of Illinois at Chicago/Jane Addams Memorial Collection at Hull House; p. 13 © Rouchon/Explorer/Photo Researchers; p. 16 © Bob Daemmrich/Stock Boston; p. 17 © Monica Almeida/NYT Pictures; p. 20 © Schwadron; p. 21 © R. Scott/The Image Works.

Chapter 2

Page 28 © Will & Deni McIntyre; p. 31 © Jesse Nemerofsky/Photoreporters; p. 33 © Bachmann/Photo Researchers; p. 34 © DeVore/Anthro-Photo; p. 36 © Holland/Stock Boston; p. 38 © Alan Levenson/Tony Stone Images; p. 39 © Nicholas DeVore/Tony Stone Images; p. 43 © Superstock; p. 45 © The Bettmann Archive; p. 48T © Joe Carini/The Image Works; p. 48C © Richard Dean/The Image Works; p. 48B © Bob Daemmrich/The Image Works.

Chapter 3

Page 56 © Robert Frerck/Odyssey/Chicago; p. 59 © Sam Abell; p. 61 © Kerry Hayes/The Kobal Collection; p. 66 © Freeman/Photo Edit; p. 67 © Brent Jones; p. 69 © Eiler/Stock Boston; p. 70 © Brenda Tharp/Photo Researchers, Inc.; p. 73 © Oddie/Photo Edit; p. 74 © Penny Tweedie/Tony Stone Worldwide.

Chapter 4

Page 78 © Frank Siteman/The Picture Cube; p. 82 © Jerry Irwin/Photo Researchers, Inc.; p. 84 © Stephen Dunn/Allsport; p. 85 CATHY: © 1995 Cathy Guisewite. Reprinted with permission of UNIVERSAL PRESS SYNDICATE. Reprinted with permission. All rights reserved.; p. 86 © Azzi/ Woodfin Camp & Associates; p. 89 © B. Daemmrich/The Image Works;

p. 90 © Milt & Joan Mann/Camermann International, Ltd.; p. 93 © Tom McCarthy/Unicorn Stock Photos.

Chapter 5

Page 98 © Dick Luria/Science Source/Photo Researchers, Inc.; p.101 Drawing by Hamilton; © 1991/The New Yorker Magazine, Inc.; p. 102 © Will & Deni McIntyre/Photo Researchers, Inc.; p. 103 © Laima Druskis/Photo Researchers, Inc.; p. 107 © Ron Sherman/Stock Boston; p. 108 © Crandall/The Image Works; p. 110 © Rick Browne/Stock Boston; p. 115 © Lawrence Migdale/Stock Boston; p. 117 © Paolo Koch/ Photo Researchers, Inc.

Chapter 6

Page 120 © Campbell/Sygma; p. 123 © Reuters/Bettmann; p. 126 © D. Wells/The Image Works; p. 127 "From The Wall Street Journal-Permission, Cartoon Features Syndicate"; p. 128 © David Young-Wolff/Photo Edit; p. 131 © Rodger Kingston Vintage/The Picture Collection; p. 135 © Martin R. Jones/Unicorn Stock Photos.

Chapter 7

Page 142 © Reinstein/The Image Works; p. 145 © Lewis Hine Photo/Library of Congress; p. 149T © Jeff Dunn/The Picture Cube; p. 149B © Granitsas/The Image Works; b © S. Katz/Black Star; p. 152B © Andrew Hollbrooke/ Black Star; p. 153 © M. Siluk/The Image Works; p. 155 © Joel Gordon; p. 158 © Paul Conklin/ Photo Edit; p. 159 © Bob Daemmrich/Stock Boston; p. 161 © Stephanie Maze/Woodfin Camp & Associates.

Chapter 8

Page 166 © Johnny Crawford/The Image Works; p. 169 © I. Berry/Magnum Photos; p. 171 © John Running/Black Star; p. 173 © UPI/ Bettmann; p. 175 © M. Granitsas/The Image Works; p. 176 © Hires/Gamma-Liaison; p. 178 © California Institute of Technology; p. 179 © Robert Frerck/Odyssey/Chicago; p. 181 © Superstock; p. 184 © Paul Dagys.

Chapter 9

Page 18 © Will & Deni McIntyre/Photo Researchers; p. 191 © David R. Frazier/Photo Researchers, Inc.; p. 193 © Joseph Nettis/Photo Researchers; p. 196T © David R. Frazier/Photo Researchers, Inc.; p. 196B © Erika Stone/Photo Researchers, Inc.; p. 201 © 1988 Ron Sherman/ Stock Boston; p. 203 © Bob Daemmrich; p. 205 © Nancy Coplon; p. 208 © K. Preuss/The Image Works.

Chapter 10

Page 212 © Bachmann/Photo Researchers; p. 215 © Brent Jones; p. 218 © Dan Bosler/Tony Stone Images; p. 221 © Index Stock Photography, Inc.; p. 222 © Liz Clairborne, Inc.'s Women's Work program; p. 224 © Milt & Joan Mann/Camermann International, Ltd.; p. 226 © Culver Pictures; p. 222 © M. Ferguson/Photo Edit; p. 229 © Whitby/ NST/FPG.

Chapter 11

Page 234 © David Burnett/Contact Press Images; p. 238 © Bob Daemmrich; b © Bob Daemmrich/The Image Works; p. 241 © Milt & Joan Mann/ Camermann International; p. 245 © George Chan/Photo Researchers; p. 247 © UPI/ Bettmann; p. 251 © Ron P. Jaffe/Unicorn Stock Photos; p. 252 AP/Wide World; p. 254 © Hiroshi Harada/Photo Researchers; p. 255 © David R. Frazier Photolibrary.

Chapter 12

Page 258 © Robert Frerck/Odyssey Productions; p. 261 Mabel Brady Garvan Colelction/Copyright Yale University Art Gallery; p. 264 © Frederick Ayer/Photo Researchers; p. 266 © Porterfield/ Chickering/Photo Researchers; p. 268 © Billy E. Barnes/Stock Boston; p. 269 © Nichols/Viesti Associates; p. 271C © Margaret Bourke-White/*Life* Magazine/Time Warner Inc.; p. 271CR © Henry Grossman; p. 271L © Brain Blake/Photo Researchers; p. 273 © Daemmrich/The Image Works; p. 277 © AP/Wide World; p. 279 © Alexander Zemlianichenko/ AP/Wide World.

Chapter 13

Page 282 © Carl Purcell/Photo Researchers; p. 285 © St. Bartholomew's Childrens's Hospital/ SPL/Photo Researchers; p. 289 © Griffin/The Image Works; p. 290 © Robert Frerck/Odyssey Productions; p. 291 From the Wall Street Journal; Permission, Cartoon Features Syndicate; p. 293 © Shambroom/Photo Researchers; p. 295 © McNeely/SIPA Press; p. 301 © UNESCO.

Chapter 14

Page 306 © Reuters/Bettmann; p. 310 © Adams/ Sygma; p. 311 © Berman/Copyrighted, Chicago Tribune Company, all rights reserved; p. 313R © National Institute of Anthropology; p. 313L © Haun/Stock Boston; p. 316 © Kerbs/ Monkmeyer; p. 321 © Robert Frerck/ Odyssey Productions; p. 323 © D. Young-Wolff/Photo Edit.

Chapter 15

Page 328 © Gish/Monkmeyer; p. 332 © S. Nagendra/ Photo Researchers; p. 335 © T. Orban/Sygma; p. 338 © Reuters/Bettmann; p. 339 © Dana Fineman; p. 341 © Laski/SIPA-Press.

Name Index

Subject Index